D0282524

310

REALMS OF VALUE

REALMS OF VALUE

A Critique of Human Civilization

RALPH BARTON PERRY

Edgar Pierce Professor of Philosophy, Emeritus
Harvard University

HARVARD UNIVERSITY PRESS
Cambridge, Massachusetts
1954

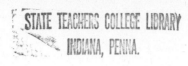

STATE TEACHERS COLLEGE LIBRARY
INDIANA, PENNA.

C.I

Copyright, 1954, by the President and Fellows of Harvard College

Distributed in Great Britain by
Geoffrey Cumberlege, Oxford University Press, London

The present volume consists of an
expansion and revision of the

GIFFORD LECTURES ON NATURAL RELIGION

Delivered at the University of Glasgow
in 1946–47 and 1947–48

Library of Congress Catalog Card Number 53–10867
Printed in the United States of America

STATE TEACHERS COLLEGE LIBRARY
INDIANA, PENNA.

121 P42
c. 1

Dedicated with fraternal greetings

to

Bernard Berenson

PREFACE

In 1926 I published a book entitled *General Theory of Value,* from which I quote the concluding paragraph:

> Having examined the general nature of value, and elucidated the principles which determine its varieties, its mutations and its grades, the next task is to employ these principles for the rectification of frontiers and the establishment of order among its historically authentic realms. Such would be the proper sequel to the present work.

If excuse for a delay of twenty-eight years in presenting this sequel were necessary I might allude to the fact that a world war, a social revolution, and a cold war have occurred since the words above were written. It would be more pertinent to plead the vastness of the task itself. It was indeed a pretentious task, and I should, perhaps, apologize for undertaking it at all. It has compelled me to enter into many fields of inquiry in which I am not a primary, or even a secondary, expert. Here I must fall back upon the usual philosopher's plea: that there is merit in attempting to achieve systematic unity in a field which would otherwise be divided among experts unaware of one another; and that even when the achievement is not achieved the attempt may still be worth the attempting. In the end I must trust, with Autolycus, that "when I wander here and there, I then do go most right."

As to the contents of the book, since the "realms" of value coincide largely with man's major institutions, and in their aggregate with civilization, the present study will traverse the fields commonly assigned to the philosophy of the natural and social sciences, and to aesthetics, philosophy of education, and philosophy of religion. Its purpose is to bring unity and order into these fields by adhering constantly to a fundamental definition of value; expounding the definition in the opening chapters, and testing it by application in the chapters that follow. I have attempted to avoid technicalities familiar only to the philosopher, in the hope that the book may be profitable to scholars in the several fields of learning which deal with man and with his major concerns. At the same time I hope that it may have something to say to the general reader. A judicious use of the table of contents will make it possible to read selectively.

I have attempted to avoid polemics, and I have, as a rule, avoided citation of writers with whom I am in agreement. Needless to say, I am deeply indebted both to enemies and to friends. Among the latter I might single out for special acknowledgment Stephen C. Pepper, Edward C.

Tolman, Gordon W. Allport, Henry A. Murray, Henry D. Aiken, and the late David W. Prall and De Witt H. Parker. I have exploited the learning and generosity of many Harvard colleagues, and throughout the years in which I have been engaged in this task I have been fortunate in having the loyal and efficient secretarial assistance of Catherine F. Lyons, Adrienne Rich Conrad, Sheila Malone, Constance R. McClellan, Alice Koller, Evelyn Masi, and others.

The present book is an expansion and revision of lectures delivered at the University of Glasgow in the years 1946–47 and 1947–48, as Gifford Lecturer on Natural Religion. This Lectureship provided me with an incentive to organize the material which I had long been gathering; and my residence in Glasgow enabled me to enjoy the gracious hospitality of my Glasgow colleagues and of the Principal, Sir Hector Hetherington, and his wife. This hospitality was none the less warm, and was doubly appreciated, because of the "austerity" which I was honored to share with my hosts.

RALPH BARTON PERRY

Cambridge, Massachusetts
     May 1, 1953

CONTENTS

REALMS OF VALUE

God has endued the soul with two faculties: one is that by which it is capable of perception and speculation, or by which it discerns, and views, and judges of things; which is called the understanding. The other faculty is that by which the soul does not merely perceive and view things, but is some way inclined with respect to the things it views or considers; either is inclined *to* them, or is disinclined and averse *from* them; or is the faculty by which the soul does not behold things, as an indifferent unaffected spectator, but either as liking or disliking, pleased or displeased, it is sometimes called *inclination:* and, as it has respect to the actions that are determined and governed by it, is called the *will:* and the mind, with regard to the exercises of this faculty, is often called the *heart.*

> (Jonathan Edwards, "Religious Affections"; C. H. Faust and T. H. Johnson, *Jonathan Edwards,* 1935, pp. 209.)

If it be possible, as much as lieth in you, live peaceably with all men.

> (*Epistle to the Romans,* 12:18)

The "remote possibility of the best thing" being better than a clear certainty of the second best.

> (Letter of Mary Temple to Henry James, quoted in the latter's *Notes of a Son and Brother,* 1914, p. 492.)

CHAPTER I

THE DEFINITION OF VALUE
IN TERMS OF INTEREST

One can generally tell a man's special field of investigation by the words which he uses carefully and the words he uses carelessly. The physicist now uses the word 'atom' carefully; that is, he is prepared to say what he means by it. The geneticist is careful with such words as 'heredity' and 'environment'; the theologian with the word 'god'; the logician with 'proposition' and 'implication'; the mathematician with the word 'number'; the economist with the words 'price' and 'demand'; the political scientist with the word 'sovereignty.' Everyone except the specialist uses these words carelessly. The philosopher who is engaged in that branch of philosophy now known as "theory of value" is distinguished by the fact that the word which he is most careful about is the word 'value.'

Everyone else uses this word carelessly. There is a usage of common sense, as when it is said that men lose sight of "higher values" when they practice power politics, or lose sight of "values" altogether in the machine age; or when it is said that it is the task of a humanistic education to make students aware of the "values" of life. 'Value' is now a favorite word among the sociologists, psychologists, and psychiatrists. The word is scattered through the text, and even mentioned in the index; but it is used like 'and,' 'but,' and the nouns and adjectives of everyday speech, as though its meaning were so well understood as to require no examination. The theorist of value, on the other hand, is one who asks, of himself and of others, "Precisely what is meant by 'value'?" It is his business to have an answer to that question. In other words, 'value' is his *careful* word.

The question, "What does 'value' mean?" is not the same as the question "What things have value?" Though the two questions are often confused, the difference is evident when attention is called to it. The statement that "a sphere is a body of space bounded by one surface all points of which are equally distant from a point within called its center" is different from the statement that "the earth is (or is not) a sphere." The statement that peace is a condition in which societies abstain from the use of violence in settling their disputes, is different from the statement that the world is (or is not) now at peace. And similarly, a statement, such as is proposed below, of what value is, differs from the statement that peace is valuable.

If the second of each of these pairs of statements is to be definitive and accurate it is clearly advisable to have in mind the first. If, in other words, one is to know whether peace is or is not valuable, it is well to know what 'valuable' is: in other words, to know what it is that is stated about peace when it is stated that it is valuable. But while the question raised by the second statement depends on an answer to the question raised by the first, the two questions are not the same question. And it is the first question with which the present inquiry is primarily concerned. In other words, theory of value ascribes value to things only in the light of what 'value' means.

Some philosophers, unfortunately, put the question concerning value in the form "What *is* meant by 'value'?" or "What *does* one mean by 'value'?" as though that meaning were already determined, and it was only necessary to call attention to it. Those who approach the matter in this way are accustomed to challenge a proposed definition of value by saying, "But this is not what is meant by 'value'" or "This is not what one means by 'value.'" The fact is, however, that there is no such established and universal meaning. Different people mean different things in different contexts. The problem is not to discover a present meaning — there are only too many meanings.

The problem is not solved, however, by simply enumerating these many meanings. This job is already done by the unabridged dictionaries which list, in fine print, all the varieties of meaning which appear in literature and ordinary speech. Theory of value is in search of a preferred meaning. The problem is to define, that is, *give* a meaning to the term, either by selecting from its existing meanings, or by creating a new meaning.

But one must not then leap to the conclusion that this giving of a meaning to the term 'value' is an arbitrary matter, dictated by the caprice, or mere personal convenience, of the author. One can, it is true, make the term mean "anything one likes," but this would not advance knowledge, or be of the slightest importance, or be capable either of proof or of disproof. The man who said "When I say 'value' I mean a purple cow" would not even be listened to, unless by a psychiatrist or a kindergarten teacher. There must, in other words, be a control or set of criteria, by which the definition is justified or rejected.

According to the definition of value here proposed, *a thing — any thing — has value, or is valuable, in the original and generic sense when it is the object of an interest — any interest.* Or, *whatever is object of interest is ipso facto valuable.* Thus the valuableness of peace is the characteristic conferred on peace by the interest which is taken in it, for what it is, or for any of its attributes, effects, or implications.

Value is thus defined in terms of interest, and its meaning thus depends on another definition, namely, a definition of interest. The following is here proposed: interest is *a train of events determined by expectation of its outcome.* Or, *a thing is an object of interest when its being expected induces actions looking to its realization or non-realization.* Thus peace is an object of interest when acts believed to be conducive to peace, or preventive of peace, are performed on that account, or when events are selected or rejected because peace is expected of them.

Both of these definitions require clarification and elaboration; but these summary statements will suffice for the present purpose of indicating the criterion by which the definitions are to be justified. These criteria are three in number, namely, *linguistic, formal,* and *empirical.* When the definition is challenged it must defend itself on three grounds: its use of words; the clarity, definiteness, tenability, and fruitfulness of the concepts which it employs; and its capacity to describe certain facts of life, to which it refers, and by which it is verified. The definition is designed, in other words, to be at one and the same time, a nominal definition, an abstract or *a priori* definition, and a "real" definition.

2

In the first place, then, definition names, or affixes a verbal label; and in thus creating a verbal usage it has to take account of existing verbal usage. The fundamental purpose of naming is "ostensive"; that is to say, it identifies some object (thing, quality, act, relation, region, event) so that it may be subsequently recovered, and referred to in communication with others. It serves the purpose of directing the attention of several minds, or of the same mind at different times, to the same locus in the mind's environment.

Pure naming is conventional, that is, no account need be taken of any antecedent ostensive meaning, but only of brevity, euphony, and duplication. But naming is rarely, if ever, pure. In order that it should be pure the name would have to be new, that is, an arbitrary symbol invented on the spot. Verbal names, however, are usually secondhand; that is, the name has an antecedent usage, which renders its present usage appropriate or inappropriate. Even proper names, such as 'Rose' and 'Violet,' are commonly secondhand names. It is true that their use as proper names may become wholly, or almost wholly, divested of their original meanings; so that it would be absurd to dispute their application to a given person on the ground that she was in fact not rose or violet in color, but white or brown. But there is nevertheless a suggestion of flow-erlike fragility which would render it inappropriate to give the name of 'Rose' or 'Violet,' except in an ironic sense, to a heavyweight prize fighter. Place names — of mountains, rivers, cities, and countries — arise from mixed motives. They are not merely labels by which the place is marked on the map for future reference, but, like 'Rocky Mountains,' ascribe to it the characteristics already designated by some common name; or, like 'America,' they say something about its history by borrowing the ante-cedent name of its supposed discoverer.

The words 'value' and 'interest' which are used in the present defini-tion are secondhand names. Although they are here given a sharper meaning, to be consistently maintained, their appropriateness must be judged by their history and suggestiveness. In the light of existing usage do they serve well as pointers to focus the discussion on a certain region of inquiry?

In the present writer's early Harvard days the word 'value' was first beginning to become current in American philosophy, largely through the influence of Hugo Münsterberg, who, in addition to being a psycholo-gist, was also a follower of the neo-Fichtean school of Windelband and Rickert. In fact, since Münsterberg learned to speak English fluently be-fore he learned to pronounce it correctly, his students heard of "walues" before they heard of "values." Münsterberg would be scandalized by the liberties which have been taken with the word since his day. For with Münsterberg and his school, "values" possessed an exalted dignity tran-scending both nature and sense-perception. They have since become completely secularized, mingling with the affairs of everyday life, and consorting intimately with the vulgar facts of sense-experience. They have even been desecrated by psychologists, in violation of that *Anti-Psychologismus* which was once with German philosophers a sort of Oath of Hippocrates.

Before the word 'value' could acquire that generality of meaning re-quired for a philosophical theory of value, it was necessary to overrule the economists who had become accustomed to claim its exclusive use. But Adam Smith and John Stuart Mill had distinguished "value in use" from "value in exchange," and, in so using the same word twice, had already broadened its meaning to apply to a field of which economic value was only a circumscribed part.

Since the beginning of the present century, the word 'value' has ac-quired a popular use which has eclipsed its transcendental use by neo-Fichtean philosophers and its technical use by economists. The conscious employment of propaganda has called attention to the diversity of creeds and codes by which different human societies are governed, and these are frequently referred to as different beliefs concerning what has "value," or "supreme value." At the same time the word 'ideology' has acquired vogue as the name for a set of ideas which concern "values" as distinguished from matters of fact. The signal failure of natural science to save mankind from war and its destructive effects is often attributed to the fact that science ignores "values"; and the world looks to religion or liberal education to restore them.

The word 'value' is, then, a good name, because its history suggests that there is something common to duty and piety, price and utility, ideals and codes. At the same time it points toward that aspect of human life for which it is customary to employ the eulogistic-dyslogistic vocabulary. It points to other pointers, and borrows the ostensive meaning of such adjectives as 'good,' 'best,' 'right,' 'ought,' 'worthy,' 'beautiful,' 'sacred,' 'just,' and such nouns as 'happiness,' 'well-being,' and 'civilization.' As a common name for what these words name, it suggests a common meaning, or the attempt to find a common meaning. Of the words which already have such ostensive meaning, and which will therefore serve as guideposts, 'value' best combines specific reference with breadth and flexibility.

The word 'value' has also a grammatical convenience, in that it possesses substantive, adjectival, and verbal variants. We can speak of "values," of "valuable," and of the act of "valuing." This is, however, a dubious advantage, since it has given rise to serious ambiguities. Thus *a* value, in the substantive sense, may mean either *that which* has value, such as gold or justice; or a *kind* of value which it has, such as economic or moral. These distinctions are analogous to those between the determinable 'color,' the determinant 'red,' and the instance, such as 'the rose.'

'Valuable' like 'value' suffers from the defect that it is sometimes taken to refer only to what is "good," "right," etc., and to exclude the opposites, 'bad,' 'wrong,' etc., which clearly belong to the same field of discourse. There is no way of escaping this difficulty except by the awkward expedient of distinguishing the "positively" and "negatively," or "eulogistically" and "dyslogistically," valuable, thus giving a broader meaning to the unmodified adjective when it refers to both.

Most insidious and disastrous of all is the ambiguity attaching to the verb 'to value,' which may mean *making* valuable, or *judging* to be valuable. Similarly, to "value a thing highly" may mean either to care greatly for it, and thus to *give* it great value, as when one loves money; or it may mean to *ascribe* great value to it in some scale of comparative magnitude, as when one judges money to be more precious than sleep. And sometimes 'to value,' or 'to evaluate,' means to assign value to an object for *reasons,* that is, because it possesses certain characteristics, as when one values money for what it will buy. These differences must not be overlooked as a result of economy of speech.

3

The second of the words employed in the proposed definition of value is the word 'interest.' Here, again, the word selected is an old word, already used as a name, but selected because of all the old words it seems the best word to substitute for a class of words — 'liking,' 'desiring,' 'willing,' 'loving,' 'hoping,' etc., and their opposites; and to suggest a common ostensive meaning as distinguished from that of another class of words embracing 'sensing,' 'perceiving,' 'thinking,' 'judging,' etc. If the word is to be used in this sense, however, it is necessary to exclude certain senses which are either too broad or too narrow.

In its broader use 'interest' is a synonym of attention; and the adjective 'interesting' is applied to any object or topic which attracts attention or excites curiosity, such as the sudden, novel, surprising, or contrasting. In this sense, a noise breaking into silence, or one's own name unexpectedly pronounced, immediately draws attention to itself and alerts the hearer. No doubt interest in this sense is commonly associated with feeling, desire, etc., but there is a difference nonetheless between sheer attentiveness — the turn of the head, shift of the eye, or focusing of consciousness — and the liking, desiring, etc., by which this may be conditioned, accompanied, or followed. This broader reference being eliminated, the word 'interest' points to attitudes of *for* and *against*, or what are sometimes called "motor-affective" attitudes, as when one says, "I am interested in the outcome," or "all interested parties should be excluded."

But here we encounter a sense of the word that is excessively narrow, its reference, namely, to self-interest or selfishness, which is a special case of interest. We need a use of the word such that the nurse's interest in her patient's recovery or relief from pain is as much an interest as her interest in gainful employment. The latter, or selfish, meaning is reflected in the use of the word 'disinterestedness' to signify interest directed to others. This word involves a flagrant ambiguity. There is a crucial difference between the absence or subordination of self-interest, and that state of apathy in which there is no interest at all. It is unfortunate that the word 'disinterested,' as when we speak of the disinterested judge, is used to mean breadth and inclusiveness of interest. It would be less misleading to say 'all-interested.'

A second excessively narrow use of the word 'interest' is that in which it refers to the collective, and more or less permanent, interest of a social group, as when one speaks of "the interest of labor" or "the interest of the consumer." The expression '*the* interests,' used in a political context, suggests interest that is both selfish and collective or permanent. But if the word is to be used in these restricted senses, then there is need of another and broader use which makes it possible to speak of interests which are generous, or fleeting and individual.

Despite these ambiguities, the word 'interest' is the least misleading name for a certain class of acts or states which have the common characteristic of *being for or against*. The expressions 'motor-affective attitudes' or 'attitudes of favor and disfavor' serve as its best paraphrases. 'Caring' and 'concern' are also convenient synonyms. The absence of interest is indifference, as when one says, "It makes no difference to me," "I do not care," or "It is of no concern to me." Indifference is to be distinguished from negative interest. Thus one speaks of not caring, or of its making no difference "one way or the other," implying that interest embraces both ways. It is especially significant to note that the words for which 'interest' is substituted come in pairs of opposites, which are not related simply as grammatical positives and negatives.

'Interest,' then, is to be taken as a class name for such names as 'liking'-'disliking,' 'loving'-'hating,' 'hoping'-'fearing,' 'desiring'-'avoiding,' and countless other kindred names. What they all ostensibly mean is what *it* ostensibly means. It invites attention to that to which they in their severalty and community already invite our attention. It will occasionally, for reasons of diction, be convenient to use some one of these more restricted names to stand for the rest. But if the term 'interest' is used with reasonable consistency to stand for them all then these richer words can be used as names for the different species of the genus which will be introduced in the further elaboration of the subject.

4

Definition does not merely name, it also *conceives*. It fixes upon an intelligible meaning. It may put together old meanings, so as to create new meanings. Although the mind may conceive freely — that is, may conceive or not, and may conceive an infinite variety of abstract or ideal objects — when it does conceive, and whatever it conceives, it is subject to certain requirements which are inherent in the nature of conceiving. These may be referred to as the "formal" requirements of a definition. They are the conditions which a theory must satisfy *qua* theory; that is, in advance of being verified. Are the concepts here employed "intelligible?" How are statements about interest as here conceived to be translated into statements about value? Does such a translation result in contradiction, confusion, and sterility? Is it fruitful and illuminating? Does it violate any fundamental logical or epistemological requirement? But at this point it is appropriate to introduce certain objections which, if valid, would save the trouble of proceeding further.

It has been objected, in the first place, that all or most of the words of the class here represented by the word 'value' (words such as 'good,' 'bad,' etc.) have *no* conceptual meaning, but only a so-called "emotive" meaning.[1] In other words, statements in which such words appear as predicates are not statements at all, but utterances. They have no objectivity, and are neither true nor false; but merely express the attitude of the person who makes them, and his desire to convert others to the same attitude. They are communicative and persuasive, but they are not cognitive and informative. Thus it is held that the word 'good' in the judgment that "Francis of Assisi was good," refers to no Franciscan characteristic, actual or alleged, but merely reflects the fact that the maker of the judgment esteems Saint Francis, and desires that others shall also esteem him.

There is no doubt of the fact that words are commonly used with an expressive, commendatory, or disparaging intent. A love poem or a political diatribe is not the same thing as a mathematical theorem or scientific statement. Words such as 'fascist' and 'red' lose their conceptual meaning and degenerate into smear words; "the land of the free and the home of the brave" may serve only to express and arouse a love of country. Most verbal statements, however, have *both* an objective and an emotive meaning. The mixture of meanings appears in the fact that either of two retorts is appropriate. Thus if a man is called a "red" in a community in which this word is offensive, he may either become angry, or affirm his belief in capitalism. Ordinarily he will do both: that is, angrily affirm his belief in capitalism. If a man is called a "reactionary" he is no doubt condemned; but he is also conceived as wedded to the past. He can defend himself either by retaliating upon his accuser with the word 'radical,' or by pointing to his interest in the future.

A word having only an emotive meaning like the word 'fie!' is the extreme opposite of a word having only a conceptual meaning, like the word 'ellipse.' The great body of human discourse, however, lies between these extremes. If verbal usage were to be so amended as to leave only exclamations, exhortations, compliments, and insults, on the one hand, and rigorous scientific concepts, on the other hand, most persons all of the time, and all persons, including scientists, most of the time, would have to remain mute. Statements which employ such terms as 'good' and 'bad' may, and usually do, convey objectively meaningful concepts, either expressly or by implication. Thus when Saint Francis is judged to be good, the fact that he fed the birds, and thus manifested loving-kindness to living things, is taken as *constituting* his goodness. Or, suppose that A, addressing himself to B, states that Lincoln was a "good" man *in that* he hated war, felt compassion for soldiers, and emancipated the slaves. A is not simply expressing his admiration for the kind of man Lincoln

[1] Cf. C. L. Stevenson, *Ethics and Language*, 1948, *passim*. Much of the ethical controversy which this book has excited would have been avoided if the book had held strictly to its title. It would then have been treated like a book on "physics and language" — interesting, but not physics.

was, and his desire that *B* shall feel likewise. He is identifying the concept of good with the concept of humanity, and ascribing it to Lincoln on the objective evidence of Lincoln's behavior.

The fact is that what force the argument has arises not from the absence of objective conceptual meanings, but from their abundance and variety. The argument reduces, then, to this: that there are no *invariable* objective meanings attaching to such terms as 'good' and 'bad' in common usage. Sometimes they mean one thing, sometimes another. Well, what of it? It is the business of theory of value to define such an invariable meaning. It is unlikely that because the word 'matter' has no common objective meaning as currently used it therefore has only a subjective or social meaning. Similarly, there is not the slightest reason why theory of value should be limited to ready-made meanings; should, in other words, be content to be a contemporary history of ideas, instead of undertaking that systematization of concepts which is the essential task of theory of value, of physical and chemical theory, in short, of all theory.

To reject the extravagances of the emotivist theory does not imply that judgments employing value terms are not peculiarly likely to be imbued with emotive meaning; nor does it forbid the supposition that judgments employing these terms may, in certain contexts, be wholly, or almost wholly expressive and persuasive in their intent.

5

It may be objected, secondly, that while the word 'value' does have an objective, conceptual meaning, that meaning is indefinable. According to one variety of this view, value, or some equivalent, such as good or right, is a specific, irreducible, "non-natural" characteristic.[2] Its being "non-natural" means that it is neither physical nor mental, and therefore cannot be empirically observed. It can, however, so it is alleged, be seen by the eye of the mind, and, when so seen, it is seen to be unique and unanalyzable.

Although volumes have been written for and against this contention, it should require no argument whatever. If unanalyzable value is *there* within the range of intellectual vision, it should be possible, after a reasonable amount of effort, to bring it into focus. He who fails to find it cannot but conclude that there is no such thing; especially when the authors of the doctrine do not agree among themselves on what they find.

According to another variety of the view, value is an indefinable empirical quality, or a class of indefinable qualities such as pleasant, enticing, fascinating, awesome, revolting, etc.[3] These qualities are in

[2] This is the position taken by G. E. Moore, W. D. Ross and others of the so-called "Cambridge" or "Intuitionist" school.

[3] This view is to be found in G. Santayana, *Sense of Beauty*, 1899; and in J. Laird, *Study in Realism*, 1920.

some way connected with feelings — either they consist in feeling, or are apprehended through feeling — hence they may be designated "affective qualities." Since, like the "secondary qualities" color and sound, they have a *prima facie* objectivity, they are sometimes called "tertiary qualities."

This is not the place to examine the merits of this view, except as concerns the question of analyzability. As sensation blends with sensation to create a new quality (such as a fused tone or color), so sensation blended with feeling possesses an integral character which is distinguishable from the characters of its constituents. But this can scarcely be cited as evidence against analyzability since it is a statement of precisely what, in the field of sense-perception, analysis is. The problem presented is the problem presented by all analysis. There is a sense in which nothing is analyzable — namely, if it is assumed that analysis must leave things precisely as it finds them. Analysis here as elsewhere destroys beyond recovery the first blush of the immediately presented. But if all this be true, and if it applies to value, it is already too late to speak of value as unanalyzable or indefinable.[4]

The history of human knowledge creates a presumption against indefinables. At the outset of any inquiry its subject matter is, as yet, undefined; nothing is, as yet, said about it; it possesses the character of a questionable vagueness located in a certain indefinitely bounded quarter of the field. When the definition takes place, this pseudo-simplicity of ignorance is superseded by articulate complexity. There is always something which escapes the final knowledge of a given subject matter, namely, the antecedent phases of ignorance. But to allow this to deter us from definition would be a cognitive defeatism. Self, activity, causality, substance, matter, force, heat, have all appeared in the role of indefinables only to prove definable. The history of thought is strewn with abandoned indefinables; and it seems highly probable that the value-indefinable will shortly come to rest among these relics of man's unfinished business.

There is a further meaning of 'indefinability' which can, for present purposes, be eliminated. Logic and mathematics employ so-called indefinables in a sense which is relative to their own systematic procedures. Certain terms are *taken* as indefinable. The choice of the word 'indefinable' in this sense is unfortunate, since it appears to say that the concepts in question *can* not be defined, when it really means only that they *are* not defined. Their selection as indefinables within the system is quite independent of definable meanings which they may or may not have outside the system.

The final proof that a conceptual definition of value is possible is to provide such a definition. The definition here proposed must satisfy two

---

[4] The Author has discussed this question in "Value as Simply Value," *Journal of Philosophy*, 28 (1931), pp. 522–6.

sets of requirements. In the end it will appear that it must be descriptive, that is, must fit a certain selected body of facts. But in advance of this empirical test the definition must satisfy certain formal, that is, logical and epistemological, requirements. These requirements have to do with the *framing* of the theory — with its internal structure. It must be "theoretically" acceptable. The concepts which it employs must not only be clear and intelligible, but must lend themselves to judgments which are capable of systematization and elaboration. More specifically, the present definition must be capable of defending itself against charges of circularity, self-contradiction, and sceptical relativism.

6

The charge that the definition is *circular* consists in pointing out that when a thing is affirmed to be good because it is an object of positive interest, it is always possible to raise the question of the goodness of the interest. Thus it is generally agreed that the goodness of drugs is questionable despite the intense craving of the addict; and it is usually concluded that the drug is bad because the craving is bad. It would seem to follow that in order that a thing shall be good it must be the object of a good interest, in which case 'good' is defined in terms of good.

But this objection loses its force altogether when it is recognized that an interest may itself possess value, positive or negative, by the application of the same definition as that which is applied to its object. While the craving does invest its object with positive value, the craving may be invested with negative value from the standpoint of other interests; and this second value may be considered as overruling the positive value owing to its taking the higher ground of health or morals. The appetitive goodness of the drug does not include or imply the hygienic or moral goodness of the appetite. There are two goods, one of which is, in some sense yet to be examined, superior to the other. In other words, the definition does not state that a thing is good only when it is the object of a good interest, but when it is the object of any interest, good or bad. When the interest is good, its object is thereby enhanced, but there is no circularity.

But in escaping circularity does one not fall into *contradiction?* Is it not contradictory to affirm that the same object is both good and bad? The charge of contradiction is lightly made and, as a rule, superficially examined. The important thing is to discover just what propositions would, and what propositions would not, be contradictory. It is sometimes supposed that the expression 'one man's meat is another man's poison' involves a contradiction. But there would be a contradiction only provided the same proposition was both affirmed and denied. Thus is would be contradictory to say that one man's meat was not that man's meat, or that another man's poison was not his poison. Meat to one man and poison to another are not contradictories, but are two different and consistent propositions.

By a kind of grammatical license the term 'contradiction' is sometimes applied to interests. Strictly speaking, interests do not contradict, but *conflict*. Only propositions contradict. But interests are sometimes allowed to borrow the contradictoriness or consistency of their objects when these are stated as propositions. Thus the interests in preserving and in destroying the life of the same individual are said to be contradictory, because the will of one can be expressed by the resolve "he shall live" and the will of the other by the resolve "he shall not live." But to speak of interests themselves as contradictory is confusing and misleading. Two contradictories cannot both be true, but two conflicting forces can coexist.

To assert of the same object that it is good and that it is bad *seems* to be contradictory, because the two assertions are elliptical, that is, because of the omission of the axis of reference. It may seem to be contradictory to assert of the same body that it is "above" and "below" when one fails to specify *what* it is above and below. Similarly, it seems to be contradictory to say of the same thing that it is both good and bad when one omits to specify the interests from which it derives its goodness and badness. The interests being specified, there is no contradiction whatever in asserting that the same object is practically useful and aesthetically ugly, or that the same act is selfishly beneficent and socially injurious.

But is not contradiction escaped only by falling into *relativism?* Well, if one may be permitted a vulgarism, and so what? The word 'relativism' has a bad sound; even the word 'relativity,' despite its association with the latest physics, conveys a suggestion of philosophical untenability. But suppose that one substitute the more colorless word 'relational' and, instead of rejecting it as a fault, boldly affirm it as a merit; since it provides not only for value, but for ambivalence and multi-valence.

Many of the most familiar characteristics of things are relational. There is no disputing the fact that brother and son are relational characteristics. In other words, when one describes a man as a brother or a son, one states his relation to another human being. For any man, there is someone to whom he is related: "God gives us relations." So, according to the theory here proposed, when one describes a thing as good or bad one describes it in terms of its relation, direct or indirect, to a second thing, namely, an interest.

This, be it noted, is not the same as to say that one value is definable only by its relation to another *value*, which may or may not be the case. There is nothing in the relational view which forbids a thing's being conceived as absolutely valuable; that is, valuable regardless of the value of anything else.

There is only one kind of relativism which is epistemologically objectionable, and which is commonly known as "vicious relativism." The

viciousness lies in its scepticism. It consists in the doctrine that all statements are elliptical unless they are introduced by the words "it seems
to me at this moment." Were this the case I should not even be stating
what I am saying now. I should say, "it seems to me that it seems to me
that it seems to me," etc. *ad infinitum;* in which case I would never get
to *what* seems to me, and I might as well have saved myself the trouble
of making any statement at all.

Suffice it to say that the theory of value here proposed is no
more relativistic in this vicious sense than any other theory, whether of
value or of any other matter. The supposition that a relational theory
of value is peculiarly vicious in its relativism rests on a confusion. It is
mistakenly supposed that because objects derive their value, positive and
negative, from interest it is implied that the interest from which they
derive value is the interest of the knower or judge. This would mean that
if I am to judge that an object possesses positive value to me *I* must like,
desire, will, or love it. When, however, value is defined in terms of interest, then *any* interest will satisfy the definition; and if I observe that anyone else likes, desires, loves or wills a thing, then I am bound by the
definition to judge it good. The evidence of its goodness or badness is
the observable fact of interest, which is just as objective, and just as open
to agreement, as any other fact of life or history.

7

The present definition of value is proposed not only as a nominal and
conceptual, but as a "real" or "descriptive," definition.[5] Its justification
requires that the names which it employs shall be well selected in the
light of verbal usage; and that its concepts shall yield judgments which
are free from circularity, contradiction, and sceptical relativism. But
these are only preliminary considerations. A descriptive definition, in
short, is an hypothesis. Its crucial test is its bringing to light the systematic structure of some realm of fact — some state of affairs *of* which
it is true. As will appear more clearly in the sequel, this does not imply
any fundamental antithesis between the descriptive and the normative,
but rather that norms themselves are also describable.

As here conceived, theory of value refers to a peculiarly pervasive
feature of human existence and history, namely, the emergence of interests having objects; in which interests combine, wax, wane, and disappear; in which certain things are qualified to become objects of interests; and in which there are things and events which promote or defeat
objects of interest. It does not deal, except for purposes of illustration,

[5] Cf. S. C. Pepper, "The Descriptive Definition," *Journal of Philosophy,* 43
(1946); A. Kaplan, "Definition and Specification of Meaning," *ibid.,* 43 (1946);
M. Weitz, "Analysis and Real Definition," *Philosophical Studies, 1* (1950).

with particular historic societies and epochs, but with general types and structures of interest.

But while the field of personal and social events, like that of physical events, is inexhaustible, it is proper to select major events, or certain human enterprises and pursuits that have a claim to special attention because of their universality or importance. Referring to these as "pursuits," "enterprises," or "institutions," one may then test the theory by its providing a systematic description of morality, conscience, politics, law, economy, art, science, education, and religion. When the master concept of such a description is given the name of 'value,' then these major realms of human life are specifically describable as realms of value. In their aggregate these realms constitute what may properly be given the name of 'civilization,' that total human adventure whose rising and declining fortunes give significance to human life upon this planet.

Theory of value so conceived is a bold and far-flung program which cannot be undertaken without a humble awareness of its immense complexity. It requires the philosopher to enter fields in which specialists have already staked their special claims, and where the philosopher finds himself an amateur among professionals. He cannot hope to do their special work better than they do it, but only to incorporate their results and add items and relationships. The philosopher is accustomed to this somewhat shameless role. He does not, however, undertake the task arrogantly or overconfidently. For it is the philosopher who, having undertaken the task, is most acutely aware of its difficulty.

Before turning to the description of the major human pursuits which constitute civilization, it is necessary to amplify the definition of interest which has thus far been only abstractly formulated. It is necessary to relate this concept to the findings of psychology, taken as a description of human nature. This phase of the inquiry will serve to clarify what is meant by an *object of interest,* and will reveal certain general *modes of interest,* which will be employed in the ensuing description of civilization and its several realms.

CHAPTER II

MOTOR-AFFECTIVE PSYCHOLOGY[1]

In employing the concept of interest the present theory enters into the domain of psychology. But unhappily the science of psychology does not provide a ready-made consensus on this matter, and the result is that the philosopher finds himself compelled in some measure to do his own psychologizing, in the hope that the experts will eventually correct his lack of precision, and fill in the gaps. The philosopher is not the only foolish amateur who rushes in where the professional psychologist has not yet trod. Historians, critics, men of letters, religious thinkers, economists, politicians, sociologists, teachers, physicians, and parents, are compelled to deal with human nature, and would like to be able to draw upon certified conclusions similar to those provided by physics, chemistry, and biology. But the psychologist has an accumulation of unfilled orders and his customers cannot wait.

The concept of interest overlaps the very part of psychology on which the experts are most divided and inconclusive, that part, namely, which deals with the "motor-affective" aspect of man. 'Motor-affective' is a loose expression designed to cover instinct, desire, purpose, will, feeling, emotion, motivation, etc.; whatever, in other words, constitutes man as a being who *acts* in behalf of what *concerns* him. Perhaps the best thing about the expression 'motor-affective' is the hyphen, which suggests, if it does not reveal, the unity of concern and action. But this historic and dramatic unit, this man in the concrete, this active pursuer of interests in a natural and social environment, tends in modern psychology to be lost to view, owing in part to a hold-over from the past, and in part to an urge to be scientifically modern.

[1] For an earlier, but more detailed, presentation of the topics contained in the immediately following chapters, cf. the Author's *General Theory of Value*, 1926, 1950, chs. vi-x.

From the past, psychology has inherited a dualistic view of man, which has assumed several forms. There is the duality of esteem, in which the "higher" man is distinguished from, and set over against, the "lower": the human in man against the animal in man; the ennobling faculties, such as reason and conscience, against the baser appetites; the immortal soul against its perishable incarnation; "spirit" against "body."

With this distinction between exalting and debasing views of man is linked a difference of method. Spirit, when opposed to body, is known "internally," or in self-consciousness; while body is known "externally" through the sense-perception of a second observer. When body is conceived in Newtonian terms, this same duality comes to be expressed in terms of the antithesis of teleology and mechanism. There is the man governed by purpose and choice; and the man composed of material particles governed by the laws of motion.

Since the purposively choosing man is a comparatively late and complex product of nature, the duality of teleology and mechanism can also be expressed by a duality of approach. One approach, following in reverse the line of evolution, reduces man, or levels him down, to his natural origins. "All are of the dust, and all turn to dust again." The opposing approach levels man up to the plane of his distinctive prerogatives, which are taken as signs of his supernatural origin and destiny.

Thus, man has been split in two, and presented in terms of opposites: higher *vs.* lower; spirit *vs.* body; internal *vs.* external; teleology *vs.* mechanism; upgrading *vs.* downgrading.

Desirous of being admitted with physics, chemistry, and biology to the select circle of the natural sciences, modern psychology has gravitated to the second term of each of these pairs of opposites and rejected the first, regardless of the apparent facts. For psychology was not compelled to choose. The most indisputable fact about man is that he is a union, and not a disjunction, of these contrasted aspects; which are complementaries and not mutually exclusive alternatives. Man is *both* lower and higher, *both* body and spirit, *both* outer and inner, *both* mechanical and purposive; to describe him it is necessary to grade him *both* down and up.

Dualistic views of man end in one or another of three forms of futility. The two terms of the antithesis may be left standing — disjoined and irrelevant ("parallelism"); or one of the terms may be chosen and affirmed to the exclusion of the other ("materialism," "spiritualism," "idealism"). In each case there is an object of study which is neglected and which is left to literature and history, and to the man in the street — namely, the man in the street himself: man in the round; the man who lives and moves among his neighbors in a space-time environment, and yet can contemplate eternity; the man who is familiar both to himself and to others of his kind; who ascends to heights considerably above the brutes, and falls to depths considerably lower than the angels.

2

Both in philosophy and in psychology there is evidence of increased attention to the integral man. Philosophers speak in terms of "emergence," "continuity," and "neutralism." [2] 'Emergence' means that while the "higher" processes develop from the "lower," they nevertheless possess, once developed, characters and functions of their own, which can properly be formulated in their own terms. 'Continuity' means that between any two levels of complexity it is ordinarily possible to discover an intermediate zone which it is equally legitimate to characterize in terms of the lower or in terms of the upper. The term 'neutralism' is used to mean that the physical and the mental are homogeneous and overlapping, being composed of terms which in themselves are neither physical nor mental, but acquire this difference by the forms of organization into which they enter.

At the same time that philosophy has shown signs of undercutting traditional dualisms, psychology has moved in the same direction. The term 'functional' is the most widely accepted name for this tendency, meaning that man is conceived neither in terms of self-consciousness and inner states, nor in terms of the minute physiology of bodily movements, nor in terms of a double entry system embracing both; but in terms of types of activity in which an agent engages its environment, or action systems of ascending complexity, the more complex being superimposed on the less.[3]

Applied to psychology the principle of emergence implies that the higher levels of human nature do not annul the lower, but embrace them and stand upon them. The nature of the higher complexes is obliged to conform to the nature of the lower, but this is a reciprocal obligation.

[2] This tendency is exemplified by H. Bergson (*Matter and Memory*, 1911); W. James (*Essays in Radical Empiricism*, 1912); S. Alexander (*Space, Time and Deity*, 1920); L. Morgan (*Emergent Evolution*, 1923); J. Dewey (*Experience and Nature*, 1925); A. N. Whitehead (*Process and Reality*, 1929); and many others.

[3] "The genius of American psychology lies in its stress upon action"; G. W. Allport, "The Psychology of Participation," *Psychological Review*, 53 (1945), pp. 117–8. This tendency was foreshadowed by James (*Principles of Psychology*, 1890) and more completely developed, with differences of emphasis, by J. R. Angell (*Psychology*, 1904, "The Province of Functional Psychology," *Psychological Review*, 14, 1907); by E. B. Holt (*The Concept of Consciousness*, 1914; *The Freudian Wish*, 1915); by E. C. Tolman (*Purposive Behavior in Animals and Men*, 1932); and by many others. The trend is the convergent effect of a number of causes — including the "behavioristic" emphasis on bodily action; the *Gestalt* school with its emphasis on the total field; the Freudian and other schools of psychiatry; social psychologies, with their emphasis on personality; and the organismic emphasis of modern physiology and biology.

Because man achieves the level of reason, purpose, and choice, he does not cease to be determined by drives, reflexes, and habits. On the contrary, these lower or more elementary processes must be so conceived as to enable them to continue to operate in the more complex organizations and unities which give to human nature its distinctively human character.

The principle of continuity does not forbid that there shall be critical regions within which specific types of process, such as reason, purpose, and choice, arise for the first time; but only that these arise gradually, rather than precipitately; and that in all probability there are intermediate types of process still to be discovered. The sharp boundaries of concepts must not be allowed to falsify the blurred boundaries of nature.

When the principle of neutralism is adopted the physical is no longer non-mental, nor the mental non-physical. Physical and mental are drawn together not only through a sameness of elementary constituents, but even through a partial similarity of form. It becomes intelligible that minds should dwell in bodies, and bodies in minds, and that they should both exist in a common natural world.

The first conclusion to be derived from these broad generalizations is that each science may examine its own subject matter without awaiting the final conclusions of other sciences. There is an order of complexity, and inquiry may address itself to any point in that order. Chemistry did not wait until physics had advanced from the atom to the electron; biology did not wait until chemistry and physics had been extended to organisms; psychology need not wait until chemistry has caught up with mind; nor need theory of value wait until the more elaborate functions of mind have been approached from the standpoint of vegetable tropism. Indeed, if theory of value is clear and consistent in its concepts, and scrupulously faithful to the facts within the domain of human interests, it is entitled to demand that other knowledge shall conform to its findings.

3

The integrating trend in psychology appears also in the reduction of the number of "schools of psychology" and in the building of bridges between them. In a recent survey of psychological theories of feeling and emotion, the number of schools is reduced to four: "introspective," "dynamic," "behavioristic," and "physiological." [4]

The introspective theory, now more commonly known as "phenomenology" or the "cognitive" theory, presents subjects with stimuli and compiles their reports. Applied to feeling and emotion, this means that the primary data are confined to the individual subject. He is supposed to recognize within the enclosed and private domain of his own conscious-

[4] J. G. Beebe-Center, "Feeling and Emotion," in H. Helson (ed.), *Theoretical Foundations of Psychology*, 1951, ch. vi. For a general consideration of the present predicament of psychology, cf. G. Murphy, *op. cit.*, ch. 41.

ness specific elements or characters denoted by the current affective vocabulary.

The "dynamic" or "depth" psychology, notably represented by psychoanalysis, concerns itself with the interplay of motivating forces from which arise tensions and alterations of personality, most notably manifested in the field of mental pathology, but then extended from the abnormal to the normal. Feeling and emotion, conceived (by Freud) in terms of the pursuit of pleasure, the adjustment to reality, and the inverse will to die, become underlying and hidden or "unconscious" compulsions which explain the personal life and provide therapeutic keys to the cure of its derangements.

The behavioristic theory, absorbed into the "stimulus-response" psychology, or into the broader tendencies of "operationalism" and "positivism," extends inquiry from the human adult laboratory to the cage and the nursery, where the unselfconscious and inarticulate organism is observed — no questions asked. Psychology is what the animal or infant does, or learns to do, under such and such conditions, or when subjected to such and such stimuli. Feeling and emotion become specific modes of performance such as grimaces and twitches; or movements toward and away from stimuli; or the complex operations of fighting, food-grasping, sexuality, or escaping.

The physiological theory has continued to deal with the old problem of "localization," employing greatly improved surgical techniques. For obvious reasons it has found the rat, the guinea pig, the dog, and the cat, more convenient laboratory materials than the human adult. Its refinements have extended to the minute physiology of nerve, muscle, and gland. Thus, in the area of feeling and emotion, it has adopted, though inconclusively, the hypothesis that affectivity is associated with the autonomic nervous sytem and the optic thalamus.

But despite their differences and claims of autonomy these four psychologies are not independent of one another. The introspective data of feeling and emotion — the feel of feeling, and the inner experience of fear and rage, serve as the primary data for which the physiologist seeks to find the physiological correlates. Thus when the outward manifestations of rage are supposed not to be accompanied by the feeling of rage, it is called "sham rage" or "pseudo-rage." In other words, it is not a true emotion, or even, strictly speaking, a manifestation of emotion at all, but merely a form of behavior similar to that of emotion. The physiology of emotion tends, furthermore, to depart from specific localization, and to interpret emotion in terms of the interested behavior of the total organism in what are called "appropriate situations." The several emotions owe their identity to their functions; and merge into a state of general arousal, or mobilization of energy, which is canalized according to the requirements of self-preservation in a specific environment.

The dynamic and clinical approach seems also to rely on introspection for the identification of affective subject matter. The motivating forces whose interplay constitutes the theme of Freudian psychology — "pleasure," "wish," "desire," "libido," "*id*," etc. — derive their positive meaning from the individual's consciousness of his own states. When they operate in the "unconscious," there is no evidence of their unconsciousness except the *absence* of introspective data. The only evidence of their unconscious existence is the fact that they are brought into consciousness in dreams or through "free-association" and in the fact that the subject is observed to behave in a certain manner.

Behaviorism has not replaced introspection, but has chosen to ignore it. But here too, the inner data are perpetually intruding; giving meaning to the "mental" and to its subdivisions, and increasingly inescapable as one rises from the comparatively simple animal or infantile mind to the comparatively complex mind of the human adult.

At the same time that it seems necessary to retain introspective data, introspection itself continues to prove its unreliability. Thus there is a growing doubt as to whether feelings of "pleasantness" and "unpleasantness" have any specific introspective qualities that are invariably present to the subject when his affective behavior is in evidence. When a group of subjects is instructed to judge degrees of pleasantness or unpleasantness it is assumed that they, together with the experimenter, mean the same by these terms. But what evidence is there of such community of meaning?

These considerations suggest that feeling, emotion, and other variants of the motor-affective life, whether in animals or in men, can be described only in terms of several dimensions or variables. No simple datum, no minimal end product of analysis, no narrow location within the envelope of the skin, no specific neural event, no movement of body or state of mind will in itself suffice. What is required is a concept which will embrace and fit together the certified conclusions of the introspective, dynamic, behavioristic, and physiological schools of psychology, and relate the whole, composed of these parts or aspects, to an environment of stimuli and objects. The concept of interest affords the best promise of meeting these requirements.

4

Contemporary psychology suffers not only from an inheritance of dualism, and from multiplicity of schools, but from a methodological fallacy. This fallacy is so frequently committed as to justify its being given a name. It may be termed the "Regressive" or "Atavistic" Fallacy.

In a temporal order of causes, conditions, or complexities, each term proceeds immediately from its next predecessor and indirectly from its remote predecessors. The fallacy here in question consists in supposing that the remote antecedent functions directly, and that it derives additional weight from its remoteness. The fallacy is analogous to the superstition of ancestor worship. It is as though one were to assume that, having produced their first effects, causes then go underground and continue to exert force. Or, to change the figure, it is equivalent to supposing that past events are present — buried, to be sure, under subsequent accretions, but buried alive, and capable of shaking the superstructure by turning in their graves.

The fallacy has its phylogenetic and its ontogenetic applications. Assuming that sensation and the motor reflex are the earliest phases in the evolution of mind, psychology has sought to reduce the "higher processes" to these terms. The conditions of the laboratory, the use of controlled stimuli, and the desire to obtain quantitative results, also conspire to emphasize the more rudimentary mental processes and to base psychology on psychophysics. In depth psychology, the Atavistic Fallacy has assumed the ontogenetic form of infantilism. The earliest influences and experiences are held not only to condition the later from next to next through youth to maturity, but to continue to haunt the scene in the subterranean quarter of the unconscious. Psychoanalysis is largely founded on this fallacy. According to Freud, "this oldest portion of the mental apparatus [the *id*] remains the most important throughout life." [5]

The Atavistic Fallacy appears in the conception of "primary drives," which are taken as prior both phylogenetically and ontogenetically. Fetal psychology is the ontogenetic equivalent of the phylogenetic rat psychology. The fallacy consists in supposing that despite his racial evolution and personal history man remains at heart a fetus or a rat. Drives such as hunger, thirst, sex, maternal care, etc., appear early in animal evolution and early in the life of the individual. Through the processes of conditioning and learning, the individual's behavior is varied and new motivations are engrafted, but these are held to remain on the original stem which still provides their sap. There is, however, no reason to assume a necessary correlation between originality and forcefulness. Later experiences and influences may count far more than earlier in mature behavior; "primary drives," having been succeeded by "secondary" and "psychogenic," may drop out and cease to count for anything. The explanation of adult human conduct by "tissue needs," or "viscerogenic needs," or by "toilet training" is merely the fantastic extreme to which psychology has been led by its sacrifice of subject matter to technique; or by its borrowing of its paradigms from the more "scientific" sciences. [6]

---

[5] *Outline of Psychoanalysis*, tr. by J. Strachey, 1949, p. 14 (note).

[6] Cf. R. R. Sears, "Personality Development in Contemporary Culture," *Proceedings of the American Philosophical Society*, 92 (1948), pp. 368–9. The child psychologist, like every other species of psychologist or social scientist, naturally thinks that *his* methods provide the key to human nature. When geriatric psychology is more fully developed it will perhaps make a similar claim.

Physiological psychology affords a parallel case — both the tendency to substitute psychophysiology for psychology and the tendency of psychophysiology itself to exploit its limited successes, rather than to admit its limitations.[7] Its atavism appears in that onesided bargain known as "parallelism." Body belongs to the physical world, which antedates the mental and from which the mental has sprung. After the mental has sprung it still remains dependent — a second class reality, unworthy of the attention of science. "Mentalism" becomes a scientific heresy.

The Atavistic Fallacy appears not only in psychology, but in the other human sciences as well. The most notable example is afforded by anthropology, which is still mainly preoccupied with primitive social groups. Such groups resemble animals and infants in that, owing to difficulties of communication, reports of self-observation cannot be relied on. It is necessary to observe externals and gross behavior. But this is taken as an advantage rather than a disadvantage, because it is more in keeping with orthodox scientific procedure; and because when a social group is thus seen at a distance it composes a coherent and readily describable unity. A primitive society, perhaps only because it escapes intimate understanding, resembles a physical organism, preserving itself by adaptation to its habitat. The description of a static, primitive society provides only an indecent covering for an advanced, progressive, and individualistic society governed by interests and purposes; but, corrupted by the same Atavistic Fallacy, the scientific sociologist tends to assume that all societies remain, at bottom, primitive societies.[8]

5

The title of a well-known book,[9] suggested to its author (no doubt ironically) by Santayana, illustrates the awkward predicament in which the habit of separating a man's mind from his body has placed the student of human nature. "Why the mind has a body" could have been matched by the inverse, and equally unanswerable, question, "Why the body has a mind." Why, indeed? When mind is purged of all bodily characteristics and body of all mental characteristics it means nothing to say

[7] K. S. Lashley, a distinguished representative of the physiological school, concedes that "physiological studies have as yet made *no* progress toward analysis of the less primitive motives of human behavior"; but this did not shake his firm adherence to the school; cf. his "Coalescence of Neurology and Psychology," *Proceedings of the American Philosophical Society, 84* (1941), p. 467 (italics mine).

[8] The emancipation of psychology from the restraints of an atavistic methodology has been impressively advocated by G. W. Allport in a Presidential Address to the Division of Personality and Social Psychology of the American Psychological Association in 1946; and published under the title of "Scientific Models and Human Morals," *Psychological Review, 54* (1947). Cf. also this writer's "The Trend in Motivational Theory," in *American Journal of Orthopsychiatry, 23* (1953).

[9] C. A. Strong, *Why the Mind Has a Body*, 1903.

that one "has" the other. To say that the two run along "parallel" and non-intersecting routes, or that they are twin manifestations of x, is not illuminating. "Pure" mind and "pure" body can have neither possession, intercourse, companionship, nor affinity.

Observation discloses no such purities. The relation between a man's ideas, feelings, and purposes and his brain, heart, hands, and feet is, as a matter of observation, so intimate that in all the characteristic functions of human life the two are inextricably commingled. Disjunctive dualism is a confession of failure. The question, "Are a man's body and his mind related?" is not a real question. No answer to this question, after discussion, can be more certain than the fact, given in advance, that they *are* related.

The natural and historic human individual — known to himself as well as to others, the topic of biography and autobiography alike, the participant in affairs, public and private, the theme of literature and the arts, the author of science as well as a part of its subject matter, is a physical organism. So much is unquestionable. He may be more than, but he is *at least*, a physical organism. The question, then, is how to conceive the human individual so that he can be *both* a physical organism and also a mind. There are certain criteria of mind which psychology employs in its procedure, and which are at least consistent with the integral view which is here proposed.

Psychology accepts as evidence of mentality the fact that the organism can communicate, that is, refer, by words or otherwise, to objects common to the observer and to his interlocutor. This is also the accepted criterion of mind in everyday human relations. If an organism is addressed with the words "What a brilliant sunset!" and responds with appropriate comments of its own, it is assumed to be seeing the sunset. The organism's mind, when so identified, consists of three factors, the brilliant sunset, the seeing, and the verbal communication. None of these is necessarily, or by nature, non-physical. The sunset certainly occurs in the physical world. Its brilliancy may consist in an intensity of light; or, if it be construed to involve feeling as well as sensation, it may be partially allocated to the internal state of the organism itself. The "seeing" and the "communication" are readily identifiable as the exercise of the appropriate organs and neural apparatus of vision and speech.

What, then, becomes of mind? Its content is, or may be, bodily. What would become of physics if the physical could not obtain access to the physicist's mind? Its agency is, or may be, bodily, otherwise what would be the meaning of blindness, deafness, and anesthesia? But to suppose that mind has then disappeared because it is analyzable into parts none of which is intrinsically mental, is as though one were to suppose that there were no triangles because they are analyzable into non-triangular elements such as angles, number, and intersection. Similarly, mind appears to consist not in the intrinsic mentality and incorporeality of its constituents, but in the way in which its constituents are functionally related.

To clarify this doctrine further one may begin with a man's mind as revealed to the man himself. At what point does he distinguish his perceptual field as content of his mind from the same field as part of his physical environment? At what point does he recognize it as private? At the point, apparently, where there is a shift of attention by which a limited area is marked off within an enveloping area which succeeds it. One is looking, let us say, at a landscape spread before him, and as the disclosure spreads, the earlier disclosure emerges in its aspect of limitedness — in its containing only so much and no more, or in its angular perspective or distortion.[10] Thus construed the contents of mind possess no common character except their exclusive togetherness within a selected aggregate. They are not "within" or "before" a mind otherwise defined, but they *constitute* mind by virtue of this togetherness. It is this which is *meant* by saying that they are mental.

So far as its contents are concerned, then, mind is an excerpt from the field of physical or other entities. But mind is more than its contents; it is also action. It is the act which defines the excerpt. A seen, for example, is distinguished from the unseen, or from another seen, by an act of seeing; and similarly with other contents of mind. They derive an inclusiveness and exclusiveness, and a mutual togetherness, from a selective act or orientation. It is this selective act which gives the point to a point of view. Which suggests that the conception of interest, instead of being derived from a preconceived idea of the mental as non-physical, may itself describe that physico-mental concreteness which is characteristic of human nature.

The same doctrine can be approached from the side of the body. The human organism is food for physiology, and through physiology, for chemistry and physics. Of that there can be no question. But by virtue of its nervous system the body is integrated, and raised to a functional level called "mind."

The body rises to the level of mind when it acts on its environment in a peculiar way — when by sensing, perceiving, remembering, thinking, planning, it pursues interests. These and like activities *set* apart that part of the total environment on which they act, and which then, without ceasing to be physical (if such it be), assumes also the role of mental. This, then, is the answer to the question whether interest is bodily or mental. It lies upon that level of complexity in which body has become mind.

[10] For a fuller statement of this view, cf. the Author's "Conceptions and Misconceptions of Consciousness," *Psychological Review*, *11* (1904).

STATE TEACHERS COLLEGE LIBRARY
INDIANA, PENNA.

121 P42
c.1   25

6

Mind, then, is not to be defined in terms of an incorporeal substance, or in terms of elements which in their severalty possess a unique "mental" character. It is a peculiar process, a train of events, operating within a surrounding field called its "environment" and distinguished by its consistency and perseverance through time.

Psychology of diverse schools, and especially in its most recent developments, recognizes the existence of action systems which, when released or evoked, impel the individual to conduct himself in a certain specific manner. There are various general names for these action systems — 'drive,' 'driving adjustment,' 'need,' 'purpose,' 'motor attitude,' 'set,' 'governing propensity,' 'determining tendency,' — of which 'drive' is here selected both because of its dynamic suggestiveness, and because of prevailing usage in the literature of the subject.[11]

The drive involves several factors. There is a neuro-muscular prearrangement or coördination, which is provided with stored energy. It is this motor equipment which distinguishes the drive from the skill. A drive, in other words, is not a mere apparatus, but a force, capable of motion and work. It contains, furthermore, not only a capacity and readiness to operate, but a tendency to operate. The drive is both a capacity and an impulse.

Corresponding to the prearrangement there is an exciting occasion by which the prearrangement is brought into operation. Both the prearrangement and the exciter are specific; the specific prearrangement is called into play by the specific exciter, and the exciter calls the specific prearrangement into play. The prearrangement is internal to the organism, while the exciter may be either internal or external. When the prearrangement is excited it usually takes command of the total organism, diverting its available energies from other possible uses, and thus requiring an adjustment and subordination of rival demands. The drive, as distinguished from the mere "reflex" is variable and modifiable, in respect of the intermediate phases through which it passes on its way to its more or less distant goal. Driving *toward* a goal, it learns *how* to reach it.

Social and personality psychologists recognize certain common drives by which to explain the conduct of individuals and groups. Animal psychologists, engaged in the study of learning, recognize the necessity of

[11] The differences of terminology are in large part due to emphasis on different aspects of what is a complex affair. As the term 'drive' calls attention to its forcefulness, and treats it as a *vis a tergo*, the expression 'governing propensity' refers to its continuing control of the intermediate stages of the process (subordinate acts, stages, etc.). The term 'purpose' emphasizes the peculiar role of the terminal or culminating phase as determining its antecedents — in short, the teleological character of the process; while the term 'need' refers to the impulsions created by a deficiency in the existing situation — which may be an urgency or "pressing need." These aspects are complementary and not mutually exclusive.

assuming impulsions, such as hunger and pain-avoidance, which underly the process of trial and error — without which the animal would not try, and without which success could not be distinguished from error. Freud's concern was not with the comparatively simple behavior of animals in an artificial maze, but with the complexities of human behavior in the labyrinth of life. The Freudian "wish," with all its variants, which impels to action, which conflicts with other wishes, which, when unable to execute itself overtly, goes underground and finds indirect or disguised modes of expression in dreams, wit, and slips of the tongue, which may so far ignore "reality" as to create hallucinations and incapacitate a person to live in his physical and social environment — the wish, which plays this dramatic role, is essentially the same thing as the drive recognized by the social and animal psychologists.

The current psychology of drives raises, and leaves unsettled, several questions affecting the nature of interests. There is, in the first place, both indefiniteness and disagreement as to what, and how many, drives there are. The recent history of the subject began with William McDougall's conception of "instincts" or forms of striving. His list, in which each instinct was accompanied by an emotion, comprised flight-fear, repulsion-disgust, curiosity-wonder, pugnacity-anger, self-abasement–self-assertion, parental love and tenderness, and others, major and minor.[12] After McDougall, the study of "learning" had the effect of casting doubt on all such lists of innate drives. Learning was invoked to explain, and remained to explain away, until nothing was left except several dubious reflexes such as the grasping and withdrawal reflexes of the infant. But since it was evident that learning itself could not be explained without drives, the pendulum swung back again, and new lists appeared.

Thus E. C. Tolman enumerated "appetites" of thirst, hunger, sex, play, "avoidance" of cold, heat, and obstruction, and "social" drives, such as gregariousness.[13] Tolman, be it noted, is primarily a student of animal behavior. Robert R. Sears, a child psychologist, named "hunger, sex, sleep and fatigue, elimination" as the "major primary drives." [14] There would appear, in other words, to be some relation between the list of drives and the special field examined by the psychologist. Thus McDougall takes his cue from the adult human; Tolman from the rat; Sears from the infant.

The second question which is left in doubt is that of innateness. Often a drive is taken to be innate by definition. But, the child psychologist

    [12] *Social Psychology*, 1910.
    [13] "Motivation, Learning and Adjustment," *Proceedings of the American Philosophical Society*, 84 (1941). In 1943 this writer's "appetites" had increased to twelve; "A Drive-Conversion Diagram," *Psychological Review*, 50 (1943), p. 504. For another complete (?) list, cf. H. A. Murray, "Proposals for a Theory of Personality," *Explorations in Personality*, 1938, ch. ii.
    [14] "Personality and Culture," *Proceedings of the American Philosophical Society*, 92 (1948), p. 368.

quoted above speaks of "major primary drives" and "major secondary drives." The minor drives are not enumerated, but appear to provide a sort of "*et cetera*" — lest otherwise the list appear too rigid. The primary drives are original, and the secondary are derived from the primary by "social interaction." The secondary drives (aggression, dependency, independence, status striving) presumably provide their own motivation once they are created.[15] E. C. Tolman, on the other hand, adopts a division into "Biological Drives" and "Social Drives," and then goes on to state explicitly that: "The basic energy comes from the Biological Drives. The Social Drives or techniques are secondary motives which are derived from the Biological. . . ."[16]

In this context the Atavistic Fallacy consists in supposing that the Biological Drives continue to provide the driving power which the Social Drives merely canalize. This would mean that the original drives are the only independent drives; meaning that if they ceased to operate the wheels of action would cease to turn. This is plainly contrary to the fact of development. Or it would mean that a present drive can be explained only as the repetition of a past success.

This last interpretation is, on the face of it, paradoxical, since it seems to say that doing something new consists only in doing something old, but doing it as well or better; which does not account for the genesis of new drives or of ways of meeting new situations. The principle of the conditioned reflex helps to explain *some* new drives, but there is no reason to suppose that it is the only explanation or a sufficient explanation. Imitation, random activity, imagination, and, above all, the total personality (whether internally unified or conflicting) constitute drives and generate them. As to ways of meeting new situations, surely thought, and learning by example or precept to *avoid* error, play a role not less important than trial *and* error.

Fortunately theory of value need not await a final verdict on these controversial topics. It is important for theory of value, and for the art of control in the sphere of human institutions, to know what drives can be assumed to be comparatively universal. But universality does depend on origin. It is important, for example, to recognize that all men are impelled by the drives of hunger and pain avoidance; but if these were *learned* by all men in infancy as a result of conditions common to all living organism, they would for all practical purposes *be* as universal as if they were innate.

It is also important to know what drives are the most powerful and deep-seated; but this, again, does not depend on innateness. Indeed it is characteristic of man that many of his most powerful drives, such as patriotism, ambition, and love of money, are clearly acquired. Drives may

[15] R. R. Sears, *op. cit.*, pp. 363, 364, 368.
[16] *Op. cit.*, p. 510.

become deep-seated, in the sense of perseverance and mastery. Hence it is not in the least prejudicial to man's higher or more idealistic purposes that they should have been developed rather than original. Human interests can rise above their source. Indeed it might be said to be the very essence of man that both phylogenetically and ontogenetically he *does* rise above his source.

7

The tendency to deal with human conduct in terms of what is observable by vision, hearing, or touch at the periphery of the body has proceeded so far as to make it necessary to affirm what was once thought to be self-evident, namely, that there *is* an affective content observable at the center. The statements "I feel a liking," "I feel pleased," or "disgusted," or "angry," or "happy," are just as reliable reports of observations as the statements "he shows a liking," "he acts pleased," or "disgusted," or "angry," or "happy." Furthermore, the terms 'liking,' 'pleased,' 'disgusted,' 'angry,' and 'happy' must be supposed to refer to the same conditions or activities in these two sets of statements. The problem is to fit them together; and the concept of interest affords the best promise of its solution.

The topic of pleasure and pain, which figures so prominently in discussions of value, lies at the heart of this problem. These terms may denote qualitatively different somatic sensations, as when 'pleasure' refers to peculiar titillations of the sort occasioned by the scratching of an itching surface, and 'pain' refers to the sharp pang or the dull ache. The sensory interpretation of pain has been universally accepted by psychologists since the discovery of pain receptors embedded in bodily tissues; and a similar interpretation is widely conceded in the case of pleasure, despite doubts as to the locus of the stimulus.

What, then, becomes of pleasure and pain in the sense of a pair of opposites — positive and negative? Does their opposition lie only in the opposed attitudes *taken toward* them, pleasure being pursued and pain avoided? They would then be like smells, some of which are attractive and some of which are repulsive. There would be nothing intrinsic to their natures which implied the correlative attitudes: it might have happened that man was impelled to pursue pain and avoid pleasure.

Such an external connection of pleasure with pursuit and of pain with avoidance would suffice to explain the place of pleasure and pain sensations in the economy of biological survival. It is useful to the organism that the sensation of pain should be avoided, when, as is frequently the case, it is a sign of bodily injury or malfunctioning. It is useful to the reproduction of the race that the sensations of pleasure associated with sexual intercourse should be pursued. The same external connection of pleasure with pursuit and pain with avoidance serves likewise to explain control by rewards and punishments. Assuming that pleasure is always pursued and pain avoided, pleasure becomes the carrot and pain the stick, which can be counted upon as an incentive or deterrent to whatever act may be conjoined with them. This interpretation also accounts for the fact that it is *possible* (though not usual) to pursue pain and to avoid pleasure.

But while this analysis is acceptable so far as it goes, it yields no meaning of pleasure and pain which would provide for the peculiar affinity between pleasure and pursuit, and between pain and avoidance — as when 'taking pleasure in' is synonymous with 'inclination' or 'liking,' and 'finding painful' is synonymous with 'disinclination' or 'disliking.' And there would be no explanation of the connection of pleasure and pain with *all* drives, and not merely with these drives of which they are the stimuli or objects.

When it became apparent that pain must be regarded as a somatic sensation, and when pleasure seemed to be following suit, so that feeling would drop out altogether, psychologists substituted a new duality, namely, 'pleasantness' and 'unpleasantness.' These were supposed to be "attributes" or "hedonic tones," present in all sensation, but not themselves sensations. It was at first assumed that these attributes were recognizable and irreducible data which needed only to be named. But once this assumption was challenged it grew more and more questionable. All that remained unquestionable was the subject's reply given in response to the question, "Is it pleasant or unpleasant?" Hence the inquiry took a new direction, and addressed itself to the subject's interpretation of the question. When does a subject, being questioned, call a stimulus or object 'pleasant' or 'unpleasant'? The answer given by the so-called "judgmental theory" is that his use of these words reflects the subject's knowledge of his own normal "reaction tendency." The following is a representative statement of this view:

> Pleasantness and unpleasantness "are attributes which we ascribe to any stimulating situation in virtue of our normal reaction tendency toward it." If the individual normally makes a positive reaction to an object, he labels it pleasant; if he normally makes a negative reaction to it, he calls it unpleasant. The *sine qua non* of affection is the judgment, pleasant or unpleasant, which the individual makes of objects in the light of his knowledge of his own reaction tendency toward them.[17]

[17] H. N. Peters, "The Judgmental Theory of Pleasantness and Unpleasantness," *Psychological Review*, 42 (1935), copyright American Psychological Association, pp. 356–7. The included quotation is from H. A. Carr, *Psychology*, 1925, p. 290. Cf. also the following: "Situations that normally arouse a positive reaction, i.e., one tending to enhance, maintain, or repeat the situation, are judged pleasant. Situations which arouse negative reactions, i.e., ones which minimize or rid the organism of the situation, are judged unpleasant. Situations which normally arouse neither positive nor negative reactions are regarded as lacking in affective tone"; J. G. Beebe-Center, "Feeling and Emotion," in *Theoretical Foundations of Psychology*, H. Helson, Editor, copyright 1951, D. Van Nostrand Company, Inc., p. 258.

There remains a serious doubt as to the precise meaning of the theory. Although the relation between the subject's judgment and his reaction tendency is variously described by such expressions as 'sine qua non,' and 'in the light of,' it is supposed to be the knowledge relation. Inasmuch as the object known is a "reaction *tendency*," or a "*normal* reaction," the judgment is no doubt a generalization which may be affirmed independently of the subject's particular reaction at the moment. But on what is the generalization founded if not on such particular instances? How can a man know whether his normal reaction or his reaction tendency is positive or negative if he does not know his reactions when they are taking place? In other words, there is an event which the judgmental theory implies but does not make clear, namely, the subject's immediate knowledge of *his own* present reaction. And this provides a place for introspective affective content; which differs from the externally observed reactions only as proprioception differs from exteroception of the same thing. The common entity is the reaction itself, reaction for or against.[18]

'Pleasure' and 'pain' will then be ambiguous terms. Taken as the names of feelings they denote awareness of the positive and negative reactions respectively — awareness of the subject's own response tinged with positivity or negativity. Taken in their non-affective meaning, they will refer to specific somatic sensations (rubbing, stretching, pressing, tingling, tickling, thrilling, sharp, dull, etc.). When there is a pursuit of pleasure and avoidance of pain, pleasure and pain will be present in both senses. Otherwise they will be present only in the first sense. In either case the sensation may be so fused with feeling as to beget new qualities such as hopefulness, delightfulness, charm or their opposites.

8

Recent discussion of the topic of emotion has been focused on three doctrines, bold and persuasive in their day, already traditional, and all persistent despite the criticisms to which they have been subjected. These three doctrines are historically associated with the names of Darwin, James, and Cannon.[19]

---

[18] Provided one is permitted to substitute 'revealing' for 'resulting from,' this seems to be the view held by W. A. Hunt — in "The Meaning of Pleasantness and Unpleasantness," *American Journal of Psychology*, 45 (1933) — who identifies pleasant and unpleasant with "the bright or dull pressures which are organic sensations resulting from bodily adjustments of approach and withdrawal." It is substantially the view held by P. T. Young, in his "Studies in Affective Psychology," *American Journal of Psychology*, 42 (1930), and other papers. Cf. also the view stated in a standard textbook: "All the theories depend on the correlation of pleasantness with seeking, approach, acquisition; and the correlation of unpleasantness with avoidance, withdrawal, rejection." E. G. Boring, and others, *Psychology*, 1935, pp. 391, 392, 395.

[19] C. Darwin, *Expression of Emotion in Man and Animals*, 1899; W. James, *Principles of Psychology*, 1890, and *The Physical Basis of Emotion*, 1894; W. B. Cannon, *Bodily Changes in Pain, Hunger, Fear and Rage*, 1929.

The Darwinian theory correlated certain major emotions (fear, rage, etc.) with instincts, and explained their outer bodily manifestations by their usefulness in earlier stages of animal evolution. The so-called James-Lange theory of the emotions identified the content of the emotional state with the organic sensations, such as contracted muscles or accelerated respiration, induced by emotional behavior. The criticism of the James-Lange theory by Cannon and others charged the exponents of that theory with neglecting the feeling component of emotion; finding this to be associated with the thalamus and hypothalamus, and to be prior to the muscular and visceral reactions.

Whatever be the conclusions reached in this as yet inconclusive controversy, the James-Lange theory appears to be modified and amplified, but not excluded. The way is left open to distinguish "feeling" as awareness of the attitude immediately provoked by the object or stimulus, from emotion as the more complex and prolonged sense of a more diffused and massive response. This would account for degrees of passion, from a relatively cool attitude of favor or disfavor to the frenzies of rage or terror, from liking and disliking to ecstasy or deep antipathy, reflecting the extent to which the total organism was involved. The difference between feeling and emotion becomes a difference of depth and spread, represented by a fan-shaped area, in which the apex is "pure feeling," and the outer perimeter the more violent or intense emotion.

It is a corollary of this view that *emotionality* replaces a specified number of emotions. Emotion becomes commotion. The several emotions differ not so much emotionally, as in their modes of external behavior, and in their appropriateness to given situations. Emotionality itself is an auxiliary engine or supercharger which can be linked with any activity, when as we say one "gets excited" or "worked up" about it. The standard emotions, such as rage and fear, are distinguished by their relation to the primitive animal needs for food-getting, reproduction, care of the young, safety, and conquest of rivals. They will appear, as Cannon pointed out, when violence or other unusual physical exertion is required. Emotionality, however, will not be limited to such situations, but may, in human conduct, be linked with acquired purposes. It will be reminiscent of these more primitive forms, and may still bear their names, as when we speak of "hungering and thirsting after righteousness," or of "moral courage," or of "fearing God."

This conception also provides for the fact that emotionality instead of acting as a reinforcement may usurp control, as when the individual is said to "lose his temper," or to be "carried away," or "swept" by emotion. The emotion then loses its direction, as when a train, through excess of speed in rounding a curve, jumps the rails, tears up the roadbed, and works general havoc. The difference here lies not in the degree of emotionality itself, but in the degree to which it has become disassociated from any guiding idea, or from the lessons of the past.

It is a quite gratuitous violation of observable facts to deny the existence of introspective emotion. Felt emotion, that is, emotion in the sense in which the subject has to *have* it in order to know it, is as good a fact of life as any other. Any musical connoisseur knows the difference between comparatively emotional music, such as that of Brahms, and comparatively "intellectual" music, such as Bach. Every man knows what it is to feel angry or afraid in a manner that cannot be shared immediately by one knower with another. Each knower is the accepted, as he is the privileged and unique, observer.

The rejection of introspective emotion is peculiarly wanton in the case of *moods*. Words such as 'sadness,' 'cheerfulness,' 'loneliness,' 'hopefulness,' 'discouragement' are on every man's lips every day of his life. When he uses them he is understood by his fellow men. They signify something — otherwise a great part of literature would be nonsense. They are states, activities, qualities, or events, and they have the character of being known only to one who *is* sad, cheerful, lonely, hopeful, or discouraged.

There is nothing in recent psychology which casts doubt on such privately known emotional facts. Thus an accepted authority in this field tells us that emotion is "an acute disturbance or upset which is *revealed* in behavior *or* in conscious experience, as well as through widespread changes in the functioning of viscera (smooth muscles, glands, heart, lungs), and which is initiated by factors within a psychological situation." [20] Thus anger, for example, in the substantive sense of *being* angry, includes both the look of it, and the feel of it — its outward combative movements, its massive and diffused organic involvements together with the immediate awareness of them, and the attitudes of favor and disfavor which distinguish interest as here defined.

Thus far a survey of the findings of psychology confirms the conception of interest as an activity or attitude having the characteristic of favor or disfavor. It exhibits interest as prior to the abstractions and dualities which have handicapped psychology in its dealing with the integral man. It not only verifies the conception of interest, positive and negative, as descriptive of human nature, but suggests that man is essentially *an interested animal*, a natural being having interests, and being governed by interests. Interest appears as a unifying concept, which gives a common meaning to instinct, drive, feeling, pleasure and pain, emotion, and other divisions of the motor-affective life which are otherwise left to stand as miscellaneous items.

But thus far there is a signal omission in the account. The definition

[20] Reprinted with permission from P. T. Young, *Emotion in Man and Animal*, 1943, John Wiley and Sons, Inc., p. 51. (Italics mine.)

of value in terms of interest requires that interest shall have an *object;* for it is its object which is judged to possess value. To clarify this aspect of the matter, it is necessary to bring to light and explore the role of cognition in interest.

CHAPTER III

THE OBJECT OF INTEREST

Since, according to the present definition, value is the character which a thing acquires by being an object of interest, it is necessary to decide precisely what is to be *meant* by a thing's being an object of interest. It is cognition that *gives* the interest its object, and the character of the object of interest is essentially the same as that of the object of cognition. Hence it is necessary to examine the role of cognition in interest, and then to examine cognition itself so far as may be necessary to discover the character of its object.

Much of what goes by the name of 'theory of value' is devoted to a discussion of "judgments of value." The discussion abounds in confusion and ambiguity. The unfortunate verb 'to value' serves only to obscure the difference between judgment and interest. Further confusion arises from the different uses of the word 'subject.' A judgment of value, in the sense of a judgment which attributes value to an entity, embraces three elements, all of which are sometimes called the "subject." There is the person who makes the judgment — the judge, or the judging subject. There is the interested subject who imparts or gives the value. And there is the grammatical or logical subject to which the value is attributed. Thus if I judge that bread is good to or for a starving man, I am the judging subject, the starving man is the interested subject, and the bread is the logical subject. The judging subject and the interested subject are different persons, while the logical subject is not a person at all.

It is important to recognize that the judging subject may not be interested at all, except cognitively. Otherwise he may be as indifferent in his judgment of value as in his judgment concerning *pi*, or the craters on the moon; caring only that his judgment shall be true. When one judges that bread is good for the starving millions in India, one does not need to judge hungrily or even sympathetically; statisticians can so judge without indignation or regret. Once the character 'valuable' is defined, then a judgment of value is a judgment in which this character is itself further characterized, as in judgments of kinds and degrees of value; or is attributed to any logical subject, whether an act, or a person, whether oneself or another, whether a physical thing or a social institution. In short, judgments of value are formally like any other judgments. Their difference lies in what they are judgments about, or in what they judge about it. Like judgments of color or number, judgments of value are distinguished by their matter.

Unhappily, however, there is an expression 'value judgment' which confuses judgments of value in this plain sense with judgments which are internal to interest itself, and which *condition* value. Thus to rejoice in the victory of the Allies in 1945 it was necessary to judge that the Allies *were* victorious. The rejoicing was founded on this judgment, but it was not itself a judgment of or about value, since it simply ascribed victory to the Allies, and did not ascribe value to anything or anything to value. If such conditioning judgment is to be called a 'value judgment' because it plays a necessary role in value, then one must be perpetually on one's guard to avoid confusion. It is safer to find another name, and to refer to judgments which condition value as 'mediating judgments.'

Judgments of value, in the sense of judgments about value, *may* serve also as mediating judgments; as when the sending of wheat abroad is favored on the ground that it is desired by hungry Indians, or the export of Hollywood films is condemned because they are aesthetically repugnant. Most mediating judgments are judgments of cause and effect, as when I desire a drug, deeming it a cure for insomnia. But there are as many varieties of mediating judgments as there are characteristics which when ascribed to an object qualify it for favor or disfavor. The mediating judgment will be any judgment whatsoever which represents the object to the interest; as when a man's love of his mother is mediated by the judgment that 'this is my mother.' The judgment is internal to his interest, since he would not love his mother unless he judged somebody to be his mother.

It would be a serious mistake, however, to restrict the role of mediation to judgment. This role may be assumed, and usually is assumed, by the less formal varieties of cognition. It is sufficient that the man who loves his mother shall recognize, perceive, or take, her as his mother. The essential thing is that the mediation in all these varieties shall possess the character of cognition, namely expectation, and, by implication, the alternatives of truth and error. The simplest kind of taking may always be a *mis*taking.

2

Mediating cognition provides interest with an object. What, then, is meant by this word 'object'? Common usage, unhappily followed by many philosophers and psychologists, fails to distinguish between the more general 'entity' and the less general 'object.' But the word 'object' is the Latin *objectus*, which is derived from the passive participle of the verb *objicio*; and while this word was sometimes used by Latin authors interchangeably with *res*, its distinctive meaning was something cast, thrown, placed, or lying, *before*. It conveyed the idea of opposite, or over-against; and clearly implied the other term of a relationship.[1]

This correlative term is ordinarily taken as an *act of mind*, of which the object is denoted by the passive participle. So construed in terms of object to or for a mental subject, 'object' becomes a general concept under which to subsume the more specific meanings of the passive participles of verbs such as 'to sense,' 'to perceive,' 'to think,' 'to judge,' 'to believe'; that is, it embraces 'sensed,' 'perceived,' 'thought,' 'judged,' 'believed.' The grammatically passive meaning of these concepts is obscured through the use of abstract nouns such as 'sensation,' 'perception,' 'thought,' 'judgment,' 'belief,' which may denote either the *acts* of sensing, perceiving, hoping, thinking, judging, the passive correlative of these acts, or the total transaction.

Assuming 'object' to refer to the passive correlates of cognitive acts, we may appropriately look to psychology for further light on the topic. Unfortunately the light is dim, owing, no doubt, to the psychologist's hesitation to enter the alien field of "epistemology." The psychology of the matter[2] suggests that cognition is not a specific state of mind on which introspection, however delicate its touch, can place its finger. It is a going-on, a pursuit, which is complex, fugitive, and often totally blank on its introspective face; and which reveals its nature only when other dimensions are included, and the total process is seen as having a determinate direction amidst variable detail. Nor can cognition be identified with any cross section or region of the physical organism, or with a physical stimulus, or with a causal relation between the two. The inadequacy of these methods of approach lies in their failure to provide for precisely what is here in question, namely, the *object*.

There was, it is true, a school of psychologists with whom this topic was the primary concern. According to Brentano and his followers, cognition is an "act" which refers to an "object" which is said to be "intentionally inexistent," or "immanent." Thus there can be no perceiving that is not a perceiving *something*; to speak of the perceiving without the "something" is an incomplete statement.

But the object of cognition is not necessarily inexistent, nor does the intention of the act forbid its existence; the act itself does not imply

---

[1] This meaning is even more explicit in the German *Gegenstand*.

[2] For its earlier history, cf. E. G. Boring, *History of Experimental Psychology*, 1929, pp. 395–9, and consult Index. For more recent references, cf. *The Harvard List of Books in Psychology*, 1949, pp. 28–32; and J. S. Bruner and D. Krech, *Perception and Personality*, 1950.

either its existence or its inexistence. As part of the act (the immanent object-of-the-act) it is existentially indeterminate. Furthermore it must not be supposed that the psychologist can learn this by simply looking into the act. It is not contained in the act as a private state or content. What is intended is not a simple datum, to the intender or to anyone else. It is not an accident that answers to such questions as, "To what do you refer?" or "What are you thinking about?" take time and pains, and frequently fail. The object is identified by the convergence of a complex of events (word, gestures, consistency of behavior). The immanent object is not revealed, displayed, or exhibited unless such performance is elaborated; and the performance by which it is revealed is essentially the same as that by which it is constituted.

The psychology of the laboratory, even when it abandons the static approach of introspection and construes cognition in terms of intelligent behavior, it is tempted to confuse the object with the *stimulus*. It is easy to understand why this should be. The experimenter hopes to conduct "controlled" experiments, after the manner of the reputable sciences. He confronts his subject (animal or human) with situations which he can precisely determine as regards their physical and chemical characteristics. He can create light, heat, sound, shapes, and colors in accurately measurable amounts, and to these he can expose his subject so that they impinge on his sense organs; whereupon he can observe the subject's bodily changes.

But there is something that he cannot control by such comparatively simple methods. This relatively uncontrollable factor is the most important factor of all, so far as it concerns human life; and, indeed, animal life as well, except on the lowest levels where it shades imperceptibly into the life of the plant. This factor is the stimulus *as it is to the subject,* or what the stimulus *means.*

Even sensation is a meaningful act and not a passive effect. That sensation implies reception of light or sound waves, or of chemical changes, or of pressures, is not to be questioned; but sensation is *re*action, and begins with the second phase in which the action reverses its direction, and proceeds outward. That *toward* which it proceeds is the sensory object. "Pure" sensation would be the case in which the reaction returns to its source, and the stimulus and the object differ only in time, as when contact stimulates a sense of hardness. Pure sensation, even in this qualified sense, rarely, if ever, occurs. Impure sensation rises to perception, in which the "from" and the "toward" differ to an unlimited extent.

All studies of perception recognize the fact that the stimulus is a small and even accidental factor in the perceptual object. Thus when one perceives a ball, the *ball* is constituted in part by its flat shape seen against a background, but also, in larger part, by its solidity, its hardness, its weight, its path of impending motion, and other visual and non-visual characters which are not sensed. One is then said to "see" the ball only because it is customary to name the perception by its sensory component. Indeed, the stimulus may serve only to touch off the reaction, and then disappear from the object; and it may finally become unnecessary altogether. Perception is then superseded by thought, which is now action, but no longer *reaction*: having an object, but no stimulus.[3]

That the stimulus and the object are not identical is now explicitly recognized even by experimental psychologists who, for reasons of method, would find it convenient if they were identical. The following statement is instructive:

> While the nature of a reaction is determined by the drive, the reaction is elicited by an object. A complete definition of reaction tendency requires a statement of exactly what is meant by an object. The object is not the physical stimulus, but what the stimulus means.[4]

The difference between the stimulus, and the object or the meaning of the stimulus, is implicitly recognized in both parties to the controversy over animal intelligence. If it be claimed, according to the more orthodox view, that animal intelligence is reducible to learning by trial and error, conditioning, associative memory, or the "law of effect," then each successive stimulus is assumed to be invested with a meaning derived from the experience of the past. If, on the other hand, it is contended, as by the Gestalt psychologists, that the animal can solve problems "all at once" by "insight," then it is assumed that each stimulus is invested with a meaning derived from its relations within a survey of the total situation.[5]

3

Psychology thus supports the contention that the object of cognition is what it means, that is, what is expected of it; or, to eliminate the "it," a system of expectations, where 'expectation' is to be construed as the expected, the *what is expected*.

When the object of cognition is conceived in terms of the expected, the analysis of expectancy becomes the key to its understanding. Here the psychologists have again been handicapped by their self-imposed limitations of method even when the role of expectancy has been properly emphasized.[6] Expectancy cannot be described by any set of concepts

[3] The difference between stimulus and object was instructively elaborated by E. B. Holt, who spoke of "the recession of the stimulus" and pointed out that this begins at a very early stage of evolution; *The Freudian Wish*, 1915, pp. 75 ff., 164.

[4] H. N. Peters, "The Judgmental Theory of Pleasantness and Unpleasantness," *Psychological Review*, 42 (1935), copyright American Psychological Association, p. 361.

[5] W. Köhler, *The Mentality of Apes*, 1925.

[6] Cf., e.g., O. H. Mowrer, "Preparatory Set (Expectancy) — Some Methods of Measurement," *Psychological Monographs*, 52 (1940), No. 2.

which omits its future reference. Expectancy looks forward, and does not disclose itself except through a train of subsequent events. The description of expectancy in static introspective terms, or in static physiological terms, violates the temporality of what is essentially temporal. It attempts to confine the process to the moment — to a momentary inner state, or to a momentary arrangement of nerves and muscles. It substitutes the beginning for the end, the first step for the course; as though one were to describe a journey not in terms of its destination but in terms of its point of departure.

It is also to be noted that expectancy is not a mere movement, or set of movements. It is movement selected and organized with reference to a destination. It is going somewhere, and to discover where it is going it is necessary to let it go long enough to mark its path and define its destination. To discover the object of expectation one must follow and project its pointing. To construe what is expected in terms of a present state or act of expecting is as though one were to look for New York City in the timetable, or Chatham Center in the signpost.

But it is to be noted that in all its phases the cognition *has* its object. It has it *here and now* if the cognition exists here and now. That to which the signpost points is a part of the present pointing of the signpost. Every directed operation has its *ad quem* from its incipient beginnings. Similarly, *what* is perceived, thought, intended, meant, or otherwise expected, qualifies the expecting whenever this occurs; even though what is expected has not yet occurred. There is no escaping this fact; the seeming paradox can be escaped only by distinguishing between the object which is "internal" to the act of cognition, and its "external" referent.

The difference between the mind's object and its external referent lies in the role which they play in truth and error. It is characteristic of expecting that things may or may not "turn out *as expected*." The expecting may be confirmed or it may be "taken by surprise." That which turns out, and confirms or surprises, is different from that which is expected in that the latter necessarily possesses precisely this ambiguity or dual possibility. While this is essential to the expected object, it is only accidental to the confirming or surprising event. The clap of thunder which confirms or surprises the expected clap of thunder, *need* not do either, since its occurrence does not depend on its being expected.

Here is the crux of the matter, ordinarily stated as the fact that cognition may be *either* true or erroneous. It is always questionable. Thus peace believed or judged must be so defined as to admit of both possibilities. It must have a kind of being that is independent of either alternative but provides for both. It is that which can be true or can be erroneous; its possibility of error is the price which has to be paid for its possibility of truth. The object of cognition, so characterized, may properly be designated as the *problematic object*.

It remains only to be said that this problematic character attaches
to all cognitive objects — to cognition all along the line from sense perception to meaning and the most articulate forms of thought. It is the
defining characteristic of cognition, which marks the place in the ascending complexity of life and mind where cognition begins.

4

The problematic character of the object of cognition is reflected in the
problematic character of the interest which it mediates.

The term 'interest,' in the sense in which the term is here used, is
awkward because it has no verb form having a passive participle. The
object of interest is *that in which interest is taken*. 'Object of interest'
in other words, is a general name for the passive participles 'liked,' 'desired,' 'enjoyed,' 'sought,' 'willed,' 'avoided,' 'hoped,' 'feared,' etc., throughout the whole gamut of mental acts embraced within the general concept
of interest. It may be objected that there are interests which have no
objects; such as the diffused states of joy or misery. But these states are
more correctly described as having a multiplicity rather than an absence
of objects. Joy is a condition of enjoying everything; misery is a condition
of finding everything distressing.

The object of interest is furnished to that subject by cognition. The
object of interest, whether presented or represented, is something expected; and possesses the questionable or problematic character of the
expected. It may be confirmed or surprised. But interest, while it embraces expectation, is something more than expectation: it is for or
against the expected. The object of interest is the *moving* or *prepotent*
expectation; the inciting prospect; the expectation which attracts or
repels. The object of interest both preserves and supplements the problematic character of the object of expectation. As expecting may be
surprised or confirmed, so interest may be disappointed or fulfilled. This
ambiguous destiny, this exposure to vicissitude, is common to both. In
both cases the outcome hangs in the balance, and the object must be so
defined as to leave both alternatives open. As an hypothesis has a determinate being of its own whether it is verified or disproved, so an interest
may never reach the crucial point of success or failure; and yet it is
indescribable without introducing its object of endeavor — its ambiguous
prospect.

In cognition and interest there is the same risk; in both cases the reach
exceeds the grasp. And in both cases there are degrees of risk. In the
case of cognition, intuition incurs the least risk; in the case of interest
the least risk is incurred by enjoyment. As in sensory intuition the expectancy is so promptly verified as to leave little room for disproof, so in
sensory enjoyment there is little room for failure or disappointment. But
even so, the enjoyment may be interrupted: the end of the world may

catch it suspended in mid-air about to take its next step. At the other end of the scale lies the interest in a remote object requiring a long chain of causal relations and mediated by a system of interdependent judgments each of which is vulnerable to error. But whether the prospect be short and narrow or long and wide, whether the confirmation or fulfillment comes promptly or tardily or not at all, there is still some degree of futurity and fallibility.

The close interweaving of interest and cognition must not be allowed to obliterate their difference. To expect something and be prepared to cope with it is one thing; to view it with favor or disfavor is another thing. An expected event may be hoped for, or dreaded, or viewed with indifference. Surprise may be attended with rejoicing, or with dismay, or with neither. Whatever the bias or absence of bias with which expectation is attended, the expectation remains the same, as to its truth and erroneousness. The same rumor of impending events may hearten or dishearten those who hear it; some may seek to hasten, others to prevent, the occurrence of the rumored events; still others, impelled by mere curiosity, may await them without taking sides. Whether the rumor is true or erroneous has nothing to do with these divergent attitudes, but only with the expectation's confirmation. Expectancy purged of all motor-affective attitudes save the cognitive interest itself is the last refinement of "pure" cognition.

There are two contemporary views to which the present view is opposed: the view which would identify the object of interest with its satisfaction or fulfillment, and the view which would identify the object of interest with the conditions by which it is satisfied or fulfilled. These views agree in placing the object at the terminal, rather than the initial, phase of the activity. Neither, however, is tenable.

The first is untenable because it cannot be stated without a circularity or endless regress. Hunger is an interest in *food,* and not an interest in the appeasing of hunger; love of peace is an interest in peace, and not an interest in the satisfaction of the love. Fulfillment in each case implies a prior object of interest without which the fulfillment itself cannot be explained. If the interest is in its own fulfillment, then it would be necessary to introduce an interest in the fulfillment of the interest in fulfillment and so *ad infinitum.*

The most plausible form of the second view is that which identifies the object of interest with "quiescence" or "achievement." [7] The drive of hunger, for example, is initiated by a lack of food: the "quiescence" is then the supplying of food in which the drive comes to rest. The deficiency causes uneasiness and random movements *until* it is removed; its removal then causes the cessation of the uneasiness and random move-

---

[7] This view is ably expounded by a philosopher-psychologist with whom the Author is largely in agreement; cf. S. C. Pepper, *Digest of Purposive Values,* 1947.

ments. But so construed the "until" of quiescence is not prospective, but a *fait accompli;* it designates cause and effect, and not object of endeavor. There is no excuse for applying such terms as 'goal' or 'purpose' except to states of *dis*quiet. The same argument applies to 'achievement.' Taken as the condition of things in which the achieving is complete, it is like any other state of affairs. A house, once built, has weight, shape, magnitude, and divers physico-chemical properties; but it is the object of the constructive interest, and derives value therefrom, only so long as it is as yet a project *un*achieved.

The object of interest belongs neither at the beginning of the activity, as when it is identified with a stimulus or state of deficiency, nor at the end, when it is identified with the quiescence or achievement. It is neither, and it is both. It is essential to the object of interest that it should pervade the entire activity from its incipient to its culminating phase. Its advent marks the beginning and its disappearance marks the end of the interest, and hence of value. The only way of meeting this requirement is to conceive the object as the ideal or problematic object which like a law is immanent in the process and determines its movement and its direction.

5

Every interest involves a specific form of consummatory activity, or class of activities. Thus hunger disposes to the *eating* of food, thirst to the *drinking* of water, aesthetic interest to the *contemplation* of the landscape, curiosity to *discovery* of the answer. This specific mode of activity, which is an inferent part of every interest, requires a name, and will hereinafter be referred to as the 'dealing.' A more familiar synonym of 'dealing' is 'using' ('utilizing,' 'making use of'). At the same time it is necessary to give a name to that *on which* the dealing impinges, or which the dealing engages, and the object, when it plays this role, may be called the 'occasion.' *All* interested activity, in other words, comprises a dealing which requires a correlative occasion; and an occasion which conditions a correlative dealing. The economic equivalent of the distinction is that between the consuming and the commodity to be consumed.

The distinction between occasion and dealing provides for the fact that qualitatively different interests may be taken in the same object. Thus food, for example, is ordinarily desired to eat. But it may be desired for any one of a number of other uses — to paint, to look at, to hoard, or to sell. Or, an object may be desired for *all* of its uses. Thus, home-loving involves a consolidation of the many home-occasioned dealings — *any* dealing of which home is the correlative occasion. Similarly, the love of peace comprises all the diverse dealings whose common occasion is the absence of violence. In weariness *any* occasion which requires effort is repugnant. The pugilistically inclined, who is "spoiling for a fight," will create enemies in order to combat them — anybody will do, provided he will put up his fists.

The distinction between dealing and occasion makes it possible to classify values in terms of the one or the other. Thus there are the domestic or local values distinguished by the proximity of their occasions; and the values of nature distinguished by the physical externality of their occasions. On the other hand the aesthetic and intellectual values are distinguished by their different modes of dealing with the same occasions whether local or distant, physical or mental.

Interest being so conceived as a commerce or transaction, involving both a mode of dealing and an appropriate occasion, one may describe the shifting of the focus from the one to the other. A mountain climber, let us say, is interested in a specific mountain-to-be-ascended. But he becomes progressively interested in climbing "for its own sake." He will spend his holidays seeking out mountains, *any* mountains which provide an occasion for the climber's mode of dealing. The focus of the climber's interest may oscillate between the mountain and the climbing, or the two may be commingled. There is a similar oscillation between the desire to defeat a specific enemy, and the general liking to win victories — "more worlds to conquer"; or between the desire to solve a problem and the zest for investigation — "the more problems the better."

The difference between positive and negative interest is a difference of dealing. The same distinction between dealing and occasion throws light on the difference between the two major types of negative interest, escape-fear and combativeness-anger. The former is focused on the dealing, and seeks to prevent or terminate it by withdrawal; the latter is focused on, and seeks to destroy, the occasion.

Since the dealing characterizes the interest rather than its object, it is to be assigned to the predicate, rather than the subject, of the judgment of value. Thus it is not the contemplation of the work of art which is beautiful; the work of art is beautiful — beautiful to contemplate. Similarly, it is the food which is good: good to eat — good because edible.

In the case in which the dealing is said to be exercised for its own sake, it is still usually the occasion, and not the dealing, which is the object. Thus if one walks to a destination for the purpose of walking rather than for the purpose of reaching the destination, the object is a class of destinations defined by the fact that walking is their correlative dealing. Any destination will do, provided, and only provided, that it entails walking.

There is, however, a type of interest in which the dealing itself *becomes the object*. A bodily dealing with a suitable occasion may itself become the occasion for another, and superimposed dealing. The climber's mountain may become accidental, or drop out altogether; he becomes aware, let us say, of the expansion of his lungs and a tingling of his muscles, and seeks to prolong this awareness. This attentive sensibility is now the dealing, and the bodily activity the occasion. In the interplay of these motivations, the striving for the goal and the enjoyment of the striving, the latter acts as a sort of supercharge to the former, and enriches the totality of value.

The problematic character of the object of interest attaches to the dealing and its occasion. During the life of the interest the dealing is not executed, but is prepared in advance, or anticipated. There is nothing mysterious about anticipation. There is present a "set" which is appropriate to a possible future occasion. In the case of bodily dealings, anticipation is a coördination of nerves and muscles together with whatever inhibitions are required to clear the way for a specific dealing. I am eagerly looking forward, let us say, to greeting my friend. I cannot greet him, and my interest cannot be fulfilled, until he is present. But I may here and now rehearse my words of greeting, have my hand half-extended, wear a smile on my face, and expel all incompatible attitudes and postures — so that only a short step is necessary for the consummation of friendliness.

6

The examination of the meaning of 'object of interest' serves to clarify the question of "motivation" — which is, in fact, only the same question expressed in other terms. This question is divisible into two questions, on neither of which is contemporary psychology prepared to deliver an altogether satisfactory answer: what is the *meaning* of 'motive,' and what *are* the motives?

The first step toward clarification of its meaning is to distinguish between 'motive' in the specific sense applicable to human conduct, and 'motive' in the generalized sense applicable to whatever generates motion. This distinction clearly excludes the auto*motive* internal combustion engine as irrelevant to the present context; but the distinction has become blurred owing to the subservience of psychology to physiology, and the subservience of physiology to chemistry and physics. Thus Lashley speaks of three variables which "contribute to the dominance of a pattern of behavior," namely: "chemical activation, adequacy of the stimulus situation, and amount of available nervous tissue." These are "actual processes involved in motivation at least at a primitive level." In the same context we are told that "the sexual interest and activity of the castrated male animal is restored by injection of testerone," and that waning maternal interest may be strengthened by an extract from the hypophysis.[8]

Are we, then, to suppose that testerone and extract of hypophysis are

[8] K. S. Lashley, "Coalescence of Neurology and Psychology," *Proceedings of the American Philosophical Society*, 84 (1941), p. 466.

specific motives because they are causes of specific activities? Are we to suppose that a vitamin is a universal motive because it "contributes" to all activities of the organism? Surely there is something radically wrong or confusing in an analysis which even raises such questions. The motives of human conduct are not coextensive with the forces or energies which determine human conduct, but constitute a specific form of determination, ordinarily referred to as "ends" or "purposes." If, owing to basic mechanistic convictions, one denies that ends or purposes do determine human conduct, then one should reject the concept of motives altogether: which is a step that no psychologist is prepared to take.

It would be unprofitable to pursue the confusions which obscure this subject in contemporary psychology.[9] The only escape from this jungle of words and ideas is straightway to identify motive with the problematic object of interest; that is, with the not-as-yet-realized occasion for a consummatory dealing.

When 'motive' is so construed, what are *the* human motives? There is no answer to this question, because the number is unlimited. This conclusion disposes, once and for all, of the venerable and widely accepted doctrine of teleological monism, to the effect, namely, that there is one and only one motive.

Teleological monism is divisible into two types, supernaturalistic or metaphysical monism, and naturalistic or psychological monism. To the first type belongs, for example, the doctrine that there is an entity called 'God,' which is endowed with all the perfections; and that all interest is "love of God." Whether there is or is not such a being is a question of theology which does not here concern us; but whether all interest is love of such a being is a question of fact to be answered by an observation of human interests. And here it is plain that even those who praise the love of God above all loves are compelled regretfully to admit that human affections are unfaithful, and need perpetually to be redirected to their "true" object.

Teleological monisms of the naturalistic or psychological type form a familiar chapter in the history of human thought. The commonest of these is the doctrine that pleasure and pain constitute the only motives of conduct — the only objects pursued and avoided for themselves. A second such monism is the egoistic doctrine that the only motive of any agent's conduct is himself, or his own preservation. These two monisms are commonly combined in the view that the sole motive of any interested subject in his own pleasure or pain.

These doctrines are so palpably contrary to fact, and so perpetually contradicted even by those who profess them, that their plausibility can be explained only by carelessness or confusion. The fact that interest is

---

[9] For the best general review of the literature, cf. P. T. Young, *Motivation of Behavior,* 1936.

in some vague sense intimately associated with pleasure and pain, and that every interest which occurs is somebody's interest, does not in the least prove that either pleasure-pain or self is the sole motive. *My* interest, attended with pleasures and pains, may be an interest *in* some other person, *in* food, wealth, sex, power, beauty, truth, or anything whatsoever — including pleasure and pain. The widespread acceptance of the pleasure-pain theory of motivation is largely due to the confusion, noted above, between the somatic sensations of pleasure and pain, and the feelings of positive and negative interest. Pleasure and pain in the first sense may be objects of interest, but are by no means the only objects of interest. Feelings of pleasantness and unpleasantness, on the other hand, construed as the inner awareness of positive and negative interests, commonly attend them, but *not* as their objects.

Contemporary psychologists are likely to argue not for the reduction of human motives to one or two but to a limited number of primitive motives. They reach this result by committing the Atavistic Fallacy; by assuming, in other words, that such motives as hunger, thirst, etc., coming first in the order of individual and evolutionary development, are the only independent motives, and persist in the dependent motives which develop from them. This view has been unqualifiedly rejected by Gordon W. Allport:

> The . . . type of dynamic psychology . . . here defended, regards adult motives as infinitely varied, and as self-sustaining, *contemporary* systems, growing out of antecedent systems, but functionally independent of them. . . . Each motive has a definite point of origin which may possibly lie in instincts, or, more likely, in the organic tensions of infancy. Chronologically speaking, all adult purposes can be traced back to these seed-forms in infancy, but as the individual matures the tie is broken. Whatever bond remains, is historical, not functional. . . . Earlier purposes lead into later purposes, and are abandoned in their favor.[10]

This writer may be said to make unnecessary concessions to that "geneticism" which on the whole he so stoutly repudiates; there is no decisive proof that independent motives may not arise in later life. But on the main point he is clear and persuasive: the motives of the human adult are indefinitely many. It is in fact this variety of motives that gives to human action its inscrutability; it is a part of the meaning of human freedom. As George Meredith says of one of his characters, "One can never quite guess what he will do, from never knowing the heat of the centre in him which precipitates his action." [11]

The Freudian and other contemporary dynamic psychologists have

[10] *The Nature of Personality*, 1950, Addison-Wesley, Cambridge, Mass., pp. 78–9; cf. *ibid.*, p. 172. The chapter here quoted appeared originally in *American Journal of Psychology*, 50 (1937). This essay should be read entire for an impressive presentation of the doctrine of "functional autonomy," as opposed to "geneticism."

[11] *The Egoist*, ch. xxx.

renewed the earlier assault upon reason; and have reinforced the broad trend of "irrationalism" which began in the nineteenth century and is still running strongly, both in "scientific" and unscientific circles. Insofar as 'irrationalism' means that human conduct is generated by feeling, emotion, and desire, or that the motor is inseparably linked with the affective — no exception can be taken. Insofar as it means that human conduct is largely erroneous, incoherent, illogical, and uncalculated, it is based upon fact; and is a wholesome corrective of that self-flattering fiction of man as a being who deduces his acts in an orderly manner from a true idea of the supreme good.

But it does not follow that man is not a "rational animal," if this is taken to mean that he has reasons (good or bad) for his actions, and acts because of such reasons. The term 'rationalization' betrays the confusion. Finding reasons for action is one of the conditions of its performance, and giving reasons for action is one of the conditions of its acceptance by others and by society. The modern age, in which man is held to be governed by irrational forces, has at the same time witnessed a refinement of the art of propaganda and the development of the science of semantics. It has become a commonplace that "words are weapons"; which implies that ideas are weapons, that is to say, forces, which direct and intensify conduct.

In other words, the cult of unreason has reaffirmed, amplified, and strengthened the thesis that human action is mediated throughout by cognition, and that the degree to which this factor is present is a distinguishing characteristic of action which is deemed human. This does not mean that reason is by itself a motive of action, still less the only motive, but that if 'reason' is taken to mean cognition in all its wide range from sense-perception and meaning to formal thought, and whether true or false, then reason is a condition of all motivation, since it provides interests with their objects.

7

Interest as here defined is distinguished by the pervasive factor of mediating fallible cognition. Mediated interest must be conceived, however, not as dwelling in a world apart, aloof from the physical and vital processes of nature, but rather as a superimposed and more advanced stage of complexity. There are antecedent and underlying levels, and there is a threshold which marks the advent of cognition, and hence the level of interest "proper," that is, intelligent or expectative interest. Like the threshold of life, and all other lines of demarcation in an order of continuously developing complexity, the threshold of interest, though definable, is hard to place.[12]

[12] For a discussion by the Author of the biological level of interest, *General Theory of Value*, 1926, 1950, chs. vi, vii.

Thus there is no interest in the sense here adopted without organization, spontaneity, and tendency, that is, directional or progressive change having a culminating phase. The level of complexity approaches more nearly to that of the interested action of men with the appearance of adjustment and adaptation. Then, within a phase of advance that cannot be sharply delimited, there begins a new and crucial form of complexity. Its distinguishing feature is cognitive mediation. The stimulus becomes a perception, or retires altogether; the acts become tinged with expectancy; the end result becomes an idea or meaning, having a forward reference, and capable, in the sequel, of being either realized or not realized.

In the heliotropism of the plant the sun stimulates growth toward the sun, and thus provides the plant with a necessary condition of its survival. The human sun worshiper, on the other hand, having the idea of the sun, responds to what means sun in a manner which he believes will procure its aid. Similarly, on the level of mere tendency and adaptation, hunger is a state of organic deficiency which stimulates movements which continue until the deficiency is made good. Add the factor of cognitive mediation and the process is differently describable. The state of deficiency is sensed as distress, and acts are performed which point to its relief. The stimulus is taken to be food; that is, it acquires the meaning of edible, and the promise of relief. The organism by now may be referred to as a "subject," in the psychological sense. He may be said to "seek" relief, and act "for the sake" of obtaining the food; and the successive activities of food-taking can be said to be adopted "in order to" reach ulterior stages in the series.

At every point where cognition is inserted it brings with it a problematic object, having a future reference and a dual possibility of truth or error. There may be no sun, or something may be mistaken for it. Or the sun may or may not exercise the power and beneficence attributed to it. There may be no actual state of deficiency, the exciting stimulus may not in fact be edible, the acts performed for the sake of food-taking in its various stages may not have the effects which are expected of them. The whole process, in short, may be permeated with mistaking. Similarly, it is quite possible that peace-loving mankind should be deceived all along the line: doing what did not in fact promote peace or negate war; resting in an illusion of peace, or acting upon the mistaken supposition that peace had come.

There is an option as to the level where the terms 'interest' and 'value' are introduced. If one desires to call a tendency an interest, and its equilibrium or culminating phase an end, and to give the name of 'value' to this end, or to the reactions of the organism or machine by which it is maintained or attained, there is nothing to prevent. It is a matter of the definition of words. Wherever a more advanced type of complexity emerges from a less advanced type, the name given to the former may, if one chooses, be extended backward or downward. It is this option which has led to the use of prefixes such as 'quasi,' 'sub,' 'near,' or 'proto.' There is nothing either illogical or contrary to fact in speaking of "quasi-interests," "sub-interests," "near-interests," and "proto-interests"; and values may be construed accordingly. But this is permissible only provided distinctions are not blurred. In the present case such an extension of meaning is permissible only provided it is clearly recognized that the extended meaning would not describe that which is distinctively characteristic of human nature and human history.

CHAPTER IV

GRADATION, INTEGRATION, AND MUTATION

A definition of value must give meaning not only to value, but to comparative value; not only to value, but to the grading, ranking, or critique of value. It is easy to understand why this question should absorb attention. Men are less excited about their values than about what they claim for their values. That which is held up before men by churches, cults, and by hortatory discourse, is not the good, but the supreme good. Thus, for example, Marcus Aurelius:

> Do thou therefore I say absolutely and freely make choice of that which is best, and stick unto it. Now, that they say is best, which is most profitable. If they mean profitable to man as he is a rational man, stand thou to it; but if they mean profitable, as he is a creature, only reject it; and from this thy tenet and conclusion keep off carefully all plausible shows and colours of external appearance, that thou mayest be able to discern things rightly.[1]

When men's values conflict, each endeavors to prove that his is superior. The problem of the critique and grading of value is properly emphasized in that important branch of theory of value which deals with morality; for morality is not only a domain of value but a level or plane of value, claiming preëminence over other value. Similarly, the practical problem of everyday life is not to find goods — there is, in fact, an embarrassment of riches. The difficulty is to choose among goods, and define principles by which such choice is justified.

The object of positive interest is better than the object of negative interest, or of indifference, by definition. And analogous statements may be made concerning evil — that an object of negative interest is worse

---

[1] *The Golden Book of Marcus Aurelius*, tr. by M. Casaubon, 1925, Bk. III, Sec. VII, pp. 22–3.

than an object of positive interest or of indifference. But these self-evident facts throw no light on the comparison of good with good and of evil with evil. For such light we must look to the ways in which one positive interest may be compared with another positive interest, and one negative interest with another negative interest.

There are certain preliminary considerations that will help to clear the way for the examination of this question. In the first place, theory of value cannot be satisfied by merely adopting ready-made rankings that rest upon habit or on verbal associations. Thus, for example, it is customary to refer eulogistically to "human" values as superior to "animal" values; but if this is not to reflect a mere pride of man in his own species, there must be some reason *why* the one is superior to the other. The same is to be said of the alleged inferiority of "physical" to "spiritual" values — an echo of traditional dualism, and religious disparagement of the "flesh." *Wherein* is the spiritual "superior" to the physical? — that is the question.

Another traditional and superficial disposition of this matter is the view that final ends are superior to means. The difficulty is that there do not appear to be any interests that are inherently independent rather than dependent. The basic biological interests may play either role: one may live to eat and drink, or eat and drink to live. Games may be played for themselves or for money. Even self-preservation may be a dependent interest; otherwise there would be no meaning in the question, "What is it that makes life worth living?"

If, as is commonly held, the intellectual and aesthetic interests are higher than the interests in food or drink, this is not because they are invariably ends and not means. On the contrary, it is commonly argued by their advocates that they *ought* to be ends in themselves because they *are* higher. They *may* be ends in themselves, and no doubt they are peculiarly qualified to be, but the fact is that they may also be means. Indeed it is widely maintained that intellectual interests are *always* instrumental; aesthetic interests may be pursued for hygienic reasons, artistic creation may be pursued for commercial reasons. It has been shown beyond doubt that ends are constantly becoming means, and means ends. This does not imply that there is no difference, but only that any interest, or mode of interest, may shift from the one role to the other.

The commonest form of the ranking or critique of values is that in which the critic takes his own interest as a standard; as, for example, when one musical connoisseur, in terms of his taste, condemns or approves the taste of a second musical connoisseur. But this implies either that the object of a negative interest is better than that of a positive interest — the principle already considered — or that the preferred is better than that to which it is preferred, whoever does the preferring — a principle to be considered below. Or, it implies that the second interest, the interest of the judge, is superior to the interest judged; which may or may not be the case. Only arrogance or dogma can claim that it is invariably the case. The last word possesses no greater weight than the first. The "low-brow" can rate himself above the "high-brow." The man of bad taste can despise the taste of superiors; the lowest sinner can curse God, and die.

Whether the grading of interest and value is or is not quantitative, whether interest and value can or cannot be measured, is a question that turns upon the definition of quantity and measure. It cannot be irrelevant that the only universal comparative and superlative forms of an adjective are those in which the positive form is preceded by 'more' and 'most,' 'less' and 'least,' or by other words which *prima facie* signify increase or decrease, that is to say, magnitude. It is optional whether the terms 'quantitative' and 'measurable' are used in a broad sense to embrace all such meanings, or in more restricted senses characteristic of mathematics and the exact sciences.

It is necessary, here as elsewhere, to hold fast to the distinction between the fact of value and the cognition of value. To judge truly that one value is more or less than another implies that one value *is* more or less than another, whether so judged or not. Unless we accept this implication we are on the slippery incline to an untenable solipsism. The point is blurred by the use of such hybrid words as 'appraise.' The present task is to determine what *makes* one thing better or worse than another.

The comparative magnitude of value must not be confused with the comparative magnitude of the valuable object. The magnitude of the value corresponds to the magnitude of the object only when magnitude itself is an object of interest. If there is a desire for a *large* house, then a house of eight rooms will be better than a house with seven. If there is a desire for *quick* arrival a plane having a speed of three hundred miles per hour is better than a train with a speed of only fifty miles an hour. But if one preferred a small house to a large, or slow travel to fast, then the magnitude of the value would be *inversely* proportional to the magnitude of the object. Three persons are more than two; but not necessarily more enjoyable: sometimes, "the more the merrier"; sometimes, "two is company, three's a crowd." To a competing athlete whose ambition is to exceed his opponent in points, the longer jump and the faster run will be better. To the candidate for election the greater number of votes will be better; to the profit-seeker the greater number of dollars; to the hungry man half a loaf is better than no bread, and to the family provider a whole loaf is better than either. But in each case the comparative magnitude of the value reflects the magnitude of the interest and not of the object.

The difficulty raised by the grading of values lies not in their *immeasurability*, but in their *commensurability*. There are various senses in which it is meaningful to speak of a more and less of interest which may be imputed in terms of value to its objects. All of these meanings are, as they should be, relative to interest, but they differ in the range of comparison which they permit. Preference, intensity, strength, duration, number, enlightenment, and inclusiveness of interest are all legitimate, and more or less explicitly recognized, modes of comparison. Intensity and preference provide comparison between different objects of the same interest; strength provides comparison between the interests of the same subject; number, duration, and enlightenment provide comparison *in these respects* between any interests of any subjects; and inclusion, or the whole-part relation, provides comparison between any interests in all respects.

In human history sometimes one and sometimes another of these several standards is in the ascendant, and is taken to define 'the higher' and 'the lower.' They are used to justify the causes in which groups of men unite, and to which they subordinate their particular interests. They create the issues on which ideological rivalries and struggles for progress are fought.

2

The clearest instance of a comparison within the range of a single interest is preference. From among its eligible objects, in all of which it is interested, a single interest sets one above or below another. By virtue of being so ranked the objects compose an order, which is quantitative in the sense that it can be represented by a line with different stretches or intervals lying between the object which is preferred to all the others (maximum), and the term to which all the others are preferred (minimum). So long as this comparison is not confused with others, such as intensity or strength, it may be said that there is a "greater" interest in what is preferred, than in that to which it is preferred.

While the order among the objects of preference is relative to a single interest, two or more such relative orders, comprising the same class of objects, and defined by the same type of interest, may be compared and found to agree. Thus two aesthetic interests may both prefer Titian to Picasso, or Matisse to Murillo. Using this method of parallel rating it is possible to say of a certain object that it is "unanimously" or "widely" preferred to others. The danger in employing this method lies in the difficulty of determining that the preferences compared are in fact governed by similar interests — both, for example, by the aesthetic interest, and not one by the aesthetic, and the other by the collector's, interest.

Two interests of the same type may also be compared as regards their capacity for discrimination; or the extent to which, in any given situation, the interest is alerted and reflectively aware of the qualifying attributes of its objects. This comparison is important in the education of taste; it is implied in the professional capacity of "tasters" of wine or perfume, and in the connoisseurship of art critics. It constitutes a part of what is meant, in the derogatory sense, when certain objects are said to be "popular" or to have a "mass appeal."

The act of preference gives a meaning to 'better' and 'worse'; but so do intensity, strength, duration, number, enlightenment, and inclusiveness.[2] The implicit or unjustified rejection of all standards save preference is often the premise of certain further mistaken conclusions. Thus it has led to the conclusion that values are not measurable at all; or, because preference is a matter of degree, to the conclusion that they are measurable only "intensively" and not "extensively." It has lent plausibility to the "viciously" relativistic view that all judgments of comparative value are relative to the preference of the judge. This would imply that it means *nothing* to state that the happiness of a society is better than the happiness of one of its members, except in so far as the person making the statement prefers the first to the second. This would exclude the possibility of basing a comparative judgment on other people's preferences, or on the preferences of experts. It would exclude the possibility of a preference which justified itself on the ground that the preferred is "objectively" better than that to which it is preferred. It would render meaningless, for example, the statement that even when the general good is not preferred to the good of an individual or group, it *ought* to be preferred because there is a greater volume of good in the former than in the latter.

A single interest varies in *intensity*. Food gains and loses value with the waxing and waning of appetite or hunger. Every interest is capable of rising to different heights above the zero of apathy or the threshold of bare awakening. 'Better' and 'best,' in the senses conveyed by such terms as 'transport,' 'ecstasy,' and 'rapture' in all their wide range of applications, from primitive bodily pleasures to aesthetic and intellectual enjoyments, and to religious exaltation, derive their meaning from this mode of variation.

The term 'intensity,' as employed by psychologists, was transferred from sensation, where it appears as a dimension distinguished from "quality"; as the same tone may be comparatively loud or soft, the same color comparatively bright or dull, the same taste or odor comparatively faint or strong. The just noticeable units of sensory intensity are not equal in any sense other than that each represents a limit of discrimination. But the series as such has its stretches or distances, and each unit is a "more" relatively to its place in the series. Comparative "pleasantness"

---

[2] For views which adopt the preferential standard to the exclusion of others, cf. C. I. Lewis, *An Analysis of Knowledge and Valuation*, 1946, pp. 550 ff., and *passim;* De Witt H. Parker, *Human Values*, 1931, ch. iii and *passim.*

and "unpleasantness" is not proportional to degrees of sensory intensity; indeed it is said to reach its maximum with a moderate sensory intensity. But the conception of magnitude is similar, in that it is a serial magnitude, in which a second object is judged to "feel" more or less pleasant or unpleasant than a given object. If the feelings of pleasantness and unpleasantness are taken, as has been here proposed, to mean the internal awareness of positive and negative interests, then the relative felt intensities of feeling reflect the relative intensities of the interests themselves.

Insofar as interests express themselves overtly, they enter into the common physical world. One may then choose as the index of intensity some manner of speech, or liveliness and volume of response. If tears are taken as the index of sorrow and laughter or gaiety of manner as the index of joy, then the sorrow of the man who "weeps quarts" can be said *in this sense* to be more intense than the "glistering grief" and "golden sorrow" of a king; and loud hilarity more intense than "laconic and Olympian mirth." But the scale of privately felt intensities may or may not correspond to that of such physically measurable manifestations; as when doubt is raised as to whether the one who wears his heart on his sleeve does or does not feel as intensely as one who is more inhibited or reticent. It is clear that there are great individual differences in the extent to which the intensity of interest, that is, the much or the little which one *cares*, or is *concerned*, is open to general observation.

Contemporary psychologists speak freely of the "strength" of reflexes, needs, tensions, drives, motives, or strivings, and of factors of "reinforcement"; as earlier psychologists and philosophers once described choice in terms of the comparative strength of desires.[3] There appears to be no clear line of demarcation between intensity and strength, nor any clear definition of either. A leading student of personality, to whom reference has already been made, emphasizes the "energic or quantitative aspect" or "needs" or "drives." Among the psychical manifestations of the organism's "vital energy" are "zest," "intensity," and "strength." But there is, alas! no consistent use of these terms:

> Evidently we are dealing here with a continuum between two extreme states, subjectively and objectively discernible: *zest* and *apathy*. The various aspects of zest may be designated by such words as alertness, reactivity, vigilance, freshness, vitality, strength, 'fire,' 'pep,' verve, eagerness, ardour, intensity, enthusiasm, interests; whereas under apathy may be subsumed lassitude, lethargy, loginess, 'brain fag,' indolence, ennui, boredom, fatigue, exhaustion. The former state yields prompter, faster, stronger, more frequent and persistent reactions.[4]

[3] Cf. C. L. Hull, *Principles of Behavior*, 1943, p. 369, and "Mind, Mechanism, and Adaptive Behavior," *Psychological Review*, 44 (1937); and the writings of B. F. Skinner and W. K. Estes.

[4] H. A. Murray, *Explorations in Personality*, Oxford University Press, 1938, pp. 129, 208.

It is to be noted that here 'intensity' and 'strength' appear in the analysis of 'zest.' Presently, however, we learn that the opposite of apathy is intensity (rather than zest), and that intensity is an index of strength, and strength of intensity. One's despair of discovering a consistency of meanings is complete when one reads that there are thirty-two criteria of "need strength." [5]

The comparative strength of interests can scarcely be defined in terms of physical force or work done (obstacles overcome), as that would imply that the elephant's weakest interest was immensely stronger than the strongest interest of an insect or even of a man. The number of times an animal will cross an electrically charged grill to obtain food measures hunger not by the amount of the electric charge but by the particular animal's repugnance to pain. The measure in terms of punishment endured, commonly employed in experiments on animals or in observations on man, measures the strength of a positive interest by the strength of a negative interest, and does not measure the strength of the negative interest itself, or the greater strength of one positive interest as compared with another. Similarly, when it is said that an appetite is strengthened by deprivation,[6] this can only mean that it approaches its full strength in proportion as it is deprived of its object. But then what is the *measure* of its full strength?

There is a measurement of interest which contemporary psychologists tend to neglect, and for which (since psychologists have not clearly given it any other clear meaning) the term 'strength' seems most appropriate. The individual has during his lifetime, or at any given period, a certain fund of available energy, for which his several interests compete. The appropriation of it by one interest diminishes the supply available for others. The strength of an interest, then, is its precedence in this rivalry.

This conception of strength provides for the fact that any interest may acquire superior strength. It also provides for the fact that the stronger or strongest interest may employ a small degree of physical energy. Its strength may lie in the fact that it inhibits the use of energy for other purposes. To employ the language of the physiologist, it is "prepotent in competition for possession of the common paths." [7] One of the several interests of an organism may "take possession," or enjoy a potentiality of such possession without exercising it.

The scale of *strength*, so defined, is relative to a single subject or

_____

[5] *Ibid.*, pp. 209, 251, 253, 255. The value of this work lies in its richness of empirical observation, and in its multiplication, rather than in its ordering, of distinctions. 'Persistence,' 'endurance,' and 'frequency,' which play important roles in this writer's analysis can, I think, best be considered under the temporal aspect of interest.

[6] Cf. G. Murphy, *Personality*, 1947, p. 140 ff.

[7] Cf. the physiologist C. S. Sherrington, *The Integrative Action of the Nervous System*, 1906, p. 231.

organism. But while it would not do to say that one man's interest was stronger than another's, it would be meaningful to say of mankind that hunger or sex tended to be among the relatively strong interests in all men. It would also be meaningful to say that one subject's appetite for drink was stronger than another's, if it was meant that this type of appetite tended to assume command in the former, but not in the latter.

3

There are two standards of comparison which appear to be applicable to any two interests, namely, time and number. Any two interests may be compared as regards their duration, or frequency of manifestation, if it be assumed that the time in which they occur is the same, or public, time. It is permissible to say that one interest, or one type of interest, lasts longer than another, and that its object therefore possesses a value that is "more lasting" — less ephemeral and transitory. The object of abiding love derives increased value from this fact, as compared with the object of a "passing fancy." It has been claimed (which is meaningful, whether or not it is true) that the aesthetic and intellectual interests yield more "durable satisfactions." The more enduring interests are sometimes described as the more "constant" or "stable." [8]

This must not be taken to mean that the greater duration of any interest implies a greater good in its object, but only the greater duration of *positive* interest. A long life is better than a short only provided there is a continuing love of life. In proportion as a negative interest is temporally extended the object varies from bad to worse. If life is evil, then the shorter the better, that is, the less evil.

The use of the standard of duration has to be guarded against the objection that "hope deferred maketh the heart sick." It might be supposed that, since the purpose is to reach the goal, the briefer the delay the better. To a considerable extent the virtue of technology lies in its abridging the time between the beginning and the end of endeavor. This objection is urged by a writer already cited:

> Intuitively, we judge that the longer one wants positively or negatively the worse it is. But this judgment cannot be derived from conation alone, but only by implicitly setting the standards of achievement above those of conation.[9]

This transition from conation to achievement does not solve the problem in terms of the present theory, since it fails to adhere consistently

[8] F. L. Wells, "Value Psychology and the Affective Disorders, etc." *Journal of Abnormal and Social Psychology*, 21 (1926–7), p. 146.
[9] S. C. Pepper, *Digest of Purposive Values*, 1947, pp. 83–4. This writer makes a similar "intuitive" leap from the standard of achievement to the standard of affection (pleasure).

to an identical concept of that which these standards measure — namely, value in terms of interest. The solution lies in recognizing that a protracted pursuit is commonly attended by negative interest — avoidance of obstacles, or hostility to opposition; and these negative values have to be subtracted from the positive value generated by the pursuit itself. The more protracted the interest the greater the chance that impatience and temporary defeats will arise. Furthermore, the longer the time which is taken to realize an object, the longer its *instrumental* values are postponed, or the greater the risk of their being lost altogether. Money cannot be spent until it is acquired, and if a lifetime is taken in its acquiring, there will be no spending; and the less of what can be bought with it has to be balanced against the value of its being acquired. Similarly the longer the time taken to realize an object the longer is its *enjoyment* postponed, if it be enjoyed.

But in the hypothetical case of a positive interest unattended by defeats or frustrations, and considered independently of the use to which the products may be put, and the subsequent enjoyments which they may subserve, the longer duration of the interest may properly be said to confer greater value upon its object. Whatever value it possesses, it has that value longer. Furthermore, the long-range interest — the durable pursuit of truth or beauty, the cause which requires time for the assembling and organization of means, or the life purpose gradually developed and realized, gathers values as it proceeds. Dependent interests, passing enjoyment, incidental values of many kinds, enrich the passage and are to be credited directly or indirectly to the remote object of endeavor.

Thus when Hobbes described life in the state of nature as "solitary, poore, nasty, brutish and short," [10] he properly reckoned its brevity among its *shortcomings!* It is this same counting of duration among the standards of value which justifies self-preservation and the prolongation of life — the prolongation of life because of the lasting and multiplying positive interests of which life is composed.

Two or more aggregates of interests can be compared numerically for the simple reason that they have the abstract character of number in common. This gives a meaning to comparative interest which is entirely unobjectionable so long as it is not confused with, or substituted for, other meanings. Four interests are greater than three interests numerically, because the numerical factor is present in both cases. But the three interests in question may be greater than the four interests in all other respects — preference, intensity, strength, duration, or enlightenment. The illicit substitution of one of these measures, such as intensity, for the numerical measure creates the seeming paradox that while there is "more suffering" when the whole population of a bombed city suffers than when a single victim suffers, nevertheless the whole population does

[10] *Leviathan,* Oxford, 1909, p. 97.

not "suffer more." There can be no objection to the numerical mode of comparison provided it is not taken to imply more than it states: provided, in other words, it is taken to mean only that there is more of interest in four interests than in three *numerically speaking*. The numerical comparison leaves other standards of comparison indeterminate, and therefore proves nothing as to total magnitudes of interest.

4

The receptivity of interest to changes of knowledge, so signally illustrated by the development of modern technology, defines a cognitive standard by which one interest may be deemed superior to another. The optimum interest judged by this standard would be an interest purged of error, and knowing truly whatever was relevant. Since all interests are cognitively mediated, and since the same standard of truth is applicable to all cognition, all interests, whether of the same or of different subjects, are commensurable in respect of intelligence and enlightenment. The only additional assumption to be made is that it is proper to speak of more or less of intelligence. It is safe to say that this assumption is correct in some sense — such as relative absence of error, possession of truth, or amount of knowledge.

A familiar application of this standard is the so-called "enlightened self-interest" which is often taken as a norm of national conduct. The object of national interest, let us say, is power or territory. The interest induces actions of which power or territory is expected. But the expectations may be either true or false; and if false the interest may be condemned on that account.

This type of critique is applicable to all interests insofar as their objects are held to possess qualifying attributes. Thus in the aesthetic field the interest may be directed to objects deemed to possess certain formal attributes, such as unity and balance, and criticism may take the form of determining the truth or error of the deeming.

Interests are allowed to borrow the attributes of the mediating cognition. Thus one speaks of interests as "true," "erroneous," "apparent," or "illusory." But this is a dangerous procedure since it tends to involve a confusion between the cognitive mediation and the cognition of value. An interest whose cognitive mediation is erroneous is nonetheless "truly" an interest; and though its object's good or evil is founded on error, it is not erroneous to judge its object to be good or evil.[11]

While the standard of enlightenment is a proper and significant standard of criticism, it is not the only standard of criticism — though this has often been held to be the case.[12] Other standards of criticism can be

---

[11] For a fuller discussion of this matter, cf. the Author's "Real and Apparent Value," *Philosophy*, 7 (1932), pp. 1–6.

[12] In general by the Socratic tradition, and more recently by adherents of the Pragmatic school.

excluded only on the assumption that there is only one good and one evil, other differences being differences in the degree to which these are known for what they are, and in the degree to which their means are correctly judged. But the plain fact is that there are many goods and many evils, and that some goods are better, and some evils worse. The less estimable characters are not distinguished wholly, if at all, by their ignorance, or the more regrettable events by the backwardness of science. Indeed evil is often distinguished by the fact that the evildoer knows only too well what he wants, and how to get it. The wolf is not less intelligent than the sheep, or the aggressor than his victim; nor is the philistine less clearheaded than the poet or mystic.

The several magnitudes of an interest obtained by the application of different standards of measurement can be multiplied by one another, and the product so obtained can be compared with the similar product of a second interest, but only when the factors are commensurable; as in the case of two volumes having similar dimensions. Unless the factors are themselves commensurable, *inter se,* the amounts assigned to them are quite arbitrary. Where, as in the case of awarding total merit, "points" are assigned, the weighting of the points is either arbitrary, or is determined by some external principle — such as commercial, athletic, or scholastic standards. The magnitudes of value enumerated above — preference, intensity, strength, duration, number, and enlightenment — are incommensurable, or commensurable within a certain range, or in a certain respect. The quantity obtained by multiplying them together would not describe a total value unless they were "weighted." The amount of intensity to be equated with an amount of enlightenment or duration, would be entirely arbitrary, or it would reflect some interest imported from outside and introducing a new dimension of value.

There is, however, a method of comparison by which one aggregate of interests can be compared with another, or with a single interest, regardless of these incommensurabilities. A totality of interests is greater than any of its parts in all respects; that is *whatever* the magnitudes of preference, intensity, strength, or duration, number, or enlightenment. The incommensurability of co-exclusive interests or aggregates of interests does not apply to the comparison of the inclusive with the included. This may be expressed by stating that if a certain interest is included as part of a totality of interests, then, however, the magnitudes are measured, there is an excess, a "more-besides," in the totality as compared with any part.

The standard of inclusiveness is the standard implicit in the superior claims of the total "personal will" as compared with any of the several appetites of the same person; and the claims of the total social interest as compared with those of its several personal or class interests. The application of this principle requires an examination of the nature of such personal or social totalities; and the sense in which their parts may be said to be included when they are "integrated." [13]

5

The "soul," thought to have been banished forever from psychology, has reappeared in the more innocent guise of "personality." The literature of the subject embraces several distinct questions. The term 'personality' is sometimes used, as in common speech, to refer to the peculiarities by which one human individual differs in a more or less marked way from another. But it also refers to a mode of integration or structural unity which is characteristic of human beings as distinguished from lower forms of mentality and from the "impersonality" of social processes and institutions.[14] It is this second, and more fundamental, question with which we are here primarily concerned.

While these two questions are distinct, they are closely related, and the answer to one will affect the answer to the other. For it is by virtue of the architecture of his interests that the more important of a man's individual peculiarities arise. One person may be distinguished from another by trivial idiosyncrasies: presumably no two individuals sneeze, laugh, or talk in precisely the same way, and a tic or accent may be the mark by which a unique individual is most easily identified. But personal character, in the more serious sense, consists in the way a man is organized and unified.

If the term 'person' is used to signify a type of structure, and the term 'individual' to signify that which distinguishes one person from another, there remain two cognate terms which demand a clarification of meaning; though it would be pedantic to adhere rigidly to any assigned usage. The term 'self' properly suggests a reflexive relationship. A person who is conscious of himself has a "self" — otherwise not. Thus the different "selves" which John Smith has are the various ideas which John Smith has of John Smith (his body, his property, his reputation, etc.), and with whose fortunes John Smith's sense of well-being rises or falls.[15] If John Smith has a highly unified personality his dominant life purpose, as he is aware of it, will be his essential self; and his reckoning of that purpose, his auditing of its accounts, his measurement of its successes and failures, will be his "self-interest." Since the term 'ego' is literally the first personal pronoun, as distinguished from the second and third persons, it would seem appropriate to use this term to emphasize the antithesis — the "I" *rather than* the "you," "we," "he," or "they"; in short, to signify the ab-

---

[13] The topic of integration, together with its personal, social, and world applications, will be resumed in Chs. VI, IX, and other later chapters.

[14] This is also the meaning when a state or a person is said, metaphorically, to be a "person."

[15] Cf. James's famous chapter on "The Consciousness of Self" in his *Principles of Psychology*, 1890, ch. x.

sence or the negative of benevolence. As has been properly recognized by child psychology from its beginnings, the ego — the "I," the "my," and the "me," develops when the individual asserts his will *against* the wills of those about him.

These terms 'person,' 'individual,' 'self,' and 'ego' all refer to different aspects of the same characteristic of man: 'person' to a type of structure; 'individual' to the differentiation of particulars or singulars of this type; 'self' to a person's being both object and subject of the same mental act; and 'ego' to the antithesis between one person and another.

There is more to a person than his personality. There are necessary conditions of personality, such as habit and temperament — but which do not *make* him a person. That which makes a man a person is the integration of his interests, both time-wise and space-wise. The person can look ahead, and plan accordingly; he can launch upon trains of purposive activities; he can relate his past to his future fortunes, and the distant to the near; he can keep his bearings; he can manage the household of his diverse interests; he can put first things first; he can hold in mind the wood, despite the trees; and all this he can do because of his cognitive capacities.

E. B. Holt conceived personality as the relatively total adaptation of the organism to a relatively large and comprehensive situation — to a "bigger section of the universe." He conceived this totalization or integration of behavior in terms of "synergy," that is, the consolidation of the individual's several motor sets. As a result of "cross-conditioning" [16] a response to one stimulus is evoked by other stimuli with which this first stimulus is frequently associated.

But as in the case of interest, so in the case of personality, it is necessary to recognize the pervasive factor of cognition. At a certain stage of complexity inter-conditioning of reflexes is superseded by meanings and judgments — the meanings which one interest possesses for other interests of the same subject, and the judgments pronounced upon one of the subject's interests in behalf of his other interests. In other words, his interests mediate one another, and the usual name for this inter-mediation is 'reflection.' Thus, it is a mark of personality that a man driven by hunger should "consider" the effect of its appeasement upon his subsequent discomforts (such as tomorrow's hang-over); or upon his health and general condition, and so indirectly upon all the other interests which will require his bodily energies. Or, it is a mark of personality that a man driven by ambition should judge this interest in the light of his family attachments or friendships. A man is a person insofar as there is a central clearing-house where his interests thus take account of one another, and are al-

---

[16] *The Freudian Wish,* 1915, pp. 196 ff. Cf. also Gardner Murphy, *Personality,* 1947, p. 619, and § 26 *passim.*

lowed to proceed only when the demands of other interests are consulted, and wholly or partially met.

The same thesis can be stated in terms of the "appeal" of the object of interest. Insofar as the appeal is to a single interest, as when the edible object appeals to hunger, there is as yet no personality. The appeal is a "personal appeal" when it is the resultant of two or more such single appeals, as when the edible object appeals not to hunger merely, but to avarice or maternal love. Insofar as its appeal is to all of the interests of a given subject, one may speak of its appeal to "him." When a person, so defined, acts on each of his interests "in the light of" the rest, all of his interests may be said to share the control of his action. He has a "will of his own," a "personal will," which exercises a lordship over his several interests. There is a central locus of responsibility, a human integer, a component of a distinctively human society, and a rational participant in its several social institutions.

6

Recent psychology has contributed richly to the study of personality. Indeed, some psychologists, such as H. A. Murray, have adopted the "point of view" that "personalities constitute the subject matter of psychology." [17] This writer, in his "Proposals for a Theory of Personality," has presented a doctrine which approximates, without explicitly stating, that which is here defended. "A human being," we are told, is a motile, discriminating, valuating, assimilating, adapting, integrating, differentiating and reproducing temporal unity within a changing environmental matrix." The problematic object of interest becomes the "press"; which is neither the external physical event, nor the sensory stimulus, but a meaning, a "sign of something that is to come," a "threat," or a "promise." The press, combined with a drive, need, or propensity, constitutes a "thema" — which appears to be the equivalent of the interest as here defined. "With age . . . conflict comes and after conflict resolution, synthesis and creative integration. . . . Action patterns are coördinated, enduring purposes arise and values are made to harmonize." With integration comes "regnancy," signifying the domination of the organism by some one of its purposes; and the regnancy, or hierarchy of regnancies, constitutes the essence of personality. The person is also "time-binding," "which is a way of saying that, by conserving some of the past and anticipating some of the future, a human being can, to a significant degree, make his behavior accord with events that have happened as well as those that are to come." [18] All of this is consistent with, although it does not explicitly recognize, the central role which in the present theory is assigned to cognition.

[17] H. A. Murray, and others, *Explorations in Personality*, 1938, p. 3.
[18] *Ibid.*, pp. 4, 36, 49, and ch. ii, *passim*.

In Gordon W. Allport's Presidential Address on "The Ego in Con-temporary Psychology" we are told that

> Ego-involvement is . . . a condition of total participation of the self
> — as knower, as organizer, as observer, as status seeker, and as socialized
> being. . . . Under conditions of ego-involvement the whole personality
> manifests greater consistency in behavior, reveals not specificity in conduct,
> but generality and congruence.[19]

This view of personality appears to differ in no essential respect from that presented above. Its central theme is that form of human life in which there is solidarity or total commitment, each motor-affective component of the individual supporting, and being supported by, the rest. It is of a person, so construed, that one says that he acts with his "whole heart," or "puts his whole self" into what he does.

Emotionally, personal behavior is accompanied by sentiments of pride, self-respect, or humiliation, or by the general feelings of happiness or unhappiness. It creates a susceptibility to insult — a "face" to be "saved." It culminates in a supreme interest with which the individual identifies himself, whose prospects are toned with optimism or pessimism, whose uncertainties beget that "anxiety" with which the existentialists are ob-sessed, and in whose decisions, according to the existentialists, a man actually lives.

The psychoanalytical school has contributed richly to the empirical knowledge of personality.[20] If the Freudian 'id' be taken to mean the aggregate of elementary impulsions, whether innate or acquired, and 'ego' the organization and mobilization by which these impulsions are enabled to present a common front to the environment, then this teaching may be cited in confirmation of the view of personality presented in the present study. E. B. Holt, following Freud, and interpreting him freely, emphasized the role of the ego in relieving the individual of conflict and suppressions. Personality becomes a hygienic and moral norm in which, through being recognized, blocked drives are freed and their energies released.[21]

7

Since society is their subject matter, the social sciences have naturally become its partisans against the partisans of the individual person. But the relation between the individual and the social totality is not to be un-

[19] Reprinted in *The Nature of Personality*, Addison-Wesley, Cambridge, Mass., 1950; cf. pp. 122, 135. This address was originally published in *Psychological Review*, 50 (1943).

[20] The Author has discussed the views of Jung and Adler, together with those of Freud, in *General Theory of Value*, 1926, 1950, §§ 77, 157–60, 237–8.

[21] E. B. Holt, *op. cit.* Freud's view is fully presented in his own *The Ego and the Id*, tr. by J. Rivière, 1927.

derstood by adopting either the individualistic or the totalitarian approach exclusively. According to the first of these doctrines, society is only a word: there is no such thing as a society, the word 'society' being only a name for an aggregate of individuals. According to the second doctrine there is no such thing as an individual, but only the word 'individual' used to designate a part of a society. Neither of these doctrines is the truth; they are both distortions of half-truth.

A society is composed of real individual persons, and can be analyzed into individaul persons *together with their interrelatedness.* But that which is analyzable is already a synthesis; and a social synthesis, having a total character of its own not possessed by any of its parts or relations severally, is something in its own right.

The distinction between the elements of analysis and the totality of synthesis has no necessary relation to the question of priority in time. It is quite conceivable that a plurality of individuals, existing first in isolation, should then become related and compose a totality. But it is equally conceivable that a social totality, existing first, should later be broken up into unrelated individuals. Which of these has as a matter of fact happened is a question for historians and prehistorians, and not for logicians.

In order to understand this empirical question it must be recognized that totalization is a matter of degree. Every society is composed of individual persons, but there will be differences in the degree to which these are describable in terms of the characteristics of the whole. Thus, for example, an army is composed of individual men, but one army will differ from another in the degree to which these individual men can be exhaustively described in terms of their army. The modern social sciences make much of the "role" with which the individual is identified in an organized society. But no human individual is ever completely identified with any role. The very fact that he plays several roles, and has somehow to reconcile them, gives him an "individuality of his own."

It is proper to ask whether comparatively early societies are comparatively "totalized." They look so, but then we are looking at them from a distance, and distance lends uniformity. It is also relevant to observe that what we now call "totalitarianism" can scarcely be said to be obsolete.

The tendency of the totalitarian emphasis is to conceive the individual as a merely passive product, channel, or locus of social forces. This error is analogous to that of the older empiricisms in which knowledge was conceived in terms of the imprint of sensation. The individual is not a blank sheet of paper, a tablet of wax, or a receptacle, in the area of action any more than in the area of cognition.[22] To weigh the rival claims of

[22] This reaction against prevailing tendencies in social science is clearly recognized by those social psychologists who begin and end with personality. Cf. G. Murphy, *op. cit.,* Part IV; H. A. Murray, *op. cit.,* pp. 719–22.

the total society and the individual as though they were mutually exclusive alternatives is to neglect the fact that the behavior of man is essentially individual response. The anthropologists speak of "culture," and
they emphasize its pervasiveness and uniformity. But the heart of the
matter is to determine how one mode of individual behavior becomes
normal and another an abnormal deviation.

The underlying causes of uniformity are the human nature, and the
physical environment which men have in common. Next in order are the
common necessities which connect these two — the necessary common
measures of adaptation. When these act as a social coercion upon the
individual they present themselves as number and prestige — the number
and prestige of other individuals. That which the individual then feels
impelled to do is what "everybody does," and especially the "important
people." To understand this we have only to observe the creation of
schools of art and letters, prevailing tastes, fashions, idioms, and sentiments, common sense, and public opinion, all of which are limited and
transient cultures. Prestige or eminence is due to many causes — to
power, office, aggressiveness, manner of bearing and speech, and exceptional capacity. Attitudes are spread by prestige, and accumulate impressiveness in geometrical ratio. But when their spread reaches a certain
point they exert an almost irresistible stimulus to the remnant.[23]

In the case of social analysis, as in the case of the analysis of personality, the unit is somebody's interest. As personal integration is to be
found in the interrelations of the several interests composing the same
person, social integration is to be looked for in the interrelations of the
interests of different persons. But here we encounter the important but
much neglected fact that the integration is achieved *within* persons. It
would be generally admitted that there are many connections which
occur only between parts of the same person. This is true, for example,
of memory, of habit-formation, of learning by experience, and of reasoning. One does not remember another person's past or form habits or learn
as a result of another person's experience, or draw conclusions from another person's premises — unless the other's has first been made one's
own. Similarly the connections which are essential to social integration
— the continuity of purpose, the dependence of one interest on another,
the mediating function of ideas, the dominance of one interest over others,
the control of acts by motives, the "therefore" and the "because" — obtain
only between parts of the same person. Hence, social integration is dependent on the sociality of the persons who compose society; that is, their
interest in one another's interests.

---

[23] This is the explanation offered by earlier social psychologists, such as Tarde
and Le Bon. Social and psychological anthropologists today do not deny it, but they
tend to ignore it or perhaps assume it, while they discuss the nature and interplay
of the different cultural systems themselves, taken *in abstracto.*

Interest in interest arises from, but does not consist in, the dependence of one individual on another. Thus a contemporary psychologist describes as follows the interdependence of the mother's "nurturant drives" and the child's hunger:

> The instrumental activities of each have been required for the production of the environmental events needed by the other. This situation describes the fundamental unit of social interaction with reference not only to arguing social behavior, but also to the formation of motivational systems involving interdependence between people.[24]

This description of the interlocking needs of mother and child is defective only in that it does not make it sufficiently clear that there is no social relation between mother and child until there is an interest of each in the other's interests; and it is because this factor is heavily weighted on the mother's side that the relation of mother and nursing infant constitutes an asymmetrical social relationship.

Such is the case with those forms of social integration with which the social sciences are primarily concerned — the family and friendship, the institutions of conscience, polity, law, and economy, the church and school, and with most of the more informal and transitory social organizations. Broader social integrations such as the "general will," the "national purpose," or the "good of all," are to be explained similarly in terms of the interests in one another felt by the several personal members of society. The precedence which is conceded to the public over the private is a precedence *within* persons of their "public spirit" over their private concerns.

8

Value taken as a function of interest reflects changes of interest. Change of interest is perpetual and all pervasive, and its causes are manifold. There is no fundamental or all-sufficient cause. It must suffice here to call attention to certain forms or types of change, and to single out a few generalizations which will best serve the purpose of its present inquiry.[25]

The object of interest is supplied to the interest by cognition, and will therefore change with the ceaseless advent of new perceptions or ideas. An interest which is directed to a class of eligible objects, will move from one member of the class to another, or it may enlarge the class. Hunger may assume the form of a preference for certain forms of food to which the subject has become habituated, or it may be expanded to embrace

[24] R. R. Sears, "Personality and Culture," *Proceedings of the American Philosophical Society*, 92 (1948), p. 365; cf. *ibid.*, p. 367.
[25] For a more detailed examination of this subject by the Author, cf. his *General Theory of Value*, 1926, 1950, ch. xviii, xix.

new edible possibilities. The musical interest may, as a result of musical experience, be narowed or broadened. Personal love may render the lover invulnerable or vulnerable to others of the sex or type. In other words, as through its mediating cognition more objects come within the range of an interest, it may become more "canalized" [26] or it may flow over a larger area. Experience not only narrows interests or broadens them, it also consolidates them. The same objects, such as home, country, or possessions, become the objects of different interests.[27]

The development and play of interests is governed by a principle which is loosely analogous to that of the conservation of energy. As one interest grows stronger it tends to weaken other interests, as though there were a limited fund of interest to be divided. It has been remarked by a recent writer that a service of too many good causes tends to reduce the service of each to a level of indifference and ineffectiveness:

> Perhaps I had travelled too much, left my heart in too many places. I knew what I was supposed to feel, what it was fashionable for my genera- tion to feel. We cared about everything: fascism in Germany and Italy, the seizure or Manchuria, Indian nationalism, the Irish question, the workers, the Negroes, the Jews. We had spread our feelings over the whole world; and I knew that mine were spread very thin. . . . What is the use of caring at all, if you aren't prepared to dedicate your life, to die? [28]

Just as there may be a dissipation, so there may be a concentration, of interest. In fanaticism, the strength of a particular interest exhausts the subject's motor-effective capacity. The censorious or prudish indi- vidual may be so preoccupied with the violations of a code of personal morals as to render him blind to a poet's or artist's creative genius.

A new object of interest may be acquired by the principle of the con- ditioned reflex. Interest is transferred from an original object to an adjoin- ing object. When this occurs there is a tendency to impute to the new object the attribute which qualified the original object. An individual is hated, let us say, for good reason; the attitude of hate is transferred to the members of his family; and these, however innocent, are then deemed to possess the hateful attributes. It is this mode of transfer, carrying ob- jective as well as emotional meaning from next to next, which is psycho- logically responsible for so-called "guilt by association," for race hatred and misanthropy, and for other wholesale and undiscriminating attitudes. But it is well to remember that precisely the same process produces in- nocence by association, love of family, and a diffused philanthropy. The extreme case of this transfer is seen in the emotional *creation* of the ap-

[26] In a somewhat broader sense than that here considered, this term is employed (with acknowledgments to Janet) by G. Murphy, *op. cit.,* ch. vii.

[27] The classic treatment of the subject under the name of "sentiments" is A. F. Shand, *The Foundations of Character,* 1914.

[28] Isherwood, *Prater Violet,* Random House, Inc., 1945, p. 104–5.

propriate object. Fear, hate, or love having been induced by a fearful, hateful, or lovable object, may then imagine lurking dangers, malignant spirits, or good fairies, to provide suitable occasions for the dealing in question.

Widely pervasive, and highly important in its social effects, is the change of interest in which means become ends in themselves. Substituting the terms to be employed in the present analysis, this means that dependent interests become independent. Especially notable in moral development is the fact that dependent benevolence, or regard for another for one's own sake, may become independent benevolence, or regard for another for *his* sake.

This form of mutation is a special case of a phenomenon that may best be described as the generation of new interests by *interpolation*. The simplest form of the process is the development of dependent interests themselves. Every interest involves subordinate acts, that is, acts performed because of what is expected of them. When these acts encounter resistance, or are protracted or repeated, they tend themselves to become interests; and having become dependent interests they may then become independent interests; and the new independent interest thus generated may then supersede the original interest by which it was generated. New values are substituted for old. There is a disposition among psychologists to hold that most of the mature interests of man have developed in this way.[29] Acquired skills, disclosing and expressing capacity, become enjoyable in and for themselves. The collective action originally organized to serve a need other than itself becomes itself the supreme value of the group. This mutation occurs every level of mental life, including the so-called "secondary drive" of the chimpanzee who, having become accustomed to using poker chips to obtain the desired food from a vending machine, "would work for the chips and would hoard them when the vending machine was not available."[30]

A notable case of interpolated interest is the contemplative enjoyment of the prospective object: as when the candidate for office "likes to think of himself" as in possession of his goal. This immediate interest, even could it be shown to be invariably present, is not the same thing as the interest which moves to achievement. It is a notorious fact that endeavor may be weakened, or superseded altogether, by the comparatively effortless pleasures of the imagination. Here lies the crucial difference between the dreamer and the man of action.

Interpolated interests, whether dependent or independent, are often of the opposite sign — involving a change from positive to negative or

[29] Cf. G. W. Allport's principle of "functional autonomy," as set forth in his "Functional Autonomy of Motives," in *American Journal of Psychology*, 50 (1937), reprinted in his *Nature of Personality*, 1950.

[30] R. R. Sears, "Personality Development in Contemporary Culture," *Proceedings of the American Philosophical Society*, 92 (1948), p. 364.

from negative to positive. Thus the animal's hunger for food generates his combativeness against the intruder who takes the food away; the love of a person generates anger against his enemy. Every interest generates fear when its object is in jeopardy. Frustration leads to aggression.[31] Or, the interpolation of interest may take the form of a shift from negative to positive. When fear is protracted, safety becomes a positive good — a "haven of refuge"; a struggle to avert defeat becomes a love of victory; the negative interest of malice may generate the positive satisfactions of sadism.

The interpolation of interest may take the form of a shift from prolonging to altering interest. Thus when the conditions of enjoyment are disturbed or removed, the interest assumes the form of an intervening effort to restore them. The reverse change, from altering to prolonging interest, may be described as extrapolation. The new interest grows out of the old at its moment of consummation. There is a tendency to have and to hold, or to find enjoyable, that which has been realized. This has much to do with the psychology of property. It is a mistake, however, to suppose that what is hopefully achieved is invariably enjoyed. Wealth, power, security, may all lose in possession the attractiveness which they had in prospect; this fact is a principal cause of human disillusionment.

A further type of change having a major social importance is the incitement of interest in a second subject by its manifestation in a first subject. Thus the sight, or other sensory evidence, of fear or of rage tends to arouse these passions in the observer. This may occur within the same subject: emotional expression tends to be circular, the expression serving as itself a stimulus to further excitement, as when one is said to "goad oneself" into fury. The more familiar occurrence is the social effect in which a demonstration of interest spreads to those who are aware of it; and is intensified in each by its extension among many, as the virulence of communicable diseases is proportional to their extent. This effect may be designed. The art of persuasion embraces the *exhibition* of the attitude of interest or conviction which is to be implanted in others; the eloquent man must be, or at least seem to be, himself wholehearted if he is to stir the hearts of others.

Any form or train of action due originally to an accidental combination of circumstances, or to natural selection, may become endeared by habit. There is, on the other hand, a restlessness, or interest in general activity for its own sake, which is constantly enriching life through the adventures on which it embarks. Whether the change of interest and of values is a change for the better or the worse can be determined only by the application of criteria of rank or gradation. If a servant of the

[31] Cf. Stuart Chase's discussion of "the blocked goal" in *Roads to Agreement*, 1951, ch. iii.

public grows ambitious until the motive of public service loses its force altogether, there has been a change for the worse, morally speaking. If an artist, being seduced by money, loses his devotion to art for its own sake, he has been degraded, judged by aesthetic standards. But if a man having practiced some form of skill as a means to his personal advancement comes to delight in craftsmanship, the elevation of a means into an end has been a change for the better; whereas a physician who, having practiced his profession for the sake of a financial reward, comes to be moved by compassion for human suffering and disability, has risen in the scale of disinterestedness. Noble enthusiasm as well as panic or mob violence may be spread by contagion.

These and other changes of interest give to the motor-affective life of man a character of perpetual mobility. It resembles a sea, rather than a river: an uneasy sea made up of tide, breaker, undertow, billow, ripple, and spray — full of cross-currents and counter-pressures. Life is a perpetual intermingling and alternation of pro's and con's. There is always some plus and some minus. It blows hot and it blows cold.

CHAPTER V

MODES OF INTEREST

Interest will hereinafter be employed as the unit in terms of which to clarify values. It will not be necessary to break interest down into ulterior elements of micro-psychology or micro-physiology. Its characteristic modes yield a vocabulary in terms of which to describe the historic values which play the major roles in the life of man. These do not as a rule coincide with the modes here distinguished, but are mixed, complex, and organized rather than pure or simple. The listing and definition of these modes at this stage of the inquiry will serve as a brief recapitulation of what has gone before, and at the same time as an introduction to what comes after. The verbal and conceptual apparatus here presented will not be rigidly employed; the language of common sense, or of the established sciences, is to be preferred when it is not flagrantly misleading.

The terms 'primitive' and 'advanced' as applied to interest refer to several distinctions which, while they tend to coincide in their applications, are not strictly identical. Thus the "primitive" interest may be taken to mean the "original" as opposed to the "acquired." This is not precisely the same as the distinction between 'inherited' and 'non-inherited,' since it is possible that an original interest should be non-inherited: it might arise as a "spontaneous variation" or mutation. 'Advanced,' furthermore, may be taken to be the opposite, not of 'original,' but of the relatively "less advanced." And while 'primitive' and 'advanced' do (by definition) refer to "early" and "late" in *some* order of progression, there are many such orders which give different meanings to the distinction. All interests, even original interests, are advanced in the order of cosmic or biological evolution. When interests are referred to as 'advanced' they are so considered in relation to the order of mental evolution. Their advancement refers to a degree of complexity such as distinguishes perception from sensation, or conscious purpose from tropism, reflex, or "instinct" in the loose use of this term. Taken as signifying a degree of mental complexity interest implies a lesser degree which falls just short of interest, and which may be termed 'near-interest.' It is in this sense that interest may be said to be advanced because of the emergence of mediating cognition on its successive levels. 'Sub-interest' then refers to that which possesses the other characters of interest but lacks mediating cognition. As applied to interest, furthermore, the term 'acquired' refers not to its being attained by nature at large, but by mind in the course of its own operations. It may, therefore, refer to an interest acquired by the exercise of interest.

The phylogenetic meaning of 'primitive' or 'advanced' is not the same as its ontogenetic meaning. The theory of recapitulation to the effect that the history of the individual repeats the history of the race is at best a plausible hypothesis. The "childhood of the race" is a figure of speech. Primitive societies, like all societies, are made up of adults. There is nothing peculiarly childish about them, nor does the behavior of the child (naïve, elemental, appetitive) resemble what we know about aboriginal tribes.

'Primitive' and 'advanced' in all their varieties and ambiguities of meaning are to be distinguished from 'strong' and 'universal.' There is no presumption that the original or early in the history of either race or individual is stronger than the acquired or late. To assume this is what has been described above as the Atavistic Fallacy. The primitive does not necessarily coincide with the universal. Even assuming that all men have a "common ancestry," it does not follow that all inherited traits are universal, since there are different *lines* of ancestry, and since inherited traits may cease to be inherited. Similarly, the original may disappear and the acquired may, by imitation and suggestion, *become* universal. In short, although strong and universal interests such as hunger and sex are primitive, primitiveness is not a decisive or final test as to what interests are either strong or universal.

2

There are various descriptions of interest that imply a deficiency of the interest as interest. Thus interests may be dormant or *latent*. Cain's hatred of Abel did not cease when Cain slept; but it then differed from his *activated* hatred as this occurred at the moment of fratricide. Most interests are latent most of the time — for reasons of fatigue, surfeit, inopportuneness, or the limitations of the span of consciousness, but they nevertheless exist as *dispositions*, to be reckoned with against the moment of their awakening. Their latency is analogous to that of stored memories, as distinguished from "calling them to mind." Latency itself differs in its proximity to enactment. A disposition may be in reserve or it may be alerted; in the rear, or advanced toward the firing line. Interest varies between complete latency, and some residual degree of latency mingled with activation, as is the case of the coiled spring which is partially released.

"Unconscious" or "subconscious" interests, or "hidden motives," may be interpreted in terms of latency. Their condition may be taken to mean that they can be brought to the surface by certain techniques, and that meanwhile they exist in the form of dispositions, like untapped memories. More than this is implied in the doctrine of psychoanalysis. It is supposed that they operate as forces when they have not as yet been brought to the surface. But this does not require that they shall at such times be active *as interests*. A great deal goes on in the unconscious organism which affects consciousness, such as circulatory changes or muscular tensions and relaxations.

The psychoanalytical doctrine is not clear on this point. Sometimes it may be taken to mean that the subject is not aware of the interests which consciously move him. He may be consciously afraid in that his objects are tinged with fearfulness, without his attention's being drawn to the fact. Sometimes the unconscious interest is a conscious interest which is charged with erroneousness, as when it is pointed out to the subject that it is not love but hate which "really" moves him; or that his hate is based on erroneous assumptions or "fixations."

There is a difference between latency and *potentiality* of interest. In the first case the interest is existent, whereas in the second case all conditions required for its existence are present, save one. Sub-interest may be said to be potential interest, when it is conceived as lacking only the factor of cognition. But there is a second and more important sense in which one may speak of "potential" interest, when, namely, there are entities which are qualified to be its objects. Interest, whether activated or latent, may be directed to objects of a certain class, but not to a given member of the class. If "gentlemen prefer blondes," any given blonde is qualified for preference, but may not in her individual capacity be an object of preference because no gentleman has met her. Any cause of an object of interest is thereby qualified to become the object of a dependent interest; and becomes such when its causal virtue becomes known to an interested subject. So-called "natural resources" are potentially useful because of the demands for which they are qualified.

Closely related to potential interest is *playful* as distinguished from *executive* interest. Every interest has its phases of incompleteness to which it extends something of its own motivation. The kitten sheathes its claws, and the puppy bites gently, thus carrying the predatory impulse *to a certain point*. The boy who plays at war, or the girl who plays with dolls, is not merely imitating the behavior of others, but is enacting an interest which can only be conceived in terms of combativeness and maternal solicitude. The materials of play — the wooden gun or the plaster doll — the social situation in which play occurs, and an inner check which arrests the activity short of the actual injury or feeding of its object, thus combine to define a limit at which the playful activity desists from its course.

Life abounds in unfinished activities, in beginnings which are not carried through, in experiments without commitment. Seriousness is mixed with playfulness, and playfulness with seriousness. But amidst all this interweaving the difference remains. The difference can be stated only in terms of the partial and the complete; and the partial can be stated only in terms of that specific completeness of which it is a part.

Interests may be described as "unreal," "non-existent," or "false." [1] Without at this time entering into refined distinctions it is to be pointed out, in the first place, that the status of value shall follow the status of the interest. If the interest is unreal, then so is the value. It is essential, in the second place, to distinguish the status of the act of interest from the status of its object. Thus an existent interest may have a non-existent or problematic object; the object may be unreal when the interested activity is real; a real interest may be engaged in "realizing" its object.

The case of 'truth' is troublesome because this term is often used to refer to being, rather than to knowledge. If one corrects this unfortunate habit of saying 'truly is' when one means simply 'is,' and confine the term 'truth' to a characteristic of cognition, there remains the confusion between the cognition of interest and the mediating cognition which conditions interest. The judgment that there is such and such an interest may be true when the interest in question is founded on error. One judges, for example, that there was great rejoicing in 1918 over the "false armistice." It was not the armistice that was false, but the rumor; it is true that there was rejoicing mediated by this false rumor. If truth is to be strictly conceived as a characteristic of cognition, it can be attributed to an interest only by reference to its cognitive constituent. The "true interest" is then the interest whose mediating cognition is true, and the "false interest" is the interest whose mediating cognition is erroneous.

3

Interest may take the form of *prolonging*, or of *altering* (making different); and an altering interest may be achieving or *terminating*, as when one sets a definite goal, or *progressive* as when a longing is insatiable. Thus he who enjoys the landscape is moved to continue it as it is; the landscape gardener is interested in bringing about something which as yet does not exist; the man who is greedy for land is interested in its endless increase.

Prolonging or recurrent interest has been thought to contradict that prospective character which the present definition imputes to all interest.

[1] For a discussion of the "ontological" distinctions, "being," "existence," "real," etc., cf. below, Ch. XXII.

Does not the futurity of the object of interest exclude being "pleased with things as they are"? Does it provide for that dwelling on the present state of affairs which is characteristic of joy and sorrow, or of liking and disliking?

This difficulty arises from two sources: the mistaken view that feeling is passive; and the failure to distinguish the sameness of an object through time, with the sameness of time itself. Enjoyment is not instantaneous — it *goes on;* and insofar as it is interested it looks ahead. If a situation is to be enjoyed as it is, both the situation and the activity which engages it must persist through time. A man who says to himself, "I like this as it is, and would not have it otherwise," does not arrest his dealing, but arrests, preserves, or reinstates the occasion so that the dealing may continue. That which is prospective is the prolongation through future time of that which already is. If an interruption or obstacle intervenes or threatens, the activity then takes the form of removing it, in such wise as to enable the activity to be resumed.

Lest it be supposed that the prolonging form of interest is merely static or repetitive it must be further recognized that the occasion is extended and complex, and therefore takes time for its exploration. In order that a landscape may be enjoyed the observer must move his eye from one part to another, and discriminate its details successively. He may then retraverse the same content, or pass from a given content to a different content, but within a whole which persists or is being completed. Or, it may take time to exhaust the whole, as when the heard part of the melody is accompanied by the impulsion to hear the parts as yet unheard. This incitement to "more of the same," "the same again," or "the rest of the same" is to be distinguished from the incitement to create, annihilate, or modify.

When a terminating interest is fulfilled it ceases, and when it ceases the value which it confers ceases with it. It is to be noted, however, that the terminating interest is often, though not necessarily, succeeded by a prolonging interest; and that as the end-point is approached the two types of interest tend to overlap. One begins to enjoy that which is partially achieved; and the altering interest is thus reinforced during a protracted period of effort.

4

The antithesis of positive and negative interests is recognized by common sense in the verbal 'yes' and 'no,' in the nod and the head shake, and in the double incentive of the "carrot and the stick." While psychologists also recognize this pair of opposites there is no agreement on its precise meaning. 'Adience' is sometimes construed as activity giving more, 'abience' as activity giving less, of the stimulus; but this distinction is designed to apply only to drives oriented to the external sensory environment. E. C. Tolman distinguishes between *appetites*, which are "set in motion" by an internal condition, and culminate in a specific "consummatory response" — a "getting to"; and *aversions*, which are "set off" by an environmental object and culminate in "getting away" from an internal state of "sufferance." But this distinction fails to take account of the fact that there is a getting away, and a getting to, in all drives; as, for example, in hunger, which may be excited either by pangs, or by the smell or sight of food; and which manifests itself equally in a relief of pangs and in an enjoyment of food.[2]

The distinction can be adequately described only in terms of the realization or de-realization of the object, which is problematic in the sense that it permits of either of these alternatives. All interests, whether positive or negative, are subject to the vicissitudes of fulfillment and non-fulfillment, success and failure. Positive interest is characterized by actions which promise to bring the object to pass, negative interest by action which promises its prevention or undoing; and each is successful or unsuccessful accordingly. It is essential that the positivity and negativity should be thus conceived as attaching to the act of interest and not to its object; otherwise it would not be conceivable that the same object should have both positive and negative value.

Positive and negative interests cannot be distinguished, as has been frequently proposed, by simple direction of motion, such as approach and withdrawal. Movement from may be a manifestation of love, movement toward of hostility, and immobility either of fascination or of fear. There is no way of describing the difference save in terms of consistency of behavior. Thus the movements of fear and combativeness may be in large part the same — running, hiding, climbing, manipulating tools — but they are both negative not because of these movements which they share with many positive interests, but because they both have the character of negating an object. Combativeness goes about it by destroying the occasion, fear by removal to a distance at which it no longer has to be dealt with; and this difference can be discovered only by plotting the total operation, and noting what it is headed towards or leads to.

It may be thought that negative interest can be converted into positive interest in a negative object, but this would be a hasty conclusion. The real merits of this question are empirical rather than logical or dialectical. Peace and not-war, war and not-peace, may mean the same thing; but peace *may* mean home and "business as usual," and war may mean violence and military routine, in which case to love peace and to hate war are not the same thing. To desire and like the life of peace is

---

[2] The double aspect of drives is recognized by this writer in the case of "social drives"; but why it is restricted to these, he does not make clear; cf. his "Motivation, Learning, and Adjustment," *Proceedings of the American Philosophical Society*, 84 (1941), pp. 543–55.

not the same thing as to avoid and dislike the life of war despite the fact that, practically speaking, they are allied. Love of life, and fear of death, or finding the thought of death repugnant, are not the same thing. There is a perpetual interplay of positive and negative motivation in most, if not all, trains of action; but this must not. be taken to mean that the motivations are the same — if they were, there could be no *inter*play. It is to be further noted that persons may be classified according as they are characteristically positive or negative: some are lovers, some are haters, regardless of their objects.

Combining the distinctions between prolonging and altering, and realization and de-realization, with the distinction between positive and negative, clarifies these distinctions and at the same time reveals other distinctions. Thus positive prolonging interest starts with the realization of its object and moves from realization to realization. *Avoiding* or preventive interest starts with the non-realization of an object and moves to its non-realization: it is a negative prolonging interest. Positive altering interest starts with its object's non-realization, and moves to its realization. *Interruptive* interest starts with the realization of its object and moves to its de-realization.

It is sometimes contended that only positive interests are original, and that all negative interests are acquired; or that only negative interests are original, and that all positive interests are acquired. Both of these opposite contentions represent the prejudice in favor of sweeping generalizations. It is quite true that negative interests are generated by the frustration of positive interests, but it is equally true that positive interests are generated by negative interests, when these proceed to their end by a series of positive steps. The positive interests of hunger and sex and the negative interests of aversion to pain and flight from danger are equally original. There is no evidence of absolute originality that does not apply to both.

5

The modes of interest which follow embrace the several senses in which interests may be broadly classified as *primary* and *secondary;* meaning that one interest takes precedence of another. Interests may be independent or dependent. The test of an interest's dependence lies in the observable fact that it would not be save for another interest. An independent interest is automotive, from which it draws its motivation. It is to this distinction that we must look for clarification of the distinction between final and instrumental interests, familiarly known as the distinction between end and means.

The distinction between ends and means must not be confused with that between occasion and dealing. Because both the ends and means are objects of interested activity each has its own occasion and dealing. Nor, for the same reason, must this distinction be confused with that between the consummatory act and the subordinate or transitional acts. Nor must the distinction between ends and means be identified with the case in which the mediation of interest is relatively formal. The relation of means to end may or may not be "calculated"; it appears just as truly on the level of perceptual meaning as on the more articulate level of concept and judgment.

A *means* is the object of an interest which is asymetrically dependent on an ulterior interest whose object is the *end*. Thus a man may covet wealth in order to achieve political power. He does covet wealth, and adopts a course of action which promises this object. But he would not covet wealth unless he coveted political power. His acquisitiveness flows from his ambition. Extinguish his ambition and his acquisitiveness ceases. The reverse is not true: if his acquisitiveness were extinguished his ambition would still remain. Both ends and means have value — the one independent or *final* value, the other dependent or *instrumental* value.

If this usage is to be employed we must be prepared to say that all ends are "ends in themselves." This is what we mean when we call them "ends." We must also be prepared to say that all means are justified by their ends; that is, their value as means is derived from the value of their ends. When the means to an end is repudiated, it will be because of another end. Or, if the means affects the choice of ends this will be because the means is also an end and not a means only.

There is nothing of which it can be said that it is *the* end; namely, the only thing that can fill this role. There is nothing of which it can be said that being an end it may not become a means, or being a means may not become an end. Such fluctuation is perpetual and all-pervasive. But when such changes occur it is the thing which has shifted roles: what was end has become means; what was means has become end. The roles themselves remain distinct: means does not become end, or end, means.

Since in the present view an object's value is defined in terms of the interest taken in it, there is no such thing as "intrinsic" value, if this is taken to mean an object's possessing value in the absence of relations to an entity other than itself. *Intrinsic* becomes the same as 'independent.' The intrinsic value is the value which an object possesses by virtue of the interest which is taken in it "for its own sake"; its *extrinsic* value is that which it borrows or derives from other value. When, for example, food owes its value to hunger, its value can be said to be intrinsic; whereas its value is extrinsic when it is derived from the desire of profit from its exchange for other commodities. Money desired for what it can buy possesses extrinsic value; it acquires intrinsic value for the miser.

'Intrinsic' is sometimes identified with 'immediate': with the felt value, which is supposed to be unquestionable, as distinguished from the judged value, which is liable to error.[3] This identification of intrinsic value with the manner of knowing it does not agree with the present analysis; according to which all value is fallible in some degree, and sensory cognition of the external manifestation of interest is just as immediate as affective cognition of its internal manifestation.

The distinction between dependent and independent interests is often confused with another and no less important distinction which applies to interests whether dependent or independent. Two independent interests may be so related that the first overrules the second. Thus a man's love of his friend may be so related to his ambition that he will sacrifice the second to the first. His ambition is not dependent on his love of his friend; if he did not love his friend he would still be ambitious. But the love of his friend sets bounds to his ambition; the ambition stops at the point where it violates the love. The love operates on the ambition negatively, but not positively; it censors, but does not induce. The overruling interest is the stronger interest, whenever the two compete for the energies of the organism. It is the dominant, ruling, or governing interest, as distinguished from submissive or obedient interest. It is to be noted that neither the independent nor the ruling interest is on that account "superior" in the sense of comparative value.

An interest which is independent may nevertheless reinforce another interest; and may then be designated as an *auxiliary* interest. Thus combativeness may reinforce any interest which requires the removal of an obstacle. Curiosity plays a highly important role as an auxiliary interest, since the mediating cognition of interest may always provide an occasion for it. Scarcely less notable is the role of emulation as auxiliary to any interest which operates in the competitive situation.

6

All interests are *personal,* in the sense that they are the interests *of* some person, and in proportion as the individual achieves a certain degree of integration. Some interests are personal in another sense, in the sense, namely, that they are interests *in* a person. When we speak of a certain person's interests as "impersonal" we mean that he is characteristically interested in objects other than persons — objects such as art or science. It is in this sense that women are said (whether rightly or wrongly) to be more personal than men. When the person 'of' and the person 'in' are different persons the interest belongs to the social mode of interest, which will be examined below.

There remains the case in which the possessor or subject of the interest is the same as its object: when the person that the interest is "of," or to whom the interest belongs, is the same as the person "in" whom

[3] Cf. C. I. Lewis, *Analysis of Knowledge and Valuation,* 1946, pp. 382, 388–9.

the interest is taken. In this case, the personal interest is *reflexive;* and the term 'self' becomes appropriate. If the idea of personal reflexive interest is to retain any meaning there must be a duality of role played by the same person. The problem is the same as the problem of self-consciousness, which can mean nothing unless the person who is conscious is the same person as the person who is the object of consciousness. There is every likelihood of confusion, but there is no logical impediment, if it be recognized that the two terms of a relationship may be regarded as in one respect the same and in another respect different.

The expressions 'self-interest,' 'self-love,' and 'selfishness' have a morally disparaging meaning when the self in question is comparatively devoid of social interests. Apart from this social aspect of the self there remains the difference between a subject's total *self-interest* and his *partial self-interest*. The former requires an idea of his integrated personality — not only of what his self comprises, but of the order among his interests. The latter requires only that his object shall be one of his own states or activities.

Inasmuch as the interested subject or agent is a whole of many parts, he lives in an internal as well as an external environment. Each activity of the organism has its repercussions within the body; each organ is interdependent on other organs; each interest of the subject has its commerce with other interests of the same subject; sensory experience embraces somatic or interoceptive, as well as exteroceptive, sensations. This distinction is not to be confused with the distinction between the dealing and its occasion. The dealing is always internal, but the interest as a whole is internal only when the occasion is also internal, as when a person is impelled to remove his own pain, or restrains his impulse to sleep in the interest of his own ambition. The social consequences of the distinction are far-reaching. Insofar as the objects of a person's interests are internal they are not of immediate concern to others; they do not impinge on the common environment, and create no occasion for dispute or necessity of social regulation.

Social interest, in the broad sense, is interest of one person in the interest or interests of a second person. As in the case of personal interest, interest "in" must not be confused with interest "of." All interests are of society, in that they are interests of persons who are members of a society. And when the interests of the members of a society are organized, and find modes of collective expression, then we may speak of an interest *of* society as a whole; though such organization would be impossible if there were no interests of its members *in* one another. As in the case of personal interest social interest may be total, as distinguished from partial; there may be an interest *in*, as well as *of*, the whole of society.

Social interest is to be distinguished from interest in a second individual where this second individual's interests are disregarded. If

Diogenes was interested, as Plutarch said, in having Alexander "stand a little on one side, and not keep the sun off," he was not interested in Alexander's interests but only in his body. "Cupboard love," so-called, is the interest of the child in an indulgent person as a mere source of supply.

Interest in another's interest may be positive or negative, and dependent or independent. The child's affection for his mother after it has passed the stage of mere interest in the warmth or food of her body, is likely at first to be a gratitude for past favors or a bribery for favors to come — for what "he can get out of her." The mother's love is likely to be an independent interest, an interest in the child's interest "for its own sake," no benefits received or looked for; whereas the father may be thinking of the child as a potential breadwinner. Most positive social interests are a mixture of dependent and independent.

The term 'benevolence' which plays so prominent a role in the literature of ethics, had best be reserved for positive, independent interest in the fulfillment of another's interest, whether this be positive or negative. To seek to discover another's interest, or to seek to implant it, is not benevolence: benevolence is to seek to further it. Malevolence is negative interest in the fulfillment of another's interest; or the desire to frustrate it.

Personal benevolence or malevolence (personal love or hate) is a relation of person to person, rather than of interest to interest. The benevolence of one person towards a second person means, in the extreme sense, that the first person is positively interested in the fulfillment of the totality of the interests, positive or negative, of the second person; the malevolence of one person to a second person means that the first person is interested in the frustration of the totality of the interests, positive or negative, of the second person. The same principles may be extended to the interests of all persons of a group; or, in the limiting cases of universal benevolence (philanthropy) and universal malevolence (misanthropy), the interests of the total aggregate of persons. A person may be characterized as benevolent or malevolent on the whole when his independent and overruling interests are benevolent or malevolent.

It is to be noted that benevolence and malevolence as here defined are distinguished from *beneficence* and *maleficence* by the presence of the *will* to fulfill or frustrate the interests of others. They are quite distinct from mere helpfulness and hurtfulness, and imply an attitude of friendliness or enmity. It is to be noted, furthermore, that the 'good' component of *bene*volence and the 'evil' component of *male*volence are relative to the interest of the second person and not of the first. The determining factor in both cases is the interest of the second party as it moves *him*, and not as it is imputed or projected by the first party.

Selfishness is clearly not the same as malevolence. Malevolence is selfish, but selfishness need not be malevolent; it consists in the mere absence of benevolence. In this sense every interest is selfish which does not consist in, or is not modified by, a positive, independent regard for the fulfillment of another's interests. The common appetites, taken in themselves, are of this sort; as is the person who is completely indifferent to the interests of others. It is quite possible that a selfish person should be entirely free from "thought of self."

7

There are two senses in which interests are *conflicting,* namely, contradiction and incompatibility. *Contradictory* interests are positive and negative interests in the same object. We have seen that positive and negative interests are not distinguished by their objects, but as the realizing and de-realizing of the object. It follows that the positive and negative interests in the same object cannot both be fulfilled. But they can coexist. The explanation lies in the fact that their contradiction is prospective — they are on their way toward a point at which the contradiction would take effect. Two projectiles moving in opposite directions toward a point of junction can coexist, despite the fact that the occupation of that point by one implies its non-occupation by the other. Similarly, two propositional attitudes ("I hope that it will rain," "I hope that it will not rain") can coexist when the propositions are contradictories. The object of both is a problematic future raining.

The conflict of interests in the sense of contradictoriness is to be distinguished from their accidental incompatibility. Two non-contradictory enjoyments of the same monument may be incompatible when one enjoyment interferes with the other through requiring the exclusive occupation of the same post of observation. Contradictoriness and incompatibility are further distinguished by the fact that while the former requires that their objects shall be the same, the latter is independent of the object. Thus an interest in the contemplation of the landscape may be disturbed by the noise of building or traffic.

There are two spheres of incompatibility, the social sphere and the personal sphere. The most notable case of social incompatibility is provided by acquisitive or "preëmptive" interests, which are distinguished by the fact that their dealings require the exclusive use of their external occasions. At least in degree there is a difference between the interest which usurps its occasion, cannot share it with others because it alters it, and the non-preëmptive interest which leaves its occasion as it finds it. The preëmptive interest leads to the institution of property, and is one of the most prolific causes of quarrels. But the principle of incompatibility is of scarcely less importance in describing the relation of the several interests of the same person, which, though they be directed to quite different external occasions must nevertheless in their dealings employ the time, energies, faculties, and other resources of the same organism.

Incompatible interests tend to become contradictory. Thus when the aesthetic interests of the two subjects are incompatible because of the requirement of the same post of observation, each tends to assume the form of preventing its occupation by the other. And when this situation arises, contradictoriness tends to pass over into malevolence or enmity, in which each person is interested in the frustration of the interest of the other.

Harmony, taken as the opposite of conflict, is to be explained in the same terms. It means non-contradiction and compatibility. Interests may exist, relatively to one another, in a state of innocence, which enables them both to be fulfilled without interference. Such a state of affairs exists whenever interests are sufficiently separated in space and time. Harmony in this sense is diminished by propinquity, and by all the technological advances in transportation, communication, and range of action, which bring men together into a single interactive system. But the same conditions which diminish the innocence of remoteness make possible that organized harmony which distinguishes the personal and social life of man on the level of conscious will. When men's interests are so related as to create incompatibility and contradiction they devise methods of achieving compatibility and consistency which in turn breed not only non-hostility, but benevolence and coöperation.

8

Interests can be ranked, so as to give meaning to 'higher' or 'lower,' or *superior* and *inferior* values. This question has been obscured by the assumption that there is only one ranking of interests, so that the so-called "supreme good" is supreme absolutely, or in all respects. As a matter of fact, however, interests can be ranked by many standards. This does not mean that interests have no rank, or that they do not really and objectively possess the ranks imputed to them; nor does it imply that one or more of their rankings may not have certain peculiarities which qualify them to be singled out for special emphasis.

Good, or the object of positive interest, is better than evil and worthlessness, the objects of negative interest and indifference. The objects of greater interest, however measured — as by preference, intensity, strength, duration, and number — are better than the objects of lesser. The object of true or enlightened interest is better than the object of false because there is a positive interest in truth, and because the fulfillment of true interests is more likely to lead to enjoyment, and to promote other interests. There is no objection to the admission of all these standards provided they are not confused with one another.

If objects are to be deemed better in terms of comparative interest, then no standard should be invoked unless it is definable in terms of interest. Such standards as "modern" and "human" must be viewed with suspicion. "Modern" is not better than ancient when this means merely a historical difference, but only when it implies a greater magnitude of interest, as for example, through advancing enlightenment or social organization. These considerations apply equally to the standard of "human." Objects of interest to men are not to be accounted better than objects of interest to animals, unless human interests can be shown to be higher on some ground other than biological species.

There is an inveterate tendency to assume that an interest that is superior in one respect is superior in all respects. There is only one respect of which this can be said, namely, inclusiveness. If one interest includes another interest it possesses and exceeds all the magnitudes which the included interest possesses. A whole must be more than its parts — otherwise the term 'partial' would lose its meaning. The standard of inclusion escapes the problem of commensurability by not raising it. To say that a total interest is greater than any of its partial interests *whatever their magnitudes* escapes the necessity of comparing these magnitudes among themselves.

Here again it is necessary to resist the temptation to claim too much. The standard of inclusiveness does not annul or supersede other standards, but omits them without prejudice. It defines the framework within which life may rise through other rankings of inferiority and superiority. It is the principle of inclusiveness which provides the warrant for the claims of morality — to which we now turn.

CHAPTER VI

THE MEANING OF MORALITY

Morality is something which goes on in the world; or, at any rate, there is something which goes on in the world to which it is appropriate to give the name of 'morality.' Nothing is more familiar; nothing is more obscure in its meaning. Moral science, moral philosophy, or moral theory consists in the investigation of this going on. The term 'ethics' is not here introduced for reasons that will appear more clearly in the sequel. Suffice it to say, at this stage of the inquiry, that 'ethics' is being reserved for a study of a special moral institution, namely, conscience, sometimes called 'custom' or 'mores'; meaning the attitudes of approval and disapproval which occur at any given time or place.

If there is any doubt as to the correctness of this statement that morality is something that goes on in the world, and which appears in all societies and in all periods of history, it rests on an ambiguity. It may, indeed, be doubted whether moral ideals have ever been *realized* in any historic society: misanthropy, pessimism, cynicism, and the doctrine of original sin, have all challenged this claim. But it cannot be denied that morality exists as a *pursuit*, having its own ideal by which a certain kind of human success or failure is judged.

The emphasis on the ideal rather than its realization has led to the wide acceptance of the view that morality and having an ideal mean the same thing. Thomas Mann, in his *Magic Mountain*, had one of his characters, the brilliant and voluble Hans Castorp, propound the paradoxical opinion that morality is to be looked for not "dans la vertue, c'est-à-dire, dans la raison, la discipline, les bonnes moeurs, l'honnêteté" but rather in their opposites — "le péché, en s'abandonnant au danger, à ce qui est nuisible, à ce qui nous consume." [1] A similar paradox is to be found in Nietzsche's view that morality lies "beyond good and evil." Later days

[1] Modern Library Edition, 1927, p. 430.

have seen the rise of cults such as fascism, nazism, and bolshevism, which have derived their morale from their defiance of morality. If such confusions are to be avoided it is necessary to distinguish the qualities of fidelity, discipline, perseverance, and enthusiasm which lend vigor to *any* cult, from the specific content of the moral cult. One must be prepared to reject the edifying associations of the word 'ideal,' and recognize that ideals may be moral, immoral, or unmoral. Similarly, morality does not consist merely in having principles and scruples, but in the nature of that to which obligation is felt and sacrifice is made.

Morality can be initially identified by a set of terms used as predicates in moral judgments: terms such as 'ought,' 'duty,' 'right,' 'good,' 'virtue,' and their opposites. It is essential here, as in general theory of value, to distinguish between the predicates and that *of which* they are predicated. There are two questions: "What is morally good?" and "In what does moral goodness consist?" Moralists of the past have usually been concerned with the first of these questions, and have sought a summary answer. Thus the ancients reduced the virtues (the things held virtuous) to justice, temperance, courage, and wisdom; while the Christians reduced the duties (things held dutiful) to faith, hope, and love, and "the two great commandments," love of God and love of neighbor. The four ancient virtues were then reduced to justice or wisdom, and the Christian duties to love; or both were reduced to happiness.

When this line of thought arrives at a supreme generalization it tends to pass over into the second of the above inquiries, with which it is easily confused. When it is affirmed that only wisdom or justice is virtuous, or that the only duty is love, or that the only good is happiness, it is natural to equate the meaning of virtue, duty, and good with these unique exemplifications. Despite this natural presumption, however, there are two distant questions, and it would be impossible without redundancy to give the same answer to both; that would be to say "virtue is virtuous," "duty is dutiful," or "goodness is good." The first question is answered when the predicate of virtuousness, dutifulness, or goodness, whatever it means, is assigned to a certain grammatical subject; the second question is answered when the predicate itself is analyzed or clarified. It is the second question and the discussions to which it gives rise that constitute the primary subject matter of moral theory.

2

It is an open secret at this stage of the discussion that morality takes conflict of interest as its point of departure and harmony of interests as its ideal goal. Before expounding this ideal it will be profitable to examine certain widespread misconceptions of morality which have lowered its prestige not only among moral sceptics and cynics, but, to no inconsiderable extent, in the popular mind. It is one or more of these miscon-

ceptions that have given morality its bad name, as when Disraeli is reported to have said of Gladstone that he was "a good man in the worst
sense of the term." Among these misconceptions there are four which
lead all the rest: asceticism, authoritarianism, preceptualism, and utopianism.

These misconceptions of morality arise not from sheer blindness but
from an exaggerated emphasis on some one of its aspects. Since these
misconceptions are half-truths their correction throws light on the whole
truth. Every solid entity can be approached from different sides, and its
many-sidedness tends to escape knowledge through abstraction of one
of its sides: the elevation is mistaken for the building. So morality, having
many sides, yields distortions. But the one-sidedness can be explained by
the many-sidedness — the misunderstandings can be understood.

The first and commonest of these misunderstandings is asceticism.
Morality does not coincide with the inclination of the moment, or with
any particular inclination. Owing to the fact that it requires inclinations
to be overruled and disciplined, duty comes to be identified with *dis*-
inclination — with doing what one does not want to do or leaving undone
what one wants to do. When this aspect of morality is erected into its
supreme principle, the good life becomes a life "against" — a substitution
of negative for positive interests. Every interest which raises its head is
regarded as an enemy, or at least a danger. This is what is known as
asceticism.

The truth of the matter is precisely the opposite of this — namely, a
life "for," the substitution of positive for negative interests. It is the
original conflict, and not the moralization, of interests that multiplies
negations. Morality is an organizing of interests in order that they may
flourish. The denials derive their only *moral* justification from the affirma-
tions for which they make room. The purpose of morality is the abundant
life.

A second aspect of morality arises from the fact that men learn it from
some authority — domestic, civil, social, or religious — which issues commands and enforces them. *Authoritarianism* is the name given to the view
which identifies morality with the acceptance and obedience of authority;
with uncritical acceptance, and passive obedience. But authority ceases
to be an ultimate principle at the moment when attention is directed to
the credentials of the authority and the motives by which acceptance and
obedience are dictated. It then appears that the authority of the authority requires that it shall be powerful, or wise, or good; while obedience
is dictated by fear, or the need of guidance, or by love and gratitude. In
other words, authority ceases to be absolute, but rests on ulterior grounds
which displace its sheer authoritativeness. And these ulterior grounds
involve some idea of good: when governed by fear, the obedient subject
himself "knows what is good for him"; when governed by the need of

guidance he assumes that the authority knows what is good for him; when governed by love he attributes goodness to the authority itself. Each good turns out to consist in interest — whether selfish interest, or self-interest, or disinterested benevolence.

Authoritarianism is the aspect which morality presents to dependence and immaturity. It is the morality of childhood — whether of the individual or of the group. The child learns morality at his mother's knee, or upon his father's. This childhood is never entirely outgrown. The parent is replaced by the policeman, ruler, or priest. Men are always in need of authority, and require to be controlled by the power, wisdom, and example of their betters. They have to be threatened, bribed, or seduced if they are to behave as the moral ideal requires. But this fact, important as it is for explaining the causes of human conduct, does not define the ideal itself; nor does it account for that mature phase of the moral life in which having understood the moral ideal men are persuaded to adopt it and to observe its requirements for the sake of its ideal end.

A third misconception of morality may properly be called *preceptualism* — morality as identified with a set of precepts. It is analogous to what in the realm of law is called 'legalism' — which is substituting the letter for the spirit or intent of the law. Moral organization like any organization requires its rules; which must be observed by the members if the purpose of the organization is to be served. Just as the law may be abstracted from its social utility and taken as an absolute, so the moral rules may be similarly abstracted.

The taboos and other customs which are unquestioningly accepted by social groups, are either arbitrary conventions resulting from accident, tradition, imitation, and habit, or can be traced to an apparent utility, formerly discovered by experience and subsequently forgotten. They are either quite indefensible, or defensible only in terms of the rediscovery and confirmation of their utility. When they are merely arbitrary conventions they cease, like fashions, to have any moral force; when their apparent utility is disproved and they are still taken seriously, they are called *"mere* taboos."

Precepts are usually expressed, like the scriptural commandments, in the imperative voice. They assume the form of injunctions: 'thou shalt,' 'thou shalt not.' But while the grammatical voice is imperative, the real voice has disappeared: the "stern daughter of the voice of God," has become an orphan, retaining only the sternness. Commandments are left without a commander. The authority has faded until nothing is left of it but its utterances tinged with an echo of authoritativeness.

When precepts are thus explained they are not explained away. Morality continues to embrace positive and negative generalizations of action, such as justice, veracity, murder, theft, but instead of being taken as the ultimates of morality, shining in their own light, and having their force in themselves, they are seen to be the instruments by which the good life is achieved, as the rules of hygiene minister to personal or social health.

The fourth of the common misconceptions of morality arises from the gap which separates its ideal goal from its achievement. It is of its very nature that there should be such a gap, that the "reach" *should* "exceed the grasp," but it is equally essential that the gap should be recognized and bridged. *Utopianism* stands for a divorce and not a gap. It does not mean that the ideal is too high, for all moral ideals are counsels of perfection, but that no route is plotted from the present actualities to or toward the remote ideal. It is this path, or series of steps, or chain of intermediaries, which makes the ideal, however exalted, a "practical possibility."

When the ideal is disconnected from the field of present action and transplanted to another world, it ceases to play its role of ideal-to-be-realized. Men then tend to be divided into two opposing camps, those who ignore the ideal through preoccupation with present action, and those who cease to be active in the practical sphere through dreaming the ideal. The first are the "opportunists" who act without purpose or direction. Since they have no ideal by which to judge their shortcomings they become the servants of things as they are. The second, the utopians, tend to substitute the image of the ideal for its realization and to become "visionaries." Seeking to correct the myopia of the opposing camp they acquire the defect of presbyopia, and become so farsighted that they cannot deal with what lies about them. The moral life requires that men shall be able to shift their focus between the near and the far, and to engage in short-range segments of long-range endeavor.

The correction of these four misconceptions throws light on the true conception of morality. In order to promote an organized harmony of life men must limit and adjust interests without destroying them, submit to authority without slavishness, conform to rules for the sake of the end which these subserve, and seek the ideal goal through a succession of effective acts departing from the here and now.

3

Morality is man's endeavor to harmonize conflicting interests: to prevent conflict when it threatens, to remove conflict when it occurs, and to advance from the negative harmony of non-conflict to the positive harmony of coöperation. Morality is the solution of the problem created by conflict — conflict among the interests of the same or of different persons. The solution of the personal problem lies in the substitution for a condition of warring and mutually destructive impulses a condition in which each impulse, being assigned a limited place, may be innocent and contributory. For the weakness of inner discord it substitutes the strength of a unified life in which the several interests of an individual make common cause together. The same description applies to the morality of a social group, all along the line from the domestic family to the family of nations.

Such a moralization of life takes place, insofar as it does take place, through organization — personal and social. This crucial idea of organization must not be conceived loosely, or identified with organism. In organism, as in a work of art, the part serves the whole; in moral organization the whole serves the parts, or the whole only for the sake of the parts. The parts are interests, and they are organized in order that they, the constituent interests themselves, may be saved and fulfilled.

When interests are thus organized there emerges an interest of the totality, or moral interest, whose superiority lies in its being greater than any of its parts — greater by the principle of inclusiveness. It is authorized to speak for all of the component interests when its voice is their joint voice. The height of any claim in the moral scale is proportional to the breadth of its representation. What suits all of a person's interests is exalted above what merely suits a fraction; what suits everybody is exalted above what merely suits somebody.

Certain philosophies and religions of the past have conceived the world as originally a moral order, that is, as *constitutionally* harmonious, all desires and wills being so fitted to one another that each acting for itself is at the same time harmless or helpful to the rest. Such a guarantee of cosmic harmony has been an article of faith in Christian theism, as exemplified in the terrestrial and celestial paradises. In the thought of the eighteenth century this was represented in terms of an idyllic "state of nature." In Kant it was a "kingdom of ends" ruled by the moral imperative. After Kant it assumed another form in the idealistic doctrine of an "absolute spirit." Still later it found expression in the Spencerian doctrine of a "perfectly adjusted society," conceived as the end product of natural evolution.

But Christian theism and the eighteenth century doctrine of nature both found it necessary to acknowledge an unfortunate lapse or "fall," from which men must be redeemed through salvation or through civil institutions. The Kantian kingdom of ends was assigned to a "noumenal" world beyond the reach of knowledge, and affirmed by an act of faith. The idealistic philosophy found it necessary to acknowledge the disharmony of the phenomenal world and to transpose the realization of harmony to a supersensible realm. And science has long since abandoned the idea that harmony is a predetermined outcome of the evolutionary process. Whether as recovery from a fall, or as a bridge from the temporal to the eternal, or as a conscious control of natural forces, it is now recognized as necessary to invoke the human will in order that harmony shall be *made out of* disharmony. Harmony thus becomes an ideal future good; a goal the attainment of which is conditioned by plasticity of circumstance, fidelity of purpose, efficiency of control, and growth of enlightenment.

Morality conceived as the harmonization of interests for the sake of the interests harmonized can be described as a cult of freedom. It does not force interests into a procrustean bed, but gives interests space and air in which to be more abundantly themselves. Its purpose is to provide room. And ideally the benefits of morality are extended to all interests. Hence moral progress takes the double form, of liberalizing the existing organization, and of extending it to interests hitherto excluded. Both of these principles have important applications to the "dynamics" of morality, or to the moral force in human history. The extension of moral organization is made possible by increase of contact and interaction, which, however, then multiplies the possibilities of conflict. Hence the peculiar destiny of man, whose ascent is rendered possible by the same conditions which make possible his fall. There can be no development of a unified personality or society without the risk of inner tensions; no neighborhood, nation, or society of all mankind, without the risk of war.

Morality as progressive achievement requires the integration of interests. They cannot be simply added together. If they are to compose a harmonious will that represents them all, they must be brought into line. At the same time, if such a will is truly to embrace them, which is the ground of its higher claim, they must themselves accept the realignment. Morality is an integration of interests, in which they are rendered harmonious without losing their identity. The procedure by which this is effected is the method of *reflective agreement*, appearing in the personal will, and in the social will.

4

Interests are integrated by reflection. In the creation of the personal will there occurs a thinking over, in which the several interests of the same person are reviewed, and invited to present their claims. Reflection overcomes the effects of forgetfulness and disassociation. It corrects the perspectives of time and immediacy, anticipating the interests of tomorrow, and giving consideration to the interests which at the moment are cold or remote. It brings to light the causal relations between one interest and another. From reflection there emerge decisions which fulfill, in some measure, the purpose of harmony: plans, schedules, quotas, substitutions, and other arrangements by which the several interests avoid collision and achieve mutual reinforcement.

The personal will which emerges from reflection is not, as has sometimes been held, merely the strongest among existing interests, prevailing after a struggle of opposing forces. It is not a mere survivor, other contestants having been eliminated. It does not intervene on one side or the other, but takes a line down the middle, analogous to the resultant or vector in a field of forces. It makes its own choices, and sets its own precedents. Its accumulated decisions, having become permanent dispositions, form a character, or unwritten personal constitution.

The achievement of such a personal will cannot be indefinitely postponed. The exigencies of life are imperative, and have to be met with whatever personal will can be achieved. There is always a dateline for action. Any given personal will is thus inevitably premature, provisional, and subject to improvement. But insofar as it is enlightened and circumspect this personal will is considered as finally justified, except insofar as it neglects the similar personal wills of others. Within the domain of its included interests it is a moral ultimate. The several interests which it embraces have no moral cause for complaint insofar as they have been given the opportunity of contributing to the purpose to which they are subordinated.

The relation of the personal will to the person's several interests is primarily one of government, overruling, or dominance. It serves as a check or censor called into play when any of the particular interests tends to exceed bounds. Like a sentinel it challenges each passing interest and requires it to show its credentials.

The similarity between the personal and social forms of the moral will must not be allowed to obscure their profound difference. It is true that as the personal will emerges from reflection so the social will emerges from communication and discussion. In both cases the emergent will represents a totality of interests, and achieves by organization a substitution of harmony for conflict. The difference lies in the fact that whereas the personal will is composed of sub-personal interests, the social will is composed of persons.

But while the social moral will is a will of persons, society is not a person. Excluding fictitious persons, corporate persons, legal persons, and every metaphorical or figurative use of the term, the only real person is that being which is capable of reflecting, choosing, relating means to ends, making decisions, and subordinating particular interests to an overruling purpose. It follows that there can be no moral will on the social level except as composed of several personal wills which are peculiarly modified and interrelated.

The ramifications of this fact pervade the whole domain of morality and moral institutions. It is echoed in all of those doctrines which exalt the person as an end in himself. It gives meaning to fraternity as the acknowledgment of person by fellow-persons. It gives to the individual man that "dignity" of which we hear so much. It provides for that unique role of the person as thinker, judge, and chooser, which lies at the basis of all representative institutions, and determines the moral priority of individuals to society.

5

The creation of a social moral will out of personal wills depends on benevolence, that is, one person's positive interest in another person's interest. To be benevolent here means not that I treat you well so far as it happens to suit my existing interests to do so; my concern for your interests is an independent interest. Taking your desires and aversions, your hopes and fears, your pleasures and pains, in short, the interests by which you are actually moved, I act as though these interests were my own. Though I cannot, strictly speaking, *feel* your interests, I can acknowledge them, wish them well, and allow for them in addition to the interests which are already embraced within me. When you are at the same time benevolently disposed to my interests, we then have the same problem of reconciling the same interests, except that my original interests form the content of your benevolence and your original interests the content of mine.

In this pooling of interests I am ordinarily concerned that your benevolence shall actually embrace my original interests; and you are similarly concerned to accent yours. Each of us assumes that the other can safely be trusted to look out for his own. Assuming that each will be biased in favor of his own interests, the bias of each will tend to correct the bias of the other. Each will be the special pleader of his own interests, and his insistence on them will reinforce the other's weaker benevolence.

There will be a further difference. Your interests are best and most immediately served by you, and mine by me. I can for the most part serve you best by letting you serve yourself. The greater part of my benevolence, therefore, will take a permissive form. I will sometimes help you, but more often will abstain from hurting you; or will so follow my own inclinations as to make it possible for you also to follow yours; or accept your inclinations as setting a limit to mine.

No will is here introduced over and above the wills of the two persons, but since the two wills now represent the same interests, they will have achieved a community of end and a coöperative relation of means. In each person the new socialized purpose will have become dominant over his original interests. Neither will have become the mere means to the other since the common end is now each person's governing end. Each can speak with equal authority for that end, and may legitimately use the pronouns 'we' and 'our' in behalf of both. Each, speaking for the common end, can approve or disapprove the other's conduct without arrogance or impertinence.

The social form of the moral will is an agreement of personal wills of which independent benevolence is the essential condition. There are many other factors which conduce to such agreement, and which in their totality make up the method or art of agreement.[2] The first prerequisite of agreement is a desire to agree, rather than to "get the better" of the other party. To induce this attitude it is necessary that both parties should be conscious of the wastefulness of conflict, and the gains, even if they be selfish gains, of peace. The Quaker idea of achieving unanimity, or a "sense of the meeting," which leaves no slumbering grievances and seeds of fresh dispute, is precisely the moral norm which is here defined. The further Quaker idea of periods of silence may or may not be taken to imply a religious doctrine of "inner light"; it may be taken to mean only that an interval of meditation will serve to cool the temper of acrimony.

Agreement is often promoted by shifting the emphasis from points of disagreement to matters in which there is already agreement. This area of agreement may be found either in subsidiary matters or in a common ideal goal. In either case there is created a mood of agreement which is favorable to further agreement. Since interests embrace a factor of cognitive mediation it is always possible to find occasions for cognitive agreement. There are always questions of fact and logic which can be made the focus of discussion. But though this conduces to an agreement of wills, it does not suffice. For practical or moral agreement it is necessary that each person should be *moved* as the other is moved, so as to achieve a harmony of purpose and action.

In the personal will it is sufficient that all of the person's interests shall be represented, whatever they be. Some of his interests may be benevolent, and no doubt will be, human nature and the circumstances of life being what they are; but benevolence is no more essential to the personal will than is hunger or an interest in collecting postage stamps. The social will, on the other hand, *must* be benevolent. Thus the social will is subjected to a double requirement, personality *and* benevolence.

When there is a social will among several persons the conduct which it prescribes will coincide with that which is prescribed by the personal will of each, but that will be only because benevolence has already been introduced into the personal will. This is a very different matter from the coincidence which *may* occur when the requirements of the personal will with or without benevolence, and the social will embracing benevolence, are applied independently. In the latter case the coincidence is accidental, that is, it cannot be deduced from either set of requirements taken separately. If it should occur invariably, it would be a happy miracle of the sort which is credited by the exponents of laissez-faire — an echo of the optimistic theism of the seventeenth and eighteenth cen-

[2] The best discussion of this topic is to be found in S. Chase's *Roads to Agreement*, 1951, cf. especially ch. 6, on "Quaker Meeting." Chapters 2–4 contain an admirable account of causes and levels of conflict.

turies. Whenever an act dictated by the social will happens to be dictated also by the personal will, this coincidence will serve to give it a double support. Either principle may be invoked to augment the justification afforded by the other.

6

Reflective agreement between persons confers on each the right to speak for all. But there are degrees of reflection. It may be comparatively hasty, shallow, impulsive, irrational; or it may be comparatively deliberate, deep, wholehearted, rational. These different levels of reflection define a norm by which the social will can be appraised. Since the person is the seat of reflection it is to the personal will that we must look for an understanding of this difference of level.

If the word 'we' is the most presumptuous word in the English language, the word 'I' is a close rival. The word 'I' claims to speak for the whole of the person to which the moment of its utterance belongs. When my hunger speaks, it says, "*I* am hungry"; momentary appetites and impulses say "I" even more carelessly and shamelessly than persons say "we." But the first person singular means, ideally, the totality of the person who is the user of that pronoun. It claims agreement on the part of the whole company of his interests, most of which will at any given moment be unconscious. This claim is warranted only insofar as these interests have been consulted and, after whatever transformations may have been necessary, have acquiesced.

In the light of this norm it may now be seen that social agreement will vary in the extent to which it expresses the total persons of the agreeing parties; and this will depend on the process, whether *more or less* reflective, by which the agreement is made. By the same token, representative agreement will vary in the degree to which the spokesman, when he uses the pronoun 'we,' can speak not only for all, but for all of all — that is, with the "full consent" of all.

It is possible to give an external, verbal, or silent consent when there is inward dissent. Such mendacious consent has social and political importance through disguising tyranny or selfish exploitation under a cloak of unanimity. Mendacious consent assumes crucial importance when a person has an interest not only in securing the agreement of others but in determining what their opinion shall be. When the opinion which he wishes to implant in others is his own opinion, we call him "sincere"; reserving harsher condemnation for him who seeks to implant in others an opinion which is not his own, but which it suits his purpose that others should hold, or seem to hold. In this case his own assent is mendacious, and the consent of others may be a mendacious means of escaping persecution; but it will be to the interest of the leader that the consent of others should be veracious, since in that case he can relax the pressure of intimidation without fear of losing support. The term 'propaganda' may be used in the larger sense to mean *any* dissemination of attitude by a person who desires to be the spokesman of those who assume it; or, in its disparaging sense, it may be reserved for the case in which the propagandist induces others to *appear* to agree with his own *pretended* attitude.

Since the unscrupulous propagandist is usually concerned with *immediate* support and control, he is inclined to be indifferent to the *manner* in which the consent of others is obtained, provided it *is* obtained. It is comparatively easy for men to agree superficially; when men think for themselves they tend for a time to take divergent paths. The method best calculated to secure a prompt unanimity is the one way passage — the spoken or written word by which the propagandist "holds the floor," while his spellbound victim assumes a passive role. He who would quickly possess men's minds will not stir their depths. The unscrupulous propagandist will not excite the critical faculties. He will appeal to ready-made opinions and to common appetites. When these existing agreements do not suffice he will induce a state of suggestibility. The essential condition of suggestibility is dissociation; which isolates some part of the person, and exposes this part helplessly to contagion and fixation by cutting its interior controls.

In short, by non-reflective propaganda men are united with one another by being divided from themselves. It is true that the effects of such suggested or passionate unanimity are sometimes benign, and its motive may be noble. But whether it be a lynching party or a crusade, a drunken debauch or a religious revival, agreement obtained by methods thus deliberately contrived to inhibit reflection does violence to personal integrity. Of such agreement it is not strictly correct to say "you agree" or "we agree." It would be more correct to say "it agrees" — referring to some fragmentary item, some accidental part, some particular impulse, some isolated idea.

It is commonly supposed that there is virtue in passionate unanimity. As a matter of fact there is more of the substance of the moral will in conflicting egoisms, where each ego is at least a reflective person. The spread of identical passions instead of justifying these passions only renders them more resistant to reason and conscience, increasing the very blindness, narrow insistence, and ruthlessness which constitute the essence of original sin. The complete social agreement which takes the supreme place in the moral order requires two components, the horizontal component of spread and the vertical component of depth.

7

Morality may be illustrated by the actual complexities of social life arranged in spheres of expanding inclusiveness. In the more intimate

family or local circle there are several persons within the range of familiar acquaintance, each with interests of his own. Through communication and benevolence each adopts as his own the interest of father,
mother, son, daughter, brother, sister, friend, neighbor; integrates them,
speaks for the family or local group as a whole, and himself accepts this
voice as authoritative over his original interests.

When representatives of capital and labor sit around a table and
engage in what is called "collective bargaining," and insofar as this is a
moral transaction which achieves a "right" solution of the problem of
conflict, the process is similar except that the interests are represented,
instead of being immediately present "in person." Each representative
enters the conference as the advocate of one of the conflicting economic
interests, and he is expected to advocate it. But he is also expected to
take the view of the opposing advocate. He must listen to him, be impressed, concede his point, acknowledge his claims. In proportion as
there is this exchange of interests, both parties tend to be actuated by
both interests. Their two attitudes tend to converge and to approximate
that of a third party, such as "the representative of the public," the
judge, or the arbitrator, whose role it is to be equally considerate of both
interests, and the partisan advocate of neither.

The procedures that are proper to collective bargaining are those
which enable each finally to decide for all. The first step is the desire for
agreement. Other proper procedures would include the discovery and
amplification of the facts relevant to any of the interests represented; the
invention of methods by which interests at present conflicting can both
be fulfilled; the recognition of partial agreements already existing and of
the commitments which these imply. Actually, other factors come into
play — stubbornness, a war of nerves, the relative strength of war chests,
endurance, threats, lung power, scowling eyebrows, appeals to the galleries. Undoubtedly the decision is forced and premature, and may have
some day to be reopened. But when we speak of a solution of industrial
problems which is better than brute force, or say that capital and labor
should be partners rather than enemies, or praise the participants as
more or less "fair," or judge the outcome to be more or less "just," it is
this ideal solution that is appealed to as a standard. Each party makes a
personal decision in the light of the interests represented by both, and
the decisions tend to agree.

A political will differs from more limited collective wills only in its
complexity and in the comparatively long chain of intermediate steps
which it requires. It is achieved by discussion, taken as an interchange of
personal interests, and of the collective interests of classes or groups. The
ruler is the guardian not only of his individual interests and the interests
of his group, but also, through benevolence, of the interests of all fellow-
nationals. Whether it be the private citizen or the public official in whom

this multiplicity of interests is assembled and harmonized, the ultimate decisions are made by a person. The political will is a political form of personal will, repeated among the members. When all agree, each can speak for the rest, and the authority for all; but the voice which speaks is a personal voice, and the agreement must be a personal acceptance. This is the moral core of politics, and the germ of political democracy.

In the judicial process the presiding judge, and the law which he applies and interprets, are supposed to represent both the defendant and the plaintiff. But it is deemed important that each litigant should plead his own case, directly or through an attorney who has identified himself with his client's case. When the decision is left to a judge he must be disinterested not only in the sense of excluding his own personal interest, but in the sense of taking account of all the interests at stake. When the decision is left to a jury it is assumed that this will afford the best guarantee that the interests at stake are sympathetically understood and have reached a unanimous agreement.

What reciprocal and sympathetic acquaintance achieves in the narrower circles of home and neighborhood, what collective bargaining achieves in the reconciliation of economic groups, what popular discussion, campaigning, and elections achieve in the civil polity, what pleading, argument, and judicial decision achieve in the field of law, is achieved in the international area by diplomacy, negotiation, treaty-making, and conference.

In this area one is painfully aware of a mixture of methods. Nations still practice war and power politics. But intermingled with this nonmoral heritage from the past there is now an increasing and not wholly unsuccessful attempt to find a moral remedy. This remedy is achieved insofar as nations and peoples "understand one another," that is, benevolently share one another's interests, and seek a harmonizing purpose in which all the interests of mankind are embraced. Insofar as this occurs there can be said to be an international will or a will of mankind; which by virtue of its maximum breadth of representation stands at the summit of the moral hierarchy.

Such a will, like every lesser will, is a will of persons. International will consists of international-mindedness on the part of nations whose national wills consist in turn of the national-mindedness of their subgroups and individual members. It is insofar as each person is directly or indirectly represented that the inclusive requirements of international organization can be said to take precedence of those of any lesser group. Morally speaking international organization is a community of persons, in which because of the identity of their ends millions of men agree upon means; and are thus brought into relations of innocence and mutual aid. Each member of such a universal community of persons would be authorized to say "we" or "our" for all men. There is no other being, unless it be God, that can speak for mankind; no other situation in which this pretension is warranted.

8

Such is the principle of reflective agreement. No claim is here made for the frequency or success of its application. But it means something, it is humanly possible, and it is successfully applied in some measure. If reflective inter-personal agreeement be the moral principle, one must be prepared to admit that there is not always a moral solution of a problem of conflict. There is, however, a *way* to such a solution — a *line of effort.* Morality is a *pursuit,* not an infallible recipe. The conflicting parties may not try at all, or they may try and fail. All that moral philosophy can do is to define the moral goal; all that moral prophets can do is to exhort men to aim at the goal; all that moral sages can do is to cite the experience of those who have been successful. If the conflicting parties do not look for agreement, there is no moral solution; if they do not succeed in reaching agreement, there is no moral solution. In case of unwillingness to agree, or in case of failure to agree, the action of the parties in question must take other grounds — partisanship, egoism, passion, whatever it be.

Morality is like a cultivated field in the midst of the desert. It is a partial and precarious conquest. Ground that is conquered has to be protected against the resurgence of original divisive forces. The moralized life is never immune against *de*moralization. At the same time that morality gains ground in one direction it may lose ground in another. Changes in the natural and historical environment and the development of man himself are perpetually introducing new factors and requiring a moral reorganization to embrace them. In the last analysis all depends on the energy, perseverance, and perpetual vigilance of the human person.

CHAPTER VII

THE INTERPRETATION OF MORAL CONCEPTS

There are certain terms of discourse, such as 'good,' 'right,' 'duty,' 'responsibility,' and 'virtue,' which are commonly recognized as having to do with morality, and to which a theory of morals must assign definite meanings.

Two meanings have already been assigned to the term 'good.' In the most general sense, it means the character which anything derives from being the object of any positive interest: whatever is desired, liked, enjoyed, willed, or hoped for, is *thereby* good. In a special sense, 'morally good' is the character imparted to objects by interests harmoniously organized.

In terms of these definitions the famous triad "the True, the Beautiful, and the Good" requires reëxamination and clarification.[1] In the first place, it must be rid of its echo of Platonism. The use of the definite article gives a substantive meaning to these three terms, and thus obliterates the distinction between *that which* is good, and the *goodness* which it possesses as an adjective. In the second place, the triad must be rid of the odor of sanctity which it derives from the use of capital letters. The conceptions of *superlative* truth, beauty, and good are legitimate conceptions, but if these are intended they should be so named; otherwise the distinction between the character and its ranking is lost, or it is implied that there is *no* truth, beauty, or good except the superlative. In the third place, there is a logical difficulty. If True and Beautiful are instances of Good, then either the three members of the triad are not coördinate, or there must be two meanings of 'good,' that which all three

[1] For illuminating discussions of this question, cf. W. P. Montague, "The True, the Good and the Beautiful from a Pragmatic Standpoint," *Journal of Philosophy, 6* (1909); G. Murphy, *Personality,* 1947, pp. 283–4.

members have in common, and that which distinguishes the third from the first and second.

These amendments being accepted, what remains of the triad? Shall it be abandoned altogether, or does it still represent a triadic distinction in the world of value which it is important to preserve? The first and second difficulties are avoided by construing the terms as adjectives rather than substantives, and by substituting lower case for capitals. The logical difficulty is avoided by making the double meaning of 'good' explicit. The triad would then read: 'cognitive good,' 'aesthetic good,' and 'moral good.' It may, then, be argued that these three kinds of good have a universality, an inter-connectedness, and a dignity in human life which sets them apart from other values.

The cognitive and aesthetic interests are simple and irreducible. Truth in itself is not a value, since it consists in well-founded expectation, and expectation is a neutral attitude; one may expect with indifference, and the verification or surprise to which it leads may be a fulfillment or defeat of hope, or it may be neither. There is, however, an interest *in* truth: ranging from primitive curiosity to the acquired and advanced pursuits of science. Similarly, there are certain characteristics which it is agreeable to contemplate. While truth is a qualifying attribute of the object of cognitive interest, beauty is the qualifying attribute of the aesthetic interest.

The cognitive and aesthetic interests have an important character in common; a character which is ordinarily designated as 'non-practical,' the term 'practical' being used to designate interest whose realization involves an alteration in the common existential environment; or interest in which the consummatory dealing excludes other interests from its occasion. Practical interest is externally preëmptive. The natural appetites of hunger and thirst, the use of tools, the appropriation of territory, and all the countless possessive interests of everyday life, are practical in this sense. The cognitive and aesthetic interests, on the other hand, do not necessarily enter into the external causal field. They take and leave external objects as they are, and do not interfere with other interests in the same objects. Two ambitions which seek the same throne are practical interests and tend to collide: but there is no such collision when two cats look curiously or admiringly at the same king, when two political scientists explain his reign, or when two connoisseurs appreciate the pageantry of his court.

Practical and non-practical interest are interconnected because each tends to generate the other, and they are universal because this transition from practical to non-practical or from non-practical to practical tends to occur in all interests. The transition from practical to non-practical interest arises from the factor of mediation. The sensation, perception, meaning, or judgment which is embraced within practical interest invites attention to itself, and may divert the interest from its original direction. Thus, alarmed by a smell of smoke, I run to the fire-escape or seize a bucket of water. So far the interest is practical. But unless the emergency is too pressing, I may be attracted by the pungency of the odor and fall to savoring it. I have then entered on the path of olfactory connoisseurship. Or I may become interested in the cause of the fire, and in the methods of extinguishing it, and so become, according to my lights, and so far as time permits, an expert in the science of pyrotechnics. Thus temptations to aesthetic and cognitive interest beset the path of every practical interest.

The reverse tendency — from the non-practical to the practical — is also universal. The Cynic philosopher, however he may seek to disengage himself from affairs, gets himself a tub and needs the sunlight which an Alexander may obscure. The devotee of solitude has to guard himself against intrusion; and he has to be lived with by family and neighbors. He gives or withholds his services to others. There is no privacy that may not become a public nuisance. Cognitive interest disposes to communication, written or oral, and fills the world with libraries and laboratories. The aesthetic interest disposes to art, which reshapes existence in order that its contemplation may be better enjoyed; and fills the external world with monuments which assail the senses.

Cognitive and aesthetic interest not only generate practical interest, but also generate one another. Aesthetic contemplation of the landscape arouses curiosity or presents a problem to the geologist. Any field of inquiry may present an aspect of beauty. It is a well-known fact that scientific theories are valued for their orderly form as well as for their truth. Moralists, philosophers, and religious teachers have repeatedly taught men that they can escape the clash of interests by reducing their external commitments. There is, however, no interest that does not give hostages to fortune, and depend in some measure on circumstances which it must control if it is not to be at their mercy. Like the proverbial ostrich a man can blind himself to surrounding and oncoming events, but his actual exposure and vulnerability are not thereby avoided or even diminished. He may run away from fortune but by so doing he only encounters other fortunes impinging upon him from a new direction.

Although the cognitive and aesthetic interests are comparatively free from the possibility of conflict in the common external world they enjoy no such immunity within the personal life. All of a person's interests draw upon the same common fund of time and energy, and what is expended for one is preëmpted from the rest. This holds equally of practical and non-practical interests. In other words, even when the pursuit of truth and beauty serves as an escape from the requirements of social morality, the personal problem remains as acute as ever.

2

An object is *good* in the generic sense when it is the object of a positive interest; it is *morally good* in the special sense when the interest which makes it good satisfies the requirement of harmony, that is, innocence and coöperation. This requirement may be met in one or both of two ways. In the first place, it may qualify any interest when that interest is governed by a concern for other interests. Thus the object of a person's sensuous enjoyment acquires a moral character when it is governed by his concern for his health or practical achievements; and a person's ambition acquires a moral character when it is governed by his concern for the interests of other persons. Or, in the second place, the moral requirement may qualify a special interest — the moral interest — by having harmony as its object.

In other words, one may state of any object of interest that it is morally good when the interest is endorsed by other interests; and one may state that a total life in which all interests endorse one another is morally good when it is the object of the moral will.

The "good life," morally speaking, may be described as a condition of *harmonious happiness* — a condition in which, through the increase and coöperation of its members, all interests tend to be positive. This description throws light on the meaning of the familiar but obscure idea of "happiness," and on the traditional claim of happiness to rank as the supreme moral end.

Happiness is attributed to a person as a whole, as distinguished from his momentary or partial interests. He is happy insofar as every outlook is auspicious; he can face many prospects and face them all cheerfully. His present interest is accompanied by a sense of the applause of all his other interests, brought into consciousness by imagination and reflection. When it is said that no man can be completely happy it is meant that every man's interests are so numerous, and his remoter interests so hauntingly present, that he is never free from some sense of negation. Happiness is "shallow" when it is an effect of blindness or cowardice; of an inability or unwillingness to extend the range of his awareness to embrace all the interests at stake together with the actual circumstances which confront them. When it is said that progress does not make men happier, it is meant that it brings new interests which have to be reconciled with the old. Real happiness cannot be achieved by anaesthetics or intoxicating drugs. Thus a man who loves life, as most men do, cannot be said to be happy when he forgets the inevitability of death, but only when he can bear to face it.

There is a traditional art of personal happiness, which can be similarly understood. When the objects of interest lie in the remote future, the interval is likely to be filled with negative interests. There are obstacles to be overcome, temporary defeats to be endured, delays to be suffered. It is for this reason that it is important to relish the means as well as the end, to find good in the routine and personal contacts of everyday life, and to cultivate cognitive and aesthetic interests, which can be immediately realized and which are comparatively independent of circumstances. In a continuously happy life long-range and short-range interests will be happily commingled.

In common discourse, and in the moral theory known as 'utilitarianism,' happiness is identified with pleasure. This identification reflects a careless use of the term 'pleasure.' If pleasure is taken to be a bodily sensation, then it is a part of happiness only because pleasure is liked and enjoyed. If, on the other hand, pleasure or 'pleasantness' is taken to mean the individual's awareness of his own positive interest, then his happiness differs from his pleasure only in its pervading and qualifying the totality of his life. Similarly unhappiness will consist not in the sensation of pain, but in the feelings which reflect the negative quality of his interests.

This analysis must not be taken to imply the unimportance of *sensations* of pleasure and pain for happiness. Because pleasure is normally liked and pain disliked, the presence of these sensations is a constant factor in happiness and unhappiness. The sensation of pain will interrupt any form of enjoyment or prosperous achievement and substitute negative for positive interest. Sensation of pleasure, on the other hand, may substitute positive for negative interest, or reinforce a positive interest which already exists. The internal environment of the organism is carried into every external environment; wherever, whenever, with whomsoever and with whatsoever, a man lives, he must live with his own body. Its pleasures and pains, its health or malaise, will affect the tone of every interest and of life as a whole.

As happiness reflects a harmony of interests, so unhappiness is an effect of conflict, as when a man is said to be "at war with himself." Insofar as this condition prevails, each interest sees the others as its enemies, and is moved to defeat them. Each positive interest — each enjoyment or prosperous achievement — then begets a negative interest on behalf of the other interests which it jeopardizes.

The application of similar principles to inter-personal relations gives meaning to such expressions as 'the general good.' The happiness of a society or a family, or nation, or mankind, is morally good insofar as its personal members live together as friends, so that each regards the others' interests as harmless or helpful to his own. The interests of the several members are so happily attuned that each person in willing his own happiness wills also the happiness of his fellows. The happiness enjoyed is the happiness of each; its sociality lies in the fact that the several happinesses are conditioned by benevolence. The happy society is a society of happy men, who derive happiness from one another's happiness.

It is generally conceded that as the personal good is morally better than the good of one of its constituent interests, so the social good is morally better than the personal, and the good of mankind than that of any narrower human group. Interpreted in terms of harmonious happiness and the standard of inclusion, this means that the greater harmonies must include the lesser harmonies. There must be a harmony of harmonies.

There are two common views which fail to satisfy this condition: the extreme "individualistic" or atomic view, in which the good of the whole is sacrificed to the goods of the members; and the totalitarian or organismic view, in which the goods of the members are sacrificed to the good of the whole. The principle of moral organization requires that the good of the whole shall take precedence of the several goods of the members, when and only when it embraces them and provides for them. There is only one way in which this can be achieved, namely, by a universal social will arrived at by reflective social agreement. Such a will exists distributively in each human person; while at the same time it represents all personal wills because the harmony which each person has achieved for himself then embraces every other person within its benevolence.

3

According to the theory here proposed, 'right' means conduciveness to moral good, and 'wrong' means conduciveness to moral evil: the one to harmony, and the other to conflict. So construed, right and wrong are dependent and instrumental values. That which is right or wrong may, however, like all objects of dependent interests, come to be loved or hated for its own sake, and thus acquire *intrinsic* value.

The view here advocated, sometimes known as the teleological or consequential theory of right and wrong, is in modern times most familiarly identified with the utilitarianism of Bentham and John Stuart Mill, but it is much more widely represented, both in the history of moral theory and in common sense.

Rarely, if ever, has it been held strictly that there is *no* connection, direct or indirect, near or remote, between right and happiness, and between wrong and unhappiness. Even philosophies or religious dogmas which preach "justice though the heavens fall" do not expect the heavens to fall in a just world. It is deemed reasonable that evil should follow upon wrong-doing, even if it is necessary to invent the evil in the form of divine punishment. Kant, who firmly refused to derive right from happiness, nevertheless was so sure that right-doers *earn* happiness that he considered this a sufficient argument for believing in a God who sees to it that the happiness is gratuitously provided. It is certainly a doubtful compliment to the right to deny that it does not of itself do good. It is to be noted, furthermore, that this expedient, which leaves the link between right and happiness to divine intervention, has commonly led men to belittle the humanly controllable causes of happiness, with the result that morality fails to reflect advancing enlightenment.

An act [2] is right when it conduces to the moral good, that is, to harmonious happiness; and it is wrong when it conduces to disharmony. The right may conduce to the good as antecedent cause to subsequent effect, as when a humane act leads to the happiness of the other party; or as part to whole, as when a man's humane act is embraced within his happiness, or when a man best serves a happy society by being happy himself. In both cases, whether the act "makes for," or "goes into the making of," its rightness consists in its *contributing to* harmonious happiness. This is the root meaning of 'right' and 'wrong.' There are several derived meanings: *superior* rightness; *intentional* rightness; *apparent* rightness; *formal* rightness; and *interim* rightness.

An act may conduce to a greater or less harmonious happiness. It may yield good in the long run or in the short run, for the person or for society, for the nation or for mankind. When the good is greater the right is superior, and is entitled to moral precedence in case of conflict.

An act may conduce to harmonious happiness or to conflict and unhappiness when these results are unforeseen. When they *are* foreseen the act's rightness or wrongness is intentional. But it should be noted "the right thing" or "the wrong thing" do not derive their ultimate meaning from intentionality, but from the nature of the *consequences* intended.

It is a notorious fact that things rarely turn out precisely as expected: the result is more or less other than is reckoned for. An agent may think his act contributes to moral goodness when in fact it does not; that is, it may be erroneously mediated. In that case it is apparently, but not truly, right. There is no contradiction provided the two 'rights' are distinguished. It is the true rightness which defines the standard by which even the apparent rightness is deemed right; and by which it is right to correct the error, if any, of the mediating cognition. It is truly right that the man who does right "according to his lights" should cultivate enlightenment.

There are certain generalized rules of conduct which experience proves to be conducive to harmonious happiness. These tend to become stereotyped and familiar, and an act may be judged according as it does or does not conform to them. The word 'right' suggests alignment, and is therefore peculiarly applicable to the relation of an act to a rule, judged by which it may be straight or oblique. When it is straight it may

[2] That to which the adjectives 'right' and 'wrong' can properly be attributed, whether act, agent, motive, interest, disposition, etc., will be examined below, § 5.

be termed "formally" right. But if the act is to be morally right the rule to which it conforms must be a morally right rule, that is, a rule the observance of which conduces to moral goodness. To ignore this requirement is to fall into mere casuistry.

A further distinction is necessary to provide for the fact that conduct on the social level often fails to promote the good life unless it is adopted jointly and reciprocally. Veracity does not work, morally speaking, unless both parties practice it. Or, it takes two, as is said, to make peace; a one-sided peacefulness may invite aggression and so precipitate war. Therefore it may be right to make war in order to bring about a situation in which pacific conduct will be effectual. It is right to create the possibility of acting rightly. The circularity is escaped provided a distinction is made between transitional or "interim" right, which is right because it brings moral organization about; and the ultimate rightness which is right because it is suitable to a moral organization when realized. In case the two rights do not agree it is clear that the former takes precedence in time. Action or inaction which conduces to a situation in which no action is morally futile cannot be justified on moral grounds.

There can be no objection to this variety of meanings provided they are not confused. It would be verbally permissible to confine the word 'right' to some of these special meanings, but it would be unprofitable since it would ignore their variety and relatedness of meaning. They belong together as varieties of beneficence; that is, conduciveness to good; that is, conduciveness to harmonious happiness.

The full meaning of substantive "rights" can be understood only in the context of polity and law, in which this idea plays a fundamental role. It is, however, a basic moral concept, and should receive its initial interpretation here.

Rights are sometimes considered axiomatic, but in a consequential theory such as is here proposed they must be explained by their conduciveness to the good life. Harmonious happiness is justified by its provision for the several interests which it harmonizes. The claim which *each* of these interests has upon the bounty of the whole is its "right." Harmonious happiness is achieved by organization, and it sets limits to the interests for which it provides. A right is therefore not the unrestricted demand of the component interest but a *right* demand — a demand the fulfillment of which is consistent with the fulfillment of other demands. Each interest is entitled to an area within which it enjoys liberty to follow its own inclination; but it is a limited area, bounded by the areas of other interests within a system which provides for all interests.

While the right of a person is similar in principle to that of any particular interest there is an important difference. The bounds of the right of a particular interest are set by the reflective will of the person to which it belongs — as regards the relative claims of his own interests the person is the autonomous and final moral authority. It follows that where the interests of another person are concerned that other person, being similarly autonomous and final, must agree. Hence within a social moral good there is a double right: a right of each person to be considered and provided for, and a right of each person to be consulted and to assent to the provisions.

4

There is a basic idea common to 'ought,' 'duty,' 'moral obligation,' and 'moral imperative.' To clarify the subject it is necessary not only to provide such a basic meaning, but also to account for various shades of meaning and meaninglessness.

On the level of everyday discourse what ought to be done is what is called for by some end; it is the converse of the right. The moral ought is what is called for by the end of the moral good, that is, by harmonious happiness. The act which ought to be performed may or may not be a necessary or sufficient condition of the good. The obligatory act may or may not be a unique act; in any given situation there may be many acts which satisfy the condition of conducing to the good, one of which ought to be performed.

That moral obligation is commonly expressed in the form of a command and therefore in the imperative voice is an accident, due to the fact that right action is associated with political, parental, or other authority. Or, the imperativeness of obligation may be an after effect of the logical necessity by which the rightness of the act was inferred from its consequences. Just as the "thou shalt" may remain after the authority has ceased to utter it, so the "therefore" or tone of necessity may remain in after the premises have disappeared.

The term 'duty' is applied primarily to the moral agent, and only secondarily to acts which are "in the line of duty." It is a stronger term than 'ought' since it is associated with an implied promise by which the agent has bound himself. When it is said that every right has its associated duty, it is meant that in claiming his benefit as a moral right he has committed himself to allotting some equivalent benefit on the other party. If he does not fulfill his part, not only as beneficiary but as benefactor, he incurs the charge of inconsistency, as well as the justifiable resentment of the other beneficiary. There are as many duties as there are rights, and there are as many rights as there are moral systems with delimited spheres and mutual engagements. There are duties as well as rights associated with every role in organized society — the parent, the neighbor, the soldier, the employer and worker, or the citizen.

When it is said that an act "ought" to be performed, it is meant that the act is called for by some good to which the act is conducive. In this basic sense the ought is sufficiently determined by the good, the act, and the circumstances. This analysis provides for "real obligation" and "real duty," as distinguished from, and antecedent to, the mere "feeling of obligation" or "sense of duty."

This distinction is plain and explicit in the case of contractual obligation. Whether a man does or does not really owe another man a sum of money is quite distinct from the question of his subjective attitude. He may blithely ignore his obligation, but he is not released on that account. His obligation is *there*, in the past undertakings and present relationships, whether he acknowledges it or not. But precisely the same holds of all moral obligation. It is implied in the total situation: a man has it, or does not have it, whether or not he experiences its compulsion. If this were not so it would be meaningless to call a man's attention to his obligations, or adduce proofs in their support, or to instill a consciousness of obligation where it does not already exist. When expecting "every man to do his duty," England was not creating the duties, but calling attention to them and demanding their performance. The latest example of this is afforded by the extension of morality to the interrelations of all mankind. When the nations of the earth are exhorted to take account of one another's interests this does not mean that they are to acquire new duties, but a new acknowledgment of old duties hitherto ignored.

Since ought, whether recognized or unrecognized, is by nature an implication, there is an ultimate premise which is not similarly implied. That from which all moral oughts are derived is not itself a moral ought. Hence if all moral oughts are deduced from the good of harmonious happiness it is meaningless to ask whether men ought to be harmoniously happy. This does not argue against the present theory except on the dogmatic assumption that the good means what "ought to be."

According to the view here adopted, ought, obligation, and duty, are not moral ultimates but are proved by the good. The influence of Kant among philosophers, and the influence on popular thought of the "stern" or "rigorous" school of morals, have conspired to create a presumption in favor of the view that the moral ought is "categorical" or "unconditional," rather than "hypothetical" or "conditional."

But there are many possible interpretations of this grim and uncompromising aspect of ought. Human opinion abounds in categoricals and unconditionals which signify only the limits of knowledge. Most opinions have this absolute character not because there *is* no ulterior ground, but because it is forgotten or ignored, or is as yet undiscovered, or lies beyond the capacity of the person who holds the opinion. Thus a man's opinion that he ought not to lie is for most persons a simple mandate, with no "why or wherefore." This does not imply, however, that there *is* no why and wherefore. It does not imply that the obligation to speak the truth may not rest on the fact that veracity is a fundamental requirement of communication, and is therefore conditional on the purpose of social

INTERPRETATION OF MORAL CONCEPTS

organization; but only that most people, most of the time, are unaware of this condition.

Or, duty may present itself as unconditional when the condition is taken for granted. Thus if it is said that a man ought to obey some precept of thrift or hygiene, it is not necessary to specify that such conduct will save him from bankruptcy or death, because the good of solvency or survival is so generally recognized that it does not need to be mentioned.

Ignorance and unconscious assumption are not the only causes of this uncompromising aspect of the moral ought. It often expresses the pressure of the social conscience. The sentiment of the community speaks peremptorily to the individual, and will listen to no excuses. He then speaks the truth because he desires the esteem of his contemporaries. Or the ought may express what the individual person demands of himself. A person cannot "bear to think of himself" as a liar; he has acquired an ideal of himself which forbids it. This does not argue against the social beneficence of truth-speaking, but only that this appeal is reinforced by another appeal, namely, self-approval. A man has to live with himself as well as with others.

In an earlier chapter some attention was given to the theory that the words of the moral vocabulary have an "emotional," as distinguished from an "objective," meaning. While this theory was rejected in its sweeping application, it was acknowledged that although these words do have an objective meaning they may be, and frequently are, used with a merely emotive intent; that is, to express an attitude and to induce a like attitude in the person to whom they are addressed. This is peculiarly true of the word 'ought.' When a person is told that he "ought to speak the truth" this is often in order that he may feel impelled to speak the truth; and insofar as this is the case the ought is not arguable. The imperative is then categorical in the sense that it is uttered categorically, and demands unconditional obedience.

The uncompromising demands of conscience, whether personal or social, while they may be first in the order of psychological motivation, are not first in the order of justification. When an obligation is imputed to a moral agent, no reasons being given, or when he is exhorted to do as he ought, or appeal is made to his sentiment of self-esteem, or to his regard for the approving or disapproving attitudes of others, it is always appropriate for the agent to ask, "Why ought I?" and it is the answer to this question, the ultimate *why* of the obligation, which reveals the fundamental meaning of the concept.

Objection to any theory which makes moral obligation conditional or hypothetical is largely due to the supposition that it is then translated into terms of egoism. It is true that the theory may be, and commonly is, presented in this form. It is then taken to mean that the duty of any person is conditional on *his* existing interests. Thus the full meaning of 'this is your duty' would be 'this is your duty if such and such is your aim.' You would then escape the duty if such and such were not your aim.

This is not the view here proposed. Duty is derived from the good, and the good is relative to interests, but not merely to the interests of the agent whose duty is in question. The good result which determines the duty may relate to the interest of another, or to all interests concerned; even when they are not sympathetically felt, or even acknowledged, by the performer of the act. My duty is conditional on *the* purpose of harmonious happiness, not on *my* purpose. When so construed, duty possesses a certain unconditional character relatively to any given person. It cannot be escaped by his ignorance, inattention, indifference, or selfishness. This interpretation is consequential or teleological, but it is universalistic and not egoistic.

It is because of the fact that the call of the greater good overrules the call of the lesser good, and often has to assert its mastery, that duty acquires its forbidding aspect. Duty is independent of present inclination, and, if needs be, stands against it. This is where duty hurts. But the hurt is not the duty any more than martyrdom is piety; duty can be painless without being any the less dutiful.

5

The meaning of the moral predicates, 'good,' 'right,' and 'ought,' having been examined, there remains the question of the subject to which, in moral judgments, these predicates are properly assignable. *Of* what kind of being is it proper to state that it is morally good, right, or obligatory?

The essential qualification of any entity to possess moral characteristics is interest. It is meaningful to ascribe moral characteristics to Mahomet or to the mover of mountains, meaningless to ascribe them to the mountain. But in order that an entity may be a subject of moral judgment, something more is required, namely, the interaction of interests. Mahomet is not only interested, but possesses two or more interests which affect one another and which affect the interests of his associates. The field or realm of moral discourse is limited to the field of beings prompted by interest, and whose interests stand to one another, internally and externally, in relations of harmony or conflict. In a world without mind there would be no morality. There would be no morality in a world, were such a world possible, in which minds held expectations, true or false, but without *caring* one way or the other. Nor would there be morality in a world in which there was only one interest, or in which interests were so insulated as to make no difference to one another.

But the field of morality is further restricted to beings which are capable of understanding the bearings of one interest on another, and of being governed accordingly. The member of a harmoniously happy society must attune his interests to the interests of others; and to do so he must be aware of the social meaning of what he does. To act rightly or wrongly he must predict (correctly or incorrectly) the consequences of his act. To have duties and obligations he must be capable of inferring what the moral end requires, and requires of him. In other words, moral judgments presuppose the presence of certain distinctively human capacities. Conflict and harmony do exist beyond these limits: peace is peace and carnage is carnage wherever they occur, and the one may be praised and the other dispraised. But morality requires that the agent shall know them for what they are, and incorporate them as the mediating cognition of his interests. It is only on this level of capacity that the agent becomes morally "blameworthy" and "responsible."

Where conflict exists, morality requires that it be removed; where conflict is possible it requires that it be avoided. Actual conflict is condemned on the assumption that it could, by the agent's taking thought, have been avoided; and the agent is blamed for having failed to avoid it. Harmony, on the other hand, is not merely praised, but is deemed meritorious, as having been attained by foresight and inference. Morality subsumes particular acts under maxims, such as the Golden Rule, and at the same time this act of subsumption is imputed to the agent. The moral agent is judged to love or not to love his neighbor as himself; but at the same time he is judged as though he possessed the capacity to grasp the meaning of the rule and to conform himself to it. Similarly morality not only judges mankind to be in a state of deplorable war or admirable peace, but assumes that the same mankind who suffers or benefits is capable of entertaining these ideas and applying them to themselves. It is on the same assumption that moral agents are "held responsible," or "assume responsibility," or are "deemed responsible" or "irresponsible."

In short, moral judgments are pronounced upon beings which, through the mediation of their interests, are themselves competent to pronounce them. Judge meets judge. The responsible and blameworthy moral agent is in this sense a rational being, that is, capable of entertaining general ideas, fixing them by words and other symbols, making inferences from them, recognizing them in particular instances, and proving them from evidence. And this is the sense in which the moral agent is "free," that is, capable of acting from deliberate choice, and not merely from the immediate incitements of appetite, or from habit, or from physico-chemical causes lying below the threshold of mind.

It is sometimes held that moral judgments are pronounced upon motives rather than acts, but when a motive is judged morally right it is because the act which it prompts is right — right in the sense of conducive to personal or social harmony. A right motive tends to good so

far as it goes, but it does not go as far as the act. To stop with the comparatively easy and painless motive is so common a way of falling short
of rightness that "hell is paved with good intentions." But while right is
primarily an attribute of action judged by its consequences, it may be
extended to motives, to dispositions, to policies, to characters, to persons,
institutions, and to societies — in short, to whatever interests, potentialities, or organizations of interest, are conducive to harmonious happiness.

If morality requires universal benevolence, then it requires a concern
for the interests of all beings that have interests. It does not permit of
limiting the objects of benevolence to responsible moral agents. This
implication raises the troublesome question of the moral status of animal
life. Lewis Carroll's parable of "The Walrus and the Carpenter" in which
the walrus "deeply sympathizes" with the oysters whom he devours with
"sobs and tears" and "holding his handkerchief before his streaming eyes,"
may be taken as a parody of the false sentimentality which attributes
personality to the oyster. But it has a deeper meaning. It symbolizes the
contradiction between man's profession of pity and his carnivorous
practices; his habit of evading the contradiction between his moral sentiment and his appetites.

The relation of man to animal life, is one of the areas of life as yet
most imperfectly moralized, both in theory and in practice. It is in his
treatment of the beast that man most clearly resembles the beast. The
solution of the problem does not lie in a vague extension of morals to
"life." Morality does not begin with life, but with personality; however
difficult the application, this is where the line is to be drawn.

Animals come within the scope of the moral good insofar as they
are interested beings. That on this score the pain of animals is evil is
not open to doubt. So far as it is possible to judge, they do not possess
wills in the full sense of the term, implying reflective agreement. They
cannot enjoy happiness when happiness is taken as a condition of persons.
But they can suffer pain, and they manifest that suffering unmistakably.
They can feel dislike and aversion, hunger and thirst, fear and rage —
and the objects of these negative interests are evils to be placed on the
debit side of the account of value. They are evil in precisely the same
sense ascribable to the objects of similar negative interests in man. This
being the case the animal's goods and evils fall within the domain of
morality when this is conceived as a reconciliation of interests. The pain
of animals is not evil merely because it is painful to the tender-minded
human being. Pain is evil primarily because of the negative interest of the
being that suffers it; and it would be evil were there no sympathetic by-
stander whatsoever. There is no escaping this conclusion once it is affirmed
that interests are objective facts which a judge of value is compelled to
recognize whether or not they be his own interests.

It does not follow, however, that there is no moral difference between men and infra-human animals. Animals are moral objects, but they are not moral subjects. Kindness to animals is morally the same as kindness to humans, and cruelty is as vicious in the one case as in the other. But the problem of reconciling and integrating animal with human interests is a problem on which only man is qualified to pronounce judgment.

The relation of the human person to an animal's interests are like his relation to his own particular interests, rather than to the interests of another person. Of his own interests he is the final arbiter, whereas the final disposition of another person's interests require that other person's agreement. While the moral agent owes kindness and consideration to every interest, including those of animals, he owes *deference* only to beings capable and willing to reciprocate. The moral agent's relation to infants, to criminals, or to the insane is a mixture of two relationships. It would be like that between men and animals were it not for the fact that human beings, however imperfectly human, possess some potentiality or vestige of personality.

6

In Act IV, Scene 2, of *Henry VIII*, Shakespeare lists the "faults" and "evil manners," and the "virtues," of the deceased Cardinal Wolsey. Queen Katherine begs leave to speak of him, "and yet with charity":

> He was a man
> Of an unbounded stomach, ever ranking
> Himself with princes; one that by suggestion
> Tied all the kingdom: simony was fair play:
> His own opinion was his law: i' the presence
> He would say untruths, and be ever double
> Both in his words and meaning: he was never,
> But where he meant to ruin, pitiful:
> His promises were as he then was, mighty;
> But his performances, as he is now, nothing.

Griffith, the gentleman-usher, coming to Wolsey's defense, then speaks of the great Cardinal's scholarship, wisdom, eloquence, amiability, princely generosity, and public benefaction. There is no difference between the Queen and her interlocutor as to the kinds of conduct which are praiseworthy and blameworthy, and they seem agreed, furthermore, that it was quite possible for Wolsey to combine them.

It is characteristic of morality that certain varieties of action are generally recognized in any given age or society as right and wrong. The words which designate them constitute the vocabulary of moral praise and blame; and while they are indefinite in number,[3] and reflect a great

[3] There is no list of virtues which can be said to be final and all-inclusive. They may be classified in many ways. For *one* classification, cf. the Author's *Moral Economy*, 1909, ch. iv.

variety of personal and local conditions, they are to be construed as the products of the moral experience of mankind, or some considerable portion of mankind. They epitomize the funded moral wisdom of the ages.

It is convenient to divide these moral stereotypes into three groups: virtues, precepts, and codes. 'Virtue' refers to acquired dispositions, habits, and fixed attitudes of society or of the individual. The assemblage and balance of his virtues and vices constitute a person's moral character; when a character, such as Wolsey's is analyzed there are the moral "characteristics" into which it is broken down. The "precepts" assume the form of rules, which prescribe or forbid. In their more primitive and negative form they are known as 'taboos.' A "code" is a system or hierarchy of precepts, more or less unified by a dominant ideal.

Virtues, precepts, and codes will have more or less of universality. Some will be relatively universal because they conduce to harmony whatever the interests involved. The moral quality of an act lies in its regard for interests other than those which immediately incite it. *Temperance* and *prudence* apply to the interrelations of the interests of the same person. Thus insofar as the appetite of hunger is affected by consideration for physical fitness, and for future practical successes which are conditioned by such fitness, its objects acquire a moral value over and above their hunger value. Temperance is moral by virtue of the element of restraint and moderation so induced. In this case both interests are independent interests of the same person. Prudence does not differ from temperance except in its emphasis on self-regard. It commonly refers to the situation in which the interest of a first party in the interest of a second party is a dependent interest — dependent on some interest of the first party, as when he so acts as to avoid the other's hostility, or secure some benefit in return. When, on the other hand, a regard for the other's interest is an independent interest, it rises to the level of *independent benevolence* — usually referred to simply as 'benevolence.'

Benevolence owes its high place among the virtues to the fact that it promotes the interests of others, whatever and whoever they be. It is applicable to all inter-personal situations. As benevolence is said to be a cardinal virtue, so selfishness is said to be the original and most deadly sin. It means, as has been pointed out, not the being governed by one's own interests (by what else could one be governed?) but the absence of independent benevolence. If it is a universal sin it is because independent benevolence is always imperfect in its weakness or in its limited extent. But there is a worse sin than selfishness, namely, malevolence (including hate, envy, and jealousy). It is worse than selfishness because it is hostile, and not merely indifferent, to the interests of others. It strikes most directly at the good of social harmony.

Justice is commonly defined to mean that each person shall receive what is "due" him. When it is assumed that wrong-doing deserves punishment and right-doing deserves reward, "retributive" justice is a form of "distributive" justice — one of the procedures by which a person gets from society what he is entitled to. In proportion as criminology becomes more enlightened it becomes increasingly clear that all justice is distributive.

But then what is the principle of distribution? The traditional formulas for distributive justice usually omit the heart of the matter. Granting that each person is to obtain what is due him, how is this to be determined? The answer is flagrantly circular when it is said that each is to obtain his "just dues" — or when synonyms such as 'fair' or 'equitable' are introduced. There are various specific formulas — to each according to his needs, or labor, or contribution — all of which turn out to be questionable in their application. The most simple answer to the question is the appeal to the existing body of law — a man is entitled to that to which he is legally entitled. But this is *too* simple, since it evades the question of the justice of the law itself.

It is evident that the question is not settled until it is referred to some final *moral* court of appeal; and there is no such court of appeal short of the reflective social agreement in which all persons acting as representatives of their interests, and expanding their interests to embrace the interests of others, arrive at a unanimous decision. This is the principle, never fully applied, which serves as a guide to the creation of a society that shall be as just as possible.

Veracity is less universal than benevolence because it is confined by the need of communication. Similarly, *courage* is applicable only to situations in which there is a danger to be met. But veracity and courage, while not universal in principle, can be said to be empirically universal, because, as a matter of fact, and humanly speaking, there always *is* a need of communication and a need of meeting danger. Similarly, *thrift* can be held to be universal on the ground that there are always future needs to be provided for in advance.

Among precepts the "Golden Rule" holds a unique place. Its wide acceptance in both ancient and modern times, in paganism and in Christianity, and among moralists otherwise as different as Locke and Kant, is not a coincidence. For it is of the essence of morality that each moral agent should accept the interests of others as he accepts his own; that he should put himself in the other's place, and the other in his place, and so recognize an interest as an interest in its own terms no matter to whom it belongs.

Among codes the highest place must be given to the "humanitarian" code, which adopts the fulfillment of the interests of all persons as the ruling purpose, to which all virtues and precepts are subordinated. This may be said to be *the* moral code.

Although certain virtues, precepts, and codes are comparatively universal they are never wholly freed from particular circumstances. And there are many virtues, precepts, and codes which are clearly of limited application. Some are relative to the condition of the individual, such as age or sex. Some are relative to a social function, such as the virtues of the mother, the precepts of citizenship, the code of the physician. Some in a high degree, and all in some degree, reflect the total culture of the society in which they find expression. The pagan virtues of Aristotle reflect the antique world and the Greek city-state; the Christian virtues of Augustine and Aquinas reflect a world in which a supernatural order has superseded, or is superimposed upon, the civil order. It is the task of the moral historian to trace the thread of moral organization through a succession of concrete situations, and to distinguish what is morally universal from what is local and epochal.

The prominent role played by the virtues, precepts, and codes tends perpetually to obscure the moral ideal. They tend to be divorced from that end of harmonious happiness which gives them their ultimate meaning. Becoming stereotyped and rigid they tend to stand in the way of moral progress.

It is customary to list "conscience" among the moral concepts. But the *content* of conscience — that which conscience authorizes and imposes — consists of precisely such virtues, precepts, and codes as have here been discussed. Otherwise, taken as a force or "sanction," conscience is an institution, and as such it will be discussed in the later chapters which deal with institutions.

CHAPTER VIII

THE PROOF OF MORAL KNOWLEDGE

The moral good has been defined as harmonious happiness, or as that organization of interests in which each enjoys the non-interference and support of the others, whether within the personal life or the life of society. This becomes the moral "first principle." It sets the standard by which objects are deemed morally good or bad, and is the premise from which right, duty, and virtue are to be derived. It provides the most general predicate of moral judgment and the basic concept of moral knowledge. How is it to be proved? The moral philosopher is compelled not only to produce evidence, but to decide what kind of evidence may properly be demanded.

Opinion on the question of moral knowledge oscillates between the extremes of dogmatism and scepticism. There are no judgments which are held with a greater degree of commitment and sense of certainty by the layman, and with a greater acknowledgment of ignorance by theorists. Moral beliefs are in the strange position of being held with passionate conviction despite apparently unanswerable doubts. It is easy to understand why the layman, compelled to meet the deadline of action, should resort to dogmatism; but why is it that moral theory, relieved of the exigencies of action, and emancipated from dogmatism, should move to the opposite extreme of scepticism?

Moral scepticism, or the view that moral judgments cannot be proved true, usually takes one or the other of two forms: the assertion that there are, strictly speaking, no moral judgments; and the assertion that moral judgments are relative or circular.

It is held, in the first place, that so-called moral judgments, although they assume the verbal form of sentences, having subject, predicate and verb, are not really judgments, accountable to evidence and demonstrably true or false. This most radical form of moral scepticism takes two forms:

the dismissal of moral judgments as failing to satisfy the requirements of verification, and the interpretation of moral judgments as merely acts of self-expression and social control. These two views are usually held jointly, the one discrediting moral judgments as "nonsense," the other explaining the role of such nonsense in human life.

The denial of the verifiability of moral judgments is based on a certain conception of what knowledge is, derived from the more "exact" sciences, and followed at various distances by other sciences which call themselves by the name of 'science.' The philosophical exponent of this cult is known as the logical positivist, according to whom knowledge is of two kinds, a logico-mathematical knowledge, which is "analytical," that is, yields no more than is put into it by definitions and postulates; and experimental knowledge, which is "synthetic," that is, yields new discoveries, and which consists of hypotheses verified by data of sense in certain controlled, repeatable, and measurable situations.

Before accepting this strict interpretation of scientific method as a definition of knowledge in general there are certain considerations to be weighed. In the first place, since the method is derived from physics, it is not to be assumed that it should be applicable to non-physics. In the second place, the method itself creates problems which the method itself cannot solve: problems such as the precise nature of verification, or of the activity of constructing hypotheses. Indeed the central thesis of logical positivism itself — its exclusive claim to the title of 'knowledge' and its description of the process of knowledge — is not proved by the logico-positivistic method. The literature of logico-positivistic philosophy is not a part of the corpus of physics. And in the third place it is to be noted that no science except physics (and possibly chemistry) employs the method of physics; so that the strict application of this standard would exclude the social sciences, and even the biological sciences. Whatever be the role assigned to these sciences, whether that of autonomy, or of half-finished physics, a theory of morality has every right to a similar role.

The other part of moral scepticism, namely, its interpretation of so-called moral judgments in terms of self-expression and social control, has already been examined in its application to judgments of value in general.[1] It is argued that moral judgments, like other judgments of value, have the intent not of describing an object but of conveying an attitude. The fact is, however, that this is not peculiar to moral judgments, but applies to all judgments in some degree, and to moral judgments only in a comparatively high degree. Judgments are not uttered in a vacuum, but are appropriate to some particular context, and since they are uttered in words, they are a form of communication, even if they are uttered "to oneself." Any verbal utterance, whether or not it employs such words as

[1] Cf. above, Ch. I, § 4.

'right,' 'ought,' and 'good,' may serve as a mere gesture, epithet, threat, command, or enticement. And it may be freely conceded that moral judgments since they closely concern action and human relations are the most likely of all judgments to be used with such an "emotive" intent. But that moral judgments do sometimes assert propositions which can be argued and more or less successfully demonstrated, is incontestable; and it is the business of moral theory to look to those moral judgments which *do* assert propositions, and to inquire concerning the evidence which can be cited in their support. The question is, "What and how do moral judgments know, when, and insofar as, they *are* acts of cognition?

The second argument for moral scepticism is the charge of relativity. Moral judgments are held to be peculiarly or fatally relative. But, as has been pointed out, relativity is vicious only when it is concealed. Moral judgments commonly apply a standard without stating it; as when a hurtful act is simply pronounced "wrong," when it should be pronounced "wrong-by-the-standard-of-harmonious-happiness." Generally speaking the standards of a person or group are so ingrained and habitual that they are brought to light only by a detached observer, or by a prolonged process of self-justification; with the result that the judgment affirms an absolute when it really means a relationship. This, again, is not peculiar to moral judgments. Men speak of a tree as "big," without specifying whether they mean height or girth; or refer to a man as "great" without specifying whether they mean powerful or wise; or characterize an event as "novel," without specifying the accustomed events with which it is contrasted.

Moral judgments are also relative in the sense that the meaning of the predicate is ambiguous and variable. Acts are declared right or wrong without any clear awareness of what is meant by 'right' and 'wrong,' some men meaning one thing and some another, or nothing at all; with the result that it is impossible to determine which of two opposing moral judgments is true and which false. But this, also, holds in some degree of all judgments, even of those carefully considered judgments which are called 'scientific' and in which undefined terms are reduced to a minimum. Are sun spots a cause of weather? This depends on what is meant by 'cause,' and it is quite possible that a conflict of opinion on the subject should be insoluble because of a difference of meaning.

Moral judgments can be challenged or postponed by substituting for the question, "Is it so?" the question, "What do you mean?" But so can any judgment. And even when they mean the same, men hold different opinions relatively to their degree of capacity and access to evidence. No doubt such conflicts of opinion are peculiarly common in the area of morals, where bias is passionate, where the unknown factors are numerous, and where the trains of reasoning are long and complicated. But there are such differences of opinion in every field of inquiry.

2

The knowledge of morality differs from other kinds of knowledge not *qua* knowledge, but in its subject matter. Before this thesis can be proved certain common misunderstandings must be removed.

It is sometimes contended that the knowledge of morality differs radically from all other knowledge in that its data are feelings. But this contention is equivocal. The datum of feeling may be taken to signify the state or act of feeling; or it may be taken to signify what is felt. In the first case, it is the feeling that is observed, whether introspectively or behavioristically; in the second case, it is the object of the feeling which is observed, and the feeling is the observing. In the first case the data do not differ from those of psychology, which embraces feeling along with sensation, and other modes of the mental life, within its subject matter. In the second case the data are those qualities or other "neutral entities" which are immediately apprehended by feeling, as colors are immediately apprehended by visual sensation, and tones by auditory sensation. In either case there are empirical data by which hypotheses can be verified.

Closely allied with this misunderstanding is the contention that moral knowledge, unlike other knowledge, must move the will at the same time that it convinces the intellect.[2] It is held that the judgment "This is right," or the judgment "I ought to do this" cannot be true unless one is *disposed* to act accordingly. But this would exclude the possibility of being inclined to a certain performance *because* of seeing that it is right. It would render meaningless the judgments "This would be the right thing to do under the circumstances," or "You ought to do this," or "He ought to do this." It would not provide for moral education, which, having first judged what a man's duties are, then seeks to inculcate living up to them.

The ground has now been cleared for the positive statement that moral knowledge possesses the same general characteristics, and is subject to the same discipline, as all knowledge. It is true or false according to the evidence. It must avoid contradiction. It must invent and verify hypotheses. It must be faithful to the specific purpose of knowing, despite all temptations to the contrary. It must be self-denying, and accept the verdict pronounced by the facts or necessities of its subject matter. It must define its terms. These and all other formal criteria, or maxims, which are applicable to knowledge in general, are applicable to moral knowledge in particular, and in the same sense.

Subject to these generalities which characterize all knowledge, there are two kinds of moral knowledge, derivative and basic. When an act of homicide is judged to be wrong it is ordinarily sufficient to call it

---

[2] For a more detailed examination of this question, cf. the Author's "Value and Its Moving Appeal," *Philosophical Review, 41* (1932).

'murder.' That is deemed sufficient, since it is assumed that murder is wrong. This judgment may be subsumed under some other accepted generalization, such as the right to life, or the goodness of security and order. But if one follows this line from premise to premise, and if one avoids circularity, one arrives eventually at an ultimate premise or first premise which cannot be similarly deduced.

The application to the standard of harmonious happiness is evident. It is judged that things are morally right and wrong, good and bad, obligatory and forbidden, judged by the standard of harmonious happiness. There are two judgments, the judgment which adopts the standard, and the judgment which applies it. The fundamental question of moral knowledge is the question of the proof of the first or basic judgment. It is a judgment about a standard, and to the effect that a specific standard, such as harmonious happiness, occupies a peculiar place among standards, and is entitled to be designated as "the moral standard." This is not a moral judgment in the sense of assigning such predicates as 'good,' 'right,' and 'ought.' Moral theory, whether it asserts that the ultimate moral standard is happiness, or that the moral right or good is indefinable, or that duty is obedience to God, or that the right is the reasonable, stands outside the whole circle of such judgments, and makes non-moral statements about them.

The first condition which such a theory must satisfy is that the proposed standard should be in fact a standard, or qualified to be a standard. If harmonious happiness can be truly affirmed to be the moral standard, it must so agree with human nature and the circumstances of human life that men can adopt it by education, persuasion, and choice; and, having adopted it, can govern their conduct in accordance with its requirements. It must be qualified to serve as a criterion by which human interests, acts, characters, and organizations can be classified and ranked. The evidence that it satisfied these requirements will be found in the fact that it is so adopted and employed.

If, however, harmonious happiness is to be proved to be *the* moral standard, to the exclusion of other standards for which a similar claim is made, it must possess further and unique qualifications. Otherwise it will be merely one standard among many, differing only historically. There would be no ground of persuasion by which the adherent of another standard could be converted to this standard. It could be judged *in terms of* this standard, but there could be no judgment *between* them. The standard of harmonious happiness would have no *theoretical* precedence.

3

Before formulating and defending a conclusion as to the ultimate proof of moral knowledge, it will be profitable to review and criticize certain traditional doctrines which have been widely held, both by

philosophers and by common sense. The most notable of these are the
intuitionist proof, the rationalistic or logical proof, the metaphysical proof,
and the psychological proof. The very shortcomings of these doctrines are
instructive.

The first and most familiar of these alleged proofs is the appeal to
intuition, or to a moral absolute pitch. There is, it is claimed, a sheer
rightness of the right, or a sheer oughtness of the ought, or a sheer goodness of the good. He who knows where to look for it and is properly attuned will find it, and that is the end of the matter. The proof that an
act is right is that it is seen to be right; the proof that one ought to perform an act is that one is aware of the obligation to perform it. The
proof that a state of affairs is good is that its goodness shines forth.

This view has a pre-critical form which appeals to common sense
because it escapes the pangs of thought and analysis; it coincides with
habit or the intellectual line of least resistance. Post-critical intuitionism
gives a philosophical sanction to this non-philosophy. It accepts a now
largely discredited notion of self-evidence. In modern geometry, the
"axiom of parallels" is taken as a "postulate"; but the intuitionist in geometry held that it is self-evident that two parallel lines *can* never meet: it is
plain that it is so. According to this view, syllogistic reasoning in general
is a chain suspended from some first premise which is self-evident, and
which transmits its manifest truth to all the conclusions which follow
from it. Similarly, according to moral intuitionism, when one considers
a statement in which 'good,' 'right,' or 'ought' appears as the predicate, one
sees both what the predicate means and that the statement is true. It
needs no further evidence that what it contains within itself.

In current discussion of moral matters, intuition is commonly invoked
against the hateful thesis that "the end justifies the means." It is held that
the means plainly is or is not right or obligatory, independently of good
or evil consequences.

The question of means and ends is never, in human life, a simple
relation of a single means to a single end. The means to one end invariably affects other ends. Even so trivial a choice as means of transportation to a given destination, whether one travels by train or by plane,
has anticipated consequences over and above the arrival at the desired place at the desired time — consequences for one's pocketbook, or
for one's enjoyment of the landscape. In political action a means to an
end, such as the peace of Europe, or the supremacy of Germany, or the
triumph of socialism, at the same time crosses, cancels or confirms the
means to a hundred other ends. When the means is condemned on moral
grounds this does not imply that it is not justified by its end, but that
the means to the end of harmonious happiness is to be given priority
over all the means to all other ends.

Arthur Koestler discusses this issue in a brief, but impressive article entitled "The Dilemma of Our Times," with the subtitle "Noble Ends and Ignoble Means." [3] He first illustrates the "dilemma" from the tragic fate of Captain Scott and his four companions who perished because they refused to abandon one of their number who fell ill. The writer then finds the same dilemma in modern political action, and points out that Chamberlain's sacrifice of Czechoslovakia and Hitler's and Stalin's purgings of their opponents represent the opposite procedure, parallel to what Captain Scott *would* have done if he had sacrificed Petty Officer Evans to the safety of the rest.

This analysis illuminates the difficulties of the moral life, but throws no light on the principles involved. It is evident that to disregard consequences would not have provided a solution; for then there would have been no dilemma and no tragedy. It is implied that if it had been possible to bring all of the party to the destination, though at the cost of delay and suffering, or if Evans had willingly acceded to his own sacrifice, that would have been the solution, since the deed would then have represented an agreement of all persons whose interests were at stake. In that case, apparently, the end *would* have justified the means.

If the end does not justify the means, what does justify it? The bare dictum that the end does not justify the means has no force whatever. At best it is a confused expression of several truths: that a means is ordinarily a means to many ends; that a given end does not justify its means regardless of other ends; that the means to a higher end overrules the means to a lower end; that a means is sometimes also an end.

The intuitionist may select one of several concepts as the moral ultimate. This role may be assigned to right, to ought, or duty, or to good, better, or best. The judgments, "England was right in declaring war on Germany," "Hitler ought not to have invaded Poland," "A world subjugated by Hitler would have been an evil and not a good world," are all moral judgments. The intuitionist chooses one as the basic intuition and derives the others from it. If he chooses "good," then the "ought not" of Hitler is argued from the comparative good of the state of affairs which would have resulted from his non-aggression, and the "right" of England is argued from the comparatively good effects of her intervention. When right or ought is selected as the basic concept, the ensuing state of affairs is argued good from the right or ought of the act which brought it about.

The most serious weakness of the intuitionist view lies in the plurality and inconsistency of these basic intuitions. What one intuitionist holds to be basic another holds to be derivative. That the same intuition should be affirmed and rejected by equally attentive and scrupulous intuitionists,

[3] *Commentary, 1* (1946).

cannot but create a suspicion that they are all mistaken, and that their alleged intuitions are not intuitions at all, but dogmas, assumptions, or meaningless words.

Except among doctrinaire intuitionists there has developed a justifiable scepticism of intuitions. The justification lies in the historical fact that so many intuitions have failed to stand the test of time, in the increased understanding of the way in which pseudo-intuitions are generated, and in the appeal of the intuitionist himself to supporting evidence for what, if it were intuitive, would need no support.

4

As moral intuitionism derives its philosophical repute from Plato, so moral *rationalism* owes its prestige among philosophers to the influence of Kant. It would be unprofitable to embark on a meticulous examination of the Kantian doctrine. Many scholars who have been tempted into this labyrinth have disappeared and have never been heard from since. What Kant *has come to mean* (whether he *did* mean it or not!) is most instructive when it is most freely interpreted.

Kant defined the moral first principle in terms to which no exception can here be taken. To paraphrase the several statements of his "categorical imperative," morality prescribes that all human persons shall be treated as ends in themselves, and that life shall be organized accordingly. Each person shall subordinate the pursuit of his own end to the requirements of a harmonious society of such persons. A follower of Kant has expressed this ideal in terms even closer to those used in the present exposition:

> If we cannot perfectly realize this new ideal, if absolute harmony is unattainable, one can still walk in the light of the ideal. One can say: "I will act as if all these conflicting aims were mine. I will respect them all. . . ." This ideal . . . says: "The highest good would be attainable if all the conflicting wills realized fully one another." [4]

But this definition of the moral ideal, acceptable as it is, does not touch the question of proof. It is the contention of Kant that this ideal of a harmony of persons is the only ideal which agrees with reason. The faculty of reason is identified with logic, and logic in turn is construed to mean two things: consistency, taken to include implication as well as non-contradiction; and universality, taken to mean the subsumption of

---

[4] J. Royce, *The Religious Aspect of Philosophy*, Houghton Mifflin Company, 1887, pp. 144–5. Since Royce was one of the teachers who most influenced the Author during his student days it is quite possible that the present work reflects his influence. The Author is more conscious of the influence of William James, whose principle of "inclusiveness" (cf. his essay entitled "The Moral Philosopher and the Moral Life") so strikingly resembles the thought of Royce as represented in the above passage.

particulars under generals. In short, it is argued that the above ideal is the only ideal which can be adhered to consistently, and under which all acts of all persons can be subsumed.

As a matter of fact, however, there is no principle of conduct which cannot be adhered to consistently — even the principles which Kant and his followers would most stoutly have rejected. It is possible, theoretically, to adhere consistently — all too consistently — to the principle of personal aggrandizement or the principle of race supremacy. It is theoretically possible that these principles should be practiced by all persons; the result would, it is true, be deplorable, but it would not be illogical. Nor can it be said that a person who practiced one of these abhorrent principles could not will that others should practice the same. He might prefer a power of ascendancy gained by overcoming resistance to one in which the rival tamely submitted. To use Kant's famous example, one *might* adopt the maxim of mendacity and at the same time prefer a company of rival liars to a company of the credulous.

One may argue that there are certain kinds of rules which are such that their social benefits accrue only in proportion as they are generally observed. This would be the case with most of the familiar moral maxims, such as veracity, honesty, and respect for life. But then the proof of these rules lies not in their logic but in the social benefits which accrue. Or, one may argue that what people really want is the kind of society in which what is good for one is good for all. But do they? And if they did, the proof would be an appeal to what people actually want, and not to the formal principles of consistency and universality.

The fundamental flaw in the rationalistic theory is its failure to distinguish between logic and the facts of life. The latter have been smuggled in, thus creating the false impression of deriving a *moral* principle directly from logic. Kant confused logical universality with social universality and inconsistency with conflict, and therefore found it illogical that different persons should practice different codes. But he himself spoke of man's "unsocial sociability," [5] meaning that man's ideas of social organization spring from his actual experience of social conflict. This is a profound observation. The strength of his position lies not in his futile attempt to "deduce" his moral imperative from reason, but in his ideal of a harmonious society in which persons are moral finalities, and which not only serves all persons but commands their assent.

5

Authoritarianism, taken as moral theory, can be briefly dismissed. It may be combined with any moral principle, providing incentive, enforcement, or "sanction" for a right or good determined on other grounds. Sheer authoritarianism, authoritarianism pure and simple would define

[5] *Eternal Peace and Other International Essays*, tr. by W. Hastie, 1914, p. 9.

right, ought, and good as obedience of command. If 'right' be taken as the fundamental moral term, an act is right because commanded, and not commanded because it is right. And the same is true of 'ought' or of 'good,' if one of these be selected as fundamental. It is doubtful if sheer authoritarianism has ever been consistently maintained. It should demand "passive obedience," obedience without asking the reason why. But every authority — God, priest, ruler, teacher, or parent — has been justified as *worthy* of obedience, because of his knowledge or power, or because he himself conforms to the moral value which he is supposed to create by his command.

Even a so-called "absolute" authority such as the Christian God, is commended to those who obey him, by certain qualifying moral attributes. He may be deemed all-wise, in which case he is taken as the supreme expert or guide in the moral practice; or he may be deemed all-powerful, and hence the giver of happiness or unhappiness to those who obey or disobey his will. He may be taken as the Creator and Providence by whom right and good are realized in nature and history, and by whom their triumph is guaranteed. Or, finally, he may be taken as himself the supreme embodiment of moral perfection, a model to be emulated or loved. In each case some prior moral standard is introduced. In each case there is a moral *ground* for obedience; a judgment of right, ought, or good by which the authority is accredited.

6

The authority of God may be justified on the ground that God is the ultimate being. This is a variety of the *metaphysical* proof, to which attention is now directed. Such a theory, if it is to mean anything, requires degrees of being, or a difference within what is, between that which "really" is, and that which "apparently" is. If moral value were simply equated with what is, then the difference between right and wrong, ought and ought not, and good and evil, would be obliterated; since both terms of these antitheses *are*. Granted some difference between appearance and reality, 'right,' 'ought,' and 'good' may then be defined as agreement with reality *versus* appearance, or with the deeper, broader, total, more fundamental, and more long-range, aspect of things, and their opposites with what is superficial, transitory, and partial.

There will be as many varieties of this theory as there are varieties of metaphysics, whether materialistic or idealistic, pluralistic or monistic; but to present the theory in its generality these varieties must be disregarded. Its adherents must be prepared to say, "Right, obligation, or goodness, whichever is taken as the moral first principle, means agreement with the fundamental nature of things, *whatever it be*": whether the mechanical order of a physico-chemical world, or a Darwinian evolution by the survival of the fit, or a Marxian course of history determined by economic forces and class conflict, or the progressive unfolding of a beneficent purpose, or the realization of a perfect spiritual being, or an infinite substance, or a congeries of accidents and unrelated items.

This view, like authoritarianism, is rarely if ever held in its purity.[6] Ordinarily agreement with reality is *justified* by ascribing some moral value to reality itself. But the theory then becomes circular. Right, ought, or good are defined as agreement with a right or good world or with a world which is what it ought to be.

If moral value is taken to mean agreement or disagreement with the deep, long-range, or total aspect of things, whatever it be, it is possible to preserve a distinction between positive and negative moral value, but the implications are strange indeed. Morality then requires that a man be "in tune with the infinite" whatever tune the infinite plays. It implies that one ought to mount the Cosmic Bandwagon whatever its route and destination. It implies that *if*, broadly speaking, the world is in fact a jungle, under the reign of tooth and claw, then it is right and dutiful to sharpen one's teeth and claws and participate to the best of one's ability in the general carnage.

The metaphysical theory of morality most widely held at the present time is known as the theory of "self-realization." It is divisible into two doctrines, anthropological and cosmological. They may be combined, or the first may be held without the second.

The anthropological doctrine identifies morality with realization of human nature. That man possesses certain peculiar faculties which distinguish him from other animals, and that individual men may differ in the degree to which they manifest these faculties, is indisputable. But it is to be noted that the human faculties singled out by the self-realizationist are his moral faculties, so that the doctrine contains a disguised circularity: morality is to consist in the realization of man's moral nature. Men have many characteristics, morphological, anatomical, physiological, and psychological, which are not found in other animals. Man is sometimes defined as the "laughing animal," but no self-realizationist has ever argued that the more one laughs the better, or that the perfect man would be he who laughed longest and loudest. The human faculty which is commonly selected for emphasis is "reason"; which, in this context, is referred to as man's "ruling faculty," designed to preside over and regulate his passions. But when so conceived as the faculty for introducing unity among diverse interests and correcting their mutual conflict, reason is man's moral faculty. Morality is not deduced from human nature, but human nature is selectively defined in terms of morality.

[6] Perhaps the nearest approach to such purity is to be found in Jonathan Edwards: "This is an universal definition of Excellency: — *The Consent of Being to Being*, or *Being's Consent to Entity*. The more the Consent is, and the more extensive, the greater is the Excellency," C. H. Faust and T. H. Johnson, *Jonathan Edwards*, 1935, p. 35.

Self-realizationism of the cosmological type asserts that in proportion as man develops his characteristically human parts or his whole self he coincides with an Absolute Being, which is supremely good because it is supremely real. But this view, also, is ordinarily circular, and contrary to fact as well. Thus it has been contended that there is only one will — a universal or divine will — which is the moral will. All will, insofar as it is understood, or insofar as it is "really" will, is a will which chooses the moral good. To this view there is a double objection. If there were such a will it would not be moral because it was real, but, being real, it would also be moral on other and quite different grounds. The second objection is that there is no such all-comprehensive single will, actual, virtual, or implicit. There are many wills, one of which is the moral will, or the will to harmonious happiness.

7

The *psychological* proof is the most ancient and the most persistent of the proofs of morality, and the proof that is most readily accepted by laymen as well as by philosophers. By the psychological proof is here meant the argument that human beings are so motivated that morality will serve them best — if they only know it. To whatever person one addresses the argument, one can prove morality to him as the intelligent way by which to promote the interests by which he is already governed. It is not necessary to change his heart, but only his head.

The psychological argument has taken two forms, the most venerable of which is known as "egoistic hedonism." According to this view, which is now generally discredited, all men are governed by the motive of private pleasure. According to the second view, men are governed by a variety of motives, some of which are innate and universal, others of which are acquired and variable. Whichever view of motivation is adopted it is held that morality can be proved to any doubter by showing him that it will give him what he wants. If he wants his private pleasure, morality will give him that; if he is moved by any one of a number of interests, then, whatever its object, morality will give him that. Morality, in short, is the universal instrumental good.

It is this second theory of motivation which is usually assumed when it is argued that morality and "enlightened self-interest" coincide. Taken as a proof of the moral standard this view is ambiguous. It may mean that the standard is *defined* as that principle the adoption of which will promote every man's interest as it stands. But there is no such principle. Or it may mean that a certain principle *otherwise* defined will, in point of fact, coincide with every man's interest as it stands. As regards the principle of harmonious happiness, however, this is not true.

The psychological proof owes its vogue to the fact that if successful it would induce not merely intellectual acceptance, but the corresponding performance. If a man can be shown that morality will give him what he already wants he will not only assent to it theoretically, but will pursue it. Right, ought, or good is grafted upon the stem of his existing motivation. He is at one and the same time both convinced and incited. The term 'persuasion' is often used to embrace both effects, being deemed incomplete until it is translated into action.

But when the proof of morality is required to appeal to the existing inclinations of the person to whom it is addressed, the evidence must vary in each case. It is not possible to argue to a second judge in terms of the self-interest of a first. A principle proved by appeal to the self-interest of Hitler could not be proved to Churchill, since it would not appeal to *his* self-interest. Or would it? Is it not possible that if Hitler's self-interest and Churchill's self-interest were both *sufficiently* enlightened, their requirements would coincide? Might it not be that if every man's self-interest were enlightened it would agree with the self-interest of every man and so with the general good? Possible, yes, but highly improbable. There is a presumption against it, as there is always a presumption against a sameness of conclusions deduced from different premises. The coincidence of each self-interest with all self-interest would be a *remarkable* coincidence.

As a matter of fact this coincidence does not occur, or occurs only occasionally, partially, and under special conditions. Thus, for example, while the interests of most persons are promoted by peace, the interests of some persons are better promoted by war; if, as sometimes happens, they prefer the fish that thrive in troubled waters. In that case the more enlightened their self-interest, the more persistently and methodically will they trouble the waters. The militarist who promoted humane feelings, or the racist who promoted justice and humanity, would be a fool; he usually knows his business better. No moralist, in the ordinary sense of the term, has anything to teach *him!* There is an enlightenment for every self-interest, narrow and broad; and the conflict of self-interest with self-interest is not annulled, but may be sharpened, by increased enlightenment.

How far the principle of individual self-interest and the principle of harmonious happiness coincide depends on how the self in question is constituted. Given a man whose interests are already harmoniously attuned to those of others it is then a matter of indifference whether the argument for morality is presented in terms of his self-interest or in terms of the interests of all. But since unhappily there is no guarantee that self-interest is so attuned, it must be morally certified before it can be taken as the premise of the argument. Morality can be argued *from* self-interest only when it has already been put into self-interest.

That men should be inclined to accept the coincidence of self-interest and the general happiness is easily intelligible. It eases the strain of effort. A high officer of the American army is quoted as saying, apropos of the atomic bomb:

> We must have a group study the problem and decide what is best for the people of the United States — and that means what is best for the people of the world.[7]

In other words, for an American to serve the people of the world, it is only necessary to serve the American people, which is easier and simpler — although not so easy or simple as is usually supposed.

8

The rejection of the traditional arguments may be taken to imply that there are no arguments for the moral standard or first principle here proposed, and that no alternative is left but to postulate it or abandon it altogether. But there still remain arguments to be advanced in its support — arguments which, though they may not satisfy everybody, at least have the merit of being appropriate to the thesis which is to be proved.

In the first place, the standard of harmonious happiness is *capable* of being agreed on — both theoretically and practically. It satisfies the requirement of cognitive universality and objectivity; that is, it is the same for all knowers who address themselves to the subject. Since the norm of harmonious happiness acknowledges all interests, its affirmation is free from the so-called "personal equation." As the astronomer recognizes all stellar facts regardless of the accidents of the observer's history, and thus overcomes the geocentricism which has led men to affirm that the heavens move about a stationary earth, so the theory of harmonious happiness overcomes that egocentricism which has led moral observers to subordinate all interests to their own, or to those of their neighborhood, class, or nation. It embraces human perspectives within a total system of relationships. It places itself in all points of view, and fits them together. It discovers alien and remote interests, and makes allowance for the ignorance which it cannot wholly dispel. It is impartial. It says, in effect, that since it is interest as such which generates good, and a harmonious relation of interests which constitutes moral good, to him who makes the judgment *his* interest is just one among the rest. Since the principle of harmonious happiness deals with the nature of interest in general, and with its types of relationship, it is applicable to all interests and persons.

But while the theoretical proof of the moral principle is obliged only to satisfy the knower as *knower*, the principle here proposed will tend also to appeal to each knower's will. The good of harmonious happiness, since it embraces all interests, is *to some extent* to everybody's interest, and thereby obtains a breadth of support exceeding that of any other

---

[7] Attributed to Gen. L. R. Groves, *New Republic*, Jan. 28, 1946. Similarly, Secretary of Defense Charles E. Wilson is quoted as saying that what is good for General Motors is good for the United States.

good. Every person, including the person to whom the argument is addressed, has some stake in it.

The extent to which the harmonious happiness of all men will reward any given man will vary widely. In the absence of propinquity, inter-action, and communication, and so long as this condition prevails, it may not reward him at all. When this aloofness is diminished, its reward will depend on how his particular personal happiness is constituted. All men, no doubt, have some spark of humanity, and are affected by the happi-ness or misery of others — but some men more than other men, and some men scarcely at all. The same is true of the extent to which men's means and ends reinforce one another. This varies with men's vocations, all the way from the recluse who is interested in solitude to the man of busi-ness whose affairs are complexly intertwined in a network of employers, workers, buyers, sellers, producers, consumers, and bankers, which now extends around the earth.

The norm of harmonious happiness, furthermore, is the only norm which is capable of appealing to all men not only severally but jointly. It is the only norm which promises benefits to each interest *together with* all other interests. It does not rob Peter to pay Paul, but limits Peter in order to pay both Peter and Paul.

Hence the norm of harmonious happiness is doubly universal. It is universal in the theoretical sense: its nature and its implications are objective, and the judgments in which it is employed are equally true for all judges; and being abstracted from particular interests, it is ap-plicable to all human situations. It is also universal in the social sense; its promised benefits accrue to all men, and to all men collectively. It is a norm on which all men can unite and agree — both theoretically and practically.

9

Making due allowance for the possibility of error in general, and for the degree of its probability in any particular field of inquiry, it may properly be argued for any theory that it agrees with widespread opinion. Opinion concerning the physical world is trustworthy in proportion as it can be attributed to observation. The relation between the sun and the earth, for example, reflects the observation of the alternation of day and night. This opinion has to be corrected to take account of the place of the observer, and the influence of the religious dogma which made the earth the scene of the drama of salvation. But whether the sun moves about the earth, or the earth about the sun, or the two move relatively to one another, the empirical fact of the periodic rising and setting remains undisturbed. And so with moral opinion. It has to be corrected to take account of non-evidential influences; not only such general influences as also affect physical opinion, but the peculiar pressures which arise from the fact that moral opinion is so closely connected with action as to be of special concern to society. These non-evidential influences being discounted, there remains an "experience of life" which has taught men the consequences of action and the ways to live prosperously together.

Again and again, in all spheres of life, and in all the ages of man, has been observed that there are certain procedures by which the destructiveness of conflicting interests can be mitigated, and by which they can enjoy the benefits of peace and coöperation. Overlaid as it is by prejudices of many sorts, this lesson has been repeatedly learned, extended to new situations, and transmitted to future generations.

In spite of the marked differences of moral opinion which appear in different social groups and historical epochs there is nevertheless a notable amount of agreement. The disagreement is notable only because there was once an expectation of perfect agreement, and because of the shocked surprise with which the unfamiliar is always greeted. Language provides an analogy. The first stage is the assumption that all people speak the same language; the second stage is the discovery that there are strange, absurd, and unintelligible languages; the third stage is the discovery that all men use language, and that all languages have their common laws and meanings. In the matter of moral opinion the extreme relativists are those who have reached only the second of these stages.

If morality is taken as that organization of life by which conflict is escaped and by which coöperation is achieved, then the moral problem is universal; and it is, after all, not surprising that amidst all historic, ethnic, social, economic, and evolutionary aberrations there should emerge a broad knowledge of the points of the moral compass. This knowledge appears in generally accepted maxims, precepts, and virtues.

The theory here proposed reaffirms the standard virtues of antiquity — courage, temperance, wisdom, and justice. The good of harmonious happiness requires, like any end, a brave will that is not dismayed by obstacles, and effort sustained without complaint through long stretches of time. It requires a moderation of appetites lest in their excessive indulgence they should rob one another. It requires enlightened mediating judgments, that is, a true representation of ends and an intelligent choice of means. It requires a distribution of goods to each interest in accordance with a judgment which represents all interest. Christianity did not reject these virtues, but added faith, hope, and love; and these, also, are endorsed by the present theory. Harmonious happiness is an ideal, and if an ideal is to be pursued there must be a steadfast belief in its attainability by means that lie beyond present knowledge, and a confidence in its actual attainment in the future. The pursuit of the harmonious happiness of all requires a sympathetic concern for one's fellow man — a sensitiveness to their pains or frustrations and an impulse to help.

Other funded moral wisdom falls into line. The most generally accepted of all maxims, the Golden Rule, is justified because the harmonious happiness of all requires that each man shall put himself in the place of other men, and recognize their interests, however cold and remote, as of the same coin with those warm and intimate interests which he calls his own. Veracity signifies the need of communication as the condition of all human intercourse. Honesty is that keeping of agreements which is essential to security and to concerted plans. Selfishness is that preoccupation with the narrower interests of self, family, class, or nation which obstructs the longer and wider vistas demanded by universal happiness.

These maxims and virtues are not invariably accepted. They are sometimes defied and they are frequently ignored. It cannot, however, be said that they are peculiar to Western Europe, or to capitalistic societies, or to Christianity, or to the modern world. They cross all such divisions, and when, as today, life is organized on a wider scale, to include all nations, all dependent and backward groups, and all hitherto unprivileged persons and classes, it is to this body of moral opinion that men appeal. Equally significant is the fact that when men differ as to the specific applications of moral opinion it is to the standard of harmonious happiness that they look for common ground. And it is by this standard that men criticize and justify their major social institutions — conscience itself, polity, law, economy — and by which they define the places in human society that are to be allotted to art, science, education, and religion.

10

The proof of the moral standard is "empirical" in the full, rather than the limited, sense of that term. In the limited sense, the term 'empirical' is sometimes applied to that part of science which consists of a summary of observations, rather than to that whole in which a conceptual theory is framed in conformity with the requirements of logic and mathematics and then verified by observation. If the theory of morals is to be considered empirical in the full sense, it must be a system of concepts verified by the data of human life.

There is much talk at the present time of a "scientific ethics": an urge to make ethics scientific, and a discussion of whether ethics *can* be scientific. There is no doubt that there can be a science which deals with *conscience*. This is now a recognized part of a scientific sociology, or social psychology, or of a scientific history. There is a certain propriety in giving this inquiry the name of 'ethics,' but if this nomenclature is adopted, then ethics must be distinguished from the science of morals.

The ultimate data of moral science are not men's approbations and disapprobations, but conflicts of interest, and the organizations of interests by which they are rendered non-conflicting and coöperative. The proof of any theory of morality is its adequacy and correctness as a description

CHAPTER IX

SOCIAL ORGANIZATION

In its most general sense, 'society' names the fact that there is more than one human being in the world, and that the several human beings are related to one another. Theory of value (fortunately) is under no obligation to say all that there is to be said about society in this broader sense. It is concerned only with the role of value in society, or with the extent to which social organization is describable in terms of value. In accordance with the present theory, this implies that society is to be considered in terms of the organization of interests and interested persons. All that has been laid down in earlier chapters concerning the personal and social integration of interests, the principle of reflective agreement, and that mode of organization which has been designated as 'moral,' is relevant to the present topic.

Society is not a mere collection, or even a conglomerate or pudding stone. Neither, on the other hand, is it an indivisible entity. Merely because there is a single name for it, it must not be hypostatized, whether as a substance or as a force. It is a complex, a one composed of many, and therefore subject to analysis. It possesses certain formal characteristics. It is a "class," that is, an aggregate of individuals having some characteristic in common. It is a "whole"; that is, it possesses certain characteristics which are not ascribable to its several components; as an army possesses characteristics not ascribable to its personnel.

Society is also a "system," that is, its members occupy certain interrelated places or roles, in the whole; and these roles can be abstracted from the individuals who occupy them. When a systematic whole, such as an army, loses its network of relationships, it is dissolved or disintegrated into a rabble. Any society is thus at one and the same time a class of individuals and a system of abstract relationships in which the terms can be named for the relationships, as 'ruler,' 'employer,' etc. A society is, or may be, a "compound," that is, composed of subsocieties. And finally, a society is, or may be, "singular"; meaning that it possesses its members and their relations uniquely or exclusively. While these formal characteristics of society are by no means adequate for its description, they form an indispensable part of the conceptual apparatus for such a description.

2

Society, in the full sense of the term, is united by the interaction of persons. But interactive relations are built upon non-interactive relations, such as similarity. Human societies are bound by the tie of common anthropological characteristics — the characteristics of the species *homo sapiens;* and they may be subdivided in numerous ways, such as male and female, black, white, brown, and yellow; or brachycephalic and dolichocephalic, etc. Anthropological similarities are reflected in a similarity of interests. Thus human beings by virtue of their common reproductive mammalian characteristics, will possess the sexual and maternal interests; and by virtue of their higher capacities they will possess some degree of moral, cognitive, and aesthetic interest.

An "ethnic" society may be based on such similarities, or on consanguinity. 'The human race' is sometimes taken to designate the descendants of common parents, such as Adam and Eve, but the original parentage of men is now shrouded in obscurity, at the same time that it has lost its importance. In spite of the cult of "racism," race in the sense of consanguinity is no longer a term to conjure with among social scientists. Hereditary characteristics are recognized as of less importance than acquired or "cultural" characteristics.

Consanguinity is a significant social bond only when it is associated with proximity. Blood may be thicker than water, but there are many things that are thicker than blood. Cultural similarities depend on proximity, and consanguinity itself generates similarities by *close* proximity. If anything were needed to show the priority of proximity both to consanguinity and to similarity, it would be proved by the fact that the highly intimate relation of co-parentage obtains, not only between individuals of dissimilar sexes, but (through exogamy and prohibition of incest) between individuals of dissimilar sexes and of different heredities.

There is another of the many non-interactive human relations which is deserving of special mention, namely, community of objects, whether of cognitions or of interests, and reflecting community of environment. All human beings, however remote in space and time, occupy the same planet, and therefore perceive, think, imagine, fear, desire, dread and hope for, the same objects or classes of objects — sun, moon and stars, the elements, food and drink, birth and death, and animals and human beings of the same or the opposite sex. This sameness of objects will be multiplied in proportion to proximity in space and time.

These non-interactive relationships derive their full social significance from the fact that they condition interaction. They are the static relationships which underlie social dynamics on the level of interest. Thus similarity of interests, when combined with proximity, conditions the sense of fellowship among persons engaged in the same occupations — fellow workers, fellow artists or scientists, co-religionists. Community of objects conditions communication and united action in a common cause. The significance of the family lies not so much in a common blood stream, as in the continuous and pervasive interaction between husband and wife, parents and children, brothers and sisters. The same is true to a lesser extent of neighbors and friends. Human beings, however similar as human, or as having similar interests, however numerous their common objects, and even though they might be descendants of common ancestors, would not constitute a society if they were widely dispersed in space or time. By reason of remoteness and non-interaction, men of historic times do not belong to one society with their prehistoric ancestors; and the inhabitants of earth do not belong to one society with the human inhabitants of Mars, if there be such, even if Martians are descendants of Adam and Eve. For the same reason Eskimos do not compose a society with South Sea Islanders.

A society, then, is a neighborhood of partially similar beings, having some community of environment, and to some extent related by blood. But these relations are social relations in the full sense of the term 'social,' because they condition, and are accompanied by, interaction.

3

A human society is a society of persons, united by the modes of interaction characteristic of persons. Human beings who act on one another through their bodies only, as when they jostle, elbow, push, or pull one another in a crowd, do not constitute an interpersonal society. The minimum condition of interaction on a personal level is intercognition, and the simplest form of this is the situation in which two or more persons perceive one another. In a society of any size the range of intercognition is extended beyond the narrow limits of perception by a knowledge *about* one another by hearsay or testimony. Community of objects, combined with intercognition, yields communication, in which two or more persons through language or more primitive signs know one another's objects, and know them to be such. For communication it is not sufficient that the sun, for example, should be known to two or more persons, but that each should know that it is known by the other. Communication is consciously shared knowledge.

There are societies, in a limited sense of the term, in which this is the sole interpersonal bond. An audience, in which a number of persons are listening to the same speaker and are at the same time aware of one another's listening, is such a society. An eclipse of the sun witnessed together by a number of persons who at the same time witness one another's witnessing, is a very different situation from that in which the spectators are isolated. When a society is said to be united by "common memories" or a "common tradition" more is meant than a sameness of memories, or of inheritance; there is also an exchange of memories and a mutual recognition of one another's inheritance.

Language serves through written records or through oral tradition to create a set of permanent social objects. Words and other signs refer not only to objects, but to common objects known to be such. These objects remain the objects of other subjects, or of other possible subjects, when any given person ceases to perceive or think them. They constitute an environment, communicable if not actually communicated — an environment already there, and to which new individuals and generations who acquire the language are introduced. This body of common and relatively permanent meanings or ideas is sometimes known as "objective mind," or "collective representation."

Mutual awareness tends to create community of objects, and community of objects tends to create mutual awareness. This is seen most clearly on the perceptual level. When a person is seen looking at an object, an observer tends to follow the looking to its object. Stand on the street corner and gaze at the sky, and others will soon gather about and gaze in the same direction. And the perceiving of an object is likely to attract attention to its other perceivers. This occurs also on the level of meanings and ideas. The thinker calls the attention of others to his thought, and the thought calls attention to the thinker.

While a merely intercognitive society is not only conceivable, but is actually approximated in special situations in which discussion takes the form of an exchange of ideas, on the whole the social importance of intercognition lies in its conditioning *interinterest*. Persons not only *know* one another, but are interested in one another's interests. This is not the same thing as to be interested in another person considered merely as a physical organism, as when persons are considered as members of a "labor force," or as "cannon fodder." Nor is it the same thing as to be cognitively interested in another interest, as when the child psychologist seeks to describe the child's hunger. Interest in an interest is here construed to mean interest in its being fulfilled or thwarted, as exemplified by the mother's interest in the appeasing of the child's hunger or the genocide's interest in starving it.

Cognition of interest, while it does not constitute interest in interest, does tend to create it. Awareness of a second person's fear tends to kindle the same fear in the first person, and so to reinforce it. Similarly, the emotion of rage is "contagious"; not in a chemical, but in a psychological, sense. Panic and mob violence are to be explained in these terms. But all interests, even the gentler aesthetic responses, are strengthened by mutual awareness, proportionally to the number involved. When all of the interests within the range of observation are similar and directed to the same object their influence on any given observer becomes almost irresistible. This effect occurs upon two levels. In the case of the crowd, the mob, or the audience, the other interest is immediately presented, and the effect, like the presentation is transitory. In the case of what is called "public sentiment" the more stable interests of others are objects of judgment based on report. The effect of the multiplication and extension of the media of communication has had the double effect of bringing more distant interests within the range of immediate perception (by radio or cinema), and also of extending the range of report.

Community and mutuality of interest constitute that *interdependence* for which intercognition and interinterest pave the way. This is a matter of degree. It may be partial and transitory, or it may be total and durable. Human societies may be of either type, or of a type intermediate between these two extremes. The members of human groups may be interdependent in respect of some fraction, great or less, of their interests. The members of a crowd attending a public spectacle are interdependent. The excitement of each is influenced by the excitement of those about him — he is aware of them, and is interested in their interest. But this interdependence lasts only during the spectacle, and leaves unaffected the main body of his familial, occupational, and ideological interests to which he returns when the spectacle is over.

4

Interdependence is not the ultimate social bond, nor is it a step towards "a more perfect union," but rather a critical point at which a society may move in either of two opposite directions. From interdependence may spring either harmony or conflict, and the social interrelations thus far recognized lay the ground for both.

Hate, equally with love, springs from propinquity, and from those relationships of consanguinity and neighborhood in which men are aware of one another, and are interested in one another. Interdependence breeds quarrels as well as alliances. There are no quarrels more bitter than family quarrels, and no rivalries more implacable than those between societies which have a common frontier, or dispute a common territory, or compete with one another for the possession and use of the same natural resources. Interdependence in itself does not generate harmony; if it does generate harmony rather than conflict, it will be because of the introduction of new principles — agreement, benevolence, and co-operation. In other words interdependence creates the problem, but does not provide the solution.

The significance and gravity of this point are driven home by the present plight of mankind.[1] There is unquestionably an historical trend towards interdependence, so that men and societies are now interdependent even for their independence. Conflict is no longer to be escaped through isolation and non-interaction. Mankind has been somewhat slow to recognize this fact, but it is now so inescapable that political isolationism, economic *laissez-faire,* and the cultural "ivory tower," do not need to be refuted: they are obsolete.

The most spectacular evidence of this trend is to be found on the level of international relations. The modern technology of communication and transportation has brought all of the inhabitants of the globe into one neighborhood. The change is so conspicuous and so revolutionary as to mark the beginning of a new epoch. But there is still a lingering and fatuous belief that this change is automatically unifying, or that, in order to meet the troubles generated by technology, all that is needed is more technology. The bitter truth is that world-wide interaction in itself has not prevented war and destruction, but has substituted world-wide war for local war, and catastrophic destruction for limited destruction.

Conflict is not prevented or resolved by intercognition or by inter-interest. It is sometimes supposed that the remedy lies in "understanding one another." But enemies develop "intelligence" agencies in order to make their enmity more efficient; if one wishes to offend one's enemy he can then discover the weak points in his armor, and if one wishes to injure him one can learn what it is that he wants — and deprive him of it.

While the antisocial effects of interdependence are most conspicuous and most devastating on the international level they pervade all of life. Within each society individuals and subgroups are progressively more interdependent. The modern economy makes the rural areas dependent on urban, and urban on rural, and all forms of enterprise dependent on common markets, common raw materials, and the interchange of manu-factured products. Labor is dependent on labor, employer on employer, and each group on the other. Mass production is interdependent with mass consumption. Even the needs of the artist or scholar are supplied from a thousand sources. But at the same time that this interpenetration of individual lives and social groups has developed each society is shaken to its foundations by internal rivalries and threatened by civil war. Even persons are divided within themselves by the interdependence of their several special interests. It is clear, then, that socialization requires further principles over and above those which create interdependence. And the first of these is agreement.

[1] Cf. the Author's *One World in the Making,* 1945.

In order that two persons shall agree in opinion they must both say "yes" or "no" to the same question. They must both expect affirmatively or negatively of the same object. Or, the same event must confirm or surprise the expectations of both. When two persons are said to agree with one another in opinion there is a further requirement: each must be aware of the opinion of the other. When this occurs each finds his opinion doubly proved or disproved.

Transferred to the relation of interests, the analysis is more complicated; but essentially the same. Both interests must be for or against the same object. The same event must fulfill or defeat them both: the same news will be "good news" or "bad news" for them both. Furthermore, their proposed dealings with the common occasion — their expectations and its uses — while they need not be the same or even similar, must be compatible. Thus two persons were in favor of the election of Eisenhower; one because he hoped to be appointed to office, the other because he sought to profit by the state ownership of tidelands oil. The one dealing, it may be supposed, was not incompatible with the other. Under these conditions, being aware of one another's attitudes, they could come to agreement. Not only were their interests allied but they could regard one another as allies. They were mutually sensible of their mutual support; and having reached this point, the election of their common candidate, they wished one another well. Each desired the other's interest to succeed whether as a condition of his own, or for its own sake. In other words, agreement implies dependent benevolence, or on a higher moral level, independent benevolence.

On a more extensive social plane, the members of the "class" of labor, for example, take the same positive interest in an increase of the wage scale; their uses of the increased wages are compatible; they are aware of their common cause and possess a sense of partnership; each desires the success of the others' endeavors as a means to his own; and may (though he need not) develop a favorable interest in his partner's interests regardless of his own.

5

Agreement on a large scale, such as characterizes a social class, or a total society, requires representative agreement. One must be entitled to speak for others. The meaning is best understood by reëxamining the situation in which it is permissible for an individual to use the first person pronoun in the plural and not merely in the singular.

The small word 'we' has weighty implications both in its use and in its abuse. Except when (as is sometimes the case with the "editorial we") the term is used merely as a symbol of anonymity, he who commences a sentence with the word 'we' embraces in the grammatical subject persons other than himself. They need not be named, for their identity is usually understood from the context. The other persons may be an audience; or the fellow-members of some recognized class, such as a family, locality, or nation. To be explicit one should say "we who are here today," or "my wife and I," "we of New England," or "we Americans." The term is sometimes used, however, with an unlimited denotation, as when one says "we don't like to see the strong exploit the weak," meaning a class larger than any specifiable class. 'We' is thus carelessly used — sometimes with a studied carelessness.

The range or definiteness of the group, however, is not the important point. Compare the two statements: 'We are friends of freedom,' and 'Americans are friends of freedom.' These statements are sometimes equivalent, in which case the first can be reduced to the second, the personal pronoun being eliminated. This second statement, 'Americans are friends of freedom,' must, like any statement, be made by some *person*, but it *can* be made by any person; the fact that I make it is accidental. When, on the other hand, the first statement is distinguished from the second by the use of the pronoun 'we,' the meaning of the statement embraces a relation between the person who makes the statement and the persons concerning whom it is made: the first is claiming to represent the second. This claim is eliminated when everyone is allowed to speak for himself. If all Americans were gathered in one place, and those friendly to freedom were instructed to say "aye," a unanimous response would involve no use of the pronoun 'we.' Every "aye" would mean "I." There would be no claim on the part of any person to speak for any one other than himself.

The pronoun 'we' derives its peculiar meaning from a specific situation in which the user of the pronoun is a member of a group — such as "those present," family, fellow-partisans, fellow-nationals, or "all concerned" — the other members of which have the same opinion as his own, and *consent* to his expressing it for them. A man's interest or other attitude is his to take; it ceases to be his when he changes it. What is his to take or change, is also his to delegate. This means that whether the interest which I express for you is or is not yours is for you to say. If you recognize your interest in my expression of it and acknowledge it as yours, then it is your interest which I express. You certify to its authenticity; so that I am then, if mine is the same, justified in referring to it as "ours." There is thus a mode of relationship between the several persons of a group such that the interest of one vicariously represents the interest of the rest, and may legitimately express itself in the first person plural.

The idea of representative agreement is a philosophical commonplace, but many atrocities have been committed in its name. There is, for example, the notion of an "overindividual" subject, or super-person, of which the several individuals are dependent and inseparable parts, and which is therefore entitled to voice their interests. Such a notion is not only fictitious, but it fails to serve the purpose, since it has no organ of expression except individual human persons. It leads, therefore, to a second notion, the notion, namely, of an individual human person intrinsically qualified to be the spokesman of the group.

The qualified representative may be one who speaks with an inner sense of authority, convinced that he taps a subterranean spiritual level which underlies the superficial desires and judgments of less "inspired" men. But this qualification leads to a conflict of claimants. Instead of expressing actual agreement it creates a more passionate and tragic disagreement, each man imputing a universal vicariousness to his own private attitude. To meet this difficulty the qualified individual may be assumed to be the ruler, who speaks for all *ex-officio,* being the organ of that greater being, the State. Actual agreement may now be obtained by force, and this forced agreement may then be interpreted as a submission of each person's empirical or apparent will to his more "real" will, the will, namely, of that superbeing of which he is a part. This solution rests on three fictions: first, the fiction of a greater being with a will of its own; second, the fiction that the acts of the ruler necessarily express such a will; third, the fiction that forced obedience is the same thing as agreement.

These fictions being rejected there remains a representative agreement — an interest having the weight of many — when a person presents his own interest as the interest of others who acknowledge it as their own. Consent may be "silent," when the persons represented are aware, and make no protest. Or they may not even be aware. The legitimacy of the pronoun 'we' would then consist in the truth of the proposition that if I should consult those in whose behalf I speak they *would* consent. In using the pronoun 'we,' one counts on consent which one does not obtain, just as in one's perceptual beliefs one counts upon sensible verification which one does not obtain. One must be prepared to withdraw or modify a perceptual belief should a contrary sensible datum appear, and the belief therefore enjoys a more or less precarious security. Similarly, when one claims representative agreement, that agreement can be disproved by any person for whom one presumes to speak. His dissent is decisive.

6

Social unity culminates in coöperation — the last step in a series of successively conditioning relationships. Coöperation is organized agreement, or agreement supplemented by the coördination of means to a common end. Coöperation is not, as is sometimes supposed, the only alternative to competition and rivalry; it is quite possible that two or more persons should avoid striving against one another, and yet not strive together. Society is full of such peaceful and yet non-coöperative relations. In international organization it is recognized that coöperation for security or prosperity is a step beyond the sheer elimination of war.

Nor is coöperation the same thing as mutual aid. The dancing bear and its owner aid one another: the bear obtains food, and the owner obtains money from the onlookers. It is quite conceivable (though this may be to underrate their intelligence) that they should have no common goal at all. Or (to give them the benefit of the doubt), it is possible that both should be interested in "putting on a good show," and that the owner should provide the music and pull of the chain, and the bear the steps, as means concerted to the same artistic end or financial profit. They would then be said to coöperate.

The mother satisfies the infant's craving for food and at the same time obtains the satisfaction of her own maternal instinct. They aid one another, and their activities are, through the wisdom of nature, nicely adjusted. But they do not coöperate, because they seek no common end. The mother is not hungry and the infant does not feel maternal. They may begin to coöperate at some later time when they are governed by the common end of a happy life together, in which they recognize one another as collaborators.

The place which the common end occupies in each hierarchy of goods is independent of the fact of coöperation. Two or more persons bent on different destinations find themselves obstructed by a barrier; they both desire to remove the barrier, and work together to remove it. The removal of the barrier may be "a matter of life and death" to one, and a matter of trivial importance to the others. It may be an end in itself to one (who is governed by the love of freedom), and merely a means, or a means to a means, for the others. The common end may be the overruling end for all participants, as when men subordinate all of their individual interests to the defense of their country against an invader.

It is because of the common end that "division of labor" is a unifying and not a divisive relationship. The efforts of persons united in a common cause, and *by* a common cause, are not merely added together, but are complementary. They collaborate by their differences of choice, skill, or aptitude.

In coöperation, as in all agreement, community and mutuality of interest so act and react upon one another as to increase them both. The creation of what is called "morale" relies largely upon these effects. Awareness that another person is collaborating in the pursuit of the same end creates an interest in that person, which is likely to be a favorable interest. There is a sense of comradeship which springs from being devoted to a common cause, and which is heightened by its symbols; and comradeship is independently, as well as dependently benevolent — partnership develops into friendship. At the same time whatever promotes friendly relations and mutual good will among the participants intensifies their devotion to the common cause and to that which each contributes to its realization.

7

A person is not a society, and a society is not a person. It would not be necessary to reaffirm this thesis were it not for the perpetual confusion which arises from the important fact that both persons and societies are organizations of interests.

The analogy between persons and societies is an ancient habit of mind, reflected in habits of speech. It is customary to describe the personal life in terms drawn from social organization, and to speak of a man as "enslaved by passion," or as "keeping order in his own house," or as "living under the rule of reason." This analogy is instructive and affords the basis of the comparison between personal and social morality, both being species of the same moral genus. But analogy means *partial* similarity, and analogies are always dangerous because of the tendency to suppose that similarity in some respects implies similarity in all respects.

The similarity between persons and societies embraces relationships which lie at the root of morality. The several interests of the same person, like the interests of different persons, may be conflicting; and by organization they may be rendered harmonious. Thus a man's hunger which moves him to eat his cake may contend with his avarice which moves him to have it; or his play and his work may dispute the use of the same hours. He may solve his problem by developing an over-all interest in his own interests, and by uniting them in the pursuit of a common end which provides for both eating and having and for both work and play. These types of relationship and organization occur also as between the hunger or play of one man and the avarice or work of another.

But, as has been pointed out, there are certain operations and relationships which are *exclusively internal* to a person, and whose exclusive internality affords the best description of what a person is. Among these are verification, learning by experience, inference, the mediation of interest; the relation between independent and dependent interest; and between the overruling and subordinate interests. These are forces which operate only among the parts of that dynamic system which coincides physically with the neurally centered organism, and on that high level of complexity which characterizes the individual person.[2]

It follows that insofar as a society derives its unity from thought, from the control of action by ideas, from the relation of means to ends, and from the control of higher interests, it borrows these unifying prin-

---

[2] This analysis does not in principle exclude the possibility of two personalities associated with a single body. Insofar as a "split personality" is wholly split, it illustrates, and does not contradict, the conception of personality here set forth.

ciples from its members. They unify the interests of different persons only when through sympathy, imagination, representation, and benevolence these are brought together vicariously within one person. This holds of any society, however extensive, however small and intimate, however infused the members may be with devotion to common ends, or by participation in coöperative endeavor.

A society, such as a corporation, may be said to have a "legal personality," in the sense that it possesses one of the characteristics of personality, namely, liability; but it is not implied that it possesses the other and crucial characteristics. It is appropriately described as "soulless." Although no society is a real person it is permissible to use the term to symbolize its unity, or to evoke attitudes of loyalty and obedience. The "Leviathan" of Hobbes is such a symbol. Similarly, when Milton said that "a commonwealth ought to be a huge Christian personage, one mighty growth of stature of an honest man, as compact of virtue as of body" [3] he used language appropriate to civic reform, but not to psychology. The state or nation may be referred to by a personal pronoun, and represented by a human figure, for the sake of endearment. Christ, according to St. Paul, represented the Church as his bride "that he might present it to himself a glorious church, not having spot, or wrinkle, or any such thing; but that it should be holy and without blemish." [4] Such statements are permissible by poetic license, but they are not descriptions of fact.

To conceive a society as a person literally and in all seriousness, is doubly disastrous. It leads to idolatry, that is, the transfer to non-persons of the attitudes appropriate only to persons. It invests non-persons with a specious dignity,[5] and leads to such distortions as ecclesiasticism and statism. In the second place, to conceive society as a person stands in the way of understanding either personality or society. By resorting to metaphor and loose analogy it diverts attention away from the internal structure and dynamics of personal integration; away from the real locus of social integration, which derives interpersonal structure from the intrapersonal structures of its members.

8

All of the interpersonal bonds which constitute a society provide at the same time for a plurality of societies — for societies within societies,

---

[3] *Of Reformation Touching Church-Discipline in England, Works,* 1931, Vol. III (Part One), p. 38.

[4] *Ephesians,* 5:27.

[5] It has been said that the nearest analogue in the animal kingdom to a society is not a man, still less an angel or deity, but the formaniferous rhizopod, which closely resembles the ant-colony, and which is classified among the lowly protozoa. The society of ants stands upon a lower level of organization than the individual ant. Cf. the Author's *General Theory of Value,* 1926, 1950, pp. 451–2.

and for societies among societies. A *singular* society is distinguished by the singularity of its members, and this in turn consists in their unique locus and orientation in space and time. It consists of human individuals who coexist within a certain area, or succeed one another during a certain lapse of time. This spatial contiguity and temporal continuity is the condition of the interactive relations between the members. It gives to the individual members of society their living-together, and their tradition and common memories. Within such a spatial and temporal framework individuals may be replaced and superseded like the cells in a body, without loss of historic identity; the spatio-temporal locus of its members makes a society *this* society, not to be duplicated, however much it may be resembled, by other societies. In this sense of singularity America is the society composed of Americans, that is, of persons residing throughout the Western Hemisphere between the thirtieth and forty-ninth parallels, between the Atlantic and Pacific Oceans, continuously from the seventeenth and to the twentieth centuries. No other society, however American in its *characteristics,* could constitute America.

Such a territorial-historical classification is legitimate and fundamental, but it falls far short of exhausting the full concreteness of a singular society. There are other bonds which are either presupposed or superimposed. It is presupposed that all members of a singular society are of the human race, and of one or more ethnic species. They will be distinguished by their common environment, and in some degree, at least, by common descent. Because of their spatial and temporal proximity they will interact among themselves, and from this interaction will emerge those close bonds of agreement and coöperation which create a society in the full sense of the term.

In other words, a singular society will be a spatio-temporal sub-class of mankind which coincides with sub-classes otherwise defined. All societies are exclusive in some respect: there must be some bond which unites the members with one another, but which unites none of them with non-members. But the extent to which a historic society is also exclusive in other respects, will vary. In short, singularity is a matter of degree.

The limiting case of a society having the maximum degree of singularity is approximated by human societies remote in space or time, such as Eskimos, Australian aborigines, or prehistoric man, before their discovery by voyagers or archaeologists. Few of the internal bonds of such a society were, it may be supposed, shared with persons outside the society. Its relations of ethnic characteristics, community of environment, consanguinity, proximity, interaction, interdependence, agreement, and coöperation were confined to its own circle. The opposite extreme, possessing the minimum of singularity, would be represented by a section of mankind having no exclusive bond save place and time. This is said to have been the case when North and South Korea were divided by the thirty-eighth parallel. Otherwise the North Koreans and South Koreans shared the same internal relations. This situation was changed at the moment when the two sections acquired separate governments and ideologies; and it would not have existed at all if, as is sometimes held, the peoples of these areas already possessed different economies.

Between these two extremes there is room for indefinitely many degrees. It would be contrary to sociological usage to consider a merely spatio-temporal section of mankind as a society at all; but precisely what, and how many, further peculiarities or exclusive bonds are required is a matter of arbitrary definition. One might insist on a peculiar language or a peculiar descent, or peculiar marriage customs, or a peculiar economic organization, or a peculiar art or science, or a peculiar government. Using the term 'culture' to embrace any acquired peculiarity, it is assumed that a singular society must possess *some* cultural idiosyncrasy.

It is to be noted that when one looks for examples of extreme singularity one finds them in primitive societies. This suggests that the characteristics of an advanced society tend to be shared with other societies, or that in proportion as a society advances it tends to lose its singularity. That is one reason why sociologists are fascinated by primitive societies. When a society advances — becomes more mobile, more enlightened, more efficient, more progressive — it is faced with a dilemma: either it loses its singularity and is merged into a larger society; or it struggles against this tendency, and attempts to give a unique flavor to all of its cultural achievements. Hence there arise the cults of nationalism and totalitarianism, which were not necessary in earlier stages of development.

Within any given historic society there will be relationships, of any type, non-interactive and interactive, which unite some but not all of its members. In proportion as the society has a high degree of singularity these sub-societies will share its singularity; that is, their bonds will obtain only between members of the society. But when the society possesses a low degree of singularity the bonds which unite members of the sub-society may also relate them to members of other societies. This is the case, for example, with the Catholic Church and with the Communist Party. In other words, societies can overlap and interpenetrate through having sub-societies in common.

Implicit in the above analysis is the fact that a sub-society may consist either of a fraction of the members of the total society, or of a fraction of their interests. Organized amateur sports, for example, embrace *some* Americans in respect of *one* of their interests, and this is ordinarily the case with organized science, art, or religion. It is conceivable that a highly "decentralized" society should consist of sub-societies whose exclusive bonds embraced the greater part of their interests. They could not embrace *all* their interests, for they would then no longer be parts of one society. Local autonomy carried beyond a certain point, as in the extreme Southern sectionalism at the time of the American Civil War, would dissolve the Union. There is a similar crucial point at which nationalism would prevent the creation of a world society. The more familiar case is that in which the members of a sub-society are united by a special interest, but are left free to be united with other persons in their other interests.

There are "special purpose" organizations, and there are "all-purpose" organizations. The latter would be illustrated by a marriage bond embracing not only the purpose of procreation but the total lives of both partners. A similar situation exists when the interest which binds the members is their only independent interest. The common interest then indirectly motivates all of the interests of each. This is approximated when the members are governed by the same political, economic, tribal, or religious, piety and the society becomes a statist, communist, capitalist, racist, theocratic, totalitarianism.

Finally, it is necessary to reaffirm and emphasize the idea of *system,* by which the social relationships can be abstracted from the particular individuals whom they unite. A society is then conceived as a system of systems; as when America is taken to be divisible into characteristic political and economic structures, and a characteristic relation between the two. Such systems can be duplicated in other societies where they are embodied in other singular members. Thus the United States and the United Kingdom can both be said to be capitalistic democracies.

The distinction between the social system *in abstracto* and the class of its members explains the difference between the idea that all societies should be democracies, and the idea that all societies should be brought into a single world democracy. The failure to make this distinction is a frequent source of confusion in the area of international thinking.

When a society is taken as a system of systems the individual member may be characterized in terms of the multiple roles which he assumes: the same individual may be citizen or ruler in the political system; judge or defendant in the legal system; teacher or pupil in the educational system; producer or consumer in the economic system; priest or layman in the religious system.

These, then, are some of the ideas which it is necessary to have in mind for the understanding of social institutions. At the same time they discredit views of human history which liken societies, in other than the loosest sense, to physical organisms. There is no equivalent of a central nervous system which controls all of the functions of a society and terminates at its periphery. There is no unambiguous boundary corresponding to the skin, which separates a society from its surroundings and enables

CHAPTER X

SOCIAL INSTITUTIONS

Neither theory, nor dictionary definition, nor common usage provides for any absolute distinction between a society and an institution. An institution is a psychological, and not a merely physical, entity. It is not to be identified with the building which houses it — like the hospital, art gallery, or Capitol in Washington. This needs to be said because to the occupants of a sight-seeing bus an "institution" is often an architectural monstrosity pointed out by the barker. An institution is not a physical product, such as a book, a picture, or manufactured commodity. An institution, in short, is a relation of meanings, ideas, and interests residing in men's minds. It is an organization of persons, based on formal, non-interactive, and interactive relationships, culminating in agreement or coöperation. But all this can be said of any society. If the term is restricted to its accepted meaning in the literature of the social sciences, an institution is a *kind* of society, distinguished by several more or less explicit characteristics.

In the first place, an institution is a social structure organized by men for the sake of a purpose which it serves. In other words, an institution is *instituted*. Though it may have been anticipated by nature, it is reaffirmed and maintained by culture. Thus the political institution of government can be traced back to the fact that by virtue of their comparative power or self-assertiveness one or more individuals of a group possess a natural ascendancy over their fellows; but the institution begins when this control is recognized, accepted, and perpetuated as a social utility. Though it may have arisen, and may be perpetuated, by habit and instinct, an institution is endorsed by the wills of its members, who identify it with their interests.

So to conceive an institution is to identify an institution with its rationale, rather than with the accidents of its origin. It is a social organization which members of a society justify to themselves as useful and good. They say, in effect, that if they did not happily possess such an institution they would inaugurate one. And the purpose which is served by the exercise of its function provides the standard by which they reshape and seek to perfect it.

In the second place, an institution is a sub-society, embraced within a larger society. Thus a nation-state embraces several institutions, as a physical organism has several organs. And finally an institution is a system which can be abstracted from its members, thus enabling it to be repeated in several singular societies, and enabling the same individual to be a member of several institutions.

In principle, there is no limit to the number of possible institutions, even with the above restrictions. If an institution is a specific way in which the members of a society organize for the promotion of common interests, there can be as many institutions, in the broad sense, as there are interests which are thought to be promoted by organization. But there is a further restriction which is commonly recognized, namely, importance or eminence. While there is no list of institutions of which it can be said that they, and only they, are *the* institutions, there is a difference between those institutions which play the major, and those which play a minor, part in human life.

2

There are several principles by which institutions can be ranked as major and minor. The first of these principles is universality. Eligibility for participation in an institution is more or less general or restricted. Thus, the society of the Veterans of the Spanish War is restricted to those who have had a certain common military experience, and will lapse when such persons no longer exist. A society of philatelists admits only persons qualified by the special interest of a small number of persons. An antivivisection society embraces only persons who are governed by a certain particular sentiment, and desire to spread it and translate it into legislation. A social club is organized for the purpose of joint amusement or edification: and is limited to residents of a certain country, or city; or to persons who find one another congenial; or to persons of a certain caste.

The degree of an institution's generality is reduced when a constant is substituted for a variable; that is, when the requirement of eligibility contains a singular individual. A personal dictatorship, such as the dictatorship of Hitler, ceases to exist with the death of the dictator. A reigning house, that is, rule by a class of descendants, is more general than a personal dictatorship. One ruler may be replaced by another so long as the qualification of descent is satisfied; but this class of eligibles can be exhausted, and the institution then ceases to be. More general is the British monarchy, because there is a constitution which provides for succession under all circumstances. But British monarchy is still restricted in its membership, and it would cease to exist if the residents of the British Isles should perish. "There will always," it may be hoped, "be an England," but this is an expression of faith and resolution rather than a statement of theoretical possibilities. Monarchy in general is more general, and government in general is most general; the class of eligible persons is inexhaustible save by the annihilation of all persons.

All men have neighbors, but it does not follow that all men are *my* neighbors. All men are linguistic, but they do not speak my language. The institution of the family is universal because every man, by virtue of the fact that every man has parents, belongs to some family, or has the familial relationship; the institution of *my* family, on the other hand, is restricted to consanguinity with me. The term 'mankind' has, therefore, a double meaning. All men are members of mankind by virtue of being men; but when they are considered to be descendants of Adam and Eve, or to be the children of God, and therefore brothers or cousins, it is implied that they constitute a single family by common descent from a particular historic ancestor. Similarly, racism may refer to common ethnic characteristics or to common parentage.

There are institutions of which there always have been, always are, and always will be, eligible members. All men, by virtue of their conflicting interests, are eligible for membership in a moral system. All men are qualified to be either ruler or ruled, and therefore to fit into some political system; all men are subject to regulation, which they impose or to which they submit; are consumers or producers or both; are makers or beneficiaries of knowledge; are creators or enjoyers of beauty; have something to learn and something to teach; are finite creatures subject to ultimate cosmic forces. Hence all men are qualified to belong to *some* ethical, political, legal, scientific, aesthetic, educational, or religious institution. Of these institutions, to some variety of which all men belong because they are men, it may be said that they possess universality — universality restricted only by the qualification of human personality.

When it is claimed, as, for example, by Marxism, that economic institutions determine the form of political, legal, social, and cultural institutions, economic institutions are given causal priority. Certain sociologists, such as Max Weber, have claimed that religion (Protestant Christianity) has been causally prior to the economic institution of capitalism. This question is different from the question of which institution overrules other institutions. Thus even though it were conceded that economic institutions were prior causally, any given society might place its political institutions in the position of command, and subordinate all other institutions to its control. Each person living in such a society would give his first obedience to the state, regardless of his legal rights, his economic needs, his cultural preferences, or his religious faith, all of which would give way in case of disagreement. In a theocracy, on the other hand, prior allegiance would be given to religion. And an institution which possesses prior allegiance ordinarily *claims* such allegiance on the ground of its superiority of rank.

More important than any of these distinctions is that between moral and non-moral institutions which will presently be examined. Judged by these and other criteria, there are certain institutions which are by general consent regarded as the great or major institutions: conscience or custom, polity, law, economy, science, art, education, and religion. They are all universal; that is, rooted in the common characteristics of human nature and human life. They are comparatively basic, that is, they rank high in the order of causality; and they are comparatively eminent, in that some one of them is given priority, actual or ideal. These are the institutions by which societies are deemed more or less "advanced," and which furnish the criteria of civilization and progress. It is in terms of these institutions that the rival claims of East and West, or of antiquity and the modern world, are disputed and judged.

3

The distinction between moral and non-moral and super-moral institutions has been anticipated in the distinction between moral good and the non-moral goods of truth and beauty. That difference lies in the fact that certain interests, commonly called "practical interests," are preëmptive, whereas others, such as the cognitive or aesthetic interests, are relatively non-preëmptive. The consummatory dealings of practical interests, such as the appetites and worldly ambitions, operate causally on their occasions, and hence disturb the external environment which is common to them and to other interests. In appropriating, they at the same time expropriate. The moral institutions are those modes of social organization whose purpose it is to render interests of the several members of society mutually innocent and coöperative. Their *ratio essendi* is moral. The achievement of social harmony is their proper business — if there were no such business to be done they would be out of business. Such are the institutions of custom and conscience, polity, law and economy.

That the aesthetic and cognitive interests provide a retreat from the scene of practical conflict is a part of man's immemorial wisdom. All interests affect one another directly or indirectly, in the short run or in the long run. But the consummatory dealings of cognitive and aesthetic interests do not necessarily involve the preëmption of their objects. They are comparatively innocent, and do not require social organization in order to obtain harmony. Nor, to achieve their purposes, do they require coöperation.

Cognition invites its object to assert itself. To experiment with things for cognitive purposes is to evoke, and not to alter, their properties. If a hypothesis is to be verified one must not tamper with the verifying event, but merely note that it does or does not occur. Whether knowing be considered as an instrument of practical interest, or as an independent interest in its own right, the principle remains the same, for when practical interests seek to change their objects, they are effective only when their mediating cognition takes account of the objects' independent natures. The satisfaction of curiosity, the agreeable sense of being fortified against surprise, the enjoyment of a familiar acquaintance with reality — these are interests which are capable of fulfillment without inducing causal changes in that aspect of the environment to which they are directed; in fact, their fulfillment is proportional to the extent to which this aspect is "brought to light" without being deformed in the process.

Aesthetic like cognitive interest abstains from causal action on its object. Insofar as it addresses itself to the realm of sense-perception, aesthetic attitude is one of voluntary exposure. It is delighted with what it finds, and would not have it different. This is true of the aesthetic interest when it is independent; and is wholly consistent with the fact that the dependent interest which it generates, namely, the creation of art, does alter the face of things so that they can then be enjoyed without alteration.

Cognitive and aesthetic interests are similar in that the changes which they require are changes in the interested subject itself. Cognitive interest creates and alters expectations; aesthetic interest creates and alters states of attention and awareness. And since all changes in the existent world have their causal reverberations throughout that world, cognitive and aesthetic interests cannot be said to make *no* external differences. But such differences are indirect and incidental. Cognitive and aesthetic interests do not of themselves make a difference to the environment common to themselves and to other interests.

An orange as object of knowledge is an orange fulfilling my expectation of its color and sphericity; or begetting expectations of sweetness and juiciness which the future will confirm. So far as this attitude is concerned, nothing happens to the orange; it continues to exist, to be circular, sweet, and juicy, and to lead its own proper citrous life. As an object of aesthetic enjoyment the orange evokes an agreeable play of my perceptual faculties. My eye dwells caressingly on its color and texture, follows and relishes the lines of its shape. Again, the orange remains undisturbed. If, however, it is hunger rather than curiosity or the love of beauty that prompts me, the satisfaction of my interest requires that I shall grasp, rend, masticate and swallow it. The orange progressively loses its properties, and is eventually annihilated altogether. In short, the practical interest "consumes" its object in the full sense of the term — in the sense namely of "using it up" and thus depriving other interests of its use.

The social implications of this distinction are of the first importance. Since a given person's cognitive and aesthetic interests primarily concern himself, and are not matters of primary concern to other persons, they do not require coöperative organization in order to be realized, nor do they require control by, and in behalf of, society at large. They constitute a realm in which a high degree of tolerance is socially tolerable.

4

The difference which distinguishes practical from cognitive and aesthetic interests affects the necessity of agreement and the methods by which agreement is brought about. While cognitive and aesthetic disagreement is notorious, it differs from practical disagreement in being less violent, less grave in its consequences, and less disturbing in the means required for its removal. Two or more persons can think differently of the same object, or the one can find it beautiful and the other ugly, without mutual interference. The methods of cognitive and aesthetic agreement will be dictated by this fact. They will require communication, testimony, sympathy, assent, correction, changes of inner attitude, but they will not require physical alterations of the common environment or a rerouting of overt behavior.

Cognitive agreement consists, as has been pointed out, in a situation in which two or more persons, mutually aware, say "yes" or "no" to the same question. When both are governed by the cognitive *interest* they both desire truth, and their agreement consists in their being mutually aware of being for or against the same idea or hypothesis on the ground of its truth. In order to bring this about it is necessary that each should first organize his own judgments or expectations. Each must then consider the testimony of the other, and arrive at a more inclusive synthesis. When, proceeding in this manner, the two have arrived at the same acceptance or rejection, either may then express it in the first person plural. Either may then take it as a premise for further persuasion or as an assumption for any joint enterprise. In the course of the process each may insist on his own view until he is satisfied that the other has taken account of it. His testimony constitutes evidence which the other, if he desires the truth, and is to speak for both, is forbidden to neglect. The effort to persuade implies an openness to persuasion; in other words, cognition being what it is, two knowers *ought* to agree. This assumption is involved in the reference of cognition to common objective evidence.

The case of aesthetic agreement is less conclusive. One person enjoys the contemplation of a given object and at the same time acknowledges a second person's similar enjoyment of the same object, or his distaste for that object, or his enjoyment of another object which the first does not enjoy. Or the two persons may agree or disagree in their order of preference — addressed to the same, or different, objects. Where agreement does not exist it may be brought about by the first person's calling the second person's attention to the object's qualifying attributes. When two persons are agreed in advance as to the qualifying attribute, or definition of beauty, disagreement is cognitive; that is, it concerns the truth or falsity of judging that the object answers the definition. Where there is no such underlying agreement as to what makes an object beautiful aesthetic agreement can be reached only by each party's learning to enjoy what the other enjoys — "see in it" that which the other sees in it; or by yielding to the contagion of the other's manifest enjoyment; or by tolerating the other's difference, and "agreeing to disagree." In short aesthetic agreement is brought about, when it is brought about, by an intercommunication of aesthetic appreciations, and the attempt of the part of each person to reconcile his original personal tastes with his imaginary adoption of the tastes of others. Only in this way can he feel for all, and substitute the plural for the singular pronoun. But the imperfect and wavering character of such agreement is reflected in the widespread doubt as to whether there is such a thing as public taste.

Practical agreement, on the other hand, requires more drastic measures. The following example will illustrate the difference. Two persons disagree cognitively as to a certain church building: one judges it to be built of stone, the other judges it to be built of concrete. They may reach agreement by discussion, that is, by an interchange of ideas or perceptions, continued until each has fitted the other's ideas or observations to his own. They differ aesthetically: one finds the building ugly, the other finds it beautiful. They may reach agreement through such an understanding and adoption of one another's appreciations as leads to a more comprehensive identity of taste, or to a common hierarchy embracing their differences, or to a mutual respect for one another's incurable idiosyncrasies. But if they do not reach cognitive or aesthetic agreement by these methods, and the disagreement stops at that point, "no great harm is done" — they do not "come to blows."

But now suppose that one is a park commissioner who proposes to raze the building, while the other is a good churchman who proposes to retain it and use it as a house of worship. The two interests are incompatible: if one has his way, the other cannot have his. The train of causes and effects by which the one fulfills his secular desire collides with that by which the other fulfills his piety. Each, following the path of his interest, sooner or later encounters the other moving in an opposite direction, so that he finds the defeat of the other's interest to be a condition of the fulfillment of his own. The only way by which this mutual destructiveness can be avoided, is, let us say, to provide facilities for worship or for recreation elsewhere. In any case, "something has to be done about it." The problem requires a moral solution.

5

Society is moralized through its moral institutions — conscience, polity, law, and economy. It is to these same institutions that men look for the moralization of international relations, or of a total, global society. These institutions do not exist to serve special interests, but to harmonize all the interests of a society. This they do in their different ways, and with their appropriate functions or instrumentalities.

To classify conscience as an institution is a departure from existing usage; but it is often so classified under the name of 'custom.' It consists of a community and agreement of approbation and disapprobation, together with the correlative of being approved or disapproved. These complementary roles, active and passive, are not separately embodied — every man exercises them both. He is both approver and approved, disapprover and disapproved. It is true that certain persons such as parents, reformers, or preachers sometimes arrogate to themselves the role of approver and disapprover; but they do not preoccupy this role, and when they do exercise it they appeal to the consciences of those to whom they address themselves, every man at some stage of his personal development being assumed to have a conscience of his own. There is no recognized keeper of another's conscience. It is because it is distributed among all persons that its claim to be recognized as an institution may be disputed.

There is no doubt, however, that conscience speaks in behalf of the general social good. A person's conscience approves with the expectation that others will share, confirm, and reinforce his approbation; and it approves disinterestedly, that is, for all interests concerned. It is this disinterestedness which distinguishes "righteous indignation" from mere anger; as when non-Jews are righteously indignant toward Nazis in behalf of Jews. It is this which distinguishes shame and remorse from mere regret.

Conscience is also a social control, and has its own peculiar weapons of enforcement which it employs when its control is insecure. Men fear the disapproval of others because it cuts them off from friendly and coöperative relations and carries a hint of overt hostility. For converse reasons men seek and enjoy the approval of others. Men also fear their self-disapproval, that is, they suffer from "pangs of conscience" and seek to avoid them; and are induced to earn self-approval by the hope of enjoying a "good conscience."

Among social institutions conscience is the most direct expression of the requirements of morality, and it is through conscience that the general principles of moral organization, such as justice and humanity, ordinarily reach the other moral institutions of polity, law, and economy.

Polity differs from custom or conscience in that the function of control is assigned to special functionaries, called "rulers," who constitute a government. It is frequently defined in terms of the employment of penalties to compel obedience. The need of such compulsion arises from the requirement of reciprocity. If any measure for preventing conflict is to be effective it must be participated in jointly by both parties. If one person executes his part, and others fail to execute theirs, he has not achieved harmony but has only submitted to exploitation. If the purpose of a coöperative enterprise is to be realized, the partial performance of one must be supplemented by the corresponding performance of his partners. If they "let him down," he has been guilty of folly. Government can provide the surest guarantee of reciprocity because it alone draws upon the power of the total group and employs this power to deprive an offender of that which his interests require. Its penalties and rewards are effective upon all persons because it has the power to inflict pain, which all men avoid; and to grant or withhold the basic conditions of all interests, such as property, liberty, and even life itself.

But enforcement is not the essential function of polity. If men were constitutionally trustworthy, that is, reliably disposed to make and keep promises, being moved by good will, or controlled by reason and conscience, there would still be need of polity because there would still be need of *policy*. The essential function of polity is to provide a comprehensive plan by which the interests of all members of a society can live and work together. Government decides upon, decrees, commands, executes, and administers such a plan in behalf of all and for the benefit of all — by force if necessary, but if without force so much the better.

Law is closely related to polity. It ordinarily operates through a judicial system which is a branch of government. But the role of lawmaker and judge could be assumed by another institution, such as religion. Law like polity is often identified with enforcement by government. Law *is* enforced by government, but if it were not enforced, or were enforced, as has presumably happened in the course of human history, only by the milder sanction of custom, it would still be law.

For the essential function of law is regulation. The law creates assurance regarding certain classes of human relationships, and thus defines a broad frame within which particular human enterprises can be confidently undertaken. The binding force of the particular is derived from the binding force of the general. Thus persons can know in advance that a particular promise will be kept because it belongs to the category of contract. By the subsumption of the particular under the general it is possible to deal all at once with an infinitude of hypothetical situations.

Beyond its immediate purpose of regularizing social life, the law has its ulterior moral purpose, which is to be found in the *content* of its regularities. Its regularities are not for the sake of regularity, but for the sake of adjusting human interests, and thereby achieving the good life of harmonious happiness. The ideal content of the law is justice and welfare.

The ulterior purpose of economy, like that of conscience, polity, and law, is essentially moral. It is a coöperative organization which provides for the needs of all at the least cost "all around." It arises from the fact that needs are preëmptive; that is, in taking for themselves they take away from others. Where rivalry for possession and use is unorganized it takes the form of plunder, which, since it deprives the plundered interest altogether of its object, is highly costly, that is, uneconomical. The most obvious method of avoiding plunder is the substitution of equivalent goods. When, owing to scarcity, there are no equivalent goods, then rivals unite their forces to increase the supply. Or, each supplies the other's deficiency out of his own superabundance. Or, the first party, having no superabundance of what the other needs, gives his services instead. Thus production, exchange, and labor develop as methods of escaping a situation in which one interest can secure satisfaction only at the expense of another.

These basic devices have undergone so great an elaboration, and have become so rooted in habit and tradition, that their moral purpose is obscured. But the idea of their harmonizing effect and general utility — their usefulness to all concerned — is never wholly obliterated. It is acknowledged whenever an economic system is justified or condemned.

6

Science and art satisfy the criteria of major institutions. The interests which they serve are universal, take a prior place in the causal order, and frequently serve as the supreme or ruling end. Their claims of science and art to be included among social institutions rests on their major importance in society, on their communicative character, on their ideal of agreement, on the social character of their products, and on their tendency to coöperative organization.

The universality of the cognitive and aesthetic interests is unquestionable. Taken as special interests they are to be found in all men and in all societies, and actually or potentially in all interests. This is due to the fact that all interests are mediated. Every interest embraces a content which is "before the mind." The cognitive interest develops when this content is believed, questioned, supported by evidence, proved true, and related to other beliefs. The aesthetic interest develops when this content is contemplated and enjoyed for its own sake. Thus the cognitive and aesthetic interests are perpetually generated from practical interests by a shift of direction.

Because of their mediating function they exercise a profound influence upon human action — so great a function that they are sometimes taken to be the most basic causes of human history. The values which they generate are often taken to rank highest among cultural achievements.

The cognitive and aesthetic interests derive their social character primarily from the fact that they assume the form of communication. They convey meanings by expressing themselves externally. The cognitive interest employs speech or some other outward medium, and addresses itself to the sensory capacities and the understanding of a second party. And, similarly, the aesthetic activity embraces the creative part and the appreciative part. These may fall within the same person, as when the painter looks at his own work; or the composer hears his own music, in the course of its composition; or they may be divided between two persons, the artist and his spectator or audience.

The cognitive and aesthetic interests are further socialized in their ideal of agreement. The knower expects his judgments to be shared by others; their proof is confirmed by the findings of other knowers. The analogy of the aesthetic is imperfect. While a belief, owing to the "objectivity" of its evidence, is disproved, or at least rendered questionable, by dissent, the object of contemplative enjoyment would still possess its aesthetic value when not enjoyed or even when disliked by persons of different taste. Nevertheless the aesthetic interest asks for agreement, and endeavors to bring it about.

The products of the cognitive interest, assembled, revised and supplemented from age to age, and interchanged by different human societies, constitute a corpus of truth; the products of the aesthetic interest constitute a gallery of monuments which through their translation, reproduction, and exhibition, minister to the enjoyment of all mankind. Taken together, science and art create a public treasury and inheritance, and a lasting environment into which successive generations of men are born.

The cognitive and aesthetic interests need not, but may, assume the form of coöperative undertaking. A solitary person may know truly, that is, test his belief by evidence. But as time goes on there is increasing collaboration and division of labor in research. Scholars profit by the work of other scholars. Laboratories are constructed and manned by a varied personnel, and their results are promptly reported for the benefit of other laboratories. Scientists organize themselves into learned societies and publish journals. The aesthetic interest may occur and may realize its object in personal solitude. But some of the arts, such as the dance, the drama, pageants, orchestral and choral music, are essentially and originally coöperative; and artists tend to organize themselves in studios, museums, festivals, and societies.

While cognitive and aesthetic pursuits are not intrinsically coöperative, nevertheless, because they are parts of personal and social lives they fall within the domain of moral organization. They must be harmonized with other interests. This follows from the fact that they employ physical means and embodiments. In order to exercise them a person makes use of the same body for which he has other uses. When his cognitive and aesthetic interests are personally harmonized he may still be brought into practical collision with other persons.

A man's curiosity may prompt him to invade another person's privacy, or he may dispute the occupation of some place of observation. In order to devote himself to knowledge he may be compelled to withhold certain services which are required by the interests of others. In order to consummate his scientific inquiry he needs certain physical appliances, which are then withdrawn from uses to which other persons might like to put them. Similar practical incompatibilities arise in the course of the fulfillment of a person's aesthetic interests. There is a practical difficulty when the family breadwinner spends too much time enjoying movies or admiring the scenery; or when a visitor to an art museum obscures the view of others. Such practical implications of the aesthetic interest lead those who can afford it to own works of art or natural landscapes which they can enjoy without interference.

Only in the light of such considerations is it possible to understand the relation between moral and non-moral institutions. The cognitive and aesthetic interests are comparatively innocent, but they do not exist in a world of their own. They lead indirectly, if not directly, to effects in that common external world in which conflict implies frustration and destruction. They need to be protected from practical interests, and practical interests need to be protected from them. Their *comparative* innocence and invulnerability creates the delicate problems of liberty, control, tolerance, and censorship; which must find their solution through the moral institutions, whose business it is to create harmony among all interests, none excepted.

If human life be likened to a garden, then morality and its institutions represent the fencings, spacings, and arrangements by which the plants, such as truth and beauty, and divers special and personal interests, are enabled to flower most abundantly. Morality does not germinate the plants, but makes room for them — for each according to its peculiar requirements. This would have no meaning were there not interests demanding room. To consider morality as the supreme end in and of itself reflects a profound misunderstanding of its role. Its values are compounded of other and prior values; its claim to control rests on its provision for these values, and for their several forms of perfection.

7

As there are institutions which are non-moral or only secondarily moral, so there are institutions which are supermoral. They are at the same time moral and more than moral. The prime examples of such mixed institutions are education and religion.

Education concerns itself with learning, whether by experience, by hearsay, by book reading, by the now multiplied and far-flung channels of mass communication, or by formal instruction. Education is an institution insofar as any of these kinds of learning are socially organized for an educational purpose, as in the school, college, or university. But what is one to learn? In the first place, one must learn how to live with oneself and with others; that is, one must learn morality. But this, even though it be of first importance, is only a part. One may learn anything "there is to learn," directly or indirectly, and within the limits of time and space: art and science, health and play, vocation and avocation.

Religion, likewise, is an institution insofar as piety and worship are socially organized. Religion, like education, both embraces and transcends morality. It overlaps morality in its affirmation of the good of harmonious happiness, and of the rights and duties which this good defines. It exceeds morality in its ideal of perfection. Whether in its conception of God or in its standard of human saintliness, it sums up and carries to their maximum all of the values of life. And, to this sum and all-embracing hierarchy of values, religion adds a recognition of cosmic forces, or relates the total realm of value to the existent universe at large.

There is a human tendency which might be described as a flight from social morality. Because men's personal lives can be distinguished from their public affairs, men have sought to retreat into themselves, purify their own personal characters, and ignore the social conscience, polity, law, and economy. But they have invariably found that the threads of their personal lives intertwine with those of others, and that life cannot be moralized within merely personal limits. Men have sought to escape moral responsibility by absorption in the non-moral vocations of science and art; but have found that the exercise of these vocations are subject to conditions which can be provided only by moral institutions. Similarly men have sought to rise above morality into the higher regions of education and religion — devoting themselves to the cultivation of their personal talents, or to communion with God, or to association with the elect; but they have discovered that these activities, while they may rise *above* morality, must rise *from* and *through* it; since whatever men do they must do it among men, and however exalted their vocations these must first achieve a working harmony with the interests, however humble, of their neighbors.

It cannot be too strongly stated that there is, in principle, no limit to the number of institutions. Apart from the need of brevity in a study of general scope, there are two grounds on which institutions may be excluded without serious objection. Many, such as sport or war, may be excluded on the ground that they are minor rather than major institutions, judged by the criteria defined above. Other institutions such as property, capital punishment, monasticism, and medicine may be excluded on the ground that they are branches of major institutions.

There are two institutions which cannot be excluded on these grounds — namely, marriage and language. One can only offer excuses and apologies for omitting them. The most justifiable excuse is the fact that these institutions derive their universality from nature rather than culture. The family is a system of biological relationships, derived from bisexual reproduction and the comparatively long period of human infancy. Marriage, on the other hand, is clearly an institution; but though of wide generality it is not strictly universal. Language is also a product of instinct and habit. Neither language in general, nor any particular native language, is instituted by men. Literature, as a product of language, is more clearly institutional, but it may be divided between the major institutions of science and art.

These considerations are by no means decisive, but the general principles involved in social institutional organizations can be sufficiently demonstrated by an examination of the seven major institutions of conscience, polity, law, economy, science, art, education, and religion.

8

Although social institutions can and must be distinguished, they are not, in actual life, separate. They interweave and interact within one continuous medium. Since the same persons are members of all the major institutions here enumerated, their requirements meet and interact internally, within each personal life. A person's economic activities are affected by his political and legal activities; his artistic or scientific activities affect, and are affected by, his economic or religious activities; and so throughout all the multiple roles which the same individual plays. In the second place, the institutions themselves, as organizations, interact with one another. The economy of any given society reflects its polity or its religion; its art reflects its conscience, its education, and its science. These interrelations will be all-pervasive, reciprocal, and multilateral. The influence of science is especially widespread, since it determines the mediating judgments of all interests. At the same time the several institutions are jointly influenced by forces which impinge on society as a whole, such as race, climate, population, and public health.

Each institutional organization contains other institutions within itself, and will even contain itself within itself. A university or a church has its internal economy and polity, an industrial corporation has its own constitution and by-laws, and its corporate consciousness; a judicial system has its regularized procedures, its own hierarchy of control, and requires salaries and supplies; a political system will have its internal polities, determining the relations of its official personnel, or of members of a party machine, or of branches of government.

Moral institutions define the limits of all other institutions. There is also a reverse influence. When men try to moralize international relations they create a UNESCO, in order that cultural agreement may reinforce political, legal, and economic agreement. The deeper interrelations among the moral institutions themselves spring from their common moral purpose. This purpose may be voiced by any one of them, and be thus indirectly applied to the rest. Because the moral institutions are engaged in promoting the same end they are brought into relations of collaboration. Conscience, whether in the form of public opinion and sentiment, or in the form of the more reflective judgments of officials and leaders, is summoned to the aid of politics, law, and economy. The state enacts, interprets, administers, and enforces law; gives to economy the form of public policy, and through public education, debate, and popular appeal, contributes to the making of conscience. Law defines the regular processes through which governments are instituted, sets limits to their constitutional prerogatives, and defines the fundamental human rights which they respect; it regularizes and sanctions economic procedure; and through judicial decisions applies and enriches the judgments of conscience. Economy provides the national wealth and taxable resources which government employs; creates major groupings of agricultural or industrial enterprise which polity and law are obliged to reconcile; and constitutes a large part of that social experience through which conscience is formed and reshaped. No one of these institutions works alone; each is allied with the rest.

CHAPTER XI

THE CULTURAL SCIENCES AND THEIR METHODS

Because value is conferred on objects by interest, because institutions are complexes of interests, and because the "cultural sciences," in an acceptable sense of that expression, are the branches of knowledge which deal with the major institutions, an examination of the cultural sciences will serve to distinguish "realms of value."

A classification of the sciences will never fit their subject matter, because the several sciences were pursued before they were classified. Nature and society themselves are not neat and tidy. There is no mode of scientific classification that will tuck in all the wisps and shirttails, and leave no remnants; or which will not dismember some recognized unity. The better acquainted we become with the world we live in, the less probable it appears that it was produced from a blueprint and that it can be faithfully represented by a chart. Nevertheless the attempt to chart it not only is useful as an economy of thought, but brings to light certain distinctions, which would not be remarked if they were not marked.

The first maps of human knowledge represented the more gross regional and topical divisions of subject matter. There were recognized sciences of the stars, the sea, the earth, the plants, and the animals. As knowledge of these areas became more refined they were seen to have common elements — such as atoms and motions. There remained the broad division between the physical world and the world of mind. But here again the subject matter proved to be intermingled — in perception, will, and emotion. Human nature was not purely physical or mental, and the sciences of man, such as psychology, anthropology, and sociology, could not limit themselves to either set of terms. The persistent but unsuccessful attempts of religion to divide a free and imperishable soul from the accidents of the body only made it more evident that observable and describable man was inextricably entangled with the physical world.

Although the confused duality of mental and physical is still used as a principle of division among the sciences, it has recently shown signs of giving way to the duality between the world which man takes as he finds it and the world which he has made for himself. The structure of the atom, for example, would belong to the first, and the structure of the state would belong to the second. For this difference it is customary to employ the terms 'nature' and 'culture,' and the sciences so classified would then be grouped as natural sciences and cultural sciences.

The notion of what is man-made requires further elucidation. Culture does not embrace all of the effects of man's presence on earth, but only those which are the expressions and embodiments of his mind, that is to say, of his interests. Casual deposits of waste matter are not culture, nor are mere traces or footprints, trampled on the ground by a human herd; but a sewage system or a road is culture because it has been made to serve an interest. Even when a "gift of nature," such as a river or a mountain, is taken as it is found, its being possessed or put to use is sufficient to bring it within the domain of culture.

The distinction between the cultural and natural sciences clarifies the sciences of man, such as biology, anthropology, and psychology which are otherwise left in an ambiguous position. Insofar as his reproduction is due to will man himself is man-made; hence such phenomena as control of population and the organization of the family belong to the cultural sciences. The place of heredity will depend on whether acquired characteristics are or are not inherited. Insofar as inherited traits are purposively regulated, as in eugenics, they fall within the cultural sciences; otherwise within the natural science of biology. Physical anthropology and ethnology will be natural sciences as distinguished from cultural anthropology.

The products of human interest imply human capacities to produce them. Insofar as these capacities are themselves the products of antecedent interest they belong to cultural science; as when men employ previously invented tools, skills developed by education, or habits resulting from past performance. The equipment *given* him to use, his so-called "original capacities" or "faculties," belong to the subject matter of psychology conceived as a natural science. Sociology is similarly mixed, since it partakes of all the human sciences — biology, anthropology, ethnology — in both their natural and their cultural parts.

The "social sciences," in the ordinary acceptance of the term, taken as dealing with certain social organizations which men have created among themselves, or which they have adopted and rationalized in obedience to their interests, are clearly cultural sciences. But cultural sciences embrace not only the social sciences in the conventional sense, but also the sciences of art, education, and religion, and the *science of science*.

For science itself is a branch of culture. This fact creates confusion but no insuperable difficulty. The role of nuclear physics in war and industry is a topic of cultural science, with which thoughtful mankind is at present greatly concerned. This topic does not belong to physics, because the physicist is concerned with entities which are not of man's making; war and industry are not his affair. When he discusses the latter he changes his role. Thus the expression 'science of physics' is ambiguous; it may mean that cognitive inquiry whose subject matter is the corporeal world; or it may mean that cognitive inquiry whose subject matter is the above inquiry.

The cultural scientist ordinarily plays both roles. The economist, for example, examines the economic effect of an economic theory such as the classical economies; and the political scientist examines the part played in political life by the political doctrine of popular sovereignty. But all of these inquiries into the cultural effects of the knowledge of nature or of culture may be segregated, and assigned to a specialist in the science of science who is better equipped for the task through his broader acquaintance with several sciences.

The fact that science is a part of culture has a bearing on the question of freedom. The laws of social or cultural science differ from those of natural science in that they can be changed by the human will. Since natural science deals, by definition, with those events which are not man-made, their laws will be beyond human control. When their laws are described as "unalterable" this is what is meant. If they change, as they may, it will not be owing to the intervention of the human will. The cultural sciences, on the other hand, participate in the making of their own subject matter, and hence of their own laws.[1] This does not contradict the fundamental principle of knowledge, namely, that it discovers things as they are independently of itself. He who uses his knowledge to make things different does not make them different merely by knowing them. It is not the knowledge which accomplishes the change, but the act which the knowledge mediates.

2

It is now possible to clarify the relation between cultural sciences and the cultural institutions. Each institution is a man-made organization for the promoting of a purpose. With each institution there is a corresponding procedure, more or less methodical, by which the purpose is promoted. There is no institution without some "know-how" — some degree of knowing how to obtain the desired result. As every interest has its mediating cognition, so the purpose which distinguishes each institution has from the beginning its own characteristic mediating cognitions. Like all mediating cognitions, these will vary in the degree to which they are

[1] For a development of this thesis, cf. R. H. Tawney, *Equality*, 1929, pp. 44 ff.

generalized and systematized; and insofar as generalized and systematized they will merit the name of 'science,' and will constitute that
particular cultural science which is named for the corresponding institution: conscience-ethics, polity-political science, law-jurisprudence,
economy-economics, science-science of science, art-aesthetics, education-
educational theory, religion-philosophy and science of religion.

These considerations throw light on the question of the relative
priority of the institutions and the social arts and the social sciences. It
is evident that men were institutionally organized before the cultural
sciences, in the accepted sense, were recognized, and entrusted to their
several theoretical experts. But such organizations were not possible without some appropriate knowledge in the minds of their members. If the
sciences are taken to embrace such knowledge, that is, the knowledge
which mediates social action, then it is meaningless to speak of priority:
no institution, no science; no science, no institution. If, on the other hand,
the name of science is reserved for a highly articulate form of this
knowledge, and its extension far beyond the requirements of immediate
practice, then the institution comes first and the science second: the
science is a development and perfecting of knowledge which already
exists. The relation between the cultural science and the pre-scientific
knowledge from which it developed is precisely similar to that between
the natural sciences and man's pre-scientific knowledge of his physical
surroundings — that knowledge of sky, earth, sea, weather, and human
nature, which men already possess as the condition of their adaption to
their environment. Minerva does not in any of the forms which she assumes spring fully armed from the head of Zeus, but develops from the
embryonic wisdom of everyday life.

Ethics, or the science of conscience, springs from the pre-scientific
knowledge implicit in conscience itself — some understanding of the
effects of attitudes of approbation and disapprobation, some recognized
code, and some belief that the observance of it is beneficent to the total
interests of the group. Men have always lived under some form of polity
and have accepted some set of laws. If so, they have always in some
degree understood, and taken measures to escape, the evils of disunion
and anarchy. They have learned something of the procedures that will
induce collective obedience and order. However incomplete or erroneous
this knowledge, it constitutes the germ of political science and jurisprudence, and differs from these only in degree.

All economic life involves some modicum of knowledge of how to
meet human needs, some justifiable suspicion that if you give a man
something he needs he will, if he can spare it, give you something in
return, some acquaintance with the fact that today's labor and saving
will provide for tomorrow, and with the fact that men can produce more
by combining their efforts. There is, in short, an economic common sense,

so directly based on the most primitive experience of life, that its absence is unimaginable. The science of economics differs from this economic common sense only in its being more complete, more precise, and more alert to possibilities; and in its providing the vocation of a certain class of scholars and expert advisers known as 'economists.'

Similarly, there is a knowledge of how to know by those who are curious, a know-how acquired by artists, a wisdom of those who teach, and a grasp of the meaning of religion by the pious, which antedate that division of intellectual labor which creates specialists in the methodology and sociology of science, aesthetics, pedagogy, and the science of religion.

3

The exposition of morality, the definition and enumeration of institutions, and examination of their relations to science, pave the way to a brief summary and classification. If the cultural sciences are to be distinguished by the cultural character of their subject matter, their classification will reflect the divisions of human culture, with emphasis on the differences which illustrate the general theme of the present study. Its theme comprises the role of morality in human life, the norms of the major institutions, and those eminent values which in their aggregate constitute what is called 'civilization.' The lines of demarcation will be drawn accordingly.

First, then, there are those cultural sciences which correspond, one to one, with the moral institutions. These will differ among themselves in that each deals with a special function or instrumentality by which their common moral purpose is served. To this group belong, as we have seen, ethics, political science, jurisprudence, and economics.

Second, there are those cultural sciences whose subject matter is not in itself moral, but which, having its moral effects and relations can be examined and judged accordingly. When these subject matters are studied, account must be taken of the distinction between their non-moral meanings and their moral implications, and of the relation between the two. To this class of cultural sciences belong the science of science, and aesthetics or the science of art.

Third, there are certain cultural sciences whose subject matter while in part moral, at the same time transcends morality. So much of their content as is moral must be examined in the same manner as that of the strictly moral sciences. Their moral parts are not accidental — they belong to it; but they do not exhaust it. It is a peculiar task of these sciences to deal with the manner in which their moral and non-moral parts interact and blend. To this class belong the sciences of education and religion.

Over and above the special cultural sciences, there are certain branches of knowledge which concern the subject matter of culture, but which are unclassifiable *among* the cultural sciences because of their

peculiar range. Cultural, as well as natural, phenomena have their quantitative aspects, as is proved by the cultural scientists' use of the statistical
method and the theory of probability. Mathematics intersects all sciences,
and differs from them only in the degree of its abstractness. In this it
resembles logic, which deals with even more abstract relationships, such
as contradiction and implication. Thus sociology and history deal with
all of culture. Their task is to depict the plenum of particularity.[2]

Neither sociology nor history is allowed to isolate the parts of human culture — which is the privilege and the advantage of every special
cultural science. What these special sciences remove for concentrated
study, sociology and history must restore to the context in which they
are in fact embedded and enmeshed. Thus these more general cultural sciences act as a perpetual corrective of the partiality of the
special social sciences. At the same time each serves in its own way as
an *omnium gatherum,* to which residua are allotted. They provide the last
refuge of neglected items. There are certain sciences which deal with
both nature and culture. Mathematics, because it is so closely related to
physics, is sometimes placed among the natural sciences. But this unduly
restricts its scope. It does not provide for "pure mathematics."

Philosophy is an amorphous and sprawling subject. It is man's
perpetual and always premature attempt to imitate the Creator on the
Seventh Day. It attempts to put all things together when there is still an
infinitude of things that are not yet known, and an infinitude of things
which have not yet come to pass. Philosophy is a provisional last word.
It is a perennial, inevitable, legitimate, and impossible enterprise in which
human faculties are strained to their utmost and at the same time are
brought to a realization of their insuperable limitations. There is no last
word for mankind at large, but for each man there is *his* last word, and
for each age *its* last word, by which to come to terms with the universe.[3]

Since the present book has been written by a philosophical addict it
is to be hoped that it will illustrate philosophy's humble audacity, by
which a small part endeavors to surround the whole: endeavors to take
into one account not only the cultural sciences, but the natural sciences
as well; not only the several realms of value and their combined realm,
but also the relation of value to non-value and of man to not-man; not
only the world to be known but the knowing of it, and not only knowledge but faith. It ranges from the extreme limit of abstractness in its
logic, to the extreme limit of concreteness in its depicting of the cosmic
panorama.

[2] It is here assumed that the history of a special human institution, as distinguished
from general history, belongs to the special science which deals with the institution.
[3] If this classification appears to omit the study of "literature," it is because this
form of culture is divisible. Insofar as it consists of "belles-lettres," it belongs
with aesthetics; otherwise it covers all forms of culture insofar as they are expressed
in language.

4

An examination of the method of the social sciences[4] raises the question whether, judged by the standards of certain of the natural sciences, a social science is a "science" at all. The more man knows the more he knows how to know. The advance of knowledge is double accelerated. As its circumference increases and the front of its advance into surrounding ignorance grows more extended, the scientists who occupy the front grow not only more numerous, but more skillful. The history of modern science properly stresses the perpetual refinement of its technique.

This emphasis suggests that science should be defined by its technique, and that on this ground cultural science should be excluded. But this is to put the cart before the horse. For technique is justified by its product: by its contribution, namely, to knowledge. The underlying motive in the improvement of technique is increased fidelity to the purpose of knowing. This is the only proper meaning of the term 'rigorous' as applied to modern science. It means only that science has become more careful and more accurate, and has freed itself to an increasing extent from prejudice and superstition. Thus rigor does not imply the use of mathematics except insofar as mathematics does, in fact, represent things as they are. The same is true of mechanics. There is no exclusive validity in the concepts of motion, force, and energy; their virtue for science consists wholly in their fitness to the physical subject matter which physical science seeks to know. And it is because of this fitness, and not because of its specific concepts, that physical science is to be accepted as a model for scientific procedure elsewhere. As things stand today the social sciences are more in need of emancipating themselves from the bigotry of natural science than of adopting its method.

Science is simply knowledge; or, in a more restricted sense, knowledge when this has reached a certain pitch of perfection. Since knowledge consists in well-grounded expectations, it submits itself to what is called "the facts"; which is simply a name for an existing state of affairs when taken in relation to the hypotheses which men entertain about it. When the state of affairs to be known is culture its method must be adapted to its cultural subject matter, and not to the fashionable methodology of the day. A science is hand in glove with its facts; the method of cultural science is the glove, and culture is the hand.

The method of the cultural sciences, like that of all sciences, is *descriptive*. If knowledge consists of well-grounded expectations, then there is one over-all method of knowing, which is to form expectations

<hr>

[4] A view of the method of social science broadly similar to that here presented, but set forth in greater detail by one who is himself a social scientist, will be found in J. Mayer's *Social Science Principles in the Light of Scientific Method*, 1941, Part I, and *passim*.

and then look to see whether things are or are not as expected. Descriptive science formulates theories in general terms, and accepts them when verified by given particularities or data. It consists of representations, or systems of representations, checked by presentations. The application of the descriptive method to the subject matter of culture encounters certain difficulties and raises certain objections. The difficulties are to be admitted, and the objections have to be met.

A major difficulty is complexity. Any part of culture contains many factors, and any statement of it will contain many variables. Culture cannot be studied experimentally in the usual sense of the word, not only because it is too vast in its range to be isolated and reproduced in a laboratory, but because its agents are human beings who cannot be treated as guinea pigs. A political, legal, or economic hypothesis can be tested by its adoption as public policy, but this involves human commitments of a wholly different order from those which occur when physical or chemical research is artificially insulated. Men can learn from social experience but they cannot create social experience merely in order to learn from it — the consequences are too grave. There is more at stake in living than merely learning about life. The greater part of culture is qualitative and non-measurable. This fact, together with the difficulties enumerated above, results in a total difficulty, the difficulty, namely, of arriving at laws in terms of which the cultural future can be predicted. But these limiting considerations, while they are relevant, and do affect the procedures of the cultural sciences, do not raise any fundamental question of principle. That which is hard to describe, or which cannot be described as precisely as one would like, is not on that account to be considered as indescribable. In fact, since these difficulties arise from the subject matter, the recognition of them is part of its description.

Over and above these difficulties, there are two main objections of principle to the use of the descriptive method in the cultural sciences. First, it is argued that they deal with wills and attitudes, which cannot be observed, but only "appreciated." It is quite true that the cultural sciences deal with interests, and that the immediacy of feeling, and a sympathetic "entering into" the center of another's life, play an important role in the knowledge of interests. It is well that this should be emphasized. But feeling and sympathy are forms of observation as good as any others, and which, like other data, can play the role of verifying hypotheses. Every time the physician, the lover, or the orator forms a judgment of another's attitude, every time a social reformer frames a theory of human happiness, he relies on such data.

It is objected, in the second place, that the interests with which the cultural sciences deal have norms and ideal objects which, being nonexistent, are therefore indescribable. But this objection not only is untenable, but is contradicted on almost every page of the literature of

cultural science, however scientific it professes to be. The customs of
primitive societies and the ideologies of advanced societies are describable both in their breach as in their observance. It is of their nature that
they should be problematic objects — it is this which makes them ideals
and norms; but since one ideal or custom differs from another, it must
have peculiar characteristics; and when these characteristics are set down,
the ideal or norm is described. Furthermore, though ideals and norms do
not in themselves exist, the *pursuit* of them and the *use* of them as
standards of comparison do exist, and the ideals and norms are a part
of their description.

The recognition of these difficulties and the removal of these objections support the general conclusion that all cultural science is descriptive,
including those parts of social science which are commonly excluded as
"normative."

5

When an object of interest is taken as a standard with which to compare an achievement, or by which to compare two achievements with
one another, it becomes a "norm"; the judgments which make such comparisons are "normative judgments." Since the norm and the achievement
are both describable the comparison is a description of the achievement.
In other words a comparative success or failure as judged by an end or
ideal — differences of level between the two, and its being "up to," or
"falling short of" — are matters of fact; since culture is made up of interests and complexes of interests having ends or ideals, these matters of
fact fall within its description. When science so describes it employs the
normative method.

When, on the other hand, the object of interest is taken as something-
to-be-realized, and it is stated that a certain achievement would realize it,
or make for its realization, the method employed is the technological
method. The normative method characterizes an achievement by a norm;
the technological method characterizes a norm by an achievement.

The normative and technological methods do not exhaust cultural
science; in fact they omit that very method which the cultural sciences
most frequently employ, and which they pride themselves on employing.
It will not do to designate this third method as the "descriptive" method,
since the normative and technological methods are also descriptive. In
the present context the old, and still persistent, controversy as to whether
social science is descriptive *or* normative and technological, no longer
has any meaning. Description can no longer be identified with the non-
normative and non-technological. The least misleading designation for
the third branch of the descriptive method is 'explanatory.' This method
takes the total fact of interested endeavor together with its object, and

makes statements concerning its origins, constituents, conditions, and causal relations.

The judgment that the creation of the United Nations is a step toward the realization of universal peace, is a normative judgment; the judgment that the elimination of the veto would promote the peaceful purpose of the United Nations, is a technological judgment; the judgment that the longing for universal peace reflects the state of insecurity resulting from the Second World War is an explanatory judgment. The basic judgment says, "Salvation is desirable"; the normative judgment says, "Your soul is damned"; the technological judgment says, "Faith is what you need in order to be saved"; the explanatory judgment says, "The quest for salvation arose in the Hellenistic Age as a result of the breakdown of the Greek city-state."

This methodology of the cultural sciences has the merit of distinguishing different methods while at the same time showing that they are prescribed by the subject matter and intimately connected. An institution is a complex of interests having some common object of agreement or cooperation. The institution has somehow come to pass and somehow occurs within the field of existence. But being what it is, it is equipped with a norm, with which its own achievements (as well as those of other interests) can be compared. And when such critical or appraising judgments are made, the transition to technology is easy and continuous; for if one knows that the norm is served well or ill by this and that, this knowledge already begins to be a knowledge of how, given the norm, it can be served better.

Thus it is not surprising, but, on the contrary, inevitable, that in the study of the cultural sciences the explanatory, normative, and technological methods should be mingled. Any sharp line of demarcation would be artificial; that is, alien to the subject matter. To examine in fuller detail the meanings and implications of these three methods is the next task.

6

Beginning with the explanatory method, it is first to be noted that while the peculiar subject matter of the cultural sciences is culture, culture embraces parts of nature; that is, certain natural materials have assumed the form of culture. Hence any explanatory description of culture will overlap natural science. Human interests on every level, from raising crops to writing poetry, employ the human organism, and involve parts of its surrounding natural environment. The creations of the fine arts require pigments, musical instruments, and printer's ink. Even worship of God is commonly on bended knee, and kneeling requires a physical surface on which to kneel. Schools and churches are constructed of building materials. All interests employ the organs of the body and the native capacities of the mind. Whatever science deals with these natural parts of interest, is drawn upon for their explanatory description. There is, in short, a physics, a chemistry, a biology, and a psychology of every human institution. The explanation of an institution in terms of race, climate, soil, natural resources, disease, hereditary traits, constitutional characteristics, belongs to this branch of cultural science.

Institutions are in large part products of human *nature*. The instinct of fear plays an important role in conscience and religion; self-assertion and docility are peculiarly characteristic of man's political and educational life; physical needs and incompatibilities of his economic life; curiosity of his intellectual life; playfulness of his aesthetic life. For the explanation of all of these components of man's institutional life cultural science must draw heavily on the natural sciences which deal with man.

Culture is also to be explained by culture. The parts of any given institution act and react on one another. The personal conscience is causally related to the social conscience; the executive branch of government influences its legislative branch; one judicial decision serves as a precedent for another; trade has to be explained in terms of monetary exchange; the science and art of different periods are chapters of a continuous scientific and aesthetic history; one kind of educational practice determines another; religion reflects changes of dogma and worship.

But the explanation of any institution will also include its relations to other institutions. No explanatory description of polity would be complete that did not report its dependence on economy, law, or religion, and otherwise pass beyond its bounds to the broader cultural context, and each institution in turn is similarly dependent. Thus the explanatory method of the cultural sciences is not only naturalistic and intra-institutional, but also inter-institutional.

The difference between the explanation of any institution in its own terms, and the explanation which includes factors taken from other institutions, distinguishes the aim of any branch of culture to arrive at its own laws, such as "purely" economic, or "purely" political, laws, from the growing disposition to emphasize mixed laws. In the one case the law would embrace only political or only economic variables; in the second case it would involve both. In the latter case the independent variable of an economic law might be political, or the independent variable of a political law might be economic. It might be held that economy was a function of polity, as in the commonly accepted theory of Western democracy; or it might be held, as in the Marxist view, that polity was a function of economy.

This distinction between the intra-institutional or pure, and the inter-institutional or mixed, is of equal importance in the normative and technological methods, and in order that it may have a designation that can be consistently employed, it will be hereafter referred to as the distinction between the autonomous or *internal,* and the heteronymous or *external.*

7

Since there are divers branches of culture, each with its own norms, the normative judgments pronounced on them may be either internal or external. The internal normative judgment of any unit of culture is in terms of its own aims; that is, in terms of the function or purpose which distinguishes it from other institutions. Does it or does it not do that which *it* is "supposed" to do? When it is said that each institution has a purpose of its own, so that it may be judged internally, it is not meant, that all of its instruments and components owe their existence to that purpose. It is only necessary to suppose that the structures which constitute the institutional achievement are used for a purpose, that they are from time to time adapted to it, and that they are referred to it for their perpetuation and justification. There is an application of this to all institutions. The first ruler may have been the strong man, provided by the accident of biological variation; the law may have begun as an arbitrary habit; conscience may have originated as a sheer prejudice; production may have arisen as a form of enjoyable exercise. Science may have begun as sensation, art as an accidental daubing, education as imitation, and religion as dreaming. All that is necessary for internal normative judgment is that these arrangements and practices should be "valued" by their participants for a certain purpose, and referred to that purpose as a reason for retaining them, and as a guide for their improvement.

Institutions are artifacts by adoption and modification if not by origin. It might, perhaps, be said that the whole meaning of culture lies in the difference between clothes and feathers. Feathers, provided by the bounty of nature, would become clothes at the point where their possessors consciously employed them for protection, concealment or appearance, and looked to them for these uses. If birds maintained feather-dresses and beauticians, they would fall within the domain of cultural science, and their covering would be a proper subject of internal normative judgment.

The purpose of any unit of culture may also be applied as a norm beyond that unit of culture, that is, externally. There are, in other words, inter-institutional normative judgments. There is no restriction of such judgments except that the achievement and the norm shall be in fact comparable. An actual government may be compared with its own proper political norm, that is, by the ideal end of government; but since the government embraces within itself persons who have rights and property, it may also be judged by legal and economic standards. Similarly, a theory may be judged not only by its own proper standard of truth, but also by the standard of beauty. A work of fine art may be judged internally, that is to say, aesthetically, but it may also be judged externally, by the norms of morality or commerce. Religion may be judged to be "good for business."

Both internal and external normative judgments are legitimate, and yield conclusions that are true or false. There are two procedures, however, which are notoriously illegitimate and inconclusive. The first of these is the concealment of the norm, so that the critical judgment has an aspect of absoluteness; as though one were judging by no norm. This concealment of the stand is especially common when the judge is so accustomed to it, employing it constantly and living among people who constantly employ it, that it has become an unconscious assumption.

Equally illegitimate and inconclusive is the procedure in which an external standard is confused with an internal standard. This is the so-called "pathetic fallacy." The judge imputes his own purpose to the achievement judged, and judges it as though it were intended to be what he praises it for being, or condemns it for failing to be. In the extreme case a judgment may be taken to be internal when there is no purpose at all; as when the sun is applauded for benevolently providing man with warmth and light. More common is the case in which an external norm is substituted for the internal norm. Thus another's artistic production may be judged by the standard of piety, that being the standard by which the critic is judging his own affairs; whereupon the object of the judgment may properly object that fine art is not religion, but has another and quite different purpose. These forms of illegitimate criticism would be avoided if every normative judgment *specified* the norm to which the comparison is made.

8

There is a second distinction within the normative method which arises from the fact that each institution has not only its proper end, but its peculiar agencies; and each of these is subject to criticism, whether internal or external. In the chapters that follow this distinction will be designated by the terms 'final' and 'instrumental' or 'functional.'

This distinction has special importance in its application to the critique of moral institutions. The moral institutions are so classified because they all have the same final moral end, by which they may be judged. President Roosevelt was appealing to this common end when in the last speech before his death, he referred to "the science of human relationships" as "the ability of all peoples, of all kinds, to live together and work together in the same world at peace . . . if civilization is to survive."[5] Thus a conscience, polity, law, or economy may be judged ac-

---

[5] *The Public Papers and Addresses of Franklin D. Roosevelt*, 1950, Vol. XIII, p. 615.

cording as it does or does not promote harmonious happiness. The radical criticism characteristic of revolution tends to assume this form. Widespread discontent among the relatively unprivileged groups, or the thwarted ambition of rising men, or the shock and demoralization resulting from external war, leads men to ask themselves what, ultimately, their institutions are *for*, and to demand this of them. Whatever be the institution first attacked, whether it be the conscience of the times, or the existing political, legal, or economic system, men go back to its fundamental moral purpose and apply it as a norm.

But each of these moral institutions has its peculiar function, mechanism, or instrumentality, by which it promotes the moral end, conscience by approbation, polity by centralized direction and control, law by regulation, economy by production, distribution, and countless other devices. Each such institution can therefore be judged *finally*, by the common moral purpose, or *instrumentally*, by the efficiency of its special mechanisms. It is to be noted that the distinction between internal and external is applicable to both forms of normative judgment.

The internal critique of an institution takes two forms. It may be judged by its *rationality*, that is, by its fidelity to its purpose and enlightenment in its pursuit. When the purpose is the moral purpose, its faithful and enlightened pursuit — its rationality — will involve the moral principles of *liberality* and *universality*. These are the canons ordinarily invoked by social reformers — who complain that the institution is "harsh," or restrictive of freedom to a degree not required for order and justice; or too narrow and exclusive in its jurisdiction.

The distinction between instrumental and final normative judgments also applies to non-moral and super-moral institutions. The final end of science is truth, but the pursuit of truth requires its own instruments; and there is a tendency to neglect one through preoccupation with the other. The final end of fine art is aesthetic enjoyment, and it may be criticized as failing to realize this end. But art, and each particular art, has its specialized skills, and these may be emphasized at the expense of the end, or neglected by those who think only in terms of the end. There is a perpetual dispute between the craftsmen and the experts, the technicians, the virtuosos, the academicians, who insist that the scientist or artist must be schooled in the tools of his trade, and those devotees of truth and beauty, who would fly more directly and freely to the mark.

There is the same interplay between the instrumental and the final in education and in religion. There are the professional educators who emphasize the arts of pedagogy, curriculum, and administration, and those who with an eye to the terminal value, stress all the more informal and spontaneous ways in which the minds of men can be molded. In religion the ecclesiastics and systematic theologians may be opposed to the pietists and mystics.

9

Wherever normative judgments are applicable there is also a technology. There is, in short, a constructive and not merely critical aspect of normative situations.

The test of technology is its effectiveness for the purpose for which it is invoked. It does not follow, as is claimed by "operationalism" in its extreme form, that all knowledge is technology. Because true knowledge is effective, effectiveness serves as a good criterion of truth, but not as its final proof. Technology selects from knowledge what promises to prove useful in practice. But in knowledge, including the knowledge of practice, it is theory which speaks the last word. There is an independent, and not merely a dependent, cognitive interest.

The mediation of interest provides the entering wedge of knowledge, and there is no kind of knowledge that may not enter. Thus technology may be drawn from natural knowledge, as when the judments of chemistry mediate the interests of industry. The term 'technology' is sometimes used in a restricted sense to refer only to such naturalistic technology. But this restriction is arbitrary and serves only to obscure the essential principle. That institutions which discover and inculcate naturalistic technologies should have come to be considered as institutes of technology *par excellence,* was a historical accident. In the fields of management and labor relations, for example, economy makes use not only of psychology and other natural sciences of man, but of the cultural knowledge of the acquired beliefs and interests of employers and employees. "Ideologies," so-called, are systems of normative judgments. The end of racial purity pursued by the Nazis, was used by them as a norm by which to approve or condemn; and knowledge of it formed part of the technology of any nation hoping to have successful dealings with them. The judgment borrowed was, in this case, a final normative judgment; but the American advocate of white supremacy could with equal reason borrow the instrumental judgments by which the Nazis justified their genocide or spurious anthropology.

While it is true that technology lends itself to base uses, it is not confined to such uses. There is a technology of money-grabbing and a technology of military conquest; but there are also technologies of truth, beauty, enlightenment, and piety. These higher pursuits can profit by technology derived from the lower. And conversely the ethical, scientific, artistic, educational, and religious technologies may be put to uses of every level, including the uses of material gain and selfish aggrandizement. It would be unduly laborious to recite all of the schematic possibilities. Suffice it to say that there is no knowledge of any kind whatsoever, and borrowed from whatever source, that may not play the role of technology for cultural institutions.

These distinctions of method in the cultural sciences will presently be applied to particular institutions. It is hoped that their meaning will become clearer and more significant. But they are not to be taken too rigidly. Nor are they to be taken as of equal importance. Since the purpose of the present lectures is to set forth certain standards by which civilization and its several parts are justified and appraised, the normative method will be emphasized and the explanatory and technological methods will be subordinated. The moral institutions come first in order of treatment, beginning with conscience, which is closest to morality itself.

CHAPTER XII

CONSCIENCE AND ETHICS

It is not usual to number conscience among the social institutions. The term has been, and still is, widely used to designate the mind whenever it addresses itself to moral matters. In a still more restricted, but equally familiar, sense 'conscience' is taken to designate a distinct cognitive capacity; a "moral sense," that is, a form of sensibility specifically attuned to moral qualities, as is the ear to sound; or a faculty competent to deliver itself of intelligible moral judgments or intuitions.

Moral intuitionism has already been examined.[1] It has been generally discredited owing to the discovery that moral intuitions, despite their subjective sense of certainty, vary from one society to another, and are often flatly contradictory. This evidence of relativity has been reinforced during the last century by the explanation of the alleged moral intuitions in terms of the social conditions of time and place. Conscience has not lost its oracular quality, but its oracular claims are no longer accepted.

When subjected to criticism, conscience assumes the character of a cultural product, composed of attitudes of approval and disapproval, together with their correlative codes, creeds, and ideals. Even when so conceived it may be denied a place in the list of institutions on the ground that it has no special functionaries such as rulers, judges, employers, scientists, artists, teachers, and priests. Conscience is everybody's business. But under the names of 'custom' and 'public opinion' it has long been recognized as a form of social control. It satisfies the criteria of a major cultural institution. It has a specialized function and instrumentality of its own. It is universal — arising out of conditions which prevail in all social groups in all periods of human history. It consists of organized relationships, by which persons play reciprocal roles. It is durable, in that its interrelated attitudes or systematic characteristics are perpet-

[1] Cf. above, Ch. VIII, § 3.

uated by tradition through successive generation of particular members.

While conscience is customary, it is not coextensive with custom. Dialects, manners, dress, and countless other idiosyncrasies characteristic of a social group, are customs, and are imposed on its members by the same sanction that is employed by conscience. But they fall outside the institution of conscience as here conceived because they are accidental, conventional, or arbitrary. Conscience, on the other hand, is distinguished from custom by its *moral* content, by the fact that it expresses itself in moral judgments employing the moral predicates of good, right, and duty. It serves the moral purpose of social harmony. It submits itself to moral criticism. As is the case with other institutions its purpose is revealed in its self-justification: by the fact that when called upon to defend or reform itself it takes moral ground.

2

If conscience is to be considered as a cultural institution, then there is a science of conscience, which is related to this institution as political science is related to polity, jurisprudence to law, economics to economy, and the other cultural sciences to their corresponding forms of social organization. All things considered, the best name for this science of conscience is 'ethics,' despite the fact that this word has not been invariably so used.

The very ambiguity of the term 'ethics' is instructive. If there is an appeal from conscience to its underlying moral principles, and if there is a similar appeal from polity, law, and economy, then it is necessary to recognize a branch of knowledge which shall discuss the moral principles common to those moral institutions, which may be called 'moral philosophy' or 'the science of morality.' But this basic and common subject of morality may be approached from any one of its institutional embodiments, and may be named accordingly. It may be, and was in antiquity, called 'politics.' It might with equal justification be called 'jurisprudence,' or 'economics.' The ideal polity or republic, the ideal system of law, and even the ideal economy, will at their limit of ideality become indistinguishable from the moral ideal.

The peculiar priority of ethics among the moral social sciences is due to the fact that conscience is ordinarily the channel by which moral judgments are applied to polity, law, and economy. Owing to the fact that conscience is less elaborately organized than these sister institutions, and is less preoccupied with instrumentalities, it represents morality more directly — so directly, in fact, that it is often *confused* with morality.

The common moral basis of conscience, polity, law, and economy was recognized until modern times, when emphasis on the explanatory method, together with the general tendency to scientific division of labor, led to their separation. But as physics, once the only natural science, later one of many, is again the recognized mother of the brood, so moral science, often disguised under other names is resuming a similar role in another family. Whichever member of the family — whether ethics, politics, jurisprudence, or economics — is taken as its representative, its fundamental analysis will reveal the moral principles common to all — the principles, namely, of reflective agreement and harmonious happiness.

The subject matter of ethics, then, is conscience, taken as a cultural fact, having its own peculiar instrumentalities by which it serves the purpose of morality. It is to this fact that ethics looks for the verification of its judgments. It is quite true that conscience is so intermingled with other parts of human life that it is difficult to disentangle it. There is no such event as a pure state of conscience. But it is meaningless even to ask of any state whether it is or is not "conscience" until in the early stage of inquiry a decision has been made as to what the term shall mean. This decision is arbitrary, but only in the sense of a selection of subject matter and choice of words. If it be objected that too much is here claimed for conscience, it must be remembered that it is conscience as here defined for which the claim is made.

3

Expressed loosely, conscience is a widespread collective approval or disapproval expressed through individual persons. The definition of conscience consists in tightening this statement, beginning with the meanings of the words 'approval' and 'disapproval.' Approval is an attitude of favor, and disapproval is an attitude of disfavor, but this is not all. To approve is not the same thing as to like, desire, or love; disapproval is not the same thing as disliking, avoiding, or hating. It means something to say, "I like it, but I don't approve of it."

The difference begins with the restriction of approval and disapproval to personal objects (total persons, groups of persons, acts, or dispositions of persons). But the personal object is further restricted by a qualifying attribute: it is approved or disapproved, on social grounds; that is, it is favored or disfavored as morally qualified. Thus, for example, when the aggression of the North Koreans was disapproved, this means that it was the object of a negative interest *because of* its supposed injury to the South Koreans, or to the generality of mankind who desire peace. In other words, approval and disapproval embrace a factor of independent benevolence or disinterestedness.

It is for this reason that Westermarck's definition of approval and disapproval as "retributive emotions" is not satisfactory.[2] *Righteous* indignation is not simple anger, nor is it a resentment of injury done to the indignant person, but a resentment of injury done to some third person, or to a group of persons which, while it may include the indig-

_____
[2] E. A. Westermarck, *Origin and Development of Moral Ideas*, 1912, Vol. I, p. 21.

nant person, must look beyond to other persons. Insofar as the condemnation of North Koreans by Americans expressed concern for American interests alone, it would be a natural and common attitude but it would not be disapproval. But conscience is a socialized attitude not only in its object but in the attitude itself. One who approves considers himself, and is considered by others, as representing an agreement. He demands the confirmation of others, and the outward expression of a personal attitude is given the weight of a collective attitude.

The structure of conscience may be briefly summarized in terms of an *agent,* a *patient,* a *client,* and an *associate.* The agent is the person in whom the attitude of approval or disapproval is enacted; the patient is the person to whom the attitude is addressed; the client is the person or persons in whose behalf the attitude is taken; the associate is the person or persons who share the attitude. Each person plays all four of these interchangeable roles. He is approver and approved; client and intercessor; principal and associate.

Through his conscience a person not only approves others, and is approved by others, participates in the approval of others, and suffers it with others, but, as part of the approving group to which he belongs, imposes its collective approval on himself. He enjoys an "easy conscience" or he suffers remorse. When a person is thus himself a channel by which the social conscience is applied to himself, he is a party to it. He joins the ranks of his friends or his enemies; like the man within a stronghold who takes the side of the besiegers, the social conscience bores from within. This analysis recognizes no separation of the social and the personal conscience. There is no conscience that is not both. An attitude which is only personal, plays a highly important role in the disruption or alteration of conscience, but until it has won a widespread agreement it is at most a conscience in the making.

Conscience taken as a sanction, that is, as a mode of social control, is distinguished by the fact that the attitude of favor or disfavor is unexecuted. It is a sign, and not a fulfillment — a hint, intimation, threat or promise, conveyed by a word, or gesture. "A word to the wise is sufficient." The attitude of conscience may be conveyed by the subtlest facial expression, by the jaundiced eye, by intent watchfulness, by ironical laughter, by sly insinuations.

The degree of the force of conscience is increased rather than diminished by its lack of explicitness. The manifestly directed blow is less dangerous than the blow which may fall one knows not where; the specified injury is less menacing than the general attitude of hostility, whose applications are variable. Similarly, friendship is better than any particular kindness, and a hostile god, whose all-pervasive disfavor may manifest itself anywhere at any time is more to be feared than a god who will send you to hell if you break one of his specific commandments. The latter can be appeased, circumvented or endured; the former leaves no avenue of hope. By the same token, if God thinks well of you, is your friend, is on your side, who or what can prevail against you? This intimation of diffused friendliness or enmity is so powerful a force as to suffice for long periods of time, and for the majority of mankind, to control conduct in the total absence of overt rewards and penalties.

The pressures of conscience are proportional to the resistances which it has to overcome. Because there is an inertia of selfishness, conscience bestows a premium on unselfishness and self-sacrifice. Because certain appetites are strong, their excesses are severely reprobated. So conscience tends to be associated in men's minds with the enjoyment of public applause or with the pangs and shames of remorse. But these extremes of emphasis (reflecting the ratio of moral demand and supply) do not measure the moral value of conscience. If it so happened that men, whether by nature or by education, were so happily attuned to the collective approvals and disapprovals as to require no penalties and bribes, but only guidance, they would be ruled by conscience none the less.

4

Ethics, construed as the cultural science which takes conscience as its subject matter, employs the explanatory, normative, and technological methods. Under the present scientific division of labor the explanatory account of conscience is widely distributed, being largely entrusted to anthropology, psychology, sociology, and history. There is a structural aspect of conscience which deserves special emphasis, because it is usually slighted. When there is approving, there is something approved; and when there is something approved, there is an approving of it. There is, in other words, an objective and a subjective aspect of approval, and this duality is of its essence. Whereas anthropologists and sociologists are disposed by their scientific habits to ignore the subjective aspect of conscience, so psychologists are sometimes disposed to ignore its objective aspect.

Furthermore, the distinction between approving and being approved must not be allowed to obliterate the distinction between the *persons* approved, and *that for which* they are approved, in other words, their qualifying attribute. If the latter is to be termed the object or objective of approval, then it is necessary to introduce another term such as 'patient' to provide for the impact felt by him to whom the approving is addressed. The difference is analogous to that between the crime and the criminal.

The term 'mores,' as commonly employed, observes these distinctions. Customs are objects of approval, and except insofar as approved they do not deserve to be considered as manifestations of conscience. But they are commonly abstracted, and treated as though they were independent entities. This procedure arises from the fact that the object of approval is more easily identified, being recorded in words or monuments, or observable in gross behavior. Thus anthropology is largely preoccupied with primitive societies, and since there is an almost complete ignorance of the psychology of primitive men, anthropologists describe *what* is sanctioned and are able to throw little or no light on those states of mind which gives the sanction its force. But the total situation, in the case, for example, of exogamy, involves the act of approval, the family relationship approved, and the person approved for conformity to the relationship. Similarly, incest or any other taboo is not merely what is prohibited, but also the act of prohibiting and the deterrent effect of its prohibitive pressure.

Taking any given historical conscience as a uniformity of approval it will reflect underlying natural uniformities, such as climate, habitat, food supply, health, and inherited ethnic traits. Acquired uniformities are also to be explained psychologically. There is sufficient evidence to warrant the broad statement that there are in all human beings certain dispositions to conformity. These dispositions are based on man's peculiar sensitiveness to the presence of his fellows. There is a discriminating alertness not only to the presence of a fellow man, but to his whole range of attitudes. 'Gregariousness' is the name given to the fact that human individuals, like members of a herd of animals, tend to take refuge in a group. They shrink from being conspicuous. There is in all men, and in some to a higher degree than in others, also a tendency to suggestibility and submissiveness; they tend to believe what they are told, and to do what they are commanded. And, as in the case of communicable diseases, the force of these impulses is proportional to their spread, and thus increases in geometric ratio.

But conscience is, as has been seen, a promise and a threat. It operates, therefore, through exciting hope and fear. The range of fear and hope is extended far and wide by association or the conditioned reflex. And here again the force of the stimulus is proportional to its volume. The hope or fear excited by the approval or disapproval of many is stronger than that excited by the similar attitude of a few.

When one inverts the relationship, and considers what it is that prompts men to act approvingly or disapprovingly, it is evident that many of the same principles apply. One approves because other people approve, or from hope of benefit, or from gratitude, and disapproves because others disapprove, or from fear of injury, or in retaliation. The tendency to censoriousness owes something to the love of power, rooted, perhaps, in a more elemental impulse of self-assertion. Even approval, when it takes on a patronizing tone, may flatter the ego of the approver, as indicating the other's deference to his opinion. The disinterestedness of conscience, on the other hand, arises from sympathy or fellow-feeling for the client.

The importance of "prestige" is evident. The sources of prestige are manifold, but once an individual or a group achieves a position of superiority for any reason whatever their approval is especially coveted, and their disapproval especially feared; their attitudes are supercharged, as though they represented the group as a whole. And those who enjoy prestige themselves feel a peculiar disposition to express their approvals and disapprovals. They find it natural to cast themselves in the role of wise men, moral leaders, makers of opinion or elder statesmen.[3]

Of all the causes of conscience, however, the most important is the sense of solidarity, that is, the belief that when one offends, all will suffer. This may take the form of a religious belief that the guilt of one will bring down the wrath of God on all; or it may reflect the more or less instinctive recognition of interdependence. Hence to the question, "Am I my brother's keeper?" the answer is "Yes." Together we stand, together we fall. The benefits which each individual derives from collective action are threatened by the deviationist, and he becomes the common enemy. It is this which makes the group particularly approving or disapproving in time of crisis. For examples one does not have to look beyond the censoriousness of Americans towards Communism, or towards anything which is associated with Communism; and the corresponding applause of orthodox Americanism.

The conditions which give rise to conscience are cultural as well as natural; and its cultural conditions are both internal and external, that is, they may consist of conscience itself, or of other forms of culture. Conscience itself, once it is created, has effects upon other conscience. Thus to explain the origin of an American conscience it would be necessary to refer to the Puritan conscience. But each institution has effects upon other institutions, and a genetic explanation of the American conscience would take account of democratic political institutions, the Common Law, and the capitalistic economy, as well as of the characteristics of American science, art, education, and religion.

Closely related to this genetic question of origins is the evolutionary question of change. That a social conscience should come to pass, and that it should be perpetuated, are less difficult to explain than that the cake of conscience once it is baked should crumble. To explain the dissolution of conscience reference must be made to commerce, war, and

---

[3] It has been pointed out that in a certain tribe of American Indians the susceptibility to cataleptic seizures has been taken as a mark of distinction by which certain women have become "the pathway to authority over one's fellows . . . the most respected social type . . . which function with most honour and reward in the community." (R. Benedict, *Patterns of Culture*, 1934, p. 267; qu. by E. C. Tolman, in *Science, 101* (1945) p. 161.)

other intercourse with alien groups; and to the independent development of other institutions within the group. Two causes deserve special mention. In advanced societies, perhaps, for all we know, in all societies, there is a certain free play of individual thought and imagination despite the reign of custom. From this source there springs that independent moral insight which distinguishes the "great" founder or reformer.[4] A second important cause of changes is the "revolutionary" force, the protest and revolt which arises when repression is felt as oppression, and when the resistance has gathered sufficient force. There are revolutions of conscience as well as political and economic revolutions.

The subject matter of conscience lends itself to the comparative, as well as to the morphological, genetic, and evolutionary methods, with an unavoidable overlapping similar to that which attends these methods in biology. A survey of human history and of the human groups which coexist upon the earth reveals notable diversities of conscience. In the comparison of different types of conscience attention may be focused on its object, as when one says that lying was approved by the ancient Spartans whereas it is disapproved by modern Christian nations. But it is equally possible to distinguish consciences subjectively. It is probable that the approving of lying in a military state such as Sparta differed profoundly from the countenancing given to mendacious advertising in a modern industrial society.

5

In passing from the explanatory to the normative method in ethics it is to be noted that the critique of conscience also operates as a cause. Thus a dietary taboo may be explained by habit, but it may also be explained by the judgment that it is hygienic and therefore good. The disapproval of incest may be explained by the fear of God, but it may also be explained by the judgment that it produces weak offspring. And once such judgments are admitted as causes, it is impossible to exclude the evidence on which they are founded or by which they are proved. A cause among others by which taboos or codes are brought into existence is their "apparent utility," and appearance of utility already embraces some evidence of utility. Once this is granted, further evidence, positive or negative, enters by the same door, and conscience is thus conditioned by its own criticism. It makes claims and its claims are more or less supported, and its continued existence, its modification, and its disappearance, are effected by the renewal or withdrawal of that support.

The normative science of ethics may be either instrumental or final, internal or external.

Judged internally, that is, by its own peculiar instrumentality, conscience may be deemed strong or weak, as when it is said of a person that

[4] This is the second of Bergson's "deux sources de religion et de la morale."

he is "highly conscientious," or, at the other extreme, that he has no conscience at all. Similarly, one may speak of a group as having a powerful collective sentiment and opinion which acts as an effective coercive force upon its individual members; or as having little or no conscience, as when one says of the totality of mankind that their world conscience is as yet unhappily feeble and intermittent, as compared with their several nationalisms. Similarly, one speaks of the presence or absence of a "code" which binds the members of a group engaged in specific collective activity, and recognizes that it may be present in greater or less degree. Thus the British are supposed to have a strong code of sportsmanship, as compared with other nations; the medical profession has its code, imposed by the approval of its members, whereas the profession of business is said to lack such a code; or the military class, which once had a strict code of "honor," is said, under modern conditions of warfare, to have lost it.

It is required of a conscience that it shall be not only strong but sound. Its critique embraces a pathology of conscience; or an examination of the several ways in which it may break down and cease to function, through disorganization.

In order that a conscience shall be sound or vigorous several factors must be present in balanced proportions. Thus a conscience may be deficient in its act of approving and disapproving through lack of forcefulness in its personal channels. The social group may lack "leadership"; or its titular leaders may be lacking in that so-called "force of personality" which is compounded of articulateness, aggressiveness, decisiveness, attractiveness, oddity, or latent power. Where this lack occurs there is a corresponding lack of respect on the part of those to whom the approving or disapproving is addressed. But, on the other hand, the voice of conscience may be excessively arrogant, and breed sycophancy in the party of the second part. A tyrannical conscience "makes cowards of us all."

Or, the source of the unbalance may lie in the passive member of the relationship, who may be either constitutionally resistant and unassimilable, in which case the authority of the other party is weakened; or he may suffer from an "inferiority complex." A too passive acceptance of the moral code, as was pointed out by the Sophists of old, exposes the more naïve to the exploitation of unscrupulous tyrants who do not feel bound by the code themselves. It is this excess of submissiveness which is the burden of Nietzsche's charge against morality. In relation to his self-approval a man may be conscience-ridden, or overconscientious; or he may expend too much time and attention in perpetual self-examination. He may engage in a sort of self-flagellation, in a masochistic indulgence in tortures of remorse.

A sound conscience will address itself both to others and to self.

When the emphasis on reproving others is excessive a person renders himself vulnerable to the *tu quoque* argument; he is accused of intrusiveness and censoriousness, and it is suggested that he look to his own conduct. If through reticence or humility he utters no judgment on others, he fails to play his part in the creation of the collective sanction. If the emphasis on self-judgment is excessive, he becomes an "introvert." If he is excessively approving of himself, he is called "self-righteous"; and this self-approbation is likely to be imputed to him if, through preoccupation with judging others, he fails to judge himself. When his disapproval of others is coupled with self-approval, he is considered a hypocrite, on the ground that no person can *really* be as blameless as he takes himself to be.

Conscience may fail to be in balance through a too great reluctance to agree. There is an excess of individual independence which may take the form of "negativism," that is, a pride in being different. On the other hand, there is an excessive readiness to agree, a lack of "sales resistance," which is not agreement at all, but merely a reflex of conformity or chain reaction, like the process of crystallization in a liquid medium.

And, finally, conscience requires a balance of self-interest and disinterestedness. A person who has no independent benevolence, that is, no concern for the fulfillment of the interests of others for their own sake, is incapable of conscience. He may use its language and tone of voice but his approval and disapproval are no more than instruments by which he hopes to persuade others to serve his own interests. An absorption in his own interests is likely to weaken his interest in the interests of others. There may, however, be the opposite form of excess. The use of the term 'altruism' is unfortunate. The client of conscience, in whose behalf a person approves or disapproves, includes himself as well as others. The omission of this self-reference in conscience has no recognized name unless it be 'folly' or 'fatuousness.' Excessive unselfishness is a rare disease which society is under no great necessity of preventing. Nevertheless, the question "Where do *I* come in?" is a legitimate and sometimes a timely question.

The diagnosis of conscience can be approached from another angle with similar results. All of the parts of conscience, its active assertion, its passive acceptance, its application to self and to others, its benevolence and disinterestedness, call into play certain deep-seated human propensities; and these may pervert conscience as well as nourish and sustain it. The indignation in righteous indignation is a form of anger, and the anger once kindled may consume the righteousness. The line between strong disapproval and anger is sometimes a fine line, but judged by the standard of conscience it is a frontier. A mass demonstration of mere anger, regardless of the innocence or culpability of the victim, is not a manifestation of conscience, though it may sometimes feel so and call itself by that name. Similarly, fear plays an important role at the opposite side of the relationship, and fear may run away with any state of mind, individual or collective, of which it is a part. But yielding to approval or disapproval merely from timidity or panic, is not conscience. In short, conscience intimidates, but it is not the same thing as intimidation.

Approval and disapproval constitute forms of power, and may be fed by ambition. Those who play important roles in setting the patterns of approval and disapproval are likely to be prompted in some degree by self-assertion, and are likely to profit by their ascendancy. Here again human nature, admitted as an ally of conscience, may usurp its role. The Puritans, who were experts on conscience, were well aware that the Devil may enter by this door.

Disgust and repugnance may enter into the act of disapproval, and they may invigorate it; but in themselves they cannot constitute it, and must not be confused with it. A disgust for tobacco not infrequently expresses itself in the judgment that smoking is wrong. This emotional compulsion of conscience appears in what is sometimes described as "appetitive inversion." When sex is frustrated it may take the form of a strong repugnance, and this in turn may take the form of excessive disapproval. What sounds and feels like a declaration of conscience may then be nothing more than a form of psychic nausea. Prudery is a perverted and corrupted form of conscience.

Finally, a sick conscience may be a divided conscience. This is a vast topic ranging all the way from schizophrenia to the normal problems of divided allegiance. The reference here is not to the conflict between conscience and the appetites and desires which conscience in some degree represses; or to the external conflict between different communities, each with its own conscience. By conflict of conscience is here meant that internal conflict which arises from the fact that a person belongs to several communities of opinion and sentiment, in each of which he plays all the different roles which conscience implies. In this sense race-conflict is not a conflict between the white's conscience and his greed or sadism, or a conflict between whites and blacks. It consists in the fact that whites are at one and the same time members of a special caste and members of a community with a traditional Christian code. The conflict of conscience is the conflict, within the breast of the white person, of the requirements of these two consciences.

The most persistent and widespread conflict of conscience is that which arises from the coexistence within the same society of the two communities of church and state. Each has its own conscience, and they create a tension within the personalities of their common members. The conflict between the Catholic's religious conscience and his secular conscience is a widespread and momentous phenomenon in the modern world. The "conscientious objector" illustrates the same type of conflict.[5]

6

There is a final, as well as an instrumental, critique of conscience. The second means that the conscience is or is not in good working order and capable of exercising its specific function; the first means that it satisfies or does not satisfy the requirements of that moral good, which is its ultimate purpose. It is true that this line cannot be sharply drawn; nevertheless the distinction serves to clarify and amplify the normative method in the science of ethics.

Without this distinction it is impossible to describe the fact that an institution can stumble over its own feet. Its instrumentalities may through their specialization, their internal complexity, and their inertia, become vested interests, and stand in the way of the very purpose of which they are the instruments. The institution may, in short, defeat itself. This is illustrated by situations in which a society which has achieved a high morale is nevertheless morally objectionable. Let us assume that at the outbreak of the Second World War the Nazi Party had succeeded in imbuing the German people with a strong social conscience, so that all Germans shared the same approvals and disapprovals, applied these to themselves, and through a sense of solidarity were concerned for one another. And let us suppose, on the other hand, that the social conscience of France was comparatively feeble; in other words, that its morale was "low." [6] Despite the superiority of the Nazi conscience on instrumentalist grounds, the conscience of Germany is not thereby exonerated. It may still be condemned not only externally, on the grounds of the injury to its victim, but internally on the ground of its own ulterior purpose, namely, by the moral purpose which it is the function of conscience to serve.

· The final normative critique of conscience is not a judgment of conscience by conscience; it is a judgment of conscience by the principles of morality; or by the critic's conscience only insofar as this has itself been already examined and certified by these principles. It is only by the common moral standard that it is possible to judge finally between one conscience and another.

[5] A study of American conscientious objectors at the time of the First World War revealed the fact that 90% based their opposition to the civil requirements of military service on sectarian religious grounds. Cf. "Testing the Conscience of the Conscientious Objector," *Literary Digest*, April 5, 1919.

[6] It is interesting to note that Count Keyserling, writing in 1929, found Germany notably lacking in *tenue* (meaning possessed of a unifying code of honor) as compared with other European nations with the exception of Russia. Had he been writing today he might have found in both Nazism and Communism attempts to overcome this weakness. Cf. his *Recovery of Truth*, 1929, pp. 517 ff.

The difference between criticism by conscience and criticism by morality is exemplified by the present necessity of *creating* a conscience that shall support other international institutions, also in the making, and designed to promote general peace and welfare. Such a conscience of mankind would not be justified because it was approved by the existing consciences of narrower scope; on the contrary, these may be condemned because they are disapproved by a higher, that is, more inclusive, conscience which has yet to be created. Both the positive judgment that a world conscience *would* be good, and the judgment that existing consciences *are* defective, appeal for their evidence, not to any existing conscience, but to the moral purpose.

The question is clarified by the analogy of scientific doctrine. Anybody of scientific opinion can be judged by any other body of scientific opinion, as being in agreement or in disagreement. Thus the Ptolemaic astronomy can be criticized in terms of the Copernican or the Copernican by the Ptolemaic, or both by the opinion of naïve common sense. But when one judges between these astronomies the appeal is not from opinion to opinion, but from opinion to true and certified knowledge.

7

The moral critique of conscience is divisible into two parts: a critique by the canons of rationality, and a critique by the canons of reform. A conscience may be said to be rational insofar as it is "true" to its moral purpose; 'true' being taken to mean both fidelity and also enlightenment. It cannot be too strongly affirmed that the fidelity of conscience here means fidelity to its own purpose. It does not mean fidelity to the purposes of science, art, education, or religion. Conscience *can* be criticized by such extra-moral standards; such external criticism has meaning and is of common occurrence. But conscience owes no allegiance to these external purposes; it cannot on such grounds be convicted out of its own mouth, that is, on the terms which it offers for its self-justification.

It may be said to be the role of the moralist to remind conscience of its moral purpose. It brings the moral purpose of conscience into focus, making men more consciously aware of it, and more methodical in their pursuit of it. Reflection broods upon the utterances of the existing conscience, and interrogates its exponents; seeking to clarify the meaning of the terms which it employs, and to systematize its judgments under some conception of the moral good.

The most famous instance of this procedure is to be found in the Socratic dialogues of Plato. The critic and his interlocutors start with the existing social conscience; for which it is assumed that any man may speak, whether he be an illustrious Sophist, or an unsophisticated Athenian youth. But while Socrates, thanks to his place in history and to the literary art of Plato, is considered as the founder and prototype of the critique of conscience, the same procedure appears throughout the ages in every highly developed culture. The conscience of the Hebraic-Christian world, thanks to the prophets old and new, moved from the ancient tribal mores to the Ten Commandments, and from the Ten Commandments to the "Two Great Commandments," and from those to the supreme good of universal love. Modern criticism moved from the several duties of feudalism to a supreme duty to society as a whole, conceived in terms of "the greatest happiness of the greatest number," or the total national interest, or the welfare of mankind.

The rationalization of conscience is said to be a sign of social weakness, as demonstrated by the appearance of Socrates on the eve of the collapse of Greece. There is no doubt that the critical attitude taken in itself does reflect a lack of uniform and certain conviction, and that this, if carried beyond a certain point, may diminish a society's cohesiveness and power to survive in a struggle for existence. But it is quite possible, indeed usual, for this self-criticism to serve as a leaven, directly engaging only a small portion of society, or others only in their occasional "lucid intervals." In any case it is the price which has to be paid for moral progress, and affords the only escape from the tyranny which develops whenever the instrument loses sight of its end.

The term 'tyranny' is derived from the political context where it is most notorious. Governing officials, in whom the function of political control is vested, seek control for its own sake, or for the sake of the ruler's private good, or for that of his friends. But there is a like tendency to tyranny in all institutions; there are domestic, legal, and plutocratic tyrannies; scientific, artistic, educational, and religious bureaucracies. Among all the tyrannies which man creates and from which he suffers, there is none more abusive than the tyranny of conscience. This tyranny may be embodied in certain persons who assume the role of the keepers of the social conscience; each man harbors a potential tyrant within his own personal conscience.

The canon of enlightenment as applied to conscience does not mean any enlightenment, but moral enlightenment. Assuming a conscience which is faithful to its moral purpose it may fail to serve that purpose through fallacious judgments of what will fulfill that purpose. The "folkways" of primitive societies provide abundant illustrations of the fallacy of *post hoc ergo propter hoc.* Judgments based on a single instance which happens to be striking and memorable are thereafter hardened by habit and tradition and become impenetrable to evidence. The following examples are provided by Sumner:

> In Molembo a pestilence broke out soon after a Portuguese had died there. After that the natives took all possible measures not to allow any white man to die in their country. On the Nicobar islands some natives who had just begun to make pottery died. The art was given up and never again

attempted. . . . Soon after the Yakuts saw a camel for the first time small-
pox broke out amongst them. They thought the camel to be the agent of
the disease. A woman amongst the same people contracted an endogamous
marriage. She soon afterwards became blind. This was thought to be on
account of the violation of ancient customs.[7]

The importance of these examples lies in the fact that they differ
only in degree from what is of daily occurrence in societies which pride
themselves on their enlightenment. *Post hoc propter hoc* is still perhaps
the commonest form of so-called reasoning and Cyprian's dictum that
"custom is often only the ambiguity of error" is still applicable — despite
the development and vogue of science, and sometimes, indeed, within
science itself. The social thought of everyday life, even in the twentieth
century, abounds in areas which are impenetrable to light — slogans and
clichés which divert social action from its true end. Perhaps for mankind
the more decisive struggle is not that between morality and immorality,
or between mores and mores, but between mores and morality: between
the established approvals and disapprovals of the group, and its rational
pursuit of the moral good of harmonious happiness.

8

The moral ideal is the organization of interests for their greatest possible benefit, and embracing as many interests as possible. It is this
maximum and optimum fulfillment of the moral purpose which inspires
reform, and provides its justification. The reformer says "This is good,
but it might be better." In the name of *liberality* it condemns repression,
and in the name of *universality* it condemns exclusiveness.

Moral organization requires the limitation of the interests organized,
and conscience tends to freeze the limits, even when they are excessively
narrow. The so-called "social Gestalt," that is, the existing system of
attitudes, and the scale of values into which successive generations of
individuals are initiated, imposes restrictions on individual freedom
which exceed the requirements of social order. The moral purpose requires that the conscience of the group shall be perpetually liberalized,
lest it shall give interests less than their due. Its inertia evokes a legitimate protest in behalf of interests that seek more room within the moral
household.

This protest, whether from the aggrieved parties or from disinterested
reformers who take the aggrieved parties as their clients, is the moral core
of that "social revolution" which is more conspicuous in its political, legal,
and economic manifestations. In this struggle the resistance of the existing conscience, which is satisfied with the benefits of the *status quo,* and
neglects its costs, is known as "conservatism" or "reaction." Liberalism, or
progressivism, on the other hand, insists that no social organization is

[7] W. G. Sumner, *Folkways,* Ginn and Company, 1907, pp. 24–25.

acceptable so long as there is a possible reorganization which would provide for interests more abundantly.

The moral ideal implies universality — it implies, in other words, that all interactive, and therefore potentially conflicting, interests shall be brought in. Morality "begins at home" — that is, it spreads from narrower to wider circles. The psychological factors which create conscience — gregariousness, sympathy, fear, suggestibility, prestige — all operate more strongly within the narrower circle, and stand in the way of its extension. As a local or class conscience creates a barrier to a wider social conscience, so this wider social conscience in turn creates a barrier to a still wider conscience embracing two or more societies. In augmenting the solidarity of a single society, conscience may arm it against another, and thus aggravate that very conflict of human interests which it is the purpose of morality to resolve. Hence the conscience of a nation, which is an essential part, if not the core, of its nationalism, may be attacked on moral grounds; or in the name of those universal moral principles which apply to all human relations, international as well as national.

When conscience becomes identified in men's minds with its abuses, they forget its uses. It would generally be granted in a cool hour that men cannot live without government, law, and economy; but when these institutions become symbols of conservatism and reaction men may propose not to correct them, but to abolish them altogether. Similarly, the complaint against the evils of harshly repressive conscientiousness tends to assume the form of an attack upon conscience in general. But it is as unthinkable that men should live harmoniously and happily together without the force of collective and personal approval, as that they should live without government, law, and economy.

The moral critique of conscience, the normative judgments passed upon its approvals and its disapprovals, will attempt to remove the abuse while preserving the use. It will recognize that while conscience tends to be misguided and ignorant, illiberal and narrow, and cannot, therefore, be accepted as it stands, it is morally the most fundamental of all institutions. It is the institution on which society must place its chief reliance for bringing the sister-institutions of polity, law, and economy into line with the purpose of harmonious happiness.

9

Since there is need of conscience there is a demand for the methods and arts by which it can be created. Hence there is a technology of ethics, as there is of every other institution. The discussion of the explanatory and normative judgments which are applicable to conscience has already trespassed on the domain of technology — not by inadvertence, but by necessity. For, as has already been pointed out, all explanatory judgments yield matter for technology, and all normative judgments can by a mere change of direction be converted into technological judgments.

Conscience as a system of approving and disapproving attitudes, in which sentiment and opinion are conjoined, can be implanted. To him who is engaged in this task recipes can be supplied by the various sciences, natural and cultural, which deal with man, and no science of man is wholly irrelevant. Insofar as such recipes are made to order, and fitted to their specific uses, they constitute ethical technology. What is known about past or existing conscience can be employed in the making of new conscience. In the implanting, strengthening, or modification of conscience use can be made of biology, anthropology, sociology, and psychology. Use can be made of other cultural sciences, such as linguistics, politics, jurisprudence, the sciences of education and religion, the science of art, and the science of science; provided only that their products are selected and adapted to the use in question.

Conscience being a form of control the technique of its implanting is sought whenever and wherever this control is desired, and for whatever purpose it is desired, whether personal or social, selfish, or moral. Thus businessmen in a capitalistic system are interested in implanting or conserving the code of free enterprise, that is, a social approval of thrift, labor, sobriety, and emulation. Ambitious rulers or military leaders in their desire for power seek to implant a code of loyalty. Priests, in their desire to glorify the church, may seek to promote a cult of supernatural, to the neglect of natural and worldly, values. Parents or teachers may seek to inculcate a cult of obedience as a means of promoting their own ascendancy. These and all similar functionaries who desire to create approvals and disapprovals that accord with their designs, create a market for the "know-how" of conscience.

Technology of conscience can be put to a great variety of uses, bad as well as good, low as well as high, but it must not be supposed to have any predilection for the bad and the low. There is a technology of a morally good, as well as of a morally bad conscience. The implications of this for propaganda and education, all along the line, are evident. If the conscience implanted is to satisfy the requirements of morality, the moral end itself must be implanted. The lover of peace and human welfare must learn how to cultivate these ideals, and to create a conscience in which they will be so strongly approved, and their opposites so strongly disapproved, by the aggregate of society, as to lay the ground for the more palpable moral institutions of polity, law, and economy.

A polity is an over-all plan, adopted by all for all, and imposed by all on all: a plan by which the members of a group live together for their joint advantage; to escape mutual conflict, to pool their resources, and to enjoy the benefits of coöperation. If such a comprehensive plan is to be effective, it must be not only contrived and formulated, but obeyed, and obeyed by all. The members must be able to count on one another. So essential is this assurance of reciprocity and so great is human unreliability, that it is humanly necessary to enforce obedience. Hence men unite to create an irresistible instrument of enforcement, and reserve its use to the political authority. They create inducements so strong that they will exceed any probable temptation to disobey: inducements of the same order as the temptations; inducements which appeal to those primitive interests such as pain, life, property, freedom of bodily movement, which can be assumed to actuate all men and particularly those men who would be disposed to disobedience.

These extraordinary and artificial instruments are introduced to supplement prior inducements. The first inducement, commonly called the inducement of reason, is the desire for that end of harmonious happiness of which obedience is seen to be a necessary condition. The second inducement is the collective approval or disapproval; that is, conscience. When these do not suffice men resort to more tangible and palpable rewards and punishments. The importance which any given social philosopher attaches to such enforcement will reflect his view of the generality of mankind; that is, his view of the extent to which men will probably remain incorrigible despite the first and second inducements. If he has an extremely low view of human reason and conscience he may go so far as to identify polity with enforcement. This view, however, is clearly untenable. Polity implies policy-making and administration, and it implies obedience; but voluntary obedience is no less obedient, and is in the long run more trustworthy, than compulsory obedience.

If it be the purpose of polity to create harmonious happiness by the adoption of a common plan, then when such a plan is adopted and its fruits enjoyed, polity exists: it exists when and insofar as it serves its purpose. The mythical "state of nature," when human affairs were ruled by reason and conscience, was not pre-political, but ideally political. The "fall" symbolizes not the beginning of polity but its failure. To deny this is in effect to say that a ship which steers easily has no helm, or that lungs do not begin to be lungs until they require the assistance of an artificial pump. To say that polity is measured by the imposition of rewards and penalties is as though one were to say that the ship's discipline is measured by the suppression of mutiny, or that conscience is measured by remorse, or that piety is measured by repentance, or that law is measured by the prison or concentration camp, or, in short, that government is a reign of terror.

Enforcement is not of the essence of government, but is an insurance against its failure. It is the mopping up which takes care of remnants of resistance which mark the partial failure of government to be what it ought to be, namely, policy made and policy obeyed, for the common good. So conceived, enforcement may be recognized as a proper and humanly indispensable adjunct of government. For if men are to enjoy a *guarantee* of reciprocity, and not a mere hope or probability, there must be provision against the contingency of disobedience, however infrequent or sporadic its occurrence.

If organized society is to serve its purpose, there must be an over-all public policy, that is, a policy for all; which requires a central command obeyed throughout the entire body politic. Decisions must be made by a recognized authority, and these decisions must be followed and carried into effect. There must be a head who lays the course, steers the ship, gives orders, permits and forbids, and quells insubordination. These conditions are never completely met, but in proportion as they are, a society is a polity or state.

2

Because the function of ruling is assigned to certain specialized functionaries, constituting the government, there is a tendency to divide a political society into two groups, the rulers and the ruled. In principle this division does not hold, inasmuch as rulers are also ruled and the ruled are also rulers. But the fact that there is a duality of command and obedience, if not a dual classification of persons, has created a fundamental problem of political theory.

What person or persons are properly entitled to exercise the function of political direction and control, and under what conditions? This is the so-called problem of *sovereignty*, notable for its importance, and notorious for its misunderstandings. The literature and discussion of the subject persistently confuse two quite different questions: sovereignty *de facto*, and sovereignty *de jure* — "where lies the control?" and "where ought it to lie?" The actual center of political control may be located anywhere, in a person of superior strength or cunning, in a crowned head, in a leader of the armed forces, in the rich or in the poor, in the privileged or in the unprivileged, class. But he who exercises the control, and his associates who share it, justify their control; arguing that they not only exercise it but have a right to exercise it.

The question of the "legitimacy" of the ruler may be argued on merely constitutional grounds, as when the monarch's title is proved by his parentage, or the elected official's title is proved by counting the votes. But then there remains the ulterior question of the right of the recognized heir or of the duly elected official. Why *should* a person or person, however accredited, exercise unique and irresistible power over the other members of society? There is no answer to this question save in terms of moral priority; and there is no morally justified control except the control of the included part by the more inclusive whole. The control by a part is justified only when delegated to that part by the whole; or only insofar as the governing part expresses the agreement of all parts. This is the meaning of the doctrine of natural (inborn or divinely created) political equality: as affirmed by John Locke and embodied in the American Declaration of Independence. Prior to the organization of a polity of agreement, the rights of men to rule over other men are equal; that is to say, there is no such right.

The acceptance of the principle that the right of sovereignty consists in the priority of the whole over the part has led social philosophers hastily to conclude that where there is a whole of wills there is a will of the whole. As has already been argued, however, there is no will except a personal will, and there is no will of a whole composed of persons except insofar as there is an agreement of personal wills. The claim of government is disproved by the dissent of any person whose agreement is claimed. The failure to recognize this very simple fact has led to the assumption of a popular will as a postulate or fiction which is contrary to the facts of psychology; or to such purely theoretical inventions as a "vicarious," "imputed," "ex-officio," or "virtual" agreement.

The so-called "compact theory" of government, despite its shortcomings, is to be credited with recognizing that the right of government to govern rests on the real agreement of the governed. A compact in its simplest form is a voluntary agreement entered into by two or more parties for their joint benefit. Each party is at one and the same time a maker of the agreement and a beneficiary. Its authority over each consists in the consent of both to a plan which is for the benefit of both. All parties create a joint power from their several powers, and bind themselves to obey it for the sake of the security and coöperation which its obedience will enable them severally to enjoy. Compact, in this sense, does occur in human history between man and man, or within small uprooted groups, such as the voyagers of the *Mayflower*, or the settlers on a new frontier. But as a principle of political theory it is a model, invoked when a polity is called upon to justify itself. This doctrine is personalistic in its conception of will, inter-personalistic in its conception of the social will, and moralistic in its conception of the right of sovereignty.

These same considerations serve to correct the widespread but erroneous supposition that the right of popular sovereignty is the right of a majority to govern a minority. As there is no right of one person to rule over another, so there is no right of 51% of the members of society to rule over 49%, or of any fraction to rule over any other fraction. The right of government is the right of all members of society over any fraction, large or small. The decision by a majority vote is a device by which to reach a decision of policy at any given time. There are many such devices — a two-thirds vote, a plurality, a majority of those present, or of a quorum, a majority of two or more successive votes — all of which are compromises between the principle of unanimity and the exigencies of action.

All of these devices are, theoretically, assented to by all. The collective will which authorizes government is the will which supports the general system or constitution and not the will which supports particular decisions made under the constitution. The will of the defeated candidate for office and of his adherents, or the will of a member of a defeated legislative minority, has in an immediate and limited sense been denied. But he has also willed the system within which he has been outvoted, and with this will even his defeat is in agreement. Constitutional changes affecting the terms of the fundamental agreement must approximate unanimity more closely than changes of official personnel or of legislative and administrative policy. On this account they are made more conservatively either through the prolonged operations of constitutional amendment or judicial review, or through profound alterations of public opinion and sentiment. Or when the system is too inflexible to permit of orderly and continuous change the system itself breaks down and polity is suspended during a period of revolution and civil war.

Polity as a morally justifiable institution rests on the thoughtful agreement of those who live under it: a coöperative organization entered into by persons in whom the interests of all overrule the interests of each. This overruling occurs only within the several persons, who by virtue of this prerogative become "citizens." A man who obeys government from fear of the penalties of disobedience, is not ruled by the whole, but by his own fear. All government is thus personal self-government distributed among a number of persons who have come to agreement.

As we have seen, the rule of one interest over another within a person is essentially permissive. This is reflected in the fact that the minimum condition of political leadership is that it should define limits to which the interests over which it rules must accommodate themselves. To the prohibitive authority it may add more or less of "enabling" authority: it may, in other words, assist members of the group in the fulfillment of their interests. It is this difference between the minimum of permissive authority and the maximum of enabling authority which defines the range of possibilities between little government and much government. Within this range the choice rests not on the general principle of polity, but on expediency. How much shall be prescribed by public policy and how much shall be left to private initiative and enterprise is determined by what, in the light of experience, proves best for all.

3

Such being the nature of polity in general, political science will explain its forms and origins. Morphology will compare and classify the different species of polity which appear in human history, varying among themselves in size, in structure and mechanism, in their organs of policy-making and control, and in their procedures — patriarchal monarchies, constitutional monarchies, absolute monarchies, aristocracies, oligarchies, dictatorships, direct democracies, representative democracies — with countless other forms and blends, and innumerable minor differences of detail. In its genetic and evolutionary branch political science will examine the genesis of polity, and the causes by which it is modified. How does polity come into existence? On what conditions does its existence depend? What are the forces by which it is changed? No attempt will here be made to enter into these complexities, except insofar as may be necessary to demonstrate the method.

The limits of the explanatory method are illustrated by the widespread and persistent misunderstanding of the doctrine of the political "compact." This doctrine, as has been pointed out, is primarily a justification of polity and not an account of its origin. Government has a right to the control which it exercises only so far as the governed see such control to be good and on that ground consent to its exercise. When, as at Dumbarton Oaks and San Francisco, an attempt was made to inaugurate a limited world polity, or when as at present, certain persons advocate a "world government," this principle is recognized as the proper ground on which to persuade nations to adopt it. Ordinarily, however, men *find themselves* under such a control without their leave, and accept it, if at all, after the fact. The earlier proponents of the compact theory, reflecting an excessively rationalistic view of human behavior, played into the hands of their opponents by asserting that all government has, at some time in the past, been consciously contrived and has come into existence as a consequence of having been agreed upon. In other words, they shifted the question from justification to causality, and suffered defeat at the hands of the historians and psychologists who recognized the extent to which human institutions arise from irrational causes.

The centralized control of human affairs may actually come about through any of the causes which give one man or class of men ascendancy over their fellows. Under primitive conditions the ascendancy may result from sheer bodily strength, or from superior cunning. As society evolves the control will fall to an increasing extent into the hands of those who excel in the personal aptitudes, such as a capacity for leadership, which enable their possessor to exert influence. And in either case polity may spring from a love of power. Control implies not only the giving of commands, but also their obedience. Why do men submit to government?

This also has its natural explanation in terms of fear, submissiveness, and the sense of inferiority; both command and obedience being confirmed and crystallized by habit.

From the beginning of human history political control has arisen from cultural as well as from natural causes. The superior man is measured no longer by his muscles, or merely by his inborn traits, but by his skills, social status, wealth, and other acquired advantages. And for every such superiority there is a corresponding inferiority, which impels to obedience.

Polity consists not merely in command and obedience, but in some measure of agreement on a common end. How do men come to agreement of opinion and sentiment? To answer this question it is necessary to traverse the whole field of man's sociability, natural and acquired, embracing his communicativeness, gregariousness, racial blood-stream, fellow-feeling, sympathy, imitativeness, and whatever like causes there be, and called by whatever names.

The making of public opinion and sentiment involves a vast set of acquired instrumentalities. It is possible to treat public opinion and sentiment as a gross emergent phenomenon, tested by a Gallup poll, or described like a cloud in its broad contours and distributed densities. But as a cloud consists of drops of moisture, atoms and molecules, wind currents and relative temperatures, so public opinion and sentiment consist of related and interacting individuals, together with the entire social equipment for the making of minds. Its adequate explanation must take account of language and of public speech, and, in these modern days, of the vast ramifications of press and radio and television, and of the operations of subordinate organizations such as public parties and private "movements" contrived for the express purpose of disseminating political opinion and sentiment. It must take account of the psychology of give and take, of discussion, bargaining, and compromise.

Polity, like every social institution, is conditioned by its sister-institutions. In certain periods of human development it was profoundly affected by the institution of the family and tribe; and even in later times to call the ruler the "father" of his country, or to call the country the "mother" country, is not a verbal accident. Those who affirm the economic foundations of polity err, if at all, only in the degree of their emphasis. Polity is influenced not only by those institutions most closely allied through their common moral purpose — conscience, law, and economy — but by art and science, by tradition and education, by religion and the church, and by all the elements, and by the composite whole, of culture.

In polity, as in conscience, internal normative judgments act as causes. Political institutions rise and fall according as they are deemed good or bad by those who live under them. They are put to the test, and are acquired or abandoned by trial and error; that is, according as they succeed or fail in realizing their end. Because of the extravagant claims once made for the role of reason in human affairs, it was necessary to bring to light and stress the operation of other causes — unreason, selfish and unscrupulous ambition, the primitive human instincts, the struggle for existence, the physical conditions of soil and climate. This needful corrective has led to the rejection of facts which are no less actual because they are less unsavory. It does sometimes happen that the wise man is chosen for office because of his wisdom. It does sometimes happen that changes occur, whether of constitution or of policy, because of judgments in which they are compared with political norms, and praised or condemned accordingly.

Thus the explanation of polity provides the starting point for its critique. The self-critcism which operates as a cause becomes, when elaborated and systematized, the normative branch of political science.

4

Polity has its own distinctive instrumentalities for policy-making and control. When these fail, a government collapses; when these are efficient, a government "works." Such judgments constitute the instrumental part of normative political science.

It is said that the minimum requirement of a government is that it shall govern. A government which is not obeyed is therefore rightly condemned as non-government. A weak government is subject to a like indictment in lesser degree; it requires to be strengthened. The weakness of a government may be due to a variety of causes; for example, to the lack of coördination between the several branches. It is then like a defective or broken machine. Its parts, instead of working smoothly together, annul one another, as may be said of the American government when its executive and legislative branches are in stalemate.

The weakness of government may be due to functional disputes within the government itself, to the multiplication of small parties, to sectionalism, or to deep social cleavages, such as that between clericals and anti-clericals, or between labor and employers. It may be due to a lack of forcefulness and leadership in its official personnel. It may be due to a temper or habit of insubordination on the part of the people. The failure of many South American nations to create firm and durable governments is a familiar fact, which has never been satisfactorily analyzed. It is commonly said that Anglo-Saxon peoples, whether owing to tradition, social traits, political experience, or a code of sportsmanship, accept party defeat in good temper and resort to constitutional methods to retrieve it; whereas Latin Americans, despite a similarity of institutional forms, resort to revolutionary violence and military dictatorship.

A government represents the wills of the governed. Unless there is some degree of representativeness, there is no polity at all, but a mere exploitation of the weak by the strong. This form of failure in government is commonly due to the unique advantage which the government enjoys in influencing the popular mind. If government derives its right of sovereignty from public opinion and sentiment, it must not itself create them; for this would be to say that it derives the right from itself; which is equivalent to no right. A self-perpetuating government is not a government. A government can perpetuate itself by controlled indoctrination, by intimidation, or by hysteria.

It is an ironical and revealing fact that the very polities which pride themselves most on unanimity and organic unity are those which find it necessary to cast out their own members. In antiquity the dissenter was sent into exile; in more recent days he is forced to exile himself. The states which claim to be organic unities are known by the inorganic ingredients of which they continually purge themselves and with which they enrich less organic societies in various parts of the world. In these days they are called "refugees" and they prove themselves remarkably assimilable by societies based on voluntary agreement. It is evident that if two parties disagree, *dis*agreement can always be removed by the elimination of one of the parties. But this does not bring about agreement; it only accentuates its failure. The logical outcome of agreement pursued by the method of ex-clusion, ex-pulsion, or ex-communication is the isolation of a small surviving remnant, weakened not only by its own isolation but by the strength which it supplies to its rivals.

When a government perpetuates itself by intimidation, the consent of the people is dictated by a narrowing of the range of choice. They consent "or else" — as the victim of a holdup consents to hand over his purse when he is given no alternative but "his money or his life." While it may be said that the people obey of their own volition, their choice is reduced to a choice of evils: they choose to obey rather than to suffer torture, fines, imprisonment, or death. They choose to avoid the penalties which the political system imposes, but they do not choose the system which imposes the penalties. They are revolutionaries at heart if not in deed. A government can perpetuate itself by terror through its monopoly of weapons and the disorganization of its opponents. It can deal with revolutionaries one by one, and nip revolution in the bud. But even with the improved technique of terror which such a government now has at its disposal, its situation is precarious, and it commonly resorts to the technique of hysteria — as old as the technique of terror, and, like the technique of terror, now much improved.

The term 'hysteria' is here used not in any precise psychiatric sense, but to signify that form of consent which is obtained by the incitement of sheer emotionality. It takes many forms, well-known to the demagogues of all time, but now refined by the modern arts of mass appeal — rhetorical eloquence, reiteration, the use of slogans and symbols, public

meetings held in vast amphitheaters and subjected to the carefully calculated effects of lighting and music, the dramatization of public issues,
the arousal of primitive instincts and passions, the personal magnetism
of leaders, the use of radio, television and newspaper headlines. Whatever the means employed, and they are many in kind and number, they
have this in common, that they inhibit reflection. Their intent is to secure
agreement without thought — second thought, and even first thought. To
prevent that disagreement which arises when men stop to think, they
prevent men from stopping to think. They hypnotize, intoxicate, carry
men away, sweep them off their feet.

In proportion as consent is secured by hysteria men do not really
agree. A government which rests on such superficial agreement does not
represent the wills of the governed but only their passions. Their assent
is a reflex rather than a choice. Insofar as this is the case, a government
forfeits claim to be so named.

All of these instrumental defects of government reflect political incapacity on the part of its personnel. It is a recognized fact that the
eminent "statesman" may be lacking in political shrewdness or wisdom,
and may require the services of a "professional politician" to supply the
lack.

Such are some of the normative judgments which can properly be
pronounced on a polity when measured by its own instrumental standards. They indicate some of the ways in which the instrumentalities of
polity can, through their disuse, misuse, or abuse, fail to be effective
political instruments.

Polity can be judged by norms drawn from non-political institutions.
The application to polity of the norms of law and economy is familiar.
The history of political thought abounds in the interchange of normative
judgments between polity and religion, or state and church. The most
conspicuous example of such inter-institutional criticism at the present
time is the dispute over control of education. The scientist or artist may
praise democracy because it permits him to pursue science for science's
sake, or art for art's sake, condemning totalitarian government on the
same grounds. He may praise aristocracy because it accords special
privileges to a cultured elite, or praise a paternalistic government because
it subsidizes scientific research, patronizes music and drama, builds monuments, and rewards the creative genius; and condemn democracy on the
ground that through its emphasis on equality it destroys standards of
scientific or artistic excellence.

Of such cross-judgments, deriving their standards from non-polity and
applying them to polity, there is no end. They are meaningful normative
judgments and each may be true or false in its own limited terms; provided the judge makes clear the norm by which he is judging. The danger

lies in the fact that in such external judgments the norm employed is commonly concealed.

5

The final normative judgments of political science invoke the moral purpose of polity. Lord Acton quotes Burke as saying: "The principles of true politics are those of morality enlarged." [1] This is well said, provided morality is rightly conceived. If morality be conceived as the effort to achieve harmony of interests then the polity provides its most conspicuous and unmistakable example. Failure to recognize this is due not to a lack of moralizing but to misconceptions of morality which divorce it from public affairs.

The interest which is served by the state is sometimes called "the public interest." The state is not owned by, nor is it designed to serve, any particular interest. No person can properly call it his, nor can any limited group of persons properly call it theirs. It belongs to everybody and is designed to profit everybody. The public interest is composed and compounded of private interests. If government is dedicated to public service, no private individual can ask it to serve him, but only him *together with the rest*.

The expression "welfare state" has recently come into vogue as referring to certain services which the state renders over and above providing a frame within which private interests can coexist and coöperate — certain added services, such as social security, favorable working conditions, rural development, housing, health, and education. [2] The question of the extent to which government shall undertake such services is not a question of principle, but only a question of method. Whether welfare shall be promoted by government directly, or only indirectly, through allowing and safeguarding private efforts, is to be determined by the results, experienced or predicted. In principle all polities are devoted to the welfare, well-being, or happiness of their members.

This moral purpose of polity has been recognized from the beginning of political thought. [3] It appears in every act of policy-making, when the proponents of a new measure are obliged not only to prove its workability and its profit to those special interests on which it immediately impinges and who perhaps instigated it, but also to reconcile it with all other interests. The heavy burden which is carried by the ruler, and which

---

[1] *Lectures on Modern History*, 1906, p. 28.

[2] For an admirable summary of these extensions of government in the United States, cf. H. S. Commager, "Appraisal of the Welfare State," *New York Times Magazine*, May 15, 1949.

[3] Hobbes is no exception. For the "peace" which is the purpose of the state ("*Leviathan*") is a blessing to everybody — not to the timid only; and still less only to the bold, who might enjoy greater advantages in a state of war.

proverbially interferes with his sleep, consists in precisely this necessity of taking every interest into account — the interests of all persons, localities, and sections, and interests of every variety.

This moral purpose of polity creates a dilemma for its members: they must either impose its rule on themselves privately through reason and conscience, or submit to its being imposed on them by the public authority alone. Any person or group of persons who conduct themselves irresponsibly, that is, without regard to the effect of their conduct on interests other than their own, have to be restrained by government, as the child is restrained. Insofar as all members of society claim for themselves the privilege of doing as they like, they invite the paternalistic role of the state as the only agency in the community whose business it is to see that they do not become a nuisance to others and so forfeit the benefits of collective action.

There is a profound paradox in the fact that democratic communities tend through excessive emphasis on individual self-interest to create the necessity for that very overlordship against which they protest. Those who would reduce the control of the state to a minimum are often those whose conduct requires that it be increased to a maximum. The most vigorous proponents of free enterprise, those who most resent the interference of government, are often those who need most to be interfered with. Similarly, the most radical advocates of a free press, or a free art, or a free science, or a free religion, are often those who create the necessity of censorship. In short, public responsibility is the sequel to private irresponsibility.

6

Polity, like conscience, is rationalized by fidelity and enlightenment. Most of the notorious evils of government arise from the fact that in polity the role of policy-making and control is set apart, and vested in certain individuals in whom there is a mixture of motives. Hence it may defeat its moral purpose through the infidelity of the official to the ultimate purpose of the office. There is no such thing as a ruler who is only a ruler, any more than there is such a thing as a scientist or poet who is only a scientist or poet. To describe a person as a scientist or poet is to describe only a part of him which interacts with his other parts. Similarly, a ruler is "human."

Political disinterestedness is a specific attitude which may sometimes be found in certain persons, but it is inevitably related to other attitudes found in the same persons. When it does occur in a ruler, it may be reconciled with his other motives; but there is always a likelihood of contamination. When the ruler's official duty is compromised by his desire for personal gain or for the gain of his friends, the government is said to be "corrupt"; when it is subordinated to his personal ambition, he is said to be a "tyrant." [4] The experience and perpetual fear of this infidelity has created a distrust of rulers, and has led to the creation of checks and safeguards; such as the definition of civil rights to freedom of speech, press, and assembly, and of other rights which protect individuals and minorities; the control of military by civil authority, and of the executive by the legislature; and the opposition party which is peculiarly alert to the corruption and tyranny of the party in office.

A government may lose sight of its ulterior good through habit and inertia. It is easier to repeat than to innovate, and the traditional and familiar acquires a factitious value. Ruling officials become captives of their own past declarations of policy, or to party commitments. The multiplication of instrumentalities blocks the view — which is the common charge against "bureaucracy" and "red tape."

The infidelity of government is due not only to the contamination of the public purpose by the private interests of the officials and to the rigidity and decay of the political instruments, but to mistaken ideas of the meaning of the moral end. When these mistaken ideas prevail in a community at large, a public servant who violates his trust is often deemed morally blameless provided he obeys sex taboos, exhibits the domestic virtues, accepts the edicts of an authority such as the church, or pays lip-service to ideals. But when morality is understood as the organization of interests for their joint and total benefit, there is no longer any difference of principle between public and private morals. The public official differs from the private individual only in the scope of his responsibility, and in the instrumentalities employed. His conduct cannot be right or dutiful in any of the proper senses of these terms, except insofar as it is conducive to the good of the community over which, on a higher or lower level, he rules.

If government is to be faithful to its moral purpose it must possess a clear conception of that purpose, and an understanding of the means by which it can be realized. In other words, it must be not only purposive, but also enlightened. The political evil known as "statism" consists in a false idea of the public purpose. It substitutes the greatness and glory of a fictitious corporate entity for the interests of individual persons; the real purpose of polity is superseded by a pseudo-purpose. This displacement may occur only in the minds of the ruled, and be used as a means of exploitation by the ruler. Or it may occur in the minds of both ruler and ruled: both being victims of the same idolatry, and equally eager to offer themselves as human sacrifice to Moloch. To be an "enlightened" ruler is not the same as to be a merely "intelligent" ruler, who "knows the game," or is skilled in the art of political organization; it implies a states-

---

[4] As distinguished from the "despot" or "dictator" whose fault lies in his ruling by personal fiat, without representation. But the ruler who is guilty in one of these respects is likely to be guilty in the others.

manlike grasp of the remoter moral goal. Statesmanship, in other words, requires *moral* knowledge. The statesman is the ruler who is both farseeing and wise. He sees the good of the whole and not merely of the part, and the good of the total community in the long run, rather than merely in the short run; and he keeps this object firmly in view. But he is also wise: he understands in what this greater good consists, and he knows the means by which it can be achieved. This was Plato's idea, when he said that the "philosopher" should rule — the philosopher being conceived not as the professor or writer, but as the man who knew the way to the true good.

When the role of ruler is distributed among the people in their capacity of citizenship, the same norm of enlightenment is applicable. Political democracy in the justifiable sense, is not the rule of the mass, but the rule of the wise. No increase of numbers compensates for lack of enlightenment. Imbecility multiplied is still imbecility; wisdom multiplied yields a product which arithmetic cannot measure.

7

The moral purpose of polity is to serve men's interests by enabling them to live peacefully and fruitfully together. It may be excessively repressive, as judged by the norm of *liberality;* or excessively exclusive, as judged by the norm of universality. These are the norms which are invoked by political reform.

Polity promotes harmony not for harmony's sake, but in order that the elements harmonized may live as abundantly as possible. In fulfillment of this task it is therefore the first duty of government to acquaint itself with the interests of the governed, and to take account of their claims. If a first person, the ruler, is to discover the interest of a second person, the ruled, he must in the last analysis accept the second person's testimony. This does not mean that the second person may not be reminded of his interest, or taught his interest, but that if in the end he does not recognize and acknowledge it as his, it is *not* his. His testimony need not be verbal. Other forms of testimony are often more trustworthy; Caesar may deny that he desires the crown, and yet if he reaches for it his action may be said to speak louder than his words. But he must himself reach for it. It is not his ambition if his friends grasp it for him — it is *their* interest in him.

The confusion between the interest which a person himself has or takes, and the interest which a second person has or takes in him, is one of the pitfalls of parentage, teaching, religion, and all the varied forms of professed benevolence. In order to discover whether professed benevolence is really independent benevolence, ask the beneficiary rather than the benefactor. The parent's mistaking his own interest for the child's interest, is notorious, and is one of the chief causes of domestic revolution.

The teacher tends to confuse the interests of his pupils with his own ambition. The priest may be concerned to spread his own gospel. This is the root of the religious proselytism and inquisition which ends by burning heretics "for their own good."

Government is afflicted with the same error. The ruler may claim to serve the interests of his people when he is in fact ignoring their interests altogether. To slip into this egoistic dependent benevolence he need not be governed by base motives, such as avarice or lust for personal power. He may be, and often is, animated by high ideals; and yet identify the interests of others with his own. Insofar as this is the case the government is said to be "paternalistic." In order that this insidious error may be avoided, government provides for channels by which the governed may voice their own interests, each person his own, each class or group or vocation, their own. They are given a hearing; and in order to assure their being heard they are given the power to challenge, remove, and replace their representatives — when these prove to be hard of hearing.

This obligation to serve the interests of the people as they define and assert their own interests, rounds out the full meaning of representative government. A polity which realizes its moral purpose will not only derive its control from the collective decision of the members but, returning again to the source, will facilitate the fullest expression of members' interests in order that it may serve them. Hence polity is committed to two freedoms — the freedom of each member to think and judge, and contribute the making up of his own mind to the making up of the collective mind; and the freedom to pursue his own interests, so far as this is consistent with the similar freedom of others. The first of these is the freedom which is a condition of government; the second is the freedom or liberty which government bestows. Government creates this second freedom either by protecting it from invasion by other freedoms, or by assisting it to help itself.

The priority of all to each is the only moral ground on which any freedom can rightly be abridged or denied. The negation of interest is justified only by its wider affirmation; the "no" has to be translated into "yes."

It follows that whenever the restraint upon interests severally exceeds the requirement of their totality, these interests have a justifiable grievance. If any reorganizaion of interests is possible which diminishes the cost to each, then polity is bound to adopt that reorganization. If, consistently with its purpose of housing all, society can provide more spacious mansions for its members — its component persons and their interests, — then it is bound to rebuild. There is thus an expanding pressure from within each included interest against the restraints of organization, and it is this pressure which creates the perpetual social revolution. A wise polity will anticipate and relieve this pressure before it becomes an explosive force. It will not defend the *status quo;* it will be continuous but not unchanging, firm but not rigid. It will perpetually contrive new measures by which order and stability can be reconciled with the enlargement of freedom. In short, it will be liberal and progressive.

8

There are many polities, and each government is under obligation to promote harmonious happiness by removing conflict and facilitating coöperation among its own people. It is also bound to enable its people to defend themselves against attack from without, and to represent its people in their relations to other governments and peoples. But through its preoccupation with these tasks it may create a form of selfishness which, even though it be on a higher level, is identical in principle with any selfishness. It may properly be judged by the norm of *universality.*

Morality is a bond between man and man. It does not stop at any frontier provided there are human persons on the other side. Conflict and non-coöperation *between* polities create the same problem as that created by conflict and non-coöperation *within* polities. The dividing line between one singular society and another may be geographical, racial, ethical, political, legal, economic, or cultural, but it is not moral. Two or more men whose interests interact, whatever otherwise they may be, compose one moral field. Their aggregate life together is morally good or bad; their conduct relatively to one another is subject to judgments of right or wrong; they have moral duties to one another and to their greater totality. If this is not conceded and if human life is not organized accordingly, it is not the fault of morality but of man's failure to understand and achieve it. For the idea that international relations or "foreign policy" are in principle non-moral, there is no justification whatever.

International or universal polity is the theme of a vast literature, reflecting both the urgency of the problem and its bewildering complexity. The idea of such a polity is ancient and persistent.[5] The evident fact that mankind at large constitutes an aggregation of interrelated persons, whose diverse interests bring them into disastrous conflict, begets the ideal of a universal harmony. The greatness of the success hoped for is proportional to the gravity of the failure suffered. Until the moral problem is solved on the world-wide scale all lesser solutions are provisional. Narrower resolutions of conflict may only aggravate the destructiveness of wider conflict; while the wider conflict may undo the good of the narrower.

The very fact that there is no world polity at the time that the need for it is recognized brings to light its purpose. In this case there is no historic institution which can obscure the norms by which polity is

[5] The great modern classic on this subject is Kant's *Eternal Peace and Other International Essays,* tr. by W. Hastie, 1914.

justified; there is no confusion between what is and what ought to be. The existing situation defines both the problem and its solution. It clearly reveals the difference between the inferior rightness, defined in terms of a lesser good of the nation, and the superior rightness defined in terms of the greater good of mankind. It focuses attention on the difference between the final or ideal rightness which would be appropriate for a universal moral organization once achieved, and the interim or transitional rightness which is required in order to bring such organization into being.

How long it will be before the problem is solved, whether, in fact, it will be solved before its non-solution will have destroyed the means of its solution, is the question which is now uppermost in the minds of morally responsible men. Advancing technology not only has created more devastating weapons, but through extending and multiplying human contacts it has created more occasions of conflict — more situations in which men are faced with the alternatives of working against one another or working together with one another. The greater the causal unity of the world, the greater the necessity of its moral unity. The first is an accomplished fact, whereas the second is a dubious project.

But the same changes which have made a universal polity a desperate necessity have contributed to its attainment. The idea of the totality of mankind once rested on the fragmentary evidence of the stranger beyond the borders — the recognition of Gentiles by Jews, of Mediterraneans by Greeks and Romans, of barbarians by Mediterraneans, of heathen by Christians, of aborigines by invaders, of East by West. Now the experience and imagination of men have traveled around the earth and returned to the starting point, enveloping the whole earth's surface and all its peoples. The increased facilities of communication and movement provide instruments of agreement as well as of disagreement — possibilities of friendship as well as of hostility.

From the least aggregation of interests to the greatest the principle of moral authority is the same; the principle, namely, that the requirements of a totality of interests take precedence of the requirements of any part. In accordance with this principle the totality of the interests of mankind should govern the interests of any constituent society. If the whole is to govern the part there must be a plan or a policy of the whole, and that policy must be adopted by the parts. There must be a global agency of policy-making and control. On the level of world polity, as on other levels, the necessity of enforcement would argue the imperfection of polity. Obedience of the world polity would be essential, but if it were obeyed without artificial penalties and rewards, so much the better. The "international police force" would be accidental; arising from the fact that the several societies of mankind were reluctant to obey, so that it would be their fear or greed rather than their moral will which consented.

As the universal policy rests on the same ground as other policies so it would be subject to similar normative judgments. Its instrumentalities could be judged by their strength or weakness; and the degree to which they reflected a freely formed opinion. It would be praiseworthy or blameworthy according as it was or was not faithful to its moral purpose of achieving non-conflict and coöperation; and according as it did or did not serve this purpose with enlightenment.

The justifiable authority of a world government would lie in the superiority of the whole to the part, and not in the superiority of one part over another part. The self-interest of a nation-state is not a moral finality; but neither is it rightly overruled by the self-interest of any other nation-state, but only by benevolent agreement among all nation-states. In this consists the equal sovereignty of all self-governing societies, large or small; which is the international analogue of that "natural equality" which underlies all polity.

9

Having, by definition, satisfied the canon of universality, the world polity would still be subject to the canon of liberality. This canon argues for the preservation of as much national freedom as is consisted with international order and coöperation. It justifies not only the aspiration to independent nationality on the part of colonies and "dependent areas," but the reluctance of nation-states to yield their present sovereignty to a super-state.

Nationalism, whatever the excesses to which it gives rise, and of which mankind are painfully aware — aggression, isolationism, egoism on the grand scale — signifies a like-mindedness and intimacy, growing out of common territory, language, race, tradition, and a hundred other causes all of which increase the likelihood that a national government will express the wills, and understand the interests, of its people. It is improbable that internationalism would have reached even its present imperfect stage of development had it not been for nationalism. The next forward step in political organization is not to destroy or thwart nationalism, even if that were possible, but to support it while at the same time adapting itself to the requirements of internationalism.

If universal polity is to work with and not against nationalism it must assume a federal rather than a monolithic form. The requirements of international polity will take precedence of the requirements of national polity, but will affect only a small fraction of national polity. There will be loyalties within loyalties, and the wider will be less pervasive than the narrower. The general maxim that government should be permissive rather than enabling will apply in an increasing degree as its spheres enlarge. There will be a world polity which frames world policy and imposes it, if needs be enforces it, upon any fraction of the world; but this policy and control will be so devised as to leave the greatest possible latitude to the self-direction of the national members. It will concern itself with facilities by which nations and private interests may coöperate, and above all it will provide a broad frame of security within which nations and private interests can fearlessly conduct their own affairs. International polity, like all liberal polity, will be an organization in which men unite in order to create the opportunity to differ amicably.

A liberal world polity will promote and not annul the liberality of its constituent nation states. It will not through attention to national governments encourage these to be deaf to the protests of the persons and groups which they in turn are bound to serve. In short, a world polity, if it is to serve its moral purpose, must be liberal, both directly and indirectly. From the top to the bottom of the political hierarchy it is the individual and his interests that finally count. So as polity arises from self-rule to national rule, and from national rule to super-national rule, it must perpetually look back to its personal members both for the refreshment of its rightful sovereignty and for the distribution of its benefits.

10

The origin of war is no mystery. There is no need of tracing it to any peculiar instinct, or of imputing it to a law of history, or a fall from grace. A war is merely a big quarrel, and it is not difficult to account for quarrels. There is no human interest which may not bring men into conflict, and no conflict that may not break into violence. War is on the broader view unreasonable; and the greater its costs the more unreasonable. But this does not make it inexplicable since it is characteristic of men that they do not take the broader view and count the ultimate costs. Over and above the tendency of any interest to assert itself regardless of the cost, and the tendency of two interests to assert themselves regardless of the cost to both, there is the tendency of each interest to anticipate the other's ruthlessness and to initiate violence as a measure of protection. The difficult thing is not to explain the occurrence of war, but to justify it. It is a direct violation of the moral principle of harmony — in short, war *is* moral evil, and peace *is* moral good.[6]

The moral evil of war does not consist merely in the injury inflicted on the external enemy. It is an internal evil. Of all the collective passions which inhibit reflection and blind men to their several interests the fever of war is the most blinding. For the manifold economic and cultural values of individuals and groups it may substitute the unsubstantial and

---

[6] It is evident that the view here presented resembles that of Hobbes without Hobbes's egoism (either psychological or moral), and without his political absolutism: the state of war is the essence of moral evil; the first maxim of morality is "seek peace"; the moral virtues are the dispositions or modes of behavior which are conducive to peace.

transitory value of "glory," and even this is enjoyed by a small fraction of those who pay the cost. It sharply abridges the domestic liberties. By forcing the entire population to the single occupation of war it narrows or destroys every personal choice, and thus arrests or reverses the growth of liberality.

Despite the fact that war in itself is flagrantly contrary to the moral ideal, it may partake of morality. It illustrates the tragic irony that morality within limits may serve as a means to immorality beyond. Loyalty to the country's safety or even to its aggression may cause persons and groups to be less sordid, less egoistic, irresponsible, quarrelsome among themselves, than in time of peace. But when the narrower unselfishness strengthens the broader selfishness, the greater evil outweighs the lesser good.

The waging of war today, because it is apparently the only means to the enjoyment of peace tomorrow and thereafter, affords the most signal example of interim morality. But if war is to be justified as a regrettable necessity imposed by the ulterior purpose of peace the necessity must in fact be a necessity, every peaceful alternative having been considered and tried. And if the necessity is to be construed as regrettable it must be in fact regretted, that is, subordinated to the love of peace, that love being kept alive in the heart, ready to resume full control whenever circumstances permit. This puts a severe strain on human sincerity. Pious protestations of peace may mask imperialistic appetites. But that it is not impossible to combine war with a sincere desire for peace, is illustrated by those who, like Lincoln or Woodrow Wilson, wage war with firmness but without gladness, suffering within themselves the conflict between the ideal good and the means which they find themselves compelled to employ.

Threatening war in order to prevent war, or making war to end war, is psychologically treacherous, but it is not morally contradictory. Harmonious happiness as a goal to be achieved by the organization of nations and mankind, may at a given time be better served by present violence than by evasion or submission. When, and how far, this is the case is a material question, depending on the existing situation and on the available possibilities of effective action. Morality dictates the broad principle that evil when used shall be used for good ends; combining insistence that it shall never be used except for good ends with due regard to the danger that by using it the good end may be forgotten, the good will corrupted, or some better end defeated.

Diplomacy may be judged by the same standards as war, when it is, as it often is, a kind of war — a war of words or nerves, a war of intrigue, deception, and veiled threats. Diplomacy in this sense is, like war, at best a morally regrettable necessity. But there is another sense in which diplomacy is itself a moral process — of the very essence of the morality;

namely, the sense of discussion with a view to agreement. Diplomacy is then, like collective bargaining, a process of reflective agreement — a meeting of minds, each of which is the trustee of interests; but at the same time sympathetic with rival interests and capable in some degree of both magnanimity and impartiality.

11

Political technology consists of judgments borrowed from any branch of knowledge and shaped to a political use. All human knowledge is available for political use, and because of the great complexity and range of political action, there is no branch of knowledge which may not serve some political use. The political arts are served by a knowledge of nature and of human nature, all the way from rules of thumb to nuclear physics and psychoanalysis. They are served by a knowledge of men's acquired interests and forms of social organization; not only political organization itself, but non-political organization — whether family, school, church, economy, law, fine art, or science. An all-wise and superlatively skillful maker, director, and enforcer of polity requires so vast an equipment that men have identified him with deity or with some human person or class of persons inspired by deity. In the long run, however, men have preferred their own imperfect mastery of the political arts to dogmatic or mystical abdication. For deity or its agents they have substituted the staff of experts.

The malodorous term 'Machiavellian' signifies that political expertness is relative to the use to which it is put. The original of this name gave advice to an Italian prince, actual and supposititious, who desired to achieve and maintain power. Like any consultant he adapted his advice to the interest of his client; and he suffered the reputation of any expert, whether military strategist, psychologist, lawyer, or professional politician, who is employed for a specific purpose, and who is worthy of his hire regardless of the worthiness of that for which he is hired.

The fact that political success may be achieved on the low level of the narrowest self-seeking and rankest demagoguery, must not be allowed to obscure the fact that politics on its highest level also requires mastery of its appropriate tools. Ideal polity, that is, polity whose instrumentalities of government are strong, durable, and representative, which is faithful to its moral purpose, enlightened, liberal, and universal, requires more and not less technique than the unsound and perverted polity which is unfortunately called "politics."

The very difficulties with which political action is in the present age beset confirms the basic truth that polity is an organization contrived by men to realize their interests, and not a pre-existing organism or mere historical legacy. The almost insuperable obstacles with which men are confronted in its making and remaking prove that polity is man-made, and neither natural nor divine; and at the same time reveal the way in which it must be made if it is to be well made. If polity is to be well made it will strain all human capacities to their utmost, including, at the present time, the untried capacity of the human mind to extend itself beyond the accustomed limits of the nation-state.

But there is no third alternative: either despair and surrender; or patient effort, embracing larger and larger circles of men and extending over as many years, decades, and centuries as may be required to execute the task. The fact that government when instituted is liable to its own characteristic failures, abuses, and shortcomings, should not be allowed to obscure the fact that government is in principle the best friend of every man — his ultimate insurance, indispensable, even when it is his last, resort.

CHAPTER XIV

LAW AND JURISPRUDENCE

Law, like polity, is one of those familiar things which are rarely defined, and, like polity, it touches human life at all points. The difficulty of definition is here aggravated by the fact that, while polity is clearly a cultural institution, law belongs also to the realm of nature. Nor is this merely an accident of verbal usage: there is a community of meaning.

The search for this broader meaning in terms of which the laws of physics and the laws of society, the laws of God and the laws of man, are all "laws," carries us back to a basic distinction of thought, and, if thought be taken to reflect the character of what is thought about, then to a basic distinction within being itself. The interpretation of this distinction has divided philosophers from the earliest times because, while they differ in what they make of it, they cannot ignore it. The distinction in question is the distinction between the universal and the particular. The concrete persons, things, objects, or events, which occur uniquely or only once, and which in their aggregate constitute nature and history, fall into kinds or classes of similars. That which is *perceived* in its particularity can be *conceived* in its generality — in diverse generalities, and in a series of broadening generalities.

The relation between the particular and the universal can be taken in either of two aspects, both of which it actually presents. It can be taken in the aspect of subsumption, and used for purposes of classification; or it can be taken in the aspect of determination, and used for purposes of explanation. The particular belongs to its universal; and it is thus correct to say of any particular that it is a certain general; as when we say of Socrates that he is a "man." But the universal possesses its particular; and it is then also correct to say of any general that it prescribes what its particulars shall be or do; as when we say that "man" manifests itself in

Socrates. These statements are not symmetrical: man is not a Socrates; nor is Socrates manifested in man.

We have already reached the point at which the term 'law' and kindred terms can be introduced without violation of usage. Taken in the second of its aspects, the relation of particular and universal can be expressed by saying that the universal controls, governs, regulates, or *is a law of,* its particulars.

But universals are also related to other universals, and particulars are related to other particulars through their common or related universals. Thus the universal teacher is related to the universal pupil; and this relation will hold of Socrates and Plato. If these particulars are correctly conceived then they can be counted on to be and to behave as the concept and related concepts require, regardless of their other characteristics and regardless of varying and changing circumstances. If Socrates was indeed a teacher, and if Plato was indeed his pupil, then no matter what other conditions may have affected either party or the relations between them, Socrates will have formed the mind of Plato. It is the aspect of the situation expressed by the terms 'regardless,' and 'no matter what,' which constitutes the element of constraint in law. The particular cannot escape its universal; those of its characteristics which fall outside its universal are helpless to prevent.

Taken in respect of their connecting threads of universality, particular things and events compose an "order." Nature is an order, and the knowledge of its orderliness is the knowledge of its laws. The laws of nature consist of the relations of the universals which are particularized in the existing things and events which are not of man's making; the formulations of these laws by the knowing mind constitute the "scientific laws," such as the laws of physics and chemistry. The law of nature belongs to nature, the scientific law belongs to culture.

But culture like nature has its laws. Human artifacts are particulars of universals, and are related and describable in terms of *their* universals. They are not usually mathematically describable — at least in terms of any mathematics as yet available. But there are laws, however incompletely discovered, which determine human affairs, and these are the laws with which the cultural sciences are concerned insofar as they employ the explanatory method.

It is evident that some term is required by which to distinguish laws which "belong to" the realms of nature and culture from the scientific laws by which they are known and formulated. The term 'law of nature' will not suffice since there are also "laws of culture." They may be designated as the real, operative, actual, governing, or "determining" laws. They are related to scientific laws as an event is related to the idea of it. In proportion as the idea is true it will become identical with the event.

Similarly, in proportion as the scientific law is true it will become indistinguishable from the law of nature or of culture of which it is true.

2

Jural law, the subject matter of jurisprudence, is determining law which shares with all law the general character of binding particulars through their universals. Its distinguishing character lies in its being both a law of wills and a law by wills. It is voluntary both in the application and in the making. The resulting order is self-imposed.

Men are bound by jural law, and conform to it by their choosing, that is, through the balancing and integration of their interests. This does not mean that they do *not* conform; if they did not there would be no order. Choosing is not to be defined by its vagaries and irregularities; choosing the same is not less a choosing than is choosing the different. When men choose the true or the good it is to be expected that their choices will agree. The supposition that difference rather than sameness is evidence of will means only that when men agree voluntarily their sameness is *not* due to certain other causes, such as habit or imitation, by which it is more easily and more commonly brought about.

A jural order, then, is an order in which the universality of the members consists in the universality of their wills. The stars in their courses obey the laws of astronomy, but they do not choose to do so. Thus, if Joshua, instead of commanding the sun and moon to stand still, had commanded them to move in their orbits, and if they had then obeyed from choice, their laws of motion would have become jural laws. If, as on the creationist hypothesis, the laws of celestial bodies were imposed on them by God, these laws would not be jural laws unless it is assumed that the planets had to be persuaded to obey them. Observance of the jural law has to be induced. It operates through choosing; its being universally chosen is what brings it into being.

The second characteristic of jural law is that it is made not only *of* men but *by* men. The jural law is in society in the same sense as the law of nature is in nature; but it is *put into* society. Men adopt by choice the law which they obey by choice; and they adopt it for what seem to them good reasons. In other words, jural law is for something, and it is made for that something. It has a function — which is to introduce *regularity* into human life. A jural law, is a system of universals — such as voter, citizen, property-holder, taxpayer, husband and wife, landlord and tenant, plaintiff and defendant, creditor and debtor, and countless others — which are exemplified in the particular members of a society; and which, when the members are thus conceived, renders their conduct predictable. Insofar as men live lawfully they are dependable, not as automatons, but as beings who act from choice.

This is the primary and immediate function of law. When this function is exercised, the law is; and an explanatory jurisprudence will seek to discover how it comes to pass. The fuller examination of this function will disclose the instrumental or purely legal criteria of law, and at the same time will lead on to the disclosure of its ultimate moral purpose.

3

That law is intimately related to polity is evident — so evident that the two are often identified, to the confusion of both. The public agencies of law are a part of the frame of government. The legislative and judicial branches of government make law, and the executive branch of government administers law. Law, like the decisions of government, is enforced, and when it is enforced, it is the political authority which serves as the agency of the enforcement. But however much law and government are thus intermingled in actual social organization, their essential ideas are nevertheless distinguishable. If this were not so it would be meaningless to speak of "government by law"; which implies at least the theoretical possibility of government without law. There is a similar possibility of law without government.

Polity without law is what is called "personal government."[1] There has presumably never been a government wholly without laws, but such a government is definable as a government in which the government is itself above or beyond the law, or in which it governs by edicts (such as "bills of attainder" or "private bills") addressed only to particular persons. When a ruler's authority is itself generalized so that it can be assumed by a succession of "legitimate" rulers, the government is a "legal" or "constitutional" government, and when it is addressed to categories of persons which can be exemplified by many particular individuals, it is a government by law.

The idea that there can be no law without polity is argued, first, from the fact that if law is to be obeyed by choice it has to be known. From this it is supposed to follow that it has to be promulgated and commanded by the head of state. But however commonly this occurs, it is not necessary. Customary law is not promulgated from any central seat of authority, but is made known to each individual by his own social conscience. It is communicated from next to next by suggestion or tradition, or by literature, monuments, or symbols. So important is this way of knowing the law that it has led some social philosophers to derive all law from custom; and other philosophers to affirm that the fundamentals of law are revealed to each individual by the "natural light" of reason. Even when law is promulgated, it need not be promulgated by the political authority: it may be promulgated by seers, by "sacred" books, such

---

[1] "We must not rend our subjects from our laws
And stick them in our will. . . ." Shakespeare, *Henry VIII*, Act I, Scene 2.

as the Koran or the Scriptures, or by a priestly authority speaking in the name of God. And when promulgated by a central authority, whether political or non-political, it need not, though it usually does, assume the form of command. It may be hortatory rather than imperative, or it may be declaratory, with little or no emotional intonation.

The argument most commonly employed to prove the dependence of law on polity is the requirement of enforcement. If law is to confer on society the benefit of order and regularity it must be generally observed; without assurance of its observance by others, there is no reason why an individual should submit to it. Human nature being what it is, he cannot possess that assurance without a guarantee. During a recent meat shortage the mayor of New York issued a "plea" for a "conservation Monday" to be observed by the restaurants. The newspapers reported that many restaurants ignored the plea, and that the others complained; or, as the headlines ran, THOSE WHO HEED IT IRKED. SPOKESMAN SAYS OBSERVANCE MUST BE GENERAL OR PLAN SHOULD BE DISCARDED.[2] The implication was that the rule should be enforced by penalties; otherwise there would be no public advantage and those who did observe it would be placed at a disadvantage by their own observance. The same reasoning applies throughout the entire range of law from this more trivial level all the way to the laws governing men's most sacred liberties and rights. So to the primary law, or law of first intent, there is annexed law of second intent — a penal law, which provides that all who break the primary law shall be made to suffer.

Thus the penal law prescribes that the murderer shall be executed or imprisoned for life. The primary law prescribes that men shall respect one another's lives and avoid injury to each other, so that all may go about their business unarmed and enjoying a sense of bodily security. Owing to the violence of hate or the temptation to profit by another's removal, men will still, despite the beneficence of the law and the precepts of conscience, occasionally take one another's lives. Murder is exceptional, but one murderous individual at large in the community is sufficient to create a panic. Hence there is a secondary law imposing a severe penalty on the hypothetical murderer who now "knows what to expect"; those who *define* law in terms of enforcement would then be obliged to say that there is no law *for* bodily security, but only a law *against* murder; no law of the innocent but only of the guilty — than which nothing could be more fantastic and illogical. For the penal law derives its meaning from non-penal law. If there were no law to break there would be no lawbreaker to punish.

Punishment, or threat of punishment — punishment by school, by parents, by church, by God, by social disapproval, or by government — is evidence of the law's failure and not of its success. It is an instrument

[2] *New York Times*, February 6, 1945.

for dealing with lawlessness: the more punishment the less law. Punishment is an auxiliary buttress which proves the weaknesses of the legal structure. In an ideal legal order, that is, a society which was legally perfected, no sanctions would be necessary; it would be *"law-abiding."* Men would choose not only obedience of the law, but the law which they would obey.[3]

It should now be possible to answer the question, "When can there be said to *be* a law?" There are several answers to this question. The jural law is, in the first and most fundamental sense, when it is obeyed: when it actually regulates human conduct — when men conform to it and when, therefore, their voluntary action is predictable. But it may also be said to be when it is promulgated. In these two cases the law becomes a part of the description of a historical event, the act of obeying it or the act of affirming it. But there is a common factor in these two acts — namely, the law as it is conceived, or the law as idea or meaning. This is the corpus of the law, or the code, which may or may not be recorded. It is *what* the lawmaker wills or intends, the "decision" which the court affirms. It is the "objective" law, in the sense in which the term 'problematic' has already been introduced in defining the object of interest.

But while the law in this last and abstract sense does not *exist* in itself, it *is* in itself, that is, one can say that it is what it is, or that "there is" such a law. It can be interpreted, compared with other laws, judged by precedents, inferred from other laws, taken as the premise from which other laws are deduced, and applied in the adjudication of particular cases. This is the formal, and relatively static aspect of the law, which is emphasized by the "analytical" school of jurisprudence.

4

Law may be discovered or "found" in two senses. Its conceptual content may be explained in its own terms and compared with the content of other conceptual law. It has, in other words, its abstract morphology, as when one compares one set of marriage laws with another. Or law may be found where and when it is made, uttered, promulgated, commanded, enforced, or observed. Emphasis on law as it is observed — that is, on determining law, underlies the contention that a law

---

[3] For the classic statement of this view, cf. the following passage from Kant: "A constitution allowing *the greatest possible human freedom* in accordance with laws by which *the freedom of each is made to be consistent with that of all others* . . . is . . . a necessary idea, which must be taken as fundamental not only in first projecting a constitution but in all its laws. . . . The more legislation and government are brought into harmony with the above idea, the rarer would punishments become, and it is therefore quite rational to maintain, as Plato does, that in a perfect state no punishments whatsoever would be required." (*Critique of Pure Reason*, tr. by N. Kemp Smith, Copyright 1933, p. 312; reprinted by permission of the Macmillan Company.)

is finally identified with its interpretation by the courts. It is impossible to know precisely what a law is until its application is decided, and those who make the decisions then make the laws. A considerable body of law, such as the common law, begins with judicial decisions, and is afterward generalized, systematized and codified. This is what is meant by speaking of "court-made law." Through its making and through its observance law takes its place in the stream of existence, and is influenced by existing conditions. The examination of these conditions constitutes the explanatory part of the science of jurisprudence.

The modern insistence on the explanatory method signifies an antecedent neglect not of the conditions of law altogether, but of certain *kinds* of conditions. The doctrines that the law was given to man by God through Moses, or that it has been created by the political ruler, or by the courts, or by conscience, or by reason, have been found inadequate because the law has so many other conditions.

Law as an historical product [4] reflects all of the factors and forces which enter into human life. It reflects human nature in its original and inescapable social characteristics, and social development in all its broader phases. It is conditioned by man's irrational propensities, his instincts, habits, emotions, appetites, and prejudices, and not merely by his higher faculties of conscience and reason. It corresponds to the diverse forms of social structure. It is influenced by the political, economic, domestic, educational, and religious forces exerted by its sister-institutions, and by the scientific or artistic characteristics of that concrete culture of which it forms a part. And law has its internal, legal, as well as its extra-legal, conditions. This adds up to the summary conclusion that jural law does not dwell in a world apart, but is embedded in a social and historical context.

The acceptance of the explanatory method in jurisprudence must be guarded against two improper inferences. Because legal institutions are historical, it does not follow, as has sometimes been affirmed by the so-called "historical school," that they are merely historical — devoid of conceptual content and purposeless. Historical jurisprudence is not to be argued against analytical and normative jurisprudence, but as a supplement which provides answers to a different question.

In the second place, the recognition of the irrational causes of law does not exclude rational causes. There is a natural but indefensible tendency to suppose that because the lucid intervals of reason are rare, or are contaminated by unreason, they are therefore ineffectual. Just as those who have wished to exalt the law have tended to dwell excessively upon its more august connections — so their critics have fallen into the opposite error of dwelling excessively upon its less respectable connec-

---

[4] This shift of emphasis in jurisprudence, as in political science, is due largely to Sir Henry Maine. Cf. his classic *Lectures on the Early History of Institutions*, 1875.

tions. This tendency to give excessive weight to whatever has a flavor of scandal, appears in recent explanations of constitutional law in terms of the personal characteristics or bias of judges — as though because judges are often motivated so there is no such thing as a judicial mind. Similarly the explanation of "due process" by the interest of the propertied classes is true insofar as it does explain; but this does not imply that there is no principle of due process — no objective meaning and norm on which disinterested judges can agree, and by which they can be guided.

5

The law taken as itself a standard provides for normative judgments which may apply to any person or act falling within its jurisdiction. The great body of legal judgments are of this type. Judged by the conceptual law as it is, what men do is either legal or illegal; that is, agrees or disagrees with the law. Normative jurisprudence, however, is concerned not with applications of the law, but with the law itself — to the effect that it is good or bad. As in the case of polity, so also in the case of law, the institution may be appraised in its own instrumental terms; or in ulterior terms, including its external appraisal by the standards of other institutions, and its internal appraisal by that moral standard which it shares with conscience, polity, and economy.

The first of the instrumental requirements of law is that it shall be obeyed. When law is disobeyed with a frequency that destroys the mutual confidence of those who nominally live under it, then law ceases to fulfill its function of regularity and predictability. It is bad law, in the sense of weakness and inefficiency. The law "breaks down."

Disobedience of the law may be ascribed to the refractoriness of those to whom it applies, but the probability of its being obeyed is a criterion of the law itself. Law may be bad law because of failing to take sufficient account of human nature or of the strength of human sentiments. Law must be capable of being observed and also, when necessary, of being enforced. This requirement has been brought to public attention by the experience of "sumptuary legislation" in which the law has proved an ineffective instrument for controlling certain powerful human appetites, such as the consumption of alcoholic beverages. When a law is unenforceable it may put a premium upon the very practices which it is designed to prevent; and beget new forms of crime.[5] There is, in short, an economy of law, lest it undertake more than it can effectually achieve. Excess of lawmaking may not only overburden the agencies of law, but

---

[5] It has been alleged that "in five short years the Capones of our cities took over the billion-dollar rackets growing out of four specific prohibitions: the Harrison Narcotic Act, the Volstead Act, Legislation outlawing Prostitution, Legislation outlawing Gambling"; D. P. Wilson, *My Six Convicts*, 1951, p. 329.

through the spread of disobedience develop a resentment of the law's intrusiveness, and a general habit of disobedience and disrespect.

The usefulness of a judicial order, like that of the order of nature, consists in its implications for tomorrow. Nature can be counted on to remain what it is long enough for the desired consequences of action to accrue. The jural order, unlike the order of nature, is a part of human history. It is a succession of orders, and not a changeless order; if it were not a succession of orders, it would not be capable of correction and growth. But there is a minimum of change, beyond which it cannot exercise its function of making human conduct predictable: legal changes may result in no constancy, no dependability, and hence no possibility of long-range plans. The rules of a game need to be changed, but if they are too frequently changed it is impossible to play the game.

For similar reasons law may be praised or condemned according as it is or is not consistent with other law within the same area of jurisdiction. New law must be consistent with old — if a man is to "know where he stands." It is a defect of the law that the divorce laws of the several states should be in conflict, since they apply to citizens of the United States who move freely from one area to another within its boundaries. A society whose laws are unstable or conflicting is as anarchical as a society which has no laws.

The law may fail to do its job through the very proliferation of its instruments. It may fail through its complexities and delays, or through its procedural clumsiness. It may fail through its rigidity — a hardening of its arteries — its inertia, its substitution of the letter for the spirit. The law consists in its meaning and not in the words in which it is recorded and communicated. Words in themselves are never a perfect vehicle of meaning, because meaning depends on context. The words may remain when the original context has been forgotten and no new context has been introduced to give them fresh meaning.

The law through its mechanisms may become mechanized and over-mechanized. It may also fail through the inability of individuals, whom it is designed to serve and to protect, to invoke it. The jury system, the idea of presumptive innocence, the right to be represented by an attorney, the cross-examination of witnesses, and all the ritual of public trial, are designed to safeguard the individual against the law's arbitrariness or dictatorship. The costs of litigation are notorious, and often prohibitive.[6]

6

A legal system may be judged externally by any non-legal interest or institution. Such criticism of the law may lie upon any level from the

---

[6] For an excellent presentation of this general topic, cf. A. T. Vanderbilt, *Men and Measures in the Law*, 1949. Cf. also, M. Radin, *The Law and You*, 1948.

self-interest of an individual or class to the higher norms of conscience, polity, economy, science, art, religion, and education. He who condemns the law because it forbids his doing what he would like to do or forces him to do what he is disinclined to do, is judging it normatively. When a man condemns the tax law, as men usually do, because he dislikes to pay to the public treasury what he might otherwise spend on himself, or condemns a draft law because he dislikes the risks and sacrifices of military service, or condemns the food regulations because he has a taste for meat and butter, his judgment is likely to be true on *his* grounds: the objection is to the grounds he takes.

The existing legal system is open to criticism in terms of the prevailing conscience. The law of capital punishment or the laws of war may be condemned because they violate the widespread sentiment of humanity. This is the characteristic normative judgment of the so-called "pacifist" who takes the precept of non-violence as his standard. There is no doubt that the law *does* reflect the existing social conscience. When the Mormon practice of polygamy was prohibited by law, the decision did not rest on arguments for monogamy. It was sufficient that polygamy should be deemed an open offense "against the enlightened sentiment of mankind," where 'enlightened sentiment' meant the sentiment prevailing in the United States in the year 1889.[7] Similarly, the legal prohibition of nudism, indecent exposure, drunkenness, profanity, and irregular sex relations does not rest on judgments concerning the hygienic or social effects of such practices. It is sufficient that they should offend the prevailing social conscience, even when they are supported by a sectarian or cultist conscience of their own.

The ultimate connection of law and polity leads to a critique of law on political grounds. The approval of law as an instrument of government — of government by law — is such a judgment. There is a perpetual exchange of critical judgments between the maker of public policy who complains of the law's delays or anachronisms, and the exponent of law who complains of the haste and opportunism of the executive or legislature. The existing legal system may be judged by its consistency or inconsistency with a particular political standard, as when the laws regulating suffrage are condemned as violations of democracy when they are too exclusive, or as violations of aristocracy when they are too inclusive.

The exponent of a particular economic system finds grounds for praise or condemnation of the law. Thus if he is an exponent of laissez-faire capitalism he will think well of a legal system which emphasizes property and inheritance, and ill of a legal system which "interferes with business." An advocate of a socialistic economy, on the other hand, will

[7] Latter Day Saints vs. U.S., *U.S. Reports, 136* (1889), p. 50.

complain of a traditional legal system as a bulwark of capitalism, and advocate laws which regulate business and provide for a "planned economy."

The law may be judged by the scientist. An anarchical society is as repugnant to him as chance and chaos in nature. He will look to the law to protect his freedom of inquiry and perhaps subsidize research; or he will deprecate such regulations as make science dependent and create a scientific bureaucracy. Order is one of the qualifying attributes of aesthetic enjoyment, and a law-abiding society may be deemed beautiful or pleasing to contemplate. The artist, like the scientist, may judge the law in terms of his vocation — demand legal privileges, or resent legal restrictions.

The law may be judged from the standpoint of education. Public education, in its modern developments, invokes the compulsion of law; private education may complain of such compulsion or of its exclusively secular character. Similarly the law may be appraised in terms of religion, as promoting, or failing to promote, religion in general or any particular religious cult. Such judgments may vary all the way from a theocratic demand that the law shall be subordinated to religious dogma and worship, or that a church shall be "established," to the protests of those who would tolerate any and all religions and confine legal control to the guarantee of religious freedom.

7

The final internal critique of the law is its moral critique. It takes as a standard that moral purpose which law shares with conscience and polity and economy. A decision of the United States Supreme Court supports this view, though in language somewhat different from that here employed: "The function of jurisprudence is to resolve the conflict of opposing rights and interests by applying in default of a specific provision of law, the corollaries of general principles." [8]

The immediate and specific function of law is to create an orderly society. But something more may properly be demanded of it; it is the business of law not only to create order but to create a morally beneficent order. There are two distinct questions that it is proper to ask of law: "Is it good *law?*" and "Is it *good* law?" This distinction is of grave importance. Without it legal conformity is likely to be substituted for morality; and law itself is likely to become static and arbitrary, for lack

[8] N. J. vs. Delaware, *U.S. Reports*, 29 (1934), p. 384, note 7. Those authorities in jurisprudence who reject or play down the moral principle of the law appear to accept it under another name. Thus Justice Oliver Wendell Holmes: "I think that the judges themselves have failed adequately to recognize their duty of weighing considerations of social advantage." Qu. in Max Lerner, *The Mind and Faith of Justice Holmes*, 1943, p. 81. Cf. *ibid.*, pp. 76, 396–7.

of a principle by which old law can be revised and new law rationally created.

The ulterior moral purpose of the law is revealed at the point where law is created: when a decision is made as to what law shall be created, or why one law should be created rather than another, or, fundamentally, why there should be any law at all. There are many such points, official and unofficial. An informal group of persons may agree among themselves on the adoption of a set of rules to govern their behavior one to another. A parent, tribal head, priest, teacher, elder, or king, may act in a judicial capacity, that is, be called upon to settle disputes or grievances; and insofar as his decision serves as a precedent and defines general rules applicable to similar situations he is a maker of law. Statutory law, that is, the law created by legislatures, arises similarly from translating policy into rules.[9] In all of these situations the nature of the problem and of its successful solution is similar. The ultimate reason for having law is that it removes conflict, and enables men to live at peace with their neighbors; or enables them to coöperate, that is, live happily and fruitfully with their neighbors. This is the "why" of the law in general, and of laws in particular; it serves as the principle by which law is justified, and by which, when it is not justified as it stands, it is revised.

There is nothing revolutionary, or even new, in the moral interpretation of law. Law is traditionally associated with moral ideas such as justice, rights, and equity.[10] In some languages it is named for these ideas. This is not a verbal accident. It is the purpose of law to provide justice and to define rights.

'Justice' means the morally right allotment of the benefits of social organization or of its penalties. It does not mean *any* allotment, for an allotment, in the moral sense of the term, is that which is prescribed by the principle of harmonious happiness. The judgment of Solomon would, if possible, send both disputants away happy. The term 'rights' in general

---

[9] Historically speaking, of course, there is no society without law — as is the case with all the major institutions. The creation of law in general, *de novo*, can be described only hypothetically, in terms of the motives which *would* impel men to make law if they did not already have it.

[10] It is well in this context to recall the words of Magna Carta: "To no one will We sell, to none will We deny or defer, right or justice." For present purposes the term equity need not be separately examined. It is sometimes used as synonymous with justice, or with the fundamental moral principles of the law; sometimes to designate the special jurisdiction of the English "Court of Chancery," which was originally designed to correct the "injustices" resulting from the law's rigidity. Cf. J. B. Ames, *Lectures on Legal History*, 1913, pp. 233–4: "Equity lays the stress upon the duty of the defendant, and decrees that he do or refrain from doing a certain thing because he ought to act or forbear. It is because of this emphasis upon the defendant's duty that equity is so much more ethical than law." There is a famous passage in Aristotle's *Rhetoric*, in which he says that "equity is a kind of justice, but goes beyond the written law." *Rhetoric,* tr. by R. C. Jebb, 1909, p. 58.

signifies a recognized sphere within which a person acts and may enjoy the liberty of acting upon his interest unmolested. But a justice of the United States Supreme Court has referred to such liberties as "privileges long recognized in common law as *essential to the orderly pursuit of happiness by free men*." [11] The term 'rights' is correctly borrowed from the moral vocabulary because a right must be *right*. The claim of a right rests on the assumption that the system of rights of which it is a part serves the good of the total community, that is, the moral good. It is an adjustment of each to the requirements of the whole. In this consists the rightness of rights, namely, their justice.

The number of rights is in principle limitless. It reflects the advancing complexity of human culture, the division and specialization of human activities, and the increasing stress on the individual. Potentially there are as many rights as there are interests, provided these interests are sufficiently general and sufficiently insistent to require that the social order shall recognize them and explicitly provide for them. Insofar as rights are guaranteed by the public authority their number is determined by the "limitations upon effective legal action." [12]

The current distinction between "property rights" and "human rights" is misleading. All rights are human rights. Property has no rights, but persons have limited rights to *possess*. The antithesis of human to property rights has no meaning except as a protest against undue emphasis on this right to possess what one has, and to accumulate and bequeath possessions, to the neglect of other rights, such as the right of free speech or the right to education.

The drafting of new lists of rights for the purpose of international organization attests to their increasing number and variety. Thus a "Bill of Human Rights" proposed in 1946 by the Commission to Study the Organization of Peace, included the following rights as applying to all persons "without distinction as to race, sex, language or religion," and as limited "by the rights of others and by the just requirements of the democratic state": protection of life and liberty under law; freedom of conscience and belief; freedom of religious and other forms of association; religious teaching, practice and worship; forming and holding of opinions; receiving opinions and information; freedom of expression through all means of communication; peaceable assembly; petition for redress of grievances; participation in government; freedom from searches, seizures, and other interferences with person, home, reputation, privacy, activities, and property; fair and prompt public trial when charged with criminal or civil liabilities; conviction and punishment only under domestic laws in

---

[11] Quoted by C. Warren, "The New 'Liberty' under the 14th Amendment," *Harvard Law Review*, 39 (1925–6), p. 454 (italics mine).

[12] R. Pound, "Interests of Personality," *Harvard Law Review*, 28 (1914–5), p. 344.

effect at the time of the alleged offense; freedom from arbitrary arrest or detention; education; social security; stability of employment under proper conditions and with standardized compensation.[13]

There have been various proposals for the classification of rights. A contemporary jurist of the sociological school classifies the interests which rights are designed to protect under the heads of "interests of personality," "public interests," and "social interests."[14] Public interests are those of the state considered as a "juristic person"; and "social interests" are those of the "community at large." This classification does not contradict a fundamentally individualistic conception of rights if it be admitted that the state and the community are composed of persons. Other proposed classifications distinguish between "substantive" and "procedural" rights, and between "civil," "political," "economic," and "social" rights.[15] While no such classifications are conclusive they illustrate the thesis that wherever there is an interest there is a potential right, provided only that it satisfies the principle of equality and the criterion of expediency.

While all such classifications are more or less arbitrary, there is one distinction which has the double merit of emphasizing the recent trend toward the multiplication of rights and of revealing their essentially moral purpose. Rights are *permissive*, meaning that certain interested activities *may* be pursued, or are *enabling*, meaning that certain interested activities *can* be pursued. The permissive rights guarantee noninterference, and entrust the fulfillment of interests to the existing private resources of the persons interested. Certain of these permissive rights are universal or "inalienable": the right to "life," the right to control the movements of one's own body ("liberty"), and the right to such happiness as is attainable by one's own efforts ("the pursuit of happiness"). They are "inalienable" in the sense that they constitute those values of the person short of which no social organization whatever is justified.

Enabling rights, on the other hand, require that the public shall provide private persons with resources by which their permissive rights become effective; and include such rights as the rights of education, and health, or the right to a job — rights of the type characteristic of a comparatively collective society. It is the inclusion of enabling rights, or the claim that all rights are enabling in some degree, that has led recent jurists to affirm for each right a corresponding duty on the part of organized society; as the right of education implies an obligation to provide

---

[13] *International Conciliation*, Carnegie Endowment for International Peace, New York, 1946. Cf. also the "Statement of Essential Human Rights," prepared by a committee of the American Law Institute, and published by Americans United for World Organization, Inc.

[14] R. Pound, *op. cit.*

[15] Cf. Q. Wright, *Human Rights and the World Order*, Commission to Study the Organization of Peace, New York.

schools, the right to health implies an obligation to provide hospitals and medical care, and the right to life implies an obligation to provide the means of subsistence.

This growing recognition of enabling rights is a characteristic feature of the present epoch even among societies which profess to reject collectivism in their fundamental ideology. It is generally acknowledged that the purpose of rights is to create opportunity, and not merely to fence off a space within which the person is left to himself. Whatever misgivings may be felt are justified on the ground that legal rights must be limited by what public institutions can and cannot do, or can do better than private agencies, or can do without destroying the incentive to private initiative and effort. In any case the acknowledgment of enabling rights implies that the fulfillment of private interests is a matter of public concern. It implies that the law is to be judged not merely by its setting bounds, but also by its promotion of interests *within* bounds — that is, has a duty not merely to peace, but also to welfare and prosperity.

8

There is a rightness of rights which do not yet have the force of law. It is necessary, in short, to recognize the claim of ideal rights as well as legal rights.

There are rights which ought to be, in advance of their embodiment in organized society. When rights such as women's rights were argued for, their proponents claimed that they had such rights, or a right to such rights — nor can this be attributed to mere naïveté. And the same is true of all law: it may be deduced, and correctly deduced, from the moral purpose, before it is "made law." Not only the adoption and the enactment of law, but the discussion of the merits of law, whether by courts or by legislatures, presupposes this distinction. The term 'higher law' has been used in jurisprudence to indicate such ideal law, or the law that ought to be, as distinguished from such law as is carried into effect. While jural law cannot be said to exist until it is realized in a social order (and this ordinarily implies promulgation and enforcement) it is deducible from moral premises in advance of being so realized.

It is customary to use the term 'positive law' to designate such law as exists or is realized in some historical society, and the "positivistic" doctrine of law is the untenable doctrine that there is no law but positive law.[16] Higher law, then, is law which satisfies, or would satisfy the requirements of morality, and which thus serves as a norm by which to judge the positive law.

---

[16] It is, of course, possible to reduce this question to a merely verbal question by choosing to confine the word 'law' to positive law, and to substitute such a term as 'legal principle' for ideal law. But this is highly unsatisfactory because the ideal law has the same justification as positive law, and need not be of a more general character, or play the role of a first premise, as is suggested by the term 'principle.'

"Natural law" as it appears in political and legal thought is a hybrid conception, but it is too ancient and persistent to be lightly dismissed. It is deeply rooted in pagan, Hebraic, and Christian thought, and is still widely accepted despite its repeated rejection. In various wordings and philosophical interpretations, this idea has consisted in the union of two statements: that there is a higher law which is entitled to overrule the positive law; and that this higher law is actually operative in the nature of things at large. It claims a double priority — moral and metaphysical, representing what ought to be in a world in which things are, in the last analysis, what they ought to be.

The doctrine of natural law is sound doctrine insofar as it admits an appeal beyond the positive to ideal law; and at the same time recognizes that the law's realization lies in its actual observance, and therefore requires that it shall be consistent with human nature and with the human environment. But because it unites these two ideas it is in unstable equilibrium; it tends to fall into either dogmatism or positivism: a dogmatic affirmation that what ought to be is, or a positivistic affirmation that what is ought to be. The first was the besetting sin of the eighteenth century, while the latter was the besetting sin of the naturalism and historicism of the nineteenth.

The way is thus paved for a doctrine which will escape both horns of this dilemma. There is an ideal law which defines a standard by which the *de facto* law may be normatively judged. But ideal law does not exist merely because it is ideal; it induces men to act in its behalf, but they may or may not succeed. Here, as elsewhere, endeavor is conditioned by the possibility of success. In the realm of law this faith expresses itself in the conceptual and imaginative representation of a perfected legal order in which the members would enjoy the benefits of justice, living peacefully and prosperously within their rights.

9

Law, like polity, may fail of its moral purpose through the infidelity or ignorance of its agents. Like polity, and unlike conscience, the law has its own specialized functionaries: judges, legislators, jurors, attorneys. The moral purpose of law requires that these agents shall hold this purpose firmly in mind, and not allow themselves to be deflected by their personal interests. Such infidelity is explicable, as is any form of bias, but it is not excusable. The agent of the law who allows his prejudice to color his judgment is an unfaithful servant of right and justice.

As the judge or the juror may allow his personal interests to displace his legal role so the lawyer may violate his code, however that may be defined. Assuming that it is the function of the lawyer to acquaint his client with the law — to enable him to obtain its benefits, and to protect him against the law's abuses — he may from the ardor of his partisanship or professional zeal teach his client how to evade the law. Or the prosecuting attorney in his eagerness to secure conviction, whether to enhance his reputation or simply because his combative instincts prompt him to defeat his opponent and "win his case," may act as the law's enemy rather than as its friend.

The weakness and ambiguity of the code of the lawyer and business man, as compared with the code of the medical profession, is a topic worthy of reflection. The physician sometimes sacrifices the cure to the fee, or loses sight of the health of the community in his preoccupation with a selected clientele, but since the time of Hippocrates the institution of medicine has on the whole been governed by a mandate to heal the sick. He is judged by his mandate both by his colleagues and by the community at large. The lawyer is less unambiguously devoted to the social purpose of law, and may be honored for the zeal with which he serves his client even when its effect is to promote wrong and injustice.

But the "upright judge" must also be the "learned" judge. Like the proverbial Daniel he merits his high office by wisdom and understanding, as well as by integrity. Orientation to the moral good is not sufficient. Solomon not only faced the problem objectively, but found a solution. Moral enlightenment is not to be identified with all forms of intellectual capacity. There are words such as 'sharp,' 'expert,' 'shrewd,' and 'clever,' which are commonly applied to agents of the law who exhibit intelligence on its lower levels; where its moral purpose is ignored, and it becomes "a combat of wits" in which the criterion of success is to "win the case."

10

The legal reformer, looking to the optimum legal system, will apply the principle of liberality. Morally speaking, order does not exist for the sake of order, but for the sake of the interests of the persons ordered. The restrictions imposed by the law are justified only by their benefits to the persons restricted. The burden of proof is on the restriction of interests; freedom is innocent until it is proven guilty. A society may be legally ordered at unjustifiable cost to the persons ordered; that is, when rights are negated beyond what is required by the like rights of all. This illiberality may be due to its inertia or rigidity. Prestige and tradition beget an idolatrous worship of the legal *status quo;* which, under the name of "The Law," or "Law and Order," may borrow the reverence which is due only to its benefits. Such causes work together to close the door to a fuller provision for interests.

The existing legal order may be illiberal owing to the influence exerted by those who profit from it unjustly. It is essential to the law that it should prescribe limits — that it should deny interests as well as affirm them; but at any given time in the course of human history this cost of the legal order is likely to be unevenly distributed among its beneficiaries, and those who pay least will be its friends. Paying least they acquire a power to prevent its revision in favor of those who pay most. The sick man who most needs health is most handicapped in the pursuit of it. To him who hath it shall be given.

As in polity so in law, there is a right of protest from those who demand a more liberal allowance and argue that it would be consistent with the requirements of a legal order in general. And there is a "moral right of revolution," that is, a right in extremity to resort to lawlessness. Revolution is illegal, by definition. The moral case against it does not lie in any absolute prohibition but in its costs, which are likely to outweigh, even to the least privileged, the gains of anarchy. What these costs are need not be urged in an age in which all mankind has suffered or observed them.

An ideal legal system will be a system possessing the maximum of liberality. In order that this maximum may be approximated without violent revolution, the legal system must be flexible; it must without loss of the essential benefits of order yield to the expansive pressure of interests. The house of law must not be built once and for all with an unalterable architecture, but must have movable partitions and be capable of new stories and wings, so that it may afford ever more roomy quarters.

It is this demand which creates the gravest difficulties in the restoration of order after war. Those whose interest is in domestic peace, and in rebuilding the mutual confidence between man and man which is the condition of all the mechanisms of daily life, and indirectly of food, clothing, health, transportation, and communication, become the exponents of order — order first, and at all costs. Those whose interest is in a more liberal order, being those who have hitherto suffered most from the illiberality of the old, are disposed to regard the post-war condition of anarchy as *opportunity* — and to profit by the fluidity of society in order to shape its future crystallization. To find the right balance between these counter-claims is beyond any man's impromptu wisdom. But one thing is clear, namely, that to advocate either legal *status quo* or anarchy without weighing the costs of both is to be blind to the meaning of law.

11

Finally, a legal order falls short of the optimum and is open to moral criticism when it fails to embrace all persons, or lacks all-inclusiveness. If law is good as between the persons of one society, it is also good as between the persons of different societies and between the organizations which represent them. From remote antiquity men have recognized that in principle law is human, and not merely domestic, tribal, racial, or national. This does not mean that all men should live under some law, but that there should be one system of law under which all men live.

The preoccupation of the present age with international law is due, in the first place, to the fact that from the earliest history of man the anarchy *between* social groups has been a running sore. Societies have to a large extent achieved and enjoyed internal order; but while this has promoted an understanding of the law and an appreciation of its benefits, it has often aggravated the evils of the large-scale disorder. It has enabled men within legally organized societies to live at peace, and to pool their efforts for the general good; but at the same time it has intensified the shock of intersocietal war and facilitated the conquest and exploitation of weak societies by the strong.

Meanwhile, in the second place, the development of the technical arts has multiplied the occasions of conflict and increased its destructiveness. Man has overrun the planet on which he lives, and men encounter each other everywhere throughout its diminishing surface. But since every encounter *may be* a quarrel, so the moral problem now occurs more frequently, and calls more frequently for solutions by the social institutions, such as law, which are designed for the purpose. International law has become not a mere logical implication or counsel of perfection but an imperative necessity.

The benefits of international law are parallel to those of domestic or municipal law. It enables, or would enable, men of different social groups, however otherwise divided, to trust one another abroad as well as at home, and engage together in long range, large-scale enterprise for the greater good of mankind at large. Rights of every type — civil and social, permissive and enabling, moral and positive — have their international equivalents, and preserve the same essential meaning. There is the same equality before the law, implied in the nature of the law. Nations which qualify under the general terms of the law are equally entitled to its benefits and equally subject to its prescriptions — despite their inequality in other respects.

The expression 'international law' must not be allowed to obscure the fact that the rightful beneficiaries of law, as of all other moral institutions, are persons — those beings, namely, whose interests are at stake and who possess the faculties which distinguish the moral agent. International law applies to nations only when nations are conceived as aggregates of persons; and to governments only insofar as these represent those whom they govern. The idea that international law obtains between sovereigns and other personal rulers is as obsolete as the authoritarian political doctrine on which it rests.

Those who urge that international law should concern itself with the rights of individuals, and not merely of governments, are too modest in their demands. In the last analysis only individual persons have interests, and only individual persons have the capacities required for the enjoyment and exercise of that freedom which rights guarantee. The interest of the government in its official capacity is a representative interest, which owes its superiority only to the individual interests for which it speaks. Otherwise the interests and freedoms of governing officials have no higher title than that of any other persons.

While international law imposes additional restrictions, the principle which justifies them is precisely the same as that which justifies the restrictions of domestic law, namely, the priority of all to each. If men are to enjoy the benefits of world-wide peace and coöperation, each person's rights must be fitted to the rights of all other men. The broader moral base implies more far-flung obligations. It is, however, a mistake to suppose that such restrictions are cumulative. The positive benefits of the wider system outweigh its sacrifices: it gives more liberty than it takes away. This holds in the world at large precisely as it does within any given society. A man who is in conflict with his neighbor nominally does as he pleases, but in fact he is obliged to devote the larger part of his energies to the negating of what his enemy pleases. When members of a group are lawless they spend their lives not in doing what they choose but in pursuing, without ever capturing, the opportunity of doing what they choose; which state of affairs suits no one but the warrior, and no interest of any man save his combativeness.

The supreme example of the negation of liberty through lawlessness is international war. It is one of the paradoxes of international law that until recently it has consisted largely of the laws of war, that is, in the regulation of man's lawlessness. War in its modern phases absorbs the total energies of a nation, superseding the preferred occupations of its members, or forcing all of its members into activities congenial only to a few; and at the same time it paralyzes the coöperative activities by which the interests of its members are enhanced. Lawlessness on the world-wide scale creates a situation in which the maximum of persons are to the maximum extent doing what they prefer not to do, and losing the opportunity to do what they prefer to do. This loss of liberty through war pervades every corner of human life, descending from the action of nations to the immediate and private action of the least of its members. By the same token the relief from fear and distrust on the international level through international law would relieve pressures all along the line. It would free nations, free the members of nations, and free the interests of the members.

The objection that international law, by piling law upon law, merely multiplies restraints is further met by the fact that as the law is broadened in its scope it is at the same time diluted. However much human contacts may be extended and multiplied by technological advances, degrees of proximity and intimacy will still remain. The family, the neighborhood, the province, the nation-state, the region, and the international community, represent a succession of wholes in which the parts become progressively autonomous or self-regulative; or in which the legal jurisdiction of the whole is progressively attenuated.

The criterion by which to judge what should or should not be embraced within international law is the degree of interdependence. That international law should embrace health and security is undisputed, because it has become increasingly clear that disease and violence anywhere concern men everywhere. That it should embrace trade or access to raw materials is urged because every economy is in some measure dependent on every economy; so that the maximum of welfare and prosperity for all mankind can be achieved only through world-wide cooperation. That international law should embrace civil rights is argued on the ground that no international law is possible where it is plainly desirable, as in the areas of security, health, and trade, without world-wide freedom of thought and communication.

International law, then, is to be finally judged, like other moral institutions, by the standards of unversality and liberality. It is generated by the principle of universality; and when so justified it serves to correct the morally indefensible exclusiveness of municipal law. But at the same time it is pledged, like all law, to liberality, that is, to the maximum enlargement of the spheres of interest, regional, national, cultural, and personal, which are embraced within the order which it creates.

12

There is, finally, in jurisprudence, as in other social sciences, a technology. International law provides a peculiarly pertinent example of the technology of jurisprudence, because here it is clearly evident that man makes his laws, and makes them for the benefits which he hopes to derive from them. When man finds his institutions ready-made, thanks to God or history, so much the better; if not, he must make them to order. In the field of international law, he must, comparatively speaking, make them out of whole cloth. In approaching the problems of international law men cannot take the view that law is a natural organism, or an inheritance from the past, or a divine institution like state or church; they begin without it, and must contrive to create it. This contemporary situation renders irrelevant the attitude of jurists who say, "But there is no international law"; and feel that out of the depths of their juristic learning they have said the last word.

Fortunately the positivists and historicists are not in charge of the matter. Leadership has been seized by those who combine learning in the law with the layman's naïve idea that if there is anything man greatly needs, and he does not have it, he must devote his energies and wisdom to its making. Every agency organized or affiliated with the United Nations is engaged to the best of its ability in the making of international law, with a view to attaining through law on a world-wide scale the two great moral benefits of security and welfare.

This effort exemplifies the wide range of legal technology. The makers of international law borrow from the sciences whatever knowledge may be applicable to the matter in hand. Because the greatest present threat to safety on the international level, and indirectly on all levels, lies in the use of the atomic bomb, the maker of international law enlists the expert advice of the nuclear physicist. Because the greatest possibilities of welfare, on the international level and indirectly on all levels, lies in the industrialization of backward areas or in a freer access to raw materials, the maker of international law looks for aid to the chemist and biologist. Because the world-wide order which international law seeks to bring into being is composed of human beings and groups of human beings, its making is served by all the sciences of man — by psychology, anthropology, and sociology.

The technology of international law draws upon existing social institutions, and utilizes whatever experience and certified conclusions are to be found within the corresponding cultural sciences — politics, economy, and law itself. Since the benefits of law to each depend on its guaranteed observance by all, international law looks to enforcement as a last resort, and the military expert must be added to the staff. Because education and religion are not only embraced within the world-wide order but throw light on human motivation, knowledge of these universal human enterprises also contributes to the making of international law, and their exponents play the roles of expert consultants to the jurist.

Since the ultimate purpose of international law is a moral purpose its makers profit by moral judgments in proportion to their truth, and thus consult, or should consult, even the moral philosopher, though usually known by some other name. Since of all social institutions conscience is the most direct expression of morality, the international jurist, like the international economist or the political scientist, will look to ethics for guidance. He will appeal to the conscience of the times and at the same time employ whatever techniques are available to create a new opinion and sentiment; so that international law may enjoy the sanction of approval, within each man's breast and in the supporting attitudes of his fellows.

When law is conceived as a product of man's making, and it is recognized that it is made not only by legislatures and administrative officers, but by courts, jurisprudence is faced with a seeming paradox. How can an agency designed to apply the law at the same time make the very law which it is applying? Since the real law is the law as it takes effect, and since the law as it takes effect is the law as it is interpreted by the court, there is no escaping the conclusion that precisely this does, in fact, occur.

The question arose in an acute form in the field of criminal law, in the recent Nürnberg trials. The court presiding over these trials undertook to create new international laws — laws of peace and humanity, laws against aggression and "genocide" — in the very act of finding certain Nazi leaders guilty of their violation. But this procedure would appear to be *ex post facto*, and to deprive the defendants of a fundamental human right, which has recently been formulated as follows:

> Every person has the right to freedom from conviction and punishment except under laws in effect at the time of the commission of any act charged as an offense, and likewise to immunity from any penalty greater than that applicable at the time the offense was committed.[17]

The Nürnberg trials cannot be justified under the strict terms of this maxim. The only maxim that would be consistent with the Nürnberg trials, and with court-made law in general, would be founded on such a principle as the following, stated by Justice Cardozo:

> International law . . . has at times, like the common law within states, a twilight existence during which it is hardly distinguishable from morality or justice, till at length the *imprimatur* of a court attests its jural quality.[18]

This "twilight existence" is represented by the conscience of the community, speaking for right. When a defendant is found guilty of transgressing precepts recognized by the community of which he is a member and held to be vital to its well-being, it is reasonable to suppose that he anticipates the possibility of retribution from the community which he injures. In terms of the *ex post facto* maxim, literally and rigidly construed, it would be impossible to explain either the latitude of the judicial process, or the first steps in the development of the common law. Positive law is forever being generated from custom or conscience by application to cases deemed of sufficient importance to warrant the intervention of society as a whole.

Suppose a pioneer community in which there is no established legal system. A horse thief is caught red-handed. Shall he be expelled, hanged, confined, or otherwise punished? Or shall he be exonerated on the ground that at the time of his theft there was no law against stealing horses? No such community has ever hesitated in its answer. The horse thief was aware that his action so violated the common interest that every man's hand would be against him. He has no excuse for being surprised that having declared war on society, society in turn should protect itself against him. Such procedures of the community express the collective

---

[17] Memorandum prepared and adopted by the Executive Committee of the Committee on Human Rights of the Commission to Study the Organization of Peace, New York, 1946.

[18] N. J. vs. Delaware, *U.S. Reports*, 291 (1931), p. 383.

interest against its internal enemies; and at the same time its aspiration to become an organized community, in which justice shall prevail over vindictiveness, and cool reflection over passion. They are not manifestations of disorder, but beginnings of order.

The criminals of Nürnberg were like that horse thief, taken red-handed in conduct intolerable to the wider complex of human interests. None of those convicted at Nürnberg, despite their air of injured innocence and their legalistic protests, could have been unaware of the opinion and sentiment of the world in which they lived — repeatedly and solemnly affirmed in countless treaties and agreements, publicly professed by heads of state, and voiced by the most authentic exponents of the western and modern conscience. Had those responsible for the aggressions and inhumanities of the Nazi regime been allowed to go unpunished, mankind would have lost a supreme opportunity to crystallize in legal form a recognized and pressing moral necessity. The time was ripe to step across the line from conscience to a legal order; and to create a legal precedent for future time. Those who would have preferred exoneration, or assassination, or summary execution, were not the friends of law in principle, but the defenders of outmoded law or of the perpetuation of lawlessness.

CHAPTER XV

ECONOMY AND ECONOMICS

All societies embrace an institution called 'economy,' and the cultural science which takes this institution as its subject matter is known as 'economics.' What is that aspect of social life[1] which leads to the organization of an economy, and gives it a place beside conscience, polity, and law among the ubiquitous and perennial institutions?

As has been pointed out, all interests tend to assume a preëmptive form, that is, to demand the exclusive possession of their objects. Insofar as the interest fails unless the object is exclusively possessed, the object is said to be "needed." The effort or strength of the interest, or some fraction thereof, is then directed to the acquisition of that which is deemed indispensable. In the primary sense, an economy is an arrangement by which men, having interests, acquire what they need. It will be noted at once that this function of economy is not limited to any class of interests, since all interests, humanly speaking — physical or mental, high or low, from the basest appetites to the most soaring aspirations — generate needs and therefore fall within its provisions. Hence economy is all-pervasive and universal.

But why is it necessary that an economy should be *organized?* Because, in the first place, needs compete with one another in the field of causal interaction. They reach into the common environment, and in taking for themselves they tend to take away from others; as when the hungry man, needing food to eat, and appropriating it to his own use, deprives other hungry men of its use. Men may find themselves competing for the same external object even when there is actually plenty for all. Interests have to be organized to prevent, remove, or mitigate this in-

[1] Although there may be said to be an internal economy within each person, and an imaginary economy of a single person, such as Robinson Crusoe, for the purpose of the present discussion 'economy' is taken to mean social economy.

compatibility. There are certain simple methods by which this is attained. The same object may be used in rotation, or it may be divided; or a particular bone may cease to be a bone of contention through substituting another and equivalent bone from an existing supply of bones. By combining their efforts men can provide for more needs than they can by acting separately. But coöperation, to achieve the maximum of fruitfulness requires that the several coöperating parties shall not only supplement one another but play complementary roles which coincide with differences of talent, aptitude, and skill. Save, perhaps, on the biological level of paternity and maternity, coöperation requires an organized division of labor.

This highly simplified description of economy implies its essential features. This is its merit. It omits the details of the modern western economy, but it construes these as complexities which develop from the simplicities, and which have to be brought back to the simplicities if their meaning is to be understood.

Production and distribution perform the double function of escaping incompatibility and procuring abundance because the things which interests require are usually in some degree limited; *scarcity* is an essential, and not an accidental feature, of the economic situation. This is equally true of *cost:* production is impossible without the sacrifice of some good, or possibility of good, even if its loss is compensated. If objects are to be used they must be possessed — hence *property;* property may be accumulated — hence *wealth.* The instruments of production must themselves be produced — hence capital goods as distinguished from consumer goods. If production is to serve its purpose the products must be *distributed* among the needs which it is designed to supply. When production is organized there are those who *labor* and those who manage, with varieties of each. If there is to be production for future use there must be an *ad interim* provision for present needs; as when a man must be fed today while he is planting next season's crop — hence saving, borrowing, and eventually *banking,* with all their refinements. The possession of objects in excess of present needs leads not only to saving for the future but to the exchange of the unneeded for the needed or the *exchange* of the less needed for the more needed; and the gain of each by this transaction is called his *profit.* When needed objects are divisible into quantitatively equal units there is a ratio of exchange, or *price.* The fecundity of organized production within any community leads to an excess beyond use: hence *surplus* and *commerce.*

There is an aspect of economy which has yet to be brought to light, and which is properly associated with the word '*economy*' and all of its derivatives, such as 'economical' and 'economize.' Since economy involves cost, that is, the forfeiture, or postponement, of something needed, the norm of minimal cost is the negative implication of the norm of maximal provision for need, as the diminution of evil is implied in the augmenting of good. 'Cost' means cost to all embraced within the economy. The cost to each party — his labor at the sacrifice of leisure or of preferred activities, his surrender to others of things possessed — must be induced by his expectation of gain. An economy is an organized reciprocity, in which both the costs and the gains are shared.

The same truth may be expressed by saying that all genuinely economic relations, such as that between producer and consumer, buyer and seller, employer and worker, or lender and borrower, are partnerships; not as judged by some external humane or religious standard, but intrinsically insofar as they are not partnerships they are not economic relations. They presuppose an underlying agreement of the parties concerned to engage in a joint enterprise for their mutual and total benefit.

This reciprocity defines the dividing line between economy and certain procedures which economy supersedes — between the economic institution, and the economic "state of nature." Plunder, piracy, and banditry, that is, the dispossession of a person or group by violence, is a non-economic procedure, because the cost to the second party is not compensated and commends itself only to the first party. Loving kindness, private charity, public relief, and the care of dependents, however admirable on other grounds, fall outside of economy, because the recipient of the gift makes no contribution to its cost. Unemployment is a sign of economic failure, since the unemployed, having no opportunity to pay their way, are thereby excluded from the economy.

An economic system, once established, is thus an automotive or self-propelling system, in which the several parties are moved by their hope of benefit. It pays its costs out of its benefits. It is a system of incentives, by which in order to provide for their own needs each party contributes to the needs of others. If an economy requires external intervention, or the use of violence, or total self-renunciation, it is, for better or worse, no economy. An economy does not do its own particular work, and make its own peculiar contribution to society, except insofar as it goes of itself. An economy to be an economy must *draw;* it must generate its own power by the inducements which it offers; it must be "viable" or "dynamic."

This must not, however, be taken to imply that such a self-propelling system can be divorced from conscience, polity, law, and other institutions. It is only through these that it can be created and operated. But despite its penetration by every sort of social and historical influence, economy has its own specific function, by which it serves the moral purpose of non-conflict and fruitful coöperation, and in terms of which it can be described and appraised.

2

A considerable portion of economic theory is devoted to what is called 'theory of value' or 'value theory.' What is the relation of value in the strictly economic sense to value in general, as that has been already defined?

A New York business man once asserted that brains are cheap.[2] By way of explanation he went on to say that anyone could hire a college professor for five thousand dollars a year. It is clear that in self-defense a college professor is bound to insist that being expensive is not the only way of being valuable. He may be driven to retort that the things that are freely available, such as truth, beauty, or the grace of God, are the things that are worth most: or that the best things are priceless. Or he may retort by suggesting that a man who estimates the value of things in terms of dollars is corrupted by his occupational habits. At any rate it seems fairly obvious that what is "cheap" may yet have redeeming features. 'Expensive,' when taken as connoting value, has a special and restricted meaning determined by the economic context.

Adam Smith distinguished between "value in use" and "value in exchange" [3] to which Mill added that "the word Value, when used without adjunct, always means, in political economy, value in exchange." [4] But this is highly misleading if it is taken to mean that economics excludes value in use: value in exchange is itself derivative from value in use.

No economist treats utility as lying outside his field. He may contend that utility does not enter his domain until exchange occurs, but when it does occur it does not leave utility behind; it embraces utility, and is quite meaningless without it. Thus when value in exchange is explained in terms of supply and demand, demand is explained in terms of anticipated utility; that is, in terms of what is deemed needful.[5] And since needs are to be explained in terms of interests, economic value conceived as exchange value is a derivative of value in general, defined as object of interest.

The only serious attempt to divorce economic value from interest is the so-called "labor theory of value." Although this theory has had a long and respectable history, it would seem at best to rest on confusion and misunderstanding. If 'labor' means "work" in the physical sense of that term, that is, measurable in foot-pounds, it can be duplicated in the fall

---

[2] Portions of the text which follows are reprinted from the Author's article "Economic Value and Moral Value," *Quarterly Journal of Economics, 30* (1916).

[3] A. Smith, *Wealth of Nations*, Bk. I, ch. iv.

[4] J. S. Mill, *Principles of Political Economy*, Bk. III, ch. i.

[5] J. M. Keynes has pointed out that it is the "expected utility," and not the actual utility, which determines economic value. Cf. his *The General Theory of Employment, Interest, and Money*, 1936, ch. v.

of a body to the earth's surface, or in any other physical event involving the expenditure of energy. If, on the other hand, 'labor' means effort, that is, motivated action, or if it is taken to imply painful effort, or disagreeable drudgery, or expenditure of time, or sacrifice of any description, or if the outcome is taken as useful, or if a man is said to have earned a "right" to the fruits of his labor, then interest becomes the essential factor in the description.

Economic value, as distinguished from value in general, is commonly identified with price. And so — what *is* price? This is an ambiguous question. It might mean the question that can be answered simply by the price tag, or the price list, or the price index, or the market quotations. But no economist would admit that such information was a contribution to economic theory. The more serious question which he has in mind cannot be answered by the salesman or the statistician, in terms of some monetary standard of measurement, such as the dollar or pound, but only by stating *what it is that the price measures.*

3

Broadly speaking, the price of any given object measures what one can get for a thing if one has it, or what one can get it for, if one does not have it. The underlying fact is giving for the sake of getting, impelled by a comparison of needs. Every man has something to give, and in terms of that, he will think of the "price he has to pay" for what he gets. If he has nothing to give but his labor, he will think in terms of his time, his bodily strength, his skill, his painful exertions, and the exclusion of other things he would like to do. The man who has land or domesticated animals to give will think of price in terms of their surrender. The difference is not fundamental. The first man presumably used his hands for two purposes: to make something, or to grasp something. Whether he gave his labor for the sake of the product, or gave up his present possession for the sake of acquiring another possession, he was exchanging something he had for something he had not but which he believed he needed more.

'Exchange' in the economic sense does not mean that an object changes hands; it is not a mere exchange of place or possession, as when two men accidentally exchange hats in the coatroom, or generously exchange gifts at Christmas. To qualify as an economic exchange it must be a calculated exchange, from which both parties believe they profit. To understand 'price' as a measure of exchange it is not necessary to accept (or reject) the law of "diminishing returns," or the doctrine of "marginal utility," or the Malthusian doctrine of the subsistence wage, or the Marxian doctrine of "surplus value," or the classic doctrines of interest or rent, or any of the doctrines which have played so prominent a role in the economic theory of the past but are now matters of controversy. The meaning of 'exchange' in the economic sense does not imply any of these ideas, though its complete analysis will no doubt borrow something from all of them.

Exchange does presuppose, in the first place, two or more subjects each of whom has needs, and each of whom has resources at his disposal, which can either be used to meet these needs, or transferred to the possession and use of another subject. It presupposes, in the second place, that each subject is qualified to arrange his needs in an order of preference, and to anticipate, more or less correctly, their fulfillment by his own resources or by the acquisition of resources possessed by a second party. In other words, exchange presupposes economic agents possessing those faculties of thought and choice which are the peculiar prerogatives of a person.

It is presupposed, further, that the subject's existing resources are capable of alternative uses. The most unmistakable example of this is the subject's time, which he can employ for any of his interests, or which he can give to the service of someone else. The same will hold, in a more restricted measure, of his labor and his skill. But the principle of alternative uses will also hold, although in a still more restricted measure, of his possessions. Thus, his house and his child can be transferred to the service of another's needs when considered only as space and labor, though not when considered as objects of his domestic affection.

These are not the only presuppositions of exchange. It presupposes communication and transportation. It presupposes possession and transfer of possession. It presupposes mobility of labor. It presupposes non-interference by any agency, private or public. It is not to be argued against economy as here defined that these presuppositions are never wholly met; that there is never, in short, a "pure" or "free" economy. It is necessary, as in all science, to abstract from the full concreteness of existence in order to understand its complicating factors.

Exchange occurs, then, when there is a meeting of two economic agents, each of whom is bent on providing for needs still outstanding, who are so situated that each can give up to the other in return for what he gets from the other, and each of whom believes that he needs what he gets more than what he gives. Exchange is thus an extension of alternative uses. In the absence of exchange, a man having a cow can use the cow either to eat or to milk. Adding the possibility of exchanging the cow for an acre of land he can use the cow either to eat, or to milk, or, indirectly, to extend the area of his arable soil.

When exchange occurs the price of what he gets is what he gives, and the price of what he gives is what he gets. The cow is "worth" an acre of land, and an acre of land is worth a cow. Which is the same as to say that when two things exchange for one another their price is the same. This is all that 'price' means. 'Sameness of price' does not mean equal usefulness: as a matter of fact it arises from unequal usefulness: one party finds the cow more useful, and the other finds the acre of land more useful.

To understand how a "standard" of value arises it is necessary only to extend bilateral exchange to multilateral exchange. The man who obtains the acre of land in exchange for a cow may exchange it for a house. These future possibilities of exchange may govern both economic agents in making the original bargain, and they thus enlarge the range of alternative uses. The cow is then worth any one of the things which its owner may obtain for it; and all of the things that are thus directly or indirectly exchangeable for a cow are worth the same, namely, one cow. The economy is then a cow economy; or may be said to be based on a "bovine standard."

In other words, it is possible to substitute for the rate at which two objects are exchangeable the rate at which each is exchangeable for a third; or the rate at which all are exchangeable for one; which then becomes the medium or common denominator of exchange, called 'money.' Monetary price is thus a many-one relationship, which can be represented as a circle with the chosen medium at the center and radii to all other goods on the periphery. The relation of the center to the periphery represents the command, through exchange, of a variety of goods obtainable by him who possesses some one. What object shall be selected by the purpose is determined by reasons of convenience: it might be a cow, which would be highly inconvenient, or a package of cigarettes, which is said to have served the purpose in parts of post-war Europe, but it is more likely to be a precious metal, such as gold or silver, or a piece of paper which is convertible by government into a precious metal, or which is legally recognized in payment of debts or taxes.

He who has money virtually possesses all the things that "money will buy." It opens to him a vast, indeed a limitless, perspective of getting what he has not but needs more, to replace what he has but needs less. It is this power, and not because of any base appetite or hoarding mania, that men seek money and more money.

The money value of a given possession thus represents no single value computed in terms of interests and needs. To say that an object is worth one hundred dollars means that it is exchangeable for a class of objects. He who has one hundred dollars can obtain any one of this class, and he who has any one of this class can obtain one hundred dollars, with which he can obtain any other member of the class. But the members of this class of interchangeable objects will have different interest-values for the different parties to the exchange. The "hundred dollars' worth" may be of negligible value relatively to one man, while "beyond the dreams of avarice" to another. To suppose that "a hundred dollars' worth" represents a single value relatively to the interests and needs of society as a whole would be to substitute a fictitious substantive entity for a complex network of relations.

4

Since economy is coextensive with man, explanatory economics is an inexhaustible inquiry. There is no cause which affects human life at all that does not affect economy. There are, however, certain broad considerations which are appropriate to the present context. The first of these is the distinction between analytical or systematic explanation, and historical explanation.

Analytical explanation explains economy in general, and expounds the forces which are at work in all economies. It is this explanation which has been offered above in expounding the general nature of economy and of economic values. Such explanation may be pushed much further than has here been attempted. Especially inviting is the examination of "economic behavior" by social psychology and sociology.[6] Such a study would deal with the general characteristics of human nature and human relations as applied to the general characteristics of man's economic life.

Applied historically the explanatory method sets forth the particular circumstances of time and place which distinguish one particular economy from another — difference of geography, soil, climate, racial traits, social structure, scientific and technological development, custom and tradition. Unfortunately analytical and historical explanations are sometimes confused, with the result that the characteristics of a special economy, such as that of England in the nineteenth century, are taken to define economy in general.

The fact that economy is an organization of interests prescribes the manner in which its causes operate. Physical changes which diminish or increase natural resources will affect an economy through affecting human needs and the alternatives open to choice. Through the interests which it serves an economy will reflect the conscience or mores of the community: a society of ascetics will have a different economy from that of a society of sensualists and sybarites. The kind of economy a society has will reflect the character of its political institutions, whether they are democratic or authoritarian. Whether government is in business or out of business, a very considerable part of law and rights is that which regulates men's economic relations — from the laws protecting property and prescribing the keeping of contracts, to the complicated laws of incorporation, finance and trade. Science, art, religion, and education, with their differences and changes, will all determine economy whether

---

[6] For a psychological approach to this question, cf. C. L. Hull, "Value, Valuation, and Natural-Science Methodology," *Philosophy of Science*, 10–11 (1943–4).

through the interests served, or through the modes of human relationships which they create.

There is a quite gratuitous dispute over the question of the social or individual character of economic causes. When it is understood that 'social' means a plurality, agreement, interaction, or other relation among individuals, there is no problem. The following is a typical form of the argument:

> It is only changes in fashion or mode, in general business confidence, in moral attitude toward this or the other sort of consumption, in the distribution of wealth, changes in taxes and other laws, etc. — causes of a general social character — that you can count on to produce important changes in values.[7]

It is quite true that economic value, as measured by price, is an effect of many minds, and is changed only when many minds are changed. It is quite true that an individual's felt need for an object is mediated by his judgment of the attitudes of others: he wants it because others want it or admire it. It is quite true that because price is a product of so many minds it is independent of any single given mind, and that an individual is obliged to accept it as an objective fact.

5

Normative economics, or economic critique, is divisible into three distinguishable but overlapping parts: the internal instrumental critique; the external critique, instrumental or final; and the internal final, or moral, critique.

Judged by its instrumental standard the worst economy is that condition of man in which there is no economy at all. This condition has, presumably, never existed in human history, since some economy is a condition of survival. A group whose members lived by plundering one another and were deprived of the advantages of organized production, distribution, and exchange, could scarcely bear the impact of natural forces or of rival groups.

Economy of some sort or of some degree is an organization already acquired when human history begins. But a society which has economy enough to survive may yet embrace members who do not participate in its economy — that is, who do not pay their way. So far as these members are concerned there is no economy. For reasons of age, incapacity, or incorrigible selfishness, there will always be a residuum of persons remaining outside of the economy, as its wards or enemies; as there is always a residuum disqualified for political citizenship or legal rights.

[7] B. M. Anderson, "Schumpeter's Dynamic Economics," *Political Science Quarterly*, 30 (1915), p. 651.

But otherwise the presence in society of persons who neither give nor get, or get without giving or give without getting, is an indictment of that society's economy.

A highly organized economy of the modern occidental type may generate the causes of its own failure, as the bearings of a machine may be obstructed by the products of friction. The economy which has prevailed in Western Europe and the United States since the Industrial Revolution is frequently indicted on this score, even by its own friends. It is said in this or that respect to "break down" or not to "work." [8] The terms of this indictment of the capitalistic economy are familiar. It is subject to cycles and to periods of so-called "depression." It presupposes competition, but tends to monopoly because the competitive motive itself leads each competitor to weaken and destroy its rivals. The motive of reducing costs leads to combinations, and great combinations absorb the small.

Successes and failures lead to gross inequalities of wealth, breeding a class of idle rich and a class of helpless poor. Those who possess too much have no incentive to expenditure and those who possess too little have nothing to expend. Savings become stagnant at the top and dry up altogether at the bottom. Large-scale enterprise leads to aggregations of labor which by inheritance, habit, narrowly specialized skill, and the costs of migration, become immobile. Since labor is a cost of production at the same time that laborers comprise a major part of the consumers, the reduction of costs diminishes the demand for the product. In their economic action men oscillate between extremes of timidity and rash speculation — between underconfidence and overconfidence. Fluctuations of price catch men unprepared, or lead to spirals of inflation and deflation through the attempt to discount them. New inventions lead to overproduction, which leads through retrenchment to underproduction and unemployment.

As men become more and more dependent on the large-scale and delicate mechanisms of mass-production, transportation, and public utilities, they become more vulnerable. If anything goes wrong at some bottleneck or focal center, so that the great machine slows down and stops, even for a day, everybody suffers, and men may pass precipitately from affluence to privation. So that even in the midst of unparalleled economic efficiency there is a haunting sense of impending disaster.

The modern economy has its flaws and weaknesses and seeks to amend them. But judged by this same instrumental standard it has demonstrated remarkable efficiency. Its outstanding merit lies in its abundant and perpetually advancing provision for human needs by the inducements and incentives which it offers to those who pay the costs. It excludes con-

---

[8] For an examination of the "break-down theory," cf. Paul M. Sweezy, *Theory of Capitalistic Development*, 1942, ch. xi.

fiscation, slavery, forced labor, and paternalism at home, and substitutes
trade for conquest abroad. It is not surprising that it should have been
gratefully accepted as a gift of God or the order of nature.

Any economic system as well as economy in general may be criticized
on the ground of its incompatibility with democracy, and free enterprise
is defended on the ground of its unique consistency with democracy. An
economy, or any of its practices, may be condemned as violating legal
rights; or owing to its emphasis on property, approved as conducive to a
stable order.

In the history of man there has been a continuous critique of economy
from the standpoint of religion. Such is the wholesale charge that economy exalts earthly and temporal goods when man's attention should be
directed to the life to come or to eternity. Thus Christianity has taught
that the possession of riches prevents access to the Kingdom of Heaven.
Similarly, a religion of the ascetic type, such as Buddhism, condemns
modern industrialism as preventing the attainment of Nirvana. Mahom-
medanism has prohibited interest, and Christianity usury. Protestantism
has given its blessing to capitalism, as has Confucianism to the traditional
economy of China. Christianity has always felt uneasy over the conflict
between the hard bargaining of a competitive economy and its own gospel of charity; and its occasional marriage with socialism is a result of
the application to economy of the Christian parable of the Good Samaritan.

From the standpoint of higher culture, economy has been held guilty
of neglecting the pursuits of art and pure science; as when England was
slightingly referred to as a "nation of shopkeepers," and economics as
the "dismal science." [9] Judged by educational standards economy is condemned for its emphasis on livelihood and vocational subjects rather
than on "spiritual" values and the humanities.

The external critique of economy may be taken as revealing its limits
rather than its inherent evils. It is concerned with meeting the needs
which are generated by human interests, and not with the nature of those
interests. It is concerned indifferently with the tools of the artist, the
weapons of the soldier, the plow of the farmer, the vestments of the
priest, and the investments of the financier. It deals with objects which
are divisible into homogeneous and interchangeable units, and therefore
neglects or omits the unique objects of love and admiration. Its place in
life is in the market place, and goods which are not marketable lie outside
its province. But it cannot be condemned for omitting what lies beyond
its province so long as it recognizes the limits of its province. It is at
fault only when, and insofar as, it mistakes its province for the whole
empire of human life: when, through the narrowing effect of its own

[9] The first of these characterizations was Carlyle's and the second is attributed
to Samuel Adams.

habits, the preoccupation of men with the exigency of livelihood, and the inordinate passion for riches and the power which riches bring, it accounts as of no value those things whose price is above rubies or whose value is priceless.

6

An economy may qualify as an economy and yet fall short of being an optimum economy because of failing to fulfill its final moral purpose. The slogan "Business is business" bespeaks the vain attempt to evade this moral obligation. Business is a great deal more than business.

The view that economy is subject to the requirements of morality has prevailed throughout the greater part of the history of economic theory, beginning with Aristotle. After an interregnum during which the claims of morality were disputed in the name of "scientific" economics, morality again speaks with authority.

The "Beveridge Report" cites Lord Keynes's argument that accumulated savings are uneconomical unless they are expended, and then goes on to say:

> On the earlier teaching of the economists, moral and technical considerations in regard to the distribution of wealth had appeared to be in conflict. Moral considerations suggested the desirability of a more equal distribution of wealth, while technical considerations appeared to require great inequality as the condition of adequate saving. On the newer teaching of the economists . . . moral and technical considerations unite in favor of substantially greater equality of wealth than has obtained in Britain in the past.[10]

Assuming that the words 'technical' and 'social' are here equivalent to the terms 'instrumental' and 'moral' as used above, this passage illustrates the admission of a moral standard by which an economy may properly be judged. From the beginning of the Industrial Revolution the moral defects of the laissez-faire economy were noted and in some measure remedied: low wages, excessive hours of labor, unsanitary and over-congested living conditions, excessive dependence of worker on employer. The growing body of ameliorative legislation has been resisted by the proponents of a strictly "scientific" economics. But when pressed to justify themselves the proponent and opponent of reform have taken the same ultimate moral ground.

It is true that the impulse to economic reform is usually generated

---

[10] W. H. Beveridge, *Full Employment in a Free Society*, W. W. Norton and Company, Inc., 1945, pp. 95–6. Cf. J. M. Keynes, *The General Theory of Employment, Interest and Money*, 1936, pp. 372–4. Keynes's famous book is pervaded by an appeal to moral or social standards, as when in his "Concluding Notes on Social Philosophy" he remarks that "the outstanding faults of the economic society in which we live are its failure to provide for full employment and its arbitrary and inequitable distribution of wealth and incomes" (p. 372).

among those who are aggrieved; and who are open to the charge of pressing their own special interest, and engaging in reprisals against the more privileged. But in their final self-justification they take broader ground, and speak for society as a whole. The exponents of the economic *status quo* are open to a similar charge of bias, since they are usually those whose special interests are entrenched. But when pressed to defend themselves they take the same ground as the aggrieved. They do not say, "We possess economic advantages, and propose to hold them. What are you going to do about it?" On the contrary, they endeavor to persuade the aggrieved that their interest, too, lies in adherence to the existing system — that it is good for everybody. They speak of the indirect and universal benefits of the competitive system, as catering to the wants of the consumer, rewarding thrift, stimulating invention, increasing production, reducing costs, accelerating progress, and multiplying opportunities. They say to the less privileged: "We are, indeed, at the moment more successful than you. But what we have attained, you may attain; or if not you yourself, then your children."

The implication of the moral standard pervades economic thinking throughout. It appears in the assumption that there is something wrong with the feudal system, not because it did not work, but because it was authoritarian and unjust. It appears in the assumed obligation of government to control the public domain, and conserve natural resources, in the interest of the total society, present and future, and in the condemnation of "log-rolling," by which special groups exchange economic favors with no regard to the public interest. It appears in the assumption that there is something wrong with a system in which the rich grow richer and the poor grow poorer, and not merely because it reduces consumer demand. It appears in the assumption that there is something wrong with a system which fails to remedy human poverty, misery, and unemployment. It appears in the assumption that a Malthusian economy in which growth of population reduces wages to bare subsistence, or in which labor is induced only by fear of starvation, or in which survival is based on the elimination of the relatively weak by plague or malnutrition, is a deplorable state of affairs which economy is bound if possible to remedy or prevent.

This moral premise, often unspoken, is unmistakably clear in the critique of slavery — in its defense as well as in its condemnation. Slavery was attacked on the ground that slaves, being property, have no voice in the economic system under which they live. It was defended on the ground that were the slaves to know their interest, being by nature slavish, they would assent to their slavery; or on the ground that as slaves they were "better treated" than they would be as free men, or on the ground that the conditions of production were such that the wealth whose benefits they in some measure enjoyed were unattainable without slave labor.

Somehow, in other words, by direction or indirection, by hook or crook, the institution was so presented as to secure the hypothetical agreement of the slave. Such a moral justification of slavery is clearly distinguished from the narrower judgment which considers only the advantage of the slaveholder. Thus it has been argued that free labor would be more efficient than slavery; would create a local purchasing power and market for the master's goods; would enrich him more abundantly; or would deliver him from the menace of a slave insurrection. But it is the broader moral ground, the ground, namely, that it is unfair to the slaves, on which is based the final condemnation of the slave economy, however well or ill it may work.

It is one of the unhappy results of economic thinking that this ulterior purpose of economy is so often allowed to remain in the background, to be brought forward only when the system is on the defensive. Too often the economic thinker instead of surveying economy as a whole and judging its processes and instrumentalities by the moral good, puts himself in the position of adviser to a special client.

7

The ulterior moral purpose of economy may be presented by an examination of the moral limits of prudence, which is the name given to an organization of interests *however limited they may be*. It is entirely consistent with selfishness, that is, with an absence of independent benevolence. It is apparent that the ordinary processes of business and trade fall within this definition. The economic agent may not be concerned with a merely private gain: he may be the trustee of an orphan asylum, and his customer may be the director of a board of foreign missions, and each may genuinely represent the interests with which he is charged.[11] But in the strictly economic transaction the two are pitted *against* one another. The first party is at the moment ignoring the heathen, and the second is ignoring the orphan. The breadwinner of one family may be similarly pitted against the breadwinner of another family; or the director of one corporation may serve its stockholders with no consideration for the stockholders of a second corporation. When the economic adviser remarks to the physician: "You ought to charge more for your services — you could easily get it," or to a benevolent employer apropos of his high wage-scale: "This may be good religion, but it isn't good business," he is appealing to the limited prudential standard. Judged by the same limited standard the economic agent is absolved from the obligation of buying in the dearer market out of sheer goodness of heart, or of paying more than necessary in order to benefit a deserving merchant.

It is this same prudential principle which justifies a purely competitive,

[11] On this matter cf. P. H. Wickstead, *Common Sense of Political Economy*, 1933, Bk. I, ch. v.

as distinguished from a coöperative, relation between persons. Hence it is associated with mere "success," or "the Goddess of Getting On." [12] Its code of "economic virtues" emphasizes thrift, industry, and sobriety; those virtues, namely, which contribute to the conserving and increase of a person's resources regardless of other purposes. The moral purpose, on the other hand, prescribes that account shall be taken of *all the interests* which action affects, or its consequences all around. The prudential principle which serves a limited set of interests must on moral grounds be subordinated to a principle of larger scope which provides for the good of the other party to every transaction, and implies the motive of independent benevolence.

The moral economist will concern himself with those who get the worst of the bargain. He will be disturbed by the comparative helplessness of any party to recognize and press its interest. He will align himself against an economy in which advantage is taken of ignorance; and will seek to promote an economy which provides for sales resistance as well as sales pressure. He will not be satisfied with an economic system merely because those who profit by it most are enabled to drive good bargains, and induce others to accept them. He will be concerned not with bargains only, but with *bargaining power.*

Economic value as measured by price conceals inequality of bargaining power. It measures the more needed which a man gets, in terms of the less needed which he gives; but ignores the place of the needs in the personal scales of the bargainers. One party in exchange differs from another in *how much* he needs that which he needs less, and which he is obliged to surrender for what he needs more. He who possesses little is obliged to give from that little, which, though he needs it less than that which he gets, he nevertheless needs greatly. Thus the man without property has nothing to give but his labor, and may be obliged to give that in order to obtain food and shelter. The man of large property, on the other hand, has so much to give that he need not labor at all, and he may, in giving from what he has, deprive himself of what he needs slightly or not at all.

When one party is in a position to give what he needs comparatively little and the other party must give what he needs comparatively much the first party's bargaining power is superior to that of the second. He has superior *power* because he can in a higher degree control the second party's disposition of his possessions and services. He can "force" the second party to trade, and he can "dictate" the terms of the trade. Such inequality of bargaining power tends to be cumulative. Each transaction increases the advantage of the one and the disadvantage of the other. When this advantage is pressed beyond a certain point it is called "exploitation" — or in its extreme development, "wage-slavery."

[12] Cf. Ruskin, *Crown of Wild Olives*, Lect. II.

It may be objected that the terms 'force' and 'dictate' cannot accurately apply to superior bargaining power, since the weaker party is still free to work, buy, or sell, or not, as he chooses. But to condone such a system in the name of freedom is to falsify the meaning of freedom. The man who must sacrifice leisure, recreation, and self-development to bare subsistence, or the woman whose circumstances compel her to sell her body or starve, has "little or no choice." An economic system which even though it operates through the choices of its members has the effect of abridging their choices, cannot be praised on the ground of freedom. It may in fact reach a point at which it is doubtful whether it is better than no economy at all, and at which its victims are tempted to resort to plunder.

Expressed in more familiar terms, this means that great inequality of wealth indicates an unsound economy. This is not because inequality of wealth dries up the purchasing power of consumers, or removes incentives to investment, or depresses the morale of the workers, so that the system becomes less profitable to the exploiter. It is unsound for the reason that it is unjust to the exploited, that is, fails to satisfy the moral requirement that an economy shall be equally mindful of the interests of all concerned.

8

The rationalization of economy requires enlightened fidelity to its moral purpose. There must be an overruling of selfish prudence by justice and humanity — a control of limited self-interest, however shrewd and calculating, by the long range good of all. Where shall this rational control be lodged? There are two possibilities. This moral control must be lodged either in the public authority, or in the conscience and moral wills of those who participate in the economy. Economy must either regulate itself, or submit to being regulated. The "interference" which it resents is the penalty of its moral irresponsibility.

The common resort has been to government, which enacts and interprets laws to control economy in the general interest. Reliance on the intervention of government is typified in the following statement, made apropos of the widespread suffering predicted as a result of the mechanization of cotton growing in the Southern United States:

> It is not within the province of private enterprise to deal with problems of this nature. Strictly speaking, social problems are irrelevant to the operation of a private business. We cannot expect the new agricultural industrialists to have either the will or the capacity to handle them; that is a function of government.[13]

[13] J. M. Morse, "Revolution in Cotton," *New Republic*, Aug. 19, 1946.

The influential teachings of Maynard Keynes provide for the systematic, and not the piecemeal, intervention of government. If the operations of an economy are to be beneficent as well as efficient, it is necessary that government shall determine the framework within which it operates:

> Thus I agree . . . that the result of filling in the gaps in the classical theory is not to dispose of the "Manchester System," but to indicate *the nature of the environment which the free play of economic forces requires if it is to realize the full potentialities of production.* The central controls necessary to ensure full employment will, of course, involve a large extension of the traditional functions of government.[14]

But government is not an infallible instrument of moral control. It may itself be unfaithful to its trust. It is composed of human beings who may or may not be disinterested. There is danger of a vicious circle: an unregulated economy may have corrupted the very government which is called upon to regulate it. Inequality of wealth implies inequailty of influence, with the result that government tends to become the voice and instrument of those very interests whose privileges it may be required to correct. Even "public opinion" may be only the private opinion of those whose disproportionate wealth enables them to control the agencies of publicity; in which case the making of the public opinion on which government rests becomes itself a form of exploitation.

The moral apportionment of economic goods must in the last analysis be determined by a social will which expresses agreement among persons who through sympathy and benevolence take account of one another's interests. Ideally speaking, the final judgments of an economy are voiced only by persons who by consent are entitled to speak for all. If such persons are found in public office so much the better; but there is little likelihood that they will be found there if they are not widely dispersed among private individuals and groups.

A society's economy, like its other social institutions, will reflect the moral enlightenment of its members. Here, as elsewhere, there is no escape from individual human responsibility. Sooner or later, and somewhere, there must be men who play a double role, men whose prudence is subordinated in their own persons to the control of the moral purpose. Fidelity to the moral purpose cannot be imposed from without but must be implanted within; and this is a task to which *all* the agencies of moral education — parents, teachers, preachers, sages, priests, orators, journalists, officials — working together are scarcely equal.

The extreme exponents of the laissez-faire doctrine, who have entrusted economy to economic agents governed by selfish prudence, have assumed that a rivalry among such agents would be morally beneficent.

[14] J. M. Keynes, *op. cit.*, Harcourt, Brace and Company, Inc., p. 379 (italics mine).

They have assumed that men are so constituted that their intelligent self-seeking, no matter what self they seek, would be good for everybody automatically; that men are by nature so predisposed to harmony that all they have to do in order to promote harmony is to be natural.

Now that it has been proved by the sciences of human nature and by the bitter experience of conflict — between man and man — that such is not the case, it is evident that if a harmonious society is to be achieved, human nature must be fashioned to fit it. Original human nature must be transformed into human second nature, before it can be trusted to follow its own promptings. Certain primitive impulses, such as fear and combativeness, must be played down, and other primitive impulses such as sympathy and love must be played up; and the first must be subordinated to the second. Men must be socially trained. They must acquire a sense of the total community and their devotion to it must become their overruling interest. When men are thus internally governed by good will they may then seek to excel one another in good works. The self having been socialized they may then give free rein to self-interest, and drive with one another what bargains they please.

There are two forms of economic knowledge. On the one hand there is prudential intelligence — the shrewdness and foresight, the understanding and inventiveness, the specialized skills — which enables men to produce what can be sold, to sell what is produced, and to outstrip competitors. On the other hand, there is that higher enlightenment which aligns the instruments of economy with the moral purpose. Both forms of knowledge are indispensable: it is necessary that they should be combined in the same society and in the same persons, and that the first should be subordinated to the second.

9

In the case of economy, as in the case of other moral institutions, it is illuminating to distinguish two canons of reform which are implied by its ulterior moral purpose: the standard of liberality, and the standard of universality. Both have to do with the resolution of conflict: liberality is the moral standard as applied to class conflict or the social revolution within societies; universality is the moral standard as applied to war or the conflict between societies. Both principles have meaning in the field of economy.

The term 'social revolution' is commonly used to signify a revolution that is motivated by economic discontent, and which results in a radical redistribution of economic wealth and power. Insofar as groups within society are consolidated by the sense of their common advantages or disadvantages they form so-called classes, and their conflict becomes class-struggle. Marxism introduces rigidity and fatality into what is a perennial phenomenon permitting of many differences of degree. In any economy there are always those who profit more by the system, or are relatively privileged, and those who profit less, and are relatively unprivileged. This difference appears in a socialist economy such as Soviet Russia, as well as in capitalistic societies. The extent to which the privileged and the unprivileged are set apart and mobilized against each other is the accident and not the essence of the matter.

The standard of liberality arises from the fact that morality is an organization of life for the benefit of the elements organized — not for the sake of the unity of the whole but for the sake of the parts. Such an organization is morally defensible only insofar as it commends itself to its members on this ground. Like any organization, it limits the interests of the participants; but, like any moral organization, it limits each only so far as is required by the good of all.

This is the principle which defines the moral right of the relatively unprivileged to protest and demand reorganization when they believe that the limits imposed are excessively narrow. Their protest is not justified because of their poverty, helplessness, or frustration; or even because their share of the proceeds of the economy is less than that of others — although this gives them a *prima facie* case. The appeal is not to the interest of the aggrieved party, but to disinterestedness — that is, all-interestedness. The aggrieved party may rightly demand that its comparative privation shall be proved necessary in the interest of all concerned.

This analysis is applicable to the lowest imaginable economies, such, for example, as that which employs the labor of galley slaves who exchange their much-needed time and bodily strength for what they need even more — namely, escape from punishment and starvation. This is a morally bad economy, not because of the slave's hardships — it might be that no other method of transport by sea was possible, and that these hard necessities were imposed by the interests of the total group, including the slaves — but because the economy neglects the interests of the slaves, and gives weight only to the interests of the owner, the trader, or the slave driver. The exponent of the slave's interest may rightly claim that if all interests were considered the resulting economy would distribute the burden more equitably. Such a better economy would, perhaps, assign the hitherto more privileged parties a turn at the oars; or it would alleviate the burden of the oarsmen by better food and shorter hours; or it would give the oarsmen a voice in the conduct of the enterprise; or it would seek for some improved system of transport, such as the sailing vessel, by which the costs to its human participants would be diminished.

The demand for liberality finds its authentic expression not in the sheer self-assertion of the unfortunate nor in their envy of the fortunate, nor in pity felt for the unfortunate, but in the will to reform. The fault lies in the system, and remedy is to be sought in its liberalization: not in alleviating suffering, but in preventing it; not in treating the economically sick, but in economic prophylaxis or hygiene; not in visiting the poor, but in eradicating poverty; not in bread and circuses, but in social reconstruction. In this sense, in their demand that the house be remodeled rather than that its less attractive quarters be made more habitable by fumigation, incense, soporifics, or anaesthetics, the social revolutionaries are profoundly right; provided, however, due allowance is made for the losses incurred by all when the remodeling is too abrupt or violent.

Interpreted in the light of these considerations, the so-called "labor movement" was a moral movement, which applied the standard of liberality to the existing system or employment. Its exponents, whether workers or reformers speaking in their behalf, believed that it was possible to provide for human needs at less cost to those who worked with their hands. They affirmed that if the total enterprise were conceived in terms of the workers' interests as well as the employers', it would not embrace a group of persons so near to the subsistence level, and so dependent, as were the workers immediately after the Industrial Revolution. The system as it stood, they contended, was an imperfect economy which had not rid itself of an inheritance of plunder and exploitation. They asked the employer and consumer, and the disinterested judge, to design a more liberal economy.

In pursuing this goal, the labor movement encountered an opposition of special or vested interests. But insofar as the labor movement was justified, the opposing force was a species of an obscurantism, which failed to start from the true moral premises and to face their broad human implications. So conceived, the issue of principle was between the friends of justice who desired that all parties should have that to which they were rightly entitled, and the unwitting partners of injustice who were satisfied that some (usually themselves) should have a disproportionate share, or between those who proposed to equalize bargaining power and those who accepted, and profited by, its inequality.

In order to improve its bargaining power, labor bargains collectively. The employer's need of the services of a single worker is so slight, and the individual worker's need of employment is so great, that the employer can virtually dictate the terms of their agreement. When workers are organized, however, they can withhold their total services and prevent the employer from doing business at all; and meanwhile, during the period of negotiation, the needs of the individual worker can be supplied from a common fund. The workers' power to withhold or to "strike" is a weapon to be used against the employer's power to deny employment. Collective bargaining so construed is a contest between opposing interests — an endurance test, or an exchange of threats, each party thinking only in terms of its own gains and losses.

When, however, collective bargaining is looked to for a fundamental solution of the problem of conflict, the premises of the argument are shifted. Both parties appeal to public opinion, or to a third party representing the public — an official of government, a neutral arbitrator, or industrial relations expert. In the course of the argument, the issue is broadened and the representatives of employment and labor themselves develop an attitude of disinterestedness. Each recognizes the claims of the other and adds them to his own, until both participate in the solution of a common problem which is to reconcile the interests of all concerned.

To understand the motivation of organized labor it is important to recognize that it is an effort to obtain power and to obtain rights. The employer who "treats his employees well," and helps them to create a "company union," or whose wife visits their homes and dispenses charity, often exhibits a hurt surprise when the recipients of this indulgence are ungrateful, or even resentful. This unwillingness to accept gratuities is due, at least in part, to a rivalry for power, since it is more blessedly powerful to give than to receive: to give is a form of control. But the deeper reason for the attitude of organized labor lies in the fact that it is not asking for favors but for the right of workers to choose their good for themselves, and the right to a just share of the proceeds of the economy in which they participate.

When economy is considered broadly as a system devised to provide as abundantly as possible for all human needs, account must be taken of the negative effect of the pains of labor — not only pain in the strict sense, but fatigue, anxiety, and boredom. When the immediate values of labor are negative, so that a man works only in order to escape work at some future time, or in the hope of compensation, there is clearly a loss. But when work itself is enjoyed, through its appeal to pride and emulation or to the creative impulses of craftsmanship and management, there is a positive value to be added, and not a negative value to be subtracted. The recent emphasis on the psychology of the worker[15] — his motivation and the conditions of his personal happiness — thus has a moral and not a merely instrumentalist meaning. The depressing effect of modern mechanization, with its tendency to convert the worker into a robot, is to be deplored not merely because it reduces his efficiency, but because it deprives him of good.

10

The canon of universality is clearly applicable to economy. Its beneficent relationships embrace all human persons, who, having needs, are

---

[15] Cf. G. W. Allport, "The Ego in Contemporary Psychology," *Psychological Review*, 50 (1943), pp. 471–2; T. N. Whitehead, *Leadership in a Free Society*, 1937; F. J. Roethlisberger and W. J. Dickson, *Management and the Worker*, 1939; also the writings of Thorstein Veblen.

confronted by the alternatives of plundering one another or of engaging in transactions that are mutually profitable. When an economy stops at some geographical, racial, or national frontier, while other persons with interests and resources are within reach on the other side of the frontier, there is at that point no economy; and there is a loss of that moral good which economy provides, namely non-conflict and coöperation.

So strong is this extensive force of economy that international economy has been the first international institution to develop, and has paved the way for the others. The trader has sponsored or accompanied the discoverer and has often been himself the discoverer, or the crusader and missionary. And although the first contacts have assumed the form of plunder, they have led immediately to exchange, even with ignorant and defenseless aborigines. The Mediterranean world, Europe and the Americas, and finally the West and the East, have been unified by commerce when still profoundly divided in conscience, polity, law, science, art, education, and religion.

Economy tends to global economy — to an economy embracing all mankind. This does not imply, as is sometimes supposed, that worldwide business transactions are necessarily more profitable to their participants than local transactions; or that business transactions between Asiatics and Europeans who live 10,000 miles apart, are more profitable than a transaction between two European neighbors; or that multilateral business transactions are more profitable than bilateral business transactions. They may or may not be, depending on what two or more parties have to give one another in return for what they get. The members of a local economy may be cut off from possibilities of profit which would be available within a larger economy. A purely urban economy may be unable to exchange a financial or industrial surplus for the products of agriculture, and the national economy is then better than the merely regional economy; but it does not follow that a local enterprise, such as a retail store, is less profitable. Improved communications make it possible to do business at a distance or through a third party, but such remote or indirect transactions are not necessarily more profitable than next-to-next transactions. In short, the global economy merely multiplies the alternatives of economic choice.

The normative judgments applicable to limited or national economics are also applicable to a global economy. It may be criticized instrumentally, that is, as failing to work and as generating the causes of its own failure. The world-wide economy is subject to cycles, monopolies (here called 'cartels'), excessive saving, the decline of purchasing power, overproduction, unemployment, inflation and deflation. A global economy may or may not be true to its moral purpose of fulfilling the needs of all to the maximum degree. If this purpose is to be fulfilled the global economy must be controlled by international statesmen who are faithful and enlightened; or, in the last analysis, by an international economic statesmanship widely distributed among the private persons and groups or the national rulers, who conduct its economic affairs.

An economy which satisfies the requirement of universality may nevertheless fail to satisfy the standard of liberality. It was its illiberality which discredited the economic imperialisms of the nineteenth century. The European power which imported ivory from Africa or spices from the East Indies, or employed native labor for the development of local resources, often exploited ignorance and poverty. After its fashion it was an economy on the global scale; since both parties obtained what they needed more for what they needed less. But it rested on a grossly unequal bargaining power.

No doubt mere prudence would dictate an increase of the purchasing power of the so-called dependent peoples up to a certain point; but it would not close the gap between selfish economy and economy considered in terms of its advantage to both. Only the disinterested recognition of the interest of dependent peoples themselves would prescribe that they should be made independent; that is, encouraged to develop their own resources and industries so as to compete on more equal terms with the developed economies of Europe and America.

A liberal world economy will be organized in behalf of all mankind, and that which it prescribes will take precedence of an economy organized in behalf of any limited part. Its requirements will overrule those of so-called "national self-interest," if and when there is a conflict between the two. There is more lip-service to this idea than understanding of its meaning. Perhaps national self-interest is only what some national says it is — without too much protest from his fellow nationals. But let it be assumed that the standard of a national self-interest is the provision which it makes for the interests of its members, as they stand, and whatever they are. One may then inquire whether a national economy so defined will do its job better by extension of its economic transactions beyond its borders.

No one has ever doubted that this will to some extent be the case. The people of the United States clearly benefit from a mass production which is made possible only by access to foreign markets. But the world economy stands on its own independent ground, as being good for the interests of the totality of mankind, as *they* stand and whatever *they* are. All of the declarations of recent years, from the Atlantic Charter to the guiding principles of the Economic and Social Council, the International Bank and Monetary Fund, and the Commercial Charter of the United Nations, have taken this broader ground; and have affirmed that the claims made on this ground take precedence of the claim made on the narrower ground of the national interest. It is hoped, or dogmatically believed, that the two claims will agree; and for home consumption it is customary to dwell upon this agreement, so that appeal may be made to the national rather than the international claim. But there is no reason to suppose that the two claims will agree in their applications throughout unless the national interest is taken to include a benevolent interest in other nations.[16]

Thus when the exploitation of dependent areas is condemned, it is not merely because it is bad for the exploited; although in some measure it undoubtedly is. When it is conceded that all nations should have access to basic raw materials, it is not merely because this will better the position of those who have hitherto monopolized them. When an international bank is created for the purpose of making loans to backward economies this is not merely because these economies will then provide new customers for the advanced economies. Beyond a certain point, and in the last analysis, these proposals argue from the good of all concerned, and require that the participants be activated by independent benevolence. If this ground were not taken the argument could not possibly appeal to all parties; it would be meaningless to hope for agreement through a conference of all parties in the full light of the economic facts and possibilities.

It is morally admirable to relieve distress in all parts of the world, but if this is to be done by economic means the mechanisms and instruments of economy must be preserved. It is true that Good Samaritanism is in principle not confined to near neighbors: on humanitarian principles all men are neighbors, and in the age of travel by air the road from Jerusalem to Jericho encompasses the earth. But the binding up of wounds is not economy — unless, as is not recorded of the Scriptural Samaritan, it is attended with the expectation of eventually doing business after the wound has healed. In an ideal economy men and nations would still do business with each other, and do it in a businesslike manner. The interests of each man might be exalted to the highest level of humanity; and art, science, and piety might be preferred to material goods. All men and groups might possess equal wealth, intelligence, and bargaining power, poverty and exploitation having been eradicated. But it would still be good that men should exchange for their mutual profit, and by division of labor and combined effort produce more abundantly for their several needs.

[16] The convenient but unwarranted assumption that the two claims coincide is illustrated on a more limited scale by a typical statement of the economic relations of the United States and Latin America. Having laid down the principle that "in a human world . . . intelligent self-interest must be the paramount guiding force," the writer goes on to say that "no policy is satisfactory to the United States that does not redound to the common interest of the entire hemisphere — including the United States." "Is the 'Good Neighbor' Policy Sound?," *New York Times Magazine*, March 28, 1948.

11

Economic technology embraces all knowledge that is adapted to any economic use. The increase of expertness is the most unquestionable feature of economic history. The rapid advance of scientific discovery is reflected in the acceleration of industrial progress, and reflected so promptly that nuclear physics is scarcely discovered before the imagination of the industrialist is anticipating its applications to war, engineering, and medicine. Indeed technology presses so hard on science as to overrun it, and put the technological cart before the scientific horse. So far does science now rise in response to the demands of technology that the laboratories of science dwell under the same roof with engineering, and research is housed with industry.

Manufacturing utilizes applications of mathematics, physics, and chemistry. Soil culture and animal husbandry utilize the applications of chemistry and biology. Industrial management and advertising utilize the applications of psychology and sociology. Business employs lawyers and political lobbyists. All this is external technology, that is, the utilization of knowledge drawn from sources other than economics itself and devoted to economic ends.

There is also an internal economic technology in which economy profits by its own experience, or uses economic knowledge. This knowledge may be used by an individual economic agent for his own private profit, or by organized industries and corporations, or by government. It may be used to facilitate the total economy — to recover from depressions or to prevent them, to increase the national income, or to provide employment and purchasing power in order that the economic wheels may continue to revolve. Or it may be used to raise the system to a higher level of justice and humanity. All this is too evident to require elaboration.

The economies of today and of tomorrow, whether individualist or collectivist, are planned economies: proved, corrected, and developed in the light of their success in providing society with the benefits for which an economy is designed. It is true that despite the obsolescence of the metaphysical and historical myths which placed economy beyond the reach of the will, there is still a sense of man's helplessness to cope with his own product. Production, distribution, exchange, advancing technology; the specialization, segregation, and correlation of services; the creation and mobilization of capital; the financial agencies of money, banking, and credit; the organization of labor; and the countless other devices in which economy proliferates, form a system so vast and intricate that the individual born into it is disposed to accept it, for better or for worse, as a fatality to which he must needs conform himself. But while the modern economy places an increasing burden on man's power to organize himself, there is no providence of nature or history which is going to relieve him of the burden.

Here again the extension of economy into the wider international and global area points its moral meaning. There *is* no global economy, as there is no global conscience, polity, or law; or, if they exist at all, they exist only in their crude beginnings. But there is a felt demand for such institutions and a resolve to achieve them. Needing them and not having them, man must invent them. The great moral institutions are man's to make or to leave unmade; to accept as they are with all their faults of commission and omission, or to refashion in accordance with the common moral purpose which commends them to human choice. Conscience, polity, law, and economy are different branches of the same fundamental moral pursuit, employing different instrumentalities for the same end, namely, an organization of men and of human interests that shall enable them to live and prosper together. This long campaign of man against conflict and helplessness has its advances and retreats, its battles won and its battles lost or drawn; but the goal and direction of effort are clear.

CHAPTER XVI

THE CLAIMS OF DEMOCRACY

Democracy, although usually described as a "form of government," is in fact a social system, of which government in the strict sense is only a part. It may properly be called an ideology, since it defines an order of values which pervades all of the major aspects of human life.

It is characteristic of democracy, in this broad sense, that its adherents are not merely loyal to it but believe that its claims to acceptance are superior to those of any rival ideology. It is considered a mark of enlightenment in the modern age to adopt an attitude of sceptical relativism toward one's fundamental allegiance — whether it be to God, or to country, or to any other cause. The effect is strangely paradoxical. He who claims for his cause that it is in some sense true or valid offers reasons for it. He, on the other hand, who claims nothing for his cause save that it is his, looks to no proof save his own sheer assertion. Hence sceptical relativism generates fanaticism. Such fanaticism is the most terrible of all fanaticisms: since it is incorrigible and remorseless. It is blind to evidence and deaf to argument. Against opposing doctrines it brings a closed mind, and a naked will. It submits to no arbitration but that of force. Its only credential is its power to survive, and the authenticity of its credentials is established by its success in surviving. It consecrates itself, therefore, to the cultivation of power and to the destruction of its rivals.

The adherent of democracy rejects sceptical relativism and claims truth. He refuses to concede that democracy is just one among conflicting ideologies, each of which is good for its own devotees. He claims it is the optimum form of social organization, endorsed by advancing enlightenment and acceptable even to present opponents in proportion as their ignorance, inexperience, or willful perversity is overcome; in proportion, that is, as it finds entrance into thoughtful and disinterested minds.

This bold claim of democracy is based on the alleged identity between democracy and morality. Democracy is the *right* organization of society, or the way in which society *ought* to be organized, or the *good* society; the terms 'right,' 'ought,' and 'good' being given a moral meaning, and 'morality' being taken to mean the organization of interests for the purpose of removing conflict and substituting coöperation. So construed, morality is applicable to all interests, to all persons taken as having interests, and to all relations among interests. It does not depend on the particular character of the interests, or on their time and place; it does not depend on the particular subject of the interests, or on race, nationality, or condition. There is no society of men whose orbits intersect or whose interests meet to which this standard is not applicable, whether in praise or in condemnation.

Democracy is the social application of this principle, and it shows the same universality. In its fundamental meaning a democracy is a society of persons who so manage their relations and their affairs as to escape the evils of isolation, frustration, and violence, and achieve the good of living innocently and fruitfully together. It is a harmony of wills by which to achieve the maximum fulfillment of the interests of all concerned. So defined the democratic society is the ideal society, and in proportion as this ideal is achieved a society merits the name of 'democracy.'

2

Lest this definition of democracy seem to be arbitrary, or merely to represent the extravagance of its adherents, it must be tested by comparison with traditional verbal usage. Democracy has always been associated with the term 'people,' as in Lincoln's classic "government of the people, by the people, for the people." Judgments of democracy both unfavorable and favorable have reflected the meanings given to this term: the comparative ill-repute of democracy in ancient times was based on a derogatory idea of "the people," and its comparatively high repute in modern times has been based on a eulogistic idea of "the people."

The derogatory idea of "the people" sprang, presumably, from the division of society into classes or castes. Since the dawn of history, and in all parts of the world, human societies have as a rule possessed a pyramidal structure: an hereditary chieftain, a king exalted in dignity above the rest and ruling by personal command; an oligarchy or hereditary aristocracy, enjoying special privileges and forming the king's immediate entourage; and on the other hand, a residuum, larger in number and lower in privilege and dignity. The term 'democracy' (δημοκρατία) first came into vogue as the name for a society ruled by this last and most numerous class, the demos (δῆμος). The alternatives were distinguished in terms of number — the rule of the one, the few, or the many — and the many were assumed to be inferior in wealth, knowledge, talent, and prowess.

When democracy is achieved by revolution this conception will always possess a certain justification. The few who were on top will in some degree have been selected by merit, and those who are placed on top when the pyramid is overturned will retain some of the characteristics of the bottom. They will, as a group, have enjoyed less of what are called "advantages." They will be less skilled in the art of managing affairs; and less disinterested, since they are more likely to be governed by envy and greed.

This conception of democracy as the inversion of a class pyramid — as turning society upside down, and putting on top those who belong at the bottom — has never ceased to reign in men's minds. The condemnation of the French Revolution and more recently of the proletarian revolution in Russia has been largely on this ground. But there has been a tendency to shift the emphasis from a lowest and most numerous class to a type of mentality supposed to be characteristic of it. Polybius in ancient times introduced the term 'ochlocracy' as the name for the rule of the mob or crowd.[1] But the mental characteristics of the mob are no longer confined to any sharply distinguishable social class; with the spread of literacy and the rise of the general standard of living all parts of society have become vulnerable to mass appeal, and to the demagogue who debases men's minds in order to win their blind support.

When democracy is taken to mean the rule of the people, and the term 'people' is taken to mean the mass or the mass mentality its refutation is self-evident. If democracy means the rule of those who are unfit to rule, it is condemned by definition. Instead of being the best form of society it is clearly the worst.[2] If the rule of the people is to be justified, they must be believed to be the *best* qualified to rule — not necessarily well-qualified, but at any rate the least disqualified.

Democracy makes three claims to satisfy this requirement. In the first place, it takes an optimistic rather than a pessimistic view of human nature. It judges men by the capacities displayed by them at their best. No doubt modern democracy was in its rosy dawn over optimistic. Deliverance from the harsh restraints of tyranny and bigotry seemed, in the eighteenth century, to promise an immediate and glorious triumph of that faculty of reason which distinguishes the human species from the

---

[1] The term "ὄχλος" implied turbulence and unruliness, as contrasted with the less invidious term "δῆμος," frequently used to mean the multitude or the total population of a country. A similar shading of meaning appears in the English word 'populace' as distinguished from 'people.'

[2] Similarly Plato had no difficulty in proving that aristocracy is the best form of society since he took it to mean the rule of those most fit to rule. One is tempted, were it not for its cacophony, to introduce the word for the antithesis of aristocracy, 'the rule of the worst.' Unfortunately the word is 'kakistocracy'!

brute. The disillusionment which followed called for a greater sobriety and patience — a long struggle rather than an easy victory. If men were not actually rational, they were at any rate potentially rational, and could become rational through education and opportunity.

In the second place, the people are best fitted to rule because it is their good which is at stake and of this they themselves are the best judges. Experience has shown that in the long run the best guarantee that the interests of men shall be consulted and provided for by society is to put them in charge of it. When the ruler is separated from the ruled he is likely to become so preoccupied with his own interests as to forget the interests of the ruled ("the forgotten man"); or to put what he feels for them, in place of what they feel for themselves.

The final and conclusive qualification of the people to rule is their inclusiveness. There is no morally justifiable claim of one man or one group to rule over another, but there is a morally justifiable claim of the whole to rule over one of its parts. There is a finality in a human person which forbids his being rightfully overruled save with his own consent.

Hence democracy as the morally best form of organized society is a society organized and ruled by its own members, and all of its members, for their own good as they see it. If the rule of the people by themselves and for themselves is to be something more than a high-sounding phrase by which authorities soften the edge of their authoritarianism, by which a king commends himself as the "father" of his people, or a demagogue masquerades as the "friend" of the people, the wills of the members of society must be so organized as to enable them to make public policy and profit by it.

3

In the examination of the relation of the several social institutions to democracy it was well to begin with polity, because political democracy has led the way in democratic practice, and has largely determined the verbal expressions used in the theoretical discussions of democracy. Thus it is customary to speak of democracy as a "form of government," although the vogue of such expressions as "democratic processes" and the "democratic way of life" implies that polity is only a fraction of what is being talked about. It is political democracy, furthermore, which brings out most clearly the important difference between a democracy of control and a democracy of benefits. The latter is now commonly referred to as 'social democracy,' and it will be convenient to employ this usage. But if it is to be employed it must be with reservations, for evidently polity is social, both in its own peculiar instrumentalities, and in its ulterior purpose.

A polity is democratic when, and insofar as, the ruling, that is, the control, of public policy is lodged in the entire people rather than in any individual or group. Different forms of democratic polity will then be distinguished by the different methods by which the people exercise this control: the most important difference of method being that between its direct, and its indirect, exercise. The direct method of control is employed when public policy is decided by the people assembled *en masse,* or by a referendum; the indirect method when the people delegate their control, or choose representatives who act in their behalf.

Those who wish to disparage democracy sometimes refer to the second type of polity as "republican," and deny that it is democratic at all; invoking the authority of the Founding Fathers. It is quite true that James Madison and others who participated in the classic debates of the Federalist did so use the words 'democracy' and 'republic.' [3] But Jefferson, on the other hand, gives no sanction to this terminology:

> We of the United States . . . are constitutionally and conscientiously democrats. We consider society as one of the natural wants with which man has been created; that he has been endowed with faculties and qualities to effect its satisfaction by concurrence of others having the same want; that when, by the exercise of these faculties, he has procured a state of society, it is one of his acquisitions which he has a right to regulate and control, jointly indeed with all those who have concurred in the procurement, whom he cannot exclude from its use or direction more than they him . . . Hence, with us, the people . . . being unqualified for the management of affairs requiring intelligence above the common level, yet competent judges of human character, they chose, for their management, representatives, some by themselves immediately, others by electors chosen by themselves.[4]

Jefferson advocates indirect popular control, on the ground that the people at large are competent to judge of facts and of character, though not of policy. And it is this ultimate popular control, called into play when the deputy is chosen or removed, which then constitutes the defining principle of political democracy. Thus, according to *Webster,* a democracy is "a form of government in which the supreme power is retained by the people and exercised either directly (pure democracy) or indirectly (representative democracy)." [5]

In practice it is impossible to hold even to this distinction, except as a difference of degree. It is doubtful if any democracy has been pure in the sense of dispensing altogether with delegated authorities; and the delegated authority will always exercise *some* discretionary authority in the discharge of his duties of legislation, administration, or judicial decision, and in the interval between elections — otherwise there would be no reason for having him. On the other hand, every elector will, in cast-

[3] Cf. *Federalist,* IX, X, XIV, XXXIX.
[4] Letter to P. S. Dupont de Nemours, 1816; *Writings of Thomas Jefferson,* P. L. Ford (ed.), 1899, X, pp. 22–3.
[5] *New International Dictionary,* 2d Edition, Unabridged, 1938.

ing his vote, be in some measure concerned with the candidate's opinions as well as his character, and will therefore be compelled to make up his own mind on matters of public policy. In short, the popular representative is neither the mouthpiece of his constituents, nor a superior person selected to do their thinking for them: he is both — a mixture of the two in varying proportions.

All of the characteristic devices of political democracy are designed with a view to effective popular control, whether direct or indirect: the elected legislature and executive; election of the judiciary, or its appointment by the elected legislature or executive; manhood suffrage and periodic elections; the secret ballot, enabling the citizen to register his opinion without fear; the multiple party system, providing for the organized expression of group opinions; freedom of criticism of the party in power by parties out of power, and by the general public; the campaigns which precede elections; liberty of press, radio, and assembly, by which the public may be informed of issues of policy and by which both sides may be presented; public education, in order to fit the people to exercise their function of citizenship.

The device of majority decisions as applied both to elections and to the acts of the assembly is of the greatest practical importance, but must not, as has been pointed out, be mistaken for the meaning of democracy. No fraction of the people, however large, is identical with *the* people. The core of democracy is government by consent — by the consent of all who live under government. The right of any given majority lies in the underlying agreement of all parties to accept a decision by majority vote. And at the same time the minority may not be deprived of the opportunity to convert itself into a majority.

This, however, is only half of the story. A democracy is known by its fruits and not merely by its control. It is essential that another question should be asked, namely, "For whose good does a democratic government govern?" It is assumed that if the people control society they will control it not merely for the sake of controlling it, or for the sake of perpetuating their control, but in order to obtain what they desire or enjoy what they like. The ruling and the interests of the ruled — the democracy of control and the democracy of benefits — are interdependent parts of one whole. Nevertheless it is possible to distinguish them. This becomes clear when it is recognized that democracy of control *could,* theoretically, be combined with privileged benefits, and privileged control with a democracy of benefit. A government by the people, could, however unlikely, be devoted to the interests of a king or of an elite. A government by a priest or king, or by a hereditary aristocracy, or by an oligarchy of the rich, or by a single party, might be dedicated to the interests of all the people. Democracy in the full sense rejects both of these alternatives. If, then, out of respect for usage, and despite the probability of misunderstanding, the term 'political democracy' is used to designate popular rule or control, and the term 'social democracy' to designate popular distribution of benefits, then the union of the two will constitute "integral democracy." The same distinction provides for the difference, and at the same time the close relation between political rights and social rights, between the political and the social parts of freedom, and between political and social equality. One can also understand how in the history of democracy there is an opposite or alternating emphasis on these two aspects, ultimately inseparable though they be.

4

Democracy can be considered as a circle, sometimes benign, sometimes vicious. When democracy flourishes, this circle is a circuit through which democratic forces gather strength as they flow; but when democracy fails at one point of the circle, it is likely to fail throughout. Political democracy tends to promote social democracy, and social democracy tends to promote political democracy. But the lack of one tends to destroy or prevent the other, and when there is no democracy at all it is necessary to decide which shall be the first point of attack. These considerations have a pertinent application to the present, when it is proposed that democracy shall be extended to large portions of mankind who have hitherto been without it.

The absence of social democracy incapacitates a people for political democracy, and without political democracy the people are unlikely to achieve social democracy. Effective political democracy reflects social benefits already enjoyed. Without education, leisure, and economic power widely distributed, popular control can never be more than nominal. When the great majority of a people has little or no margin above the level of bare subsistence, it has neither the competence nor the inclination to assume political control, or to utilize its mechanisms when these are offered. In other words, as is now said of vast aggregates of mankind, bread comes before the ballot. They are disfranchised by their poverty.

As a consequence of this situation, political control falls into the hands of privileged monopolists of land and capital, who are disinclined to abandon their privileges. Polity then obeys the law that "to him who hath it shall be given" — and shall continue to be given. Their political exploitation of the people follows from their economic exploitation. This political exploitation need not assume the more gross and palpable forms. It may consist simply in a general disparity of all of those capacities and attainments which, in their sum, condition the influence which one man can privately exert upon his fellows. It may assume most gracious forms and be consecrated by tradition. It may be accompanied by small kindnesses and the observance of decent amenities on the part of those who exert influence, and by docility and loyalty on the part of those who receive it. But it still remains exploitation. The exploited may applaud and vote as they are told, since they know no better; and rally to slogans invented by their betters, who have the superior wit to invent them, and who occupy the key positions, and possess the instruments, by which slogans become effective. The mind of the people is made for them by those who create the ideas and the symbols which seize the popular imagination. By making the popular mind the privileged minority makes the government; and if they are human, they will be inclined to perpetuate the condition of which they are the privileged beneficiaries.

No one would give the name of 'democracy' to this state of affairs. How is a society to be extricated from this vicious circle? Only, it seems clear, by improving the social condition of the masses of the people, so that they may be enabled to profit by their numerical strength. Once in this prostrate condition the people cannot save themselves by political democracy: they need social salvation first in order to understand and achieve political salvation. They have to be helped to their feet before they can walk, or learn to walk by themselves.

The escape from this situation may take a variety of forms, the most radical of which is revolution proceeding from the more embittered and passionate of the exploited class, led by members of the intelligentsia, who from any one of a number of motives, high and low, may have come over to their side. Or the situation may be escaped, without violence, through a benevolent dictatorship at home, or through a benevolent imperial master or trustee operating from abroad. A paternalistic government is invoked to give the people what they have neither the knowledge nor the power to demand, in order that thereafter they may be qualified to prize and preserve it. Whichever form the intervention assumes it will take time to bear fruit. This is commonly called "preparing a people for self-government." There are, in other words, situations in which political democracy can be brought into being only by non-democratic procedures.

The danger of such remedies is notorious. Violent revolution tends to a general and prolonged disorder — to cruelties and reprisals, hatreds and suspicions, which are disastrous to the entire society, and from which all parties, including the exploited themselves, turn for relief to dictatorship. Paternalism once practiced at home or abroad, tends to become permanent, the time when the people are considered "fit for self-government" being perpetually postponed. To accomplish the delivery and the weaning requires a magnanimity, political craftsmanship, and forbearance which, though by no means unknown, are rare.

No such dangerous remedies are required within societies which have already achieved a fair measure of social democracy. In such societies, there is already a sufficiently wide distribution of power and understanding to justify a scrupulous observance of democratic political forms.

These then serve as the institutions through which a more or less enlightened and self-confident popular will can extend its rule. But even in
such societies there is no guarantee that these institutions will be effectively democratic unless they are perpetually devoted to the wide distribution of these conditions of life which enable a man to speak intelli-
gently and effectively in behalf of his interests, and to play his part in
the molding of public opinion. Democracy can be destroyed through a
process of social gravitation by which large groups of the community,
despite their constitutional rights, become inarticulate and impotent.

The interdependence of the political and social aspects of democracy,
with the possible emphasis of one at the expense of the other, throws
some light on the present unhappy state of the world. Two groups of
nations are aligned against one another in the name of democracy, and
each denies the other the right to the name. Thus in the Western democracies it is the common belief that the name of 'people's democracy'
employed in communist countries, is mere camouflage. But there is a grain
or two of truth in the view that the dispute is not between a genuine and
a fraudulent democracy, but between two halves of democracy, each of
which is mistaken by its partisans for the whole.

A recent cartoon by Low represents two figures labeled "Eastern View
of Democracy" and "Western View of Democracy." The first looking
into a mirror sees the second instead of seeing a reflection of himself.
The first carries a book labeled "Marx-Lenin Doctrine" and bearing the
inscription, "Government in the Interest of the People"; the second carries a ballot box bearing the inscription "Government by the Will of the
People." The first, "The Eastern View," is represented as blind in one
eye, while the second, "The Western View," is represented as seeing with
both eyes, and wears an expression of surprise at the one-sided vision of
the other. Now had the cartoonist not been a Westerner, he might have
represented both figures as defective in one eye. There would then be
two democracies, each of which sees better out of one eye than the other,
but which differ in the eye which sees better. Neither would be wholly
blind to the fact that democracy implies both "government in the interest
of the people" and "government by the will of the people," but communist countries would be credited with a clearer vision of the first
implication, and the western democracies of the second.

The Bolshevik revolution of 1917 was an uprising of peasants and
workers, under doctrinaire leadership, against extreme and long-standing
exploitation by the landowners, industrial magnates, administrative bureaucracy, imperial dynasty, and clerical hierarchy of the old Russian
regime. It was a violation of established human and property rights, and
resulted in the creation of a harsh and repressive dictatorship. The new
Constitution, proclaimed in 1936, did not represent the realities of the
situation, but it did represent the professed goal. In its definition of rights

it emphasized social rights, as being necessary to make political rights effective. Thus a Soviet apologist, having emphasized "such great rights as the right to work, to rest and leisure, to an education, and to material maintenance in old age and also in case of sickness or incapacitation," proceeded as follows:

> It is these social rights, above all, that insure the widest enjoyment of all political rights and liberties, for they provide freedom from worry about employment, freedom from fear of "rainy days," they guarantee stable earnings, provide the necessary free time to take part in political activities, enable everyone to broaden his horizon and acquire general and special knowledge.[6]

These claims are advanced to prove that "Soviet democracy is a higher type of democracy," and "a system of true popular government." The argument can be reversed, to prove that a people denied political liberties have lost at least half of their democracy, and that without their political liberties the people will lose the best guarantee of their social rights. No doubt Western democracy at present exceeds Soviet democracy on both scores, but it cannot afford to dismiss the Soviet argument lightly. There are European and American adherents of democracy who are too easily satisfied with the creed of political democracy, and who need to be reminded that social democracy is both the proper fruit and indispensable condition of political democracy.

Furthermore, in its appeal for the support of mankind, Western democracy is too likely to forget that its gospel of political democracy does not always meet the existing situation. There are multitudes of mankind for whom the first step toward democracy must be the relief of their misery, ignorance, and exploitation. The saving gospel will be that of an integral democracy comprising both a popular control, and a popular distribution of benefits.

5

Democracy will employ all of the basic moral institutions — of conscience, law, and economy, as well as polity — and each of these in turn will be democratic. A society which is democratic in any one or two of these spheres and non-democratic in the rest, will find itself in a state of uneasy equilibrium. This follows from the interdependence of the institutions themselves, and from the fact that the same persons are embraced in all, and will carry their habits and attitudes from one to another.

A democratic conscience will be distinguished from any class conscience — from any code which rests on privilege and exclusiveness, such as the code of a military caste, the code of the courtier, the code of the

---

[6] *USSR Information Bulletin*, Washington, D. C., Nov. 6, 1946, pp. 11–15, including quotations from documentary sources.

sportsman, the code of the worker, even the code of the race or nation. The democratic conscience is the code of "man to man the warld o'er." It does not contradict narrower codes provided these are subordinate. It may embrace a peculiar deference to the opinion of fellow-members of any limited circle, provided it does not supersede the deference to the opinion of one's fellow-men at large.

Law will be democratic in the double sense already brought to light in the examination of democratic polity. The people will make their own laws, and will themselves enjoy the benefits. Law made by the popular assembly will express the popular will most immediately and directly; law made by the judicial process, will provide for the rights of all individuals and minorities, and thus protect the people as a whole against the tyranny and haste of the momentary majority. In its democratic procedures law will give every litigant the opportunity to argue his own case on the grounds of fact or legal interpretation, and thus to participate in the making of the decision which finds him guilty or innocent, or by which he obtains or suffers damages. The people are also justified in insisting that the law's benefits shall accrue to all, without fear or favor, and that it shall promote their well-being and happiness. Since the ultimate premises of constitutional law are derived from a social philosophy, in a democracy they will coincide with the general principles of democracy. Every decision which is based on narrower premises will be open to challenge and reargument.

The principles of democracy have peculiar weight in their application to economy. Gross inequalities of wealth and bargaining power can arise within a society whose political constitution is democratic, and a growing awareness of this fact has shifted the emphasis of democratic gospel from polity to economy; a political democracy which is not at the same time an economic democracy is a hollow mockery. What boots it if a man may speak his mind and deposit his ballot if other private persons, through command of the resources which he needs, can make and mold his life from the cradle to the grave, and from father to child? He feels, rather, that he has exchanged one master for another — a magnate, instead of a Caesar, who bestrides the narrow world like a colossus.

As in polity the citizen plays the double role of ruler and ruled, and as in polity the ruling is for the benefit of the ruled, so in an economy each human integer plays the double role of the producer and consumer, and the producing is for the sake of the consuming. As in a political democracy the people govern for their own benefit, so in an economic democracy they produce for their own benefit. They will suffer no bondage save the bond of their own agreement. The divisions of labor and role which the economy requires will be raised to the level of voluntary coöperation and shareholding in a common enterprise.

If a society is to be democratic as a whole, the major social institutions — conscience, polity, law, and economy — must be democratic. But there is still room within a democracy for subordinate organizations which are non-democratic — provided they are not anti-democratic. It is clear that an army, for example, cannot serve its purpose without discipline, that is to say, without the prompt and invariable obedience of commands from above. But if autocratic control within a democracy is to be consistent with its democratic framework there are certain conditions which must be met.

In the first place, the authority must be a delegated authority, in fact as well as in name. The purpose for which the autocratic control is exercised must be accepted by those who are called upon to obey it. Thus an army is democratic, however autocratic the control exercised by the officers, when the necessity of such control and the purpose for which it is exercised are understood and accepted by the men in the ranks. The efforts to implant this condition of mind, however pathetic its failure, is characteristic of the so-called "popular" or "citizens'" armies of a democracy.

In the second place, the delegated control must not be interminable, irretrievable, or absolute. The man in the ranks must not lose his citizenship, and his political or legal rights; and he must have safeguards and means of redress by which these rights are protected. The same will hold of all similar organizations, or institutions, such as the church, the school, or the industrial corporation, when the internal mechanism of control is autocratic. The member must not deliver himself totally, but only partially for some limited and defined purpose, reserving his moral will for the ultimate decisions in which he participates as a citizen of a democracy.

In the third place, the social relations within the subordinate organization must be consistent with the personal dignity of its members. The members will be aware of their double finality, as ultimate sources of control, and as claimants whose interests it is the ultimate purpose of social organization to reconcile and promote. On these grounds he will respect himself and demand the respect of others. The personal relations within the organization must not violate this respect — whether they are relations between officer and private, priest and layman, director and shareholder, professor and student, or employer and worker.

In the fourth place, the subordinate organization must not so accustom men to submissiveness and subserviency as to unfit them for the exercise of their democratic roles in conscience, polity, law, and economy. They must not lose their capacity to think and choose for themselves. If the church, school, or any other private organization teaches its members blind obedience, or the uncritical acceptance of another's judgment, it unfits them for taking part in any democratic organization, large or small.

It will have killed the spirit of freedom and equality which is democracy's very life.

6

There are two watchwords or maxims of democracy, which, while they do not define it, nevertheless through their multiple meanings serve best to convey its all-pervading quality. The first of these is *freedom*.

Freedom is not doing "what one likes" or "pleases" merely, but doing what one *chooses;* and in a fuller sense it is doing what one chooses oneself within a system where other people also do what they choose. Freedom thus has both personal and social implications.

It is a mistake to suppose that doing what one chooses is a merely negative thing: it is more than the mere absence of obstacles and hindrances.

The false idea that freedom is a negative thing arises from the fact that people take their interests for granted, and focus attention on what interferes with them. There is a tendency to think of freedom as the removal of whatever it is that one finds frustrating. A conspicuous example of this tendency at the present time is the business man's idea that freedom consists in the non-interference of government; but to the growing youth freedom consists in escape from the interference of the parent or the schoolmaster, to the worker escape from the interference of the boss or employer, to the prisoner escape from jail. All of these freedoms neglect the fact that without a freedom *for,* a freedom *from* has no meaning. Positive freedom requires the possession of means and the presence of favorable conditions. There is no freedom unless there is an interest which demands fulfillment and unless that fulfillment is possible.

When it is said that freedom is doing what one chooses, there is a great deal of meaning packed into a little word 'one.' It is not a matter of doing what *is chosen,* but of what some *person* chooses. Personal choice implies reflection, that is, a capacity to select from several acts which are represented in advance by ideas. It implies calculation, that is, judgments of the results of possible acts; and it implies a weighing not only of alternative means but alternative ends. It then appears, furthermore, that the degree of freedom depends on the range of alternatives — the number and variety of the possibilities open to choice; and this, in turn, not only upon their existing but upon their being known.

But it is from its social implications that democratic freedom emerges. Man lives in a social environment — there is always more than one freedom involved. Other persons may not only present obstacles to freedom, but may have their own rival claims to freedom. Democracy proclaims the principle of the maximum freedom of each which is consistent with a similar freedom for all.

This is the point at which freedom is a product of organization — of the moral and legal institutions, which define areas of freedom, and guarantee them in the name of rights. It is not correct to say that organized society either destroys or creates freedom. Those who hold that it destroys freedom imagine men to be free in a "state of nature," being ignorant or neglectful of the fact that in the absence of custom, polity, law, and economy men would deprive one another of freedom. Those who hold that civil society creates freedom are ignorant or neglectful of the fact that in the absence of social organization men would still have interests, and would in some measure do what they chose. What civil society does is to impose public restraints on freedom, with a view to diminishing the private restraints on freedom. At the same time, through coöperation, it broadens the possibilities of choice, and provides men with the instruments by which their choices may be effective.

Because democratic freedom is a freedom for all, it is a shared freedom. The democratic will to freedom, though it animates each person, is not an exclusive or egoistic claim; it is an assertion of "our" freedom and not merely "mine." A democracy is a free society, or society of free men. The attitude of man to man, in all human relations, is flavored with respect for others' freedom. To live appropriately to a democratic society requires that one shall prefer this form of association to the company of the servile and obsequious. It is this interplay of freedoms — this living among the free — that creates the zest and exhilaration of democratic social relations.

7

The second great democratic slogan is *equality*. Like freedom, it has been widely misrepresented. Democracy is supposed by some of its critics to affirm equality at the expense of difference. But to affirm human equality without reservation is so evidently absurd that no one has seriously affirmed it.

Inequality of natural endowment is undeniable and ineradicable; and whenever the conditions of life are equalized, men will profit unequally by these conditions, as the children who inherit equal shares of the same estate will presently have achieved unequal fortunes, or as the runners in a race, having an equal start will arrive unequally at the finish. Such inequality of attainment is not only unavoidable, but desirable. To equalize attainment it would be necessary to devise a system of graduated handicaps. The result would be to reduce all human attainment to the level of the least qualified, and to deprive society of the contributions of superior ability and energy.

Where men start in the race of life is determined for them. If men are to start equal they must be *given* an equal start — this does not take care of itself. The circle which has been observed in the relation of political to social democracy has its application to equality. Inequalities of opportunity tend to perpetuate themselves, and it is the function of democratic institutions to intervene and to create equality of opportunity, for example, by public education, provisions for social security, or apportionment of the burden of taxation. Only when their condition is equalized can they preserve and perfect their own equality.

At the same time, democracy condemns *in*equality of opportunity, holding that the more flagrant inequalities among men have been due neither to talent nor merit, but to differences of station arising from the social structure itself. Kings and nobles are not inherently superior to plebeians, but enjoy a superior position, through the accident of birth; the rich may not be inherently superior to the poor, but may owe their superiority to inherited wealth and family background. Democracy attacks such adventitious and privileged inequalities. It calls attention to superior talent and merit in the humbler ranks, and to inferior talent and merit in more exalted ranks. It proclaims the general fact that when advantages and disadvantages of social position are removed, men will be redistributed in the scale of eminence. There may not be any more equality than there was before, but it will be of a different kind; and the change will be known as an equalizing change, because those who advocate it are usually those whom it will raise up, and who say in effect, to their erstwhile superiors, "We are as good or better than you."

What, then, becomes of the declaration that men are "born" or "created" equal? To understand its meaning it is necessary to understand that at the time when John Locke uttered this declaration (to be adopted afterwards by Thomas Jefferson) the authority of some men, such as kings, *over* other men, known as "subjects," was defended on grounds of birth and "divine right." The democratic contention is that the only justifiable superior authority is that which men originally equal in authority delegate provisionally to some of their own number. The same principle applied to economy means that the only justifiable inequalities of wealth are those which arise among men originally of equal wealth — entitled to equal shares of nature's bounty — but some of whom make better use than others of their opportunity.

"Equality before the law" refers to the fact that law is couched in terms of universals and is therefore equally applicable to all instances of the universal. It means that all who fall under the law are equally entitled to its benefits, or liable to its restrictions, regardless of their differences. It does not mean, for example, that there may not be one law for the rich and one for the poor: but that if there be such laws, all the rich shall be equal before one law and all the poor before the other; and that *both* rich and poor shall be equal before other laws.

However they vary otherwise — in talent, aptitude, physical characteristics, or energy — all men are men. There is an option as to whether attention shall be focused on the specific differences or on the generic sameness. Democracy emphasizes the common humanity of men, and their common potentialities, to whatever degree these may be realized. It does not invent the biological fact that men belong to one family, or the historic fact of their common inheritance and destiny, but it stresses these facts, lest they be ignored in the narrower perspectives of daily life and amidst the rivalries by which men are divided. Democracy excites the sentiments and devises the symbols appropriate to these wider relationships.[7]

Democratic equality, like democratic freedom, culminates in the feeling of participation. The vast size and complexity of a modern society make it impossible that a man should live in the physical presence of more than a small fraction of his fellow members. It becomes the more imperative that he should by imagination and understanding extend this fellowship beyond these narow limits. That which distinguishes democracy is not happines merely, but shared happiness, or happiness of the kind that is enhanced by living among the happy. In proportion as a man is democratically minded he will find it intolerable that his happiness should be enjoyed at the expense of others. Accustomed to interchanging his lot with that of other men, whether through the objectivity of thought or through sympathy, he will count the unhappiness of others as his own, and in his pursuit of his own happiness he will join his efforts to those of other men who are pursuing theirs.

This does not imply uniformity or gregariousness. It does not mean that human interests in a democratic society will be reduced to collective activities, such as social reform, choral singing, processions, games, or even dinner parties — God forbid! One may be as aloof or as fastidious as one pleases. One may prefer the company of the select rather than the company of the crowd. One may spend one's most rewarding hours in solitary contemplation. All that democracy requires is that one's enjoyment of solitude or converse with kindred spirits should be attended with a sense of innocence and of like privileges enjoyed by others. Indeed it may be argued that the consummate flower of public organization is its multiplication and protection of privacies.

These, then, are the meanings embraced within the idea of equality, when this is used as a token of democracy: the creation of a situation in which all men shall be given the same chance to prove themselves by their talents and effort; the belittling of the inequalities which are due merely to the position of the individual in the social structure; the

---

[7] The "check-up" which it is now customary to obtain at a large modern hospital, illustrates this underlying human sameness. It is not unusual to witness, in the anteroom of an X-ray clinic, a bishop, a business executive, a judge, a shop girl, a mechanic, etc., sitting patiently awaiting their turns, all clad in the same drab and shapeless robes, and holding in their laps the discarded clothes and insignia which distinguish them in the public view.

awarding to all men equally of the opportunity to demonstrate their capacities; the emphasis on the common nature and the common lot of mankind; the sense of participation and companionship in a joint effort to provide for the several and different interests of all men.

8

Democracy is a cultural product which lends itself to all the methods of inquiry which characterize the cultural sciences. It can be *explained* by attention to the conditions which give rise to it, and to its various forms, and it can be judged by standards, internal and external. It is characteristic of all ideals that their adherents fall short of their full realization — even Satan after having fallen from angelic heights presumably failed to conform perfectly to his Satanic code. If this generalization does not apply to God it is because a divine being is perfect by definition. It is evident that democracy is a counsel of perfection, and that the gap between the reach and the grasp is in proportion to the height of the reach.

Since democracy embraces all of the major social institutions — conscience, polity, law, and economy — its critique will embrace the critiques to which those institutions severally submit themselves. An ideal democracy will be efficient in its ethical, political, legal, and economic instruments, and in these several fields of social organization it will be true to their common moral purpose. It will require a democratic statesmanship in which this purpose is combined with enlightenment.

The lack of qualified leadership and direction is the besetting sin of democracy, of which it has been in some measure guilty throughout its history, and with which it has been with some justice charged by its opponents. This sin is as tempting and as deadly in the modern world as in earlier days. Democracy substitutes the people at large for the privileged person or class: the danger is that it shall then cease to be guided by those more eminent qualities of which the privileged were, if not the embodiment, then at least the symbols. Democracy incurs, as always, the risk that in rejecting the superior person and class, it shall reject superiority altogether.

In principle democracy implies that superiority shall be distributed among the members of society instead of being reserved for a self-appointed and self-perpetuating segment. For the overlord and the ruling class it substitutes the citizen. The farseeingness, all-interestedness, and steady vision of the good, which Plato ascribed to the philosophers, are supposed to exist in varying degrees in every man — at least in the form of a potentiality and an obligation. But the danger is that privileged authorities shall be superseded not by a body of more or less high-minded citizens, but by the mass, and by those who are skilled in the art of manipulating the mass.

This danger, as has been pointed out, is aggravated by the size and complexity of modern societies; and by the technologies of mass communication and mass production. The citizen as a thinking individual, who is competent to judge matters of public policy on their merits, and by discussion and persuasion to participate in the formation of an enlightened public opinion, tends to be replaced by the mass audience, the mass mind, and the mass consumer, or by the lobbyist and pressure group, who by speaking for the mass, or for some selfish interest, intimidate the public official.[8] The first concern of the friends of democracy, should be to save the thinking citizen from being thus degraded, submerged, and obliterated.

To the lack of enlightened fidelity to the democratic creed among the personal members of the nominal democracy are to be ascribed the notorious failures which have excited the scorn of its opponents. It is a wholesome and seasonable exercise of the mind for modern democracies to measure their deeds by their professions. Such a candid self-examination will reveal a widespread failure to redeem their pledges of liberality. Modern democracies abound in inequalities of opportunity, and in deprivations of freedom — of those very freedoms of thought and communication in which they pride themselves.

Democracy is an unfulfilled aspiration. Those who are underprivileged in a democracy such as the United States, are sustained by the sense that in the long run the society in which they live is theirs to make. The following paragraph was written by a sensitive and loyal American Negro, despite the disillusionment that followed the Second World War:

> I will take this that I have here. I will take the democratic theory. The bit of road of freedom that stretches through America is worth fighting to preserve. The very fact that I, a Negro in America, can fight against the evils in America is worth fighting for. This open fighting against the wrongs one hates is the mark and the hope of democratic freedom. I do not underestimate the struggle. I know the learning that must take place, the evils that must be broken, the depths that must be climbed. But I am free to help in doing these things. I count. I am free (though only a little as yet) to pound blows at the huge body of my American world until like a chastened mother, she gives me nurture with the rest.[9]

This utterance, even though it springs from a discouragement that borders on despair, and bespeaks an attitude of stubborn faith rather than a sense of triumph, profoundly expresses the motive of democracy and truly describes its saving grace.

---

[8] The Author has described this danger to democracy, and suggested means of meeting it, in *The Citizen Decides*, 1951. The expression "chain-thinking" has been used by H. Shapley, "A Design for Fighting," *The American Scholar*, 1944–5, p. 27.

[9] J. S. Redding, "A Negro Looks at This War," *American Mercury*, Nov. 1942, pp. 591–2.

9

In war, cold or hot, there are ordinarily two sides. In the world wars of the present epoch the antagonists have been groups of nations united by bonds of interest and ideology. The opposing ideologies that now divide the world are highly complex. Democracy, as understood in Western Europe and America and spread abroad from this source, being compounded of many ideas, is supported by its adherents on many grounds. The same is true of communism. As each side acquires supporters, so also it creates opponents, for different reasons. As the different elements of each ideology come to be combined under common labels and symbols, and felt as a common cause, each is further unified by its opposition to the other until there is little left but the primitive difference between friends and enemies. It is important for the future of the world that men should turn from this sheer combativeness to ideal issues so that they may know precisely what it is that they are for and what against.

The situation is confused not only by the emotion of hostility but by the fact that communism has assumed a different aspect since 1944, when it was possible for Americans and Englishmen to accept a military partnership with Soviet Russia, and, albeit with some misgivings, to look forward to coöperation in time of peace under the aegis of the United Nations. The enemy then was fascism or nazism, against which Western democracy and Eastern communism appeared to be united. Scarcely a half dozen years later, communism had replaced nazism in the role of enemy, and was commonly supposed to be essentially the same thing.

The following statement made in 1947 by an English critic of Sorel, the French syndicalist, is instructive:

> The most interesting point raised by Sorel's career is that of the resemblances and differences between Bolshevism and Fascism. If Sorel stands on the common ground where Marx and Nietzsche meet, this is also the common ground from which Bolshevism and Fascism diverge. Marx and Nietzsche, Bolshevism and Fascism, both deny bourgeois democracy with its bourgeois interpretations of liberty and equality; both reject the bourgeois doctrine of persuasion and compromise; both proclaim absolutes which command the obedience of the individual at the cost of all else.[10]

In other words, while fascism or nazism and bolshevism or communism *both* reject the libertarian individualism of the Western democracies, they still diverge. The methods employed by both were anti-democratic, but these methods were final in one case, and merely transitional in the other. Judged by its ultimate goal the one was a gospel of power and exploitation, the other a gospel of social reconstruction. So long as com-

[10] "The Adventure of Syndicalism," *The London Times Literary Supplement*, Nov. 1, 1947.

munism was so conceived Western democracy could hope that after communism had passed through its phase of revolutionary violence and fear, the communist and democratic factions of mankind could dwell in peace and collaborate in the long-range enterprise of improving the condition of mankind throughout the world.

Judging communism by the recent policy of the Soviet Union, as this appears to the now disillusioned West, there can be no doubt of its opposition all along the line to what the West calls "democracy." The democratic conscience approves the traditional virtues and maxims of the Hebraic, Graeco-Roman, Christian tradition: justice, veracity, humanity, love; the communist conscience sanctions injustice, mendacity, and inhumanity, and substitutes loyalty, orthodoxy, and obedience. The democratic polity is a popular government, resting on universal suffrage, the secret ballot, and a rivalry of parties; while the communist polity is an authoritarian monolithic state in which power descends from a single party dictator or inner circle and which permits no organized and outspoken dissent. Democracy adheres to the principle of the self-determination of all nations, large and small; while the communist state does not hesitate to impose its rule on the other nations by infiltration and conspiracy, if not by overt aggression. The democratic legal system emphasizes the rights of the individuals and minorities, and supports them by strict procedural guarantees; the communist legal system tends to paternalism, exalting social rights above civil rights, and subordinating the judiciary to political controls. The democratic economy is more or less capitalistic and individualistic relying on private enterprise and the motivation of private profit; while the communist economy is relatively socialistic and collectivistic, relying on the state control of capital, labor, enterprise, and distribution of goods.

In democracy, science and the fine arts are allowed to be governed by their own inherent standards of truth and taste; in communism, they are used as instruments of propaganda. In democracy, education aims to develop the individual's faculties so that he may think and act for himself; in communism, education indoctrinates the individual from an early age so that he may conform to authorized dogmas. In democracy, religion is accepted as an independent institution, to be either allied with the state, or encouraged by a policy of benevolent neutrality; in communism, religion is suspect, and is either forbidden altogether or reluctantly conceded provided it gives no offense and provided its gospel agrees with the communist gospel.

It is to this area of opposition that the terms 'totalitarianism' and 'tolerance' are most clearly applicable. Communism stands for the strict regulation of every branch of human culture from a common center and in accordance with a common creed. Democracy tolerates differences, not in the negative sense of permitting them, but in the positive sense of promoting them to the end of the enrichment of society and the mutual stimulation of its diverse interests.

This is the ideological opposition as seen from the standpoint of democracy; in which democracy gives itself the best of every doubt and communism the worst. If democracy were to be judged by its most ignoble practices and communism by its noblest professions the picture would be somewhat differently colored.

When communism, stripped of its unethical, authoritarian, and totalitarian features, is identified with socialism, and democracy with capitalism, there is no longer a sharp antithesis. Socialism, broadly conceived, stresses the idea that economy is a public, and not a merely private concern. From this idea it proceeds — or leaps — to the conclusion that this massive transaction should be directed and controlled from one center. In a pure socialism the public agency would be the sole owner of the means of production and the sole employer of labor. It is assumed that this power would be used to avoid the injustices arising from the inequalities of private bargaining power.

As the logic of this idea is simple and plausible, so its dangers and difficulties are evident and familiar. A supreme economic control would reach into every department of human life and it would still be a human control. It would be justified only on the assumption — the large assumption — that without the check of effective bargaining power it would be wisely and disinterestedly used.

Furthermore, a public economic agency, like any private economic agency, would be compelled to satisfy the general requirements of *economy* and induce men to give for what they get. A socialism which forced men to labor or surrender their possessions would be a form of slavery or plunder. A socialism which merely gave men what a central authority thought they needed would be a form of paternalistic benevolence. A socialism which merely combined these two functions of taking for nothing, and giving for nothing — a combination of plunder and charity — would not be an economy at all.

The opposite doctrine, known as "capitalism" or "industrial capitalism" or "individualistic capitalism" or "free enterprise" or, in its extreme form, as "laissez-faire capitalism," also has its simple logic and plausibility, and also its evident and familiar difficulties and dangers. It stands for the irrefutable idea that the only way to determine what people need is to find by experiment what they are willing to work and pay for. But such a merely prudential economy proceeds from a *given* distribution of economic power; whereas economy is ultimately concerned with the *just* distribution of this power. It requires that the social situation shall be so controlled, that the prudential motives will work for the fullest possible satisfaction of the needs of all.

Neither a pure socialism nor a pure capitalism will suffice; each must

borrow from the other, and serve as a check on the other. The characteristic charge of capitalism against socialism is that it does not function of
itself, but depends on non-economic procedures of expropriation, forced
labor, and charity. The characteristic charge of socialism against capitalism is that it enriches the strong and impoverishes the weak. The economy most consistent with democracy is a "regulated capitalism" within
which the instrument of economy is geared to its ulterior moral purpose.

10

Democracy, like the several moral institutions of which it is composed,
is in principle universal. It accepts no frontier but leaps across to mankind on the other side. Wherever there are men with human interests and
human faculties, democracy defines their ideal relationship, regardless of
differences of race or nation. Extension of democracy to embrace all
human societies raises the questions: "Should the over-all organization
be democratic?" "Should it be composed of democracies?"

The first of these questions has been answered by the history of the
United Nations. The Preamble of its Charter is a formulation of democratic principles, and the Charter as a whole is a democratic constitution.
After two devastating world wars, and in view of the growing interdependence of all human societies resulting from advancing technology,
men were faced with two alternatives — a world-wide imperialism, or a
world-wide democracy. In agreeing to create the United Nations men
agreed to choose the latter, and to reject the former. They arrived at
this choice by discussion and general consent, and the organization by
which the choice was to be implemented provided that the substitution
of coöperation for conflict should be achieved by discussion and consent.
That the United Nations has largely failed to realize its purpose does not
disprove the purpose: its success and its failure alike testify to its democratic intent.

The second question leaves more room for debate. It has been repeatedly stated or assumed that there can be peace and coöperation
between nations which practice war and exploitation at home; that governments can proceed democratically in their treatment of one another
and autocratically in their treatment of their own people. Such a view
is contrary to history as well as to logic: the grave difficulties of the post-
war settlement emphatically disprove it. When the representatives of
different nations meet to iron out their differences they bring with them
the ideologies which underlie their domestic policies, and to which they
are habituated. When these ideologies are profoundly opposed agreement
can at best be provisional and precarious.

But there is a more fundamental reason why a democratic international organization must be democratic in its parts. It rests on the agreement of nations. But nations in their composite capacity cannot agree —

only persons can agree. For agreement is a form of choosing, and only persons are capable of choice. If official delegates arrive at personal agreements among themselves, the nations do not agree; and the delegates cannot agree *for* their nations unless the personal members of their nations agree among themselves and with the delegates. Such internal agreement can occur only in the degree to which the nations live under democratic institutions.

Hence it is false to suppose that a world organization founded on the principles of democracy can be indifferent to the democratic or anti-democratic ideology of its national members. It is a mistake to suppose that democracy is only a local peculiarity, which can, in the long run, live democratically with anti-democracy. There can be no democracy on any scale, national or international, unless it reaches down to the democratic man.

The project of a democratic world society composed of national societies underscores the fact that man makes his own institutions by his recognition of their purpose and his choice of instruments. In this case, as in the case of all international institutions, man cannot rest on history and tradition. This being the case, there is a technology of democracy which draws from every branch of human knowledge, to an extent which is proportional to the vastness of the undertaking. The architects of this global structure will profit by all the sciences, natural and cultural. And they will profit by previous human experience in this very field — by the human wisdom acquired in every effort, successful or unsuccessful, to solve the problem of living freely and equally together.

CHAPTER XVII

SCIENCE AND THE SCIENCE OF SCIENCE

The explosion of the atomic bomb at Hiroshima, in its dramatic and tragic impressiveness, awoke mankind to a vivid realization of the life-and-death importance of science in human affairs. As an application of modern physics it exemplified the astonishing advance of scientific discovery and organized collaboration. It promised a great step forward in the release and control of the forces of nature — men began at once to discuss the uses of atomic energy in industry and medicine. But while these beneficent uses of atomic energy were *promised,* the first uses that were *realized* were destructive. Hence there arose the fearful doubt that this epoch-making discovery, instead of contributing greatly to human convenience and happiness, might be the instrument of catastrophe.

This danger, now so widely recognized and feared, raises in acute form the question of the good of science. There was a long period in human history when this question would have seemed quite unnecessary, if not impertinent — at least in Western Europe and the United States. During the seventeenth and eighteenth centuries the opinion widely prevailed that in order to be beneficent science needed only to be delivered from authority and obscurantism — needed only, in short, to be true to itself. During the nineteenth century the prestige of science continued to increase — through its spectacular discoveries, through the multiplication of its applications, and through its alliance with an industrialized economy.

At the same time, it is true, the position of science was becoming less tenable. Its old opponents, who accused it of stressing "material" to the exclusion of "spiritual" values, rallied against it. Along with all intellectual enterprises it was undermined by the growth of divers forms of anti-intellectualism. In its applications to man it appeared to be self-defeating; since, curiously enough, it described man in mechanical terms that made him incapable either of pursuing science or of profiting by it. Nevertheless, when the First World War, with its disastrous consequences, broke upon the world the prestige of science was still high. After the First World War social tensions and conflicts were in large part attributed to the technological developments of industry. War itself had become increasingly technological. Thus the scientist, however innocently or reluctantly, appeared in the role of the ally of the monopolist and the right hand of the warmaker. The world awoke from the Second World War as from a terrifying and unforgettable nightmare in which nazism represented the awful partnership between the most advanced developments of science and the lowest forces of bestiality. Communism, in turn, derived from science not only the tools of economic progress, but weapons of oppression and terror. And then came the atomic bomb, suggesting the possibility that science, of which man had been so proud as the one incontestable guarantee of his progress, might lead to his total and final self-destruction. The scientific laboratory, once considered as a wellspring of life, took on the aspect of a witch's cauldron where scientists brewed the elixir of death.

This is the situation which calls for a fundamental examination of the role of science in human life. Is science intrinsically beneficent or intrinsically harmful? Or is science itself merely an instrument which may be put to good or bad uses? Is there anything in science itself which predetermines the uses to which it shall be put, or by which it finds the good use more congenial than the evil? Is the scientist *qua* scientist a benefactor of mankind, or does he become such only by accident, or by forces independent of his own scientific motivation? If science contains such evil possibilities that it must be controlled, how shall it be controlled, and by what principles? How can it be controlled without depriving it of that freedom which is the condition of its development? These questions are not academic. Unless answers can be found, man may seem to be faced with the necessity of restricting or abandoning one of his greatest powers for good lest through its abuse it become a fatal instrument of evil. The cultural science to which these questions are assigned is the science of science.

2

Since science is a kind of knowledge, description of science must begin with theory of knowledge; and since knowledge is itself a form of cognition it is necessary to go even further back. This subject constitutes one of the major tasks of philosophy, and it is evident that it cannot be introduced here save in its bare essentials with little or no argument. The position taken is, in brief, that cognition is expectation, that knowledge is *qualified cognition,* and that science is *highly qualified cognition.* The first of these theses, which identifies cognition with expectation, has already been introduced in connection with the cognitive mediation of interest. This thesis requires a brief restatement and defense.

The most serious of the apparent difficulties which beset this definition of cognition lies not in the identification of knowledge with expectation, but in the temporal ambiguity of expectation itself. The time of the act of expecting and the time of what is expected are different. How can one *now* expect what has *not yet* occurred? The present act of expectation has its object now, and must be said to *have had* its object even if that later object should never occur.

This paradox rests fundamentally on the false assumption that the description of a temporal event must be confined to the contemporary, whereas it is of the very essence of temporal occurrences that they are fully describable only in terms of other times, past or future. This is the case with time itself. It is of the very nature of any specific moment that it succeeds earlier moments and precedes later moments. When one states that at fifty-nine minutes past eleven it is about to be noon, one is describing *that* moment of time. Every "now" is before and after a "then." The same analysis holds of events in time. Suppose that a broad jumper is now ready to leap. His neuro-muscular system and his bodily energies are now organized in a specific manner which can be described in terms of the present. But something has been omitted, the very fact indeed, which the expression "ready to jump" is designed to accentuate: the fact, namely, that this organization is headed towards a future act. The jumper *is now about* to jump *later.* If he should die of heart failure so that the event of jumping did not occur, it would still be the case that he *had been* about to jump. Various states of mind are thus describable only in terms of futurity: interest, will, disposition, expectation, and cognition.

The apparent difficulty of identifying cognition with expectation requires the introduction of another factor, namely, the object of expectation. There is no expecting without an expected. An expecting is always an expectation of *something;* it is always proper, when expecting occurs, to inquire, "*What* is expected?" If the answer were, "Nothing is expected," there would be no expecting. In order to take account of this fact it is necessary to provide expecting with an object which it *has* when it, the expecting, occurs, but which is itself non-occurrent, and which may or may not occur at a future time. This object has been designated as the "objective" or "problematic object."

It is not necessary for the present analysis to assign the problematic object a precise status in the realm of being. It may be supposed to belong to a peculiar realm, called 'subsistence.' It may be anchored to mental existence, as a qualification of the act of expecting; or to external physical existence as what would characterize it if the expectation were fulfilled; or it may be anchored to both, as their connecting link. It is the same kind of entity as the hypothesis, or conceptual framework, of science. The one thing that is clear, and that it is essential to note at this point, is that taken in itself, abstractly, it does not occur at the same time with the act of expecting or with the event by which the expecting is fulfilled.

These distinctions make it possible to reconcile the future reference of expectation with those kinds of cognition which, on the face of it, are nonpredictive: with sense perception, which appears to be cognition of the present; and with memory and history which are cognitions of the past.

Sense perception varies between two extremes. At one extreme, presentation serves only to stimulate ulterior expectations. At this extreme the object of perception is a physical object — a system of expected presentations, in short, a problematic object. At the other extreme, presentation itself may assume a cognitive role. Attention is then directed to the color, shape, hardness, sound, and apparent shape which are being sensed. Is there or is there not then an attitude of expectancy? The answer is clearly affirmative. The attitude of purely sensory cognition (sometimes called "immediacy" or "intuition") points to the *prolongation* of the present sensory content. The preparation for this content requires no new adjustment but the maintaining through time of the present adjustment. Because of this continuity and sameness of the content, and because its next moment is so close at hand, the future reference tends to be ignored. But when this interval of futurity reaches the zero point, when there is no expectation of the near or remote, no dwelling upon, or persistence, no return to the same, the sensory process sinks below the threshold of cognition. Most perceptual cognition lies between these two extremes — a mixture of continuing presentation with expectation of ulterior presentations more or less numerous and complex, and more or less systematic. It is this, as has been pointed out, which distinguishes the object of sense perception from the stimulus. What of cognition of the past?[1] Here also there is no escape from the fact that cognition lives in time, and points ahead in time. But there is no reason to deny that it cannot also, in some distinguishable sense, point backward in time. It is a matter of empirical fact that this does happen; it is one of the commonest, though not one of the simplest, things in the world.

To account for this possibility it is necessary to recognize, in the first place, that the past is "irrevocable." That which existed in the past

[1] For a more detailed examination of this question, cf. the Author's article, "Knowledge of Past Events," *Journal of Philosophy, Psychology, and Scientific Methods*, III, 23, pp. 617–26.

may cease to exist at some later time; indeed if it is identified with the time of its existence it *cannot* exist at a later time, since it is of the essence of time that its moments cannot persist or recur. But this does not mean that the past is excluded from the domain of existence; for existence embraces what occurs at any time. The past is "there," waiting with inexhaustible patience for the time of its discovery.

It is necessary, in the second place, to recognize that it is possible to think an idea of the past, *now:* the time of the thinking is 1953; the time of that which is thought of may be 1000 B.C.; the time of the thought, a problematic object, is neither now nor then, but is timeless.

But while this analysis is necessary to clear the ground it does not provide for the temporal reference of the idea — for the "pastness" of the past, for the "then" as distinguishable from the "now," or for the relations of "earlier" and "later" in the specific senses which distinguish these from "before" and "after." The past cannot be thought in terms of the timeless. It can be thought only because there is a "sense of time," or immediately presented temporal perspective. This sensory perspective suffices to establish a direction, called "retrospect"; which may then by the introduction of concepts of order and magnitude be prolonged beyond the range of sensation. In this way — by the extrapolation of immediate memory, the remote and intermediate past can be arrived at, and the whole assumes the form of the chronological past.

The chronological past, once it has emerged, can then be explored at any time when an explorer of sufficient diligence and capacity appears on the scene. The later explorer may visit and revisit the earlier — the order of his visiting reversing the order of events in the region visited. And if he be cognitively minded he will form expectations of what he will find there. He may find what he expected, or he may find the novel and surprising.

3

Cognition is expectation, but knowledge is not the same thing as cognition. Without this distinction it is impossible to make sense of the question, "Is knowledge possible?" Cognition is an indisputable fact, but whether it is possible that it should acquire the further requirements which distinguish knowledge is debatable. Without the datum of cognition it would be impossible to settle this debate, or even to ask the question.

It is demanded of knowledge that it shall be true, proved, and certain. Unless a cognition possesses these characters, it is cognition without being knowledge. When there is a cognitive interest these are the qualifying attributes of its object. The cognitive interest, in other words, is an interest in cognition *because of* its being true, proved, and certain; these become the standards by which it is judged. And the qualifications must be so conceived as to be applicable to cognition. True, proved, and certain cognition, that is to say, knowledge, must fall within the realm of ideally or theoretically possible cognitions, even if it should be unattainable.

Each of the qualifications of knowledge has its opposite: the opposite of truth, is error; of proof, dogma; of certainty, doubt. That which is capable of truth must also be capable of error; that which is capable of proof must also be capable of dogma; that which is capable of certainty must also be capable of doubt. The application of this requirement to truth, excludes a common use of the term, in which it is synonymous with 'real' or 'existent.' A mountain or river cannot be said to be true because it cannot be erroneous. An expectation, on the other hand, because of having a problematic object, can be either true or erroneous.

A judgment, construed as expectation, is true when that which is expected agrees with that which is *going to happen,* or when a readiness to deal fits a prospective occasion. Two series — an unfolding series of attitudes and acts, and an unfolding series of events in the environment — are convergent. The judgment is true now, when it, the judgment, occurs as a state of preparedness in advance of that conjunction with the environmental occasion in which it finds its prepared dealings appropriate. The possibility of error consists in the fact that the judgment may occur when the corresponding occasion is *not going to occur.* The judgment may be destined not to fit the impending situation. It may be headed towards surprise rather than fulfillment.

Truth so conceived as the alternative to error, and as qualifying an act which in itself can be either true or erroneous, means that truth and error are "contingent." Given a certain judgment, including its problematic object, its referents of truth or erroneousness are conditioned by circumstances beyond its control. Judgment itself is free and creative; the judging mind can form hypotheses and entertain ideas, of limitless variety and complexity. But though it "proposes," the nature of things "disposes." Which, if any, of its proposals is true as opposed to erroneous remains yet to be determined by events which are independent of itself.

The same analysis explains the conflict of judgments. In order that this shall occur, two judgments must both take place; the occurrence of the one act of judgment does not exclude the occurrence of the other act of judgment. But they cannot both be fulfilled or surprised; that which fulfills one will surprise the other. Similarly, the conflict of truth and error signifies the incompatibility of the same judgment's being both fulfilled and surprised by the same event.

If a cognition is to be said to constitute knowledge in the preferred sense, it must be more than true: its truth must be proved. And it can be true without being proved. Thus a man may judge truly that the sun will rise tomorrow, in the sense of being prepared to deal with that state of affairs, without a scintilla of evidence to support his judgment. As a matter of fact, such is the case with most cognitions, whether true or erroneous. They may be "hit upon" by accident; one may "guess the truth"; one may imbibe it unconsciously from one's surroundings, or possess it unconsciously by instinct or imitation, or adopt it more or less consciously by "wishful thinking" or submission to authority. That which is proved, the judgment, is capable of being proved or disproved, or of being neither proved nor disproved, that is, dogmatic.

Since proof is the chief criterion of that preëminently qualified form of cognition called science, this topic will be examined more fully below. Suffice it here to call attention to a broad consideration which follows from the analysis of cognition. The proof of cognition will be proof of expectation; that is, it calls for evidence that a given expectation is destined to fulfillment rather than to surprise. The proof of a cognition will look to the sequel, rather than its internal structure. This implies that of the two types of proof which are ordinarily accepted, namely, a priori proof and empirical proof, the latter must be considered as conclusive, the former only as provisional. Insofar as induction is empirical, and deduction is a priori, final proof will be inductive rather than deductive.

Certitude, construed as decision, a fixation of belief, differs from both truth and from proof. Man is often "most ignorant of what he's most assured" when 'ignorance' means the absence of truth and proof. There is a meaning of 'certitude' which has its own opposite, distinct from the opposites of truth and proof. The opposite of truth is error; the opposite of proof is dogma; the opposite of certitude is doubt. The choice of words is optional, and verbal usage is variable; the important thing is to recognize the difference between these three pairs of opposites, by whatever names they are called.

'Certitude,' as the term is here employed, signifies commitment. Cognition being defined as a set, readiness or preparedness of future response, it follows that the mind may be more or less finally and irretrievably "made up." When the mind is wholly made up in a certain determinate manner the prepared response has been carried to the point at which alternative responses are excluded; like the train which having passed all junctions and sidings is bound to follow a single track. To this is opposed that attitude in which several responses are held open; or in which each response is adopted only tentatively. The state of the believing mind is then hesitant, wavering, undecided, doubting.

Indubitability is thus a condition of the individual at the moment of judgment. *He* can no longer doubt. But *what* he is incapable of doubting someone else may doubt, or he may himself doubt later. All objects of judgment are dubitable, but the *act* of doubting may be impossible in any given condition of the individual or of society.

Although proof and certitude are different there are causal relations between them which are partially accountable for their confusion. Proof tends to create certainty, while disproof tends to create uncertainty. When proof follows fast upon judgment there is "little room for doubt," as compared with a situation in which the proof lags behind. Cognitions which are not demonstrable at all easily acquire certainty by imitation or unconscious contagion.

These considerations shed some light on the dark topic of probability. There is a probability which means degree of uncertainty; but there is a difference between this "subjective" probability and objective probability; or between psychological probability and mathematical or logical probability; or between a probable judgment and a judgment of probability. The last may be as indubitable as *any* mathematical or logical judgment.

Cognition cannot be said to have earned the name of 'knowledge' until it has reached a decision. It does not consist in merely "entertaining" judgments, or in adopting them tentatively in order to prove them, but in adopting them. The mind which is not "made up" has not concluded its cognitive business. This does not mean that the mind may not be reopened, or that it may not be ready to open itself, or that it may not be a little open, but that it must not be too wide open. Certitude plays an important role in the value of knowledge. A wholly doubting judgment is of no practical use, nor would it satisfy a lover of knowledge for its own sake. But certitude is also necessary if new knowledge is to be built on old. So much for the definition of knowledge as qualified cognition. Be it noted for future reference that these qualifications do not in themselves connote value, for which it is necessary to introduce the factor of interest. A cognition can be true, proved, or certain, without as yet being either good or bad.

4

There is much confusion at the present time as regards the meaning of the term 'science.' In the curricula of schools and colleges it is pre-eminently identified with physics and chemistry, somewhat more doubtfully with biology, and still more doubtfully (apologetically or pretentiously) with psychology, politics, economics, and sociology. It is evident that it will not do to define science in terms of a part of itself — in terms of natural science, or physical science. The historical definition encounters the same difficulty. All scientists and scientists of science agree that something of great scientific importance happened in Europe during the seventeenth century, associated with the names of Galileo, Francis Bacon, and Newton. This is often referred to as "the beginning of modern science." But though granting the importance of this period of science one cannot properly define science in terms of one of its own periods.

A more instructive approach to the definition of science is afforded by an examination of its method. Innovations of method are less precipitate than they first appear to be, and the more one learns about the history of science the more one is compelled to doubt that it began with Galileo's *Dialogues* in 1632, or with Newton's *Principia* in 1687 — there is always an Archimedes or Roger Bacon to dispute priority. But if attention is focused on method the question of dates is subordinated, and the question is shifted from "*When* did it happen?" to "*What* happened?" And here the answer is fairly clear, namely, that in the course of the development of European thought a certain human enterprise, which we call 'science,' became, after many ups and downs, more successful and progressive. It appears that what has made progress is cognition; that its progress has revealed more and more clearly those criteria which distinguish knowledge — namely truth, proof, and certitude; and that in proportion as these criteria have been explicitly recognized, the methods of satisfying them have been improved.

The emphasis on method in science must not be taken as substituting the method for the intent and the subject matter. Scientific method is not an activity to be carried on for its own sake, and to be applauded in proportion as it grows more ingenious and highly organized: if it does not yield a knowledge of something it is only an intellectual game. Nor must it be supposed that only those branches of knowledge whose methods are most highly perfected shall be recognized as knowledge. At the present time, and perhaps at any time in human history, the areas in which the most improved techniques are applicable comprise only a small fraction of the field of knowledge. The fundamental maxim of knowledge is *to know as well as possible what there is to be known*. It violates this maxim to disparage all knowledge except mathematics and physics and those parts of other branches of inquiry which employ the methods of mathematics and physics.

Science is distinguished, then, by its achieving, relatively to its subject matter, a comparatively high degree of those characteristics which distinguish knowledge, namely truth, proof, and certitude. The method of modern science enables it to satisfy these criteria. In its dedication to truth science defers to things as they are, independently of human subjectivity. Cognition is expectation, and the purpose of knowledge is that expectation shall agree with impending events not of its own making. During the modern period of European intellectual history men acquired an increasing respect for facts — otherwise the race would not have survived. But during long periods of human history certain beliefs have prevailed (very naturally and excusably) which have tended to dull the edge of their brutality.

In proportion as men have felt themselves powerless to control their environment, they have been eager to believe that it was already on their side. Having found it to be sometimes friendly they have interpreted its indifference and hostility as friendliness in disguise. As science has developed it has endeavored to rid itself of this optimistic dogma that pleasingness to man is a condition of the occurrence of natural events. Even when it has stressed its usefulness, science has come to recognize that it can serve men only when it tells them the worst. The only way men can control nature is by first letting it speak for itself.

This fundamental "realism" of science would seem to be controverted by its increased activity and inventiveness. It may be argued that if the aim of science is to discover things as they are, it should simply expose the mind to them, and submit passively to their imprint, or at most pay attention; whereas it is generally agreed that as science develops it becomes a more and more complicated "operation." But assuming that its aim is to discover, it does not follow that this is easily accomplished. Indeed, the hasty assumption that all that is necessary in order to discover things is to glance in their direction has been largely responsible for the failures of science: it has left men prey to their unconscious subjectivity, their habits, bias, and limitations of outlook; and it has led them to be satisfied with superficiality. If things are to answer for themselves they have to be asked the right questions, and devising the right question becomes a major part of the scientific procedure. The course of events has to be detected; and the deeper and more constant course of events requires a correspondingly intenser and more elaborate effort of detection.

Modern science is distinguished by its emphasis on experiment and on mathematics. These methods can be understood in terms of truth, construed as discovery. Experiment is a method of isolating or repeating certain situations — so that they may speak clearly for themselves. In the world as one finds it there are a great many things going on at the same time. Astronomy began to be scientific at a comparatively early date because the celestial bodies, in their grosser characteristics and motions, stand out by themselves and repeat themselves. The laboratory attempts to achieve something of the same isolation with events that occur on the surface of the earth. It sets them apart so that they can speak unambiguously for themselves. The so-called "controlled experiment" means precisely that: the creation of an artificial situation in which only selected factors are present, and can be repeated, and so that there can be a maximum assurance of precisely what it is that is under observation.

The contention that the fundamental purpose of science is to bring to light the independent and "stubborn" facts may seem to be belied by the appearance of mathematics on the scene, and by its increasingly prominent role. The contrary, however, is the case. Even if it be supposed that mathematical systems rest on assumptions and postulates, the "if-then" by which they proceed is more relentless than the clap of thunder; one may contrive to prevent the clap of thunder from following the flash of lightning, but there is no way of preventing a conclusion from following its premises.

But why should mathematics be conjoined with experiment and enter into the knowledge of existence? Because while mathematical entities do not exist in themselves, they are nevertheless constituents of all existent things. Mathematics comprises those formal or structural characteristics, such as number, magnitude, and order, which belong to the existent world because the existent world is numerous, large or small, and more or less orderly. While mathematics does not deal with space and time, it is peculiarly revealing of those spatial and temporal relations which do fit the realm of natural existence.[2]

The mathematical emphasis of science can be further understood as meeting the demand for generalized expectations. Knowledge of particulars is knowledge. The expectation of a particular smile from a particular friend, or of the next note in a melody can be, and usually is, an about-to-be-fulfilled expectation, and hence true. Truth does not consist in generality. But if true knowledge consists in being prepared for contingencies there is a peculiar virtue in being prepared for a class or system of contingencies. Hence the end product of science, is a law, stated in terms of universals. And mathematics serves to reveal the structures and relations of universals.

It has been contended that the characteristic feature of science as revealed in modern science is its progressiveness. That this is a notable feature of science is incontestable. The nature of science is to be found, however, not in its progressiveness, but in the reasons for its progressiveness. Science is progressive, in the first place, because of its continuity. If, as has been suggested, the latest achievements of physics would be acclaimed by Galileo and Newton,[3] this is because successive scientists are engaged in a common task of knowing, for which they accept the same criteria of success or failure. The later scientist succeeds in doing

---

[2] The same argument is applicable to logic, though it is not necessary to press the point here. There is a tissue of fact in the nature of propositions, implications, disjunctions, contradiction, etc. which confronts expectation as relentlessly as any physical boulder. Indeed, the logic of the boulder is more relentless than its mineralogy.

[3] Cf. J. B. Conant, *Science and Common Sense*, 1951, p. 38, and ch. ii *passim*. George Sarton, writing in 1941, said that "scientific activities are the only ones which are cumulative and progressive," and adds that the task of all scientists is "essentially the same . . . they are aiming at the same goal"; *The Life of Science*, 1948, pp. 24, 26.

what the earlier scientist failed to do, or he does the same thing better. But modern science is progressive, in the second place, because its theories, being proved in general terms, create a surplus, both of other theories which they generate, and of further particular judgments in which they can be applied. Because it provides explanations, and types of explanations, in excess of the requirements of the data with which it originates, every advance in science opens new vistas.

5

The thesis that science is simply knowing carried to a comparatively advanced stage of excellence, requires that it shall satisfy in a preëminent degree the criterion of *proof*.

The fundamental fact to be kept firmly in mind in the examination of this vexatious topic is the fact that the *demonstrandum*, that which is to be found, is the truth of a cognition; not the truth of a "proposition" in the purely logical sense of that term, but the truth of a judgment or expectation in the psychological sense of the term. So conceived all proof is of the same general type. An expectation or advanced preparedness is true when it is about to be fulfilled; it is proved true or proves true, when it is fulfilled, or is "verified"; having been so proved, it retains its proof in the form of verifiability. In other words scientific proof is only a more refined and elaborate form of what is called "learning by experience."

When scientific proof is so defined two important consequences follow: "deduction" and "induction" are not two distinct and opposing forms of proof, but two inseparable parts of proof; no proof can escape contingency and fallibility.

When an expectation is formulated conceptually, it becomes a hypothesis or theory. It is then possible to examine its structure and its relations to other conceptual structures. This is to discover "what a theory implies." Thus the concept "man" may be found to imply the concept "organism" and the concept "death." This procedure of "finding" is sometimes called "analytical" but it is nevertheless a cognitive procedure. There is a judgment that can be fully described only by stating that there is an expectation of one concept's being implied in another, which is fulfilled.

But in the second premise of the famous syllogism, the premise that "Socrates is a man," the procedure is similar. There is an expectation of the individual Socrates, namely, the concept 'humanity': humanity is expected of him, and if this expectation is fulfilled the judgment "Socrates is a man," is proved.

And, finally, the conclusion that "Socrates is mortal" is said to "follow from" proof of the two premises. Man's being proved mortal and Socrates' being proved a man, taken jointly, imply that Socrates is mortal. The expectation here is the implication of the conclusion by the premises.

This final proof is said to be a priori because it is not necessary to inquire further and test the judgment of Socrates' mortality by the fact of his death.

Proof, so construed, rests on the assumption that every particular is subsumable under *some* universal. Everything is a something; it remains to be seen *what*. This is the only sense in which the so-called "uniformity of nature" is assumed.[4] But it is by no means a "pure assumption." Nor is it a "law of thought." It is the most frequently and unexceptionally verified of all hypotheses. Or, it may be stated in terms of the judgment that particularity implies universality; so that to conceive Socrates as a particular is already to conceive him as subsumable under a universal.

All judgments are fallible and no kind of proof, whether deductive, inductive, empirical, or "intuitive" can relieve them of the possibility of error. Deduction is not infallible. The truth of "then" or "therefore" is attended by its own corresponding hazard of error. It is possible to "conclude" erroneously that "it follows." In deductive reasoning it is always possible, only too possible, to make "mistakes." The whole elaboration of logical fallacies, as well as the schoolboy's miscalculations in arithmetic, testifies to this fact. The possibility of such mistakes is proportional to the length of the train of reasoning, that is, to the number of "therefores" that are introduced.

Empirical knowledge is also inescapably fallible. The perception of the physical object is notoriously so — since it consists mainly of sensory expectations, which are not fulfilled. Sensation itself is cognitive only when it assumes the form of an expectation of further sensory quality in a certain quarter defined by sentient attention, or is open to confirmation by the sensory experience of other subjects. Even the so-called "mystical" experience, insofar as it is identifiable and describable, is shot through with expectancy which may or may not be fulfilled; the mystic will always assume that his experience is recoverable under specified conditions, whether by himself or by others; and will expect its persistent or unfolding characteristics.

Even the moment of verification itself is fallible. One expects a bell to ring momentarily; and one says that the expectation is fulfilled when it does ring. But this is an oversimple statement of the matter. It is not the ringing of the bell, but the *perception* of its ringing, in which the expectation is confirmed. The ringing of the bell would *not* confirm the expectation unless it were itself object, and the same object as that of the original expectation. The ideational object becomes a perceptual ob-

---

[4] The view here defended is in substantial agreement with that of John Dewey, when he says: "It is admitted . . . that propositions about singulars *as of a kind* are required in order to reach a generalization, and also that any proposed generalization must be tested by ascertaining whether observation of singular occurrences yields results agreeing with its requirements"; *Logic,* 1938, p. 437 (italics mine).

ject, but it is still a problematic object: even when the ringing of the bell is heard it is possible that the bell should not, in fact, be ringing.

Although there is no such thing as an infallible cognition, and no such thing as a true judgment which *may* not be erroneous, it is legitimate to speak of a minimum of fallibility. The common names for this are 'self-evidence,' 'observation,' 'inspection,' 'immediacy,' 'intuition.' The meaning is that the interval between the expectation and its fulfillment approaches zero, as its limit. When it reaches zero, there is no longer any cognition; when it is greater than zero there is a possibility of error. This penultimate stage of an expectation, *just short* of surprise or fulfillment, marks the maximum of proof, and is taken as "evidence" by which to prove other more remote judgments. It appears in two forms: "sensible" immediacy or intuition, such as the apprehension of a color or a tone; and "intellectual" immediacy or intuition, such as the apprehension of a mathematical or logical relationship.

Science is distinguished by the criterion of certainty as well as by the criteria of truth and proof. It takes these criteria in a certain order. Scientific proof is a proof of truth, and scientific certainty is a certainty of proof. It is still a subjective criterion, namely, the absence of doubt; but it is the removal of doubt not by default, but by evidence. In sensible and intellectual immediacy there is the minimum "room for doubt." Doubt being removed, the judgment assumes the form of commitment; and may then become a premise of other knowledge, or a part of the permanent corpus of knowledge or a knowledge on which to base action — a knowledge on which to stake one's fortunes.

6

The analysis of interest has revealed the intimate relation between cognition and practice. All interest is mediated by cognition on some level — whether it be sense perception or articulate judgment, and whether it be true or erroneous, proved or dogmatic, certain or doubtful. This mediating cognition is the entering wedge of science into action, and justifies the most extravagant claims for the utility (or disutility!) of science in human life. Insofar as it does mediate action science may be said to be "applied," as distinguished from "pure."

Technology, as distinguished from knack or skill, is a kind of knowledge, and is immediately motivated by the cognitive interest; that is, the interest in truth, proof, and certainty. But its ulterior motive may or may not be cognitive. This may be expressed by saying that in technology the cognitive interest is a dependent interest. Technologism, in one of its untenable senses, is the doctrine that the cognitive interest is *always* a dependent interest.

Technology, then, is knowledge selected and processed for some ulte-

process of knowing
knowledge or the capacity for it
a product of this process, as a perception or
notion

rior use. The captain of a ship wishes to bring his cargo to a certain port; if he employs a navigator then the navigator is proved worthy of his hire by the captain's success. But the procedure of the captain and the navigator are not the same. Whereas the captain runs the ship, the navigator has to make calculations and observations before he can offer the captain useful advice; and in these operations he is governed by criteria of knowledge rather than by the success of the captain's voyage. If the captain wishes to sail the Seven Seas at all seasons of the year he has to employ an accomplished navigator, who can impart instructions as to how to reach any one of a large number of ports under different conditions. Proceeding from this small beginning we may now imagine that our captain desires to be prepared for all emergencies on land and sea, expanding his field of action until he becomes a sort of composite man whose practical interests, present and foreseeable, embrace those of every man. In this case the qualified consultant must be able to show his client how to do anything he can conceivably desire to do. The client becomes the practical man in general, and the consultant becomes the general technologist, or walking handbook of engineering.

But the difference of motive and standard still remains. The practical man enlarges his sphere of practice, but does not become less practical. The consultant, on the other hand, becomes more and more theoretical. He must increase his general funds to cover greater and more diverse demands. He must pass beyond the scene of action, and do more and more "homework." He retreats into a laboratory where he does only the kinds of things which are done in order to know truly, demonstratively, and certainly. Eventually he ceases to be even a general technologist and becomes an astronomer and physicist. As the practical man and his consultant move away from the particular situation towards generality they nevertheless move in opposite directions — towards two opposite poles of generality. The practical man is interested in control, and ends by being a lover of power; the consultant is interested in truth, proof, and certainty, and ends by being a lover of knowledge.

Knowledge is knowledge, and power is power, but one must not add "and never the twain shall meet." Knowledge *gives* power and is a condition of its possession. It is also correct to say that power conditions knowledge. In order to know one must be *able* to know, or to do those things by which knowledge is achieved. As science advances its implementation grows more elaborate, whether it be the calculations of the mathematician or the equipment of the laboratory. There is, in other words, an industry and technology of science, in which the results of science are applied to the uses of science. But knowledge does not constitute power; nor does power constitute knowledge. Blind and unenlightened action is still action; and unused knowledge is still knowledge.

The distinction between pure and applied science would seem to be contradicted by the fact that successful application is itself a proof of scientific truth. Thus, for example, the truth of the judgment that the earth is a sphere is proved by the voyager's circumnavigating it. The same event, namely, the arrival at the place of origin by continuing to move east to west is at one and the same time a practical success for the voyager, and a verification of the hypothesis of the geographer or astronomer. But although the same event plays two roles, the roles are different and their difference becomes more marked as the theoretical and the practical intents diverge. The theoretical scientist, like the closet geographer Kant, may have no ultimate interest in trade or zest for travel. If he could remain at home and discover the sphericity of the earth by geometrical and astronomical techniques, or by collecting the reports of other observers, he would probably prefer to do so. The voyager, on the other hand, is not interested, ultimately, in making calculations, or in verifying hypotheses, but in novel experiences or in bringing a cargo to market. The successful applications of science, while they do constitute proof — so far as they go — are not selected for that purpose. The application is a relatively clumsy, wasteful, and inconclusive proof, as compared with that conducted in the laboratory or the study. It may be the last which would be selected by the devotee of science.

In proportion as the theoretical interest asserts itself, hypotheses of wider generality will be substituted for hypotheses of lesser generality. The hypothesis that "if today I sail west from Lisbon, and keep on sailing, I shall eventually find myself in Lisbon again," is replaced by the hypothesis that "if any one sails at any time from any point on the earth's surface and continues toward the same point of the compass, he will arrive at the point of departure." This second hypothesis will be elaborated by spherical geometry, trigonometry, and astrophysics, and these will yield a vast number of further implications, such as the earth's precise deviation from sphericity, which may not in the least serve the mere voyager or trader.

7

Science as something which occurs in human history has its historical conditions. How is it to be explained, that is, accounted for? The subject is vast and complex, and it must suffice for present purposes to deal with certain broad considerations. There are two general questions: first, the question of the conditions of scientific opinion; and second, the question of the conditions of the scientific interest and enterprise.

The first of these questions is confronted by the challenge of social relativity.[5] Since scientific opinion is a part of culture, it is influenced directly or indirectly, more or less, in one way or another, by all of its

---

[5] It is to be noted that the physical theory of relativity has nothing to do with the relativity of scientific knowledge. Cf. L. Infeld, *Albert Einstein*, 1950.

other parts. It does not follow, however, that scientific opinion based on evidence and comparatively free from irrelevant social influences may not itself be the product of social influences; as a monastic enclave of un-worldliness is a product of worldly forces. Indeed, this appears to be precisely what has happened. It involves no contradiction, once it is clearly understood. Disinterested science has proved as consistent with an individualistic social environment as Aryan mathematics or communist biology with a totalitarian social environment. It is a task of explanatory cultural science to account for an "atmosphere" favorable to science, and of applied cultural science to create such an atmosphere.

Scientific agreement and certainty are peculiarly affected by extra-evidential causes. Agreement is not a proof of truth. Taking the history of mankind as a whole there has been more agreement on error than on truth. *Any* opinion, however dogmatic, may be widely disseminated by habit, suggestion, emotional contagion, and artful propaganda. The fear of "indoctrination" often comes from those very scientific circles in which extreme emphasis is placed on "corroboration." The scientific value of agreement depends altogether on how it is reached. When there is appeal to the same evidence, corroboration serves to clear the judg-ment of the accidents of individual subjectivity. Judgments about the same ought to be agreed on when they are true, because when they are true they conform to the same objective evidence. Agreement of opinion is usually a mixture of these two causes: a uniformity ascribable to a common subject matter, and a uniformity ascribable to extraneous influ-ences. Similarly, there are two forms of certitude: the certitude which reflects the removal of doubt by evidence, and the certitude which is ascribable to mass psychology.

The choice of scientific subject matter is undoubtedly due in large measure to non-evidential accidents. Especially in its beginnings, science deals with those aspects which the environment *presents* to men. The fact that he occupies the surface of a particular planet, at a particular period in its history, that he became consciously and methodically scien-tific at a certain period in his own history, that he is an animal organism requiring food, drink, shelter, and all the local varieties of these and other human conditions, determine what man shall be scientific *about* — what shall be his field of inquiry, the angle from which he shall make his cognitive attack upon the unknown. Science, in short, is human; but its humanity does not prove its truth, nor does it preclude its truth.

As to the conditions of the scientific interest itself — its rising or declining fortunes — detailed historical studies[6] reveal the influence of economic and social change. War and peace make a difference to sci-ence, but in opposite ways. Economic prosperity sometimes stimulates technological advance, but sometimes retards it; and the same is true of

---

[6] Such as G. N. Clark's *Science and Social Welfare in the Age of Newton*, 1937.

economic depression — it may diminish, or it may increase, the demand for technological invention. Scarcity of labor, the price level, the distribution of wealth, the rise and fall of living standards, all affect technology, but there appears to be no constant effect. Since technology is stimulated not by the continued use of its past products but by the demand for new, not even competition can be counted on to have this effect, since competition may take the form of reducing capital expenditures. The only generalization that can safely be made is that any general cult of unworldliness or "the simple life" which rendered men indifferent to physical comforts and conveniences, or any widespread conservatism which led men to prefer the accustomed ways of life to any form of innovation, would remove a major incentive to scientific and technological activity. It would remove "a major incentive," but not all incentive. It is doubtful if any cultural change could altogether extinguish man's desire to do more efficiently what he is already doing; or his apparently innate desire to invent and contrive;[7] or his interest in knowledge for its own sake.

The most disputed question in what is called "the sociology of science" is that of the relative priority of pure and applied science. The answer is that sometimes the one, and sometimes the other takes the lead. Much of the usefulness of science has been unforeseen. The science of electricity (Benjamin Franklin to the contrary notwithstanding) has not arisen as a result of a demand for lightning rods, but from the devotion of the physicist to the solution of his own outstanding problems. Science provides the knowledge, regardless of its utility, and then, often much later, "a use is found for it": the technologist searches in the corpus of science for what will enhance the efficiency of existing practices.

The unpredictability of the applications of science is due, furthermore, to the fact that technology (such, for example, as the manufacture of motor vehicles) draws from several lines of scientific development, in which each investigator was quite unaware of the manner in which his discovery was to be combined with the discoveries of other investigators working quite independently. The synthesis of technology is not a product of scientific collaboration, but of a practical collaboration which draws upon, and draws together, many different, and originally unrelated, theoretical tributaries.

The possibilities of application would not exist if pure science had not been allowed to go its own way. Too much preoccupation with the application may result in there being nothing to apply. On the other hand, pure science is largely indebted to its applications for the support of

---

[7] "The proximate aim of all industrial improvement has been the better performance of some workmanlike task." Cf. Thorstein Veblen, "The Instinct of Workmanship and the Irksomeness of Labor," in *Essays in Our Changing Order*, 1934, p. 84, pp. 78–96 *passim*.

public opinion and for the provision made for science in the organization of a modern society. The pure scientist is maintained in his aloofness because mankind are persuaded that sooner or later he will pay his way. Again, the applications, even though dictated by practical exigencies, such as war, may open new vistas of research and suggest new hypotheses. Finally, insofar as research involves the experimental laboratory it depends on the apparatus which it derives from the applications of past science. There is, in short, not only a scientific technology, but a technology of science.

8

The values of science arise from its relations, direct or indirect, to interest. Science, like all knowledge, has its intrinsic values: in other words, there is an interest in science for its own sake. There are words which refer to the fact that man likes or desires to know, quite apart from any ulterior use to which knowing is to be put: there are belittling words, such as 'curiosity' and 'inquisitiveness' and eulogistic words, such as 'wonder' and 'love of truth.' It requires a strong scruple to outweigh the impulse (when no one is looking) to open a sealed letter, or a locked drawer or closet. One is uncomfortable in the dark, or in an empty house, or in a world bounded by a curtain of ignorance, for lack of knowing what to expect.

Despite the present emphasis on its usefulness, modern science has more single-minded devotees, even fanatical and mystical devotees, than the science of any earlier period. In proportion as truth has become not merely an object of love but a pursuit and organized enterprise, it has developed a set of activities of its own, employing both mind and body, which are enjoyable in themselves and whose joys are enhanced by participation in a common enterprise. If the demands of industry and war should cease altogether, the scientists would seek some way to pursue their vocation — some way of *being* scientists.

The extrinsic, instrumental, or utilitarian, values of science are those which are imparted to objects by the dependent scientific interest — an interest in true and proved knowledge which draws its motive from some non-cognitive interest. The test of an interest's dependence on a second interest is to eliminate (actually or imaginatively) the second interest and observe whether the first interest is still alive. Remove the greed for gold, and if the prospector does not "lose interest" but continues to explore, this is evidence that he has an independent interest in the science of metallurgy.

While the distinction is valid and important, purely dependent or purely independent scientific interest is rare: there is usually an interplay between the two. Thus though a scientist be independently and sufficiently motivated by his love of truth and experimental proof, his motivation may be augmented by an impulse to rival and excel competitors, and by the prospect of money and fame. The aesthetic interest in his theory, considered as a work of the imagination, enriches the scientist's pursuit, but is neither a necessary nor sufficient condition of it. The same may be said of all the incidental values that spring from human association in the scientific enterprise. The independent values of science consist of the qualifying attributes of knowledge, that is, those characters of truth, proof, and certitude, for which knowledge is esteemed when it is esteemed for its own sake. Judgment by these attributes taken as standards constitutes the final and internal part of the normative science of science. In proportion as cognition "measures up" to these standards, it is good cognition or knowledge; and when it reaches a more or less vaguely defined level of such goodness it is called 'science.' Thus the development of science, normatively considered, is both a progressive increase of truth, proof and certainty, and a rejection of past cognitions as erroneous, dogmatic and uncertain.

The question, "What is the value of science?" has two answers. It is intrinsically valuable because of the cognitive interest itself; it is extrinsically valuable because of the many interests which the cognitive interest affects. In the latter case it is judged externally, and it *may* be judged *either* good or bad externally, whether it is good or bad internally. "For hath not nature furnished man with wit and valour, as it were with armour which may be used as well unto extreme evil as good?" [8]

Present doubts regarding the beneficence of science do not arise from its uselessness, but rather from its excessive and indiscriminate usefulness. The "ivory-tower" scientist is at worst a harmless eccentric who has to be maintained at the expense of society; the danger arises from the scientist who descends to the plane of action and places himself at the disposal of all and sundry. The fact that useful science is not better than the use to which it is put has been obscured by a habit of dwelling on its good, and forgetting its bad, uses; and by certain fallacious but persistent philosophical trends which may be appropriately designated as 'noölogism' and 'technologism.' Noölogism is the doctrine, deeply rooted in ancient philosophy and never wholly discredited, that all knowledge is knowledge of the good, and inclines the knower to its pursuit. Technologism, the doctrine that all technology is inherently and automatically beneficent, is compounded of several errors, which at this stage of the argument it would be superfluous to discuss.

Both pure science and general technology are useful, but they are indifferent to the uses which they serve. They are capable of practical applications, but lend themselves with equal readiness to any practical application. Pure science arrives at proved truths, but is itself concerned only that they shall be proved true. The laboratory does not inquire into

[8] R. Hooker, *Laws of Ecclesiastical Polity*, 1821, Vol. I, p. 157.

the personal affairs of its patrons. A shopkeeper asks a technologist for the difference between ten and six; the technologist performs his calculations and reports that the difference is four; whereupon the shopkeeper is enabled to give his customer the right change, or to shortchange him. Which the shopkeeper does is not the affair of the mathematician; he has done *his* job when he has given the true answer. The general technologist is prepared to tell anybody how to do anything, whoever he be and whatever he does. The neutral enjoys a freedom from commitment which has its merits, but there is at the same time a suggestion of being too free, like the woman of easy virtue. Being equally accessible to all comers is admirable as a sort of large-mindedness, but of shady repute when it is called 'promiscuity.'

Between the promiscuity of pure science and the promiscuity of general technology there is a difference. It is like the difference between the man who has no friends, but may unwittingly render friendly service to all, good and bad alike; and the man who has both good friends and bad. Pure science is infinitely useful, general technology is an infinitude of utilities. The first differs from the second as the chemical laboratory, which creates the elements of both medicine and poison, differs from the apothecary who carries both medicines and poisons in stock. Pure science is indirectly capable of uses both good and bad; technology is nearer to the good use, but also nearer to the bad.

9

The most important external judgment upon science is the moral judgment — most important because the social order is at stake. While science *qua* science is not obliged to consider its moral relations, society may well consider them, and ask how far science, being what it is, tends to serve or thwart the moral purpose. In balancing its moral account, what is to be set down on the credit side, and what on the debit side, of the ledger?

When the atom bomb was first used for military purposes American nuclear physicists, almost to a man, became good citizens. They abandoned their laboratories, they scurried to Washington or other political capitals, they came out for world government, they organized among themselves to promote the beneficent control of atomic energy. It appeared that the problem might solve itself, since if all nuclear physicists were to become preoccupied with the control of nuclear physics there would soon be no nuclear physics to control. How are we to explain this sudden removal from the laboratory to the forum? What was there in the scientific vocation itself that prompted scientists, unhesitatingly, almost automatically, to concern themselves with justice, humanity, and peace?

Pure science is to be credited, in the first place, with universality.

Morality must take account of everybody, and overcome the bias of self-ishness. It relates interest to interest and man to man, and seeks agreement between them, whoever, wherever, and whenever they may be. Similarly, scientific truth, because it rests on objective evidence, is true for everybody. Science concerns itself with those characters of nature which are ubiquitous and permanent. It directs the attention of men to that which they have in common, rather than to what divides them — to the earth of which they are the co-heirs, and to that fixed constitution of things which they must all take as their point of departure whatever the divergent enterprises in which they severally engage.

It is characteristic of the theoretic pursuit, furthermore, that it is relatively non-acquisitive, or non-preëmptive. Other human appetites and purposes must annihilate their objects or appropriate them exclusively, that is, at the expense of rival interests. But one man's knowledge does not rob another's. The scientific interest, divested of its accidental circumstances, instruments, or by-products, is innocent, and is enhanced rather than diminished by being shared. It is thus peculiarly suited to a life of harmonious happiness.

Scientists are brought by their common vocation into a world-wide collaboration, for which all men are eligible. Every man is invited to re-affirm for himself, in the light of public evidence, the conclusions which the scientist reaches. While professional scientists constitute a class and, owing to the need of training and talent, a small class, this class does not coincide with, but serves to offset, those differences of class, nation, race, and religion by which men are most antagonistically divided. Scientists are predisposed to internationalism. Their learned societies tend to embrace the scientists of all societies, and have created one of the first bridges to be thrown across the chasms that divide mankind.

Finally, since the purpose of science is defeated when it is subjected to social, political, economic, religious, or other external pressures, and since it must proceed by the method of discussion and persuasion, the scientist's vocation inclines him to support free institutions.

Turning to the debit side of the account — one of the most ancient of the charges against science can be summarily dismissed — the charge, namely, that its subject matter is morally degrading. This charge arises from the false suppositions that all science is physical science, and that the physical as such is base — a supposition due to the confusion between the physical world in general and certain physical appetites which are peculiarly prone to intemperance. If the physical as such is base, then it is degrading to heal the sick, clothe the naked, feed the hungry, or contemplate the beauty of nature and the wonders of creation.

If pure science is opposed to morality it is not because of its subject matter but because of its preoccupation. The scientific pursuit has, despite its aspect of universality, also its aspect of narrowness. The scientist who in his conceit or in his unconscious absorption affirms the theoretical interest to the exclusion of others is the enemy of a morality which is bound to take account of all interests. He tends to disassociate himself from all organized enterprise devoted to the general good. And, insofar as the prestige of science affects public esteem, the scientist then tends by example to disseminate throughout society a moral irresponsibility like his own.

The cult of science also works against morality through its very dispassionateness. The scientist *qua* scientist feels himself superior to passion because he stands outside of it; he feels none of its heat, and takes none of its risks. Where interests are concerned he treats them all alike, being the observer of all and the champion of none. He derives equal theoretical satisfaction from their success and their defeat; the battle of life is his spectacle. To the devotee of science any partisan seems childlike, naïve or even contemptible. But the scientist forgets that to the man of affairs he himself, with his books and his instruments, is not less contemptible; his aloofness is seen as evasion and escapism.

10

What shall be placed on the credit, and what on the debit, side of the moral account of technology? Since general technology can serve *any* interest it can serve the moral interest, and provide the arsenal of the moral will. Technologism, or the belief that technology is automatically and invariably benign, is due largely to the existence of certain human institutions and professions in which it is linked with a moral purpose. The physician, for example, is devoted to the prevention and remedy of disease, and is governed by his professional code. In the pursuit of his humanitarian end the physician employs technologies derived from physics, chemistry, and biology. Similarly, the so-called 'engineering sciences,' are commonly associated with the peaceful and constructive activities of bridge-building, industry, and commerce. These technologies thus owe their moral quality to the personal wills or the institutional purposes by which they are controlled.

Technology in itself, in proportion as it follows its own bent, acknowledges no prior allegiance to the moral will. It lends itself without reluctance to any will, good or bad. The captive scientist is the servant of many masters, and wears all their divers colors. If, therefore, technology derives credit from those social arts by which it is linked with constructive purposes, so it derives discredit from those arts of oppression, impoverishment, demolition, extermination, degradation, and corruption in which it has been linked with destructive purposes. Technology is also the arsenal of Satan.

The cult of technology is not only the willing tool of many forces — forces for evil as well as forces for good — but it tends to focus the

attention upon the tool, rather than upon the use for which it was originally designed. Men are inclined to do what they can do easily and efficiently. The development of physical technology prompts men to do what
they are thereby peculiarly equipped to do, namely, create material
goods. Those demands which can be satisfied by material goods tend
to be affirmed and developed. As the means are perfected and new
gadgets invented, interest shifts from the end to the means. Thus piety
requires men living at a distance to come together in a common Mecca,
and this end dictates an improved technology of transportation. Presently
the pilgrims become camel-minded, or motor-minded, or air-minded, with
the result that they move about like water bugs on the surface of a pool,
apparently for no purpose whatsoever.

Men tend to do what they can do easily, and to pursue those ends
which are best implemented. It is said (perhaps falsely) that whatever
is worth doing at all, is worth doing well. In any case, it is false, but
human, to suppose that whatever can be done well is worth doing. Unhappily the things most worth doing are the things it is most difficult to
do. It is less difficult to manufacture goods or improve their quality than
it is to distribute them justly. It is easier to manufacture an improved
type of electric refrigerator than to raise the general standard of living
or achieve economic democracy. And so men tend to devote their energies to the manufacture of electric refrigerators and to the enjoyment of
them and their contents.

The art of politics, in the sense of gaining and retaining power, is
easier than the art of statesmanship: there is a proved technology of the
first, but not of the second. It is easier to wage war than it is to achieve
peace. There is a highly developed technology of war, but no equal technology of peace. Hence men tend to devote their energies to bigger and
better wars, rather than to the less efficient struggle to avoid them.

It has been argued that the cure for the defects of science is more
science — not more science indiscriminately, but the extension of science
into the domain of human relations and institutions. Despite the notable
developments of psychology and social sciences in recent times, the evils
of the day are still attributed by many to a time lag of the control of
human forces behind the control of the forces of physical nature.

But no one who has lived through the early decades of the present
century can seriously affirm that the cure for human ills lies in the development of a technology of human nature that shall parallel the development of physical technology. Enough is now known of the possibilities
of such a development to make one shudder at the thought of its success.
If man is not ready for the right use of physical technology, still less is
he ready for the right use of psychological and social technology. Hitler
was a worse monster than his generals, and a Goebbels is more to be
feared than a Goering. The destructive and corrupting uses of the arti-

facts of physical technology is childish innocence as compared with an unscrupulous manipulation of other minds. An age which has mastered, and been mastered by, the arts of deception, advertising, publicity, rabble-rousing and indoctrination is certainly no better off than an age in which "things are in the saddle, and ride mankind." [9]

There are two questions that fall within the technology of the science of science. The first is the question of "scientific method": What are the techniques by which true, proved, and certain knowledge can be achieved? Answers to this question are implicit in the discussions above of these three criteria. The second question is the question of the moral control of science, so that society may be assured of its beneficence.

The moral control of science may be entrusted to some social institution, such as conscience, polity, law, or economy. Such control is not, however, a moral control except insofar as these institutions themselves are subjected to a moral control. Science is not rendered morally beneficent merely through being brought into conformity with prevailing sentiment and opinion; for that sentiment and opinion may itself be blind and prejudiced. If the control of science by the state, or its regulation by law, is to be morally benign then these authorities must themselves be aligned with the purpose of harmony. Science is not rendered benign through being controlled by the existing economy, whether feudal, capitalistic, or socialistic; for these forms of economy may themselves be oppressive and destructive. Similarly the international control of science is morally justified only on the assumption that the international institutions in which this control is vested are themselves dedicated to the end of the just provision for all human interests, personal, class, national, and sectional. In short, if the control of science is to be normally beneficent the moral will must control its controls.

But there remains the crucial question of the kind and degree of control. When science is brought into line with moral requirements it must not be killed. Pure science is a tender plant. It cannot stand pruning or being tied to a stake. It prospers only when, being supplied with the requisite conditions of soil, and protected against winds, parasites, and extremes of temperature, it is then given a free space within which to grow after its own manner. It must be allowed to follow the evidence, and to proliferate along the lines of free inquiry.

It was only after a long struggle that pure science came to enjoy its popular privileges. Society can afford to concede them not only because science pays for them by the volume of its usefulness, but also because pure science is so removed from action. It contains immense potentialities of evil, but these potentialities are not realized until pure science is converted into technology. The control of science can be postponed until at some stage of its application it becomes dangerous.

[9] R. W. Emerson, *Ode Inscribed to W. H. Channing.*

The difference between the control of pure science and the control of technology is recognized in contemporary discussions of atomic energy. Pure nuclear physics must not be so controlled as to deprive research of its essential freedom to follow the evidence and expand the limits of inquiry; and so controlled as to deprive man of its good applications as well as its bad. It *need* not be strictly controlled because nuclear physics does not destroy cities until it has been converted into weapons. Similarly society controls, or aims to control, in behalf of the good of mankind at large, the particular technologies required for the manufacture of firearms, noxious gases, or toxic drugs, at the same time that it shrinks from controlling chemical research.

The recent controversy over genetics in Soviet Russia illustrates the confusions which beset the question of the social control of science. The issue between the supporters and the opponents of Lysenko was not whether acquired characteristics are or are not inherited. That is a question for the geneticists to decide by the most scrupulous experimental procedure. Lysenko may be right, or his opponents may be right. The issue was not whether scientists shall or shall not apply themselves to the social and economic problems of the day. It does not matter in the least whether they start with agro-biology and broaden out from there; or start with general biology and eventually focus on agro-biology; or divide themselves into agro-biologists and general biologists. The issue was not whether science shall be "classical" or modern; it should be both. The issue was not whether the U.S.S.R. is or is not a dictatorship. The issue was, and is, whether non-science shall intervene in a scientific controversy: whether a question of genetics shall be settled by a Politburo, a question of chemistry by a Secretary of Commerce. And here the answer is clear. Political judgments are simply irrelevant to genetics and chemistry; because they do not present the appropriate evidence, they are powerless to prove them either true or erroneous.

The moral control of science is peculiarly bound to the principle of liberality. If it is to serve it must be driven with a loose rein. The scientist must be free to follow the evidence wherever it leads him. He must be free to communicate his results to other scientists and thus to obtain their confirmation and their collaboration. And if his results are to be available for good uses they must be deposited in a public fund to the credit of all mankind. Happily, when he discovered fire Prometheus was not compelled to treat it as classified information, to be used only by flame throwers, incendiaries, or pyromaniacs. The moral control of science must look ultimately to the science of morals. But even a true science of morals affords no guarantee of moral beneficence. The knowledge of good *and* evil does not of itself make men good. It would seem probable that Satan, who chose the evil, was reasonably expert in such matters. Indeed there is Scriptural authority for the idea that man fell from grace, when, owing to the subtlety of the serpent, he learned too much about good and evil. Prometheus, also, knew too much, and Pandora's box was deemed a suitable punishment for his temerity. Assuming that the true moral science is that branch of science which is most fruitful of moral good, it will not bear that fruit so long as it remains *merely* science. Men must acquire a will inclined to the good, the right, and the dutiful, and opposed to the evil, the wrong, and the undutiful. The pursuit of harmonious happiness is a union of passion with enlightenment. It is the function of the science of that ideal to define its meaning, to illuminate its characteristics, to commend it to such human interests and sympathies as are sensitized to these characteristics, and to discover whatever techniques will enable men both to achieve agreement and to realize the ends on which they agree. But when all this is said and done there will still remain the task of creating the will itself. The striving toward the moral ideal is not a universal human predisposition; it is not a hardy perennial; it has to be implanted, replanted, and continuously nourished.

CHAPTER XVIII

ART AND AESTHETICS

Fine art like science derives its distinctive character from a specific independent interest, here to be designated 'the aesthetic interest.' It is this interest which motivates the "fine arts," distinguishes these from the "useful," "industrial," or "practical" arts, and confers on objects those values which are summarily comprised under the name of 'beauty.'

Men plant two kinds of gardens, vegetable gardens and flower gardens. The difference between them lies in the character of the interest which induces their planting. Vegetables are produced to be eaten; flowers, or gardens of flowers, to be looked at or smelled: in short for the gratification of sensibility. Both vegetables-to-eat and flowers-to-look-at grow wild; that is, both hunger and visual enjoyment can find ready-made occasions for their dealings. Or the occasions can be contrived, and made to fit the dealings; as when vegetable culture is generated by hunger, and floriculture by the interest of sensibility. The flower garden is a work of *art* in the sense that it is an object produced for the sake of consumption; it is a work of *fine* art because the consumption for which it is produced is the aesthetic interest of sensibility, as distinguished from the practical interest of food-taking.

This statement is a simplified first approximation. The interest of visual sensibility exemplifies the aesthetic interest but does not adequately represent its varied possibilities. The eye has its own bias and preference: there are certain objects which are agreeable *to look at,* and others which are disagreeable to look at. But the ear, too, has its bias and preferences; and so do the other senses. And other forms of apprehension — perception, meaning, and ideation — also have their own biases and preferences.

The analysis of the aesthetic interest must provide for this wide range of possibilities. It must also provide for the artist. Fine art is a dependent practical interest *immediately induced* by the aesthetic interest. If it is only indirectly so induced, the maker of it is a mechanic or a laborer. Thus the gardener, even if it be a flower garden, is not an artist if he works only for exercise or for hire. It is true that if it were not for the aesthetic enjoyment of his product at some point there would be no demand for it, and no inducement to employ him, but the hired gardener is not himself aesthetically motivated, and in this case it is the landscape architect who is the artist. Or, the gardener may be his own landscape architect, as well as the ultimate aesthetic consumer. One may contrive, plant, and cultivate a garden in order to enjoy it. Even then, his own enjoyment of it may be so postponed as not to preside immediately over its making. He is an artist insofar as his interest in the product is attended by its enjoyment; insofar as he aesthetically enjoys it in the making.

The manufacture of paint brushes and pigments is induced by the fact that somebody somewhere enjoys looking at pictures, but the manufacturer is not an artist (unless it happens that he takes an aesthetic interest in his own products, as, of course, he may) because his motivation is commercial. While this is obvious in the case of the specialized production of the painter's tools, it is also true of the activity of the painter himself, short of the actual painting. In the arranging of his studio, and the preparation of his canvas and palette, he is not the artist; he might conceivably have this "work" done for him by a studio assistant. But when he paints he becomes at one and the same time maker and enjoyer; his hand is guided by his aesthetic sensibility. Similarly, the musician listens to his own music and the poet to his own poetry, and each is governed in his composition by his own aesthetic likings and dislikings.

The dealer, the collector, the historian, the museum director or curator, the hanger or restorer, does not by these activities give objects the status of objects of fine art. Unless he enjoys the object in the distinctively aesthetic manner he is like the hired gardener. He is less vitally concerned with the fine arts than the most naïve visitor to the gallery who lingers there because he likes to look. It is the *enjoyer* of poetry, rather than the publisher, prosodist, or even the reader, who makes it poetry.

Here, then, is the substance of the matter, which must not be lost sight of amidst all the vast and intricate complexities of the aesthetic part of life: that there is a joy of apprehending — a delight in consciousness or awareness itself, which varies with its object. That which is *good-to-behold*, not good-to-do, or even good-to-believe, is *ipso facto* possessed of aesthetic value.

This analysis provides for the mutual reinforcement of fine art and useful art. A house built for shelter, so that were it not for this desire for shelter it would not be built as it is, or built at all, is a product of useful art. A house built for its appeal to sensibility, so that it would still be built as it is, were there no desire for shelter, is a product of fine art. But a house is ordinarily built to suit both interests — to provide shelter and to gratify the eye of its beholder. Or it may be that the usefulness for shelter is itself agreeable to the eye, as is maintained by the "functional" school of architects. This would mean not that its usefulness and its aesthetic appeal were the same thing, but that their requirements coincided, so that the product was doubly blessed; as when a shelter is monumental or one finds shelter in a monument. Similarly, an advertisement may serve both a commercial interest and the aesthetic interest, and may even serve the commercial interest better because of being aesthetically agreeable; but the two interests are nonetheless distinct, as appears in the fact that in the mixture one interest may be said to be "sacrificed" to the other.

2

That intimate interweaving of the aesthetic with practical and cognitive interests which makes it difficult to follow its thread, accounts for its peculiar universality and eminence. It does not suffice to say that the aesthetic interest is common to all men — there are many such interests; or that its works constitute a common heritage; or that, like all specialized interests, it has proliferated and expanded; or that it engages the organized collaboration of artistic experts; or that there has been a progressive refinement of aesthetic sensibility and connoisseurship, if such is the case. Indeed there is some ground for affirming that the effect of many of these developments may be to trivialize rather than to dignify art — to make it a mere hobby or avocation for man's idle moments. It is a common and not unjustified complaint that the aesthetic interest which was once associated with every form of utility and with the common experience of common men, has through the obsession of its devotees lost its proper place in life, at a loss both to itself and to the life from which it has been abstracted. Celibacy, here as elsewhere, may purchase concentration at the cost of barrenness.

The universality of the aesthetic interest is deep and basic. It is common not only to all men, of all ages, races, nations, and places: it is common, at least potentially, *to all interests*. Every interest, in its mediation, contains the occasion for, if not the actual presence of, the aesthetic interest. The visual sensation of the garden may be a springboard for action — the weed to be pulled, or the branch to be pruned; it may beget an expectation — the bud that will ripen tomorrow; or it may simply delight the eye. Given any scene or situation whatever, any content or assemblage of elements, sensible or intelligible, and it may be associated with any or all three attitudes: one may do something about it, as in practice; one may believe something of it, as in cognition; or one may dwell upon it aesthetically. The occasion of a serenade may be dealt with in any one or all of three ways; one may throw a boot at the sere-nader or yield to his appeal; one may seek to discover who it is, and let it go at that; or one may listen, gladly or reluctantly, to the music.

The third of these options is the aesthetic interest. There can be no practical or cognitive interest that does not either excite it or tempt it. There is no situation, practical or cognitive, which is not also an aesthetic situation. Nor is there any aesthetic situation which does not tend to knowledge or action. Whichever attitude dominates will carry the others on its back or in its train. Each attitude shifts quickly and perpetually into one of the others. This mobility and subtlety of interblending is an unquestionable fact, which, however, must not be allowed to blur the differences, and obscure the fact that the aesthetic interest has a distinct motivation of its own. Unless this is recognized it is not possible to understand either its intrinsic values or its interplay with other interests.

3

Fine art is a creation induced by the aesthetic interest; and it owes its value to the aesthetic interest which is taken in it. The crux of the matter, then, is the aesthetic interest. Further discussion begins with an examination of its specific peculiarities. One may then understand what characteristics qualify its objects, and the ground of their appeal; after which one may explore art and the aesthetic interest in terms of their causes and conditions; and then define the standards by which they may properly be assessed.

The aesthetic interest is an interested *activity* — a mode of dealing of which its object provides the appropriate occasion. As the object of hunger is food-to-eat, or of avarice is money-to-possess, so the object of the aesthetic interest is something-to-enjoy in a specific manner. The first step toward understanding this manner is to insist that it is an activity. That it is an activity is evident even in those instances of absorption which appear superficially to be most passive. A man is sitting on a hill-side in early summer, gratified by the sound of birds, the sight of green meadows, the contour of distant hills, the odor of flowers. He is not moved to alter the landscape, or bridge a brook, or build a house, or eliminate the insects which devour his trees. He is content to take things as they are. But his preoccupation is none the less dynamic. Disturb him, and one will see. His faculties are busily and intently engaged, and are on guard to protect him against interruption. "Holding the mirror up to nature" is a highly misleading description either of art or of aesthetic enjoyment itself unless one puts the emphasis on the "holding" rather than on the "mirror."

The aesthetic interest is a *contemplative* activity — there is no better word, despite its suggestion of passivity. Indeed it might be said that the very essence of the aesthetic attitude lies in its being a kind of active passivity. Although the term 'contemplation' is, in some philosophies, used as a name for knowledge, it may without too great violation of usage be taken to mean being before the mind, whether presented or represented, but without exciting the cognitive interest, or any other interest save that in *keeping* it before the mind.[1]

The simple fact is that men possess a bias of apprehension. The mind prefers to entertain certain objects rather than others; it finds some entertainments more "entertaining" than others, regardless of their truth or proof, and regardless of what, if anything, is "to be done about it." Consider Wordsworth's familiar testimony in his "Lines Written Above Tintern Abbey":

> The sounding cataract
> Haunted me like a passion; the tall rock,
> The mountain, and the deep and gloomy wood,
> Their colours and their forms, were then to me
> An appetite; a feeling and a love
> That had no need of a remoter charm,
> By thought supplied, nor any interest
> Unborrowed from the eye.

There are flaws in this statement. Wordsworth's passion for the "sounding cataract" was borrowed from the ear and not from the eye, and borrows still more freely — even "remoter charms by thought supplied." The aesthetic interest is not an appeal to any one sense to the exclusion of the rest, or to sense alone to the exclusion of the intellect. But the poet testifies unmistakably to the independent motivation of joys of apprehension — joys which are always possible, but which, owing to cognitive and practical preoccupations, are often untasted. Keats gives similar testimony in a letter to his friend John Hamilton Reynolds:

> Now it is more noble to sit like Jove than to fly like Mercury — let us not therefore go hurrying about and collecting honey, beelike buzzing here and there impatiently from *a knowledge of what is to be aimed at;* but let us open our leaves like a flower and be passive and receptive . . . sap will be given for meat and dew for drink. I was led into these thoughts, my dear Reynolds, by the beauty of the morning operating on a sense of idleness — I have not read any books — the morning said I was right — I had no idea *but of* the morning, and the thrush said I was right.[2]

[1] There is good authority for this usage. Thus Locke speaks of "keeping the idea which is brought into [the mind] for some time actually in view, which is called Contemplation"; and C. S. Peirce, in quoting this statement, adds that it is "(1) protracted, (2) voluntary, and (3) an action"; "Some Consequences of Four Incapacities," *Journal of Speculative Philosophy,* 1–2 (1867–8), p. 152, note. The Locke quotation is from the *Essay Concerning Human Understanding,* Bk. II, ch. x, § 1; cf. also Bk. II, ch. xix, § 1.

[2] From *The Selected Letters of John Keats,* copyright 1951 by Lionel Trilling, Farrar, Straus and Young, Inc., publishers, pp. 111–112.

This passage is cited for its contrast between the Mercurial "hurrying about," the "knowledge of what is to be aimed at" and the Jove-like contemplation of the given pageant. But allowance must be made for the poet's carelessness in failing to see that the receptivity of which he speaks is activity. To "open our leaves like a flower" and to keep them open, is a focusing of attention. It is not a *being* possessed, but rather a *taking possession*.

The aesthetic interest is a *prolonging* interest. That which is prolonged is not a single instant, but a whole which endures in time, and which requires an internal advance in time. In elaborate compositions, whether musical, visual, or literary, the unity of the whole may be but faintly grasped, or grasped only by subjects having a trained capacity to deal with the particular artistic medium. It will depend on the capacity of the aesthetic subject to sustain sameness through change, or to embrace "all at once" a more or less widespread complexity.

A further feature of the aesthetic activity is its *playfulness*, that is, partial enactment of the responses of "real life." It repeats forms of overt behavior, but stops short of commitment. The familiar example is that of the spectator at the play who, though he may fight for his seat or resent the man in front who obscures his view, will not intervene in behalf of the heroine attacked by the villain. He feels moved by hostility, but at a certain point he disconnects the engine, as when the clutch of an automobile is put in neutral. The difference between the competitive sport and the battle turns on the same point. There is something of the heat of combat in both players and spectators, but it is arrested at a certain point short of the injury of the opponent, and the activity is enjoyed in a manner analogous to that of a dance or pageant. The line is hard to draw and is frequently overstepped, but there is a difference of principle which distinguishes the playfully aesthetic from the "really" practical.

It is this detached or playful character of the aesthetic interest which accounts for the paradox of tragedy, and provides the true explanation of Aristotle's famous doctrine of "katharsis." This doctrine has suffered through its suggestion that emotion is an impurity of which the system must somehow be purged, or the riddance of which affords relief. The essence of the matter is that an emotion partially or playfully felt can afford an enjoyment of apprehension which overrules its painfulness. The positive aesthetic value of tragedy depends on the difference between being "really" afraid and tasting the flavor of fearfulness. Grief and rage are negative interests, and in the "real" emotion the negative response is dominant. But if the emotion is checked the distress is not weighed by the contemplative enjoyment.[3]

---

[3] The playful emotion is also less intense. Cf. H. Zinsser, *As I Remember Him,* 1940, pp. 435–6: "For the poet arrests emotions at their points of greatest supportable heat, just short of the melting point as it were, and can hold in that perfect state,

4

The first step in the analysis of the aesthetic object is to recognize that the aesthetic interest *has* an object. Objectivity in the sense which is inherently and universally characteristic of the aesthetic interest does not imply existence, but means that there is (in the most abstract sense of 'being') a passive correlate of the aesthetic act — a something aesthetically *enjoyed* — which is describable and communicable. There are three distinguishable classes of aesthetic objects: *sensory qualities, sensory relations* and *structures,* and *representations* or *ideas.*

Bernard Berenson has testified to the intensity of his interest in sensory qualities. Referring to a majolica plate from Gubbio, by Maestro Giorgio, he spoke of its "dazzling sheen of ruby and mother-of-pearl tints"; and said, "I like to sit down where I can get the light aslant on one of his plates, and then to look at it for hours." [4]

There is a sensuous relish of varying intensity and strength. Thus the psychologists have discovered certain general sensory preferences: red and blue are the most pleasant hues, yellow the least; sweet generally pleasant, bitter unpleasant; putrid and burnt odors unpleasant, fruity, spicy ones relatively pleasant.[5] Sensory qualities may themselves be aesthetic objects, as when the blank wall is enjoyed for the sake of its green, or the sea or sky for the tint of its blue, or the tone of the flute for its liquidity. And sensory agreeableness may give superadded value to objects represented in a sensory medium.

The claim that only sensory qualities can serve as aesthetic objects is clearly inadmissible. There is an aesthetic enjoyment not only of tonal qualities but of relations of tones, as in the preference of the major third to the minor third in combinations within the musical octave. Each sensory medium, over and above its specific qualia, has also its own structures; interrelations among its own qualia — contrasts, blends, similarities, repetitions, gradations, intervals, orderly sequences; and embracing all the variations, such as intensity, saturation, or duration, of each quality. The permutations and combinations of sensory differences, even within the range of a single sensory medium such as the audible or the visible, are inexhaustible, and far exceed the number for which ordinary

---

permanent in his words and meters, those feelings and comprehensions which pass too quickly to be held through the minds of the ordinary."

[4] From an unpublished letter written from Berlin, October 6, 1890. The strength of this writer's interest in the contemplation of aesthetic objects is emphasized by its overcoming of the physical fatigue to which he is peculiarly vulnerable. He speaks of himself as doing nothing for two hours but look at Savoldo's "Gaston de Foix" in the Lichtenstein Gallery in Vienna, and as hanging onto railings and trembling with exhaustion while looking at pictures in Dresden. (Letters written in October and November, 1890.)

[5] E. G. Boring and others, *Psychology*, 1935, ch. xv.

language provides. Beyond certain relatively narrow limits they are nameless and must constitute their own vocabulary.

But sensuous structures need not be confined to a single sensory medium. The dance, for example, combines audible with visible qualities. When sensory images are added to sensations a new range of possibilities is added. Poetry commands the greatest range of possibilities because to a verbal nucleus having qualities and forms of its own it annexes images drawn from all the senses. To say that the possibilities of sensory structure are infinite is only to state a fact, since all the dimensions of qualities are infinitely divisible continua. The only aesthetic limits are those which are imposed by the act of contemplation.

It is possible that an aesthetic interest should have no other objects save sense qualities and their structures. The expression 'absolute music' is used to designate the limitation of aesthetic objects to the qualities and structures of tones. Painting which as no other object save the qualities and structures of color or of line might similarly be referred to as "absolute painting." The same possibility exists in the case of each of the sensory media. Imagism and Gertrude-Steinism in poetry suggest a similar restriction in literature.

Beyond the range of sensuously exhibited objects there lies the equally inexhaustible range of represented or ideal objects. Anything whatsoever of which it is possible to form an idea may be aesthetically represented. The aesthetic interest is not subject to any imperative which regulates its choice of subject matter except its own demand that it shall be contemplatively enjoyable. It may find its objects in nature, or in human life, but there is no obligation that it shall do either. Its objects may or may not coincide with the familiar, ready-made objects of practical common sense.

The "tiger, tiger burning bright" is not a purely sensuous object, but an object of perception, having its cognitive and practical meanings. It may also be an aesthetic object. A striped apparition crosses my path. Obeying the interest of knowledge I judge it to be a tiger, that is, I expect a certain future train of appearances and prepare myself for them, so that if there should be an apparition of tail-wagging amiability I would be surprised. Obeying the interest of self-preservation I shoot my rifle in its direction, and if it should then continue to advance in my direction I would be dismayed. Or, following the aesthetic interest, I may find it agreeable to contemplate the tiger; provided I am behind a rampart, up a tree, or, better still, provided it is only a poetical or pictorial tiger. But the tiger as an object of contemplation embraces in some measure both its judged characteristics and what is to be done about it; that is, incipient expectations and trains of response — something-that-will-eat-me, something-to-be-shot. These trains of expectation and response are only partial or playful; I execute none of them, but turn from one to another, and so savor and relish the essence of *tigerishness*.

The object of the aesthetic interest need not be an individual of a recognized species, such as the tiger, but may be an abstract idea, such as lithesomeness, agility, stealthiness, power, movement, or carnivorousness. One or more of these ideas may be portrayed *through* the representation of a tiger, by subordinating the tiger's other characteristics and accentuating the "smile on the face of the tiger." But there is always the danger that the other characteristics will assert themselves and obscure the limiting intention. Doubt may arise as to whether the abstract characteristic is portrayed by the tiger, or the tiger by the abstract characteristic. So-called "abstract art" is designed to escape this ambiguity by eliminating the tiger altogether and representing the abstract characteristics directly by free combinations of line and color. This is not easily achieved since the visual structures employed will tend at the same time to suggest the familiar object in which they are embodied. The structure designed to portray the tiger-like characteristic tends to "look like" a tiger, and thus to be *perceived* as a tiger.

This difficulty can be generalized. Every language employed to represent an object, not only language in the strict sense, but every sensuous medium, will have its ready-made, habitual, perceptual meanings of which it is almost impossible to divest it. The difficulty is to be found at its maximum in literature, where the words employed can never be purged of their ready-made meanings; if they were they would cease to be words. Belles-lettres, and especially poetry, may be said to be engaged in an all-out struggle to free words from their habitual meanings by using words which *have* habitual meanings. Music lies at the other extreme, since tonal structures are not closely identified with the things and events of everyday life; though, even so, they "sound like" locomotives, cries of animals, or rumblings of thunder.

The question in the mind of the unsophisticated layman who asks of any work of art "What does it mean?" is usually "What familiar object of everyday life does it mean — is it a tiger or an elephant, a man, or a mountain?" If he is unable to identify the meaning in such ready-made terms, he complains that he cannot "understand" it. The proper answer, in many cases, is that it means some abstract characteristic, or some newly created thing for which the artistic medium itself provides the only designation. The exponents of abstract art have not clarified the situation by the use of the expression 'non-objective.' All art, no matter how abstract, no matter how far it departs from the range of existing verbal meanings, has *some* object.

This is the reason why it is a mistake to suppose that art should be easily understood, or understood by the masses. The line of least resistance is always the line of habit — the recognition of the familiar. The aesthetic object will always differ in some degree from the familiar object — otherwise the aesthetic object would never be as good as the original. Granting this, the aesthetic interest may legitimately require any degree of effort, always provided that after effort there *is* an object which is clear and unmistakable. The objection to "vulgar appeal" is not on the score of the number of those who respond to it, but on the score of its limitation by existing habits. There is a "learning to like" what has not been liked before — an annexing of fresh territory to the domain of the aesthetic. A new aesthetic object, like a new theory in science, may eventually be understood by all, although at first only by the innovators. A contemporary poet has spoken of the preference of "a difficult simplicity to an easy obscurity"; which is suggestive of mathematics — "simple when you understand it," but not simple to understand.[6]

In art and nature, however, the ideal object is viewed *through* a sensory medium. There will then be some discrepancy between the ideal object and its sensory embodiment. The act of aesthetic contemplation will *find* it, but it will never be wholly purged of the conditions under which it is found. Like the existent physical event, it will be *approximately* logical, mathematical, or conceptual. In some degree its edges will be ragged, its outlines blurred, its regularities broken. After the familiar Platonic analogy, its total aesthetic object will be the illuminated rather than the light, the reflection rather than the sun itself. The ideal object is embodied in a sensuous structure, which, in turn, is embodied in sensory qualia, and finally in the act of enjoyment. Or, the act of enjoyment reaches forward through an unfolding series of vistas — through sensory qualities to sensory structures, and through sensory structures to the ideal object, which is thus triply blest.

The aesthetic object is *that which* is aesthetically enjoyed; and it is the aesthetic enjoyment which confers on the object its aesthetic value. But at the moment of enjoyment the feeling of enjoyment and the object of enjoyment tend to coalesce, and to be distinguishable only by analysis. The object is so commingled with the feeling that the feeling appears as a "tertiary" quality of the object: the delight *taken in* the object becomes the object's "delightfulness." The exteroceptive sensory elements and the interoceptive affective elements become "fused." This mode of description is unobjectionable provided it is not forgotten that the fusion implies the elements fused. It must not be allowed to obliterate the distinction between the interested response and that which occasions the response. It is the latter which, when so responded to, becomes the logical subject of judgments in which aesthetic value is assigned as the predicate. Unless the distinction is preserved it is impossible to avoid the

[6] P. Viereck, "Pure Poetry, Impure Politics, and Ezra Pound," *Commentary*, 11 (1951), p. 346.

circular statement that it is the aesthetic enjoyment which is aesthetically enjoyed.

In proportion as the enjoyment is emotional it will involve organic reverberations, often corresponding in their structures to those of the sensible object. To stretch the point, one may say that there is in aesthetic enjoyment always some element of the dance, however subtle and refined. The beating of time to music is only a palpable and external sign of the intimate relation of the response to the object. The organism in some degree enacts in itself — in its breathing, circulation, or muscular tensions and coördinations — that which appears visibly or audibly. There is a parellelism, a harmony, a being "in tune," between the subject and the object owing to their common structure.[7]

In this review of aesthetic objects there has thus far been no mention of those physical things which hang on walls or stand on pediments, which furnish museums and houses, which men buy and collect, and which men take such pains to save from destruction. The fact is that it is only in the realm of visual art and in the enjoyment of nature that any single physical embodiment is indispensable. Needless to say the physical painting or sculpture is not an aesthetic object owing to its scarcity, or in respect of its weight, dimensions, chemical composition, or other purely physical characteristics. It is an aesthetic object because it exhibits sensory qualia and structures, and whatever ideal objects these represent: an individual painting, statue, or building is distinguishable from reproductions or replicas so far as it alone can provide such content.

We are thus brought back, after many turnings, to the fundamental fact that the aesthetic object is that which is enjoyed in contemplation, however presented or represented. He who apprehends it possesses all that the aesthetic interest requires.

5

There has of late been a tendency of aesthetic critics to prove their sophistication, if not their enlightenment, by denying that there is any such thing as "beauty." This is an unhelpful, not to say fantastic, opinion. The noun 'beauty' and the adjective 'beautiful' exist in all languages because there is a need for the words; because there is something for which, if the word 'beauty' were rejected, some other word would have to be found.

The denial of beauty owes its force mainly to the vogue of a certain doctrine: the doctrine that beauty is a simple, unanalyzable, indefinable,

---

[7] For the notion of "tertiary qualities," cf. above, ch. i, § 5; ch. ii, § 8. For the formal similarity of emotion and external sensation, cf. C. C. Pratt, *Music as the Language of Emotion*, Library of Congress, 1952; for "fusion," cf. S. C. Pepper, *Aesthetic Quality*, 1937, ch. iv, and *World Hypotheses*, 1942, ch. x.

characteristic: just beauty, beauty *per se*. But this doctrine is not consistently adhered to even by writers who are now assigned to the "classical" tradition. In his famous *Analysis of Beauty*, Hogarth wrote:

> I shall proceed to consider the fundamental principles, which are generally allowed to give elegance and beauty, when duly blended together, to compositions of all kinds whatever; and point out to my readers, the particular force of each, in those compositions in nature and art, which seem most to *please and entertain the eye*, and give that grace and beauty, which is the subject of this enquiry. The principles I mean, are FITNESS, VARIETY, UNIFORMITY, SIMPLICITY, INTRICACY, and QUANTITY.[8]

Allowing for a certain lack of precision, pardonable in an artist, and for the restricted application to the visual arts, this writer says, in effect, that beauty embraces several characteristics the possession of which qualifies an object "to please and entertain" man's sensibility. His list does not differ radically from the lists compiled by others who have asked themselves the same question, and have spoken of "proportion," "unity-in-multiplicity," "organization," "balance," "symmetry," "the golden section"; in modern criticism the words 'form' and 'composition' have acquired vogue as summarizing these and other characteristics. It will be noted that Hogarth justifies his list empirically, that is, by discovering what characteristics "seem" as a matter of fact to satisfy the condition of being contemplatively pleasing and entertaining. It is not claimed that they have anything else in common, or that they are the *only* characteristics which satisfy that condition. The list is multiple and provisional.

When it is recognized that there are as many aesthetic characteristics as make their objects aesthetically enjoyable, beauty does not cease to be, but it is definable as the class of the qualifying attributes by virtue of the possession of which any object commends itself to the aesthetic interest. Beauty is both multiple and one, in that while the characteristics are several, they all provide occasions for the same mode of positive response. It would be better to speak of "beauties" rather than of beauty. Certainly the list would have to be longer than Hogarth's.

It would include a balance of novelty and familiarity, and some idiom, idiosyncrasy, or "signature" to convey the impression of personal creation rather than of manufacture. It would include the purely qualitative characteristics peculiar to each of the senses; and the inexhaustible variety of sensible structures. The connoisseur of each art may properly come forward with his own adjectives, and who shall say him nay? Thus the man of refined musical taste who construes music as tonal mosaics, finds Brahms enjoyable for his "stateliness," Mendelssohn for his "sprightliness," Mozart for his "wistfulness," and Tschaikovsky for his

[8] W. Hogarth, *The Analysis of Beauty*, 1753, Introduction, pp. 11–12.

"vigor." [9] The list would include all the nameless characteristics for which there is no language save in their own sensory medium. The nameless characteristics must be recognized, if it be only to account for the straining by metaphor or circumlocution to name them. The list of beauties is long, and there can never be any defensible ground for closing it. For with the development of aesthetic taste it is always possible to enjoy objects for characteristics for which objects have never been enjoyed before.

The error of "formalism" consists in supposing that the characteristics which make up beauty are already finally known, having been drawn from "reason." Formalism in this sense is to forget that the proof of beauty lies in the enjoyment, and that this, even when there is reason to expect it, always "remains to be seen." [10]

For every positive interest there is a negative counterpart, and the object of negative aesthetic interest is commonly known as the "ugly." This does not signify the absence of aesthetic enjoyment merely, or the negative interest towards that which prevents or destroys beauty. The ugly is the object of contemplative repugnance. This repugnance may be as strong as positive enjoyment; indeed there are persons whose aesthetic life consists almost wholly of distress, or of pronouncing things "ugly." How strong aesthetic repugnance can be is illustrated by a statement made by Sir Osbert Sitwell about Edith Sitwell, the poet:

> My sister invariably represents the United States of America, a country towards which her innate love of liberty and hatred of oppression made her feel a tremendous attachment — and one, indeed, which never wavered until it came into conflict with her aesthetic sense some years later when, at the age of fourteen, she was taken to hear Sousa conduct his own band, and, after a march of his composition had been played, was violently sick and had to be led out of the Albert Hall.[11]

The range of the ugly is coextensive with that of the beautiful. There are simple qualities which are disagreeable or disgusting. There are sensory structures, such as musical discords, clashing colors, unbalanced shapes and forms, ideal objects, which are intolerable to contemplate.

[9] C. Pratt, op. cit., and "Objectivity of Esthetic Value," Journal of Philosophy, 31 (1934), pp. 40–5.

[10] There is an analogy between formalism in aesthetics and formalism in physical science. Formalism in science (whether Aristotelian or Kantian) affirms the possibility of laying down "categories" from which it is possible to know in advance what hypothesis will be true or false. Modern science prescribes nothing of hypotheses in advance save that they shall be verifiable by perception. Similarly, an experimental aesthetics will prescribe nothing in advance save that its judgments shall be capable of being submitted to the test of enjoyable contemplation.

[11] The Scarlet Tree, Little, Brown and Company, Atlantic Monthly Press, 1946, p. 31.

There is no abstract character of ugliness, but many characteristics having nothing in common save that there are conscious subjects which cannot bear to sense, perceive, imagine, or conceive them.

6

The aesthetic interest, together with its products, occurs in human life under certain conditions; and it is the task of the explanatory method in aesthetics to bring these conditions to light. The aesthetic has its physiology, its psychology, its history, and its sociology; in the materials which it employs, its physics, and its chemistry; and in the perceptions of nature which it reflects, its geography and climatology.

The question of the universality of the aesthetic interest has already been explored. It is a potential ingredient of every human interest, requiring only a turning from practice and knowledge to contemplation.

There is a chapter of explanatory aesthetics which has yet to be fully written,[12] namely, the explanation of aesthetic preference, or of those structural characteristics which in their sum constitute so great a part of beauty. Pending further exploration of this topic, it seems evident that what is enjoyed in contemplation reflects certain fundamental characteristics of the human organism and of its natural environment. The processes of the organism, such as breathing, circulation, and locomotion, are rhythmic. A rhythm which is interrupted awakens a disagreeable sense of suspense, like that of having an advancing foot poised in mid-air. Even the ape, the psychologists tell us, is impelled to complete a broken visual pattern by filling in the empty space. The structure of the organism is bilateral and symmetrical, and the upright human organism is equipped with reflexes which restore balance and equilibrium.

It has become increasingly evident that the mind has a bias for structure so deep and original as to have its roots in the physical organism. Perception *makes* wholes out of elements, and *brings* order out of chaos, even when the whole and the order are not there. This bias of the mind is, indeed, a common source of illusion. The most striking feature of dreams is their construction of scenes and dramatic passages out of the broken images of memory. The mind which thus instinctively creates structures, welcomes them when found and enjoys their contemplation.

The physical environment, too, has its rhythms: in the alternation of day and night and of the seasons of the year. Nature exhibits geometrical forms — the discs of sun and moon, the circumference of the horizon, the dome of the sky, the straight line, which is the shortest distance between two points. The shapes of shells and plant life provide motives of decorative design. Nature provides not only the elementary colors and

---

[12] The most promising approach to this topic is that of the "Gestalt" psychologists. Cf. W. Köhler, *Gestalt Psychology*, 1929, ch. vi, and *The Place of Value in a World of Facts*, 1938, chs. iii, ix.

their composition, but invests them with meaning, as signals of danger, safety, or utility.[13] The sounds of nature, including the calls of fellow-creatures, friend or foe, the melodic songs of birds, the confused uproar of sea and storm, are familiar experiences which reach far back in the line of evolutionary development. The centripetal pull of gravity is felt before the beginnings of architectural design. There is, in short, no sensible aspect of nature that does not contribute to the content of aesthetic objects, and attract, in some degree, favorable or unfavorable attention. It is only necessary to assume that what is interesting in practice is also enjoyable in contemplation; and that once the artistic impulse is aroused and directed, the invention of the artist operates to satisfy a growing demand.

The present emphasis in explanatory aesthetics is not on the sources of the aesthetic interest itself, but on the social conditions which determine the artistic product. It is easy to disprove the extreme claims of nationalistic relativism.[14] Of all the parts of culture, save science, art has proved itself most cosmopolitan and most susceptible of influence from abroad. It is only necessary to mention the spread of Greek art throughout the Mediterranean basin, the revival of ancient art in the Italian Renaissance, and the spread of Italian art to all parts of Western Europe. Nevertheless, art, like every branch of human culture, does reflect in some manner and degree the peculiarities of its social environment.

Beyond a certain point art is a luxury, and its great periods have coincided with accumulations of wealth, and with the large scale expenditures of rulers or private patrons. This correlation is clear in the case of great artistic monuments which are costly to produce, but otherwise it is subject to certain exceptions. The painter who starves in the garret suggests only that art does not pay its way, and that unless its costs are provided from an economic surplus, the artist does starve, and would presumably in the long run become extinct. But the starving painter also suggests that art depends on the existence of persons who are willing to starve for it. The riches of ancient Carthage appear to have produced no art — there is a widespread suspicion that the art of the United States is not proportional to its material prosperity. So much for the highly dubious generalization that wealth provides the best fertilizer for the aesthetic soil.

There appears to be a correlation between national, or possibly ethnic, characteristics, and superiority in a particular form of art. The Germans and Russians have excelled in music, the Chinese in painting, the Italians

[13] For a summary of the place of color discrimination in animal behavior, cf. G. L. Walls, *The Vertebrate Eye*, 1942, ch. xii.

[14] Of which Taine provides the classic example. Cf. his *Philosophie de l'Art*, 1865, and *Histoire de la Littérature Anglaise*, 1863–4.

in painting and sculpture, the English in poetry. The evidence is slender. It does not account for the eminence of the French in all the arts. Such historical generalizations are vitiated by the accidents of physical preservation; and the correlation, if such there be, has never been satisfactorily explained. That the instruments of art shall reflect the available physical materials — marble, metal, wood, pigments — and the development of technology, is self-evident but scarcely important.

That which *is* important is the relation between the ideal objects of art and the experience and ideology of the society or the class. The imagination, despite its freedom, derives its materials and its accent from life. What the artist represents in sensible media, and what the enjoyer of art looks for and recognizes, reflect the ideas that are most widely prevalent and the emotions that are most poignantly felt in the community to which they belong. It is no accident that the Sicilian sings of sulphur mines, or the slave of his serfdom and his dreams of release, or the troubadour of love. It is no accident that the European medieval culture embodied Christianity in all of its art forms; or that the present Western world should render into art the prevailing ideas and emotions of a machine age. By the same token it should occasion no surprise that the art of Soviet Russia should deal with the proletarian revolution or echo the past heroisms of Russian nationalism.

It is also evident that the artistic product will reflect the interests of the class from which the artists, their patrons and their enjoyers, belong. But the application to Western art is by no means clear. Its appeal has been not to the capitalist alone, but to the aggrieved and the exploited; to the artistically unsophisticated, as well as to the artistically sophisticated; to the cosmopolite, as well as to the nationalist. So-called "bourgeois" art appears to be distinguished, if by anything, by the absence of exclusive appeal to any social, economic, or cultural class. Western societies have freed art, as they have freed science, from allegiance to any motive beyond its own, allowing it to follow its own bent. Is this not, indeed, the *complaint* of the Marxist?

The explanatory method is also applicable to the personal life of the artist, a topic which has acquired increased vogue from the influence of Freud and the psychology of personality. There can be no doubt that whatever makes the man makes the artist and that what makes the artist makes his art: his heredity, his natural environment, his childhood experiences, his love life, his inner tensions and conflicts, his frustrations and triumphs. Art is intensely personal and, of all forms of art, poetry and fiction are most intensely personal. Thus it is impossible to understand the artistic creations of D. H. Lawrence without a knowledge of his relations to his parents, the setting of the countryside of Derbyshire, his passionate and intemperate nature, his revolt against the creed of Christianity, the grievances and bitterness that sprang from the intolerance of his critics. These explanations must not, however, be allowed to obscure the fact that he was governed by the motive of the artist, and it is only insofar as his personal life is seen to determine the object which he sought to express in the medium of *literature* that it is relevant to aesthetics.

How does the artist arrive at his ideal objects? Here is, indeed, a mystery. It is not surprising that many should adopt the view that the artist is "inspired" — in other words, that he derives his objects from some metaphysical source: from God, or from some Absolute Spirit. It is not surprising that the "subconscious" should be invoked, as it is invoked to explain so many things. But until "inspiration" is spelled out and clarified, is it anything more than another name for mystery, namely for that which is *not* explained?

It is well to bear in mind, furthermore, that this mystery is not peculiar to the aesthetic part of life. In spite of the Freudians, the visions of dreams remain a mystery. Daydreams, as well as sleeping dreams, remain a mystery. The vision of the great scientist, in which hitherto unrelated facts and discoveries resolve themselves into a unity — this, too, is a mystery. But there are little mysteries in everyday life — the sudden recollection of that which was forgotten; the happy phrases and original fancies of lively conversation; the process of thinking itself, in which, as one says, "it occurs to me." The most that can be said is that past experiences and stored memories suddenly crystallize into organized unities which constitute something new in the universe of consciousness. Imagination, in short, is not merely a store of fragments, but an activity of invention which appears to be spontaneous.

However complete the account of the conditions under which an aesthetic interest has come to pass, however exhaustive its personal and social history, this does not in itself constitute the normative part of aesthetics.

7

The internal critique of art judges art not by its authorship, as in "attribution," but by its own generating purpose of affording aesthetic enjoyment. This standard may be veiled by focusing attention on the qualifying attribute, which then itself becomes a criterion, which can be "objectively" applied without reference to the aesthetic interest. When the qualifying attribute is assumed it may be said that the object possessing it ought or deserves to be enjoyed, or that the object possessing the opposite characteristic ought not to be enjoyed. Assuming, for example, that a certain proportionality called 'the golden section' is a condition of the aesthetic enjoyment of visual linear structure, criticism may take the form of applying a ruler. Assuming certain conventions of versification the criticism of poetry may take the form of counting the feet or rhymes. Each of the arts — music, the dance, architecture — has its own set of established rules which constitute its discipline, and which define an area of criticism which consists simply in their application.

But these criteria are themselves justified only by appeal to the aesthetic interest itself, and it is therefore a major function of criticism to keep this interest alive. If the object is to be judged according as it does or does not meet the demands of the aesthetic interest, it must be the *aesthetic* interest, and not some other interest, whose demands are consulted. The value of an aesthetic object cannot be dismissed on the testimony of one who simply says, "I like it" or "I do not like it." The taste of the critic is authoritative only when it is both pure and developed. This is the legitimate sense of the term "connoisseurship." "I do not see it" is not evidence that "it is not there," unless "I have an eye for it," and am looking intently and alertly in the right direction. Hence the absurdity of determining aesthetic values by the questionnaire or the statistical method. The liking and preference of a single man of cultivated taste in the moments when his taste is alive and dominant, is more authoritative than a consensus of aesthetic judgments gathered at random; as the testimony of one careful and acute observer is better evidence of the occurrence of an event than that of a cloud of blind or careless witnesses.

It is a part of the task of aesthetic criticism, then, to distinguish the aesthetic interest itself from extraneous interests with which it may be mingled or by which it may be more or less unconsciously superseded: and likewise the work of art may be criticized on the ground of the purity or impurity of the creative motive. The aesthetic activity is subject to judgment by the standard of fidelity, or, as it is sometimes called, "integrity."

The aesthetic interest, like all interests, has ways of defeating itself. The interest may be deflected from its purpose by its own means; techniques may intervene between the activity and its goal, or lead to a sort of technical exhibitionism or "virtuosity." In the course of its intensive cultivation it develops intermediaries which obscure its goal, or precipitates by-products which stand in its way. Its arteries may become hardened. The so-called "degeneration" of art consists largely of the clogging of the grit produced by its own grinding. Repetition has the similar effect of a sedimentary deposit which blocks the circulation. "Staleness of language gums up transmission" says a musical critic. "Some freshness is ever required to dissolve the greases that collect in the machinery of meaning." [15]

"Modern" or "modernistic" movements of art, in whatever period of history they occur, have no aesthetic justification if motivated by a desire

[15] V. Thomson, "Copland as Great Man," *New York Herald Tribune*, Nov. 24, 1948.

to shock or to arrest attention by sensationalism, or if they rest on the assumption that what is new is *ipso facto* better than what is old. They owe their serious justification to a desire to recover the original artistic impulse when this has become overlaid by foreign matter — as when art has become merely an imitation of other art. In this, artistic reform resembles religious reform which seeks to return to the essential religious experience which has been obscured by ecclesiasticism or dogma.

If art is to fulfill the aesthetic interest it must be "interesting." An objection which does not awaken the aesthetic interest at all, or "leaves it cold," is no aesthetic object, and has no aesthetic value. Since the aesthetic interest, like all interests, is subject to fatigue and satiety there is a requirement of variety and novelty. A simple color may be agreeable to the eye or a simple tone to the ear, but the eye and ear would soon have enough, and the color or tone would lose its power to charm. Hence the superiority of the painting and musical composition which permit the eye and ear to rove. Similarly there is a requirement of freshness and invention. There is no aesthetic object so high in the scale that it does not pall, but there are differences of degree in the extent to which they reveal a new richness on each successive occasion. In art, as in science, there is a zest of discovery, and a credit to those whose originality annexes new territory to the domain of the enjoyable. On the other hand, familiarity not only breeds contempt or indifference; it also endears. The old aesthetic object is *recognized;* its aesthetic possibilities are more readily revealed, since the path to their discrimination is already broken. Hence the requirement of a balance between the strange and the familiar.

The value of the art object is proportional to whatever measure is applicable to the aesthetic interest. The aesthetic interest has its scale of preference, which makes it possible to rank works of art wherever the interests of two or more subjects are the same. The difficulty in applying this standard arises from doubt as to the sameness. Tasters of tea and tobacco, or experts in perfume, may agree; expert critics of a given artist or of a highly specialized branch of art are somewhat less likely to agree; the judgments of aesthetic subjects in general concerning objects of art in general, notoriously disagree. There is nevertheless *some* agreement among connoisseurs in the same field, even if it be only in the distinction between that which appeals to connoisseurs and that which appeals only to the taste of the vulgar.

Judged by the standard of inclusion, that which appeals to all aesthetic interests of a group has greater value than art which appeals to one or some of the group. This does not mean that number outweighs other standards: the standard of inclusion must include all standards. Whether there is any aesthetic object that suits all tastes, that suits them best in every respect, and that is repugnant to none, is questionable. The most that can be claimed is that if there were such an object it would be entitled to the claim of artistic supremacy.

8

The aesthetic life of man is embedded in his total life, and its internal standard is only one among many standards by which it may be judged. The critique of art by external standards of education has played an important role in controversy over the place of art in civilization. The critique of art by religious standards played a considerable part in the rise of protestantism, and in disputes among protestant sects. The omission of these topics here is practically compensated by the fact that these critiques are largely concerned with the relation of art to morality. The examination of the moral and cognitive critiques of art is more fundamental and calls for special consideration.

In the appraisal of man's major institutions of conscience, polity, law, and economy, the moral standard is internal. These forms of human life are essentially moral institutions, that is, their very being lies in their more or less successful solution of the problem created by the conflict of interests. The aesthetic activities and enjoyments, on the other hand, are only accidentally moral; they become so because the aesthetic interest is one among many interests with which it will conflict or harmonize, and because morality itself may be an object of the aesthetic interest.

It may be argued that these relations of the moral and the aesthetic are necessary and not accidental. Thus it may be argued that there is a positive correlation between the value of art and the moral character of the artist. But this is notoriously contrary to fact. Indeed the aesthetic interest seems peculiarly capable of flourishing in the absence of morality; indulgence of moral laxity is considered a price to pay for the contributions of artistic genius. It is by no means clear that an excess of passion beyond the bounds of virtue, and even extended to vices highly offensive to the conscience of the community, may not positively enhance artistic creativity. A distinguished musical critic has described Wagner's looseness of living, his sponging on his friends, his cruelty to his opponents, his infidelities, childish tantrums, ingratitude, egotism, insolence, and dishonesty. He was, in short, a moral monstrosity — a social parasite. It is clear that a society of Wagners could not exist. The writer goes on to say:

> And the curious thing about this record is that it doesn't matter in the least. . . . When you consider what he wrote — thirteen operas and music dramas, eleven of them still holding the stage, eight of them unquestionably worth ranking among the world's great musico-dramatic masterpieces — when you listen to what he wrote, the debts and heartaches that people had to endure from him don't seem much of a price. . . . The miracle is that what he did in the little space of seventy years could have

been done at all, even by a great genius. Is it any wonder that he had no time to be a man? [16]

It is often argued that art must choose a moral object; or that if it deals with human life at all, it must point a moral. William Dean Howells was a comparatively moderate exponent of this view:

> If a novel flatters the passions, and exalts them above the principles, it is poisonous; it may not kill, but it will certainly injure; and this test will alone exclude an entire class of fiction, of which eminent examples will occur to all. Then the whole spawn of so-called unmoral romances, which imagine a world where the sins of sense are unvisited by the penalties following, swift or slow, but inexorably sure, in the real world, are deadly poison: these do kill.[17]

This argument would seem to contradict the same writer's contention that fiction should be true to life. But are "sins of sense" invariably visited by penalties? Is the critic not representing what would happen in a just world? And if so, on what artistic ground can he demand that a writer omit the tragic fact that vice *is* sometimes rewarded and virtue penalized?

There is a persistent strain of European thought which identifies the aesthetic and the moral through the principle of harmony:

> Harmony, which might be called an aesthetic principle, is also the principle of health, of justice, and of happiness. Every impulse, not the aesthetic mood alone, is innocent and irresponsible in its origin and precious in its own eyes; but every impulse or indulgence, including the aesthetic, is evil in its effect, when it renders harmony impossible in the general tenor of life, or produces in the soul division and ruin.[18]

But the aesthetic value of harmony and the moral value of harmony are not the same value. The aesthetic value of harmony is the enjoyment of the whole in contemplation; the moral value of harmony is benefit to the parts from non-conflict and coöperation.

The distinction between the aesthetic and moral standards paves the way to the understanding of their relations. Insofar as harmony is one of the constituents of beauty a moral society is beautiful, that is, good to

---

[16] D. Taylor, *Of Men and Music*, Simon and Schuster, Inc., 1937, pp. 7–8. Beethoven provides a similar, but less extreme case. Cf. J. W. N. Sullivan, *Beethoven, His Spiritual Development*, 1947, Bk. II, ch. vi.

[17] *Criticism and Fiction*, 1891, p. 95.

[18] G. Santayana, "Brief History of My Opinions," *Contemporary American Philosophy*, G. P. Adams and W. P. Montague (eds.), Vol. II, 1930, p. 256; reprinted with permission of The Macmillan Company. Jonathan Edwards's moral value is "beauty of the qualities and exercises of the heart, or of those actions which proceed from them" — which turns out to be the same thing as benevolence. *The Nature of True Virtue, Jonathan Edwards, Representative Selections;* ed. by C. H. Faust and T. H. Johnson, 1935, pp. 349–50.

contemplate. But many, indeed most, harmonies fail to meet the requirements of morality; and are under no *aesthetic* obligation to do so. The moral standard is one of many external standards which are applicable to art.[19]

Assuming the aesthetic interest to have a peculiar and independent bias of its own, it may be asked how far this bias happily coincides with morality, and how far it diverges and resists. The aesthetic interest, like the cognitive interest, is amenable to morality because it is non-preëmptive, that is, does not appropriate its object exclusively. In the act of enjoying its object it does not deprive other subjects of its enjoyment. On the contrary, its enjoyment is enhanced by participation. Not only does it possess this original innocence, but it disposes men to friendly association. Because it does not need to take away from other interests it is unlikely to be associated with combativeness — with an impulse to weaken or destroy competitors.

Because the aesthetic interest operates in the realm of the imagination, it enjoys a peculiar freedom to multiply and entertain ideal possibilities. It tends to emancipate men's minds from habit, authority, and the *status quo,* and thus readily allies itself with the forces of progress and liberalization. It can dream utopias without hindrance, and through giving them vividness and permanence can provide direction to the moral life and to all aspiration. It can add to the attractiveness of any goal, including the goal of harmonious happiness; and can thus provide an additional motivation for ends which would otherwise suffer from their remoteness or abstractness. Art provides symbols for the moral cause. In its symbolic role the aesthetic object helps to preserve the identity of the goal amidst the vicissitudes of fortune, and to make it clearly manifest. Like the flag it can be hauled up where it can be seen; like the flag it can rally armies, regiments, and companies, and their successive replacements, to the same standard. And finally, the aesthetic interest can fortify moral courage by compensating life's practical and theoretical failures, and enable men to face the grimmer aspects of reality by presenting them in their tragic beauty. It thus contributes to that general auspiciousness of outlook which constitutes happiness.

The same traits of the aesthetic interest which render it morally propitious account for its moral dangers. Its detachment from the competitive struggle does, it is true, render art comparatively innocent, but there is a selfishness of innocence which consists in a withdrawal from affairs. The aesthetic interest does, it is true, tend to non-aggression, but it may tend to a passive complacency, a narrow absorption, and an irresponsibility toward that very social organization on which the aesthetic

---

[19] There are indefinitely many external standards which are applicable to art — including, for example, the dealer's standard, and the collector's standard.

life itself depends. In his Olympian detachment the artist or man of contemplation is likely to forget that Olympus rises from the plain of organized society and that he owes his privileges to those who guard its approaches.

Aesthetic rapture does not escape the danger which attends all raptures. It tends to be so obsessive as to make men indifferent to its evil effects — of commission or omission — on the lives of other men. Nero would not have been less morally blameworthy if he had been Jascha Heifetz.

The aesthetic interest evades the problems of knowledge and action, instead of solving them; for their real solution it substitutes that pseudo-solution which is called "aestheticism" or "escapism." The aesthetic interest may render the ideal so vivid and reassuring that it is mistaken for the real: and men may perish from aesthetic illusion, as they die of thirst in the desert through the allurement of the mirage. Because the aesthetic interest renders the evil of life palatable it weakens the will to remove it.

Aesthetic enjoyment can add to the appeal of the good and strengthen the moral passion; but it can also strengthen evil passion. It has a promiscuity similar to that of science. "Music hath charms to soothe the savage breast"; but it has other charms, and may debase the civilized man to savagery. There are "Dorian and Phrygian harmonies" which incite men to courage and temperance, but there are also Lydian, Ionian, and other harmonies which incite men to voluptuousness, to idleness, or to sexual excesses.[20] The fine arts can be used to give force to any propaganda, whether totalitarian or democratic; the actor can play any part and give it dramatic value; the poet can make Satan more appealing than God.

The fact that art can be put to bad as well as to good uses, and that the aesthetic motive cannot be trusted, when left to itself, to take the side of the angels, raises the question of its social control. It cannot be controlled as effectively as science, nor is its control so deadly. Under the present regime of Soviet Russia art is explicitly subjected to the state and to Communist ideology, but we are told that "there are thinkers and artists, living perfectly respectable lives, but forever struggling to introduce into their official epics of stereotyped verbosity disguised glimpses of an inner vision personal to themselves." [21] And in art, at least, this struggle is more or less successful. Science is more readily controlled, because it depends on access to evidence, and on the facilities of organized experimentation. The "inner vision" escapes external control, and its disguise is not easily penetrated by the grosser eye of the censor. What-

[20] Plato's *Republic,* tr. by Jowett, Bk. III, 398–9.
[21] E. Crankshaw, *Russia and the Russians,* 1948, p. 187.

ever restrictions are placed on men's overt conduct, there is always food for aesthetic contemplation, and some room for the play of the imagination.

But in principle the objection to social control is the same in art as in science. The artist renders his particular form of service through being free to follow his particular vocation. Art appraised by rulers and police is no longer judged by its own standard. Art harnessed to ideology becomes a dependent interest, deriving its motive from an ulterior end. In proportion as it is thus enslaved, art is destroyed at its source; it can no longer give other interests that very enhancement for the sake of which it was controlled. The effect of control is likely to be wholly negative. It can destroy and prevent better than it can create. Art will flourish best when it is allowed to germinate, grow, and proliferate in obedience to its own nature.[22]

9

The aesthetic interest in beauty is distinct from the cognitive interest in truth and it is not subject to the same requirements. There remains, however, the question of their relation. Is there any preëstablished harmony between these two interests, any inner complicity, whereby that which is true and demonstrable tends to be beautiful, and that which is beautiful tends to be true? Opinion in this matter has varied, all the way from the Platonic-Keatsian view that "beauty is truth, truth beauty," to the modern scientist's contempt for the poet as one who lives in a world of dreams.

The question has been, and still is, obscured by the tendency to melt the edges of all terms of eulogy in a glow of sentimentality. To offset this tendency it is well to recognize that knowledge and aesthetic enjoyment may be, and often are, opposed. Not only is the truth often unpalatable, but the love of truth requires that the mind shall subordinate the aesthetically agreeable to a respect for what are aesthetically described as the "harsh" or "ugly" facts. Error, as well as truth, can be embellished, and this may conduce to its perpetuation. The aesthetic interest may cause men to close their eyes to the more unsavory aspects of life. The historical, realistic, psychological, sociological, or pedagogical novel, which purports to be a mixture of art and knowledge, reveals the rivalry of these two interests. Its proved truth does not give it aesthetic appeal, nor does its aesthetic appeal prove it true. It can be criticized by either standard, or condemned by both standards, on the ground that the novelist has confused the two and allowed the one to compromise the other.

[22] Political and ideological controls are not the only alien controls by which the aesthetic part of life may be frustrated. There is also a commercial control, less palpable, but all the more insidious.

Insofar as the aesthetic interest *claims* truth it subjects itself to the standard of truth. There is no aesthetic commandment which prohibits an artist from painting or modeling a "likeness," whether of nature or of a human subject. He does so at his aesthetic peril, for this purpose may defeat the artistic purpose. If there is an interest that the portrait or statue should serve, like a passport photograph, to identify the original, or like a memorial to remind one of the original, then the work of art becomes a hypothesis, and the original becomes evidence of its truth or error. Similarly, if the interest of the artist is to "give" a true idea of a mountain or a ruin, or of death or justice, or any object that he selects, then it submits itself to judgments of truth or error in the light of that object — judgments which the artist himself is in a privileged position to pronounce since he is often the only person in a position to examine the evidence. But the object represented may be an imaginary object, in which case the work of art is true, not of existence, but of its own fictitious creation; as the novelist may truly or erroneously portray the character whom he has conceived.

The artist may also be said to be sincere or insincere according as he does or does not himself contemplate an object. He is not "honest" or "authentic" when he uses the language of art without himself grasping the meaning which it conveys. All art which merely imitates other art — as when the poet adopts a traditional poetic vocabulary, or the visual artist adopts a traditional style without making it his own — is a kind of parroting which communicates nothing, since the parrot does not mean what he says.

Acknowledgment of the independence or even opposition of the aesthetic and cognitive interests paves the way to the understanding of their alliance. First, truth as well as error *can* be embodied in works of art. While appeal to aesthetic enjoyment itself affords no proof of truth it may *add* beauty to truth. Scientific views of nature, man, and history will find their way into the content of poetry or the plastic arts, and thus be doubly blessed.

The aesthetic interest serves knowledge through its very license to rove beyond the limits of knowledge. The realm of the imagination is the field of man's infinite inventiveness. It extends the range of possibilities, it tends to fertility of ideas, to the enrichment of sensory experience, and to the multiplication of the permutations and combinations from which knowledge, as well as practice, make their choices.

Finally, the aesthetic interest contributes to knowledge through the concreteness of its object. The aesthetic interest, at any rate in its sensory objects, contemplates not bare relations, arrangements, organizations, variables — but terms in relation, subject matter arranged and organized, values of variables. The object so contemplated escapes both the schematic thinness of concepts, and the chaotic plethora of sense-perception.

The aesthetic object is neither the warp nor the woof, but the warp and the woof together with the nap and the dye — in short, the carpet. If knowledge is both rational and empirical, and if reality is what it is known to be, then the aesthetic object can be said to reveal a feature of reality that is likely otherwise to escape knowledge, namely its union of structure and content, or quantity and quality.

10

There are two opposed attitudes to the aesthetic part of human life — the belittling and the eulogistic. The belittling judgments are uttered from the standpoint of science, which condemns the aesthetic as irrational and illusory, and from the standpoint of practice which condemns it as evasive and ineffectual. These judgments are valid judgments in terms of the standards which they apply, but they are limited judgments. The praise of beauty, however extravagant, is deserving of respect; if it cannot be wholly justified, it must at least be accounted for. The justification of its extravagance is to be found in the role of the imagination in human life, which the belittlers are disposed to ignore.

The imagination is, of all human faculties, that which contributes most to man's escape from his sense of finitude. It breaks through the barriers of common sense, familiarity, and relevance, and voyages abroad on the limitless expanse of possibility. The imagination is the *enlarging* faculty by which the natural man, while still remaining man, seems to surmount the restrictions imposed by place and time and by his animal-bound inheritance. Whether he does or does not actually surmount these restrictions, he *seems* to himself to do so, and no account of the place of the aesthetic in human life can be complete which does not take this seeming into account. In any case, aesthetic enjoyment enlarges consciousness, both internally through increased sensitivity and discrimination, and externally through making tolerable and even palatable, the harsh accidents of life and the rude thrusts of circumstance. It enables men to "face" life with their eyes open.

Aesthetic enjoyment is characterized by a heightened sense of activity, which has led an eminent critic of art to speak of "life-enhancement" as the crucial test of beauty. Cognitive and practical interests follow a determined route from problem to expectation to verification or disproof, from task to trial to success or failure. Because they are impelled to follow through, they must be confined within a comparatively narrow area of relevance. The aesthetic interest, on the other hand, can engage in many activities because it need not complete any. The imagination has wings and can soar; cognition and practice are pedestrian. A person impelled by the aesthetic interest can imagine the movements of bodies whose actual movements he cannot share — imaginatively he can move with them. He can enter into the inner life of objects other than himself.

Hence he feels an augmented richness and fullness of kinaesthetic experience, which is in part at least accountable for that exhilaration which commonly attends the aesthetic life in both its creative and its appreciative moments.

Aesthetic enjoyment is associated with a sense of mastery. It scores victories. The aesthetic interest, even in its mature development, is like the play of a child who can live the life of a king or a robber, or whatever his fancy may hit upon, unconfined by circumstance. But this imaginative triumph may take a much subtler form. What one enjoys in contemplation is *as though* it were designed for one's contemplation. Antoine de St.-Exupéry has thus described the feeling of a group of friends who were lunching together on the banks of the Saône the day before the war:

> We savoured a sort of state of perfection, in which, every wish vouchsafed, nothing remained to reveal to each other. We felt we were pure, upright, lambent, indulgent . . . The dominant feeling was certainly that of assurance. Of an assurance almost proud.
> Thus the universe, through us, showed its kindness. The nebulae condensed, the planets hardened, the first amoeba came into being, and life's gigantic labour pains led the amoeba to man in order that all should converge harmoniously, through us, in this quality of pleasure! [23]

The aesthetic life, in certain moments, yields not only this exhilaration and sense of mastery, but that feeling of being "pure, upright, lambent, indulgent" to which St.-Exupéry refers. Selfish and sordid considerations are forgotten. Because the aesthetic interest is not competitive, and does not arouse the self-preservative and combative impulses or prompt men to fear and suspicion, it opens the floodgates to the impulses of sympathy and kindness. The love of beauty has something of the tenderness which characterizes the love of persons and the love of God. It is not envious, but worships its object in a mood of self-surrender.

The aesthetic interest tends not only to subordination of self, but because of its freedom from ulterior cognitive and practical motives it enjoys a sense of perfection — a sense, namely, that its object is all that *it* ought to be. Its value is not dependent on its consequences, but is self-contained. The aesthetic interest does not take its object as a mere stepping stone — something *on* which to act, something *from* which to expect — but rests in it, dwells on it, in order to explore the richness and nuances of its content.

These experiences, which might be summarily designated as feelings of "enlargement" or of "exaltation," are not *defining* characteristics — in the sense that there is no aesthetic value without them, but they are nevertheless characteristics, and may properly be credited to the aes-

[23] "Letter to a Hostage," translated by John Rodker, from *Modern French Stories*, copyright 1948 by New Directions, pp. 152–3.

thetic in any judgment of its place in human life. Some would say that they are distinguishing marks of "great" art, or of the "highest" aesthetic enjoyment — but that is another story.

11

The claim of "greatness," like those of "enlargement" and "exaltation," cannot be ignored, however unsatisfactory the results of any attempt to define it. The central difficulty in this case is created by the assumption that there is a one-dimensional order of greatness in which every artist or work of art can by general consent be assigned a place. No doubt it would be generally agreed that Homer, Sophocles, Dante, Raphael, Shakespeare, Goethe, and Beethoven are "great." But there is serious doubt whether this agreement is based on any single and common standard. The problem is aggravated by the fact that the fine arts themselves have become so highly specialized that even if it were possible to define a single standard of greatness for poetry or painting, it would be of doubtful application to music or architecture. The only test which is widely accepted is "the verdict of posterity."

There is no alternative but to conclude that greatness in art is a resultant effect of many incommensurable values, and having nothing in common save their effect upon the esteem of a sufficient number of persons over a sufficient length of time to warrant its being described as "the general esteem of mankind." This standard is, no doubt, circular: it amounts to saying that great art is art which is judged to be great, or which achieves fame. But it changes the question. We no longer ask the unanswerable question, "What is *the* standard of greatness?" but "What are the more important among the many considerations whose total impact finds expression in the judgment of 'greatness,' and creates the necessity for the word?"

When greatness is considered as an aggregate of incommensurables which have a joint effect upon the opinion of mankind, it is no longer permissible to narrow the judgment of greatness to the internal aesthetic standard. This would, at best, define greatness in terms of the preference of connoisseurs. No standard, however vulgar or external, may be excluded so long as it is applicable to art. Prestige, and even commercial value or collector's value, may not be excluded, since these are expressions of, or causes of, general esteem. Still less is it permissible to omit usefulness (does not its usefulness as a place of worship contribute to the greatness of a Gothic cathedral?), or moral value (does not their representation of the Christian virtues contribute to the greatness of medieval painting?), or cognitive value (does not their understanding of human life contribute to the greatness of Goethe and Shakespeare?).

Those who reject the extra-aesthetic evaluation of the aesthetic, who espouse the cause of "art for art's sake," or insist on the distinctness and independence of aesthetic value *per se,* justly protest against the *confusion* of standards. But in the extravagance or bitterness of their protest they have been led to *reject* these other values, and to prove their point by identifying beauty with immorality, with bestiality, with revolution, with cynicism, despair, and impiety, and with every form of iconoclasm. In their eagerness to disprove Aristotle's contention that the theme of tragedy must be noble, they select ignoble themes. But in so doing the aesthetic purists have overreached themselves. In order to free the aesthetic from contamination they have robbed it of all the super-added values which it derives from its place in life and its interaction with the other parts of man's total civilization.

There are certain aspects of art, themselves compounded of many causes, which are commonly cited as peculiarly conducive to the esteem of mankind: originality, perfection, monumental impressiveness, depth of appeal, depth of the object, cultural significance, universality, permanence, and mystical sublimation.

A work of art, like a discovery or generalization in science, may be epoch-making. Standing at a crossroads or turning point, where the path changes its direction, it may predetermine all future aesthetic activity or enjoyment. This gives greatness to Greek art and letters in general, or to the paintings of Giotto, or to the founders of modern music, such as Palestrina.[24]

A work of art obtains general esteem when it is superlatively good of its kind: that is, when it seems to satisfy all of the requirements of its particular medium and form. Thus one may speak of a poem of Shakespeare as a "perfect sonnet," or a composition of Beethoven as a perfect symphony, or the cathedral at Rheims as perfect Gothic, or as "Gothic of the best period." It stands as the seemingly complete solution of an aesthetic problem which is limited enough to be capable of a complete solution. It stands as that which cannot be improved upon, and thus acquires a kind of immortality.

Monumental impressiveness implies quantity and duration, as notably exemplified by the pyramids of Egypt. The work of the goldsmith or miniature painter, however exquisite and perfect of its kind, is not described as "monumental." The visual arts, and particularly architecture, here enjoy an advantage over other forms of art. They endure through a long period of time in the full view of mankind. They do not require any record or interpretation, but speak for themselves. Durability is, however,

---

[24] An interesting illustration is provided by the modern composer Arnold Schoenberg, who has proposed to free music from the tonal relationships of the traditional harmonic system. The "revolutionary" composer attempts to break habits, and to substitute new rules for old, and when he succeeds in converting the taste of his hearers, as he often does, he has at least given meaning to the term "originality." Cf. P. Yates, "Arnold Schoenberg: Apostle of Atonality," *New York Times Magazine,* Sept. 11, 1949.

a condition of greatness in all the arts, as is also quantity. It is a part of the greatness of Homer, Dante, Titian, Shakespeare, that they bulk larger in human experience through the volume of their productivity and the range of their genius.

"Depth of appeal" clarifies the meaning of what is sometimes called "spiritual significance." Esteem is here based on the extent to which art calls human faculties into play. Art which appeals only to the senses, or which satisfies only certain formal requirements, is less esteemed than art which evokes the profounder emotions or requires the exercise of the higher intellectual faculties. Great art demands more for its appreciation, and in so doing also gives more. Similarly, the ideal object may be superficial or profound. The crime story, shock thriller, and melodrama, in order to make tragedy amusing and so appeal to popular taste, miss its true inwardness. "Great" art will enable men to taste the poignancy of tragedy and yet find it palatable. The "happy ending," the sentimentalist's complacency, are concessions to the vulgar at the cost of shallowness; the satirist will reveal "the worst," and yet enable men to enjoy its contemplation.

Art is esteemed for the degree to which it sums up and "mirrors" the cultural characteristics of a society, nation, or age. It will enjoy esteem among those to whom it thus gives articulate expression, and will stand as a landmark to the rest of mankind. The Parthenon is esteemed for being essentially Greek, Molière for conveying the spirit of France in the age of Louis XIV, Shakespeare for embodying what is characteristically English or Elizabethan. Whenever any poet or painter or musician shall have succeeded in epitomizing the industrial age, or the age of the cold war, he will be esteemed as great on that account. Art thus serves the purposes of history and of education in perpetuating and concentrating the past in memorable unities.

"Universality," which is perhaps the commonest of the recognized attributes of greatness, refers to the extent to which the aesthetic interest selects for contemplation the common characteristics of human life. These may or may not be its familiar characteristics, such as home, or sexual love, or the common familiar relations, or the homely occupations of everyday life. When such familiar characteristics are selected it is assumed that they will be easily recognized, and appreciated. This is the claim made for art which is enjoyed by the mass of mankind, and which is therefore "popular." But the universal object may be that which is taken as the deeper meaning of life: accessible to every man's apprehension, but requiring penetration, insight, and generalization.

Art owes its permanence in part to the sameness of human nature, whereby men continue throughout time to enjoy the same sensible qualities and structures, and in part to the unchanging character of human experience in its essentials. But there is another sense in which great works of art are said to be "immortal." Each artistic achievement is *final*, or invulnerable to the effects of time. What does it mean, for example, to say that Homer's *Iliad* is a "joy forever"? The answer lies in the fact that its poetic value is independent of historical knowledge, and of the historical course of events. It would not have been in the least diminished if Schliemann had not discovered Troy, but had come to the conclusion that no such city ever existed. It would have been proved to be bad history, which no one has ever doubted. If the Trojan War is taken as an actual conquest of Trojans by Greeks, then in the light of later events it may prove to have been a political mistake. But such vicissitudes do not touch that realm of the imagination in which Troy *was* destroyed. Only provided human nature were so radically altered that the imaginary episode ceased to be enjoyed in contemplation would its artistic permanence be affected.

Finally, art is esteemed as great when it enables man to face the universe, and to rise above its differences and conflicts to some all-reconciling synthesis. A recent critic of Beethoven, in contending that this composer's work culminates in his last quartets, at the same time contends that this consummate achievement of music is the consummate achievement of all art:

> To be willing to suffer in order to create is one thing; to realize that one's creation necessitates one's suffering, that suffering is one of the greatest of God's gifts, is almost to reach a mystical solution of the problem of evil, a solution that is probably for the good of the world that very few people will ever entertain . . . We know . . . that Beethoven was a man who experienced all that we can experience, who suffered all that we can suffer. If, in the end, he seems to reach a state "above the battle," we also know that no man ever knew more bitterly what the battle is.[25]

This does not, however, in the least mitigate its limitations and defects, as judged by moral and cognitive standards. To see moral and cognitive evil as aesthetic good does not make them good judged by their own standards. To be "above the battle" weakens the moral will dedicated to the overcoming of evil. To achieve a state of assurance and certitude merely through the aesthetic experience weakens the faculties dedicated to the proof of truth. Nevertheless the mystical vision in which suffering is sublimated may be the most rapturous form of enjoyment.

[25] J. W. N. Sullivan, *op. cit.*, Alfred A. Knopf, Inc., pp. 223, 225, 233, 242, 252–3, 262.

CHAPTER XIX

CULTURE, CIVILIZATION, AND SOCIOLOGY

The discussion of science and art proves the inadequacy of any account of human life that limits itself to moral organization, or to the great social institutions of conscience, polity, law, and economy. Human life is more than any one of these institutions; more than their sum, or even their systematic interrelations. The moral institutions are organizations of interests, but do not specify what these interests shall be. Even when the specific independent interests of science and art are provided for, there is still a large gap between the description and human life itself. The terms which refer to the full complexity of human life, and restore the whole after the itemization of its parts, are the terms 'culture' and 'civilization.' The discussion of this topic will prepare the way for the understanding of history, education, and religion, which embrace the cultural totality in its temporal progression, its transmission to successive human generations and individuals, and its destiny in the world at large.

The term 'culture' has already been introduced as the antithesis of 'nature.' Culture is that which man has made *of* his natural environment, and *with* his natural faculties. What he makes of nature and with nature he makes in obedience to his interests. But the products of man's interested action are incorporated into his subsequent life. Hence culture is not merely what man makes *of* his culture with his natural endowment, but what he makes of culture *with* his culture, that is, in obedience to his *acquired* interests and capacities. The effect is vastly to multiply the varieties of his specific modes of cultural life, all within the broad framework of what nature permits and enables him to do.

Culture denotes the variety, totality, and mobility of what man makes of himself and of his environment. There is an aspect of sameness and repetition. All human societies comprise certain common factors which are rooted in nature and common experience. Wherever human life is found, these are found. But each of these constant features of human life appears in a number of specific forms. There are peculiarities which never repeat themselves, because of historic and local differences, and because of the unpredictable spontaneities which operate in the field of human behavior like mutations in the field of genetics.

Culture signifies not only these particularities, but also their modes of togetherness. The human face is composed of features and there are infinite varieties of each. But the face also has its physiognomy which is the characteristic effect of the combination of features. Similarly, there is a cultural physiognomy consisting of the interrelationship of the parts, their relative prominence, shape, proportion, distance and arrangement; in short, their configuration. Hence the vogue among students of culture of such terms as 'structure' and 'pattern.' But over and above facial physiognomy there are fleeting expressions, and the play and interplay of the features. Similarly, a cultural physiognomy is a dynamic and not a static thing: not a static composite of elements, but a peculiar inter-action and movement in which particular varieties of interests modify, and are modified by, one another.

Culture is doubly embodied: in the ideas, attitudes, and dispositions of men, and in the physical artifacts by which these are expressed and implemented. Strictly speaking, the latter constitute not culture itself, but its precipitate and record. The automobile as described by physics and chemistry is no part of culture. It becomes a part of culture only when it is linked with the skills of its maker and driver, with the taste of its designer, with its uses of transportation and recreation, and with its enhancement of the prestige of its owner.[1]

It is one of the ironies of human life that it should be outlasted by its own lifeless products. When, if it so happens, the last man expires on an uninhabitable earth, the ashes and broken ruins of his life will no doubt remain for thousands of years awaiting that future archaeologist who will never come. But his culture will be dead. Even though the city of man should through some catastrophic accident be preserved intact with all its streets and houses, its furnishings and appurtenances, culture would have disappeared from the earth; for culture consists not in the physical city but in the meanings and uses which it has for its inhabit-ants. The dead civilizations of the past are known by their relics, but they are nonetheless dead, as dead as the empty shell of some pre-glacial crustacean. So far as such relics belong to culture at all, they belong to the past culture of the society which created them or to the present cul-ture of the society which discovers them.

If some powerful wind should blow the gadgets of industrialized America into the desert of Central Arabia, where they became meaning-

[1] F. H. Allport and D. A. Hartman, "The Prediction of Cultural Change" in *Methods in Social Science*, S. A. Rice (ed.), 1931, pp. 325–6.

less objects of amazement to wandering nomads, there would be no diffusion of American culture: because the ideas, attitudes, and dispositions
in which culture consists cannot be carried by the wind. Culture would
have been transmitted only if and when the new society learned to use
the automobile, the radio, or the electric refrigerator, and assimilated
them into their characteristic way of living. When we speak of war as destroying culture we often refer confusedly to the ruined houses, bridges,
ships, railways, libraries, churches, and museums which the bomber
leaves in its trail. But this is a destruction of culture only insofar as men's
lives are broken. The rubble of culture is not the pile of stones and mor-
tar or twisted steel, but the rubble of men's minds.

Language, literature, and art play a unique role in the records of
culture. The vocabulary, inflections, sentence structure, idioms, pronun-
ciation, intonation, and style of language; the shapes, lines, colors, contrasts, and harmonies, the delicate strokes of the painter's brush and the
sculptor's chisel permit of an infinite variety of nuances by which the
full concreteness can be most nearly conveyed and felt. But they express
nothing and they communicate nothing except to human persons attuned
by sensibility, understanding, and sympathy.

In literature and common speech the terms 'civilization' and 'culture'
are used interchangeably. They are used either as synonyms; or, when
two meanings are distinguished, the words are used in reverse senses
by different speakers and writers. As a contemporary philosopher has
pointed out: "European critics . . . impressed by America's advanced
plumbing and (as they judge) backward arts, have divided about equally
between telling us that we have civilization but no culture and telling
us that we have culture but lack civilization." [2] There is, however, a difference, which is of the utmost importance in the present context, between culture or civilization, whichever it is called, in the broader generic
sense, and in a narrower and more selective sense. There is a level or
stage of culture or civilization, which is marked off as in some sense
superior, higher, or more advanced, and which implies standards of appraisal. It is important not to lose sight of the distinction. Hence the
word 'culture' will hereinafter be used for the genus, and the word 'civilization' or some qualified expression, such as 'humane culture,' for the
species.

2

The branch of knowledge which corresponds to culture and civilization is, or should be, sociology; but sociology tends, especially in America, to suffer from a timidity engendered by methodological scruples. To
it belongs the role of surveying the totality of man's life and keeping it

[2] W. R. Dennes, *Civilization,* University of California Publications in Philosophy,
1942, p. 163.

in view amidst the partial and one-sided glimpses which suffice for other branches of social inquiry. With certain notable exceptions sociologists shrink from this role because of the impossibility of applying to so comprehensive a whole the more precise methods which can be successfully applied to the parts. So, fearful of being criticized as "unscientific," it sells its birthright for a mess of positivism, and may by so doing end in destroying itself. For taken narrowly it dissolves into travelogues, or into psychology, anthropology, and geography, or into the several cultural social sciences.

A science of totality need not be flamboyant in design, or loose and flimsy in construction, but it should be spacious — the work of an architect rather than of a cabinetmaker. It is under the same intellectual obligations as any other branch of knowledge. But the first of these obligations is to subordinate method to subject matter. If in the case of sociology the subject matter does not permit of exactness and conclusiveness, then it does not suffice to be exact and conclusive about some other subject matter.

Contemporary sociologists are to be applauded, therefore, when they insist on intellectual scrupulousness, and on being as exact as their task permits. They are also correct in adopting the method of description. They are disposed, however, to fall into the error of assuming that if sociology is to be descriptive it cannot be normative. It suffers from the fear of being thought edifying, and in the name of description neglects the fact that values and norms are intrinsic to its subject matter. Since culture and civilization are composed of interests, and since interests cannot exist without objects on which they confer value, and since the ideal objects of interest constitute norms which acts and achievements in some degree either realize or fail to realize, it is impossible to describe culture and civilization and at the same time exclude values and norms.

Recent German schools of sociology are divided between those who insist that the sciences shall be *wertfrei*, that is, purged of all reference to value; those who insist that the data of sociology require *Verstehen*, that is, sympathetic appreciation of the internal motivation of life.[3] The confusion arises, no doubt, from the supposition that to introduce values implies that the sociologist introduces his own *personal* standards of value; which ignores the fact that there are many other standards, such as the neighbor's standard, the foreigner's standard, and the standards of cultural activities themselves.

Having recognized that culture and civilization are systems of interest and therefore embrace values and norms, sociology will then employ

[3] T. Abel's *Systematic Sociology in Germany*, 1929, gives a summary of the doctrines here referred to. For the insistence of L. von Weise and Max Weber on "*wertfrei Betrachtung*," cf. pp. 113–4; and for Weber's "*verstehende Soziologie*," cf. ch. lv. Cf. also Alfredo Pareto, *Traité de Sociologie Générale*, 1919, Vol. I, ch. i. Max Weber is both the least pretentious and the least confused.

the same methods as the several cultural sciences insofar as these methods are appropriate to its own subject matter. Thus explanatory sociology will deal with the structures and conditions of total cultures. Normative sociology will differ radically from the normative branches of the specific cultural sciences in that society is not an institution, and cannot, therefore, be said to have any peculiar instrumentality or purpose of its own. It will be especially concerned with total social value, and with those superior values which, within culture in the basic sense, distinguish that general level of eminence which warrants the name of civilization. Technological sociology will consist of whatever knowledge is useful to those whose aim is to create an integral culture or civilization.

3

Explanatory sociology will examine the natural environment which determines the character of a culture as, for example, the climate of the region in which a society exists, its geography, and its natural resources. It will take account of those elements of human nature which incline men to live together and to develop uniformity and community.

In explaining culture by the socializing propensities of human nature sociologists are in danger of falling between two stools — an unanalytical psychology and an unpsychological analysis. The psychological explanation in terms of "drives" has usually failed to analyze them. In particular it has neglected their cognitive aspect, and in so doing has failed to bring to light the ways in which life is socialized by the fact that two or more interests have common objects and take one another as objects. This neglect may be said to be on the whole characteristic of Anglo-American psychologists. The German schools of psychology, on the other hand, have suffered from a psycho-phobia traceable to their Kantian inheritance; and from an antiquated view of psychology as concerned wholly with "inner experience." Sociology rightly concerns itself with types of relationships, but only when they are *mental* relationships, and as such fall within the province of psychology — the more so since this science has now through its emphasis on social behavior acquired a competence to deal with relations between, and not merely within, human subjects.

German and French sociology has exhibited another unfortunate tendency, namely, to conceive social totalities as irreducible to personal relationships.[4] Cultures and civilizations *are* wholes, and it is the peculiar duty of sociology to see them whole. But the doctrine of emergence provides for the whole at the same time for the terms and relationships by

---

[4] For the emphasis on *"Ganzheiten"* by A. Vierkandt and other German sociologists, cf. Abel, *op. cit.*, p. 75. For a discussion of the more important French school of E. Durkheim, cf. the Author's *General Theory of Value*, 1926, 1950, §§ 191, 192, 197.

which the whole can be explained. The recognition of a community of objects accounts for whatever there is of truth in the doctrine of "collective representations," that is, ideas which are not the private possession of any single mind. The identity of a cultural system embodied in different individuals accounts for its independence of any single individual. Cultures exist in aggregates of persons, who are interchangeable and replaceable; a single individual is not indispensable to it, but will feel it as something independent of himself.

While culture embraces institutions, the sociologist is not concerned with the explanation of each in its own terms, but with the explanation of one by another. He will focus attention not on the ethical, political, legal, or economic, but on the ethico-political, politico-legal, legal-economic, etc., taking the whole society as an interaction of institutional parts.

In the explanation of culture an important place is rightly given to its own products. Pareto employs the terms 'residues' and 'derivatives' [5] to distinguish between the basic drives and their justifications or rationalizations. He has given vogue among sociologists to the idea, which he shares with Freudians, that rationalizations are essentially irrational. They are make-believes having no cognitive validity because they are not arrived at by the "logico-experimental" method; and only the naïve and superstitious will take them to be either true or false. But so to construe them is to ignore the immense role played in human culture by rationalizations which *are* supported by evidence — judgments of social utility which are rational even by Pareto's own standard of rationality.

Explanatory sociology is distinguished from the special moral sciences — ethics, political science, jurisprudence, and economics — by its recognition of major pursuits, such as science and art, which are essentially non-moral, and of those pursuits of education and religion which transcend morality. At the same time, in obedience to its aim of completeness, sociology must provide room for the thousand and one miscellaneous activities of human life — play, sport, war, marriage, etc. — which slip through the meshes of a coarser schematism. And to approximate the full concreteness of the social plenum it must recognize these values, such as personal love and happiness, which peculiarly concern the individual.

4

The question of the unity and plurality of cultures is complicated by the distinction, between individual or historical cultures, and cultural types. To speak of "a culture" may mean either of these two quite different things. Cultures in both senses, furthermore, may be overlapping. Do Italy and France, for example, constitute two cultures or one? Individually there are clearly two, since one is the culture of Italians and the

[5] *Op. cit.*, Vol. I, ch. vi.

other is the culture of Frenchmen. At the same time they are of one cultural type, which is called "Latin culture." But we can also speak of "European culture," and in two senses: the culture of the Europeans, and the set of cultural characteristics possessed by Frenchmen and Latins in common with Americans, as distinguished from the cultural characteristics possessed by Asiatics; and to this it follows that the question whether Italy and France constitute one culture or two is capable of several correct answers. There are classes and sub-classes of individual cultures, and there are types and sub-types of cultural characteristics.

There are innumerable ways in which cultural types can be distinguished, according to the factor chosen as the independent variable. Thus, cultures may be defined by the techniques employed to provide for material needs, human culture of the most primitive, or nomadic, variety being distinguished from anthropoid culture by the use of five simple tools of stone and wood. Although the tools were gradually improved, the general characteristics of group-life remained essentially the same. The people who composed such groups were "wandering hunters, who lived entirely on wild game and the wild edible plants and other products of nature . . . they could gather, and . . . their usual abode was some sunny ledge under an overhanging cliff, or the mouth of a cave. They seem to have lived in small groups," since "it is absolutely impossible to support a larger community of people by hunting." [6]

Then, between 7,000 and 12,000 years ago, there began the domestication of animals and the discovery of agriculture, which brought increased food supply, increase of population, the building of villages and towns, division of labor, accumulation of wealth, organized warfare and trade, writing and the keeping of records, increased power and complexity of government and other institutions. Then about 1500 A.D. another profound change took place due to the occurrence, simultaneously or in rapid succession, of numerous discoveries and inventions, such as the circumnavigation of the globe, Newtonian science, the steam engine, electricity, the conquest of the air. This mechano-industrial phase has not yet run its course, and the confusion and bewilderment of the present age is said to be due to the fact that human life as a whole has not yet assimilated these technological changes.

We are not here concerned with the thesis that the independent variable in cultural change is necessarily technological, rather than ethnic, religious, or political. But the illustration, assuming that it has at least some modicum of truth, illustrates the meaning of types of culture — "ways in which men live together" — in which each of the factors of human life acts and reacts upon the rest. But each such type is capable

---

[6] E. R. Wulsin, "Man and the Technics of Civilization," in *A Revaluation of Our Civilization*, Argus Press, 1944, pp. 9–17.

of being divisible into sub-types, and of being subsumed under some more general type. And each type, super-type, and sub-type is capable of embodiment in different individuals, without loss of its identical meaning. It can be transmitted vertically by inheritance or laterally by diffusion. It is clear that there is no reckoning of the number of cultures save to say that the number is indefinite since it depends on the unit with which one reckons.

An individual culture that is doubly defined as a group of interacting human individuals embodying a specific type of culture may arise in time, develop, and disappear. These ups and downs, this waxing and waning, suggests the analogy of the physical organism. From Herder to Toynbee by way of Spengler the analogy has been pressed with varying degrees of boldness and, for the most part, with an insufficiency of critical caution.

Of all the characteristics of a physical organism there are none more obscure than growth and senescence; and to transpose these characters to culture provides no understanding, but merely introduces a term having respectable scientific associations, and gives to inquiry a specious sense of scientific achievement. It is doubtful whether anything whatsoever except poetry is gained by speaking of cultures as "young," "mature," and "old." Waiving the inaccuracy of terms, cultures are always both old and young; something is ending, and something is beginning. It is doubtful if any culture has ever died of old age, that is, merely as a consequence of living too long. The oldest cultures in the world, namely, the "primitive" cultures, are at the same time the youngest — are, in fact, embryonic. Why speak of cultures as "decadent," "sick," "dying," or "over-ripe," if what is meant is that they have declined in respect of certain criteria selected for comparative judgment? Furthermore, it often happens that at the same time that they have declined in certain respects they have improved in others. Indeed it may be that their peculiar character consists in the very co-presence of the better and the worse. It is a well-known fact that great philosophy flourished in Athens contemporaneously with small politics; and it has been said that Southern California was once distinguished by its blend of medieval ideas with the latest technological gadgets.

It is no doubt true that in the field of art and letters styles tend to deteriorate when they are prolonged, whether through the exhaustion of their inventive possibilities or because the geniuses who originated them are succeeded by lesser disciples and imitators. It is no doubt true that organization tends to become increasingly complicated, and thus to break down through excessive specialization and the accumulation of obstructive by-products. But little light is thrown on these facts by merely employing the vague metaphors of decay and arterio-sclerosis.

5

The critique of cultures is challenged by a form of the doctrine of relativism. It is an indisputable fact that cultural characteristics, being integral characteristics of a given society, in some sense or to some degree qualify all of its members and all of their activities. It follows that they will qualify the judgments which the members pronounce on other cultures, whether judgments arrived at by scientists and philosophers, or the uncritical and unmethodical judgments of common opinion and sentiment. This indisputable fact creates what may be called the "culture-centric predicament." This predicament is sometimes taken to imply that no culture can be appraised in its own terms, but only in terms of the culture of him who makes the appraisal. Followed through to its extreme limit this would result in a cultural solipsism, analogous to that which is supposed to be fatal to every claim of objective truth. The predicament is indisputable, but the implication is both gratuitous and contrary to fact.

Cultural relativism or solipsism in the vicious sense cannot be stated without self-contradiction. As has so often been pointed out, the reflective act by which a relativity is discovered surmounts the relativity which is asserted. In a criticism of Karl Mannheim's *Ideology and Utopia,* the late Carl Becker called attention to the failure of a relativistic sociology to provide for itself — for its own virtual claim to have escaped the very cultural relativity which it holds to be inescapable:

> I feel that, having relentlessly pressed all our heads down below the surface of the flowing social process, he first assures us that we can never get out, and then tells us that we can after all escape drowning by frankly recognizing that we are under water. I must confess that I do not share his confidence, but if we are all under water for good no doubt something is gained by recognizing the fact.[7]

While the critic put his finger on Mannheim's difficulty, he appears in the end to have succumbed to it himself. He failed to recognize the positive implications of his own argument.

The development of cultural critique follows the same course as the development of all knowledge. It is a perpetual endeavor, never perhaps wholly successful, but more and more successful, to eliminate the distortions and limitations of experience by bringing them to light and putting them where they belong. It rectifies the distortions and supplements the limitations. It achieves this by conceptual thought and by imagination.

[7] C. Becker, "Social Relativity," in *The New Republic,* Jan. 27, 1937, p. 388. For Mannheim's attempt to escape the circularity by the notion of "the unattached intellectual," cf. his *Ideology and Utopia,* 1940, p. 140, and ch. iii *passim.* Cf. the admirable summary and criticism of this work by A. J. Melden, "Judgments in the Social Sciences," *Civilization,* University of California Publications in Philosophy, 23, 1942.

Thus ancient culture is ancient to those who live in the year 1953. Conceptual thought substitutes for this particular retrospect from 1953, a chronological scheme of years measured before and after the birth of Christ, and which includes the year 1953. One may then say that the same culture which is ancient to us was recent to the cultures of the Early Middle Ages, prospective to the Minoan Culture, and contemporary to other cultures of the years 600 B.C. to 300 A.D. And one can imagine what this civilization was like in its own time, and in the times just preceding and just following, and to the barbaric outsiders as well as to Greek and Roman insiders. In so doing one will judge Graeco-Roman culture not only from the angle of its own time and place, and from other angles, but roundly and centrally.

It is quite true that there is no critique *of* a culture which is not a critique *by* a culture. But it does not follow that the judging culture invariably or in any fixed degree modifies or misrepresents the culture judged. It may or it may not; it may in certain respects and not in other respects; it may in some degree. It may be characteristic of a culture that it emancipates itself, more or less, from its own prejudices. Granting that all culture, to be seen at all, must be seen through a cultural medium, it does not follow that the medium may not be transparent.

Insofar as the interests which compose any culture are known at all — and they are as objective facts as any other facts — they are known for what they were or are. Such being the case their successes and failures can be known for what they were or are, and the way is open all along the line to an internal critique of cultural achievements, in terms of its own standards. Or they can be judged externally in terms of the standards of the culture to which the judge belongs; and this is a legitimate and objective judgment provided the standards are made explicit.

6

Most discussions of culture, even when they profess to be "merely descriptive," introduce a ranking of cultures. This is both legitimate and inevitable, since culture consists of values, and since values are in one or more ways higher and lower. This makes it desirable to have a term which explicitly recognizes such appraisal — a term which refers, not to culture in general or to any culture, but to culture which in certain specifiable respects holds a comparatively high rank. The term 'civilization' is here set apart for this use. It is then meaningful to say that some cultures are civilized, whereas other cultures are uncivilized, barbarous, or savage; or to say that war may destroy civilization, and still leave culture.

The appraisal of types of culture, or of single cultures, is frequently concealed, especially among anthropologists, by the use of terms whose *prima facie* meaning is temporal or genetic, and which at the same time assume that what comes later, or develops out of what has gone before, is therefore better.

The most familiar instance of this assumption is afforded by the distinction between "primitive" and "advanced" cultures. Of such statements, however, it is pertinent to inquire, "Advanced in what?" "Advanced in what direction, along what route?" The answer most frequently given by anthropologists is, "Advanced in the control of the physical environment." Thus, in the order of cultural types outlined above, the first step is the discovery of fire and the invention of tools; the second is the discovery of the arts of agriculture and animal husbandry; and the third is the improved technology based on the discoveries of modern physics and chemistry.

If this history of culture is an advance from good to better, and not merely a temporal continuity, it must be because of a similarity of interests. Thus the needs of physical preservation persist throughout, and are served better in later than in earlier phases of human history. In modern as in primitive societies men need food. Given the choice they will prefer the modern way because it enables them to procure more abundant and more appetizing food, and to acquire a store of provisions by which to enjoy security against drought, flood, scarcity of game, or other seasonal or catastrophic contingencies. Similarly, throughout their history men need clothing, shelter, and weapons to protect them, and given the same needs they will choose more adequate clothing, shelter, and weapons wherever these are available.

There is a second technological criterion of civilization with which this first is commonly confused. Science yields not only specific technologies, that is, techniques linked to existing interests and created in response to their demands, but also a general technology which provides instruments for their *possible* interests. Its creation does not await, but anticipates demands; and tends to create them. For men not only prefer more effective ways of doing what they already desire to do, but desire to do what they know or believe that they can do. Viewed in this light a civilized culture is thus a comparatively resourceful culture. This is part, at least, of what is meant when civilization is identified with a progressive or "dynamic" culture.

That technological efficiency is not the only criterion of civilization is implied by the judgment that economic advance has been accompanied by cultural decline. This view has been vividly presented by Lewis Mumford:

> The goal of the eotechnic [early-technological] civilization . . . was not more power alone but a greater intensification of life: color, perfume, images, music, sexual ecstasy, as well as daring exploits in arms and thought and exploration. Fine images were everywhere: a field of tulips in bloom, the scent of new mown hay, the ripple of flesh under silk or the

rondure of budding breasts: the rousing sting of the wind as the rain clouds scud over the seas, or the blue serenity of the sky and cloud, reflected with crystal clarity on the velvety surface of canal and pond and watercourse. . . . [The] new economic men sacrificed their digestion, the interests of parenthood, their sexual life, their health, most of the normal pleasures and delights of civilized existence to the untrammeled pursuit of power and money. . . . In only the most limited sense were the great industrialists better off than the workers they degraded: jailer and prisoner were both, so to say, inmates of the same House of Terror.[8]

The standards of civilization implicit in this indictment of ruthless efficiency are the moral and humane. It is implied that civilization is marked by the existence of a comparatively enlightened and sensitive conscience; and by the degree to which a society has solved its problem of conflict by liberal political, legal and economic institutions. It is further implied that morality provides the ground plan, but not the sky-line, of civilization. The non-moral or trans-moral values are the flowering of which morality is the garden plot.

Hence civilization is marked by the development of interests which express certain human faculties having a peculiar universality and dignity, namely, the cognitive and aesthetic interests. So conceived, a civilization will be a culture which excels in the emergence of creative genius in the fields of science, art, and letters. Because the faculties engaged are distinctively human such culture is referred to as "humane" or "humanistic" culture. It is this value which is said to distinguish the civilization of Athens in the fifth and fourth centuries, B.C., and the civilization of Italy and other European societies at the time of the Renaissance.

Or, civilization may be distinguished by its eminence in education and religion. The educational criterion itself may be formulated in various terms. A civilized society may be taken to be a "cultivated" society, judged by the personal development of its members; when it not only has abolished illiteracy but has brought a considerable portion of its members to the higher levels of secondary, liberal, or professional education. Or it may be deemed civilized when, through its instruments of communication and publicity, it has created a comparatively responsible and enlightened public opinion. Judged by the religious standard a culture is deemed worthy of the name of 'civilization' when its piety has risen above the level of so-called "superstition," having been reconciled with science and with personal freedom; or when it has advanced from the worship of local and tribal gods to the recognition of a universal god of all mankind.

When one has added together the goods of organized social life, of conformity to conscience, of the security and freedom conferred by polity and law, of justly distributed wealth furnished by economy, of the indi-

[8] L. Mumford, *Technics and Civilization,* Harcourt, Brace and Company, 1934, pp. 148–9, 168, 177.

vidual improvement contributed by education, and of the ultimate faith given by religion, and when to these one has added the pursuit of truth and the enjoyment of beauty, the sum still falls short of the fullness of life. That which remains is both small and great. It is small because it is so familiar and banal; it does not need to be invoked by authorities, wise men, or seers. It is great because it is so pervasive. It fills the interstices, and gives value to what is otherwise known by belittling names such as "innocent pleasures," "routine," and "daily life." It appears on all levels of life, but because it is so familiar it is known by its more humble rather than by its exalted associations.

This remainder and concrete filling of life has no name. It embraces all the miscellaneous and unclassifiable goods — health,[9] work and play, recreation, conversation, rest, laughter, craftsmanship, the pleasures of food and drink, the feel of the breath of life, reputation, fame, the minor successes that are not recorded in history or even in biography. It is the margin of these goods over their opposite evils that makes life solvent. As life on earth is impossible, so life in any other world is unimaginable, without them. More of these things than is ordinarily supposed belong to those treasures of heaven which neither moth nor rust corrupts, and which no man could afford to leave behind in his last journey, no matter how much he is advised to lighten his baggage.

The list of the values which sweeten daily life is as inexhaustible as it is miscellaneous. It is the poet's and not the philosopher's task to single them out and do them honor, but there are two, namely, love and happiness, which will serve to represent them all for the purpose of rounding out our survey of civilized life. Both terms are here employed in their ordinary rather than in their euphemistic or "euphemystical" senses.

7

By 'love' is here meant not the esoteric and metaphysical love of God, or the abstract love of mankind, but personal love between man and man, or between man and woman. The first, which is sexless, is an intensification of the bond between fellow-creatures, and is commonly known as friendship. It is benevolence focused upon an individual; or positive interest in another's interests because they are his; it is independent benevolence mediated by recognition and familiarity.

Plato and Aristotle have exercised a forceful, but largely misleading, influence on European views of love. Whether rightly or wrongly these philosophers have been taken to mean that the object of love in the highest and purest sense is the universal idea. When, according to this view, the immediate object of love is a particular this serves as a symbol of the universal, or a medium through which the universal is to be

---

[9] For an examination of this important topic, cf. D. H. Parker, *Human Values*, 1931, ch. vii.

reached. When love is convergent, the lover and the loved are united through their common ideal object; their love is directed not towards one another, but towards a third object. It is a companionship of admiring contemplation. So to conceive love is to miss its meaning altogether. That which distinguishes love is not the movement from the particular to the universal, but the reverse movement, from the universal to the particular. This does not imply that love is not enriched by ideas, but that its ultimate object is their individual embodiment. Love is not the same thing as judgment or contemplation, however much this may be enjoyed. The loved person is not a set of attributes. It is characteristic of the lover to bestow qualities upon the object of his love. The degree of his love is reflected in the extravagance with which he heaps superlative on superlative — we do not expect him to be judicious and objective. The fact that love and poetry are so frequently combined is not an accident. But this does not mean, in either case, that attributes are substituted for the individual object, but testifies, rather, to the impossibility of such an equivalence. The very extravagance of the praise signifies the vain attempt to achieve the concrete by the multiplication of abstractions.

The lover and the loved one are, it is true, united by their interests. The lover accepts as his own the interests of the loved; if the loved had no interests he or she could not be loved. Love is essentially indulgent, and sympathetically attuned. But in love it is the individual that is the independent variable. When two persons enjoy activities together lovingly, each enjoys these activities because of the togetherness. The perfect lover will prefer any activity in participation with the loved one to any activity in which the loved one is absent, be it talking or silence, reading or domestic chores, going abroad or remaining at home, business or idleness — anything *with* rather than anything *without*.

Love is thus peculiarly fruitful. It pays as it goes. Interest reinforces interest: it can give value to activities which would otherwise be barren, and positive quality to interests which would otherwise be negative; when the end is remote it can fill the interval between undertaking and achievement. It yields benefit not only to the receiver but to the giver. Love is good to live with — it elevates the lover in his own esteem without conceit or arrogance. Love begets love in return. It is an ascending spiral or a benign, and not, like hate, a vicious circle.

Although its two great commandments are commandments of love, the effect of Christianity upon the Western conception of love has been evil as well as good. Christianity has been the great corrective of Platonism. For a supreme idea of Good it has substituted a personal God, and this has made it possible to transfer to the relations between God and man the personal love experienced between man and man — the love of a father for his children, and of a child for his parents. An Idea cannot love, nor can an Idea be loved except in the specious sense of admiring contemplation. The gospel of Jesus, furthermore, was a humanitarian gospel, not a cult of the intellect but a quickening of pity and tenderness, felt for conscious beings in their concrete particularity. All of this has been inherited in the Christian tradition, and has persisted despite the dogmatism, mysticism, ecclesiasticism, and hardenings of the heart with which, in Christian history, it has been attended.

Over against this personalization of love with which Christianity is to be credited, stands, on the debit side, its degradation of sex. This has been due to two motives: the first of which is the ascetic condemnation of the flesh. Sex, as being the most powerful and unruly of the carnal appetites, has been represented as the temptation of the Devil, opposed to the life of the spirit. The higher life of man has been identified with chastity and celibacy. The result has been to divide human nature against itself, and so to create and aggravate the tensions, neuroses, and hypocrisies which form so tragic a part of the personal life of the modern world.

The attempt of spirit to subjugate and alienate the body is a losing battle. Nature is already in possession of the field and the art of love is to win it as a friend. The only effect of attempting to disembody the spirit is to despiritualize the body. The design of the Christian God which was to implant spirit in flesh is a better design than that of Christian men who have attempted to tear spirit from its natural roots. This treatment of sexual passion as an enemy to be crushed and if possible destroyed, not only has invested it with morbid propensities but has robbed love between the sexes of its vital core and sensuous content. Following the parallel between sex and the other parts of the natural man, love should be more and not less than instinct. Its role is to contain physical passion and raise it to a human level, by compounding it with sensitiveness, generosity, loyalty, respect, and understanding.

The second and more shocking perversion of love by Christianity is the Pauline divorce between physical love and the institution or sacrament of matrimony. Official Christianity has little to say against loveless intercourse between the sexes provided it occurs within the marriage bond, and is designed for the propagation of offspring. It saves its denunciations and anathemas for sexual love which has not received the sanction of the law or the church. In the history of Christian Europe, romantic love has been extracurricular. The legendary lovers, who provide themes for literature, are, in the Christian teaching known as sinners. Tristan and Iseult, Launcelot and Guinevere, are grouped with Semiramis, Helen, and Cleopatra, among the spirits of the incontinent. Even Paolo and Francesca, though their story moves Dante to tears, are condemned to the tortures of Hell.[10] The history of Abélard and Héloïse

[10] *Divine Comedy, Hell,* Canto V.

is the story of a fatal conflict between a love which rises to the greatest heights of passionate fidelity, and the vocation of the Christian cleric.

But this is not the worst. Compelled to make terms with custom and the demands of the flesh, Pauline Christianity has conceived marriage as a hiding place where the sexual appetite can be decently veiled, and where the carnal pleasures are condoned provided they are not mentioned. It has required nothing short of a social revolution, not yet fully achieved, to bring the realities of the domestic situation, so intimately connected with personal well-being, to open light and air. There is no profounder paradox than the fact that Christianity, which has put woman on a pedestal, has done much to degrade her role in the most intimate of human relations.[11]

The character of love is revealed not only in its fruitfulness of good but in its limitations, its evil implications, and its paradoxes. Like all natural impulses it can be intemperate. Its most ugly by-product is jealousy. In the case of sexless love this arises from the excessive demand of the loved upon the interest of the lover: the greater the intensity of loving the greater the expected return. Jealousy in this sense is a form of greed, and its cure is to be sought by an infusion of disinterestedness. In love between the sexes, jealousy has stronger and deeper roots. Here the intimacy and completeness of surrender forbids its being shared. Its exclusiveness implies possession, and turns against the trespasser and even against the loved one suspected of connivance. Infidelity is resented as breach of a reciprocal commitment. There is a logic of passion by which love is convertible into hate; and there is no assured immunity to the evil without abandonment of the good.

Love, then, is a costly and dangerous thing. It makes the lover vulnerable; it gives hostages to fortune. Those who would escape responsibility and anxiety and achieve independence, will do well to avoid it. It requires that appetite shall be tempered by reason, and ecstasy by moderation. It must convert madness into sanity. It requires a reconciliation of an intense preoccupation with the immediate, and a broad concern for its wider human and social implications. Obsessive attention to one must not render the lover blind to the rights of the many. This is a counsel of perfection, rarely and only intermittently attained, but it represents, even in the application to sex, the essence of human destiny. All of the

[11] The utterances of Paul have been interpreted as above: "But if they cannot contain, let them marry: for it is better to marry than to burn" (I Cor., chs. 7, 9, and *passim*). The history of the Christian conception of marriage is complicated and confused: but there is no doubt that on the whole Christianity has sanctioned the idea that sexual desire testifies to man's "fall"; that it is excused, rather than idealized, in marriage; and that through the unilateral injunction of obedience it has created an obligation on the part of the wife to submit herself to the more insistent demands of the husband.

great and good things of human life are attended by risk, and by the certainty of partial failure; but to abandon them for that reason is the real fall from grace.

While so-called sex education concerns itself with "the facts of life," with physical and mental hygiene, with the biology, physiology, psychology, and sociology of men and women, it says little or nothing of the ideal of romantic love. It neglects the astonishing miracle of love, the most dramatic of all the triumphs of human nature, whereby it achieves the closest union between the most profound differences. It leaves to the lyric poets the vision of love as a summit of human aspiration, and, in its rare moments, one of the superlative human attainments.

8

When the moral good is defined in terms of harmonious happiness, the emphasis is on the "harmony" rather than on the "happiness." It is the particular business of morality to remove conflict, lest mankind make one another unhappy; to define and protect spheres of life within which men are free to pursue happiness; and to provide such forms of happiness as are mutually enhancing. Morality has little to say of what constitutes happiness, or of the art whereby it can be achieved. Indeed, morality has been so much occupied with the restraints that are necessary to prevent an immediate, momentary, or selfish happiness from destroying an ulterior, durable, or general happiness, that it has seemed to speak against happiness rather than for it. But the ulterior, the durable, and general happiness is still happiness, augmented rather than diminished.

Whatever, more specifically, it can be said to be, and on whatever level it lies, all happiness is personal happiness. A happy life or a happy society can only mean a happy personal life or a society of happy persons. And where the seat of happiness is, there also is its pursuit. Each man must attain happiness in his own way, depending on his temperament, his specific interests, his vocation and his circumstances. This personal locus of happiness, however, does not imply that it has no general meaning.

No word is more commonly used to describe the good life — from the most ancient to the most recent of modern times. Its very familiarity gives it a specious meaningfulness; or excuses its meaninglessness. Lin Yutang, a friendly Oriental critic, has observed that "the most studiously avoided subject in Western philosophy is that of happiness." [12] He cannot mean that happiness is not praised. It is held to be "our being's end and aim"; the "thirst after [it] is never extinguished in the heart of man." [13] Even with Kant, for all his uncompromising moralism, happiness is the *summum bonum*. With the ancients happiness was the very definition of

---

[12] *On the Wisdom of America*, 1950, p. 209.
[13] Pope's *Essay on Man*, Epistle IV; Rousseau's *Confessions*, Bk. IX.

the good. Christianity's supernaturalism conceives the future and eternal life in terms of happiness, or some more refined equivalent. It would seem reasonable to expect that so great a thing — this beacon of hope, this good of goods — should have a meaning.

Something can be learned about this meaning by a review of the critique of happiness in Western thought. At the same time that it has been so greatly praised, its pursuit and its enjoyment have from ancient times been attended with a flavor of disparagement or sense of guilt. This has been due in the main to its too common and too hasty identification with pleasure, and to confused ideas of what pleasure is. Pleasure, as has been seen, has two different meanings: a specific somatic sensation, and the feeling which attends positive interest. The interest in one's somatic sensation of pleasure tends to be selfish, that is, to preclude social or ideal interests. But the glow of favorable feeling may attend any interest high or low in any scale, from the interest in food and drink, or a crossword puzzle, to the love of mankind, the raptures of the mystic, or the bliss of Heaven. The moral danger in pleasure in this sense lies not in its tendency to selfishness, but in its promiscuity.

Happiness is not pleasure, in the sense of bodily sensation, but consists in the sense of positivity of interest. But there is a further restriction of meaning. Happiness is not an attribute of a *single* interest; one does not speak of a man's enjoyment of food, or sex, or a landscape, as happiness — but only as conducing to happiness. For happiness is an attribute of the total person. It exists, when it does exist, "on the whole," and not in the part. We are thus brought to the conclusion that happiness means the *general auspiciousness* of a person's life; or the degree to which the outlook to all parts of the horizon which bound the person's interests, is favorable. Happiness is a pervasive hopefulness, and its opposite an integral despair.

The definition of happiness in terms of interests rather than in terms of states of pleasure gives a meaning to pessimism. The judgment that happiness is impossible — so common in later antiquity and in all periods of disillusionment does not mean that there are more pain sensations than pleasure sensations, but that human interests are felt as doomed to defeat. Life is believed to be "hopeless" — which is clearly a one-sided view of life, since an equally good case could be made for the opposite thesis. Many interests are fulfilled, and this experience warrants the expectation of future fulfillments. Or it may be contended that while happiness is possible, it is a stroke of fortune — a "gift of the gods"; which is again a false generalization, disproved by the fact that many people achieve happiness by their own effort and skill.

The pessimism of Schopenhauer and Oriental religions is based on the fact that interests are no sooner realized than they are succeeded by new interests, as yet unfulfilled. This point, also, can be argued both ways; for since old interests often are fulfilled, there is good reason to hope that the new interests may likewise be fulfilled. The newest philosophical pessimism is "existentialism." It is contended that the essence of life is *anxiety* — the fear of the worst, the sense of impending disaster; and that when, despite this inauspicious prospect, men make their own decisions and commitments, they then "exist" in their own right. But here, again, the fact is open to the opposite interpretation — given other temperaments and other social situations. Life, to be sure, is uncertain, and choices must be made without assurance of the outcome; but this argues equally well for the positive sense of opportunity. Risks can be accepted with hopefulness as well as with despair; indeed if there were only despair, it is difficult to understand how decisions would be made at all.

In Latin and Latin American societies, and among adherents of the pessimistic strain in Christianity, the gospel of happiness is condemned as being contrary to human nature. This argument takes two forms. It may be held that the pursuit of worldly happiness is essentially illusory; man is by nature sinful, and can be saved only by supernatural regeneration. This judgment, again, is a one-sided judgment, since life provides examples of saintliness as well as of sinfulness; indeed, if this were not so men would not ever have imagined saintliness and pursued it as an ideal. Furthermore, all such supernaturalisms preach happiness in another world, and even, for the elect, in this. Happiness is promised to those who renounce it.

The second form of this disparagement of happiness consists in regarding it as an *arriviste* idea — vulgar, naïve, and shallow. Man, it is argued, is not meant to be happy; and he acquires dignity only when he recognizes that he is essentially a tragic being. This view that only tragedy is noble, and that all else is light or trivial, may be explained as reflecting the comparatively gloomy attitude of its authors; but the idea of tragic nobility has a deeper meaning. The gospel of happiness *may* be shallow. It may rest on ignorance or unwillingness to face facts. "Where ignorance is bliss 'tis folly to be wise"; but 'tis deeper folly to put one's trust in a bliss founded on ignorance. It is not only precarious, since the truth will sooner or later make itself known; but it is not a *human* bliss since it fails to embrace one of man's chief capacities and commanding interests, namely, knowledge. The dignity of tragedy does not lie in the evil itself, but in the courage to acknowledge it when it occurs. If evil were not inflicted by circumstances beyond the will's control, but were invented for its tragic effect, its acceptance would be more theatrical than noble.

It is also argued that man learns from unhappiness more than he learns from happiness. But what does he learn, if not that men are unhappy? And to what end does he learn of unhappiness, if not in order to remove or endure it, or for the joy of the knowing: if not, in short, to the end of happiness? Furthermore, how is one to learn of *happiness*, which is also a fact of life, if not from happiness?

Finally, it is said of happiness — both for it and against it — that it can only be attained by a denial of life. The parable of Diogenes and his tub teaches that happiness so attained is a shrunken happiness, since it reduces life to bare existence, and, at best, barely escapes *un*happiness. Every eradication of a desire is the killing of some goose which has a golden egg to lay. Tolstoi, describing Levin's experience on visiting his infant son, says: "There was nothing cheerful or joyous in the feeling; on the contrary it was a new torture of apprehension. It was the consciousness of a new sphere of liability of pain." [14] It is true that every happiness has its corresponding apprehension and sphere of liability; whether it be parenthood, or the contemplation of the universe. But it also has its safeties and its securities. Escapism, playing safe, is not only in itself an abridgment of happiness, but affords no guarantee of happiness in what is left of life.

The critique of happiness, while it does not discredit happiness, reveals its conditions and requirements. It requires health and sanity; that is, a "sound mind in a sound body." It must be reconciled with perseverance and aspiration — a perpetual discontent with imperfect achievement. It must permit of perpetual change and renewal of effort. It is conditioned by knowledge of things as they are; that is, adaptation to what lies beyond the control of the will. There is no formula for happiness. There are, however, suggestions gathered from human experience which may serve as first steps in the art of happiness. Perhaps the first of these is to recognize that there *is* no single formula but, rather, numerous lines of attack.

There is, for example, the well-known paradox that happiness is to be won not by a direct, but by an indirect, attack. Like fame, happiness is coy. For it is constituted of many interests, and not of an interest in happiness; and its interests must be given their head. Happiness is "given" to those who are too preoccupied with their several interests to give it much thought.

Since it is essential to human life that there should be far-flung interests whose realization is long postponed, it is essential to happiness that there should be interests that bear fruit immediately. To avoid boredom or discouragement there must be birds in the hand as well as in the bush; impending fulfillments, and not merely hopes of the distant future. There are many interests whose objects lie thus ready at hand. Thus there is a zest of effort, a delight in activity or craftsmanship, which is enjoyed *on the way* to a distant goal. And when effort is united effort there is the interest in participation, the liking to do things together in an atmos-

[14] *Anna Karenina*, trans. by C. Garnett, Modern Library Edition, p. 838.

phere of friendliness or love. There are the recreations and pastimes
which can scarcely fail, because the achievement is easy, or because they
are not "taken seriously," or because the joy is in the game rather than
in the victory. There are the objects and surroundings that are endeared
by familiarity — that "sweet monotony where everything is known, and
loved because it is known." [15] Aesthetic and intellectual enjoyment need
never fail for lack of an occasion. There is no aspect of nature, or of the
human environment, that may not be relished as food for contemplation
or thought.

The art of happiness must provide for failure. A wise man will not
undertake the impossible and beat his wings against invincible barriers.
He will not adopt an end for which there is no means. But he will cheerfully embark on the improbable, and entertain hopes that are forlorn.
Indeed, it may be said that in all the more fundamental adventures of
life the goal itself exceeds full attainment. It must then suffice if one can
feel that the line of effort is true to the mark and that the steps of advance, however small, move in the right direction.

There are maxims of happiness which apply to this perpetual and
inevitable defeat: profit from failure, by learning how to avoid or diminish
it in the future; turn promptly from defeat to a fresh undertaking; when
occasions prove recalcitrant, change the mode of dealing with them. The
Stoic teaching that even incurable sickness can be nobly borne can be
generalized to mean that there are few situations in life that cannot be
the object of a positive interest: even if it only be to live in agreement
with one's personal code of honor or duty; or to rejoice in necessity as
evidence of intelligible order; or to discover some hitherto hidden secret
of nature; or, in the last extremity, to draw upon reserves of faith in a
goodness of things despite appearances. And so long as one still breathes
it is possible to extract some relish from a bare sense of being alive, of
which even the capacity to suffer is evidence.

The supreme test of man's capacity to be happy is the prospect of
death. The greater the enjoyment of life the greater the loss if life is
annihilated. How then, is one to expect that loss, and still be happy?
There are two common solutions of the problem of death, which the
standard of happiness excludes. It is folly so to dwell upon approaching
death as to nullify present enjoyments, and there is a powerful disposition to ignore it. Nevertheless happiness requires that death shall be faced
without terror and with the minimum of aversion. The standard of happiness also excludes a second solution of the problem, which is so to
exploit and accentuate the unhappiness of life as to make death the
least of evils.

There remain two acceptable solutions. The first of these is to be so
interested in the future of mankind that its good outweighs one's own

[15] G. Eliot, *The Mill on the Floss*, Bk. I, ch. i.

absence from the scene. The second is to believe in a life after death. This belief may be taken as proved to be true; or it may be adopted as an act of faith — permissible in default of decisive evidence to the contrary, and justified by its present effects upon the will.

Positivity of interest tends to spread from one interest to another, by a sort of osmosis or chain reaction. Hence a cure for unhappiness is to be found in turning to some prosperous interest in order that its secretion of joy may be discharged into the wider stream. Triumph in one quarter will make obstacles elsewhere seem less insuperable.

The pursuit of happiness, like all pursuits, is subject to the moral injunction that the good of one shall be subordinated to the good of all. Personal happiness may be private, and even solitary, but it must be innocent. Moral happiness cannot be enjoyed at the expense of the happiness of others. More positively, it will be enhanced by an awareness of others' happiness.

9

Is it possible to compare one civilization with another, and judge it to be higher or lower? Does not the wholeness and uniqueness of civilizations forbid their being submitted to a common standard? The key to the answer has already been disclosed in the examination of cultures in general, of which civilization is only a higher form. Unique wholes may have similar parts; unique civilizations contain similar interests; where there are interests there are standards; therefore, the same standards are applicable to two or more civilizations — so runs the argument. All civilizations embrace the moral interest in ethical, political, legal, and economic organization, the non-moral and super-moral interests in science, art, education, and religion. Because they have these common interests, civilizations borrow from one another not merely through involuntary diffusion but through choice. Such imitation is the sincerest flattery. The civilization which consciously borrows prefers what it borrows, the culture which lends prefers what it has, and they appeal to the same standard. Through this similarity of interests and orders of preference, civilizations become commensurable and one may be considered as higher or lower than another in terms which can be employed by a neutral historian or critic.

But while these considerations are sufficient to refute the alleged impossibility of judging two or more civilizations by common standards, we are still left with a plurality of standards. It is legitimate to say that "other things being equal," a civilization which ranks higher in the order of aesthetic preference is a superior civilization; and there is a tendency in making such comparisons to assume that other things *are* equal. But suppose that other things, such as science and technology, are not equal? It is meaningful to say that Greek civilization is higher than modern

American civilization, in a certain respect, such as poetry, while American civilization is higher than Greek civilization in certain other respects, such as sanitation and social justice. But this provides no answer to the question as to which of two civilizations is higher *on the whole.*

It is customary to make loose and provisional comparisons of this type by the method of "scoring," after the analogy of competitive sports. One team "defeats" another through having a greater number of "points," and this is supposed to constitute a measure of "all-around" athletic prowess. It is this method of comparison which is usually employed when it is said loosely of a certain civilization that it ranks above others. Thus Germanic civilization may be credited with a first in music, a second in science, and a third in literature, which gives it a high total even though it may fail to qualify in painting or in politics. Similarly, the Athenian civilization of the fifth century B.C., or the civilization of the Renaissance, may be said to rank high owing to its number of "firsts," that is, its cluster of high excellence and its galaxies of genius, in the humane arts, in science, and in philosophy.

Such comparison rests on dubious assumptions. It is assumed that although the several rankings represent different forms of *specific* endeavor, they at the same time represent some common form of general endeavor. Thus the different tests of a track meet, however incomparable one with another, are taken to represent a common athletic test of "athletic ability," which includes both strength and speed, together with endurance, skill, and competitive spirit. It is assumed that the events selected in a standardized meet suffice to test this general ability. And it is also assumed that the tests selected test it equally, so that firsts in one may properly be counted for as much as firsts in another.

The doubts and ambiguities which beset this interpretation of athletic competition are aggravated in a rivalry between civilizations. It is assumed that there is a general cultural ability, which is tested, and tested equally, by attainment in the humane arts, technology, politics, and all the other respects in which civilizations can be compared. Since there appears to be no such general cultural ability it can be claimed only that civilizations are comparable in the several respects selected for comparison. There is no standard in terms of which the "respects" are comparable among themselves, so that high rank in one can be only arbitrarily equated with high rank in another.

There is a possible escape from this difficulty — in principle — even though its application must be attended with a high degree of inaccuracy. The several forms of cultural eminence may be so causally related among themselves that one or some among them may be considered as evidence of, or as affording promise of, the rest.

Some interests underlie or condition other interests. There are two such conditioning interests which underlie all interests, the self-preservative interest and the moral interest. Self-preservative and moral values may be said to be more "important," "indispensable," or "fundamental" than other values. Other values are founded on them, so that if they were removed the superstructure would collapse. Any civilization, whatever the heights to which it may rise, can be destroyed by extinguishing the lives of its members, as is attested by the graveyards of history. Nor can interests of any sort flourish and enjoy the spheres of freedom within which their special interests, such as the cognitive and aesthetic interests, can ascend to their several heights, unless they are rendered harmonious by morality.

It is this fact that justifies the statement that war is fatally and totally destructive: because it kills men by wounds, starvation, and exposure; and because it demoralizes both men and societies, that is, dissolves the organization within which their several interests can live and flourish together. In proportion, on the other hand, as a society commands the necessities of life and enjoys the benefit of moral institutions, it possesses at least the potentiality of all other values, and two societies compared in this respect are compared as wholes.

The interdependence of interests within a society suggests a further standard of total comparison, namely, the extent to which the component interests reinforce and fructify one another. It has often been held on this ground that the civilization of Europe in the Middle Ages, despite its glaring defects in this or that respect — in science or in social justice — excelled other civilizations, earlier or later, in the interfructification of its parts. So judged, the better civilization will rest on a secure biological and moral foundation, and on this foundation its special interests will not only coexist, but reflect one another's light, and each will reflect the intensified light of their concentrated rays.

Special interests yield auxiliary, as well as independent, values. As men's special interests develop they may lose connection with one another and give less to the balance of life despite the fact that they have more and more to give. Knowledge, for example, not only satisfies the love of truth, but serves as a guide of action; in "high" civilization knowledge is lived by, as well as enjoyed for its own sake. Similarly, art may not only provide beauty to be enjoyed for itself when contemplated in galleries and monuments, but embellish utilities and provide symbols and images which reinforce the appeal of all other ideals. Similarly, education and religion, instead of being confined to the school and the church, may profit by the development of the cognitive and aesthetic interests, and give back to these in return.

These considerations in their sum yield the norm of a well-ordered total civilization, with which the several historic civilizations can be compared, and through which they can be compared with one another. It would be a society healthy, well-nourished and well-equipped; non-conflicting and coöperative; brilliant in its manifestations of eminence in science, art, education, and religion; and enhanced on the whole by the cross-fertilization of its parts.

10

Culture and civilization, like all of their branches, reach out to embrace all of mankind. There is a total aggregate of cultures, and by the principle of inclusion this is something better than any of its parts. But it is better only provided it embraces all that each narrower culture yields, and supplements it with more. It would not be better in the sense of inclusiveness if its effect were to diminish the several cultural values which it embraced. When, however, one speaks of a "world civilization" one does not mean this mere sum of cultural achievements. One means an over-all *single* culture, analogous to national or other local cultures in the interpenetration of its parts and its unique physiognomy.

The general principle of inclusiveness itself does not imply any answer to the crucial question of the effect of such a single world culture upon the narrower units of culture. Since a single culture implies a high degree of internal intimacy and interaction, there is always the possibility that its expansion to global proportions would result in its impoverishment rather than enrichment. There is no general answer to this question.[16]

It is clear that moral institutions gain by being extended to world-wide proportions, since their task is to eliminate conflict and promote coöperation. A world-wide conscience, polity, law, or economy is dedicated to the preservation, protection, and increase of freedoms; and since it does not prescribe how men shall use their freedoms, it invites individual and local diversities. Science, since its purpose is to know the common objective world and since its methods are obedient to this purpose, knows no human bounds. Truth is not American or Russian, Western or Eastern, or, for that matter, even global. If left to itself science spreads out automatically to all inquiring minds — dealing with the same subject matter and being pledged to the acceptance of the same evidence. World science, and the world-wide collaboration of scientists, need no promotion or propaganda, but only facilities and the absence of obstacles.

With art the answer is different. It is of the essence of art that it should reflect the concreteness of human experience, and embrace within itself a particular medium, idiom, tradition, point of view, and emotional attitude. To reduce it to some artistic equivalent of mathematical sym-

---

[16] For a discussion of the question, cf. the Author's *One World in the Making*, 1945, ch. vi. The application to the specific branches of culture is considered in the chapters of the present book dealing with moral institutions and with science, art, education, and religion.

bolism would contradict its intrinsic purpose and deprive civilization of what it, and it alone, has to contribute.

With education and religion the answer is both "yes" and "no." These pursuits can profit by world-wide influences, but must guard against that thinness and dilution which is associated with "cosmopolitanism" and "the man without a country." Science could only gain by a world-wide extension; a world art would scarcely be art at all; a world education and a world religion would never be the whole of education or religion.

All of the evils of a national totalitarianism would be multiplied by a global totalitarianism. It would subject each branch of culture to alien controls; it would achieve oneness of culture by destroying all cultures save one. It matters not which element is chosen, whether it is drawn from conscience or some other moral institution, or from a cult of science or art, or from a school or a church, if it absorbs and assimilates the whole of culture the loss is greater than the gain.

There is a further sense of world civilization which can have no unfavorable meaning. When conceived as a wide stream uncanalized into any narrow bed, or as a stream made up of many streams, it constitutes a reservoir of which all mankind are tributaries, and a source from which all mankind draw refreshment. Or, to change the figure, world civilization is a common treasure upon which all men draw and to which they all contribute. In proportion as men become aware of a common past and a common future this possibility becomes a reality. All men share what all men give.

The idea of the totality of civilization paves the way to the understanding of history, education, and religion. In its temporal sequences and continuities this total civilization makes history, which is the subject matter of the science called by the same name. The imparting and acquiring of it, whether organized or unorganized, constitutes education, to which there is a corresponding branch of inquiry. Concern for its cosmic destiny is religion, which when organized is the church, and which when examined and reflected upon constitutes the science and philosophy of religion.

CHAPTER XX

THE HISTORY OF HISTORY

The subject of history has assumed an increased importance in modern times for a variety of reasons, all of them familiar. The nineteenth century witnessed the appearance and widespread diffusion of the idea that the understanding of any subject matter, whether it be the physical universe or the human mind and its achievements, is to be found in its genesis. It is true that Christianity had its Book of Genesis, and that primitive cultures contained myths concerning the origin of the world and the genealogy of the gods, but in the nineteenth century this emphasis and approach became in an unparalleled degree the central feature of European thought. At the same time geological, biological, archaeological, and cultural studies acquired improved techniques resulting in an immense extension of man's knowledge of the past, to the enrichment of his cultural heritage and the widening of the boundaries of his universe.

What, then, is history? This simple question turns out on reflection to be not so simple. The difficulty of the question arises in part from a verbal accident. The same word 'history' is used both for a subject matter and for a branch of knowledge. While polity is the subject matter of political science, law of the science of jurisprudence, economy of the science of economics, and society of the science of sociology, the subject matter of history is history; which is, to say the least, confusing.

The beginning of clarity in this subject, then, is to distinguish between history as a subject matter to be known, and which would have taken place if it were not known; and that branch of knowledge which is devoted to the knowing of it. Many a boulder has fallen from its place on a mountain side, leaving its chain of effects, without being known to any historian; unless a divine historian is introduced expressly for the purpose, in obedience to the requirements of a metaphysical generalization that *nothing* can exist or happen that is not known — a generalization which the occurrence of such pre-human events itself serves to refute. The same distinction between the historical event and the subsequent knowledge of it holds also of human events. Let us suppose that when "stout Cortez . . . with eagle eyes" first stared at the Pacific he was alone, without witnesses; that he did not "realize" what lay before him; and that, having stared, he was instantly struck dead or suffered a total loss of memory. His staring would nevertheless be an historical event, in the sense that it would have happened in advance of its later discovery through, let us say, his footprints in the sand.[1]

The fact that man's knowledge of history is a part of his personal history, must not be allowed, then, to blur this distinction. There is a likelihood of confusion, but there is no paradox. Historical knowledge, the science of history, historiography, historiology, historics, or whatever it be called, is one thing; the history which it knows is another thing. Historical knowledge always presupposes a history to be known; and may then itself in turn be presupposed in historical knowledge on another level. Physical nature is one thing, physics is another thing. Since the physicist employs apparatus and uses his hands there can be a physics of physics, if anyone were to take the trouble to inquire. By the same token since historical knowledge is a human happening there can, if a historian chooses, be a historical knowledge of *it*. Gibbon made history by writing it, but the history he thus made was not the same as the history of which he wrote. There is a title in the Harvard University Library which reads as follows: "*Oysters, and All about Them,* by John M. Philpotts, *being a complete history of the titular subject.*" Oysters have their history, which is a proper subject matter of historical knowledge. The knowledge of oysters, "all about *them*," is a part of human history; and John M. Philpotts, who was not an oyster, thus belongs to the subject matter of that history of molluscian zoölogy which he did not write.

What, then, is that historical subject matter, that field, which it is the business of historical knowledge to know? There are four defining principles: temporality, uniqueness, humanity, and importance.

In the broadest sense the field of history may be said to embrace the aggregate of events, that is, of existents occurring in time. This definition, unless accompanied by certain restrictions, is too broad to distinguish historical knowledge from other knowledge. If it be held, as in temporalistic metaphysics, that to exist at all means to belong to the space-time-causal nexus, and if it be held, as it is now generally held among scientists, that physical nature is composed of spatio-temporal

---

[1] The identification of historical subject matter with historical knowledge makes sense only on the supposition that a human deed embraces all of its relations, including those which unfold in later time and which are revealed to the thought of that later time. The most valuable exponent of this monistic-organicist-idealist view is Benedetto Croce, according to whom reality=history=philosophy.

events, then all knowledge of existence is temporal in subject matter, and all laws would be laws of change in time. The objection to this outcome does not lie in the definition of terms (which is optional) but the failure to give a meaning to 'history' which distinguishes the branch of knowledge *so-called*, from physics or psychology.

To make such a distinction it is necessary to introduce, first, the qualification of *uniqueness*. An "historical event" is not an event which occurs in time, merely, but which occurs only once. Contrary to the common saying, history is that which never repeats itself. Thus the great Lisbon earthquake of 1755 is an historical event insofar as it cannot have happened before the time designated, and can never happen again. As subject matter for the science of seismology, on the other hand, it is considered not in respect of its uniqueness, but in respect of certain variables of stress, temperature, gravity, mass, energy, etc., which *are* repeatable. The uniqueness of "this" earthquake consists in the totality of its particulars. As a contemporary historian has remarked: "The bombing of Hiroshima and Nagasaki is to be distinguished from the chain reactions studied by atomic physics." [2]

So identified by the time at which it occurs, or "takes place," the historical event may belong to the past, the present, or the future; unique past happenings, contemporary happenings, and future happenings all alike "belong" to history. The historian *may* occupy himself with contemporary history, or predict future history: his customary preoccupations with the past simply reflects the fact that the past as compared with the present and future, is more accessible to exploration, and more amply provided with evidence, such as records, and the data of memory, by which the knowledge of particular happenings can be attested.

A more restricted conception of the field of historical knowledge is provided by prefixing the adjective 'human' to the substantive 'happening.' This restriction excludes from the domain of "history proper" the history of the earth which would then become a part of human history when it was tenanted by man; the history of a glacier when by its retreat it rendered certain regions habitable by man; or the history of an atom when its splitting destroyed Hiroshima and brought to an end the war between the United States and Japan. The solar eclipse which occurred on May 28, 584 B.C. was a part of solar and terrestrial history; it became a part of human history when Thales discovered it, and when, as in the *Encyclopaedia Britannica*, we are invited to "see under *Thales*" for an account of it. All of which goes to show that, whatever their character otherwise, happenings become a part of history proper when they happen to man, and become a part of the life of man: when, namely, they serve or defeat, or otherwise engage, human interests.

[2] Hajo Holborn, "History and the Humanities," *Journal of the History of Ideas,* 9 (1948), p. 67.

There remains a further restriction, namely, to what is humanly important. A ballet dancer's tying her shoe at five P.M. on a certain day is a unique manifestation of human interest, and therefore falls within the domain of history as defined up to this point. It would not, however, be embraced even in the ballet girl's biography, unless, let us say, an important artist, such as Degas, painted her in the act. Otherwise it would be excluded as trivial. It will not do to say that "important" is what anybody *feels* to be important; for anything may be felt to be important by somebody. If an event is to *be* humanly important it must engage a wide range of interests; or it must occur at some crucial point or parting of the ways, or at some seat of control, so as to have ramifying influences throughout the field of interests; or it must be connected with interests of a higher order; or it must embody some eminent achievement which commends it to the preference and admiration of posterity. It is this factor of importance or significance which is conveyed by the honorific idea of history, as when one speaks of events as "historic," or refers to a person as having "achieved a place in history."

2

There remains a further restriction of the subject matter of historical knowledge, which is optional, but is justified by usage. The historian is concerned not with mere aggregates of unique and humanly important events, but complex unities which endure through time. The historical entity, in this sense, not only *is* history, but "has a history."

The characteristic of the enduring historical entity is the same as that of a singular society. Its unity consists in an interaction of interests, and is not adequately described in static terms such as similarity or contiguity in space or time. There is a fundamental difference between a so-called "history of the North American continent" and a "history of the United States of America." The first of these histories has as its subject matter a collection of historical events having nothing in common save their occurrence in the same region of the earth's surface. The second deals with an enduring unity of interweaving interests. The first suggests the second, because it is assumed that human events occurring in the same area are likely to become interactive. But it is quite conceivable that British colonists on the Atlantic coast of North America and Russian colonists on the Pacific coast should be quite unaware of one another, as was no doubt for a time the case. There would then be two histories and no common history. Or, it may be supposed, as was also the case, that British colonists from the East, French colonists from the North, Spanish colonists from the South, and Asiatic colonists from the West spread, mingled and organized their interests. There would then begin to be one history and not four. A history of the tropics, or of the arctic or temperate zones, is either a chapter of natural science, or a collection of "local histories," or implies the fact that these are areas in which men meet in war and trade. It is to be noted and reflected upon that no historian has as yet proposed to write a history of the belts of the earth's surface defined by latitude and longitude.

If it is absurd and contrary to usage to identify a historical entity with an area, it is equally absurd (though not equally contrary to usage) to identify it with a period of time. Centuries, decades, and years do not *have* their histories, though they may comprise histories or parts of histories. A temporal segment has no more historical meaning than a spatial cross section. The third millennium B.C. comprises, let us say, a chapter in the history of China, and a chapter in the history of Egypt; but they are not chapters of a common history. The supposition that a century (such as the eighteenth century) has a history is due to the habit of associating that designation with a chapter in the life of England, or in the life of a more or less integrated Europe. Because a common period of time is likely to *lead* to interaction it is assumed that it is an interaction.

History has been profoundly falsified by the motive of scholastic and textbook convenience. Having divided histories by centuries, scholars and teachers are compelled by their increasing knowledge of the historical facts to expend a considerable amount of time and energy in obliterating these divisions. It is the historian, and not history, who observes the boundaries of the calendar. History itself — *what goes on* — does not turn sharp corners. It is not divided into acts and scenes, with the curtain going down on the old and rising on the new.

The writing of history in terms of cultures, civilizations, and societies serves to identify historical objects with interactive unities, rather than with segments of time.[3] The danger is that, owing to bias or preoccupation, the historian may find such unities where they do not exist, or to separate them absolutely when they run together, or to consider them as co-exclusive when they overlap.

These considerations are illustrated and sharpened by their application to universal history. Does the totality of mankind constitute an enduring historical entity? This is often affirmed. Thus it is said that all history is a history of man, and that history may, therefore, be considered as a study of man. That history is human and that historical knowledge throws light on human nature, is not to be denied. But psychology, though it may profit by history, is not a history of man. If there is to be a history of man, man must *have* a history, which is something more than a collection of histories and biographies having nothing in common save that they are human.

[3] Cf. Arnold J. Toynbee's chapter on "The Unit of Historical Study," which he finds to be a society or culture: *A Study of History*, abridged by D. C. Somervell, 1947, pp. 1–11.

In order that man shall have a history it does not suffice that all men belong to the same species, or that they live on the same planet, or have lived on that planet during the period 1,000,000 B.C. to 1953 A.D. *If* man has a history it is because all men live together: communicating with one another, aware of common and continuing tasks, and achieving some measure of coöperation. It is evident that this describes a state of human affairs which is not primordial, but which is now coming about through widespread interaction, and through a sense of identification with the past. Up to the present mankind has had many histories, but no single, common history. Now that mankind is beginnng to have a history of its own, universal history is acquiring an object of its own and becomes distinguishable from a mere omnibus history.

As historical events are unique, human, and important independently of their historians, so enduring historical entities possess that enduring character independently of the historian who observes and records *it*. Their unities are not given to them by a unifying act of knowledge, but are found and selected, as the orders of nature are found and selected by the natural scientist.

This independence of the historical entity must not be taken to exclude the fact that historical knowledge does contribute to the creation of enduring historical entities. It is evident that the historian contributes to nationality. Knowledge of its past (its heroic days, or its "founding fathers") is a major factor in the creation of a nation's identity, as memory is a major factor in personal identity. But it is only one of many factors — together with habit, language, and interdependence. The same holds true of universal history. Shared historical knowledge converts many traditions into a common tradition. But this is only one of many forces which unite mankind in a common life, which then has its own history; and that common life if, when, or insofar as, it occurs, is the independent historical fact which verifies or disproves the judgment of the universal historian.

3

What, then, is the nature of historical knowledge? It has been contended that historical knowledge is *sui generis* — knowledge of a totally different order from that of the natural or social sciences.[4] This contention is argued on three grounds: that historical knowledge is *non-empirical;* that its object is individual; and that it is peculiarly *relativistic*.

The theory that historical knowledge is "non-empirical" assumes its restriction to knowledge of the past. Judgments of the past cannot be verified by observed facts because past events cannot be presently perceived. Hence historical knowledge is a product of the imagination

---

[4] Cf. R. G. Collingwood, *The Historical Imagination*, 1935; and *The Philosophy of History*, 1930.

and is said to be justified only on a priori grounds. But precisely the same may be held of all of those natural sciences, such as astronomy, geology, and biology, which deal with the past. It may be held, indeed, of all of those sciences which deal with the future in time and the remote in space, in short, of all natural sciences without exception. They all employ inferences from the perceived to the unperceived; their very merit lies in this enlargement of knowledge beyond the limits of present perception.

Knowledge of the past, if historical knowledge be thus restricted, argues from effect to cause, and from a particular kind of effect, namely, traces and records. In other words, knowledge of the past, once it reaches beyond immediate memory, rests on knowledge of another sort, namely, knowledge of signs. One does not have to be an expert semanticist to have such knowledge. Robinson Crusoe knew enough about the imprints left by human feet to infer that some other man had recently been present in person on his island, and he could make a shrewd guess as to his size. If he had been a Sherlock Holmes he could have inferred his age, sex, and occupation. Men have learned early that what is recollected to have happened, is likely to have happened; and, making allowance for prevarication, that what men say they recollect they *do* recollect. Relics imply the people who have left them behind, and the interests for which they used them. Out of such rough common sense there have developed the elaborate techniques of paleontology, paleography, and comparative philology. All of these techniques are based on the fact that signs point, and if "all signs point," so much the better. Effects are signs of their causes, fragments of their wholes, names of their meanings, pictographs and photographs of their originals. And when past events have been established by such inferences they serve as evidence of other past events.

But this procedure does not differ in principle from the procedures of natural science even when it is not primarily concerned with past events. The scientist relies on testimony and corroboration. In so doing he relies in turn on empirically tested beliefs concerning the credibility and veracity of witnesses. No scientist rests his conclusions wholly on his *own* observations; but accepts as evidence the observations of others, which he infers from their behavior, and, in the last analysis, from the meanings of words.

The method of historical knowledge differs from the method of every other kind of knowledge, but the same can be said of physics, biology, or psychology; for the simple reason that if two sciences differ in their subject matter, they will also differ in their methods. It is quite true that historical knowledge often lacks the exactness of certain highly developed sciences, such as physics. It is less well proved, and it is less precise. But this is due to the peculiar complexity of the subject matter, and the comparative weakness of the evidence. The knowledge that an eclipse occurred on May 28, 585 B.C. is better certified than the knowledge that Thales predicted it. While the astronomers confidently affirm even the precise time and place of the eclipse, no historian has ventured to assert on what hour of what day Thales made the prophetic utterance which established his reputation as a Wise Man. It is not even fully proved that he made such an utterance at all.

What is the reason for this difference? It does not turn on the presence or absence of eyewitnesses, or on the use of inference; these factors are present in both cases. In both cases a generalization is first verified and then applied beyond the limits of its verification. But whereas the motions of the sun, earth, and moon are affected by relatively simple and constant causes, so that the gap between the present and the past can be filled by the extrapolation of a few variables, Thales' prediction is connected with the present by a tangled web of intersecting influences. Its determination is based on empirical generalizations concerning human credibility, and the relation between events and the subsequent memory or recording of them; on the application of such generalizations to Herodotus and Diogenes Laërtius in particular; and on other inferences as to what sorts of knowledge were available to Thales at the time, and from which he could have deduced his prediction. The chain of inference is long and devious, and many of its links are weak.

It has been held that historical knowledge is a knowledge of individuals ("ideographic") while science is a knowledge of laws ("nomographic"). But this is not a difference of principle. The solar eclipse of May 28, 585 B.C., and the battle between the Medes and the Lydians which occurred on the same day, are equally individual; the eruption of Vesuvius in 79 A.D. is as individual as the death of the Elder Pliny. In all of these cases the knowledge, whether scientific or historical, is "ideographic."

Both history and natural science, on the other hand, are "nomographic." Neither relies wholly on the observation of eyewitnesses; both employ inferences from general laws. The difference lies in the fact that while natural science is primarily interested in the law itself, and in the individual only for the purpose of verifying the law, the historian is primarily interested in the individual and in the law as a means of knowing the individual.

Theory of evolution as distinguished from physiology and genetics, proves the impossibility of drawing the line between history and natural science in the score of the individuality of the object. Theory of evolution is concerned with the origins of life and with the succession of individual forms of life on the earth's surface — the when and the where, and the occasions, of their unique occurrence. "History" deals similarly with the origins of capitalism, and with the succession of individual human societies and cultures. The essential difference is not one of method, but lies in the fact that the first deals with plants and animals, whereas the second deals with important events in the life of man.

4

The topic of "historical relativism" has been anticipated in early discussions and needs only to be briefly restated. The subject matter of the history of the past is known from the standpoint of the present; the historical events belong to one age, the historian to another age. But the relativity of historical knowledge is only a special case of that "centricity" which affects all knowledge. There is a relation of the to-be-known and the knowing of it, and since the knowing is a part of some personal or social life it is exposed to modification from this personal and social context. When these "subjective" factors are imputed to the object independently of the subjective relationship there arises the difficulty, called "subjectivisim" or "relativism," where the "ism" implies the defeat of the purpose of knowledge. All knowledge is a knowing *by* somebody, in some phase of *his* life, *of* something in some phase of *its* life. Knowledge is an intersection of two planes, and leads to a confusion between what lies on one plane with what lies on the other. The criticism of knowledge and the refinement of its techniques consist in the progressive elimination of this confusion.

The simplest and most readily corrected instance of this confusion is the perceptual judgment which imputes to the physical object *where it is,* the shape which it has only from where it is perceived. Once it is discovered that the elliptical shape of the penny is a projection of its circularity to a point occupied by the observer, the confusion is removed; and the round penny can be defined in terms of equidistance of all points on its perimeter, together with the system of its projections to surrounding points, in which case the initial perceptual appearance is both included and at the same time transcended.

In its essentials this analysis is applicable to all subjectivities, including the subjectivity of the present knowledge of the past. There is the "then" of the occurrence of the event-to-be-known, and there is the "now" of the occurrence of the act of knowledge. It is erroneous to attribute to one time what belongs to the other — for example, to attribute to ancient times themselves the approach to antiquity from the time of the Renaissance. The "point of view" of the Renaissance having been distinguished, it can then either be discounted, or included in the total view of antiquity in all its temporal perspectives.[5] Similar considerations apply to historical criticism.

The way is now prepared to examine the meaning and validity of the contention that history has to be rewritten in every age. It is rewritten to embrace new discoveries, made possible by advancing historical tech-

[5] Cf. the Author's *Puritanism and Democracy,* 1944, ch. iii.

niques. Past errors are corrected and past ignorance is overcome — as will hold of all knowledge. The advance of time introduces a more distant perspective, which reveals contours which were invisible from close at hand. Events can not only be *seen* to have an importance which was not seen before, but they can *acquire* new importance. As their consequences unfold they may not only loom larger but become larger, as is the case with the Industrial Revolution, which is only today realizing its full potentialities.[6] These considerations elucidate and justify a contention such as T. S. Eliot's: "But the difference between the present and the past is that the conscious present is an awareness of the past, in a way and to an extent the past's awareness of itself cannot show." [7] They lend no weight to subjectivistic doctrine that historical events or objects have to wait for the later historian before they can be what they were in their own time.

5

The expression 'philosophy of history' has a variety of meanings. Like 'philosophy of science' it may be taken to mean a fundamental examination either of a kind of knowledge, or of its subject matter. The philosophy of natural science embraces both methodology, in its most general terms; and also nature in its most general terms, that is, what was once called 'cosmology.' Similarly, philosophy of history deals with two questions: "What, in its most general terms, is the nature of historical knowledge?" and "What, in its most general terms, is that history which is the subject matter of historical knowledge?" The second of these questions may be attacked in either of two different, but related ways, both of which have their equivalents in philosophy of science. Herbert Spencer's famous *First Principles* dealt with nature in general by assembling the results of the several natural sciences, and so presenting nature as a whole. At the same time he found a unifying principle of evolution which reigned over nature as a whole. Similarly, a philosophy of history may be a piecing together of all partial histories — histories of different epochs, societies, and institutions — so as to obtain a universal or synoptic survey. Or it may claim to discover a principle governing history as a whole and which governs all particular histories.

Philosophy of history in the synoptic sense presents no theoretical problems. There is one great stream of history, if in no other sense, then at any rate in the sense in which there is one great stream of time from

---

[6] This perspective interpretation of the facts of history suggests the value for the historian of knowing the near as well as the remote perspectives: the value of viewing the past as continuous, and thus, for example, of viewing antiquity from the standpoint of the Hellenistic and medieval periods. Many misunderstandings of history arise from "skipped intermediaries" of perspective. The past has not leaped, but has grown, into the present.

[7] "Tradition and the Individual Talent," *Selected Essays*, 1934, p. 6.

the remotest horizon of the past to the remotest horizon of the future, and embracing all important human events which have occurred or will occur between these limits. It is possible to link these events together in many ways — in space as well as in time, or in terms of interaction insofar as all humanly important events form parts of one interacting whole — a philosophy of history would be an account of mankind's history.

Philosophy of history in the second sense would be the discovery of a law or laws governing all history and peculiar to history. Claims to the discovery of such laws have been more or less dogmatic — resorting to dogmatism to eke out the insufficient empirical evidence.

It has been said that there are only two alternative interpretations of human history, the cyclical and the rectilinear. History either goes round and round, or it marches straight forward. These alternatives cannot refer to time itself, since even in the cyclical theory each turn of the circle is later than the last. Assuming that the reference is not to time, but to what occurs in time, these alternatives are not mutually exclusive, since it is quite possible that the course of events should sometimes go round and round, and sometimes straight forward, sometimes backward, sometimes zigzag, and thus, taken as a whole, in many directions.

The cyclical theory which prevailed in antiquity reflected the now obsolete cosmology of the philosophers — its doctrine of the circularity of celestial motions, and its doctrine of fixed species appearing and reappearing in a fixed succession.

The Hebraic-Christian philosophy of history is avowedly a reading into history of religious preconceptions — from the simplified history contained in the Old Testament, through Augustine's *City of God,* down to Bossuet's *Histoire Universelle* in the seventeenth century, in which the author's learned exploration of secondary causes was subordinated to Divine Providence as the First Cause. The course of human events is a rectilinear unfolding of God's dealings with man, from creation at the beginning to the Last Judgment at the end — a drama with sin, salvation, and the church as its central theme. The facts of history are selected, not to verify a hypothesis, but to illustrate a body of doctrine derived from revelation and authority.

The eighteenth century, committed to a belief in reason, saw history as a progressive emancipation from authority and obscurantism, and a predestined triumph of order and happiness. The nineteenth century witnessed an emphasis on the historical approach and the historical method in all fields of inquiry. Meanwhile from antiquity there had been a steady growth of so-called "critical history" — an increasing scrupulousness and an improved technique of historical discovery. Nevertheless the philosophy of history remained largely dogmatic: Comte, Buckle, and Spencer drew their concepts from natural science, Hegel from dialectic,

Karl Marx from economics *and* dialectic. History, in short, was fitted to a design drawn from a part of itself and imposed on the whole.

The great contribution of the nineteenth century to philosophy of history, for which credit is due primarily to German thought, was its emphasis on the solidarity of culture and civilization. But this brought with it new forms of dogmatism. The greatest of modern philosophies of history, Herder's *Outline of a Philosophy of the History of Man*[8] exercised a profound influence upon the history of the several branches of cultural history, but in its final synthesis sacrificed empirical history to an idealistic-romantic conception of the evolution of human perfection. Later writers combined "intuition" and "insight" with the analogy of the organism, and saw history as the birth, growth, senescence, and death of distinct "civilizations," each having its own peculiar genius and physiognomy. This form of dogmatism reached its height in Oswald Spengler's *Decline of the West*.[9] If the facts failed to fit his eight great cultures, it was history and not Spengler, whom the author held at fault.

The most recent, as well as the most sane and cautious, of the monumental philosophies of history, is Arnold Toynbee's *A Study of History*. But this writer's very temper of empiricism, and his scrupulous scholarship, have served to emphasize the difficulty of escaping dogmatism in the attempt to make a unified drama of the totality of historical facts. Toynbee's doubt as to just how many such civilizations there are, whether nineteen or twenty-one, or possibly twenty-six (in contrast to Spengler's eight), raises doubt as to precisely what an individual civilization is. His rhythmic formulas of "challenge and response," "withdrawal and return," "rout and rally," "growth, breakdown and disintegration," have, in order to fit the facts, to be made so verbal and so flexible that there is little left in the end but the evident generalization that a plurality of human civilizations, more or less overlapping and indistinguishable, have in the past come into existence and gone out of existence; and that their fortunes and misfortunes depend on a relation between internal and external forces. And one is left in the end with a "Western Christian Civilization," whose future, despite the author's explanation of the past, is unpredictable, and has to be entrusted to the intervention of the Deity.[10]

History itself, the complexity of human happenings, has burst the seams of all neatly tailored philosophies of history. Their great merit

[8] J. G. von Herder, *Ideen zur Philosophie der Geschichte der Menscheit*, 1784–91.

[9] *Untergang des Abendlandes*, trans. by C. F. Atkinson, 1926. Of this writer, a contemporary and more critical philosopher of history has said: "His ideas are an unexpected commingling of world-old analogies and up-to-date conclusions in art, logic and science, precariously formulated and enveloped in an atmosphere of the portentous." (F. J. Teggart, "Spengler," *Saturday Review of Literature*, January 19, 1929.)

[10] Cf. A. Toynbee, *op. cit., passim* (consult Table of Contents).

despite dogmatism and over-simplification, lies in their broad sweep, and in their emphasis on the relations, continuities, and similarities which are lost sight of in special histories. Such a masterly survey as Toynbee's is not only compendious, but brings to light certain aspects of massiveness and generality which are as solid facts as the items or limited segments with which more meticulous historians are preoccupied. They are there to be seen by one who has the far-reaching and synoptic vision to see them. But a pluralistic philosophy of history agrees better with the known facts than a monistic philosophy of history. A more modest, if less impressive, philosophy of history, reveals both manyness and disorder, threads of connection together with disconnectedness and irrelevance, false starts, detours, and vicissitudes of many kinds. Such a spectacle, despite its lack of architectural grandeur, still reminds man of his membership in the family of mankind and leaves open the possibility of a unity to be achieved by good will and enlightenment.

6

There are three distinguishable but clearly interrelated methods of historical knowledge: factual, explanatory, and normative. The first of these methods is divisible into three forms of inquiry: chronology, interpretation, and recreation. Historical knowledge thus seeks answers to five questions: first, "What occurred in a specific place at a specific time?"; second, "What is the importance of what occurred?"; third, "What was it like when it occurred?"; fourth, "Owing to what conditions did it occur?"; fifth, "Is it good or bad that it should have occurred?" These are all pertinent questions; none can properly be disqualified; and they all permit of answers more or less true and more or less proved.

Historical knowledge begins with so-called fact-finding, which corresponds to the "observations" of the natural and social sciences. The refinements of historical techniques have been largely focused on the accuracy and conclusiveness of determining the occurrence of an event or set of events at a date measured from the time of the historian, and compared with the dates of other events. The result of such inquiry is to assemble a set of certified chronological judgments which may, unless restricted by some principle of selection, be infinite in number; one item of knowledge to every past event. The emphasis on this branch of historical knowledge is not unwarranted, for while some of its results may be and are trivial, they are indispensable to any further historical knowledge. The interpretation, re-creation, explanation, and evaluation of an event do not constitute historical knowledge unless it is true that the event occurred when it is alleged to have occurred. Chronology provides the solid and reliable bricks, of which the higher orders of historiography are constructed. If, furthermore, the historian is to select, there must be a multitude of items *from which* to select; as the biographer must "know the facts" before he begins to discard. The selection will be unjustified in proportion as it merely reflects a lack of information.

Historical knowledge selects by interpretation, where the term 'interpretation' is taken to denote judgments as to what is of importance. These judgments are not capricious. The important *is* important: not because it happens to appeal to the fancy of the historian, but because of its actual relation to the large-scale interests of mankind. The newspaper fails to be history when and insofar as its headlines are designed merely to *attract* the reader's attention instead of *directing* it to events which have far-reaching implications. Only some of the events which occur are "news," and the reporter or editor must screen the happenings of the day; but news is not history until the momentous emerges from the welter of petty incidents, crimes, scandals, and other matters of merely "local" or "passing" interest. No days pass without the occurrence of infinitely many events; many days pass without events which are newsworthy; many more days, perhaps years, may pass without events that are "historic"; it is not impossible that there should be countries of whose entire lives it could be said, "Happy are the countries which have *no* history."

Distinguished achievements in historical knowledge are rare because they require over and above industry and accuracy a sense of proportion — a capacity to discover the greater movements which bear the lesser movements on their backs, as the waves bear the ripples and the tides the waves. Furthermore, historical interpretation requires foreground and background. The judgment of importance is based on a seeing of relationships. No historian can, for example, interpret the discovery of America, without knowing the later history of both America and Europe; or the assassination of Lincoln except in the light of the era of Southern Reconstruction.

While interpretation presupposes chronology, the reverse is also true. It is a mistake to suppose that chronological items are first gathered regardless of their importance. The observations of science are not made at random, but are selected by their relevance to theories already accepted, or to hypotheses proposed. Science begins with unities of common sense and looks for data which will confirm, extend, or correct them. Similarly, historical inquiry does not collect miscellaneous facts, and then discover that some are important and other unimportant. The first of these tasks could never be completed. But having assumed certain items to be important the historian then looks for further items which are related to these. This does not forbid the turning up of new items whose importance had not hitherto been suspected, but only that judgments of importance already made serve as a *guide* to further fact-finding. Chronology and interpretation interact.

In the third place, historical knowledge "re-lives" or "re-creates" the past. This method is required because the historical object is individual and unique, and cannot be adequately represented by abstract ideas. It has to be recaptured as it was in the concrete fullness. The imagination enables the historian to insert himself in the past and to follow the flow of time, from *that* time with *its* past, through *its* present, to *its* future. He achieves an imaginary equivalent of contemporary perception and feeling.[11]

This is the office of "narrative history." It may coincide with literature, as in the historical novel, provided it satisfies the cognitive requirements of truth and proof and not merely the requirements of agreeable contemplation; when history is also literature it satisfies both requirements. It is not to be supposed that what is imagined is necessarily illusory. Images constitute one of the most common forms of theory, serving the purpose of cognition by their similarity to that for which they prepare the mind. Memory constitutes the most familiar, but by no means the only, example. The knowledge which one has of familiar "scenes," the expectation of what places or persons are "like," or will prove to be "like," consists as a rule of sensory images which are verifiable when the image is succeeded by actual sense-perception. This form of cognition is peculiarly suited to concrete situations or events such as constitute the objects of historical knowledge.

7

The explanatory method in historical knowledge is of limitless scope, because the concrete and unique event which constitutes its subject matter emerges from the confluences of so many tributaries. It is not difficult to discover necessary conditions, but the discovery of its sufficient cause is an almost impossible task, aggravated by the impossibility of performing controlled experiments. This multiplicity of causes and complexity of conditions has led some to conclude, quite unreasonably, that history is not "determined" at all; or to ascribe its determination to a principle, such as Divine Providence, drawn from outside the stream of history, or a principle invented *ad hoc*, such as Fate, Necessity, or History itself, personified and capitalized.

The expression "historical determinism" is at present in bad odor because of its association with Marxism. It attributes historical events to one type of cause and ignores other types. There is a good reason for

---

[11] Dean Gilman praises Gibbon for "that truly philosophical discrimination (*justesse d'esprit*) which judges the past as it would judge the present; which does not permit itself to be blinded by the clouds which time gathers around the dead, and which prevent our seeing that, under the toga, as under the modern dress, in the senate as in our councils, men were what they still are, and that events took place eighteen centuries ago as they take place in our days"; E. Gibbon, *Decline and Fall of the Roman Empire,* with notes by Dean Gilman and M. Guizot, 1854, Vol. I, pp. x–xi.

condemning Marxian determinism in particular, but not historical determinism in general — taken to mean that historical events, like all events, have their conditions, which, insofar as they can be discovered, serve to explain them.

Looking empirically for historical causes in the stream of events itself, and recognizing their multiplicity and diversity, the explanatory method in history discovers, first, *natural* causes. There are more remote natural causes, such as the available supply of solar energy, and the general conditions of the earth's surface; and there are more immediate and variable causes such as climate, soil, topography, and natural resources. In historical knowledge it may not be assumed that any of the remote natural causes are absolutely constant. Historical events cannot be insulated from their physical environment. The descent of the icecap has something to do with man's past, and the cooling of the sun may have something to do with his future. The exhaustion of the supply of water and minerals, and the changing of coastlines, are already factors to be reckoned with. Earthquakes, volcanic eruptions, tornadoes, and other natural upheavals, intrude from time to time in a manner that leaves no doubt of their power to mold human history.

To the natural causes and conditions of historical events are to be added the cultural. Man resumes his affairs from time to time where he left off, and what he is enabled to achieve is conditioned by what he inherits from his own antecedent achievements. His history is to be explained by his comparatively stable social environment of political, legal, and economic institutions. The causes of the American Revolution, for example, may be found in the colonial form of government, the common law, or the frontier economy. There were also religious causes, such as protestant Christianity, and educational causes, such as the influence of the British university system on the New England Puritans; and there were humane cultural causes, such as the science and art which the settlers brought with them from Europe. There were not only these general causes, but the particular deeds and achievements falling within these several types. All of these causes may legitimately be invoked for explanatory purposes, and no one of them may properly be excluded owing to an historian's prepossessions. They are here cited not with the intention of exhausting them, but to demonstrate the fact of their inexhaustible number and variety.

In the case of individual events whose causes are multiple, it is customary to refer to one cause as *the* cause, when it is the precipitating or *crucial* cause or the cause through which the event can be *controlled*. This selection of one cause for special attention has an application to historical causes. The last increment of water which leads the river to overflow its banks or to break the dam, is considered as the cause of the flood, despite the fact that there would be no flood were it not for many other conditions, such as the shape and composition of the river bed, the angle of declivity, the general topography of the basin, and the volume of water up to the crucial point. The straw which breaks the camel's back would not have this important and unfortunate effect were it not for the weakness of the camel's back and the load already carried; but it is singled out for attention because it is "the last straw," whose addition or non-addition "makes the difference."

But the last straw was added by the camel driver, and if he had withheld it he would have prevented the event. The small break in the dike could have been stopped by the hand of man; and if it had been stopped the dike would not have been swept away, despite its fragility and the pressure to which it was already subjected. This was the cause through which the catastrophe was humanly preventable. The course of history abounds in analogies — the last provocation which caused the outbreak of war, the saving conciliatory gesture which prolonged peace, the arrival of Blücher which "turned the tide" at Waterloo, the death of the heir which precipitated the struggle for succession. There are throughout history partings of the way where the addition or subtraction of a slight force determines the occurrence or non-occurrence of an important event, and where the adding or subtracting is decided by one or more human individuals.

Is the individual the product of history or is he the maker of history? Stated in these general terms it is like the dispute between the environmentalists and the hereditarians: like that dispute it should never have been stated in terms of an either-or. The individual is a product of history, but, being produced, he then becomes one of its makers. This broad conclusion being admitted, there will be differences of degree in the extent to which an individual person makes history. When an historical event requires the combined action of a considerable number of units of a type of which the supply is abundant, no single unit is irreplaceable; but when the supply is limited even an individual of no eminence at all may "cast the deciding vote." Or, the individual's action may be decisive owing to his uniqueness of talent or station. Persons who sat on thrones, or who happened to be the sons of their parents, were once so placed that all of their acts were of momentous consequence; and the same has been true of our more recently invented dictators. In a more fluid society, it lies within the range of the individual's ambition to *make himself* one of these individuals who occupy "positions of power" — who have their hands on the lever.

The decisive role of genius in human history is not disproved by the fact that these exceptionally endowed individuals appear in clusters, as in Greek antiquity, or at the time of the Renaissance, or the rise of modern science. Whether there be one genius or several does not affect the argument; whether the event would not have occurred "but for *this* individual," or "but for *these* individuals," or "but for this *or* that individual," the principle remains the same.

There is another general question of historical causality which is closely related to the role of the individual, the question, namely, of the role of ideas. The contention that ideas do not act as causes, has at the present time few supporters. No balanced judgment would affirm that the religious idea of the recovery of Jerusalem was not at least a contributing cause of the Crusades, or that the idea of the Holy Roman Empire was not at least a partial cause of the eagerness of German emperors to be crowned in Rome, or that the abolitionist creed did nothing to bring about the American Civil War. Ideas, however mistaken or fictitious, have throughout history played a decisive role in major wars and historical cataclysms;[12] and "ideologies" today threaten the peace of the world, and perhaps determine the survival of civilization.

No doubt ideas which cause important events are widely disseminated, but they start with individuals, or they are spread from individual to individual, by the exercise of individual capacities. It is a common error among philosophers of history to suppose that ideas lead a life of their own, divorced from the men who think or believe them — that history skips from peak to peak, or operates in the stratosphere by an "ideal necessity." [13] The individual operates in history as the originator and carrier of ideas. His thoughts and beliefs govern his actions, which may be of decisive importance; he communicates his thoughts and beliefs to another and may thus induce *his* decisive action; or by communicating his thoughts and beliefs he may start or prolong a chain reaction resulting in a sharing of ideas by the total group.

History thus abounds in openings or points of application where the decision of the individual, made in obedience to his ideas, affects the course of human events on that level of importance which merits the name of 'historic.' It makes a difference, and it may make "all the difference." This is the sense in which the course of history is "rational": the causes of history embrace the action of individuals who act "for reasons."

Does the variety and multiplicity of historical causes mean that historical explanation is to be distributed among the special sciences, or is there still room for an over-all explanation? There is one such possibility which arises from the very multiplicity of causes itself. The major historical events are to be explained only by the *convergence* of causes. Thus the historian in explaining the French Revolution, or the Italian Renaissance, or the rise of nationalism, will not only find many causes, but will find that many causes work together, and reinforce one another. The unique historical event can be seen as the effect of a trend, in which

[12] Cf. E. A. Freeman, *Historical Essays*, First Series, 1871, pp. 133–4.
[13] F. J. Teggart, *Theory of History*, 1925, p. 87.

many forces are allied. The event will then occur *as though* the many favorable conditions had been governed by a common purpose; there need be no such purpose, but only a fortuitous alliance of many independent causes. The confluence of historical causes also permits of negative inferences. When an event has occurred under certain conditions it can be stated that they are at least consistent with its occurrence.

Although such explanations are valid, and agree with the empirical evidence, they will not satisfy those who are in search of "historical laws" — laws which operate on the historical level of complexity, laws which are peculiar to history and which exert a force which cannot be broken down into more elementary forces. The contention that there *are* historical laws, whatever they may be, has been argued on the ground that particular causes can be eliminated *one by one in turn* without affecting the outcome. Thus a recent historian, speaking of major events such as the Protestant Reformation in England, writes:

> These great changes seem to have come about with a certain inevitableness; there seems to have been an independent train of events, some inexorable necessity controlling the progress of human affairs . . . Examined closely, weighed and measured carefully, set in true perspective, the personal, the casual, the individual influence in history sinks in significance, and great cyclical forces loom up. Events come of themselves, so to speak; that is, they come so consistently and unavoidably as to rule out as causes not only physical phenomena but voluntary human effort. So arises the conception of *law in history.*[14]

The fallacy of such reasoning is apparent. If Henry VIII had not fallen in love with Anne Boleyn no doubt the English breach with the Pope would still have occurred; no doubt the elimination of any one, or of several of its conditions would not have prevented its occurrence. But the conclusion is that it took a combination of many conditions to bring about so momentous an event, and that while some of them could have been eliminated, and perhaps all *taken in turn*, nevertheless had more than a certain number been eliminated all at once the event would not have occurred. There is no justification for invoking any residual cause, any historical cause *per se*.

A more hopeful procedure is represented by those who discover, or seek to discover, certain structures of events which repeat themselves, and whose general characteristics will help to explain their particular instances. A case in point is the concept of *revolution*. There is, it is alleged, a type of historical change so named, which has its characteristic succession of phases. The French Revolution, or the Bolshevik Revolution, being revolutions, can be explained by these characteristics of revolution in general.[15] Another example is afforded by the "pendulum

[14] E. P. Cheyney, "Law in History," *American Historical Review*, XXIX, 2 (1924), pp. 234–5.

[15] Cf. e.g. C. Brinton, *Anatomy of Revolution*, 1938.

theory," especially in its application to a two-party political system: there is an oscillation between the "ins" and the "outs."

Such explanations are instructive, but lack decisiveness of proof, and afford very slender ground for prediction. The difficulty lies in the limitless number of variables involved. Though it is sometimes said that history is an experiment in living, it is far from being a "controlled experiment." One cannot limit the variables by creating an artificial laboratory situation. There is always serious doubt as to whether any given historical situation *is* a revolution, or a two-party political system. The concepts are either too loose to permit of deduction, or too abstract to fit the facts.

Such explanations are inferior to those of the special cultural sciences. Indeed they owe their explanatory virtue to what they borrow from these sciences. The tendency of revolutions to pass from a moderate phase to a phase of violence and finally to a restoration of order under authority, and the tendency of the party in power to wear out its popularity, can be explained in terms of the instincts of fear and combativeness, the accumulation of grievances, or the "looking for a scapegoat"; nothing is added by invoking general "historical laws."

In short, the best promise of historical explanation lies not in the discovery of causes *sui generis,* but in the assembling and focusing of knowledge borrowed from all the sciences of man and his environment. Even then the claims of explanation must be comparatively modest in view of the inexhaustibility of the factors involved in the concrete individual situation.

8

Historical knowledge, like all knowledge, is descriptive. To describe man's deeds and achievements in terms of his interests is at the same time to define standards by which they may be judged good or evil, more or less good, more or less evil; in short, normatively.

There are as many forms of normative historical knowledge as there are standards with which historical events can be compared; and their number is legion. Such standards may be external, as when one judges the early history of Indonesia by the standards of Western civilization; or they may be intrinsic, as when it is judged by its own standards. It is commonly said that Gibbon's history of early Christianity was "prejudiced." But this charge would have carried no onus whatever if he had *stated* his prejudice; though he could have judged early Christianity by what the Christians themselves were trying to achieve, rather than by what he, Gibbon, would have liked them to achieve. This is a familiar distinction, recognized by the great historians. The mixture of piety and ferocity which characterized the Catholic persecution of the Huguenots, and the equally fanatical persecutions by protestants, can be judged by the ends by which these persecutions were governed; or by the more

tolerant purpose of later times. Both judgments are normative, and both
are, or may be, true judgments of comparison.

But this is not a necessary disjunction, for it is usually possible to find
some standards which are common both to the age of the judge and to
the age which is judged. This is the case whenever the same interest occurs in both ages. Let us suppose, and it is not an arbitrary supposition,
that the need for polity, law, and economy, and the love of beauty and
true knowledge, and the aspirations to personal development and re-
sourcefulness, and to piety and faith, are persistent and recurrent interests. We may then say unqualifiedly that the Magna Carta was politically
admirable; or that Rome made notable contributions to law; or that the
economy of Israel has advanced beyond that of adjoining Arab countries;
or that Greek antiquity ranks high in the order of humane culture; or that
Pestalozzi and Froebel have taught us something in the field of educational endeavor; or that the history of the Hebrews and of India are note-
worthy chapters in the history of religion.

Among the standards applicable to history by the historians there is
none so decried, but none so pertinent, justifiable, and unavoidable as
the moral standard. The only valid objection to a moralizing historiography is to its naïveté and lack of discrimination, as when the historian
judges history by his personal moral bias without being aware of it, or
judges by the conscience of his own age without recognizing that it
differs from the conscience of the past.

Man is a moral being, and it is impossible to characterize a person
without appraising him morally. Indeed such appraisal is a favorite
theme among historians of recognized competence and distinction. There
is a special fascination in the attempt to describe "great men" whose
characterization requires that they shall be both admired and condemned.
Freeman, objecting to Lord Brougham's severe condemnation of the
Emperor Henry V, says that "it is seldom fair to judge any historical
character by so unswerving a standard; we must make allowance for the
circumstances, the habits, the beliefs, the prejudices of each man's
time." [16] The following appraisal of Frederick Barbarossa explicitly adopts
as its standard the conscience of the Emperor's own time:

> Possessing frank and open manners, untiring and unresting energy, and
> a prowess which found its native element in difficulty and danger, he
> seemed the embodiment of the chivalrous and warlike spirit of his age, and
> was the model of all the qualities which *then* won highest admiration.[17]

It is to be observed that with the possible exception of "warlike
spirit" these qualities still win admiration, so that the historian is in
large part judging this historic character by a standard *common* to the

[16] E. A. Freeman, *op. cit.*, p. 117.
[17] "Frederick I (Barbarossa)," *Encyclopaedia Britannica*, 11th ed. (italics mine).

twelfth and the nineteenth centuries. Frederick Barbarossa mixed cruelty with clemency; and though he wrought havoc in Italy and the Holy Land, he gave his German subjects comparative peace and prosperity. His successor, Frederick II, was licentious, quarrelsome, and inordinately ambitious, but he was learned and cultivated. Charles the Bold, in a later age, was cruel and warlike, but at the same time brave, and austere in his private life.[18] Antiphon of ancient times has been condemned by posterity as a traitor, an employer of assassins, and an unprincipled ghost writer, but was praised by Thucydides as "a man inferior in virtue to none of his contemporaries"; which means, according to Jowett, that he possessed "ability, force of character, and faithfulness to party ties." [19]

Similar mixed judgments are commonly pronounced on Alexander the Great, Julius Caesar, Charlemagne, Richelieu, Cromwell, Frederick the Great, Napoleon, and other men of action, in whom ambition and ruthlessness have been mingled with statesmanship and justice. They are commonly condemned by the standards of a later age at the same time that they are approved by standards common to their own age and the age of the historian. There is an implicit assumption that the common standard is the conscience of European Christendom, and an approximation to the conscience of mankind; and that the later standard is a more enlightened conscience.

Both of those norms (universality and enlightenment) by which conscience itself is judged, carry the criticism back to a fundamental moral norm. When morality is taken as man's effort to resolve conflict and create a harmony of interests, and thus to disperse happiness, then the events of his political, ethical, legal, economic and other cultural history can be seen in the light of this effort, and judged in its terms, quite objectively, to be successes or failures. This standard is not read into history by the historian, but is found there in the actual struggle of mankind.

The remarkable thing is not that historical knowledge should be normative but that this fact should ever have been doubted. There is scarcely a page of written history that does not record successes and failures and distribute praise and blame. This does not imply any hortatory intent on the part of the historian, but is prescribed by the nature of his subject matter. If historical knowledge is about men's deeds, their rising and declining fortunes, and their influence, *for better or for worse*, on their time and on posterity, it cannot be descriptive without being normative.

If, then, the historian is to avoid dogmatism he has only to make his standards explicit. This requires that he shall examine his own personal

---

[18] Cf. E. A. Freeman, *op. cit.*, pp. 278 ff., 290 ff., 339 ff.; Lord Acton, *The History of Freedom*, 1922, IV, V.

[19] Thucydides, *History*, trans. by B. Jowett, Vol. I, p. 594, and Vol. II, p. 502.

standards and the standards of his time and place; he must also understand the prevailing standards of the time of which he writes. Every
historian must be a social historian, and something of a psychologist;
implicitly or explicitly, he should have a philosophy of value. His "objectivity" is not to be achieved by a neglect of standards, but by an
enlargement of his field of objectivity to embrace standards. This is asking much of him, but it greatly exalts his role.

9

The question of progress arises only when the distinction is made
between later in time and better in some scale of value. It is easy to
slip into the use of the term 'progress' when it means only change, continuity, and accumulation. Thus Ortega y Gasset who says that "the error
of the old doctrine of progress lay in affirming a priori that man pro-
gresses toward the better," and who insists on the perpetual variability
of history as contrasted with the invariability of nature, also affirms that
"the same knowledge that discovers to us men's variation makes patent
his progressive consistency. The European of today is not only different
from what he was fifty years ago; his being now includes that of fifty
years ago." [20] It is evident that today does *not* include yesterday, except
in a very limited sense; and even if it did, *mere* addition does not merit
the name of progress — otherwise the increase of a sandbank or coral
island would be progress.

Having made the distinction between time and value, it is then meaningful to ask whether the later is also the better. Progress, in other words,
is a curve defined by two coördinates, a time-coördinate and a value-
coördinate. "The later the better" is thus a diagonal between these coördinates above the line, indicating that each step *forward* in time is also a
step *up* in value. Granting that there are two coördinates other curves
are also possible: a diagonal below the line, indicating that each step
forward is a step downward — "the later the worse"; or an irregular curve
indicating that as history moves forward in time it moves up and down
in value — "the later the sometimes better and sometimes worse."

This does not represent the full complexity of the question. For there
may be many value-coördinates, and as history moves forward in time
it may move up in some respects and down in others. In order that a
later time may be said to be better than an earlier time it is necessary
that their values should be commensurable. This condition is satisfied by
the continuity or identity of interest. Insofar as the same tasks are from
time to time repeated or resumed, such achievements can be judged *in
terms of such tasks* as comparatively successful or unsuccessful. Whether
there is or is not a value on the whole in respect of which history *on the
whole* can be said to move up or down, is, as has been pointed out,

[20] *Towards a Philosophy of History*, 1941, p. 218.

highly questionable. When the poet says, "Yet I doubt not thro' the ages one increasing purpose runs," the absence of doubt is due not to the evidence of events but to an optimistic faith, an echo of a religious or metaphysical dogma. Or the idea of total moral progress may be based on the equally dubious doctrine that there is some one scale of value which implies all the rest.

Granting that progress or decline is measured by two coördinates, one may inquire whether their correlation is merely a matter of fact due to no ascribable cause, or whether there is a necessary connection between the passage of time and a rise in the scale of value. It is only in the latter case that one can properly speak of a law or principle of progress.

A survey of the history of Europe and America during the last two centuries presents a dramatic picture of the improvement of "social conditions." In England at the beginning of this period hundreds of trivial offenses were punishable by death; prisons were unspeakably filthy, brutal and corrupt; women and children worked in coal pits; chimney-sweeps of six were whipped to keep them awake; press gangs were employed to recruit the army and navy; and half of the population received no schooling. Serfdom was the order of the day in Europe and slavery in America. Dueling was a common practice. Plagues were rampant, The people were politically helpless and their protests were harshly suppressed. These conditions were not greatly altered until toward the close of the century; since then their improvement has been so rapid and so radical as to merit the name of revolution. Prisons and penal laws, hospitals and public health, conditions of labor, education and political rights, have been so "reformed" that to Europeans of the present generation the misery and helplessness which were the common lot even a century ago are both shocking and incredible.[21]

This change for the better, profound as it has been, in itself implies no general principle of progress, but only a happy conjunction of circumstances. The picture portrays only a limited area of the earth's surface, a fraction of its inhabitants, and a selected aspect of their lives. It would be quite possible to draw another and less favorable picture. Suffice it to mention the changes which have culminated in the great economic depressions and world wars of the present century, the widespread evils that have followed in their trains, and the gloomy outlook for the future.

There remains the question whether there are any *reasons why* historical change should be for the better on the whole or in part, or why changes for the better should in the long run prevail over changes for the worse. The simplest view of this type is the view that good has a greater durability than evil, so that time itself will operate selectively. Thus Count Keyserling asserts that "only the true and the right survive

[21] For an admirable survey of this reform, cf. G. Trevelyan, *English Social History,* 1942.

in the long run." [22] Such a statement is either an expression of faith, reflecting the resolve of the will that "the true and the right" *shall* prevail;
or it is a dogma, deduced from the assumption of its own truth. If nature
and history are conceived as the expression of a spiritual principle which
embraces all the perfections, then these perfections will manifest themselves, if not in the short run, then in the long run. But in proportion as
they do *not* manifest themselves the conception is disproved — unless it
is to be accepted as a dogma, that is, despite the evidence to the contrary.

This is not the worst of it. For when a dogma appears to be contrary
to the facts there is an almost irresistible tendency to select and interpret
the facts so that they will agree with the dogma. The dogma of progress
thus leads to the ignoring or excusing of evil. As a recent writer has said,
with justifiable indignation:

> There is something inexpressibly brutal in the dogma of necessary uni-
> versal progress, which is simply the old dogma that this is the best of all
> possible worlds in a temporal form, to wit, that every change in the world
> is a change for the better. Like other forms of brutality, this glorification of
> the historically actual is due to a lack of sympathy or imagination which
> prevents us from seeing all the finer possibilities, hopes and aspirations, at
> the expense of which the triumph of the actual is frequently purchased.
> The doctrine that right always triumphs is but an insidious form of the
> immoral doctrine that what triumphs (i.e. might) is always right. [23]

Sober second thought has discredited all attempts to derive a general
law of progress from the Darwinian theory of evolution. There is, no
doubt, a "survival of the fit" — but fit for what? The only general answer
to this question is: fit to survive. That which is fit to survive corresponds
to no eminence in any scale of value, not even the biological scale; for
given certain conditions which it is not difficult to imagine, and which
some scientists are disposed to predict, it may be that in the very long
run it is not man or superman but the most rudimentary forms of life
that will succeed in the struggle for existence. If societies are substituted
for species the answer is the same. The kind of society which will prevail depends not only on the changing physical environment, but on the
type of competition among societies. If it be war, then the last surviving
society may be the most ruthless, in which the arts of civilization have
been eliminated or harnessed to brute force.

Another principle of progress which has had its day but has succumbed to a candid recognition of the actual course of events, is that of
a "natural" or "ideal" development, or succession of stages, through which
every society and institution is destined to pass. The supposition that
history is divisible into integral cultures which, like the living organism,

---

[22] H. Keyserling, *The Recovery of Truth*, 1929, p. 522.
[23] M. R. Cohen, *Reason and Nature*, 1931, p. 378.

are born, mature, grow old, and die, has already been examined and rejected. Even if it were tenable it would not be a doctrine of progress, but rather the opposite. At best it would promise an endless cycle of growth and decay; and since there is no guarantee that new cultures will be born to replace the old, the most certain ultimate prospect would be that of death. The classifications of societies as primitive or advanced; as hunting, nomadic, agricultural, and industrial; or as promiscuous, endogamous, exogamous, matriarchal, and patriarchal, afford no evidence that these stages succeed one another in a necessary order, or that the last is better than the first.[24]

10

If there is no over-all law of progress, there may yet be piecemeal progress — *strains* of progress, aspects of the course of human events, in which time works for the better.[25] This more modest and empirical approach to the question compels the admission that there are also regressive factors in history, as well as certain forms of historical achievement in which the passage of time can be said to make no difference either for better or for worse.

This last possibility has already been explored in the comparison of art and science. The following paragraph provides a text for further comment:

> There are in life two elements, one transitory and progressive, the other comparatively, if not absolutely, non-progressive and eternal, and the soul of man is chiefly concerned with the second. Try to compare our inventions, our material civilization, our stores of accumulated knowledge with those of the age of Aeschylus or Aristotle or St. Francis, and the comparison is absurd. Our superiority is beyond question and beyond measure. But compare any chosen poet of our age with Aeschylus, any philosopher with Aristotle, any saintly preacher with St. Francis, and the result is totally different . . . The things of the spirit depend on will, on effort, on aspiration, on the quality of the individual soul, and not on discoveries and material advances which can be accumulated and added up.[26]

There are certain forms of human achievement that owe comparatively little to the passage of time. It is necessary to say "comparatively" for there is no form of human achievement that derives *no* advantage from the passage of time. The sage, the seer, the saint, the artistic or scientific genius, lives in a society which is so developed as to permit some individuals to be freed from the exigencies of subsistence and the

---

[24] Cf. M. R. Cohen, *op. cit.*, p. 382; F. J. Teggart, *op. cit.*, pp. 93, 116.

[25] Karl R. Popper speaks of "piecemeal social engineering"; *The Open Society and Its Enemies*, 1950, p. 3. Despite many points of difference there is a fundamental bond of agreement between this admirable book and the present work.

[26] G. Murray, *Religio Grammatici: The Religion of a Man of Letters*, George Allen and Unwin, Ltd., 1918, pp. 23–4.

inflexibility of custom. The examples commonly cited to illustrate that which is "eternal" in human achievement have all occurred within a comparatively recent chapter of man's long history. It is a matter of record that genius did not flourish until human culture had already ascended to a high plateau. A considerable stretch of progress lies behind the non-progressive.

But when human life has reached a certain level which permits of what we call 'civilization,' then and thereafter there occur human achievements which owe little or nothing of their superlative quality to the time in which they occur. The saintliness of St. Francis, or the ideas of Socrates, or the plays of Shakespeare, values of love or ironical wisdom or poetic insight, depended on what is unchangeable in human nature, and on what is universal in the human situation.

When we say that the fine arts are unprogressive, what do we mean? Not that there is no improvement in the instruments of art, as there clearly is: musical instruments, pigments, chisels, building materials, printing, communication. Not that the artist of each period does not have before him new techniques resulting from past experience, and an increasing store of past achievements from which to derive stimulus or guidance. Not that modern social institutions do not, with some exceptions, afford the artist greater freedom of opportunity, a better education, and a greater recognition, than he enjoyed in the past. But that these things do not in themselves increase the *aesthetic* value of the product — its appeal to aesthetic enjoyment and taste. The factors which do count aesthetically — sensory appeal, form, the happy marriage of these with their subject matter — are independent of the particular time of their occurrence.

These same considerations apply to heroic qualities, to purity of character, to power, to daring, to inventiveness, to creativity, and to fertility of imagination, in all fields of activity. They are demonstrations of what man with his native endowment can do in *any* situation. The undated can be thus divorced from the dated; and that which is not dated is never *out*dated. It has a finality as it is: it is not disqualified by lack of that which is yet to come.

With its non-progressive aspects are to be contrasted those aspects of civilization in which achievement is built on past achievement. Insofar as past achievement is preserved (a very important condition which may always be destroyed by natural or social catastrophe) later interests enjoy an advantage over earlier, owing to the effect of accumulation. Those who come later in time possess a greater fund of resources, whether tools, or wealth, information, ideas, techniques, memories, or models. Whatever the human race learns by experience gains from "long experience." Through the community of tradition, lessons once learned by trial and error do not have again to be learned by that costly process, but provide a starting point for further experiment. Both of these principles of progress — accumulation and learning by experience — apply notably to knowledge, and in particular to the corpus and the proofs of science.

The later is better when uses are identical. What the present possesses would then *have been* welcomed in the past by those engaged in the same task. The hand plow is "superseded" by the horse-drawn plow, and eventually by the tractor, because each in turn will do the same job better and because he who has the job to do will prefer and adopt the better. Men not only learn through time to do better what they have already done, but they learn the meaning of what they are doing; and their action becomes not only more efficient, but also more rational — more consciously purposive. At the same time that men acquire improved means they better understand their ends.

There are progressive factors in the moral life which are not wholly unrecognizable even in this age of war, confusion, and gloomy forebodings. Morality is the organization of interests for their greater security and for their fuller realization. The limitations which moral organization imposes internally tend to be resisted, and from this expansive pressure arises a tendency to liberalization, or to "social reconstruction." Happy are the societies in which liberalization springs from the wisdom of statesmen. Lord Acton said of the Athenians that "they avoided violent and convulsive change, because the rate of their reforms kept ahead of the popular demand." [27]

This progress in liberality is to be credited largely to the implementation by modern technology of the fundamental human motives of self-preservation, ambition, emulation, and compassion. Those who have already risen in life are stimulated by an expectation of rising higher. Those who have not yet profited, or who have profited little, have come to believe that human misery is not necessary; with the result that world religions have shifted their emphasis from resignation to a hopeful humanitarianism. Social progress of this type, be it noted, is not ordained; but is the effect of causes that are in turn dependent on natural resources, political and legal order, public education, and the expanding economy of mass production.

At the same time there is a tendency to universality, that is, to more inclusive moral units. Existing units, such as tribes, principalities, or nation-states, come into contact with one another at their peripheries, and this contact presents the dilemma of destructive war or constructive peace. There results a situation in which men are forced to choose between anarchy — and through anarchy, annihilation — and an extension of the moral order to embrace ever larger areas of life. In short, the

[27] *The History of Freedom and Other Essays*, 1922, p. 66.

same forces which produce social revolution and international war impel the social intelligence of man to the contrivance of moral solutions as the only way of survival.

This is one side of the picture. There is another, a regressive side. In certain respects time works against, and not for, the interests of man. The increase of population is a cumulative function of time, and presents grave, perhaps insoluble, problems. There is an irreversible exhaustion of natural resources, which may or may not be offset by technological progress. Civilization is brittle, and becomes more brittle the higher its level. The best things in life are peculiarly vulnerable. Wars produce dictatorships; and mass communication, one of the proudest achievements of improved technology, facilitates war, dictatorship, and demagoguery. Problems or crises which induce successful attempts to find a solution, may also prove insoluble and induce despair.

Progress itself, because it is local or partial, may work against progress. Because different contemporary societies have reached different stages of progress they find it difficult to understand one another, and to work, or even live, together. Technological progress, which is the most indisputable of all forms of progress, has to be paid for. It tends to the production of disutilities as well as utilities; or for artifacts for which men try in vain to find a use after they are produced. Henry Ford thus reflected upon that progress to which he had made so notable a contribution:

> Progress, as the world has thus far known it, is accompanied by a great increase in the things of life . . . There is no adequate realization of the large proportion of the labour and material of industry that is used in furnishing the world with its trumpery and trinkets, which are made only to be sold, and are bought merely to be owned — that perform no service in the world and are at last mere rubbish as at first they were mere waste.[28]

A hundred years ago, when technology was in its infancy, Emerson called attention to its costs:

> Society never advances. It recedes as fast on one side as it gains on the other . . . The civilized man has built a coach, but has lost the use of his feet. He is supported on crutches, but lacks so much support of muscle. He has a fine Geneva watch, but he fails of skill to tell the hour by the sun. A Greenwich nautical almanac he has, and so being sure of the information when he wants it, the man in the street does not know a star in the sky . . . His note-books impair his memory; his libraries overload his wit; the insurance-office increases the number of accidents; and it may be a question whether machinery does not encumber; whether we have not lost by refinement some energy . . . some vigor of wild virtue.[29]

[28] *My Life and Work*, 1926, p. 268.
[29] B. Atkinson (ed.), *Complete Essays and Other Writings of Emerson*, 1950, pp. 166–7.

And so of progress: there are many questions, and there are many answers. Is there in the course of human history a progressive or a regressive tendency? The answer is yes and no. The final balance must await evidence which is not available. Time is long, and the last judgment lies beyond the range of empirical knowledge. In the absence of any a priori proof the question passes from the domain of knowledge to the domain of faith.

11

What is to be learned from history besides a knowledge of history? It does not itself define a standard of value unless on the unwarranted assumption that it is progressive. But despite the fact that history never repeats itself, it does embrace similarities, and so can reveal relationships and causal connections by the knowledge of which posterity can profit. Through their distance in time these can be objectively and coolly considered. Lessons can be learned from the past without offense to pride, and without being distorted by passion or the pressures of immediate action. One can hold human life at arm's length. Historical knowledge delivers to the men of any given time an immense legacy. They become the "heirs of all the ages." It creates a sense of identity with all mankind. It enlarges the horizon, and corrects the provincialism and snobbism of the here and now, or the modern.

Historical knowledge has its consolations. It was once supposed to reveal a better bygone past — a golden age — which bred a sense of inestimable loss. Now that, as a consequence of historical studies, the past seems less golden, men who complain of the present comfort themselves with the thought that things were once worse. A man who finds society corrupt, or men ignorant, or practices brutal, can look back to earlier chapters and find a greater corruption, ignorance, and brutality. A man who finds taxes high can read Sydney Smith's description of England at the opening of the nineteenth century:

> The school-boy whips his taxed top; the beardless youth manages his taxed horse with a taxed bridle on a taxed road; and the dying Englishman, pouring his medicine, which has paid 7 per cent., into a spoon that has paid 15 per cent., — flings himself back upon his chintz bed, which has paid 22 per cent., — and expires in the arms of an apothecary, who has paid a license of a hundred pounds for the privilege of putting him to death. His whole property is then immediately taxed from 2 to 10 per cent. Besides the probate, large fees are demanded for burying him in the chancel; his virtues are handed down to posterity on taxed marble; and he is then gathered to his fathers, — to be taxed no more.[30]

And finally, historical knowledge teaches the lesson of patience, and creates the courage to bear the short-range disappointments by taking

[30] "America," 1820, Works, 1860, p. 140.

the longer view. As it opens up the past, frees it from romantic glamor, and reveals the long road which man has trod, tortuous and uneven though it be, man is reconciled to the distance that has still to be traversed before his high hopes can be fulfilled. He does not mistake any single battle for the war. He knows that "times change," and that time may work for, rather than against, his ends. He knows that as the world of today was unpredictable from yesterday, so tomorrow is unpredictable from today; and that at least to some extent, and perhaps to an increasing extent, what the future has "in store" will be the effect not of implacable external necessity, but of his own resolve.

CHAPTER XXI

EDUCATION AND THE SCIENCE OF EDUCATION

In the fundamental sense, education is the cultural process by which successive generations of men take their places in history. Nature has assigned an indispensable role to education through the prolongation of human infancy, and through the plasticity of human faculties. By nature man is not equipped for life but with capacities that enable him to learn how to live. Since it is generally agreed that acquired characteristics are not inherited education assumes the full burden of bringing men "up to date," creating "the modern man" of the 1953, or any other latest, model. Through education men acquire the civilization of the past, and are enabled both to take part in the civilization of the present, and make the civilization of the future. In short, the purpose of education is three-fold: inheritance, participation, and contribution.

It is quite conceivable that any one of these elements should be so accentuated as to exclude or obscure the other two: as when education is conceived as a mere deposit and preservation of the past, or as a mere fitting of individuals to an existing society, or as a mere preparation for the years to come, whether in this world or the next. Its full significance rests upon the idea of human life as a going concern into which successive generations of persons are initiated, in which at any given time, they play their roles, and to which they give a fresh impulse of creative inventiveness. This statement should serve to correct the abstractions, accidents, and one-sidednesses by which the role of education in human life is belittled.

As persons are born, grow old, and die, they preserve the achievements of the race through their overlapping. The young can begin where the old left off. Were it not for education in this sense each generation would be compelled to begin the life of man all over again. There would be no continuity and growth save within that small span of years accorded to the individual.

But men are not mere depositories and channels of transmission, because of the nature of that which is transmitted. When we speak of man's inheritance of the past we do not refer to the fact that inorganic bodies outlast organic bodies. The tools found in geological deposits have endured when their users have perished, the bones remain after the flesh and blood have disintegrated, and the monuments are more enduring than their builders; but education as inheritance of the civilization of the past refers to precisely that which, in this physical sense, is least durable. The content of civilization consists not of things, like granite and metal, which are comparatively resistant to wind and weather, to pressure, erosion, and chemical action, but of ideas, sentiments, and habits whose vehicles are highly perishable; and these can be preserved only through being perpetually reincarnated in human persons. Those who inherit the civilization of the past must *live it in their own day;* hence there can be no separation between education as inheritance and education as participation.

Participation in the life of the present is likewise inseparable from the life of the future. The human inheritance embraces unfinished tasks, a doing of something that can be done better or worse. There is thus not only a continuity of achievements but a continuity of standards by which achievements are recognized as falling short — as leaving something to be desired. In different degrees, and with more or less of conscious purposiveness, men attempt to improve upon the past, and to bequeath more than they have inherited.

Because the future is only partially and uncertainly predictable, and because human faculties are inventive and resourceful, education for the future implies education for a future which is of man's own making. This has been held to be the essentially democratic and American idea of education:

> We must concentrate upon teaching our children to walk so steadily that we need not hew too straight and narrow paths for them but can trust them to make new paths through difficulties we never encountered to a future of which we have no inkling today.[1]

2

Since man's education traverses the whole content of civilization and extends throughout his life, education is capable of many divisions and subdivisions. All such divisions should be viewed with suspicion. They are necessary, but misleading, since they tend to obscure the over-all purpose of education.

Thus education is *both* personal and social: personal, because the end result is a condition of the individual and so essential to his well-being

[1] M. Mead, "Our Educational Emphases in Primitive Perspective," *American Journal of Sociology,* 48 (1942–3), p. 639, and *passim.*

as to constitute a recognized right; social, because it is a matter of such great concern to society as to require special instruments and forms of organization which justify its claim to be regarded as an institution.

The distinction between self-education and education by external agencies is permissible only if it be recognized that education is always both. Education cannot be imposed on merely passive or receptive minds. All of the figures of speech which suggest this, and which depict the mind as a receptacle into which knowledge can be poured, falsify the actual nature of the educational process. External influences obtain access to the mind only when the mind opens its doors from the inside, even if it be only by the act of attention. This is the truth proclaimed by so-called "progressive" education, and which has been perpetually proclaimed by the educational reformers of all ages. Men learn by exercising themselves, by following their interests, by trying to succeed; and if education is to educate it must release the springs of such activities.

But it is one of the immense advantages of human over animal learning that a man can learn "cognitively," that is, from what other people have already learned, and not only from his own experience. If the human mind is to realize its greatest possibilities of growth, it must be nourished from without; if its activities are not to be random and wasteful, it must be guided; if it is to find what it needs, it must be told where to look; if it is to know, it must be compelled to face the stubborn facts of nature; if it is to learn how to live, it must adapt itself to its existing social environment. Education involves restraint, redirection, and control, by those who "know better." Spontaneity and discipline are two halves of one whole, and they should not be separated by an either-or and developed into opposing educational cults.

Education is often divided into parts which correspond to the supposed parts of human nature — into education of the mind and education of the body, or into education of the intellect and education of the emotions and will. These abstractions are professedly rejected in modern times owing to the decline of psycho-physical dualism and facultative psychology; and the ancient Greeks are praised for having avoided them. But in practice, by omission if not by commission, these divisions stubbornly persist, and falsify the undeniable fact that human nature is physical, emotional, and volitional as well as intellectual.

There is a familiar distinction between that vocational or professional education by which the individual is fitted for a place in the social division of labor, and that "general education" which conduces to self-development and association with his fellows on common ground. This distinction tends to obscure the fact that by becoming a specialist the individual does not cease to be a man among men, and the fact that there can be no special education which does not affect a man's personality and fit or unfit him for human association.

Education is commonly divided into so-called formal and informal education. By 'formal education' is meant education by agencies, such as schools and teachers, expressly devised for educational purposes. 'Informal education' will then be the name given to the remainder, such as parental education, or education by friendship, religion, press, radio, theatre, books, and occupation. The merit of this distinction lies in the repetition of the word 'education,' implying that informal education is also *education*. It should be added that informal education is the greater part of education. It precedes, accompanies, permeates, and supersedes formal education. Formal education is largely forgotten, and it is a part of its task to teach men how to teach themselves and how to learn from influences which are not expressly designed for educational purposes.

Formal education leads to a division of education into "subjects," which make up the so-called "curriculum." The division of labor and the introduction of schedules has led to the illusion that nature, society, and history themselves are made up of distinct subjects; as though the pattern of creation were a sort of handbook of studies.

Grossly misleading, too, is the division of education by the age of the educated; child education and adult education, or elementary, secondary, and higher education. Most misleading of all is the idea that education comes in the earlier years and ceases at some indeterminate point between 18 and 30. There is ground for such a division. Some things are best learned in early years when the individual's instincts and spontaneities incline him to their learning; certain things are best taught before certain other things, because the later things are built upon, and make use of, the earlier things. It is well to learn to walk before one engages in field work; and it is well to learn to read before one learns from books. It is also true that habits are formed in the course of time, and that they accumulate and harden; so that the mind is more impressionable in earlier years, both in the sense that it is more open to new impressions and in the sense that what is then impressed is likely to be more lasting.

But these facts have led to an exaggeration of the differences between childhood, youth, and age. The mind is impressionable at all ages; and it is one of the tasks of education to see that it remains impressionable. The mind is not a limited space, as though, having been filled in early years, no room is left for more. On the contrary, the more one knows, the more one can learn. One can unlearn as well as learn. Old habits can be broken and new habits created so long as any time remains. That greater wisdom which was once imputed to the old consisted not in the mere deposit of years, but in ripeness and perspective, and in having acquired more to learn with, in having had more time to learn and to "learn better."

3

Since education is a public, as well as a private, concern, it is socially organized. Hence the school, college, university or other institution conducting "formal education," and hence the "curriculum." In ancient times society did not try to teach everything, even though there was comparatively little to teach. At the time of the Renaissance, and during the centuries that followed, the vast and rapid increase of knowledge broke against the barriers of a rigid and exclusive system. Until recently the history of education has consisted largely in the opening of doors and windows, so that more and more of the newly recognized knowledge could obtain admission; as though the purpose were to extend the bounds of education to the limit of omniscience.

The increase of the corpus of knowledge, together with its elaboration and specialization, has now far exceeded the possibilities of formal education. There is vastly more to know than there is time and capacity either to teach or to learn. The present problem, therefore, is not the problem of inclusion but the problem of selection.

There are two divisions of education in which the increase of human cultural achievement appears to cause no embarrassment — elementary education, and vocational education. If elementary education is taken to mean the teaching and learning of "the elements," such as "the 3 R's," there is no curricular problem. But this implies an artificial conception of childhood. "The child is father of the man," and has to be dealt with accordingly — as a growing adult. Elementary education is not a finished product, complete in itself, but a phase of unfolding. There is no fixed number of years and months at which childhood can be said to end and manhood or womanhood to begin. Elementary education must therefore be forward in its outlook, and so contrived that at each stage the child is prepared for the next. His education must not only feed his growth but stimulate it, and offer the individual something which lies at the ever-widening circumference of his existing powers. The child is also a person, or begins to be at an indeterminate age; he is never merely a reader, writer, and doer of sums. He has his world to live in; and he must live in the same world with his contemporary elders.

Vocational education is also an abstraction. The individual must at some point acquire one or more marketable skills. But no man or woman is designed to be merely a mechanic, a clerk, a tradesman, a lawyer, or a doctor. To educate him only for a division of labor is to mutilate him. As Emerson has said, organized society tends to make of its members "so many walking monsters — a . . . finger, a neck, a stomach, an elbow, but never a man." [2] Vocational education has a duty to avoid this offense

[2] "The American Scholar," *Complete Essays and Other Writings*, B. Atkinson, ed., Modern Library edition, p. 46.

to man's nature and dignity, and to educate a *man* and not a mere inter-changeable part of the social mechanism.

It is in the field of secondary and higher education that the problem of the curriculum is most acute. Since studies must be selected it is im-perative that they shall be selected for a purpose: not because they coincide with certain portions of knowledge and life, but because they serve the purpose of *education*. The question is confused by the fact that the teaching staff in institutions of higher education, if not in secondary schools, is composed of "scholars" who are at the same time devoted to the advancement of knowledge. This is not accidental or undesirable, since each activity in some degree promotes the other. It is one of the purposes of education to learn what knowledge is, and how it is advanced, and no one can teach this lesson as well as one who practices what he preaches and exhibits the methods and passion of inquiry in his own person. Nevertheless there is a conflict of interest between education and research. When they are combined in the same men and institutions there will be a tendency to reduce research to the content of the curriculum, or to expand the curriculum to the widening frontier of knowledge.

If the curriculum is to be judged by its purpose of education the admission of any subject matter must be tested by the lesson to be learned. How far, and in what respects, does it put the learner in posses-sion of his cultural inheritance, enable him to participate in the contem-porary world, and qualify him to contribute to the civilization of the future?

Thus the so-called "natural sciences" should teach two lessons — nature and science. The individual should learn that his lot is cast in a physical environment, by which he is controlled, and which he can control in turn. He should learn, in broad outline, what is known about that physical environment. At the same time, he should learn *what science is* — a body of certified knowledge transmitted and perpetually augmented; and how it is achieved — its methods and proofs. In learn-ing what is true he should learn what truth is, and acquire a respect for its objectivity. He should capture something of the spirit of inquiry. And he should learn the limits of science, and its role, for better or for worse, in civilization.

From the so-called "social sciences" — ethics, political science, juris-prudence, and economics — the individual should learn similar lessons of objectivity, rigorous thought, and intellectual invention. He should become acquainted with the general structure of his institutional environ-ment, with emphasis on the difference between the culture which man creates and the nature which he takes as he finds it. He should learn that he is what he is because of his human environment and antecedents. But at the same time he should learn that the major social institutions are moral institutions, dedicated to the purpose of peaceful and coöper-ative achievement. From sociology he should learn of the solidarity of culture, and from history the lessons of history; what history is, and enough of its content to plot the general course of man's life on the planet and identify his own place on its map. He should acquire a sense of belonging to the army of mankind — a sense of the success and failures which have attended its march, and of the unfinished tasks which are left to his own and future generations. He should learn the perspective and the patience which are required for all long-range human achieve-ments; and courage to face the indeterminate future.

Literature and the fine arts should acquaint the student with objects of aesthetic enjoyment; and excite his enjoyment of them, while at the same time developing a refined and discriminating taste. He should acquire some stirring of creative impulse, and a love of truth and beauty as ends in themselves which transcend the utilities of practical life and the bare requirements of morality.

Philosophy, in its general sense, and whether it be taught under that name by so-called philosophers or conveyed through the philosophi-cal-mindedness of teachers of other subjects, has its own irreplaceable educational values. It should fix attention on that all-inclusive together-ness of things which is both the first step of naïveté and the last step of sophistication. Its object is that dimly outlined and inexhaustible immensity which is called "the universe," or "the world." At the same time, because it takes nothing for granted, philosophy should stimulate the critical faculties and challenge every ready-made assumption.

Summarizing both what is and what ought to be, philosophy provides the basis for that ultimate synthesis of existence and value which, when converted into a faith to live by, constitutes religion. At the same time from the study of religion and of education itself, the individual should learn of those values which not only embrace the requirements of man's organized living but add some glimpse of perfection.

This summary statement of the curricula of secondary and higher education does not imply the exclusion of studies designed to provide specific information or vocational skills. It does not imply that the curric-ulum shall omit concentration of attention upon one or more of the special divisions of human knowledge and experience. It does not define a "practicable" program of study. It is designed only to provide criteria by which from a vast range of subject matter formal education shall select, within limits of time and capacity, that which will best serve the purpose of an education for all.

4

Over and above formal or organized education, there is an unorganized education which proceeds unceasingly.[3] When the child first goes to school he has already been educated. While he is in school or college he is being educated by his family life, by his association with contemporaries of all ages, and within the school or college itself by all the experiences of which attendance at school provides the occasion, but which fall outside its curriculum. And after leaving college the individual continues to be educated by his vocational activities, by his friendships and neighborly contacts, by his children and grandchildren, by his adventures with nature, by his participation in social institutions, by whatever he imbibes through his eyes and ears. He continues to be educated up to his death, his last and perhaps most poignant lesson, from which, in this world at least, he is given no opportunity of profiting.

It is an ironical and inescapable fact that while this non-formal education would be generally admitted to be the larger part of education, speaking the first word and the last word, and never remitted, it is left largely to chance. That tardy and half-hearted educational effort known as "adult education" is pitifully incommensurate with the task, and can be accounted as little more than the symptom of a remorseful conscience.

The greater part of education is educationally purposeless. This is inevitable because these all-pervasive and ceaseless educational forces are, and must be, organized for other purposes. The family, conscience, polity, law, economy, science, art, and religion have their own purposes to serve, and they cannot serve them best if they are bent to the special requirements of informing, training, and edifying the partially educated.

To canvass the influences which impinge upon the individual throughout his life, which shape and mold his mind, would far exceed the limits of a mere *chapter* on education. There is an aspect of this question, however, which merits special attention at the present time, and which is of crucial importance for the immediate future of mankind: the effect, namely, of the instruments of mass communication. The urban and national newspaper, and the weekly magazine, with circulations in the millions, the radio, the newsreel, and now television, perhaps greatest of all in its potentialities for the future, have created channels through which opinions and sentiments are carried to the listening ears and watchful eyes of vast multitudes. A man in official position, or any unofficial person who can "make the news," or a public or private agency which controls the instruments of publicity, can command the attention of a public that now embraces all the nations of the earth.

[3] Portions of this section, and of §§ 8, 9, are reprinted from the Author's *The Citizen Decides*, Indiana University Press, 1951, *q.v. passim.*

The man at the microphone or before the camera, or who sits at the editorial desk, eclipses the teacher in his classroom.

The revolutionary advance of the arts of mass communication is sometimes considered to be in itself evidence of educational progress; whereas it signifies only a multiplication of the instruments of education — *for better or for worse*. It is true that the advance of communication argues a spread of literacy, that is, of the capacity to attach a meaning to spoken and written words or to graphic representations. The minds of more men more of the time have become more accessible, and more vulnerable, to visual and auditory signs.

But if by education is meant *educational values* — inheritance of tradition, participation in the life of the present, contribution to the civilization of the future, acquisition of correct information, respect for true and certified knowledge, understanding of the moral standard of social institutions, capacity for sound judgment, refinement of aesthetic taste, perspectives of history, love of perfection, the sense of an environing universe — if education means such things as these, then there is no reason whatever to suppose that more communication implies more education. For if one were to make a list of all the opposites, and call them educational disvalues, or forms of *mal*education, then the new agencies of mass communication could serve these equally well. And this, in large measure, is precisely what they do.[4]

The sobering fact is that the agencies of mass communication do not operate under educational controls. They *can* be used for education, but they *need* not be. They provide educational facilities; but facilities which *lend* themselves to a purpose do not necessarily serve it: they may serve a quite different purpose. The agencies of mass communication, broadly speaking, serve a commercial purpose. Publicity is a free enterprise, which means that it is one of the many ways in which private entrepreneurs make their private fortunes. It prospers in proportion to the size of its public, and its concern is to reach and satisfy the largest possible number of consumers. It will excite a demand for the goods which it produces, and since it is interested in the volume of its sales it will therefore excite the sort of demand which is excitable on a large scale.[5] It moves in a circle. Having created a public demand it will then produce what its public demands. Since the creation of a mass mind

[4] Owing to the remarkable development of its techniques it is customary to refer to mass communication as a modern phenomenon; it has, however, always been practiced, beginning with the tom-tom.

[5] "News," for example, is not merely a report of events, but that which will arrest attention. Chaim Weizmann writes that the American press stated that he was the inventor of TNT, and that he tried in vain to deny it: "The initials [TNT] seemed to exercise a peculiar fascination over journalists: and I suppose high explosive is always news." (*Trial and Error*, 1949, p. 271.)

can scarcely be said to be the purpose of education, mass communication and education thus work at cross purposes.

What is the remedy? There are three possibilities, no one of which is to be neglected. The first possibility is to reform the producers. There is no maker of books, newspapers, magazines, films, or radio and television who is not at times overtaken with a sense of his educational responsibilities. But in the last analysis the producer is likely to say that in a competitive economy he is not in business for his health, or even for the health of society, but to pay wages, salaries, and dividends. The rewards of commercial success, and the risks of commercial failure, will operate as stronger incentives than his educational conscience, and the prevailing code of the economic game will justify him.

The second possibility is to place the agencies of mass communication under the control of government, acting in the interest of public education. But assuming that government is governed by such a purpose it will then create the opinion on which it rests, which violates the maxim that political authority originates with the people. This is only a fraction of the difficulty. For a public control of the agencies which affect people's minds — a control which is not unknown in certain parts of the world — kills the spirit of intellectual, imaginative, and artistic inventiveness, and erects the government into the role of a colossal demagogue who treats the people as wards to be spoon-fed by their betters.

There remains a third possibility, which is to control the agencies of publicity not directly through the reform of their producers or the control of government, but indirectly through the education of the consumers. Those who justify the agencies of mass communication as they are, pass the responsibility on to the customer, and say that the people get what they want. The third possibility, then, is to accept this transfer of responsibility, and look to the character and quality of what the people want. If they learn to want what is good for their minds and souls the agencies of publicity will then be compelled by their economic interest to cater to this higher demand, and to invent ways of satisfying it. Every rise in the level of demand will then lead to an improvement of the product, and this in turn will confirm and further raise the level of demand. The circle will be benign and not vicious.

This places immense responsibility on the educational institutions, a responsibility which they are at present not wholly qualified to discharge. The school, college, and university are non-profit-making enterprises. They owe allegiance to no end save the end of education. In forming the minds of the to-be-educated they are not usurping any other social or cultural function, but are merely doing what they are designed to do. This remedy calls for a new orientation of formal education. It implies that during the period of his education proper the individual shall be made ready for his education improper. The phrase "education to prepare for later life" will be amended to add "education to prepare for the education of later life."

It has been said that it is comparatively easy to get educated — the difficult thing is to stay educated. If formal education is to bear its fruit in after years it must be well rooted. It must be firm enough to stand against the influence of business and professional associates, the temptations to popularity, the mass opinion and sentiment of his contemporaries, the bias of political party, the reiterations of his daily newspaper or radio broadcast, and all the forces which conspire to possess and use him. As an educated man he must be a source and not a mere receptacle: he must have a mind that he can properly call his own.

But independence does not suffice. The greater part of his learning will come in these same after years in which his integrity is threatened. He must know not only how to escape from drowning, but how to swim. To this end he must be made acquainted in advance with the opportunities of his future and continuing education. He must learn how to make use of art, books, newspapers, magazines, radio, cinema, television, speeches, or the talk of the town, so that he may draw nourishment from them — nourishment without corruption. He must learn to discriminate and choose amidst the welter of publicity which will beset him. He must acquire a sales resistance, and yet know how to buy; an initial scepticism which will nevertheless permit him to accept and believe.

5

The science of education, like the other cultural sciences, will employ the explanatory, normative, and technological methods: What are the conditions and forces which bring education to pass? Is it good or bad education? What are the methods by which an educational end can be realized?

The explanatory method of educational science is beset by an ambiguity which requires clarification. If 'education' is taken to mean the process by which individuals absorb the content of social tradition, and are enabled to profit by it in their present life and their making of the future, it embraces both the content of the tradition and also the manner in which it is transmitted. Werner Jaeger has pointed out that this ambiguity attended the use in antiquity of the Greek term *paideia*:

> Originally the concept paideia had applied only to the process of education. Now its significance grew to include the objective side, the content of paideia — just as our word *culture* or the Latin *cultura,* having once meant the *process* of education, came to mean the *state* of being educated; and then the *content* of education, and finally the whole *intellectual and spiritual world* revealed by education, into which any individual, according to his nationality or social position, is born . . . Accordingly it was perfectly natural for the Greeks in and after the fourth century, when the idea was

finally crystallized, to use the word *paideia* — in English, *culture* — to describe all the artistic forms and the intellectual and aesthetic achievements of their race, in fact the whole content of their tradition.[6]

That part of the science of education which explains the content of education will be concerned with the historical and social conditions which determine the choice and order of studies. It is clear that the curriculum reflects the order of interests in any given society. In a theocratic society, first place will be given to religious studies; in a socialist society, to the social sciences; in a culture dominated by the veneration of antiquity, to the ancient languages and literatures; the increasing emphasis on the natural sciences reflects the advance of technology. In a society with a considerable leisured class the emphasis will tend to be on the educational luxuries; in a society governed by the motive of rising in life, the emphasis will tend to be placed on the educational necessities. In a political democracy special attention will be given to such studies as prepare for citizenship.

The explanation of the process of education, as distinguished from its content, has led to a present emphasis on social psychology and the psychology of personality. Plato's recognition of the educational influence of those "fair sights and sounds" to which the youth of his ideal state would be exposed, was largely blind or indifferent to the way in which the influence took effect. Modern educational science emphasizes imitation, suggestion, emotional contagion, and prestige. It attacks the complicated and subtle question of the so-called learning process.[7] It is becoming increasingly aware of the effects of language and other symbols, and of all nuances of meaning which these derive from the social context in which they are used. At the same time attention is directed to individual differences of age, sex, and right or left-handedness, to peculiarities of memory and sensory imagination, to the effects of climate and health, to the ventilation of classrooms, and to the vitamin content of the school luncheon. All the sciences of man and society, not only psychology, but biology, anthropology, sociology, and all the sciences of inorganic nature, physics, chemistry, and biology contribute to the better understanding of how the mind of any given individual is shaped and furnished. When education is organized, with teachers and students, grades for advancement, programs of studies, the science of education is called upon to explain the educational system itself. How did the role of teacher arise? Was the first teacher the parent or the priest? What conditions have defined the period of education? Is it the respect for child-

---

[6] *Paideia: The Ideals of Greek Culture,* trans. by G. Highet, Vol. I, Oxford University Press, Inc., 1939, p. 300.

[7] Cf. K. Lewin, *Dynamic Theory of Personality,* 1935; C. Kluckhohn and O. H. Mowrer, "Dynamic Theory of Personality," in *Personality and the Behavior Disorders,* ed. J. M. Hunt, 1945.

hood? The demand for child labor? The greater or less pressure of livelihood? What are the conditions which have given rise to the specialized institutions, such as primary and secondary schools, private and public schools, colleges and universities, professional and technological schools? The economical division of labor? The social and political structure? The distribution of wealth?

Education, like any social function, may be judged, normatively, by external standards. Much that passes for educational critique is of this type. The existing educational practices may be judged by the prejudices of the judge or of his class; by the prevailing conscience of the times; by political, legal, or economic standards; by aesthetic or scientific interests or scruples; by the articles of a religious faith or an ideal of piety; by the general characteristics of a social or national culture. Of such external critiques there is no end. Suffice it here to recognize the legitimacy of all such critiques, in order to pass on to the internal critique, that is, the judgment of education by what education is for.

The internal normative part of educational science is divisible into an instrumental and a purposive critique. Instrumentally speaking an educational process would be deemed to have the minimum of value when nothing was imparted and nothing learned. On the side of the agent the zero point of education would be represented by the individual who was so inexpressive, uncommunicative, and inarticulate as to exert no influence on others. Similarly the zero point of education on the side of the recipient would be represented by an individual whose mind was closed, incapable of growth, completely insulated or habituated. And from these lower limits education may rise to different degrees of effectiveness. In education, as in polity, law, or economy, the process may be blocked, and its function thwarted, by its own by-products: as when the learner through the scattering of his attention learns nothing well; or when the multiplication of educational impacts results only in confusion; or when, owing to the elaborate organization of the educational institution, the administration building overshadows the classroom.

Education, like other social institutions, has not only its specific function but its ulterior purpose. But while the ulterior purpose of conscience, polity, law, and economy is moral, the ulterior purpose of education, like that of religion, extends beyond morality. Education is concerned not only to harmonize the individual's several interests and fit him for participation in a peaceful and coöperative social life, but to develop his intellectual and aesthetic interests for their own sakes and advance him as far as possible toward their own intrinsic perfections.

Educational science has also its technology. Given any task which involves the shaping of men's minds, educational science will tell him how to do it. Nazi propaganda borrows the techniques of American advertising. Bad, that is, mendacious or socially undesirable, advertising may, up to a certain point, employ the same techniques as truthful and beneficial advertising. Education for war and conquest and education for peace and freedom draw from the same bag of tricks. In short, educational technology, like all technology, is neutral. The range of educational technology is as wide as the range of causes and conditions, mental and physical, which produce educational effects. If it be said in any given case that the arts of teaching or propaganda are not truly educational, this may mean that they are inefficient, or it may mean that they do not serve the ulterior purpose of education.

6

Education, whether formal or informal, is finally justified by its own purpose. Taking its own purpose as a standard it may be praised as faithful to its purpose or condemned as unfaithful. The teacher — using this term broadly to mean the exerter of the educational influence — may keep the educational end clearly in view and choose the appropriate means; and he is then the educational "statesman," after the analogy of his political counterpart. Or he may act blindly and shortsightedly.

Like all institutions education tends to a displacement of the end by the means, the product by the machinery, the subject matter by the method. Academicism or scholasticism is the educational parallel of scrupulosity in conscience, of statism and the spoils system in polity, of legalism in law, of "business is business" in economy, of virtuosity in art, of verbalism in literature, of technologism in science, of ecclesiasticism in religion — of all the "isms" which represent the tendency to become so preoccupied with the instrument that its purpose is forgotten and defeated.

The varieties of this self-defeat in formal education are numerous and familiar: the vested interest of the teacher, and his preoccupation with his professional interest at the expense of the student by whose education his role is justified; the substitution of the pedagogy of subjects for the subjects themselves, and the substitution of the subject of pedagogy for the pedagogy of subjects; the fitting of matters taught to methods of teaching, instead of methods of teaching to the matters taught. The last of these self-defeating tendencies deserves special emphasis. A contemporary educational leader has said:

> The proposition that what is taught should be taught as interestingly as possible does not mean that what is interesting is what should be taught. The function of the educator is to figure out what should be taught and then teach it in as stimulating a fashion as he can. The factor that should determine what is taught is not interest but a decision about how to produce individual happiness, good citizenship, and the improvement of society.[8]

[8] R. M. Hutchins, "Education for Freedom," *Harper's Magazine*, 183 (1941), p. 515.

A similar displacement of the end by the means appears in the tendency to teach what is most *easily* taught. That which is most easily communicated is information. It requires a teacher who knows more than his students, but such teachers are not hard to find, especially if they are prepared in a restricted field and are allowed themselves to arrange the schedule lest they be caught unprepared. In fact, this form of teaching is so easy that it may be superseded altogether, either by texts or by the radio and phonograph; with a resulting technological unemployment of the teaching profession. No one would soberly affirm that the stimulation and guidance of creative art or thought, the sensitization of the aesthetic feelings and the formation of taste, the implanting of the moral will or an intelligent concern for bodily and mental health, are not proper parts of education, or that they are of negligible importance. They are not negligible, but they are neglected, mainly for the reason that the educational machine is not suited to their imparting.

This tendency to fit the task to the instrument rather than the instrument to the task appears also in the shape which studies tend to assume when they *are* embraced within the formal program. They must be teachable by books; and achievement must be examinable and measurable. The extreme of this teaching appears in the reduction of the content of a subject to questions capable of a "yes" or "no" answer. The art of hygiene appears in the shape of a required, and often despised, course in human physiology. The fine arts and literature appear in the form of their history, authorship, and influences. Musicology is substituted for music. Ideas are reduced to the time and place of their occurrence, to the neglect of their meaning and proof. Religious piety is replaced by comparative religion, the history of religion, or biblical literature. And so all along the line the thing to be taught and learned, prescribed by the fundamental purpose of education, is subordinated to the convenience of teaching it. It is necessary to reflect upon what it is all *for*, lest as men learn more about the business of education they become more and more concerned with the business and less and less concerned with education.

7

When education is directed to a definite and preconceived end, it is exposed to the charge of indoctrination. Education can, it is objected, be *too* purposeful. History affords many examples of educational procedures which owe their success to the clarity of their aims; but which are said to have paid an excessive price for this success. According to Thucydides, Spartan education was eminently successful; that is, it produced results by rigidly adhering to its military purpose. But as compared with the laxer and vaguer education of Athens, it was harsh and repressive. Jesuit education in the sixteenth century was eminently successful in producing a specific blend of scholasticism, Latin humanism,

and Catholic orthodoxy which proved to be too old a bottle to contain the
new wines of science, vernacular literature, and secular thought. Cal-
vinistic education in Switzerland, Scotland, and New England succeeded
in inculcating a prescribed morals and piety, but at the price of bigotry
and intolerance. The English system of public schools and universities
in the nineteenth century was designed to produce cultivated English
gentlemen, and it accomplished its design at the cost of intellectual and
social exclusiveness.

In our own day the outstanding examples of educational purposiveness are afforded by nazism and communism. Both have succeeded, and
the latter continues to succeed, in molding the minds of youth after a
preconceived pattern. Their success is due to the definiteness of the
pattern itself, and to the harnessing of every available force that will
contribute to the result, and the relentless exclusion of every distracting
or opposing influence. Nazism employed education to implant in the
German youth the cult of racial superiority, of military discipline, of
unquestioning obedience, of devotion to the Führer; and to this end it
controlled all of the cultural forces — science, philosophy, religion, press,
literature, music, art, symbolism and pageantry — by which the mind
of youth is molded, and which in their total impact created an irresistible
spell and hypnotic fixation. Communism, likewise, discourages every
cultural development which proceeds from independent thought and
imagination, and which fails to reiterate the theme of the class struggle
and the proletarian revolution.

On a less portentous scale the same concentrated purposefulness
appears in dominating parents who make the minds of their children
from infancy, whether by intimidation or by the more disarming methods
of demanding love. Or it appears in the school in which, by prescribed
studies and the prestige of teachers, the pupils are made to be what
their elders think they ought to be. Over and over again this theme is
repeated. A fixed educational purpose is adopted, methodically pursued,
and successfully fulfilled. When such educational procedure is criticized
by the educational reformer it is not because it is purposeless or because
it is unsuccessful. On the contrary, it is held to be *too* purposeful and
only too successful.

Thus there arises the fundamental dilemma of education. To define
in advance an end result and then to seek by all possible means to
achieve it, is held to be too narrowing, too repressive, too authoritarian.
But if, on the other hand, there is no end in view, educational activity
is confused and incoherent. Its various parts and successive phases do
not add up to anything. Without a definition of the end there is no test
by which means can be selected, and no standard by which practice can
be criticized and improved.

There is an escape from this dilemma if we look to the grounds on which indoctrination is condemned. Why does the critic find the nazi method, the communist method, the strict parental or scholastic method, objectionable? Because it is narrow, rigid, and authoritarian. But if he is against these things he must be *for* their opposites: namely, breadth, flexibility, and freedom.

These opposites and other kindred ideas themselves define an end — an end that can be methodically and consistently pursued, and that must be methodically and consistently pursued if it is to be realized. The weakness of educational self-criticism is its failure to acknowledge and make explicit the positive purpose which underlies its scruples. It protests against authority, rigidity, and narrowness — in the name of *what?* It hesitates to name the name lest it be itself guilty of the same faults. And because it fails to proclaim a positive end of its own, it lacks the dynamism which springs from conviction and enthusiasm.

Educational leadership has failed to see how constructive and far-reaching are the principles which underlie its critical judgments. To enable the student to think for himself and make up his own mind; to implant in him a respect for the similar right and opportunity of others; to support institutions in which teachers and students shall enjoy intellectual and cultural freedoms among themselves; to create a society in which such institutions shall be promoted and protected, and which shall be pervaded throughout by similar freedoms — this is a positive end, than which no end could be more positive and more constructive. It defines a task calling for devotion, courage, and effort. It is capable of creating its symbols, saints, heroes, and martyrs.

Mussolini was correct in insisting that there is no subject in which the teacher's influence may not be exerted:

One will say that geography and mathematics are by nature non-political. Such may be the case, but also the contrary. Their teaching can do good or harm. From the elevation of his chair, certain words, an intonation, an allusion, a judgment, a bit of statistics, coming from the professor suffice to produce a political effect. That is why a professor of mathematics plays a political role and should be a fascist.[9]

The objection to Mussolini's idea of indoctrination does not lie in the fact of the teacher's influence but in the fact that he may misuse it, by prostituting it to irrelevant political dogma, and by distorting the subject matter. There *is* an influence of the teacher to which no exception can be taken on any grounds, which is the influence of his own scholarly integrity. The rightful freedom of minds, the maxims of consistency and experimental proof, of intellectual honesty, of tolerance and persuasion, are themselves doctrines. And they have many implications. These beliefs together with their personal and social implications constitute a body of

[9] Qu. from *Scuola Fascista,* in *Le Temps,* Aug. 31, 1932; trans. by the Author.

indoctrination to which no objection can be raised; for he who opposes such indoctrination will himself exemplify it.

There are vast bodies of attested truth, within the domain of the natural and social sciences which may properly be accepted on authority, since their proof lies beyond the capacity or the leisure of the layman. Only a minute portion of mankind can understand the evidence for nuclear physics, or the theory of relativity, or the principles of heredity, or the chemical composition of celestial bodies, or the historical causes of the French Revolution. If the educated man's beliefs were restricted to those which he can prove for himself, the effect of education would be to impoverish and not enrich the mind; the educated man would be more ignorant than the man on the street who borrows his beliefs freely from others. But while education must invoke the authority of experts, it may initiate him into the secret of their expertness, so that he becomes the vicarious adherent of the experts' spirit of free inquiry.

8

The standing paradox of education is the comparative neglect of moral education. Its importance is pointed up by the grave crises of modern civilization. The development of technology culminating in the applications of nuclear physics threatens to destroy mankind; and they can be converted to good, rather than destructive uses, only provided they are subject to a moral control. Society is threatened at home by the conflict between employment and labor, and the only possible solution of the problem is a moral solution. Mankind lives under the horrid threat of a war in which all may go down together, and the only escape lies in implanting in the minds of men good will and the spirit of justice. Political democracy is profoundly corrupted by the development of the mass mind, and the only salvation of democracy is to instill in the people at large the virtue of integrity. Civil rights are perpetually jeopardized and often destroyed because the people neither understand them nor respect them. The favoritism and venality of public officials is notorious.

These things are well-known and repeatedly proclaimed. But what is done about it? Schools and colleges, designed for educational purposes, leave it to the home, the church, the Boy or Girl Scouts, or other private and more or less impromptu organizations. But even these agencies hesitate to assume responsibility. The home passes it on to the school, and the school passes it back to the home. The churches concern themselves largely with dogma and worship. Educational agencies rationalize their evasion of the task by professing their respect for the individual's personal independence. Where in the curriculum or other organized activities of secondary and higher education does training of the moral will and implanting of moral sentiments find a place? Perhaps in occasional so-called "inspirational" addresses delivered in the chapel or at convocations. But how much do these count in the totality of the influences which operate in the community? Does not the very fact that moral education is only occasional and incidental create a sense of its unimportance?

The moral purpose of education is obscured by the tendency to fall back on the vague notion of the development of the individual's latent possibilities.[10] But it is evident that there is no educational process which does not develop the individual's latent possibilities — for better or for worse. The standard of development is no standard at all unless some idea of *what is to be developed* is introduced or read between the lines. If it so happened that man was constitutionally predisposed to good ends, as a plant is predisposed to bear a particular fruit or flower, then all that would be necessary would be to provide him with fertile soil, moisture, and sunlight, leaving the rest to the inherent forces of natural growth. But this is unhappily not the case. It is a notorious fact, reluctantly accepted by modern thought, that human individuals if merely permitted or encouraged to grow in accordance with their own innate propensities, will bear evil fruit as well as good. Even Christianity, proclaiming the extravagant dogma of man's creation in the image of God, has been realistic enough to recognize this horrid possibility, and has provided for it by the supplementary but equally extravagant dogmas of original sin and supernatural regeneration.

The idea that the purpose of education is the development of the individual's possibilities is a sound idea insofar as it springs from a recognition that education is for the benefit of the educated and not the benefit of the educator. It is the learner and not the teacher who is the ultimate consumer. He is an end in himself, and he can be reshaped only through his own responses. The fact remains, however, that moral education implies guidance and control — external guidance as a means to internal control. The teacher hesitates to exercise this guidance. Some years ago a body of educational experts recommended that children be taught that "The things that bring all men together are greater than the things that keep them apart"; and that the teacher have "a firm grasp of moral principles even accepting the risk that these may be called prejudices." But the same report contained the reservation that "pupils must not be 'conditioned' to any set and determined ways of thinking." [11] It is clear that the reservation defeats the recommendation.

The remark that the moral teacher must take the risk of being considered prejudiced is also revealing. Morality *is* a prejudice — a preju-

---

[10] It is to be noted that the word 'education' derives from the Latin *educare* ("to rear"), and not, as is sometimes supposed, from *educere* ("to draw out").

[11] *Primary Education*, Report of the Advisory Council on Education in Scotland, 1946.

dice in favor of justice and benevolence. The use of this word suggests
that it is a petty eccentricity, an arbitrary peculiarity, like preferring
blondes to brunettes or French dressing to mayonnaise. But if morality
means that "the things that bring all men together are greater than the
things that keep them apart," as indeed it does, it underlies all human
institutions, including education itself.

There would be less hesitation in teaching morality if it were thus
recognized for what it is. It does not consist in a set of ready-made abstract maxims, imposed by conscience, custom, or external authority. It
is not a mere expression of the so-called "mores" of any particular race,
nation, or state, or of any historical era. It is not a code of repression or
a mere dream of perfection. It arises from the universal human situation,
in which man finds himself confronted by the necessity of reconciling
conflicting interests. When morality is thus conceived as the form of personal and social organization which gives to individuals and minority
groups the maximum of freedom consistent with living together peacefully and fruitfully; when it is conceived as fulfillment and not as negation of life; when it encourages diverse spontaneities and aspirations,
requiring only that they shall not violate one another, and thus promises
to the arts and sciences the fullest opportunity, consistent with order, to
follow their own inherent passions for beauty and truth — when, in
short, it *makes room* and does not merely confine, or confines only in
order to make room — then it is seen to coincide with precisely those
high motives which have led men to suspect moral education.

Moral education so fashions the individual's will as to fit him for
participation in the moral institutions — the social conscience, polity,
law, and economy. It implants in the individual such dispositions as
shall enable him to live and work with others, both *in* the present and
for the future, and on every level of human interaction and interdependence. To implant such dispositions is the task of those who are concerned
with "personnel problems" and "morale," in industry, in military organization, in private associations, and in the larger fields of national and
global citizenship.

There are divers familiar ways in which this is done, differing in the
degree to which the educable individual is taken into the confidence of
the educator. The lowest form of moral education is that which relies on
punishments artificially imposed for the protection of other interests. Or
the individual can be brought to heel by the accusing consciences of
others. Or, he may be morally educated by being initiated into the partial
or prudential meaning of morality — through recognition of its so-called
"natural consequences" for himself. He may learn by word, example, or
directed experience, the destructive effects of conflict and the weakening
effects of isolation; he may learn the blessings of peace and the fruitfulness of coöperation. Finally, he may be completely moralized through

acquiring a good will, that is, an independent benevolence toward mankind and an allegiance to the goal of universal harmony.

On this last and highest level moral education relies on two forms of appeal. First, it appeals to reason, this being taken to mean men's faculty of objectivity. Thus it proclaims the Golden Rule, which teaches men to see themselves as others see them, and others as these others see themselves; it induces that attitude of detachment in which an interest is an interest whosesoever it be, and good is good to or for whomsoever it is good. Second, in its crowning phase, moral education must appeal to that natural sympathy, compassion, or fellow-feeling which moves one individual to adopt another's interest, and be moved to its support.

9

It has been amply demonstrated, if, indeed, it is not self-evident, that the education of the people at large is indispensable to democracy. Education is not merely a boon conferred by democracy, but a condition of its survival and of its becoming that which it undertakes to be.

Democracy is that form of social organization which most depends on personal character and moral autonomy. The members of a democratic society cannot be the wards of their betters; for there is no class of betters, but only a better part gathered from all the members, and finding collective expression in what is called "public opinion." This, which in a democracy is the ultimate authority, is not, strictly speaking, opinion, but an interested attitude, a being for or against, a will, which is to be judged by moral standards as good will or ill will, and by cognitive standards as mediated by truth or error. The cultivation and firm implanting of enlightened good will in the body of its citizens is, then, the fundamental task of education for citizenship in a democracy.

Democracy demands of every man what in other forms of social organization is demanded only of a segment of society. Contrary to a common supposition, democracy is especially concerned with standards. As the debasing of standards to the level of the mass is the besetting weakness of democracy, so a clear and uncompromising definition of standards is its first educational duty. Democratic education should be an education *up* and not an education *down* — in all its stages. It will always ask more than it gets and develop capacity by straining it. It will encourage rather than congratulate.

Democracy divorces standards from any particular human embodiment. It does not identify labor with a working class, or government with a ruling class, or law with the profession of law, or business with a National Association of Manufacturers, or art with artists, or science with scientists, or education with educators, or religion with priests. Ideally speaking, all citizens of a democracy exercise all of these functions in different degrees and proportions, and each is therefore an epitome of

society. It is this integral person, and not the social instrument specialized by livelihood and vocation, which possesses dignity and sovereign
authority. The plumber, or the congressman, or the lawyer, or the retail
merchant, or the painter, or the mathematician, or the professor, or the
bishop, is not the end in himself, but the *man;* not the role, but he who
plays the role, and who because of his preëminently human faculties can
achieve an integrated personality in an integrated society.

Democratic education is therefore a peculiarly ambitious education.
It does not educate men for prescribed places in life, shaping them to
fit the requirements of a preëxisting and rigid division of labor. Its idea
is that the social system itself, which determines what places there are
to fill, shall be created by the men who fill them. It is true that in order
to live and to live effectively men must be adapted to their social environment, but only in order that they may in the long run adapt that environment to themselves. Men are not building materials to be fitted to
a preëstablished order, but are themselves the architects of order. They
are not forced into Procrustean beds, but themselves design the beds in
which they lie. Such figures of speech symbolize the underlying moral
goal of democracy as a society in which the social whole justifies itself
to its personal members.

It will be seen that education for democracy implies the development
of a capacity of personal self-determination. This constitutes the distinguishing characteristic of that "Western democracy" which is so jealous
of the name, and scorns its use by totalitarian societies. All democracy
implies a raising of the material condition of the masses, and a throwing
off of the harsh yokes of public tyrants and private exploiters; but a full
democracy implies something more fundamental, namely, the capacity of
the individuals concerned to think freely for themselves, and by discussion and agreement to arrive at collective decisions by which their joint
affairs shall be governed. The exercise of this capacity and the acceptance
of the implied responsibility requires an education that goes far beyond
literacy, and beyond acquired skill in the practical or humane arts. While
it is not to be supposed that every citizen, or even a large majority of
citizens, will rise to such requirements, a democracy which educates for
democracy is bound to regard all of its members as heirs who must so far
as possible be qualified to enter into their birthright.

For this reason it is contrary to the principle of democracy that its
members should be sorted out at an early age and prepared for occupations for which there is a social demand. It matters not whether this
distinction is made by aptitude tests, or by the numerical limitations of
educational opportunity — if careers are assigned to men before they
have reached the stage of maturity and enlightenment at which they can
decide for themselves society has failed to equip them for that role of
sovereignty to which, in a democracy, they are called.

In order that its rulers shall not be recruited from an economic class, democracy provides for public education; and extends this opportunity not only through the period of secondary education but into "higher education." "Going to college" is the normal ambition of American youth not from motives of idleness and self-indulgence, but in order to postpone a choice of occupation until they know enough to choose; and in order that they may belong to that "ruling class" which in a democracy is no class at all, but the aggregate, unlimited in number, of all of those who are the makers of the institutions and policies under which they live.

10

Liberalism in education, like liberalism in the moral institutions, represents the claim of persons to as large an area of freedom as is consistent with the like freedom of others.[12] Moral education implants the code of justice and benevolence by which spheres of freedom are defined and respected; liberal education teaches men to enjoy and exercise their freedom, and to spread and extend its domain. A man is free in the proportion to which his life is governed by his own choice. Hence the specific aim of liberal education is to cultivate the art of choice, and to provide it with eligible alternatives.

Choice is a matter of degree. Education is liberal insofar as it invites and qualifies men to choose deeply and fundamentally, to choose ends as well as means, to choose remote as well as immediate ends, to choose from much rather than from little. Liberal education, so construed, makes successive generations of men aware of a wide range of possibilities, by the discovery of new and the reminding of old. It does so in order that men may enjoy the utmost amplitude of freedom — in order that their lives may to the maximum extent be what they thoughtfully and wittingly choose them to be.

Light is thrown on the meaning of liberal education by naming some of its opposite illiberalities. It is opposed to a merely occupational education, because such an education narrows the range of choices that remain open. Having adopted the occupation of a physician a man may then choose only how he shall prepare himself, and where and how he shall practice. The occupation itself may have been imposed by circumstances; he is then said to have had "no alternative" but to practice medicine, or "no choice" in the matter. Or the individual, having taken into account his capacities and environment, may have chosen to be a physician rather than a lawyer, businessman, or artist. His education is then said to have been liberal insofar as it acquainted him with these options, and opened doors to them. Liberal education in this sense properly comes

[12] Some paragraphs of this section are reprinted from the Author's lecture, "When is Education Liberal?" published in *Modern Education and Human Values*, Pitcairn-Crabbe Foundation Lecture Series, University of Pittsburgh, 1950.

at that period in the individual's life when he has not yet committed himself. Having chosen his occupation freely, that is, with awareness and understanding of the possibilities, he may then remain free; for if he has no regrets, all the narrower choices to which he is subsequently restricted partake of the freedom of his original and fundamental choice.

Liberal education is opposed to dogmatic education where dogmatic education means the imparting of beliefs without their evidence. For insofar as the individual is dogmatically educated his mind submits passively to authority — he takes someone else's word — and he does not choose his conclusions by proving their truth for himself. His mind is made up *for* him rather than *by* him.

Merely informative education, which imparts a knowledge of facts, is less liberal than the theoretical education which imparts a knowledge of principles; because he who grasps the principles can then apply and extend them for himself. He is prepared not only for this or that particular actuality but for the infinitude of possibles that are subsumable under general ideas.

Specialized knowledge is comparatively illiberal because it limits the movement of the mind, and excludes the alternative interpretations of any subject or situation which might be made in the light of a broader context. It also habituates the mind to some specific technique, and closes it to matters in which this technique cannot be employed.

If the meaning of liberal education is to be understood, it must not be identified by labels, or associated exclusively with any part of a university. Liberality is a norm or standard by which to judge educational practices wherever they occur. It will not do, therefore, to say that a professional school is *necessarily* illiberal merely because its students are acquiring a special form of expertness for which they expect to be paid. A lawyer, for example, may choose not only his profession, but the branch of law in which he specializes. He may take the law as it is, or he may reëxamine the law's extra-legal premises, and find reasons why the law is as it is or become a legal reformer. In his legal practice he may be a mere technician, operating on a narrow front; or he may participate in the making of constitutional policy. Insofar as legal education enlarges the outlook upon society and history, leads back to first principles, and reveals the ultimate purpose of legal institutions, it may be said to be a liberal education, and the legal profession may be said to be a liberal profession.

There is no occupational or professional education of which the same may not be said. Education for business is liberal when it enables a businessman to choose business for what it is, so that by understanding its underlying principles and its role in society at large, he may be creative, and not a mere cog in the existing mechanism. Even manual labor partakes of liberality at the moment when a man *chooses* to work with

his hands; or when it becomes a skilled craft requiring taste and invention; or when it is attended with a sense of coöperation and social utility.

As the professional or vocational school may be liberal, so the "liberal
arts college" may be illiberal, and will be illiberal insofar as it is pervaded with a narrow sectarian bias, or employs methods of mere popular
appeal, or reduces study to the level of drudgery and routine, or otherwise fails to create the independent and resourceful mind and exercise
the student in the art of choice. All of the studies commonly embraced
in its curriculum are capable of satisfying the standard of liberality if
they are liberally taught or taught by a liberal teacher; and there is no
subject which may not be made illiberal. A study which is liberal at
one time may become illiberal at another time.

What agency shall play the liberalizing role depends on the existing
locus of illiberality. What will emancipate depends on what the minds
of men need to be emancipated *from*. Fresh contacts with antiquity at
the time of the Renaissance served to liberate men from their otherworldly preoccupations and their slavish adherence to secondary sources
and texts. The rise and spread of modern science liberated men from
dogma. The Reformation liberated men from centralized ecclesiastical
authority, and the rise of the modern state liberated men from the yoke
of medieval imperialism. The Industrial Revolution liberated men from
feudalism and from the closed nationalistic economy.

But an agency of liberalization may become a hard master in its
turn; in a later time men sought liberation from the absolutism of the
nation-state and, paradoxical as it may seem, from the harsh restraints of
laissez-faire. Science, to which men turned to escape dogma and supernaturalism, begot a new illiberality, and men turned to religion, literature, and the arts for emancipation. And so for every age, for every
individual, and even for every phase in the individual's development,
there is a timely and suitable instrument of liberality.

Liberal studies are sometimes given the name of 'humanities.' [13]
The name 'humanism' properly suggests that attention be directed to
man and to his works. But it emphasizes that which is admirable in man
and may properly exalt him in his own esteem. Psychology and anthropology are not humanities merely by virtue of the fact that they take
man as their subject matter; nor is the term properly applicable to any
study which stresses man's baser and more contemptible qualities.

What are the attributes of man which qualify him for esteem, raise
him above the level of the beasts, and give him that "dignity" which he
claims and acknowledges? While there is a "humanism" which praises
man for his practical achievements — for the history he has made — and
worships the hero, whether he be conqueror or statesman, humanism in

[13] For a fuller discussion of the meaning of this term, cf. the Author's "A Definition
of the Humanities," T. M. Greene (ed.), *The Meaning of the Humanities*, 1938.

the educational sense praises man for his "spiritual" achievements. The mark of man in this high and estimable sense is not his *power,* but his capacity to pursue ideals — of truth, beauty and moral goodness. Construed as a cult of freedom, humanism signifies man's emancipation from the limits of finitude by the very act of discovering them.

The question of liberal and humanistic education is obscured by identifying the idea with the mechanism. Liberal and humane education is not a "branch" of education, but a set of values that should pervade all education, and to an increasing extent on its higher levels. To identify these values with a "liberal arts college" or with a set of studies called "the humanities" is to mistake the accident for the essence. The effect is to imply that a certain institution or study is automatically liberal and humane, and that other institutions and studies need not be, or cannot be, liberal and humane. It is true that certain educational fields — notably literature and the fine arts, history and philosophy — are peculiarly dedicated to these values by tradition and vocation. But they are under obligation to spread these values to all education, and to see to it that they are themselves true to their professions.

11

If education is to qualify men to live in a global society and contribute to its development in the years to come, the content of education must be correspondingly extended. In short it must cultivate global-mindedness.

This is the core of the matter. It is well enough that international organizations should seek to repair the damages of war, and restore the facilities of education — universities, libraries, museums — when these have been destroyed. It is well that attention should be given to the removal of illiteracy everywhere, and to the improvement of means of universal communication and intellectual intercourse. But all this is beside the point unless men's dispositions are altered: unless their habits of thought, their outlook, their emotional attitudes, are attuned to the moral and cultural unity of mankind.

That the achievement of this result requires the utilization of all the forces which shape the minds of men was fully recognized at the time of the creation of the United Nations Educational, Scientific, and Cultural Organization. When the United States accepted membership in this organization, President Truman made the following statement:

> UNESCO will summon to service in the cause of peace the forces of education, science, learning, and the creative arts, and the agencies of the film, the radio and the printed word through which knowledge and ideas are diffused among mankind.
>
> The government of the United States will work with and through UNESCO to the end that the minds of all people may be freed from

ignorance, prejudice, suspicion, and fear, and that men may be educated for justice, liberty, and peace. If peace is to endure, education must establish the moral unity of mankind.[14]

This global attitude can be conveyed in all the recognized fields of formal education.[15] Mathematics, and the physical sciences and technologies, contribute to internationality through their transcendence of nationalism. Their subject matter consists of a system of relationships common to all nature; and points to nature itself, which is common to all nations. This should be alluded to in the teaching of these subjects, so as to suggest both their universality as well as their infinite human usefulness. Geography extends men's acquaintance with the surface of the earth from the familiar regions where they live to distant and strange places, in order that these may become less distant and less strange. Anthropology depicts the divisive traits and customs of the many families embraced within the one great human family. Psychology calls attention to the common characteristics of mankind.

From history men learn of the life of mankind throughout recorded time, and of the interrelation of groups and nations. No doubt the balance needs to be redressed and gaps need to be filled in order to overcome a provincial emphasis — there is need, for example, of more history of Russia and China. But it would be still better both for the public mind and for the subject of history if historians introduced an international outlook and background into *all* that they write and teach. Their readers and students would then be rid of the illusion of isolationism. They would then see Greek history, American history, English history, or any other special history, as a set of local events interacting with a wider human environment; the history of the twelfth or the eighteenth, or any other century, as a phase of the advance or retrogression of human unity; the past as composed of diverse tributaries converging on the present.

There are certain branches of knowledge which serve the interest of internationality even more directly. These are the sciences which correspond, one to one, with the major human institutions, each of which has a specific function within the common purpose of morality. These sciences are ethics, political science, jurisprudence, and economics. Global unity is a work of organization, to which each of these sciences has an indispensable contribution to make. How shall all men achieve a common conscience, a common polity, and a common system of law beneficent to all mankind? How shall they produce and distribute material goods on a world-wide scale and with a view to the maximum of human welfare? How shall they live together with the least friction, with the

---

[14] News release, July 30, 1946.

[15] Portions of the remainder of this section are reprinted from the Author's *One World in the Making*, A. A. Wyn, Inc., 1945, chs. vi, vii.

least offense to human self-respect, and with the greatest spirit of mutual helpfulness? This is what learners may now expect to learn from those who are learned in the social sciences, and what the learned must be prepared to teach.

The institution which stands closest to morality is conscience, and the extension of polity, law, and economy to embrace all mankind depends on the development of a "conscience of mankind." If men are to achieve a certain kind of world, they must approve it; those in positions of power and influence, who speak for other men with other men's consent, must approve it. There must be a widespread and dominant approving attitude, which is *for* peace and *against* war; *for* happiness and well-being and *against* misery; *for* the happiness and well-being of all men and *against* the happiness and well-being of the few at the expense of the many. Men are now falteringly and feebly disposed to this attitude owing to their vivid experience of human interdependence, proved by the disastrous consequences of war.

The fundamental condition of a conscience of mankind is to that part of human nature which is variously called by the names of 'sympathy,' 'compassion,' 'fellow-feeling,' or 'humanity,' and which is excited in one man toward another regardless of the differences which divide them. The new arts of communication have enlarged and vivified the spectacle of human cruelty and human deprivation. It is true that the springs of pity dry up and that sympathy palls. It is true that the presence of a fellow man may excite antipathy as well as sympathy. It is true that sympathy may be ill-timed and misplaced. But this proves only that the right excitement of sympathy is a part of the task of education.[16]

The problem of world unity is fundamentally a moral problem and requires moral education in order that men may be brought to an understanding of the destructiveness of conflict and the opportunity of peaceful coöperation on a world-wide scale. The moral ideal makes all men of good will joint participants in a common struggle, mourning common defeats and celebrating common victories. Liberal education teaches men to sympathize with the struggle for freedom throughout the world, whether the freedom of individuals and groups oppressed by their own institutions, or of colonies, dependent areas, and weaker nations oppressed by alien empires.

The disinterested pursuit of knowledge unites all truth-seekers in a

---

[16] The psychologists and sociologists concerned with the social side of human nature are facing this problem boldly and constructively. In 1945 a group of American psychologists issued a statement entitled "Human Nature and the Peace," expressing the belief that war is avoidable by "social engineering," by cultivating friendliness, and by redirecting those human impulses which lead to hatred and race prejudice. Cf. *Psychological Bulletin*, 42 (1945); and also G. W. Allport, "Guide Lines for Research in International Coöperation," *Journal of Social Issues*, 3–4 (1947–8).

common passion, in collaboration, and in mutual confirmation. Even the aesthetic interest, while it profits by diversity and idiosyncracy, may serve as a unifying force. It calls into play the same human faculties, and in its artistic products employs similar media and structural forms. Its themes embrace the same mortal vicissitudes of love, death, hope, and despair. Religious education, despite its sectarian divisiveness, may serve the same end of universality. The great world-religions teach a god of all mankind, who respects no differences of race or nation, and who unites all men in a common dependence and adoration. At the same time there is a universality in religion itself, which emphasizes that concern which all men feel for their common destiny in a common universe.

CHAPTER XXII

VALUE AND METAPHYSICS

The purpose of the present chapter is to give an answer to the question
of the kind of being which is to be attributed to value. The word 'being'
is a participle of the verb 'to be,' and its diversity of meaning reflects
the extreme diversity of the grammatical uses of this most familiar and
most troublesome verb. He who attempts to collate and systematize *all*
of its meanings soon finds himself going around in circles. It would be
as hopeless as it would be unprofitable to attempt to fix upon a single
meaning to which all of this diversity can be reduced. The assumption
that there is such a meaning, worthy of being spelt with a capital letter
— a "Being" clothed with majesty and constituting the final goal of the
metaphysical quest — is one of the obscure dogmas which has served
to discredit that branch of metaphysics known as 'ontology.'

Whatever systematic position be taken in logic — whether a logic of
classes, relations, or propositions, whether extensive or intensive, whether
"universals" are accepted or rejected, and whatever position be taken
in theory of knowledge, whether rationalist or empiricist, a priori or
experimentalist — in any case, provision must be made for ultimate entities or terms. Thus, according to Bertrand Russell:

> Whatever may be an object of thought, or may occur in any true or
> false proposition, or can be counted as *one*, I call a *term*. This, then, is the
> widest word in the philosophical vocabulary. I shall use as synonymous
> with it the words unit, individual and entity. The first two emphasize the
> fact that every term is *one*, while the third is derived from the fact that
> every term has being, i.e. *is* in some sense. A man, a moment, a number, a
> class, a relation, a chimera, or anything else that can be mentioned, is
> sure to be a term; and to deny that such and such a thing is a term must
> always be false.[1]

[1] *The Principles of Mathematics*, 1903, Vol. I, p. 43.

This is the only meaning that can be assigned to "pure being": it is the "anything" which is repeated or assumed in every statement which is made about anything. References to "nothing" (that is, *no thing*) involve the distinction between a name and that which it names. A "nonsense syllable," exclamation, or "mere combination of words," is itself an entity, that is, a noise or mark. But there is no entity of which it is the name, and statements which deny entity are usually statements to this effect. They are made about entities, such as verbal entities, of the kind which are commonly used as names, and which therefore beget an expectation of something named; the judgment "nothing" annuls this expectation.

The terms 'real' and 'existent' refer to specific modes of being. It is because of the questions "Is it real?" "Does it exist?" that it is necessary to provide for an "it" which is other than reality or existence: a being which is unquestionable, when its reality and existence are questioned.

It is impossible to allude to entities without introducing them into the context of discourse. It is not to be inferred, however, that they are therefore terms of discourse by definition. To point them out it is necessary to use the means of pointing out. This necessity, however, attaches to the pointing out, and not to *that which* is pointed out. The *alluding* is no more a constituent of what is alluded *to* than the signpost or index finger is a constituent of that to which it points. While this *caveat* will be more fully discussed below it must be introduced at this point because certain kinds of being are distinguishable only by their relation to mental operations.

Thus the questionable *reality* of a being may refer to its independence of subjective acts. The "real" is here opposed to the construct or fiction. The fictitious may be created by intent, as the characters and action of a drama or novel are created by the writer; or it may be an unintended reproduction of antecedent perceptions, as in the case of dreams. In either case the entity in question is dependent on the act of apprehension; it would not have been but for that — it is "make-believe," an object "made up," or "dreamed up." The fictitious in this sense is to be distinguished from whatever is not so produced. This distinction applies to knowledge when the mind-constructed hypothesis is distinguished from the state of affairs by which it is proved true or erroneous. Knowledge is true when things are, independently of the expectation, what they are expected to be.

The object of interest is "realized" when as an indirect consequence of being expected, it *becomes* real. It is not made real by the expectation of it, but by the action which the expectation mediates. Dreams do not "come true" of themselves, by virtue of being merely dreamed; but they may come true when the dream becomes a goal of effort. And when an object of interest is thus realized, it is then independent of subsequent cognitions.

The notion of the real as the self-sufficient also derives from independence. The real is that which is *in itself,* and which when known can therefore be truly known independently of the knowledge of any other being. Its opposite is "appearance," not in the sense of the illusory, hallucinatory, erroneous, or problematic, but in the sense of the partially or inadequately known. It is in this sense that the organic whole is held to be more real than its parts, or society than the individual; and is one of the meanings of the reality of a substance, as distinguished from its shadow, or from its modes or attributes. It is this idea in its extreme form which has generated the monistic doctrine that because all beings are interdependent and interpenetrating the only being which can "stand alone," and be truly known, is a one great being composed of all beings.

There is also a use of the term 'real' in which it refers to the essence rather than the accident. Unless, however, the distinction between essence and accident is construed as merely "nominal," the essence of a thing being whatever it is convenient for any purpose to single out and emphasize, essence is the same as the self-sufficient or independent. When it is said that a man is "really," that is "essentially," a rational animal this means that rationality is the key to the understanding of man: he who knows his rationality knows all.

The term 'fact' is often used to mean the same thing as 'true,' as when one says "it is a fact that," meaning it "is true that." Or, this term may be used to mean the same thing as independent reality, as when one refers to "brute facts" and counsels a "respect for facts." Or 'fact' is sometimes a synonym for 'existence,' or for 'a complex of existences.'

There remains, then, the notion of *existence*. There is, in the first place, a logical meaning of existence. Members of a class, or values of variables, or terms that stand in a relation, whichever the form of logic one prefers, exist; or the classes, variables, and relations are said to exist by virtue of having members, values, relations. When one asks whether there is "such a thing," or whether there is "anything of the kind," one is raising the question of existence in this logical sense. Thus, numbers are said to exist, inasmuch as the class of numbers has members; and zero exists by virtue of being a member of this class.

Logical existence is not to be confused with the realization of an object of interest. The identification of these two notions is responsible for insinuating teleology where it does not belong. To say that nature "embodies" ideas, that is, provides them with instances, is not the same as to say that these ideas are plans which some creative will has executed. There may never have been any such will: the ideas may never have had the status of problematic objects; because nature consists of particulars of generals it does not follow that the particulars were "created" by a mind which adopted universals as its patterns.

There is a second meaning of 'existence,' which is more restricted but more important than logical existence. Whereas logical existence signifies membership in *any* class, existence in this more restricted sense signifies membership in a specific class, the class, namely, of participants in the space-time-causal nexus which is identified, though not defined, by human agency. The existent, in this sense, is the "actual" world; the world in which things "happen," or "take place"; the world in which man "lives and moves and has his being." Hamlet's "to be or not to be" signifies "to exist or not to exist," in the sense of a prolongation of his space-time life. While the existent realm is that *in* which man actively lives, it is not necessary that it should be lived in, in order to be existent. The existential axes of reference intersect the human agent's field of operation, and can be so indicated; but they extend beyond him, and beyond his horizon.

When 'existence' is thus defined, there is an option as to whether the several characteristics of an existent shall or shall not themselves be regarded as existent. A red rose, for example, exists by virtue of the fact that it occupies a place at a time in the garden, is sprung from planted seed, and goes to seed; the red does not exist in itself, but derives existence from its being a character of this particular rose, or a part of the existing purpose of the gardener.

Although the term 'existence' will hereinafter ordinarily be employed in the space-time-causal sense, the expressions 'physical,' 'natural,' or 'cosmological existence,' or, better still, 'causal existence,' may be used to avoid confusion with 'logical existence.'

Existence is sometimes identified with particularity. Existents, as here construed, are particulars; but not any particulars. There are no absolute particulars, but only particulars of some general. Particulars of the space-time-causal nexus are so "importantly" particular because of their relation to action, that they tend to be taken as the particulars, *par excellence;* as individuals of the human species tend to be thought of as individuals in a preëminent sense.

Other familiar notions of existence fall into line. "This" or "that" is existent: yes, but because these words refer to a here-now, or a there-then, indicated by the temporal-spatial orientation of the user of the words. Sensation is taken as evidence of existence: yes, because in sensation the thing sensed acts causally on the subject — which is most palpably the case with tactual and muscular sensation. And when it is held that one knows one's own existence best (however ignorant one may be of precisely what it is that exists), this is because one is here most immediately aware of action: that is, both of causing and of being caused.

The tense of the verb 'to be' creates an illuminating ambiguity. The present tense of this verb, has a double use. When one says "Churchill is Prime Minister" one means *now,* at the time of the utterance, and refers to causal existence; but when one says that "Churchill is a Prime Minister," or that "roses are red," there is no reference whatsoever to time, but only to membership in a class, and therefore to logical existence.

2

Classification of the meanings of being, reality, and existence paves the way to a résumé of the general philosophical position already fore-shadowed in earlier chapters; namely, a union of "neutralism," "realism," "empiricism," "naturalism," "freedomism," "temporalism," and "pluralism."

Neutralism [2] is neutral between the opposing parties of mind and body when those two are aligned against one another. It refuses to take the side of one against the other, nor does it leave them merely distinct and opposed; it finds a common ground between them. As distinguished from the sheer dualism of mind and body, it may be described as the commingling, or overlapping doctrine. Thus qualities, such as colors, and structural characteristics, such as number, are not peculiarly mental or bodily, but may be either or both. The difference between mind and body is a difference in the organization of such neutrals.

David Hume made the seemingly casual admission that since "what we call *mind*" is nothing but a heap or collection of different perceptions, there is "no absurdity" in separating any particular perception from the rest; in which case, being divorced from the collection, it ceases to be mental. And similarly, he went on to say, there is nothing in the per-ceived object to prevent its being admitted to the collection, and thereby becoming mental.[3] In other words, there are elements which may enter and leave the mind without forfeiting their identity. When they leave the mental field, although they cease to be mental, they do not necessarily cease to be; and during the lapse of their mentality they may still persist in another field, such as the physical world.

Neutrals in themselves exist only in the logical sense. Thus it can be said of a neutral that it is a class having members, or a member of a class; but not that it belongs to the space-time-causal nexus. This is sometimes expressed by saying that neutrals "subsist"; but such a state-ment is questionable, since it almost inevitably suggests a quasi-existence

---

[2] Cf. the Author's "A Note on Neutralism," in *Structure, Method and Meaning,* P. Henle, etc., (ed.), 1951. For the part played by E. B. Holt and H. Sheffer in giving vogue to both the term and the idea, cf. this article. Cf. also the Author's "Peace without Victory — in Philosophy," *Journal of Philosophical Studies, 3* (1928).

[3] *Treatise on Human Nature,* Bk. I, Part IV, sect. ii. Credit for emphasizing the significance of this passage is due to W. P. Montague, "A Neglected Point in Hume's Philosophy," *Philosophical Review, 14* (1905).

in some exalted realm: exalted spatially to a kind of heaven above; exalted temporally to eternity; or exalted to a world which is governed by "spiritual," as distinguished from natural or historical, laws. Or to say that neutrals "subsist," suggests that subsistence is a specific kind of being, coördinate with existence. It is safer to say only that neutrals *are,* and rest content with that.

The most serious confusion which attends the doctrine of neutralism arises from the use of the word 'experience.' William James, who is the most influential sponsor of the doctrine of neutralism, has identified it with a philosophy of "pure experience," [4] and many neutralists have taken him at his *word.* The vogue of the word 'experience' creates one of the most dangerous pitfalls of modern philosophy. It is acceptable as a word with which to refer to all modes of consciousness, including thought and feeling as well as sensation and perception. The object experienced is then distinguished from its mental act or state of experiencing — the sound from the sensing, the thought from the thinking, the felt from the feeling. But even then it will not do to identify the neutrals with experience; for the neutral, while it can be sampled from what is experienced, may or may not be experienced.

Nor will it do to say that the neutral is that which *can* be experienced, for this implies the existence of appropriate faculties of experiencing. A "possibility of sensation," or "sensibilium," for example, requires a qualified sensory subject. The most that can be claimed for the neutral is that *so far as it is concerned,* it is capable of being experienced; or that if the appropriate mode of experiencing were present it would retain its antecedent identity in acquiring the new status of being experienced.

In accordance with this analysis, physical events may coincide, in greater or less degree, with that aspect of mind which is called its "content." This provides for the limiting case of "presentation," in which the same event occurs in both the mental and the physical realms. The mental is then a selection from the physical. In this way it is possible to distinguish mental from physical disappearance. Thus when the eyes are closed, or attention is directed elsewhere, the volcano's summit is excluded from the mental selection; but when the volcano erupts with sufficient violence its summit is destroyed, that is, excluded from the spatio-temporal-causal nexus.

The same analysis provides in principle for illusions, hallucinations, and erroneous perceptions. These are composed of neutrals which are "mistaken" for parts of the physical world; or which are "taken" for parts of the physical world as they stand, whereas they *are* parts of the physical world only by virtue of certain relations, such as the relation of the colored to the source of light, or of the hard to the

[4] Cf. his *Essays in Radical Empiricism,* 1912; especially the famous essay, entitled "Does 'Consciousness' Exist?"

body of the perceiver. When these relations are ignored they beget unwarranted spatio-temporal-causal expectations.

The mental, construed as a selection of neutrals, calls for further elucidation. It may mean no more than the relation of part and whole — a circumscribed area within a larger area. The circumscription may be due merely to the station and condition of the individual. Thus what will be embraced within the mind reflects its time and place, or sensory equipment and acuteness, or waking and sleeping, or intensity of stimulation. Or, on the other hand, the circumscription may be due to interest: the cognitive interest, or the aesthetic interest, or to any practical interest which determines the relevance or irrelevance of portions of the environment.

3

Realism is the thesis that what is truly known owes nothing to that fact except that fact itself. Thus if one truly perceives that the cat is on the chair, then the cat is "really" on the chair; the cat is on the chair independently of what, in the statement, precedes the word 'that.' The cat's *being on the chair* does not imply, presuppose, or depend upon, its *being so perceived.* If it is true that hydrogen is lighter than air, then hydrogen *is* lighter than air, regardless of the occurrence of the scientific discovery to that effect. As applied to the famous controversy over universals, it means that the universal "man," for example, does not depend upon being thought, but *is* otherwise, either as a simple entity, or as the generic characteristic of individual men.[5]

The direct approach to this topic is by way of analyzing the act of knowing. The verb 'to know' is a *non-causal transitive verb.* There are many such verbs, of which the essential meaning is that while they have objects they do not produce them. They take, but they do not make. To build a house is one thing, to buy a house "as is," is another thing. To know a house is like buying a house; it accepts it as it finds it. Such verbs may be said to denote static rather than dynamic relations. When a given physical entity, for example, "differs" from another, or approaches or leaves it, or lies in a certain direction from it, or fits it, the second entity, denoted by 'it,' is not caused or conditioned by the first entity. Such static relationships may *lead to* dynamic relationships but are not in themselves dynamic.

Mental acts *may* be causal. A fiction is by definition something fashioned, and the corresponding act (of inventing or imagining) is a causative act. Noticing, mentioning, selecting, and expecting, on the

[5] Realism in this sense does not imply that universals exist "by themselves"; as is supposed to be the doctrine of Plato. Cf. the illuminating article on "The Scholastic Realism of C. S. Peirce," by E. C. Moore, *Philosophy and Phenomenological Research,* 12 (1952).

other hand, are distinguished by their non-causative character. Discriminating is non-causative: there is a considerable difference between discriminating a man's head from his shoulders, and removing his head from his shoulders. The realistic thesis is that truly knowing is of the non-causative transitive variety: being similar to, indeed comprising, noticing, mentioning, discriminating, selecting, expecting.

Since this realistic view of the relation of knowing and known coincides with the prima facie character of the knowing act, and also with the common sense view of the matter, the burden of proof lies with the opposing doctrine, commonly named 'idealism.' Realism consists largely, therefore, in showing that idealism is not equal to this burden.

The alleged proofs of idealism consist in part of two closely related fallacies: "definition by initial predication," and "the argument from the ego-centric predicament." [6] The first of these fallacies consists in a confusion between ostensive and real definition. Because everything whatsoever can be first referred to, and thus identified by its place in cognition as that which is perceived, thought of, mentioned, or otherwise experienced, this relationship is taken to constitute its basic meaning; whereas it may be only one of innumerable accidental and trivial relationships. A teacher of modern languages may begin by saying that "a triangle is that the German name for which is '*Dreieck*'"; but this statement, though correct, generates no geometrical theorems.

The fallacious "argument from the ego-centric predicament" is to confuse the redundant statement that "everything which is known, is *known*" with the statement that "everything which *is*, is known"; or to infer the second statement from the first. The same redundancy appears in a more veiled form in such statements as "only the intelligible can be known," or "only possibilities of experience are capable of being experienced." The only significance which these redundancies have is to reveal a certain procedural embarrassment. To know whether things are or are not dependent on being known it is impossible to try the experiment of removing the knowledge. This is self-evident and troublesome, but it proves nothing as to the dependence of things on being known.

There are more serious arguments for idealism. The first of these consists in calling attention to the fact that knowledge, especially in its more advanced stages, involves the construction of hypotheses. Hypotheses *are* ideal — qua hypotheses they depend on the cognitive act; and since the thing known is what the verified hypothesis affirms it to be, it is argued that the thing known is also ideal. But this inference ignores the fact that when the hypothesis is verified it assumes another role. It is no longer "a mere hypothesis"; what is hypothetically affirmed is also real in the sense of being independent of its hypothetical affirmation.

An object which is constituted by a subjective act, such as a fictitious

[6] Cf. above, ch. xviii, § 2. Also *The New Realism,* by E. B. Holt and others, 1912.

object, may then be known by a second, non-causative, subjective act. Thus the object created by the dramatic imagination, such as Hamlet, once created, becomes independent of the Shakespearian critic's true knowledge. The fiction, so far as known, is known realistically; and the critic who creates a Hamlet of his own, is not knowing his Shakespeare truly. Similarly, a problematic hypothesis, once constructed, becomes an entity in its own right, and is independent of the knowledge of the historian of science, who may then construct hypotheses about *it*. There are hypotheses about the Copernican hypothesis, which are verified only when that hypothesis is, independently, what the historian affirms it to be.

Knowledge itself can be known, and insofar as it is known it is known after the manner of all knowledge. Idealism implies that since all things are dependent on the knowledge of them, it is necessary to know knowledge in order to know anything. Realism relieves knowledge of this necessity. This is fortunate because knowledge is one of the most difficult things to know: it is much easier, for example, to know what sweetness is, or that sweet is different from bitter, or even that the rose is sweet to smell, than to know what sense-perception is. The knowledge of knowledge comes late in the order of knowledge, and profits by the fact that there is more and more knowledge to know, and by the fact that the intent and meaning of knowledge become more and more clear, and therefore more knowable. Those who first set themselves the problem of knowledge, and postpone all other problems until this shall have been solved are likely to get no further, both because of the extreme difficulty of the problem, and for lack of any knowledge to know.

One of the major errors by which traditional philosophy has betrayed confiding mankind, is the error of supposing that subjectivity in all its aspects — self, consciousness, will, and all the various acts into which these are divisible — are so evident as to afford knowledge its securest foothold. Starting with the admissible fact that whenever anything is known there exists a knower which knows it, the doctrine proceeds to the questionable statement that every time one knows anything one knows oneself as knowing subject, and that, however well proved other knowledge may be, this knowledge is even more abundantly proved, or, indeed, needs no proof. It is by this route that the idealist arrives at a metaphysical "spiritualism," according to which the subject is the one substantial reality, to which, by its knowing them, all other alleged forms of reality are annexed.

That I exist, whoever be the "I" which makes the assertion, is not likely to be disputed, especially when the question is raised by "me." But there are many other statements of existence which are equally unlikely to be challenged. The lover, for example, is equally convinced that "she" exists; or any man by the statement that his grandfather existed, or that it is raining, or that his tooth aches. In other words, the criterion of ready acceptance or certitude gives no preëminent cognitive credit to self-existence.

One is, no doubt, familiar to oneself, but knowledge is not proportional to familiarity — quite the contrary; familiarity breeds ignorance, whether or not it breeds contempt. Similarly, one is, presumably, intimate with oneself, close to oneself. But proximity may or may not conduce to knowledge. Too close proximity may prevent knowledge; as one may fail to see the wood for the trees, so one may fail to see the "me" for its multiplicity of states. Most dubious of all is the argument that the optimum knowledge is that in which the knower and the known are identical! It is a strange thing that a doctrine which is on the face of it paradoxical, if not self-contradictory, should have achieved such high respectability among serious philosophers. If there is to be a knower *and* a known they must be at least numerically two. It is, of course, possible for one part of a whole to know another part, and the whole of which they are both parts may be a self: but then the self qua knower and the self qua known are *not* identical.

So much, then, for realism. That knowledge is contaminated with subjectivity is, of course, a fact. But the realist contends that the intent of knowledge is pledged to a self-denying ordinance. This does not mean that knowledge is passive, but that its activity — its effort and its elaborate and refined procedures — are directed to the end of objectivity.

4

Empiricism has two meanings. In the most general sense it is an application of the thesis of realism to the question of proof. It means that the being which is real or existent independently of knowledge itself provides the evidence which proves the knowledge to be true. In colloquial terms this means that if knowledge is to be true, it must "square with the facts."

This statement, however, oversimplifies the matter. If facts are to contribute evidence of truth they must be *evident,* that is, they must themselves be known; and there can be no knowledge that may not prove to be erroneous. Thus when science is verified by a "pointer-reading," the pointer must be read; when observations verified Einstein's calculations there was something observed; but what is read can be misread and observations may be mistaken. The empirical thesis must be amended, therefore to state that knowledge is proved true *in proportion as* its object coincides with that to which it looks for its verification. Knowledge always retains some degree, however small, of contingency. All the refinements of technique by which knowledge is improved — the procedures of experiment and confirmation — are designed to reach a point of minimum difference between fallible expectation and the occurrence of that which is expected.

'Empiricism' is sometimes construed in a second, and more restricted, sense to mean that only sensible knowledge is true. But this is a special case, namely, the case of true knowledge of existence. When 'existence' is construed in the causal sense, and 'evidence' is construed in terms of the close approach of the expectation to the occurrence which fulfills or surprises it, then sensation assumes its peculiar authority. For sensation is not merely a disclosure of quality, but of causality: it is an impact from without; an event which thrusts itself upon the mind, as the thunder bursts upon the ear, uninvited and intrusive. In true knowledge of the physical or natural world sensation speaks with final authority.

But logical and mathematical knowledge, while it is not proved by sensation, is nevertheless proved by confrontation with being. Terms such as 'observation,' 'presentation,' 'witnessing,' and 'seeing' suggest sensation. To provide for conceptual knowledge these terms may be used in a figurative sense, as when one speaks of "the mind's eye," or one may introduce another, and less sensuously contaminated, word such as 'inspection.' Whatever the vocabulary employed, the final word in conceptual knowledge is pronounced by a meaning, a relationship, an implication, a contradictoriness, which speaks for itself. Its thrust is less violent than that of sensation — in fact it is not a thrust at all in the causal sense; but it nevertheless has its own kind of stubbornness and requires submission like any other evidence.

The causal existence of six planets, or of a spheroidal earth, is established only by the testimony of sense. The testimony of sense is decisive because it is at that point that the causal chain itself enters into the mind — or stands on its threshold. But when a theory of the space-time-causal nexus is proved true it is true in a double sense: it is sensibly true, and it is logically and mathematically true. While only the first of these truths is empirical in the narrower or sensible meaning of the term, they are both empirical in the broader meaning. The theory as a whole is true because things are, evidently, as the theory describes them.

This equating of the physical or natural world with the true knowledge of it when that knowledge is perfected is inescapable. The statement about knowledge and the statement about being are two sides of the same statement. Things are truly known for what they are, and they are what they are truly known to be. To stop halfway and suppose that sense alone reveals the nature of things, while thought is a subjective addition contrived for human and practical purposes, is equivalent to saying that the better a man knows the more does his knowledge diverge from the order of nature and history.

5

The philosophical position here summarized would no doubt be labeled 'naturalism,' and this label is acceptable on the condition that its meaning be defined. The fact is that the term 'nature' has at the present time no precise meaning authorized by etymology or by usage.[7] Even the meaning of 'physical nature' has lost its sharpness of outline since the obsolescence of the traditional dualisms.

Naturalism has in the past been held objectionable on the ground that it disparages the conscious will together with its ideals; mentalism on the ground that it ignores, or fails to do justice to, the world of matter, force, energy, and mechanical causation. When these antitheses, negations, and recriminations are abandoned, and the conceptions of emergence, continuity, and neutralism are introduced in their place, there remains a revised naturalism which is definable by the following statements: (1) the knowledge designated as 'physical science' (physics, chemistry, biology, etc.) is true, and is more true than any other knowledge, of its own subject matter; (2) mind, together with its states and activities, exists in the same sense, and belongs to the same spatio-temporal-causal nexus, as the events known by the physical sciences; (3) physical nature embraces the objects of perception; (4) physical nature embraces the ideal objects of conceptual thought. While these statements are more or less overlapping they may for purposes of exposition be divided and expanded in turn.

(1) Naturalism is distinguished among philosophies by its respect for the natural sciences. It accepts their conclusions as they stand in their latest emendation by science itself. The conclusions of natural science are not to be treated as second-class truths, dealing with merely "secondary" causes; they are not to be transformed into truths of a transcendent or supernatural order. Any conspectus of knowledge of the world in which man lives will incorporate them. Whether or not they are final, or require correction, is left to the scientist himself. Naturalism offers no escape from the truths of natural science, however unpalatable they may be. Insofar as it assigns limits to present scientific knowledge, and thus provides an area of ignorance where faith may enter, it is the same ignorance as that which science itself acknowledges.

(2) Man with all his higher faculties has emerged within that same spatio-temporal-causal manifold which once embraced only inorganic events, which now embraces only inorganic events in vast outlying regions, and which might conceivably at some time in the future cease to contain any but inorganic events. What is true of life is also true of

[7] The most illuminating treatment of the subject, in the light of recent science, and broadly in agreement with the view here presented, is contained in R. G. Collingwood, *The Idea of Nature*, 1945.

the human history which has emerged from life. The Scriptural reminder that man, having sprung from dust, returns to dust again, is usually taken as a counsel of despair, but this is to forget "how nigh is grandeur to our dust." That man should have sprung from dust speaks well for dust, at least from the human point of view. What has sprung from dust may spring again, and that man has sprung from dust is a more solid fact than that he will some day be only dust.

Man's emergence from an inorganic world argues his capacity to act upon that world; it places man and his physical environment in a relation of effective intercourse. That which emerges can act upon, modify, and even create, things of the same type as that from which it emerges. It is a commonplace, one of those commonplaces which become marvelous "when one stops to think about it," that through his body man's mind can deal with his inorganic environment, and can create inorganic artifacts.

Those who would prefer to think that man is a disembodied spirit forget that if he were he would be no more than a specter impotently haunting the natural scene, or at best observing a play in which he took no part. One cannot have it both ways: one cannot both be incorporeal and act corporeally. The possibility of succumbing to inorganic forces is the price that man pays for his capacity to wield inorganic forces.

(3) Perceptual objects are parts of nature; indeed nature may be said to be a system of percepts, if by a 'percept' is meant what is perceived. This view is opposed to the view, held by some philosophers, that percepts are not constituents of physical nature but its mental effects.[8]

That in perception the external physical world acts upon the mind through the channel of the sensory and neural apparatus is not to be denied. But neither, on the other hand, is it to be denied that the physical world is the mind's object. Starting with the physical world one can trace a causal chain to the sensory stimulus, and through afferent nerves to a cerebral center, where it assumes the form of sense perception. Starting, on the other hand, with sense perception, one can trace a train of thought which leads from meanings to judgment, and to the verification of that very theory of physical nature which describes the first process.

Neither of these accounts of perception will stand by itself. No psycho-physiologist has ever explained how a terminal nerve impulse suddenly blossoms, like a Japanese water flower, into the pageantry of qualities and shapes which constitutes the content of sense perception —

[8] The most formidable contemporary exponent of this "causal theory of perception" is Bertrand Russell; cf. his *Human Knowledge*, 1948, ch. iv. A good antidote to the causal theory is Bergson's *Matière et Mémoire*, 1906, English trans. *Matter and Memory*, 1911.

to say nothing of the ensuing elaborations of thought. No philosophical exponent of the causal theory has ever explained why one rather than another of the antecedent causes of the mental state should assume the role of its object. And when all that perception and thought embrace is assigned to the end effect, the causes are so impoverished as to explain nothing. The physical world becomes a "one-knows-not-what" which operates as a cause "one-knows-not-how."

This agnostic outcome, which is sometimes considered to be the last word of science, is, as a matter of fact, belied by science. For science looks to perception for its verification. Science says, in effect, that we know the physical world by perceptions; it is evident perceptually; in perception it is made manifest. To form a true and adequate idea of it, science teaches one to accept actual perceptual content as far as it goes, and to supplement it by analogy and extrapolation. To know physical nature is to exceed the presented by the represented; where the represented is the perceptual more or less remotely expected — infinitely varied and multiplied, but of the same texture as the perceived.

The reverse account, according to which the external world is spun by the mind out of itself, is equally unsatisfactory because it fails to provide for the outwardness of physical nature. The mind, having annexed to itself all thought and percepts, is imprisoned within its own subjectivity, and is compelled to take its surrounding environment on faith. Nature having been placed within the mind, it is impossible to assign the mind a place within nature.

There is no escape from this dilemma except to conceive of sense perception as selective response. The progression of the afferent nerve impulse does not end at the center, but returns in the direction of its origin. This second segment of its course is not confined to the innervation of muscles controlling the posture of attention or culminating in overt behavior, but embraces attitudes, meanings, interpretations — in short, expectations — oriented toward the stimulus, which then becomes the sensory nucleus of its object.

Thus when the ear is assailed by a stimulus from a certain quarter the organism listens toward the stimulating source, and acts, or prepares to act, both upon that source, and upon its context. When so reacted *toward* and *upon* the stimulus is converted into the object; one hears the sound *there*, and perceives it as a *bell* having further visual, tactual, and causal characteristics. The perceptual object embraces what is expected of the sensory object; it is that part of the total surrounding field to which the organism alerts itself.

(4) Nature as causal existence embraces ideal objects. If this were not so it would not be possible to affirm that nature is as it is represented in the finished product of scientific inquiry. As science advances, that is, more nearly fulfills the requirements of knowledge, it describes

in terms of concepts and systems of concepts. If the logical and mathe-matical structures of knowledge are to be true of nature they must be abstracted from nature, and verified by nature; if so, they must be *in* nature.

One reads in a textbook of physics that no force, however great, can stretch a cord, however fine, into a line which shall be absolutely straight. How, then, can it be said that nature is linear? There is only one solution of this apparent difficulty, which is to suppose that nature is linear or otherwise geometrical, as a limit of approximation. Similarly, the laws which natural science discovers reign in the realm of nature, and not in the realm of natural science. The law of gravitation, for example, governs bodies and not the minds of physicists. As conceived by the scientist it is exact; as resident in nature it is that exactness which is most nearly approached. The "not quite" of nature can be described as it is only in terms of the "quite."

Nature also embraces ideal ends or purposes. As goals pursued, and represented to the agent in advance of their realization, they are parts of the spatio-temporal-causal nexus because interests exist there, and because it is impossible to state what an interest is without including its problematic object. The natural interest has its ideal object as truly as — together with other natural existents — it has its logical and mathe-matical form.

6

In discussing the topic of freedom in connection with the cultural institutions and sciences it was not necessary to go to the root of the mat-ter. One was concerned with the relation of freedom to ideals and to social controls, and not with the metaphysical question of the existence of freedom.

The answer to this fundamental question is largely predetermined by the metaphysical doctrines already affirmed. Thus realism excludes the doctrine that man is free from natural causation because he creates the laws of nature and is therefore above them. Realism implies that the necessities and determinations of nature, whatever they be, obtain in-dependently of the human, or any other, knowing mind. Naturalism places man in the stream of spatio-temporal-causal events, and assigns him no habitation in a higher realm where he is free from the causes which operate in the world of physical science: in short, whatever free-dom a man may or may not enjoy is the freedom of the natural man.

Empiricism as applied to the question of freedom, means that whether there is or is not freedom is a question of fact, to be settled by observa-tion; and not a presupposition, a postulate, or necessity derived from an analysis of the moral consciousness. Whether man is or is not free, and in what sense, undoubtedly affects what can be truly said of man as a moral agent, and bears on the meaning of moral concepts such as duty and responsibility; the empiricist, however, does not deduce freedom from morality, but adjusts his conceptions of duty and responsibility to what he finds out about freedom.

In accordance with the view, already adopted, which identifies freedom with choice, the general question is divisible into two questions: "Is human choice a cause?" and "Is human choice an effect?"

In the sense of the first question, 'freedom' means that men actually choose, think as they choose, and do what they choose. While human choice is never a sufficient cause of subsequent events in the world of nature and history, it is often a necessary condition. Certain events would not have occurred but for human choosing, or will not occur unless they are chosen. Of this there can be no more doubt than attends any empirical observation. It would never have been denied save on some dogmatic grounds.

Freedom in this sense is evidence against any doctrine which denies the efficacy of human choice. Thus what philosophers call "epiphenomenalism" holds that the line of causation passes through the human body and by-passes the will, leaving it impotently fanning the air. Mechanists of the extreme school conceive causation exclusively in the terms of physics and chemistry. Animalism and primitivism in psychology and the cultural sciences limit causation to certain lower levels of interest, such as instincts or appetites, and deny it to man's so-called "higher processes" of reflective choice. The doctrine of "historical dialectic" introduces a force *sui generis*, which presides over human destiny regardless of personal choice. Finally, freedom conceived as effective human choice is evidence against all those forms of monism which limit the causation of the will to super-personal wills, such as a will of society, or of the state, or of a god, or of a metaphysical absolute, and conceive the individual will as merely executing it or riding on its back.

The affirmation of freedom in the sense of effective personal choice has far-reaching implications. It does not exclude recognition of the narrow limits of the power of the human will: its impotence to prevent or bring about the storm or earthquake, or the procession of the equinoxes; or the impotence of the single human will either to prevent or to bring about events which require a concord of many human agents. But it does imply that the human will has points of entry into the causal chain, and that it is possible to enlarge its influence. It implies that whatever influences (such as science, education, and persuasion) create, modify, or spread human knowledge, can modify the course of events through the choices which the knowledge mediates. Through knowledge men can capture and harness the forces of nature and use them to work upon nature. The very magnitude of physical forces, such as, for example, atomic energy, then works for, and not against, human control. While the power of human choice remains small, and often seems negligible, it is true, nevertheless, that it has no assignable limits of possibility.

The second question concerning freedom has to do with the causes of human choice. Are men's choices predetermined by external or antecedent conditions which are not chosen? Are there human choices which spring from nothing beyond themselves — bolts from the blue, spontaneously generated, and therefore unpredictable? Is it true to say that when a certain choice occurs some other choice might have occurred under precisely the same circumstances?

Before attempting to answer this question it is well to recognize what would be implied by an affirmative answer. It is scarcely conceivable that choice could be effective without being itself an effect. If it interlocks with the causal chain at all, it would seem to be in a position to receive influences as well as to impart them. Furthermore, if choice were undetermined then it would not be possible for one man to influence the choices of another, since will works upon will through physical intermediaries such as speech, records, and bodily action. "Fatalism" is begotten by one or both of two beliefs: the belief that what one chooses makes no difference; and the belief that things *happen by chance*. Fatalism as a sense of helplessness or an attitude of apathy and despair, does not result from the discovery of law and order in nature, but from their seeming absence. It is the assumed lawlessness and disorder in things that lead one to say, "There is nothing to be done about it; what will happen will happen; one can only await the blows of fortune." It is to be noted that the advances of science have led to a decline, and not to a rise, of fatalism.

Whatever be its practical or emotional implications, the best verified empirical generalization as of today is that man lives in a world in which there are strains of determinism, and strains of indeterminism — areas of predictability and areas of unpredictability. There is no self-evident principle by which to settle the question in advance. To state that every event must have a cause is to state a dogma. The only conclusive proof that an event has a cause is to find the cause; wherever events appear to occur in the absence of causes, the indeterministic hypothesis remains open.

The unpredictability of human conduct is notorious, and its unpredictability is proportional to the extent to which men choose. The cultural sciences, employing the explanatory method, have not eliminated the unpredictability of the behavior of an individual who makes up his mind for himself. They tend to look for statistical laws, analogous to the physical law of the diffusion of gases; and there is nothing to forbid the conjecture that there may be molecular spheres of individual choice which, like the chemical molecules, pursue "random" courses of their own.

Modern science also supports the idea of emergence, that new structures appear in the course of nature which behave in a manner that could not have been predicted in advance of its occurrence and is not implied by the parts. The choosing person may be such an emergent structure or a series of such structures each of which is a new thing in the world and a new beginning.

There is, therefore, no reason to suppose any regrettable lack of indetermination, unpredictability, and novelty; and their admixture with determination, predictability, and sameness would seem to suit and to describe that balance of the rational and the irrational, of the planned and the unplanned, of the controlled and the uncontrolled, which is characteristic of man's pursuit of his interests and ideals.

7

The metaphysical position here adopted may be described as "temporalistic" and "pluralistic." It is temporalistic because over and above logical existence, it admits no existence save that "causal existence," that stream of events, in which each occupies a particular time, and occurs before, after, or at the same time with, the rest. "Eternal" or non-temporal entities enter this stream only vicariously, through the events of which they constitute the conceptual part, or through becoming the ideal objects of interests which exist in time. They possess no peculiar dignity or eminence, no degree of value, no value of any sort, save what they may derive from the temporal interests which are directed upon them. They are not to be confused with "enduring" entities which, if they are to persist throughout time, must exist *in* time.

There are as many varieties of pluralism as there are of monism, its opposite. Its oldest form is the monism of *substance*, this being taken to mean a universal stuff or material. Monism of this kind began with familiar substances such as air, water, and fire. It was succeeded by monisms of matter, force, energy, and, most recently, electricity. Anti-naturalistic philosophers have counterattacked with the claim that there is a universal mental substance — will, mind, spirit, soul, psyche, or thought; some one of these being selected to do the work of all the rest, and to provide the inner core of the physical world as well.

Monisms of substance, physical and mental alike, have declined with the decline of the idea of substance itself. A stuff common to all existence has to be so stripped of qualities of its own that eventually it has none, and, having lingered for a time as an indeterminate "something," eventually vanishes altogether. The common substance becomes equal first to x, and then to zero.

Monisms of *cause* have been based on the notion of cause as an impulse, communicated from next to next through a train of subsequent notions. The notion of a first physical event from which all natural and historical events have followed by a sort of chain reaction fails for lack of evidence. No such first event has been discovered, and owing to the infinity of past time, it is difficult to see how it ever can be discovered. To prove it to be first it would be necessary to prove the negative thesis that no natural events preceded it, as well as the positive thesis that all subsequent events can be derived, directly or indirectly, from it. Non-naturalistic philosophies have introduced a god as first cause, and have encountered similar difficulties. It is a sound instinct which has prompted the child to ask "Who made God?" since the very principle of antecedent causation which leads back to a god implies something still further back.

The monisms of substance and cause have been superseded by the monisms of *system* and *purpose*. The monism of system consists in the assertion that there is one all-governing order, or law; a set of propositions by which all events are implied, or from which they can be deduced as necessary, and in terms of which they require to be explained if they are to be truly explained.

It has been argued that there *must* be such a total system, because all things are related; so that it is impossible to explain anything save in terms of its relations to everything else. This argument rests on the doctrine that all relations are "internal" to their terms, and that therefore nothing can be, or be what is is, in the absence of any of its relations. But it is to be noted that the only relations which are known to obtain between all things are the relations implied by plurality. If one is to speak of a multiplicity of things at all it must be conceded that they are all related to one another by such relations as "and," co-being, number, and difference. But these are the very relations which are not internal to their terms — relations which leave the terms otherwise unaffected.

It is true that causal existences will have causal relations to one another. This implies that they are all temporally and spatially interrelated. But temporal and spatial relations alone do not imply causal relations; and terms which are causally related to some other terms need not be causally related to all other terms.

Thus the question of "the one and the many" becomes an empirical question; and the answer, based on the as-yet-unascertained facts, is that there is both unity and plurality, and that it is futile to assert one to the exclusion of the other. Science and philosophy look for unity no doubt, but there is no justification for asserting more unity than is found; and there is always a residual plurality. There are laws in nature, but there are many laws, and there is also lawlessness. There are different keys which unlock different doors, but there is no master key.

Since there is no knowledge of everything, and since there is knowledge nonetheless, it must be possible to know things piecemeal. The plurality of independent truths is as well-established a fact as any other fact. Indeed, it is as important for the advancement of science to know things separately as to know them together. The controlled experiment which exact science seeks to employ depends on the possibility of repeating the experiment; which implies the isolation of limited sets of conditions from their varying contexts. And if there is a plurality of independent truths there is a plurality of things known, and of things to be known.

As to the monism of *purpose*, no such purpose has ever been verified. The poet who says "I doubt not through the ages one increasing purpose runs" expresses his own absence of doubt, but he does not state the purpose, or provide evidence which will satisfy those who do doubt. No such all-embracing purpose has ever been affirmed save on a priori grounds, or on grounds of dogma or faith. Empirically speaking, there *are* purposes, and purposes *can* be adopted and realized; but, empirically speaking, there are many purposes, and a sufficient amount of purposelessness to warrant the utterances of the less optimistic poets.

8

In terms of a neutralistic, realistic, empiricistic, naturalistic, freedomistic, temporalistic, pluralistic metaphysics what shall be said of the relation of being and value? There are two major questions: Are reality and existence valuable? Is value real and existent?

The answer to the first of these questions is clear. Reality and existence *per se* do not imply goodness or badness. Realities and existences may be good, bad, or indifferent. When they are good or bad it is not because of their bare reality or existence, but because they are objects of interest, or are qualified to be objects of interest.

No one has argued that whatever is is bad, but the thesis that "whatever is is good" has been argued on several grounds. It has been contended that since all things are created by a benevolent deity, they must be good — otherwise they would not have been created. But the doctrine of benevolent creation requires for its empirical proof the very thesis which is here in question — namely, that all existent things are good. A more formidable argument is based on the idealistic contention that all being is the product of a knowing mind, which, in turn, is governed by interest. Things are thought into reality or existence and, since thinking is a kind of interested activity or is ruled by interested activity, things must therefore owe their reality or existence to their appeal to interest, that is, to their goodness. This argument in all its forms is refuted by realism.

There remains one, and only one, sense in which all things may be said to be good. All things are potentially good-to-know, good relatively to an insatiable curiosity. It is not possible, humanly speaking, to know everything, but there are no doubt inquiring minds bent on obtaining true beliefs concerning no matter what; beliefs whose truth is verifiable by anything. Everything is "food for thought." It is not to be inferred, however, that what is food for thought is food for any other appetite, or is good in any other than the cognitive sense. The cognitive interest embraces the desire to "know the worst" — the bad as well as the good, and the indifferent as well as the good or bad. Furthermore, cognitive goodness is relative to the cognitive interest and is a comparatively late arrival in the world. There were no cognitive goods or evils during those immense stretches of time which preceded the emergence of the intellectually curious man.

If it be conceded that neither reality nor existence gives value to an object which otherwise is valueless, there still remains the question whether they may augment the value of an object which already possesses value? As has already been pointed out, the problematic object of a given interest is not better when it is realized; indeed its realization marks the point at which *that* interest is terminated, and ceases, therefore, to confer value on its object. But the realized object may, and usually does, then become the object of a new interest — a prolonging or enjoying interest. It is clear, also, that instrumental values, potential and actual, derive value from existence: potential instrumental value from causal relations that obtain in nature; actual instrumental value from mediating judgments of causal relations, which serve their dependent interests better when they are true than when they are erroneous.

The second of the two questions concerning the relation of value and being is the reverse of the first. Does value imply being? In the fundamental sense of the term 'being' the answer is self-evident. That which is good or bad is; and its goodness or badness is. Value is also real, in the sense of being independent of the judgment which affirms or denies it. In other words, values are not made good and bad by thinking them so. Both interest and its object may be fictitious. The fictitious object of a fictitious interest has value, namely, fictitious value. But fictitious values are real in the sense of being independent of judgments about them. The fictitious objects of Hamlet's fictitious hopes and fears are good and bad independently of the reader of Shakespeare.

Values have existence in the logical sense of that term — they are members of classes, values of variables, or terms of relations. The question of their causal existence is less simple and the answer is less trivial. Generally speaking, the existential status of the value follows the existential status of the interest which confers the value. When the interest is causally existent, the value of its object is causally existent. It is to be noted that negative interests have the same title to existence as positive interests (a negative interest is not the same as a non-existent interest) and that evil is existent in the same sense as good.

The crucial point is that there are causally existent human interests, which emerge within a certain phase of the advancing complexity of life and mind. When they do emerge they interact with their non-mental and inorganic environment, as well as with other interests. This is true of interests on every level, of the higher flights of creative thought and imagination as well as of the reflexes, appetites, or basic drives. Even the non-preëmptive interests of cognition and aesthetic contemplation, although they do not act causally on their objects, nevertheless interact within the organism, and tend to become practical interests. Ivory towers have their two-way passages on the ground floor which open upon the street. Man with his interests is not an exile from another home-country, a visitor with a limited visa, an unnaturalized resident from abroad; he is a native of this world, a citizen by birth. The only "other world" in which he lives or can live is an extension of this world. What his interests move him to do here, is of consequence in the business of the cosmos.

As has been frequently pointed out, the object of interest abstracted from the interest may or may not exist. Interest may take the form of prolonging the existence of that which exists; or it may take the form of realizing the existence of that which does not exist. In the latter case the object is good when it does not as yet exist. But interest may also take the form of interrupting or preventing existence; in which case the object is bad when it exists. These considerations cut the ground from under the famous "ontological argument," which correlates existence with goodness. The object of a positive interest may be said to be "fit to exist," and the object of a negative interest "fit not to exist," if these statements are taken to mean that there are interests which tend to their existence or non-existence.

The rejection of every generalization which equates the real or existent with the good leaves room for the empirical fact that some things *do* owe their reality or existence to their goodness. Interest tends to the realization of its objects, and this realization may, and often does, take the form of bringing possibilities into existence. The realized objects of interest then take their places in the space-time-causal nexus along with the products of inorganic, non-mental, and non-human causes, and have their own future consequences. The products of man's interested activities then become part of the existential environment of his subsequent interests. To some extent man lives within a world of his own making, and in proportion as his interests assume the form of choice he lives freely among the creations of his own freedom.

9

Man, together with his interests and the values which these generate, is immersed in a natural order. There is a partial agreement between man and this natural order; and if this were not so man himself would not and could not have existed and survived. Having purchased existence by accepting nature on its own terms, man is able in some measure to dictate terms to nature. These are the two sides of man, who is both creature and creator.

The power of man to shape his cosmic destiny is pitifully small, but in principle it is unlimited. For in proportion as man knows what the limits are, and what are their causes the way is open to remove them, by indirection, by organization, and by playing one natural force against another. Man can now move mountains, having found the necessary lever and fulcrum. It is not impossible that he should someday learn to abolish death itself. It does not follow that he will do so, or is likely to do so. The issue remains in doubt, and man's personal choices, together with man himself, *may* go down to defeat and to final extinction. An empirical and naturalistic philosophy justifies no more than an attitude of disciplined hopefulness.

It is proper to speak of "mother nature," if one means that man is sprung from the space-time-causal nexus which surrounds him on all sides, before and after and to all points of the compass, and which penetrates him to the core. It is appropriate to be grateful to this natural order for the extent to which it answers to his interests: because it supplies his needs; because it has implanted sympathy and love (as well as hatred and brutality) in his breast; because it in its orderliness is suited to his cognitive faculties; because in its beauties it provides objects of his aesthetic interest.

It is improper and unwarranted, however, to suppose that the goods which nature has provided owe their reality and existence to their agreement with human interests. Nature lends itself unwittingly to the human life which it has generated. Having begotten man, nature permits his continued existence and his extravagant hopes. It would be presumptuous and foolish to assume that there is a kindly indulgence at the seat of cosmic control: presumptuous because unsupported by evidence; foolish because it would weaken man's reliance on himself. Human life appears to have survived a series of hairbreadth escapes, to enjoy a slender margin of tolerance, and to have achieved a precarious footing for the future. Indeed when one considers the vast complex of conditions, celestial and terrestrial, which have combined to make it possible, human life seems so improbable as to be incredible — but for the fact that *here we are.*

Such considerations beget doubt, and rightly so. On the other hand, they may lead to the hopeful question, "If so far, why not further?" If the cosmic order is not pledged to good, neither is it pledged to evil. Existence is consistent with good. There is always room for hope, however small the room may be. And hope is itself a hopeful sign, because hope is not a mere wishing or prediction, but a cause by which things hoped for are sometimes realized.

CHAPTER XXIII

RELIGION AND PHILOSOPHY OF RELIGION

There are many religions, and there are religions of high and low degree; but there is also religion in general, which springs from the situation in which all men and societies alike find themselves. If all historic or "positive" religions were to be eradicated and man were to begin over again, facing life freshly without any religious cult, tradition, or institution, there are motives which would prompt him to acquire religion. Defined in this generic and universal sense, religion is man's *deepest solicitude,* his concern for the fate of that which he accounts most valuable. However primitive or advanced their outlook, men will always prize something above all other things; will recognize environing forces on which their fortunes ultimately depend; and will put this prizing and this recognition together in a more or less hopeful belief.

In the early phases of his development man felt himself beset on every side by overpowering and inscrutable powers. Modern man boasts of his enlarged and ever enlarging area of control. But the widening circle of what man can do for himself is at the same time a widening of his circle of helplessness. Having pushed out in so many directions there are so many more advanced stations from which he gazes beyond into regions yet untrod. The more man conquers the more there is to conquer. However full his life a man still faces approaching death as the edge of an abyss; however elaborate the structure of his civilization, man remains sensible of its precariousness.

This sense of limited power is not, like the scientists' predictions, attended with indifference. Man has interests at stake, and he is concerned in their behalf. He may be concerned with bare survival, or with some cause to which he has given his allegiance, but he is *concerned.* He sees the environing powers in their relation to that on which he has set his heart. This is his religion.

It might seem simpler to say that religion is man's reckoning with "God." But the word 'God' is not the name of an individual, such as Napoleon, Washington, or Jesus whose identity is accepted by general consent. The use of the initial capital begs several questions. It implies that the object of worship is personal and unique, and therefore entitled to a proper name. It implies a worshipful attitude on the part of the user of the word, and therefore the acceptance of *his* religious belief. That being to which the adherents of one cult will refer to simply as "God," will to the adherents of another cult be no "God" at all. When orthodox Christians refer to God they mean *their* God — a personal and benevolent creator, the history of whose dealings with men are set down in the Bible, and whose attributes and purpose are formulated in dogmas defined and taught by Christian churches. It is evident that religion in general cannot be defined as worship of "God" so conceived, for then primitive tribal religions, Egyptian, Greek, Indian, Chinese, and Arabic religions, would not be religions at all. The only small letter god common to all objects of worship or possible worship is the ultimate cosmic power or powers on which man conceives himself to depend for the promotion of that to which he attaches supreme value.

Religion in this universal sense will then include cults which, judged by Christian standards, are atheistic. Thus communism is said to be "godless" and anti-religious, because it rejects Christianity. But in the same breath the critics of communism declare that communism itself is a religion, in that it exalts the proletarian revolution above all other ends, and holds that its success is guaranteed by the laws of nature and history. Whether one says that communism is atheistic, or that it has made a god of Economic Force, depends on whether one is thinking in terms of a particular religious belief or in terms of religion in general. The god which communism denies is a particular variety of god, such as the Christian god; the god which it affirms is another variety of the universal god; both gods answer the description of god as cosmic power viewed from the standpoint of what men take to be their paramount good.

It is clear that esoteric Buddhism as well as Marxian communism recognizes no god in the Christian sense. But Buddhism teaches that Nirvana is the supreme good, and that the constitution of things — the law of Karma and the ultimate illusoriness of existence — permits Nirvana to be attained. Buddhism is thus a religion in its conjoining of a hierarchy of value with a cosmology; and it can even be said to have its god, if by 'god' is meant the saving grace of man's total environment.

The human attitudes, such as worship, hope of salvation, piety, adoration, supplication, propitiation, and faith, which are characteristic of religion, are those which are appropriate to whatever is deemed to possess ultimate power over whatever is deemed to possess preëminent value.

Religion is sometimes defined in terms of the "sacred" or the "holy."

But these are derivative and not original ideas. These terms denote the peculiar veneration or awe evoked by objects, acts, or persons associated with deity, and borrowing the deity's dignity and power. When the salvation of all is believed to be dependent on the salvation of each, these attitudes are reinforced by public opinion and sentiment and the social sanction is superimposed on the religious sanction.

"Magic" is of the accident and not of the essence of religion. It reflects a relatively unenlightened phase of human knowledge, so judged from the standpoint of relative enlightenment. What was once magic (the magnet, for example) becomes science when it is better understood, or becomes (like slaying the enemy by transfixing his image) scientific error when it is disproved. Science itself seems "magical" to the uninitiated. This has nothing to do with religion unless the magical powers invoked are assumed to spring from some deeper source of control than the familiar agencies of everyday life. It is this which distinguishes the priest from the sorcerer, and prayer from incantation.

The "supernatural" is more clearly identified with religion. The supernatural is not, like the *non*-natural or *un*natural, merely a departure from the natural, marked by its irregular, extraordinary, and inexplicable, character — but is the manifestation of a superior power which embraces and exceeds the natural, and is the ultimate determiner of human destiny.

Animism is intimately related to religion. When the ultimate forces of the environment are conceived in terms of their agreement or disagreement with human values, they are described as "friendly," "hostile," or "indifferent." When this relation is imputed to the source as a conscious intent, the religious belief is literally animistic; and may be convicted of the "sympathetic fallacy." Religion is peculiarly disposed to this fallacy. There is, however, no error when nature is "personified" by poetic license; that is one of the things that poetry is for. There is no error in referring to nature as "bountiful" or as "harsh" — as when Emerson says, "Nature is no sentimentalist, — does not cosset or pamper us. We must see that the world is rough and surly, and will not mind drowning a man or a woman, but swallows your ship like a grain of dust." [1] This means only that nature behaves *as if* it were friendly, hostile, or indifferent, and that by the same license one may respond with the appropriate retributive emotions.

To identify religion with the magical or supernatural, or with the sympathetic fallacy, is to identify religion with lack of enlightenment, as something that man outgrows the more he knows. Thus to confine religion in general with its superstitious or primitive forms is as mistaken as to identify it with "the true religion." Religions may be high or low, primitive or advanced, superstitious or enlightened, ennobling or debasing, and still be religions. Their gods may be one or many, real or unreal,

[1] "Fate," *Complete Works*, 1904, Vol. VI, p. 6.

good, bad, or indifferent, and still be in the broad sense gods. The description of universal religion must embrace them all, and then look for standards by which they can be critically judged.

Religion is organized in the social institution known as the church, but it is not institutional by definition. In this it resembles science, art, and education. Worship is the essence; the church, or organized worship, is the accident. Were there only a single human being he would still select and create objects of aesthetic enjoyment, seek truth, and learn; similarly, he would still be religious, insofar as he felt and manifested a concern for his destiny. But it so happens that a man lives in such close and inescapable intercourse with his fellows that his life, including his religion, is permeated with sociality; and religion will therefore reflect its kind and degree. Social groups which are closely bound by ties of blood will tend to worship a tribal god. Social groups in which there is a high degree of solidarity will tend to believe that if they are to be saved at all they must be saved collectively. Highly nationalistic societies will tend to worship a national god; and highly authoritarian societies will favor an authoritarian church. On the other hand, insofar as societies are individualistic, the emphasis will be shifted to personal or private religion; and insofar as the solitary genius follows his own insight, religion will express itself in religious sages, saints, and mystics.

The definition of 'religion' as man's answer to the perennial question of the cosmic fate of good makes it possible to understand its one-sided definitions. That good which a man sets above all other goods, is sometimes said to be his religion. Or his religion is sometimes identified with his belief in first causes, or the ultimate substance of things — in short, his metaphysics. Neither of these is religion unless it is united with the other, but in different religious cults or moods either may dominate. God may be adored for his goodness rather than respected for his power, or the emphasis may be reversed.

Religions also differ in the degree of their hopefulness. The cosmic situation may be deemed so auspicious that the believer invests liberally, or so inauspicious that he narrowly restricts his stake. He may hope for no more than escape from the wrath of God or achievement of a state of resigned acceptance. Most historic religions, however, promise a highly profitable way of salvation, in another world if not in this — bringing "glad tidings of great joy."

2

The study of religion may employ one or all of the methods which are characteristic of the cultural sciences. Its origins may be traced by the explanatory method. There is no single cause, no religious force or instinct, which can be taken as its taproot. To say that all men are impelled by a "love of God" is to impute to man a motive which satisfies the requirements of dogma rather than the facts of observation. Religion is an acquired attitude which emerges from innumerable experiences which lead men to summarize and order their interests and stake them against that trend of things at large which appears to speak the last word.

As a manifestation of human mentality, religion is generated and shaped by causes which it is the business of psychology to set forth. It is a product of man's thinking, imagining, and believing faculties. It draws upon his emotional resources, such as fear and love. No doubt his capacity to dream, and remember his dreams, has provided him with a seeming clue to the ulterior forces which govern his destiny; but to attribute religion solely to dreams, or to hallucinations, or to the subconscious, is to commit the gratuitous error of assuming that there must be one cause when there are evidently many. There are many things to be afraid of besides ghosts; and however great its influence on the childhood of the individual and the race, there is no need of belief in a spirit-world to impress men with their dependence or to elicit their worshipful response.

The religious attitude, comprising ideas and emotional dispositions, will be caused by whatever causes transmit and diffuse ideas and emotional attitudes — such as tradition and imitation. Men's conceptions of god reflect the character of their institutions: god is patterned on the father, ruler, judge, commander, or landowner; and the worshiper is assigned the correlative roles of child, subject, defendant or plaintiff, soldier, or laborer in the vineyard. And each particular religion will reflect the peculiar form of these social institutions which prevails in a given place or epoch.

Since it embraces a claim to know, religion will be affected by advancing science and philosophy; and since it involves the imagination it will be affected by monuments of art and changes of aesthetic preference. And finally, any given religion will be the product of its own past history, the record and memory of its failures and its triumphs. The causes of religion are thus plural and innumerable; distinguishable from other causes only by the religious attitude in which they ultimately find expression.

There is a religious technology which consists of the application of the knowledge of causes. The revivalists of all ages have been aware of the methods by which religious emotions can be excited, and religious beliefs implanted: eloquence, music, light, pageantry, symbols, confession, ecclesiastical architecture, and above all, by mass contagion. These techniques do not differ essentially from those employed by any propaganda. There is also a practical wisdom by which a church is organized, administered, and perpetuated.

The application of the explanatory and technological methods to religion may be distributed among the natural and cultural sciences —

psychology, anthropology, sociology, history — or it may be gathered together in a special "science of religion." This science, like the other cultural sciences, is often supposed to be purely "descriptive," in the sense in which that adjective excludes the normative. But religion is compounded of interests, and occurs in a context of interests, and since it makes claims, religion cannot be described without being appraised. The values of religion, arising from the interests which it embodies and touches, are, like its causes, innumerable. There is no simple independent interest from which objects can be said to derive religious value. The religious interest is, like the moral interest, an interest in interests, a resultant interest, a complex of interests. Hence the values which it generates are widely dispersed.

Religion affects all of the sister-institutions by which it is itself affected. It molds conscience, polity, law, economy, science, art, and education, lending them its sanction and its symbols, and its patterns of thought; it may, as in a theocracy, dominate the total structure of society. Religion may, therefore, be criticized by any of these institutions, taken as standards; and when so judged, it is criticized externally.

The internal critique of religion, on the other hand, consists of judgments to the effect that it does or does not, or does more or less successfully, that which is its own proper business. Its immediate business, that by which it makes its own peculiar contribution to human motivation, is the creation in the minds of its votaries of a belief concerning the auspiciousness of the world at large — a confident belief that combines the goal of the life-struggle with an estimate of the total situation. Insofar as a man has no such belief, he is an "unbeliever" — a man of no religion. Religion which fails to generate such a living belief is like conscience whose approvals are unheeded, or government that does not control, or law that does not regulate, or economy which does not produce and distribute goods, or education from which nobody learns. It "goes through the motions," as we say, but it does not do, or does only weakly and ineffectively, the minimum of that which it pretends to do. A judgment of religion by this internal standard is its functional or instrumental critique.

But religion, like other functions, has its ulterior purpose. It justifies itself by a double claim. It claims to direct the affections and wills of its adherents to the supreme good: "For what shall it profit a man, if he shall gain the whole world, and lose his own soul?" And it claims to know and reveal the state of affairs which prevails in the world at large, and of which men must take account: "The fool hath said in his heart, 'There is no god.'" It claims in these two senses to be "the true religion." The critique of religion on these ulterior grounds, which are grounds which it itself takes, is its purposive or final critique.

3

The functional or instrumental value consists in "being religious" — in religiosity, piety, or devoutness, which is to be distinguished from the extent to which the final purpose of religion is fulfilled. Getting or having religion has its own immediate values, of which 'irreligion' denotes the absence. It is a good thing, in a limited sense, to have *some* religious belief whether the belief is or is not true, and whether the interests in whose behalf it speaks are high or low. The believer is spared the pangs of indecision. The unbeliever envies the believer's comparative tranquillity, and says "I wish I could believe," because he, the unbeliever, is "troubled with doubt," and desires to escape that particular trouble. The believer escapes not only from the trouble of doubt, but from its Hamlet-like paralysis. His belief imparts to his life a certain consistency and momentum.

Piety implies not only a settled conviction but some degree of hopefulness. Irreligion is a fundamental sense of hopelessness, frustration, or despair — a declaration of bankruptcy. It is essential to piety that there should be a way of salvation for which the believer considers himself eligible. It is impiety, not piety, which "curses God and dies"; piety will extract some last consolation even on the eve of execution. It will kiss the hand that smites, or believe that heaven chastises him when it most loves. Or, having abandoned every other hope, piety will retreat into the fastnesses of the intellect and imagination, and enjoy the triumphs of detachment and contemplation.

In proportion as religious belief is not only certain but also hopeful, the believer's life is permeated with a tone of cheerfulness. Confident of the ultimate triumph of the highest good, he can discount the momentary triumph of lesser goods and bear with temporary defeats. When the object of his belief is a personal god his confidence may assume the character of trust: he can enjoy the imaginary experience of reciprocal love, and feel himself honored by the personal attentions which he receives from the most august of beings. Religious symbols, together with prayer, preaching, and collective worship, will provide a tonic for the believer's will, break his habits, reverse his order of values, and otherwise bring about those profound changes of personality known as 'conversion' and 'regeneration.'

These values of religiosity can be embraced within the general formula of *hygiene,* embracing not only moral and spiritual health, but, owing to the subtle interactions of mind and body, physical health as well. So considered, religion is a remedy, which can be "taken" as stimulant, sedative, or soporific; and religious states may be compared on the ground of these benefits regardless of the level of aspiration or of insight.

Religion, like all human functions, may suffer from its own excesses and preoccupations. Religiosity is not only a therapy, but is, or may be, also, a cause of sickness. It can be wholesome, or, in excessive doses, unwholesome. Ideas and ideals may be dissolved in an orgy of passion; and the dividing line between one passion and another, as between carnal and spiritual loves, may disappear under the heat of sheer emotional excitement. Or a way of salvation adopted as a relief from worldly anxieties may beget another and a more intense anxiety, namely, anxiety concerning the salvation of one's soul. Solicitude may reach a pitch of intensity in which the fear of hell becomes a morbid fixation.

A second form of danger to which religion like other functions is exposed, is the danger that it shall be clogged and deflected by its own organization. Religion suffers notoriously not only from over-intensity, but from ritualism and ecclesiasticism. The ceremony of loving God may beget a loving of the ceremony and a forgetfulness of God. Insofar as religion is organized and becomes a church, the business of the church may supersede the business of religion. The recognition of this danger was a major, if not the central, motive of the Protestant Reformation, and it is a recurrent motive of all religious reformations; as though people were periodically compelled to say, "Let us get back to the saving of souls — to the inwardness of religion, and away from its accessories, its agencies, its forms, its offices, its trappings, its vestments, its investments, and its vested interests."

The religious life may through its own by-products and specializations defeat not only its own peculiar function but those ulterior purposes of truth and goodness by which it is justified. This is its deeper and no less notorious infidelity. The authority of god, which is justified by definition as all-wise and all-good, is transferred to the church, and has the effect of inducing followers to accept the guidance of clerical powers who often leave much to be desired in the way of wisdom and goodness. Through its sense of certainty religion may promote that unreceptiveness to evidence, that closing of the mind which is known as 'dogmatism.' Through its collective worship and its efforts to awaken and "revive" men's concern for their salvation, religion may beget a mass emotion and opinion which clouds the mind and debases the will.

In short, religious belief, practice, and organization may deflect the will from the good and the intellect from the truth. In so doing religion defeats its own deeper purpose, and the fundamental critique of religion is that which recalls it to that deeper purpose to which it appeals for its final justification.

4

The examination of the religious values which reflect the ulterior purpose of religion, and which distinguish "true religion," or "advanced religion," will follow its two-dimensional character. Its purpose being to combine a will directed to the highest good with a knowledge of the cosmic forces which determine its fate, any given religious piety, despite the immediate values of piety itself, may yet be open to criticism on two grounds: first, the ground that it does not orient the believer toward the best; second, the ground that its cosmological teachings are ignorant or erroneous. These two standards of criticism will be herewith examined in that order.

Plato, in a famous passage of the *Republic,* condemns the Olympian gods not because they do not exist but because they are unworthy. The Olympian religion invites men to worship that which is not worshipful. The foibles, deceits, and lecheries of the Homeric gods merit condemnation, instead of which they are exalted and consecrated. The shocking brutalities narrated in the Old Testament are condoned by Hebraic and Christian piety. God has been invoked by both sides of every struggle, and has confirmed political partisanship and national aggression. Religion lends its sanction not to the best only, but to the base and ignoble.

Because it is more than moral, religion is sometimes held to be immune from moral criticism. This claim to by-pass morality, instead of passing through it and beyond, is known in the history of religion as 'antinomianism.'

Religion cannot escape the requirements of morality for the very simple reason that it is a state or activity of men living among men. The man of piety, however exalted his piety, walks the earth like other men; the earth is the scene of his salvation, even of his regeneration. Such being the case, he is confronted with the problem that confronts every man, the problem, namely, of escaping conflict, personal and social, and of achieving that innocence and coöperation which is morality. Whatever the flights of the religious imagination, whatever sense the worshiper may have of his immediate communion with god, however much he may set his heart on a life after the grave, he is none the less a member of some family, somebody's neighbor, member of some organized society, and helps others through kindness, or hurts others through unkindness or neglect. However a man may be obsessed by religion, a man must, morally speaking, achieve a balanced personality if he is not to suffer from inner tensions and frustrations.

Religion, then, though it be more than morality, cannot be less. It must contain morality, however much it may add thereto. This is, in principle, recognized by all religious cults, however much in their occasional extravagances they may appear to deny it. Primitive religions endorse the mores of the social groups in which they arise. Buddhism and Hinduism teach charity as a way of salvation. In Hebraism and Mohammedanism the commands of god and the rules of right conduct are identified. In Christianity the love of neighbor is annexed to the love of god; and god himself, though in his "glory" he may surpass morality, is benevolently devoted to the harmonious happiness of human creatures.

Assuming that religion embraces morality, there arises the further and quite distinct question, whether morality depends on religion or has its own independent, secular ground. That religion provides morality with an auxiliary motivation, and that this auxiliary motivation is often a necessary condition of moral practice, is unquestionable. Men may be induced to follow the dictates of morality by the promise of reward or the threat of punishment; adults, as well as children, may need this inducement. The appeal of morality is strengthened by a sentiment of gratitude felt towards a benevolent being, by its vivid and exemplary embodiment in objects of worship, by its association with religious tradition and symbols, and by the *esprit de corps* of a body of worshippers.

All this is important in the history of religion. But it does not imply, as has been contended, that the *force* of morality rests on religious premises. Thus, for example, the fact that men are more readily disposed to be just when they believe that god commands them to be just, does not mean that their duty to be just consists in their deference to god's commands. There would still be a duty to be just if justice were not commanded. The same holds of charity. A statement on "Man and the Peace" made in 1946 by a group of American Catholic bishops contains the sentence: "Human solidarity as well as Christian brotherhood dictates the sharing of our substance with our brothers in distress." [2] The human solidarity would be there, and its dictates would be the same, even had Christianity not proclaimed the brotherhood of men under god.

The duty to be just and charitable rests on the ground of moral goodness. The commands of a god who induced men to do what was not on other grounds their duty, would be as arbitrary as those of a capricious father or king. Only an unprincipled god can be freed from the requirements of principle; and only an abject and unreasoning worshiper can subject himself to an unprincipled god.

Morality's independence of religion extends to moral institutions.[3] Had men had no religion they would nevertheless have been driven by their conflict of interests, and impelled by the promised benefits of coöperation, to organize themselves morally, and so to acqure a social conscience, a polity, a system of law, and an economy. Thus there arises the persistent and inescapable problem of the relation of religion to the secular social institutions; and in particular to those civil institutions of polity and law which exercise the function of over-all social control.

---

[2] *New York Times*, Nov. 17, 1946.

[3] For a fuller discussion of the relation of morality and moral institutions to the religious sanction, cf. the Author's "Catholicism and Modern Liberalism," *Proceedings of the American Catholic Philosophical Association, 19* (1943).

5

The idea of religious toleration, which is now unreservedly affirmed, and more or less consistently practiced, in most of the civilized world, arose historically from religious wars. Sectarian bigotry moved each religious sect to attempt by force to dominate, convert, or destroy its rivals. The effect was to reduce society to chaos and to destroy or debase all of its cultural goods, including religious piety itself. The moral lesson, painfully learned, was the reduction of sectarian pretensions to the point at which it is possible for two or more sects to live at peace. At the same time it was discovered that there are certain things which cannot be imposed by force. Religious persecution creates more heresies than it destroys; and proves that force at most induces only an external compliance, and never that inward assent in which true piety consists. The result of religious toleration is to establish the religious neutrality of the secular state. The several religious sects accept its authority as the keeper of the peace among them, and the defender of their several rights.[4]

The question of religious liberty can be more directly approached. It is the purpose of moral institutions to create and protect, and not to destroy, freedom. If any person or group of persons chooses to conceive a god and worship him in a certain manner, morality prescribes that they shall be allowed to do so without interference *from*, or interference *with*, the choices of other persons and groups.

Religious liberty, like other liberties, not only profits him who enjoys it, but pays a social dividend. As the freedom of science and art are not only rightly enjoyed by the scientist and the artist, but enrich the common human inheritance, so religion through the exercise of *its* freedom contributes monuments of piety and insight which would be impossible were religion not permitted to obey its own genius.

The same principles which argue for freedom of religious belief and worship argue also for freedom to reject religion. This freedom is explicitly recognized in the Constitution of Soviet Russia where it reflects a widespread anti-religious cult. The First Amendment of the Federal Constitution of the United States provides that "Congress shall make no law respecting any establishment of religion, or prohibiting the free exercise thereof." This provision reflects a diversity of Christian sects to some one of which, in a more or less orthodox form, the majority of the population adhere. But American public opinion, supported by a series of decisions by American courts, has followed the logic of the principle of toleration: if religious belief is to be adopted *freely*, its total rejection must be an open alternative. Atheism, as well as any one of a

---

[4] For a convenient summary of American judicial decisions on this question, cf. G. H. Haight and C. H. Lerch, "Freedom and Religion," *Bill of Rights Review*, 2 (1942), pp. 111–18.

number of theisms, non-Christian or Christian, must be allowed the same right of profession and propagation; provided that all beliefs, religious and irreligious alike, show a proper respect for one another, and involve no "public nuisance or breach of peace or decorum." [5]

If religion were an altogther private matter, the problem of the relation of the church to the secular authorities would be comparatively simple. The fact that it embraces a moral creed, and that it is even today after the notable decline of its influence, a major instrument of moral education, gives it an important role in public affairs. Since moral institutions will serve their moral purpose only when that purpose is adopted by the members, religion has a civic duty to implant it. To perform this task of reinforcing the principles which underlie moral institutions, religion must give attention to the social virtues, and proportionally less attention to the specifically religious virtues. It must emphasize that area of morality which it shares with secular life — peace and coöperation, the Golden Rule — and without claiming exclusive jurisdiction.

The moral conception of "the dignity of man," which is unquestionably an article of the democratic creed, is rightly emphasized in Christian teaching, but there is a "natural dignity" of man as a person, which is independent of that "supernatural dignity" which is imputed to man because of his relation to God. The secular state is concerned only with the first of these dignities as a basic principle of the civil order and the common good.[6]

Thus the separation of church and state as institutions, and the obligation of the state to show no special favor to any sectarian dogma or form of religious worship, must not be allowed to obscure the fact that there is an area of morality in which they intersect. Those who in the name of religion insist that the state, as well as other moral institutions, owes allegiance to certain "higher principles," are proclaiming the same truth as that proclaimed by any cultural science which looks beyond the instrumentalities of conscience, polity, law, and economy to the good which they are pledged to serve.

6

Since religion embraces a judgment of comparative value, it invites criticism on that score. Religion contains a record of human aspiration. It

[5] Cf. A. Scott, "The Legality of Atheism," *Harvard Law Review*, 31 (1917–18). There is still a Massachusetts law against blasphemy, but it has become a dead letter; cf. Z. Chafee, *The Inquiring Mind*, 1928, pp. 108 ff. It is to be noted that a recent decision of the Supreme Court has expressed an unwillingness to allow a moving picture to be banned on the score of "sacrilege."

[6] Cf. the reply of Rev. J. J. Ryan, M. M., to G. Salvemini, *New Republic*, Sept. 20, 1943. It is to be noted, however, that this writer makes the following somewhat astonishing statement: "If the human person be not infused and endowed with a spiritual and immortal soul he has no more moral dignity nor intrinsic worth than a horse, a cow or an elephant," p. 396.

expresses that which man, by straining his faculties to the utmost, conceives to be of supreme value. In proclaiming a way of salvation it teaches men not only how to be saved but what is worth saving. Religious founders, sages, prophets, and sacred books are credited with a vision of perfection transcending the earth-bound values of the layman. In prayer the believer not only prays *to,* but prays *for* — prays for that object which ranks highest in his order of preference. The religious imagination creates pictures of Paradise which represent a condition of ideal fulfillment — a consummation most devoutly to be wished. Worship praises and reverences a deity endowed with all the perfections; the saints and the redeemed are embodiments in lesser degree of the same perfections.

In criticizing the ideals thus commended to man's adoption, the first standard is, as we have seen, the moral standard. True religion must confirm the virtues, the rights and wrongs, and the duties, which are implied in the moral end of harmonious happiness. It must ally itself with the secular conscience, polity, law, and economy in respect of their purpose of removing conflict and replacing it with innocence and coöperation. By the same standard a religion may be condemned insofar as it excuses men from moral and civic responsibilities. True piety is "above the law," only when it obeys the law; it adds to, and does not subtract from, morality; it does not grant moral immunity, but demands a greater scrupulousness.

Religion may be criticized not only for its neglect or relaxation of moral requirements, but for its moral distortions and limitations. It is largely responsible for those misconceptions of morality — asceticism, authoritarianism, preceptualism, and utopianism — which have obsured its vital importance. It has given its sanction to the half-moralities of prudence and nationalism. Religion has been guilty not only of neglecting, distorting, and debasing morality, but of giving it excessive emphasis. Religion may be the projection of a morbid conscience which tortures man with a sense of guilt and impending doom. From antinomianism it may move to the opposite extreme of legalism, conceiving god as a mere disciplinarian who utters prohibitions and is primarily concerned to detect and punish offenders. Piety may be converted into observance of rules and regulations, pervading the whole of the personal and social life, and to be observed in the letter rather than in the spirit.

Religion rightly transcends morality. For while morality organizes interests, it does not prescribe what the interests shall be, nor the level of preference to which they shall rise, nor the intensity of their pursuit and enjoyment. The religious ideal, like the ideal of a total civilization of the goal of human progress, attempts to represent an optimum of value. In so doing it has rightly emphasized those interests, such as the cognitive and aesthetic interests, which are inherently most fit for harmony, and has endorsed those values of love and happiness which pervade and crown the good life.

The only good for which it is possible to claim preëminence is that harmony of all interests, which is the object of an all-benevolent will: a will which wills the fulfillment of all wills. Such a will would not only embrace all interests by inclusion, but would will the higher levels to which the several interests could rise, in terms of their own incommensurable standards.[7] Both the object of such a will, and the will itself, are ideal, and represent the attempt to conceive an upper limit of value, or *summum bonum,* leaving open the question of its realization.

At this point an otherworldly and supernaturalistic religion, such as Christianity, is faced with a dilemma. The only definable *summum bonum* derives its higher value from its component interests, in all their particularity and diversity. But religion in its straining after an image of perfection attempts to transplant it to another realm in which the actual human interests are purged away. In excluding the natural and worldly, the good life is divested of content. At best it becomes a spectral, thin, and pallid reproduction; which is less, and not more, than the fullness of life on earth. For natural happiness is substituted a supernatural "felicity," which is a diluted or merely metaphorical happiness. For profane love is substituted a sacred love, which is profane love divested of passion and intensity — divested, indeed, of that ecstasy, tenderness, and sense of union, which if man had not known it in the flesh he would never have imagined.

The best hours of the lives of the gods of Olympus were those which they spent on earth, intervening in the affairs of men. Plato's objections to this religion of Olympus would have been met had these hours been devoted to good works rather than to frivolous pastimes or abetting the ambitions of their favorites. In the fable of Aucassin and Nicolette hell is represented as more desirable than heaven, both for the company there to be enjoyed and for its promise of prolonging or reproducing the familiar delights of the present world. This was a not uncommon theme in the medieval age, when in his more relaxed moments the Christian compared the austerities of the supernatural with the concrete and proved values of the natural, the multiple vocations and enterprises of this world with the emptiness of the next.

The Christian imagination has been more successful in depicting the punishment of the damned than the rewards of the blessed, because the former is more realistic. Dante's *Hell* and *Purgatory* are more convincing than his *Paradise.* The pains of hell are allowed to reproduce the pains of earth, but the pleasures of heaven are so exalted above the pleasures of earth as to be meaningless. The imagination fails when asked to describe what the angels and saints *do* with the leisure which they enjoy throughout eternity. The treasures of heaven may be assumed to be rustless and incorruptible; but what are these treasures? There are man-

[7] Cf. the Author's *General Theory of Value,* 1926, 1950, ch. xxi, xxii.

sions in heaven, but what does one do there? On what errands is one bent when one walks the "pavements of trodden gold"? The reunion with the loved ones who have gone before derives its value from the memories of earth. Love is an interest in the interests of the loved one; but what if the loved one has no interests? Happiness consists in the general auspiciousness of interests, and becomes empty in the absence of interests at stake and a hopefulness of outlook felt in their behalf.

Angels, saints, and the redeemed may join in the heavenly choir and otherwise participate in worship. They may contemplate beauty, and enjoy knowledge of the truth. These interests have a certain propriety in an unworldly and supernatural sphere. But waiving the question of their meaning when so transplanted, a life *exclusively* devoted to such activities would be incomparably less rich in values than the life of incarnate man in which they are supplemented by the adventures of terrestrial existence.

In short, a heaven in heaven has less to offer than a heaven on earth. There appears to be no loftier and more impelling vision of the good than the prolongation and progressive betterment of that life which is experienced and enjoyed here and now; that life of which human history may be taken to record the early chapters; and whether those who have died survive to participate in the later and culminating chapters or are succeeded by other generations of mankind.

Not only is the otherworldly and supernatural good an emasculated and diluted good, but its exaltation in esteem has the effect of depreciating the greater goods which lie near at hand. The supernatural, which offers less than the natural, deflects man's attention from the rich possibilities of nature; the otherworldly, which offers less than the worldly, deflects attention from the possibilities of this world. What, then, does it profit a man if he shall gain his soul, and lose the whole of nature and the world?

The ideal good of religion appears not only in conceptions of the state of the blessed, but in the attributes of the deity. Worship is a lavish praise of god — the imputing to its object of every perfection. Here again there appears the same dependence of the superhuman on the human, the celestial on the terrestrial. Not only are the attributes of god modeled on human attributes ("man has created god in his own image," or by raising the human to a higher degree), but they appear to derive their meaning largely, if not wholly, from his dealings with men. The object of god's pleased contemplation at the beginning of Christian history was the creation which culminated in the creature. His love is his love of mankind.

Or, to avoid this preoccupation of god with the human scene — with man's creation and salvation — god is represented as preoccupied with himself. To exalt god above human affairs and to establish his self-sufficience he is said to will only his own "glory," or to love only himself, or to know only his own being. But then it is proper to ask what it is that makes god "glorious," if not his creation; and what it is that makes god lovable, if not his loving-kindness towards his own creatures; and in what consists god's being if it is divorced from the realm of natural and historical existence.

It is characteristic of lavish praise to bestow superlatives on its object regardless of their mutual consistency. God is both infinitely just, and infinitely loving; he both punishes and forgives; and the Christian theologian has never clearly reconciled the one with the other. God is a person, and yet he is denied those relations to a social and natural environment without which personality is meaningless. God is without flaw or blemish, and at the same time he is the all-powerful and all-creative author of a world in which evil abounds.

7

The second part of the final critique of religion concerns its claim to metaphysical or cosmological truth. The object of religious belief is an object of hope or fear; and hope and fear imply not only something hoped and feared *for,* but also something hoped and feared *from.* These attitudes contain, at least implicitly, a judgment of causal existence; this judgment claims to be true; and religion is thus on this score either true or erroneous, supported or unsupported by evidence. When religion is condemned as "superstitious," "anthropomorphic," "dogmatic," or as the product of "wishful thinking," the reference is not to its ideal of the good, but to its beliefs concerning the actual powers conceived as friendly or hostile to this good. Insofar as science tends to be suspicious of religion in general it is on the ground that its judgments of natural causes are likely to be erroneous, or at least unwarranted.

The present question is not the question of god's being, for god undoubtedly *is,* in some sense of that term, even if it be only as a fictitious character; nor is it the question of god's logical existence, for the class of gods is not a null class; it is the question of god's causal existence — his entering into that same spatio-temporal-causal nexus which embraces the events and actions of human history. An eternal, non-spatial, and ineffective god will not suffice.

The religion of Baal was doubly condemned by the Hebrew prophets: because Baal was a wicked god — a god of stealing, lying, and adultery; but also because he did not answer when he was called upon. "Cry aloud," said Elijah, "for he *is* a god; either he is talking, or he is pursuing, or he is in a journey, *or* peradventure he sleepeth, and must be awaked." The true Lord God, on the other hand, was both a god of righteousness and a god who when called upon, could cause a fire to burn upon the altar.[8]

[8] Jeremiah, 7:9; I Kings, 18:27.

In order to determine the values which are involved in this cosmological critique, we may suppose that the requirements of the first critique are met, so that god is equated with optimum good. There are then three questions which may be raised concerning the causal existence of such a god: Is it good that it should exist? Is it good that it should be truly known to exist? Is it good that it should be believed to exist, whether or not the belief is true?

The answer to the first of these questions is self-evident. The ideal good would acquire confirmation and continuity through being the object of god's unfaltering will as well as of the wavering and intermittent will of man; and god's power would so ally itself with man's aspirations as to assure their success or at least render it more probable.

Such *de facto* alliance of cosmic powers with the ideal good would not in itself constitute religion: for religion, man must know about it. The second question, then, is whether such knowledge is good. The answer to this question is debatable. Such knowledge, like all knowledge, would yield cognitive value: it would satisfy man's curiosity and love of truth. Furthermore, if god is a potent ally it is practically useful to man to know the fact, in order that he may coöperate with god consciously and methodically; as the soldier in the ranks conforms himself to the strategy of the general in command, both seeking the same victory. But assuming that god's power guarantees the successful pursuit of man's ideals, it may be argued that it is better for man not to know it, for he may then be disposed to relax his efforts. Even assuming that the victory depends on human effort, it may be argued that the maximum of such effort is induced by some proportion of knowledge and ignorance which will generate confidence and at the same time avoid overconfidence and irresponsibility.

These values of god's existence, and of man's true knowledge of god's existence are to be distinguished from the value of *believing* in god's existence, whether the belief be true or erroneous. Erroneous belief does not satisfy the cognitive interest, nor is it practically useful, since it does not enable the believer to link his own action with his causal environment. It grinds no corn. But there is a subjective value even of erroneous belief. It creates a certain inner stability and peace of mind. And even when the belief is known to be erroneous or is merely "entertained," it may possess aesthetic and symbolic values. The image of god may be enjoyed in contemplation, or it may give concreteness and vividness to the ideal of the good, and thus intensify the believer's aspiration. Between belief and contemplation there is commonly a borderland, or an oscillation between letter and symbol — a half-believing and half-disbelieving, or a believing by the naïve rank and file, combined with a sophisticated disbelieving among the augurs.

8

The so-called "proofs of god" concern the second and not the first of the internal and final critiques of religion. That which they attempt to prove is not the goodness of god, but the *existence* of a being dedicated to the good and working effectually for its triumph.

Until a comparatively recent period European Christendom has been so generally convinced of the existence of its God as to ask no proof, or to accept with little critical resistance certain ready-made proofs offered by the philosophers. "Theism" was a science or subject, rather than a doctrine: a subject embracing and formulating with variations a set of supposedly demonstrable theorems, known as "the cosmological proof," "the teleological proof" or "argument from design," and "the ontological proof." Beginning with the generalization of Newtonian mechanics, followed at the close of the eighteenth century by devastating refutations by Hume and Kant, this theistic corpus has been steadily undermined until at the present time theism assumes the form of a disputed theory leaning heavily on dogma, mysticism, and faith.[9]

A proof of god is not a proof of the Christian *God*, unless the being whose existence is proved, is both supreme and good. To prove that there is a "first cause," or an "infinite substance," even if such proofs were possible, would not prove that such a ground of existence was favorably disposed to the good, and was therefore a proper object of worship. Hence the crucial point in the traditional arguments for god is the supposed necessary connection between existence and value. This connection is the core of the ontological argument, which deduces God's existence from his perfection, and which loses its force when 'existence' is defined independently of 'value.' Similarly, the cosmological argument, or argument for a First Cause, argues for a god of religion only provided the first cause is tied to goodness. If the ontological argument fails to establish this connection, the only remaining possibility is the teleological argument, or argument from design; in which the first cause is judged *by its works* to be intelligent and benevolent. This argument is double-edged; for if there are evidences of benevolent design, there are also evidences of purposelessness or of sinister design. This objection has been steadily reinforced by man's growing doubts of the beneficence of nature, and his growing suspicion of his own tendency to see nature as good or bad as suits his bias or his mood.

The argument from design has the merit of being an empirical argument. There are other empirical arguments. A personal god who answers prayer may be considered as a hypothesis, verified by the answer to

---

[9] The general philosophical position outlined in the previous chapter — neutralism, realism, empiricism, naturalism, temporalism, and pluralism — excludes by implication the traditional a priori proofs of God.

prayer. This was the proof to which Elijah appealed when he engaged in an experimental test with the prophets of Baal. In more refined forms this is still the most convincing proof, to pious Christians of all persuasions, and to non-Christian theists who call upon god for guidance or peace of mind. It is the sort of proof which in evangelical Christianity is offered by experiences of conversion.

Such an empirical hypothesis is not to be rejected in advance. It violates no law of logic or of science. If a man feels better and does better for praying, and imputes this effect to a superhuman agency having the usual attributes of deity, there is room enough in the domain of doubt and ignorance to permit of his judgments being true. The objection is that the hypothesis is not clearly defined, and the evidence is therefore inconclusive; the experiment is not a "controlled experiment." The verdict of the critic is: "Not proved, not disproved"; "improbable, but possible."

It is urged against the experimental proof of god that "the varieties of religious experience" require no theistic hypothesis, but can be explained in terms of abnormal and social psychology. There remains, however, a further possibility, which is to substitute the idea of an immanent, for the idea of a transcendent, god; and for the idea of a supernatural and otherworldly god, the idea of a natural and worldly god. God can then be identified with man's moral and spiritual history. There is an ideal of harmonious happiness which is pursued, and sometimes realized, by human wills. This ideal is an actual force; implemented by the technologies of the sciences, it organizes persons, societies, and civilizations.

It is true that the work of this will is attended with failures and is bounded on all sides by narrow limits; but it has its successes, and it has its dream of a perfected life of humanity. The most modest of theistic claims would build on this slender, but indisputable, fact. It would employ the name 'god' for the good will and aspiration to perfection which here and there, now and then, fugitively and precariously, have emerged from the flux of existence.

It is true that the bare recognition of these facts would not merit the name of religion. Human aspiration could not provide an object of worship unless accompanied by a belief in its long-run prepotency among the forces of the cosmos. It would be necessary to suppose that the known vicissitudes of human fortune were but chapters in a longer story, scenes in a larger drama. The gap between the accredited facts and such a religious claim would have to be filled by other sources of belief. But its borrowings from dogma, mysticism, and faith would be less extensive than those required for supernatural and otherworldly religions.

The belief in "life after death" is a proper sequel, both logical and psychological, to the belief in god. Death affords the most vivid and palpable evidence of man's dependence, and the dependence of all he holds dear, upon forces beyond his control. The extinction of persons implies the extinction of the goods with which the interests and aspirations of persons invest their objects; it is a defeat, or at least a momentary defeat, of value at its source. It contradicts not only the interest of self-preservation, but every interest. Interested living of every kind, and on every level, projects itself into the future; death, in cutting off the person's future, stifles even his present activity. To die in full stride is to step off into an abyss. Aversion to death argues the liveliness of present interests, indifference to death implies present apathy. It is consistent then, with the motive of religion that it should look for some more hopeful prospect.[10]

While it is natural that the individual should identify the realization of the object of his interest with *his own* consummatory act — an occasion for his own dealings — this is not necessary. He may conceive the realization of the good as occurring in his merely imaginary presence, the interest being carried forward through later time by a succession of persons. His own immortality would then consist in the continuing effects of his present life. What he has himself achieved would remain as a contribution to the progressive achievement of posterity. As for his own future, he would hope, at best, to be an object of grateful memory, not a participant. He would be obliged to resign himself to being numbered among those fallen in early battles, leaving to others the later victories.

The traditional arguments for immortality have been divided on the question of the relation of soul and body. The arguments inherited from antiquity (including those set forth in Plato's *Phaedo*) have conceived of the soul as literally "immortal" because of belonging to a non-spatial, non-temporal realm beyond the reach of natural causes. Only that which arises from natural causes can perish from natural causes. The body can die, but its death is only a release to the soul, of which the body is the temporary and alien abode. The price paid for this proud claim is evident. The soul which cannot die can never have lived — never, that is, have interacted with a natural environment. Its invulnerability implies its impotence.

The Christian teaching, on the other hand, despite its frequent lapses into Platonism,[11] has recognized soul and body as inseparable parts of the integral man; and in so doing, it has conformed to naïve belief and the religious imagination, while at the same time it has anticipated the most advanced views of modern psychology. For immortality Christianity substitutes "resurrection," and even the bold affirmation of "resurrection of the body." Man is mortal: death is a tragic fact. The hope is that having died the individual may be *revived:* if not in his present body then

[10] Cf. the Author's *The Hope of Immortality*, 1945, originally published under the title of "The Meaning of Death," *Hibbert Journal*, 33 (1935).

[11] For a clear and fully documented presentation of the Christian view, cf. G. Florovsky, "The Resurrection of Life," Ingersoll Lecture for 1950–51, *Harvard University Official Register*, 49 (1952).

in some other body, which will assure his continued membership in the space-time-causal nexus of existence. Christ is the incarnate god, and the resurrection of Christ symbolizes the belief that what dies can live again — live in the very sense of that term which makes the loss of life so profoundly regrettable. This is a hard doctrine, which, in the Christian teaching, relies on faith, dogma, and authority.

Immortality in this sense has been defended empirically by a form of inquiry known as "psychical research." This scientific spiritism, with its ghosts, its mediums, its automatic writing, its apparitions, its telepathy, clairvoyance, and communications from the dead, remains inconclusive. It is not disproved, and the door to its truth is not closed, but as yet it has not even achieved scientific respectability. Orthodox psychology does not accept its explanations, but explains them away.

Some empirical support for the idea of resurrection is to be derived from the abandonment of the older materialistic conception of the body. The physical organism serves the mind not as an identical aggregate of matter, but as an instrument of memory, disposition, space-time orientation, action, and choice. Personal identity is not an identity of substance, but an identity of content selected and organized by interest. So conceived a particular body is expendable; it is conceivable that another body could do its work. But so slim is the empirical evidence in support of life after death that even Christian belief hesitates to rely on it. Even the testimony of eyewitnesses to the resurrection of Christ is less trusted than dogma, authority, and faith.

9

The famous "problem of evil" is the lion in the path of religious thought. It is the old problem of Job, which has perpetually tortured the minds of those who have reflected upon the implications of piety. The problem is a by-product of the effort of religious belief to establish an equation between the ideal and the existent; or to reconcile the deity's cosmic control with his imperfection. There is a prima facie irreconcilability. God conceived as perfection reflects man's experience of imperfection. Practicing and suffering injustice, man dreams of perfect justice; being both hateful and the victim of hate, he dreams of utter and universal love; being ignorant, he conceives of omniscience; amidst the ugliness and drabness of life, he fancies a perfection of beauty; from his unhappiness there springs a vision of perfect and uninterrupted bliss. God being so conceived in contrast to the facts of life, the pious believer then endows him with a limitless power to achieve what he wills. But if there is no obstacle which god cannot overcome, why, then, does he not only allow imperfection, but bring it to pass?

The contradiction is inescapable unless one of the terms of the equation is altered. Something has to give way. Either the idea of the good has to be amended to suit the requirements of existence, or the idea of existence has to be amended to suit the requirements of the good. Both of these alternatives violate the evidence, or reinstate the problem in new terms.

A Spanish poet has described two false or one-sided paradises, the paradise of light and the paradise of darkness. The "total flavor" of life is to be found only in their mixture:

> When, cast on the rocks
> of sin which is living, loving each other,
> we must fight the fight which it behooves them
> to fight who lose a paradise of light,
> or a paradise of darkness,
> to find another Eden, where lights
> and shadows cross, and where lips
> which meet to kiss shall in the end discover
> that terrible roundness of the world.[12]

In other words, he who knows life will recognize that evil is as much of its essence as good. There is no silver lining without the cloud. Evil is the invariable companion of good: no evil, no good. It is a part of religion as well as of poetry to achieve this insight and to communicate it to mankind. But this statement, true as it is, does not solve the problem of evil. Evil is no less evil for being a fact — even a necessary fact. The good-*cum*-evil character of the existent world simply disproves the thesis which gives rise to the problem, the thesis, namely, that to exist is to be good.

It may be argued, however, that evil is necessary to *good,* or is a part of its very meaning; so that an all-powerful will devoted to goodness would, by implication, will the evil as its constituent. The argument takes various forms. Thus it is argued, and it is true, that for every good there is a definable evil: for positive interest, negative interest; for success, failure; for pleasure, pain; for truth, error; for righteousness, sin. In other words, there can be no good without the *abstract possibility* of evil. But it does not follow that the evil possibility need be realized. An all-powerful will to goodness would be able to take the good, and escape the evil.

Less sweeping, and more plausible, is the contention that there are certain specific kinds of goods which require evil. Thus it was held by the Stoics that "pain is no evil," since fortitude is good, and fortitude requires that there shall be pain to be endured. Or, it may be held that obstacles are no evil, since the good lies not in the success but in the struggle. Similarly, it may be held that sin is no evil, since it is required for the goods of repentance and justice; and the villain is not evil since his villainy is required for the good of tragedy or melodrama.

[12] P. Salinas, "Truth of Two," in *Contemporary Spanish Poetry,* trans. by E. L. Turnbull and P. Salinas, 1945, pp. 109–113.

But all such solutions imply that suffering, frustration, and wickedness are evil on some level of value. The higher definition of value on which they cease to be evil assumes that they are evil on the lower level. The alleged solution defines what it is *good to do* with evil, granted that it occurs, and that it is evil. Granted that suffering is evil, it is practically good that it should be relieved or endured. Granted that frustration is evil, it is practically good to overcome it. Granted that sin is evil, it is practically good that it should be repented or punished. Granted that the villain is evil, it is aesthetically good to see his dramatic relation to the hero or to circumstance. Granted that evil of any kind exists, it is cognitively good to understand it. In short, evil being given, there are various ways by which to make the best of it, and these ways constitute an important part of the art of the good life — the art of doing as well as possible, the evils of life being recognized for what they are.

Even were lower evils explained away in terms of higher goods, there would still be no solution of the problem of evil in general, because to each new good there would be a corresponding evil. While its terms are changed the problem remains precisely where it was before. When it is held that pain is no evil provided it is uncomplainingly endured, *complaint* becomes evil, and testifies to the fact that the forces of good are not in complete command. Indeed, the new evil is more common than the old, and the corresponding good more rare. Fortitude is rarer than pleasure, overcoming obstacles is rarer than their absence, repentance and just punishment are rarer than innocence, heroism than the detached aesthetic appreciation of villainy, and the facts of good than the understanding of evil. In short, when judged by standards of higher good in order to find an excuse for lower evil, the total picture grows blacker, and less, not more, consistent with the hypothesis that perfection is omnipotent.[13]

An even more desperate attempt to solve the problem of evil is that which would deny not the evil of evil, but the *facts* of evil. Thus one may admit that suffering would be evil, but simply deny that it occurs. It seems to occur, but its seeming is an illusion; or, as the Christian Scientists would have it, an "error of mortal mind." The difficulties which this view encounters are so evident and insurmountable that it is impossible to explain how men have come to hold it at all, except as the last resort of wishful thinking. It not only refuses to accept the empirical evidence for evil, but lightly disregards a new problem which it has substituted for the old: the problem, namely, of accounting for illusory appearances.

The attempt to solve the problem of evil has led men either to a denial of the facts of existence, or to a perpetual shifting of their conceptions of value. The abandonment of the attempt leaves the situation

---

[13] It is to be noted that the Calvinists who have denied all evils save sin have painted the blackest picture of all.

where empirical knowledge finds it. There is evil as well as good in the world, and the outcome of the issue between them is left to the will implemented by intelligence. How far this undertaking may properly be attended with hope is the question of optimism and pessimism.

10

'Optimism' and 'pessimism' are the names given to attitudes of hopefulness or hopelessness regarding the future — hoping the best, fearing the worst. Insofar as the first of these attitudes takes account of human interests on the whole in the light of the total or major forces of the environment, it coincides with religion. There is empirical evidence supporting both attitudes — there are grounds for hopefulness and grounds for hopelessness.

Pessimism focuses attention on negative interests, and on the failure of positive interests. It finds abundant evidence of the brutal indifference of nature, of human depravity, of cruelty, greed, war, and disease; and harps on the immense gap between man's professions and his actions, his ideals and his achievements. There is a wholesale pessimism which consists in being so obsessed with evil as to recognize no good save its avoidance. It is against this pessimism that André Gide has protested:

> Doctrine of sin: being capable of all evil and committing none; that is the definition of good. I do not like this merely negative exercise of the will. I prefer that blindness to evil should result from being dazzled by the good; otherwise virtue is ignorance — poverty.[14]

Pessimism of this negative type is sometimes taken as the premise of supernaturalism; the utter illusoriness and vanity of the values of this existent world being taken as the point of departure for some other world, which, however, possesses no predictable good except the absence of the evil of this.

Optimism, like pessimism, is based upon selection, a seeing of the silver linings rather than the clouds. Here, too, the evidence abounds. There is an auspiciousness as well as an inauspiciousness of things. There is good to dazzle the eye, and which may blind it to the perception of evil. The facts of existence lend themselves not only to a morbid preoccupation with evil, but to a sentimental or incorrigibly cheerful preoccupation with good. Which of these attitudes a man will take may reflect his temperament, his personal fortunes, and even the momentary state of his digestion. These extremes and oscillations of attitude testify to the ambivalence of life. Each, in its turn, is a one-sided distortion: there is a fallacy of "eulogism," which is to see only the good; and there is a fallacy of "dyslogism," which is to see only the evil.

An enlightened and candid reading of nature and history warrants

[14] *Journals*, Vol. I, 1948, p. 71.

neither a complete optimism nor a complete pessimism. There is a third possibility which is neither the one nor the other, nor a mere mixture or alternation of the two. This third possibility, which is closest to the attitude of common sense, combines acknowledgment of past and present evil with a hopeful resolve to achieve a better future. The name of this third religious attitude is 'meliorism.'

There is no conclusive empirical evidence that "all is for the best." The most that can reasonably be expected of the individual, and all that he needs to ask of himself in order to enjoy self-respect and the respect of others, is that he shall contribute his portion of intelligence and effort to the *cause* of the good; that, through taking account of circumstances and profiting by their plasticity, and allying himself with the like-minded, he shall make himself "count" for something on the side of "righteousness." Theory of value does not assure him of victory, but it guides him in his choice of the banner under which he will serve. To pessimists this is optimism — it claims too much; to optimists it is pessimism — it claims too little.

Pessimism is sometimes described as a sense of the "meaninglessness" of life. This was the pessimism of Tolstoy:

> "Without knowing what I am and why I am here, life's impossible; and that I can't know, and so I can't live," Levin said to himself. "In infinite time, in infinite matter, in infinite space, is formed a bubble-organism, and that bubble lasts a while and bursts, and that bubble is Me." [15]

But Tolstoy himself had a better answer. To give meaning to life, it is not necessary to deny that man is a part of the natural world from which he emerges. The human individual ceases to be a mere "transitory bubble" when he participates in a total life of mankind conceived as dedicated to the on-going cause of good.

Meliorism is not an "easy" optimism, as the pessimist charges. It does not change its allegiance in order to be on the winning side. It does not fortify itself in an ivory tower; choosing only aesthetic or cognitive goods because they are safe, and abandoning the moral and social goods because they are exposed to mortal vicissitudes. It gives hostages to fortune, and determines to retrieve them.

A religion of meliorism is not guilty of ignoring or underrating evil; or of failing to see how ineradicable it is. Quite the contrary. All triumphs of the will are attended by the risk of failure, as all cognitive judgments are attended by the risk of error. There is no infallibility in either sphere. Man's fallibility does not demean him, but raises him to the level of a seeker for truth and a pursuer of good. Indeed, a divine being who could not fail or err would cease to be a voluntary or cognitive being.

Meliorism, then, does not choose the easy way: indeed, it denies

[15] *Anna Karenina*, trans. by C. Garnett, Modern Library edition, p. 917.

that there is any easy way — any short cut, or detour, or patent remedy; and it *chooses* the hard way. It cherishes no illusions of a hollow or predetermined victory. It is aware of the possibility of failure. It accepts every evidence of the indifference of nature, of the baseness of human nature, and of the corruption of society. It chooses the hard way with its eyes open. It takes the bad news with the good; but it does not on that account surrender or leave the field of action. It summons courage to overcome discouragement.

11

Even meliorism, modest as it is as compared with the more exuberant religious optimisms, creates a gap between what is hoped for and what is proved. There are three ways by which religion endeavors to close this gap: by dogma, by mysticism, and by faith. All of these resorts of the mind are ways of reconciling religious intoxication with cognitive sobriety — ways of transcending the bounds of ordinary knowledge by taking extraordinary measures.

Religious dogma is religious belief accepted on authority. The weakness of dogmatism lies in the fact that the authority by which the dogma is justified has itself to be justified. One authority can be justified by another through a hierarchy of authorities, but in the end some highest authority, be it the church or the "revealed word of God," has to be justified on other than authoritarian grounds. There are two ways in which an authority can be justified: either by trust, which is equivalent to accepting it without justification; or by proving it trustworthy. An authority is deemed trustworthy, when there is reason to believe that its utterances are true; but then the authority is tested by the dogma, and not the dogma by the authority, and the dogma, having been proved true, is no longer a dogma.

The mystic claims to find god in a vision which transcends concepts and percepts, and which is therefore indescribable and incommunicable. But then he has no intellectual right to give the object of his vision the name of 'god,' if that name is taken to mean perfection and existence, as these are conceived or perceived. If, on the other hand, he claims to use words only ostensively, that is, to direct the vision of others to the object of his own, he cannot be said to have succeeded. There is no reason to suppose that even mystics, who should be peculiarly responsive to such directions, have the same vision; while non-mystics, with the best will in the world, do not succeed in having any vision at all.

The only accredited fact in the area of mysticism is the existence of a class of states vaguely described as "exaltation" and "rapture" accompanied by a "sense of union." No belittling of these states is here intended. They give flesh and blood to the otherwise desiccated mummy of theological doctrine. But the existence of such states does not imply the existence of beings having the characteristics which the mystic imputes to his visionary object. His claims are unverified and unconfirmed; the mystic, like the dogmatist and authoritarian, must in the last analysis resort to faith. This is the last refuge of religious belief, but it is not on that account a vain or illegitimate refuge.

Faith is not a mere wantonness or caprice of believing — believing with no control save the impulse of the moment. It is doubly controlled: by the requirement that it shall reinforce aspiration and sustained effort; and by the requirement that it shall incorporate, and be consistent with, the knowledge which it exceeds. Faith is not to be identified with a primitive mentality below reason, or with a superhuman mentality above reason. It has its peculiar content, and it has its own peculiar justification. In this specific and justifiable sense, faith is belief, beyond the limits of theoretical proof, in the realization of interests which are still on trial; it is justified by the psychological fact that belief in success is favorable to success.

If cognition is to serve interests it must assume the form of decision. The time of the decision is dictated by the exigencies of action: interest has a deadline to be met, and cannot wait for the leisurely and protracted processes of inquiry and proof. It is necessary to believe prematurely in order to act expeditiously. Faith is theoretical doubt overruled by practical urgency.

Religious faith is a special case of such precipitate belief. Belief in the long range survival and ascendancy of values in the world of existence does not permit of conclusive proof within the life span of the individual. But if his thought concerning the cosmic destiny of value is to serve as a guide and incentive to his action — if he is to "live by it" — he must resolve his doubts and come to a conclusion. If he is to profit by what his mind has to offer on this crucial question he must make up his mind, and there is little time. Since death may come tomorrow, the time for decision is today. The prolongation of doubt is itself a sort of decision — even if it be no more than a rejection of recognized alternatives. The man who cannot make up his mind whom to marry, has, in effect, decided to remain a bachelor.[16]

The religious faith here justified is not an indeterminate belief. The several terms employed — 'value,' 'accredited knowledge,' and 'existence' — are given meanings consistent with the definition of value in terms of interest, and with the general philosophical position of neutralism, realism, empiricism, naturalism, libertarianism, temporalism, and pluralism.

Faith is not a mere absence of knowledge. The faith which is not

---

[16] The classic discussion of this theme is William James's famous essay, "The Will to Believe," published in the volume bearing that title, 1898; and in his *Essays on Faith and Morals*, 1943. Cf. also the Author's *In the Spirit of William James*, 1938, ch. v.

proved is the appropriate sequel to the knowledge which is proved: it is, loosely speaking, "more of the same." Faith is an extension beyond knowledge. From knowledge faith learns where and how to look, the unknown — the not impossible — takes its cue from the actually known.

Faith, therefore, is not blind. It does not ignore theoretical evidence; it does not fly in the face of the facts or turn its back on them. There can be no justification of belief which is contrary to the evidence. Faith is a belief which agrees with the evidence so far as the evidence goes, but goes further. It lacks proof, but it may nevertheless be true and certain; for, as has been seen, neither truth nor certainty depends on proof.

Faith is not justified by the failure of knowledge, but by its only partial success. There is no hopefulness to be extracted from a general discrediting of science, but only by extending its credit. Faith does, nevertheless, profit by the limits of science. The most remarkable feature of modern science is not this or that specific discovery, but the rapidity and surprisingness of its advance. It would be a strategic mistake to build human hopes irretrievably on the latest findings of physics, biology, and astronomy, for these may soon prove obsolete. There is a broader and more permanent ground of hope in this very fact of obsolescence; for it is this which removes barriers, and extends the horizons of possibility. Science perpetually withdraws its own negations; is, indeed, increasingly chary of committing itself to negations. Its sentences of doom are so rapidly reversed that it has abandoned its role of chief executioner of human hopes.

Science no longer sounds a note of finality, but rather a note of emancipation and of imaginative inventiveness. All of its findings are open to revision; its latest word is never its last word. It grows by outgrowing; and this change occurs so rapidly that before men can unpack their belongings and begin to occupy the premises a new cosmos has been unfolded to view. The layman, plodding behind the scientist, and falling more and more behind, can gather little but a bewildered and exciting impression that nothing is any longer impossible.

Limited horizons are enclosed within successively broader horizons until it has become reasonable to expect that all boundaries are movable and that what seems to be a whole will prove to be only a part. The wave may be discovered to be only a ripple on the back of some bigger wave. Magnitudes of space and time have so increased as to make familiar systems of measurement meaningless. Macrocosms become microcosms and microcosms become macrocosms. The human scale is completely eclipsed. The old immensities have become diminutive. Similarly, the old diminutives have become immensities: the atom takes on the aspect of a galaxy. The humanly visible and audible proves to be merely a segment of qualitative differences. A matter that excluded mind, an inorganic that excluded life, a mechanism that excluded purpose, a dissipation of energy that excluded the building of new energies, an exhaustion of resources that excluded discovery of new resources, irreversible trends, an ultimate chemical alphabet of elements and an ultimate biological alphabet of species — all these old rigidities have passed away.

It is true that nature is a much less cozy abode than it was once taken to be. Even the Copernican-Newtonian world which once seemed of terrifying proportions, now wears the aspect of a Dutch interior. Nature is no longer a room or even a house, but it is all outdoors. But by the same token it is no longer a prison; there is occasion, perhaps, for agoraphobia, but not for claustrophobia. The cumulative effect of all these changes is that nature, not the idealized "Nature" of an obsolete metaphysics, but nature as it comes from physics and its sister sciences, presents an aspect of openness. It no longer wears that uncompromisingly forbidding aspect which has driven man to seek his fortunes elsewhere.

The human mind abhors a vacuum of ignorance, and fills it with the works of the imagination. There is no principle of logic or of practice which forbids man to extract what good he can from his ignorance; or which requires him to think of what he does not know as less auspicious than what he knows; or compels him, when he dreams to dream only nightmares. Nor is there any duty which forbids man to accept his good dreams as true, provided they do not conflict with his waking knowledge.

12

Religion as here defined and justified is that religion which springs from the situation which confronts all mankind — that religion in general, which gives a common meaning to all particular religions. It is that "natural religion," which is rooted in natural existence; which exists in a natural environment; which requires no human faculties save man's natural faculties; and no revelation, save empirical knowledge and a recognition of its limits. This is the religion which men would acquire if they were to start again, deprived of every inherited religious establishment.

There is religion, and there are religions. The relation of universal religion to particular religions has its parallels in every domain of human life. Every human institution has its generality and its particularity. There is a richness of value in personal friendship and love, in companionship, collaboration, shared experience and memories, historic nationality, community of culture and language, neighborhood, of which the wider and more abstract relationships provide no equivalent. Similarly, there is a fullness of religious life which is realized only among those who are united by particular creeds and forms of worship, and by membership in an historic church; no religion of all mankind, or cross section of religions, could compensate for its loss.

But there is an even greater loss in a sectarian exclusiveness in which

INDEX